Film and the Critical Eye

Film *and* *the* Critical Eye

Dennis De Nitto

The City College of the City University of New York

William Herman

The City College of the City University of New York

Macmillan Publishing Co., Inc.

NEW YORK

Collier Macmillan Publishers

LONDON

Copyright © 1975, Macmillan Publishing Co., Inc.

Printed in the United States of America

All rights reserved. No part of this book may be reproduced or transmitted in any form or by any means, electronic or mechanical, including photocopying, recording, or any information storage and retrieval system, without permission in writing from the Publisher.

Macmillan Publishing Co., Inc.
866 Third Avenue, New York, New York 10022

Collier-Macmillan Canada, Ltd.

Library of Congress Cataloging in Publication Data
DeNitto, Dennis.
  Film and the critical eye. _See slip_

  Bibliography: p. 527-536
  Includes index.
  1. Moving-picture plays—History and criticism.
I. Herman, William, 1926–   joint author. II. Title.
PN1995.D44   791.43'7   74–10310
ISBN 0–02–328370–X

Printing: 1 2 3 4 5 6 7 8   Year: 5 6 7 8 9 0

For Elisabeth:
     who endured as well as contributed
     to the making of this book
                          —DENNIS DENITTO

For Joanna Pisello:
     who knows the cost of making books
     and who gave value to this one; with
     love
                        —WILLIAM HERMAN

Preface

*T*he genesis of Film and the Critical Eye *lies in our frustration at a lack of detailed analyses of individual films. Such analyses, with a few exceptions, are either nonexistent or restricted to articles in professional journals that are difficult to locate. Authors of books on film have tended to confine their comments on specific works to a few memorable shots or significant scenes. Our volume is an effort toward filling this lacuna in film criticism.*

The most important feature of this book is Part Three: essays on fourteen separate films and brief commentaries on six additional films. Each chapter is based on repeated viewing and checking of details of the films considered. Each essay is comprehensive, so that every aspect of a cinematic work from story to the style and approach of the director is explored. We believe this type of analysis gives a critical viewer many advantages. If he has not seen a film, our essay will supply points to look for. After he has seen the film, he will find our analysis helpful in minimizing confusions resulting from the vagaries of individual memory (the analysis is especially valuable when members of a group are comparing impressions). Finally, a viewer can challenge or confirm his own insights and interpretation with those offered in our text.

Film and the Critical Eye *is confined to one cinematic genre, the fictive narrative film. This genre is presented as a fusion of two elements, narrative and its visual expression. It has occasionally been necessary in preserving the coherence of an analysis to give prominence first to one element and then to the other, but in each of our chapters we have tried to do justice to both the cinematography and the narrative dimensions of the work discussed. When exploring story, characterization, and themes of a film, we have emphasized the narrative component. Pages on the approach and style of a director are concerned primarily with cinema techniques. In the subdivision of each chapter entitled "Analysis of Major Sequences," we have sought to combine both approaches in the commentary devoted to single sequences.*

The main criterion we adhered to in chosing films is their quality as works of art. The majority of them would be considered "classics" by any standard. As far as possible they represent various types, directing styles, and themes. One restriction on the selection of films was accepted in order to make the book more useful in the classroom and for film clubs. To ensure a practical correspondence between what the book discusses and what is actually seen on the screen, we have selected films obtainable for the most part from one renting agent. There are several excellent agencies; however, we elected to work with Janus Films. Not only is their catalogue impressive and, as experience has shown us, their staff helpful and dependable, but their prints are consistently clear and complete.

Readers of this volume will vary in experience of analyzing films and familiarity with the vocabulary and techniques of film criticism. Rather than take any foreknowledge for granted, we have included introductory material in four early chapters: "Viewing a Film" and "Interpreting a Film" (Part One), "The Language of Film" and "The Rhetoric of Film" (Part Two). "The Language of Film" is a glossary of unusual comprehensiveness and detail of definition with frequent references to examples found elsewhere in the text.

The last pages of Film and the Critical Eye *provide a bibliography of material on each film and its director and a biography and filmography for the directors of those films examined in Part Three.*

It is always a pleasure to acknowledge the assistance of those who helped in preparing a book. Our thanks for advice and encouragement are due to a number of our colleagues at The City College of The City University of New York, but especially to Professors Saul N. Brody, James J. Greene, Gerald Kauvar, Edward Quinn, and Robert K. Morris. Our problems in viewing films would have multiplied without the generous cooperation of Mr. John M. Poole of Janus Films and his two assistants, Mr. Richard Evangelista and Mr. Peter Meyer. We are grateful to Mr. D. Anthony English and Mr. J. Edward Neve, our editors at Macmillan, for many things.

Of more private indebtedness, no bald statement would be sufficient. Our dedication, however, speaks, if not volumes, at least a volume of appreciation.

DENNIS DENITTO
WILLIAM HERMAN

Acknowledgment

CHAPTER 10. JEAN COCTEAU. *Diary of a Film* by Jean Cocteau, translated by Ronald Duncan. Excerpts reprinted by permission of Dobson Books Limited. From *Diary of a Film*, 1950, Dobson Books Limited, London, and Dover Publications Inc. (paper edition only), New York.

Contents

Part One

Part Two

Part Three

Part One

*T*he two essays that make up this part of our book are not intended—no matter how declaratory their titles—to be prescriptive. They are meant simply to offer suggestions as to how an individual, especially one who is unaccustomed to considering films as art, might increase the perceptiveness with which he views and interprets a film. In the second of these essays our generalizations are illustrated by references to the films analyzed in Part Three.

CHAPTER 1

Viewing a Film

Viewers of motion pictures come in various sizes and shapes, ages, and nationalities. Their backgrounds on every level, as well as their emotional and intellectual capabilities, are often different. The needs of this diverse audience have been met by different genres and types of cinema. In the face of such a complex situation, a writer who wants to discuss "viewing a film" in a couple of dozen pages or so, even after admitting that he is infected with *hubris*, must carefully indicate the limitations of his discussion. In this essay we will deal only with basic principles and premises and of necessity will ignore whole areas of the subject.

The first step is easy. An individual's experience of a motion picture involves three interrelated stages: his attitudes and responses before, during, and after viewing the motion picture. The next step, considering each stage in turn, immediately puts us on the slippery ground of distinctions and definitions.

Psychologists use the term *sets* to label the readiness of an organism to make a particular class of responses to an organization of stimuli. Although we are reluctant to describe a film as an "organization of stimuli," we should recognize that we do have different sets for different types of motion pictures. The most significant distinction is between the *class* of responses we are ready to make to the experience of watching a motion picture: is it solely entertainment or a work of cinematic art?

This distinction is not, of course, clear-cut and is even controversial. A few definitions will clarify our discussion. An entertainment amuses or frightens or titillates us, but what it does not do is to challenge our views of ourselves and the world around us. We escape from rather than confront our emotions and ideas. When we leave an entertainment, time has passed pleasantly, but our psyches have been unaffected otherwise by the experience.

A work of art engages our feelings and intellect and arouses us to ask questions about the experience and to what degree it has influenced our world view. The greatest art even communicates to us insights into human nature that we might never have arrived at without its help. All works of art are entertainment in the sense that they hold our attention and cause us to move out of ourselves during the time that we respond to them. The crucial difference between art and entertainment, however, is the intensity of the experience in the case of art and, again, the effect it has on us after we are physically separated from it.

In cinema criticism there are no universally accepted terms that differentiate between a motion picture that is solely an entertainment and one that is a work of art. We will, however, follow the lead of John Simon in the introduction to his book of film criticism, *Movies and Film* (New York, 1971), and refer to the former as a movie and the latter as a film.

The borderline between movies and films is hidden in a forest of individual tastes and judgments. To complicate matters further, a movie may contain a moving and memorable scene and a film may have arid portions. Even if we agree that it is the effect of the motion picture as a whole that distinguishes the two types of cinema, there is still the problem of individual judgment. It is not unusual for one critic to evaluate a motion picture as an artistic masterpiece and another to dismiss it as a dull movie. The same diversity of opinions may occur when films of generally acknowledged value are compared with each other to establish their relative places in a hierarchy of artistic significance.

No more than in the other media that produce works of art does cinema criticism contain absolute criteria for judging between a movie and film or degrees of success within each category. There are even those who maintain that cinema is incapable of being an art. Some of their arguments are specious; others are disconcerting in pointing out the limitations of the motion picture medium. We do not have the space to engage in a defense of our position that cinema has and will continue to give us works of art, but we will make the following points: Critical judgment is always difficult in a popular medium, especially in the case of cinema, which has created far more movies than films. We should also keep in mind that the history of motion pictures is considerably less than a century old and serious criticism has appeared only during the last four decades. In addition, motion pictures are expensive to make (which restricts the possibility for experimentation with new ideas and techniques); specific works are not the creation of a single individual; and, most important, they are not as readily available as books are in print, paintings and photographs in reproductions, and music on phonograph records (a situation that could change radically when video cassettes are perfected).

What difference does it make, though, in viewing a motion picture if we consider it a movie or film? None, if an individual maintains the same sets whether listening to a symphony by Beethoven or tunes played by Guy Lombardo and his orchestra. Most of us, however, prepare ourselves to make a greater effort emotionally and intellectually when confronted by art than when exposed to entertainment.

The precept that an artistic work requires concentration and energy

is particularly important when one is distinguishing between films and
movies because many people have developed the habit of passivity when
viewing a motion picture. Stanley Kauffmann insists on this point in the
article, "Film Negatives," *Saturday Review of the Arts* (March 1973),
pp. 37–40, although he contrasts bad films and good films rather than
movies and films. He argues that the chief problem of film appreciation
is the ease with which a viewer can be seduced into an "aesthetic sloth."
"There is something of a whorehouse feeling about this film ease, a whiff
of lazy gratification in the darkness." On the other hand, "good films
reprove us for indiscriminate rump-plumping. Good films ask us to do
something in that seat, make demands on us, help dispel that brothel
lethargy (without destroying pleasure)." (Ibid., p. 37)

There are few cinema enthusiasts who have not discussed a significant
film with a person who insists, "I don't know what you're talking about.
It was just a movie." There is nothing wrong with movies in themselves.
There are times when we want only to be entertained, and there are few
media that can give us this type of pleasure with greater vitality than
movies. To ignore films, however, is to deny ourselves the more profound
experiences that they can offer. Motion pictures can never be anything
but movies for individuals who do not open themselves to the possibility
of being moved and influenced by what they see. And it is for this reason
that there is no more important principle than the sets we have when
viewing a motion picture.

Once this principle is accepted, it is evident why an individual should
prepare himself intellectually and emotionally before viewing a film. For
new films, one should read reviews by trusted reviewers. For older films,
articles and books can be enlightening. Later we will discuss the value
of understanding cinematic techniques, but now we will simply assert
that the more one knows about these techniques, the easier it is to appreciate what a film is attempting to communicate and to judge its significance to the viewer himself. In this respect, books, film classes, and
film clubs can help immeasurably. It is also important to learn the similarities and differences in purpose and approach of various film genre,
such as fictive narrative, documentary, cartoon, and abstract film. If it is
possible to do so, actually making a motion picture, no matter how
short, can teach one more about cinema than a dozen books and lectures.

Our prepared viewer is now ready for the second stage of viewing a
film—the experience itself. He has set himself to concentrate on the screen
and to be alert to all details; now is the time to use these faculties. To
look properly at a film, the viewer must as much as possible enter into
its rhythms and empathize with the emotions it generates. At the end
of a fine film, we may be exhilarated and emotionally charged, but we
also may be as happily exhausted as after, say, two hours spent in an art
gallery or at a concert.

There is a question often asked about experiencing a film. Should one analyze a film while seeing it? Our answer is one that not all will agree with. We believe that the *first* time an individual is viewing a film, he should not consciously consider what it is communicating or the techniques used. Anything that distracts from full, unswerving attention to the experience of the film itself should be rejected. This does not mean that a viewer will not mentally note an awkward scene or a particularly brilliant effect; it is simply that he should not dissect his reactions during the viewing. This process is reserved for the next stage, when he analyzes the film. We should mention, however, that the more experienced a person is in film viewing and the greater is his knowledge of cinematic techniques, the more details and devices he will notice. It seems that the mind develops a silent critical faculty that does not interfere with one's immediate responses to what is happening on the screen.

Because a film cannot be easily re-viewed, as in the case of a novel or a concerto on a phonograph record, memory is an essential tool in studying a motion picture. There is, as psychologists have proven, a direct correlation between memory and concentration. Here is another reason for developing the ability to focus all one's psychic energies on a film during viewing.

There is an approach that we recommend when viewing a fictive narrative film for the first time. This genre by definition contains a story. It makes no difference essentially if the story is as straightforward as in a film by Renoir or as diffuse and convoluted as often in one by Alain Renais. Although it will lessen suspense, it is worthwhile to find out the plot of a film before seeing it. It is even better to go through a script if one is available. Our justification for this suggestion is that plot is the most accessible element in a narrative film and knowledge of it allows a viewer to concentrate on other aspects while watching the film. Later it can encourage an analysis to move from "what happened?" to the more important questions of "why?" and "how?"

One naturally wants to see a significant film more than once. Each viewing will reveal new implications and subtleties. Hopefully, repeated viewings of a film will not dull the excitement of the original experience, but it is almost inevitable that an individual's critical faculties will operate with greater acuteness with every viewing. A person familiar with the over-all development of a film shifts his attention from the general to the specific, from the obvious to the elusive.

Ideally, a serious student of cinema should study a film after a first viewing on a Moviola or a similar instrument that allows him to slow down a print, even to a frame-by-frame speed. In that way he can peruse the miniature images and hear the synchronized sound. This is, however, not always possible, and most viewers must settle for taking advantage of every opportunity to see a worthwhile film more than once.

We have two recommendations for a person who is watching a film for the second time beyond the obvious one of reading any critical studies available. First of all, it is helpful to write in anticipation of that viewing and based on memory of an initial viewing a descriptive listing of the sequences that constitute the film and even a list of scenes within each sequence. Having a script in hand, of course, makes this exercise easier. The purpose is to expose the skeletal structure of the film; a sequence listing also helps to organize one's responses. Secondly, a person can make use of a portable cassette recorder during a second viewing. He can whisper into the microphone of the recorder—if this can be done without disturbing others—what he observes on the screen, such as details and techniques, and his own reactions. The value of this procedure is obvious. Not only does it aid one's concentration, but it is also an invaluable record for further study.

We are now ready to consider the third stage of viewing a film—the analysis after experiencing a film. Most of us enjoy discussing a motion picture that has excited us, yet we are often unsure of how to verbalize or to write about the experience. Perhaps we can best begin by stating our arguments against those who maintain that one should not go beyond personal, immediate responses to a film. We believe that if such responses go unexamined, in Socratic terms, then the individual is seeing without perceiving. Especially in a classroom, a supposed "analysis" of a film is very often only a justification of subjective reactions rather than a questioning, probing, and challenging of those reactions. Wordsworth may have been correct in asserting about art that to dissect is to kill. Equally restrictive, however, is the view that the mind plays no role in our appreciation of a work of art. As so often is the case with two extremes, a middle ground is the most productive. The original emotions and ideas aroused by a film must be preserved as much as possible, but now, in this third stage, they must be examined, studied, and placed in contexts that lift them from the immediate to the universal.

It is debatable just what critical apparatus one uses to dissect a film without killing primal responses to it that must always remain the foundations on which an analysis is based. Obviously, as the writers of a book of film analysis we have our own answer, which is both demonstrated and justified in the book itself. Because this volume, however, is confined to fictive narrative films, our comments will deal with this cinematic genre.

If there is one premise on which *Film and the Critical Eye* is based, it is that an analysis of a film must take into account both narrative elements and visual techniques—that the two are inseparable. Let us examine this premise.

A narrative is a series of events in time involving the relations of human beings to themselves, others, and their circumambient universe. It may describe events that have actually happened or are fictive (imagined by its creator). The narrative mode of expression has certain inherent characteristics that can be analyzed: there is a story or plot (the distinction, as E. M. Forster noted in *Aspects of the Novel*, is between a narration of events arranged in their time sequence and a narrative in which the emphasis falls on causality), characterization, conflict, themes, setting, symbols, and so on.

A narrative, however, can be communicated to an audience in various media and combinations of media. A narrative of, say, a hero on a quest can be told in a novel, poem, drama, motion picture, opera, or tone poem —to name only a few possibilities. Each form in which the narrative is cast can be explored in terms of the same elements of narration, but our experience of one form will not be the same as in another. Whatever the limitations and gains in each case, surely we respond in very different ways to the narrative of the journey of Siegfried in the medieval epic, Wagner's operas, Giraudoux's play (*Siegfried*), and Fritz Lang's film (*Siegfried's Tod*). The reasons do not have to be labored. Every medium that uses a narrative mode conveys the elements of the narrative in accord with the very characteristics that define the medium.

These generalizations will become clearer if we return to motion pictures. This medium has its own unique visual language and rhetoric (which, since the early 1930s, includes the dimension of the auditory). We usually do not realize how many cinematic techniques we have absorbed unawares. We take for granted the difference between physical time and cinematic time, the two dimensions of a screen, the effect of a close-up, a cut, or parallel development. A glance at history, however, can give us perspective. There was a chorus of critics who maintained that when Edwin S. Porter used a flat cut and D. W. Griffith cross-cutting, viewers would be completely confused. This opinion proved to be wrong and audiences soon learned to accept these cinematic principles and others that were developed.

Today an audience may have no difficulties with elementary techniques of motion pictures, but a serious student of film should go beyond these basics. He should recognize the differences in the impact of a shot or scene when a director uses a high camera angle or low angle, a stationary camera or dynamic cutting, a long shot or a close-up, parallel asynchronization of sound or counterpoint synchronization, shadows or complete illumination—or any of a dozen other devices of cinema language and rhetoric. We are not referring simply to an intellectual exercise in labeling techniques, but a means of appreciating the reasons for the choices that have been made in the creation of a film. This, in turn, leads to more perceptive analyses of films.

An aspect of the language and rhetoric of film, although it is sometimes viewed as a separate area, is the role of each component of a film in its production. Film making is a group activity that requires a director, producer, actors, scriptwriter, cameraman, lighting and sound directors, composer (if there is background music), set designer for interiors, editor, and many other artists and technicians. A director is the most important figure, for he must coordinate the activities of the others. Occasionally, a director, such as Chaplin or Welles, will assume more than one role. A familiarity with how motion pictures are put together cannot help but increase a viewer's awareness of the potentials and restrictions of the medium.

Now to sum up our recommendations for analyzing a film. First the viewer attempts to recall as completely as possible his original impressions. Next he reinforces, corrects, or adds to these responses by reviewing any notes he has taken, such as a listing of sequences and what has been recorded on a cassette tape, and by rereading a script and any other printed matter that deals with what actually appeared on the screen.

The analysis itself will have as its goal the discovery of what the creators of the film were attempting to communicate and how they did it. Solid foundations for a critical study of a film require knowledge of the elements of a mode of expression and the language and rhetoric of the film (including the roles of individuals in a team of film makers). There is not, of course, a direct ratio, only a relationship between the degree of this knowledge and the quality of an analysis, for the latter depends also on the experience, intelligence, and sensibilities of the viewer.

In the case of a narrative film, one can perhaps best proceed in an analysis by examining individually each element of narrative, yet at every point considering how an emotion or idea was conveyed cinematically. The viewer should also recognize that no one element is independent of the others, and the same applies to specific techniques.

Thus far we have offered only suggestions for analyzing a film as a self-sufficient entity without going beyond—except for developing critical apparatus—what the viewer experiences directly. To complete an analysis, however, another step should be taken. It is also worthwhile to explore an individual film in larger contexts that may give insights into the "why" as well as the "what" and "how" of a film. In other words, how do we interpret a film? We feel that this complex problem must be dealt with separately, and we do so in the next chapter.

CHAPTER 2

Interpreting a Film

We will use the phrase *interpreting a film* in a special, perhaps debatable, way here: it is the application of a system of ideas or methods from outside an individual film to illuminate the content and form inherent in that film and to focus our attention on aspects of it that we might otherwise not have noted or might have disregarded. In the previous chapter we limited our discussion of analyzing a film to the elements of a mode of expression as conveyed by the language and rhetoric of cinema. A film maker, however, is affected by the events of his day, his own experiences, and intellectual systems that attempt to explain—in fact, interpret—aspects of human existence. These forces, sometimes without the film maker being consciously aware of it, influence the multitude of choices the cinematic artist makes in creating a film.

Before considering the major categories of interpretation, we will deal at some length with one approach to illustrate what we mean by this phase of analyzing a film and to suggest some of the difficulties involved.

An individual who studies a narrative film and concentrates his attention on characterization—the motives of characters and how they determine the feelings and actions of these characters—is engaged in a psychological interpretation of that film. There are, however, movements in the field of psychology that assert certain premises about the makeup of the human psyche.

The psychological movement that more profoundly than any other has influenced twentieth-century man's view of the sources of his emotions and how they affect his feelings, thoughts, and actions is the psychoanalytic. The basic tenet of psychoanalysis, to put it in the baldest terms, is the existence of an unconscious portion of the mind that is interrelated to the conscious, waking, logical part of our mind, but has a dynamics of its own. These dynamics are revealed to us particularly in disguised forms in those experiences when our conscious mind has least control over our emotions, such as in dreams, daydreams, and hallucinations. Not long after the inception of the psychoanalytic movement, however, individuals rebelled against the dominance of the postulates of Sigmund Freud and established their own schools.

10

It soon became clear that the theories of psychoanalysis could be useful in exploring not only the creative process, both generally and in the case of individual artists, but also works of art. Because, however, there are various psychoanalytic schools, there are various ways of psychoanalytically interpreting a work of art, each with its set of premises, emphases, and methods. The ones that have proven most fruitful in this respect, named after their founders, are the Freudian, Jungian, Rankian, and Adlerian.

Film criticism, then, has available to it not only the possibility of a psychological interpretation of a film, but also, to limit ourselves to a single movement, more than one psychoanalytic approach. Two problems immediately become evident that are relevant not only to this specific type of interpretation but to any type. First of all, we have defined an interpretation as using "a system of ideas or methods" to analyze a film. It is obvious that one must have some acquaintance with that "system" before being able to apply it. In the case of a general psychological interpretation little background preparation is necessary. On the other hand, one cannot use, for example, a Freudian approach without a knowledge of the tenets of Freud's psychoanalytic theories. The greater this knowledge, the more likely one's comments will be perceptive and incisive.

The second problem is how appropriate a type of interpretation is for a specific film. Do some films by their very content and form limit the type of interpretation that can be brought to bear on them? There is an analogy that might be helpful in explaining our answer to the question.

The composition and possible uses of a chemical compound can be determined by testing it with a series of reagents. Often a positive reaction is indicated by a change in the color of the compound, and the degree of brightness of that color indicates the amount of a specific substance it contains. Applying this analogy to analyzing a film, we see that the material that an interpretation is attempting to bring to light may be so slight that there is no reaction or so little that it can be ignored. In other words, an interpretation can only reveal what is already present in the film and the rewards from some interpretations may be so negligible as to vitiate the value of the approach. We should be open, however, to what seems a farfetched possibility. It is conceivable that a Freudian interpretation of a work by Eisenstein or a Marxist analysis of one by Cocteau could increase a critic's and his readers' understanding and appreciation of the film.

Having considered some principles basic to a psychoanalytic interpretation of a film, we can proceed to two examples drawn from chapters in this book. In analyzing Jean Cocteau's *Beauty and the Beast,* one of the three interpretations we discussed was Freudian. In this instance, we supplied some pertinent background material. We believe that this approach could explain some enigmas in the film, such as why the same actor was assigned to play both the Beast and Avenant and why the two characters exchange places at the end of the film.

Beauty and the Beast suggests still another difficulty involved in using a specific interpretation. Cocteau emphatically denied that he intended to accomplish anything other than to retell a fairy tale in visual terms. One should rarely take Cocteau's declarations of intentions at face value, yet a fundamental question still remains: Can we apply a type of interpretation to a film that a director insists was not in his mind when he created the film? The answer, of course, is yes. A work of art is not entirely a product of conscious effort. There are innumerable examples in the criticism of all the arts of meanings being uncovered by critics of which the creator consciously was entirely unaware. A work of art once it has left the hands of its creator has a life of its own that we must respect. In addition, as we noted earlier, theories that are the foundation of an interpretation do not in themselves create realities, but elucidate from a special point of view an area already existing in the work of art. If an artist, such as Shakespeare, is true to human nature, he is exploring the same phenomenona, as, say, a Freud. All this is very obvious, yet it is surprising how often an individual who objects to a Freudian interpretation of a film will defend his position by arguing that the film maker has specifically written that he never read Freud.

In contrast to how we deal with background material in our discussion of *Beauty and the Beast* is our chapter on Ingmar Bergman's *Wild Strawberries*. There are no introductory pages beyond a plot summary. Although we mention such terms as *archetypes* and *anima,* only once in those pages do we specifically note that we are using a Jungian interpretation. This was done purposely to demonstrate a point that will become clear in a moment. It is necessary first to indicate here briefly some of the depth psychologist's premises that were the basis of our interpretation. This will also serve as an example of what we mean by background information.

Jung asserts that a portion of the unconscious can be creative for an individual (essentially different from Freud's view). Under certain circumstances this creative unconscious, especially through dreams, will launch a self-destructive person on a "night sea journey" through the world of his unconscious in which he will be forced to confront the repressions that have vitiated his positive energies; it may even reveal the means of breaking through his emotional blocks. In his dreams he will encounter potent symbols, such as an ominous "shadow figure." One of the most important of these archetypes is the "anima figure," a woman or women, who may guide him on his inner journey. Even if a person is changed by these experiences, a psychic transformation does not affect the reality in which the individual lives, only the way he reacts to that environment with renewed vitality.

Few of these concepts are referred to in the chapter on *Wild Straw-*

berries. A type of interpretation, then, does not have to be dogmatic, obvious, and bristling with references to the theories on which it is based.

Wild Strawberries gives us an opportunity to mention yet another aspect of this phase in analyzing a film. Any number of different interpretations of the same film are feasible; one does not exclude others. Although we used a Jungian approach to Bergman's film, we noted in our analysis of the sequences the material for a Freudian one that could be equally provocative. We have already mentioned that we included more than one critical framework for *Beauty and the Beast.* Another example is our examination of Jean Renoir's *Grand Illusion,* in which we discuss both sociological and political interpretations.

It may be superfluous to say so after the way we underscored this point in the previous chapter, but a viewer should justify his approach not only by references to the elements of a mode of expression, but also by cinematic techniques.

It should be equally obvious that a specific type of interpretation is usually applied to a whole film, yet may be confined to only a portion. Wajda's *Ashes and Diamonds,* for example, contains only two sequences that suggest that religion or the lack of it plays a role in the lives of the major characters. A religious interpretation of this film, although there is little material to deal with, is valid if it is consistent with other, more predominant themes.

We have explored the *psychological* interpretation both for its own interest and as a means of considering some problems concomitant with any interpretation of a film. Although we do not have the space to do equal justice to other types, we can at least indicate them. Once again, we will illustrate each one whenever possible by referring to chapters in this book.

In an *aesthetic* interpretation of a film, one goes beyond a concern with cinematic techniques to an exclusive attention to the language and rhetoric of cinema. Theories of perception and film aesthetics supply criteria for such an analysis. Few critics, except when dealing with an abstract film, will confine themselves to this approach—and we have not in this book—but some do make extensive use of it when examining a specific scene or sequence of a film.

In contrast to the accentuation on form in an aesthetic interpretation is the preoccupation of the *sociological* on content. Sociology is devoted to the study of human social behavior, especially the ways institutions and group attitudes influence individual responses. Many of the finest of films are concerned with this subject. In this type of interpretation, knowledge of the social conditions of the period that is the setting of a film can be essential. Only by understanding proletarian attitudes in post-World War I Germany and post-World War II Italy can a viewer achieve a balanced perspective on, respectively, Murnau's *The Last Laugh* and Olmi's *Il Posto.* The same holds true for the other end of the social scale, the aristocracy, in Renoir's *The Rules of the Game*. In fact, there are few films discussed in this volume that cannot be more acutely analyzed if one considers their sociological implications.

As psychology can be subdivided into a number of schools, so with sociology. Probably the most prominent in respect to cinema is Marxism, with its emphasis on class conflict. This social perspective can be excessively dogmatic and limiting. Yet, too much fascinating work has been done by Marxist film critics to be condescending toward it.

There is not a separation of form and content in a *generic* interpretation, but one may be emphasized rather than the other. We have already devoted enough space to the fictive narrative. Each of the other cinematic genres—such as the documentary (a form of nonfiction narrative), the newsreel, the cartoon, the nonrepresentational or abstract film, the avant-garde film (a vague phrase more useful for its connotative than denotative referents)—has its own set of theories and techniques that can serve as the basis for a type of interpretation.

The term "genre" is also employed to indicate a film maker's approach to his material rather than the form used. Tragedy, comedy, fantasy, farce, romance, and the epic are also considered film genres. If a reader is bewildered by the equivocalness with which this term and others are applied, he is not alone. In using the aesthetic nomenclature of any medium one must often depend on context and connotation rather than on indisputable definitions. In literature, for instance, an epic is a literary genre, but so is an essay. The terminology of film criticism, however, is especially imprecise. Perhaps when film theory and aesthetics grow to maturity the situation will change. Until that golden age, we will have to contend with terms that repeatedly metamorphose like miniature Proteuses when one tries to grip them firmly.

During its relatively brief history, the motion picture has developed a number of *cinematic movements*. The principles of most of these movements were derived from other arts and adapted to the cinema medium. This occurred with expressionism and surrealism, less so with neorealism and the new wave. A director is usually conscious of participating in a movement, although more often than not in partial and individual ways. The tenets of a specific movement may be indefinite and controversial, but information on the major ones is not difficult to find in books and articles. In this volume we discuss four cinematic movements and their manifestations in certain films. In the perspective preceeding our analysis of *Beauty and the Beast,* we define expressionism and surrealism; further comments on expressionism are to be found in the chapters on *The Last Laugh* and Lang's *M*. Neorealism and the new wave are dealt with in the pages on, respectively, *Il Posto* and Truffaut's *Jules and Jim*.

The final form of interpretation that we will mention here is based on *comparisons*. Under this rubric are included national films, types of films, and the works of a single director. These are vague headings, yet each category meets our criterion of supplying a framework outside of a specific film by which that film can be interpreted.

National characteristics do seem to influence the content and style of films produced in a country, whether it is Germany, Japan, or Brazil. And the more unfamiliar a viewer is with the national traits of a country, the more desirable it is that he obtain information on that country's customs, attitudes, and cinematic conventions. For this reason, an essay on "national cinema" is included in our analysis of Kurosawa's *Rashomon.*

Types of films and film genres are often confused. Earlier in this chapter we identified a genre by referring to its form (for example, fictive narrative, documentary, and cartoon) or its creator's approach (for example, tragedy, comedy, and fantasy). We now are categorizing films according to their predominant content. Some of the best known types are war, crime, political, religious, Western, musical. There is, naturally, a good deal of overlapping. It can be useful, however, particularly when focusing on themes and symbols, to interpret a film by comparing it to others of the same type.

Most directors are consistent in their style and approach, although the best directors also develop as they move from one film to another. Familiarity with a director's general style can increase an appreciation of his cinematic techniques in the specific film being viewed. For example, a recognition of Renoir's tendency toward filming a scene in lengthy shots with a stable camera in *Grand Illusion* can make us more aware of this technique in *The Rules of the Game.* The same holds true for a director's favorite themes and symbols. Our analysis of the theme of loneliness and emotional passivity in Bergman's *Wild Strawberries* can be more acute if we compare that film with his earlier *The Seventh Seal.* All four films are considered in this book.

As we indicated in the foreword to these two introductory chapters, we have not attempted to be comprehensive or prescriptive. We hope, though, that the reader will find some of our suggestions helpful in viewing a film intelligently. We have intentionally avoided the subject of judging a film, for we feel if an individual views a film with the discrimination, concentration, and background knowledge that we recommend, any judgment he makes will be judicious and worthy of a respectful hearing.

Part Two

The two chapters which follow are intended to introduce the reader to the language and rhetoric of film. The language is laid out in the form of a glossary, for convenience's sake; and even a cursory reading will make clear which items are worth studying before proceeding to Chapter 4—those entries which inform the student about basic concepts of screen size, camera movement, and so forth—and which entries are intended to complete a reasonably full reference guide.

From there, the student is taken, in Chapter 4, on a brief tour of how this language is rhetorically activated in cinema. It is a brief introduction to a complex subject, but like the glossary its examples are taken from the analyses in Part Three and this, it is hoped, will make for useful clarity.

The Language of Film

The language of cinema is the sum total of its basic resources, the means by which it achieves shots, action, movement, sound, music and other effects, and the editing devices whereby all these are articulated into scenes, sequences, and films. The verbal language we use to describe these various elements is for obvious reasons inadequate to denote the cinematic material. Nevertheless, it is absolutely essential that the student of cinema acquire this language. It is the means by which he can discuss what he sees and make formal inquiry into the structure and dynamics of individual films.

In order to facilitate the student's acquisition of this language we have chosen to define its terms in the following glossary. Wherever possible, we refer to graphic illustrations from the films in Part III of our text to make things clearer. We have also thought to include here other terms of interest to a film student, such as might enhance his basic grasp of the world of films and film making. Finally, the student should be aware that all the special film terminology employed elsewhere in the book is defined here.

Adapt: To translate an original story, novel, play or nonfiction work into a **screenplay** (q.v.) for the purpose of making a narrative film.

Angle: See **camera angle.**

Art director: The member of a film production staff responsible for the conception and design of all the decor and, also, frequently for selecting the natural **locations** (q.v.) used in a film. In this sense, he is an artist in his own right, and many film directors consistently employ the same art director for all their films.

Aspect ratio: The relationship between the width and height of a projected cinema image, expressed as a proportion or ratio. Thus, the aspect ratio of a square image is 1:1; that of a standard sound-film screen is 1.37:1 and that of the Cinemascope wide-screen process is 2.33:1. Contemporary film makers have frequently preferred to work in aspect ratios somewhere between standard and Cinemascope.

Auteur: A French word, meaning *author*. The auteur theory of film criticism, evolved primarily by the French film critics writing for *Cahiers du Cinéma* from the late 1940s onward, suggests that every film in a director's canon bears the characteristic imprint of his style or artistic vision, as these have been realized by the actors and technicians working under his control. In this sense, the theory goes, the film director is as much the true author of his own work as is a poet, a painter, a composer or any other artist. Andrew Sarris, among other American critics, uses the auteur theory as his standard of criticism; to a large extent, so do we. As auteur critics, however, we do not fall into what Pauline Kael says is the trap in this theory, that is, that the use of this single standard sometimes forces its exponents to praise bad films simply because they are the work of an auteur.

Background: That perpendicular picture plane farthest away from the camera, or, behind the subject in the **foreground** (q.v.).

Back lighting: When the principal source of illuminating the subject comes from behind so that its rays are directed at his back, back lighting is said to be employed. See p. 444, *Il Posto*.

Boom: A long, flexibly geared, lightweight metal arm, on the end of which is usually fixed a microphone with which sound technicians record **synchronous** sound (q.v.) during filming. Sometimes a lighting instrument is affixed to the end of a boom in order to achieve more flexible control of the lighting of a particular scene.

Camera: The subject for a book; basically, the instrument with which **shots** (q.v.) are made; a mechanism, usually employing an electric motor and a claw engagement device (with which to grip film perforations), to advance a continuous run of film past a photographic lens. Professional film makers usually (but not always) employ cameras equipped to record scenes with synchronized sound (dialogue, principally).

Camera angle: The position of the camera vis-à-vis the subject to be filmed. See also **high angle, low angle, eye level.**

Camera leading: Denotes a **moving shot** (q.v.), in which the camera tracks backward while the subject moves forward, keeping a constant distance between himself and the lens.

Moving camera: A shot in which the camera is transported from place to place, following or leading subject action. This is to be distinguished from other kinds of camera movement, notably the **pan** or the **tilt** (qq.v.) in which the camera does not move from place to place but only pivots on either the horizontal or vertical axis.

Subjective camera: A concept in which the camera's point of view is that of the subject. For a fuller discussion of this device, see Chapter 4.

Camera operator: A technician, a photographer, who operates the camera during the shot. He is to be distinguished from the **cinematographer** (q.v.).

Cheat shot: One in which an illusion is created "cheating" the spectator; for example, an actor leaps off a "cliff," but he is actually leaping into a net placed off camera; the cheat consists in the fact that the spectator does not know about the net and therefore thinks that the leap is a real one. See the discussion of **special effects** for *Beauty and the Beast*, Part Three, pp. 239–240.

Cinemascope: A wide-screen process distinguished by its very high **aspect ratio** (q.v.) of 2.33:1. This process is effective when the subject matter is appropriate—that is, for Westerns, epics, and so on, wherever mass action and sweep or movement are central to the narrative.

Cinematographer: Synonyms are director of photography and cameraman; sometimes also given in credits as "photographed by." The principal technician in a film crew, he is in charge of all photography, responsible for lighting and for the technical setting up of all shots. Working under the cinematographer's immediate supervision is the **camera operator** (q.v.).

Cinéma vérité: The antithesis of the staged narrative film, *cinéma vérité* denotes film documentaries shot with lightweight portable equipment as the subject's life unfolds. There is no restaging of scenes from "life" in order to enhance or dramatize the action beyond its natural state; there is no elaborate postproduction **dubbing** (q.v.) or other interference with the kind of cinema truth thus made available. Indeed, cinema truth is the meaning of the French phrase, adapted from the watchword of the Soviet pioneer Dziga Vertov.

Clip: A short section of film that has not been especially made for the work in which it appears. Thus the war sequences in *Jules and Jim* (q.v.) are newsreel clips. Clips are synonymous with **stock footage** when they are obtained from a film library.

Close-up: The term derives from the fact that with a normal lens fitted to the camera the subject must be close up to the lens in order to appear very large on the screen. When the subject, usually but not always the actor's face, fills the screen in such a way as to virtually exclude everything else, we have a close-up.

> **Extreme close-up:** A shot that gets closer to the subject than the **close-up** and therefore shows us less of that subject. In this shot, we are usually so close that part of the actor's face is beyond the edges of the **frame** (q.v.). Tight closeup is a synonym for extreme close-up and, although most of the films discussed in Part Three employ shots of this type, *Beauty and the Beast* has outstanding examples.

Composition: The arrangement of scenic elements, including actors, within the contours of the **frame** (q.v.). Composition is a principal means of directorial control of the medium.

Continuity: Sometimes used in lieu of story. Continuity also denotes the unbroken smoothness of transition from shot to shot and sequence to sequence so that the spectator's attention is not jarred.

Contrast: The range of the tonal scale between the darkest and lightest values of the photographic image. The image is said to show high contrast if this range is small, with very few graded tones, and low contrast when it is wide, with a large number of graded tones. High contrast is usually employed to reflect heightened levels of dramatic action and vice versa. See the first dream in *Wild Strawberries* for an example of this.

Craning: A type of camera movement effected by mounting the camera on the arm of a flexible crane. In order to follow action up a flight of stairs or over the edge of a cliff, a cinematographer must employ a crane.

Cross-cut: A synonym is **parallel editing.** A method of intensifying suspense by cutting *across,* back and forth, between one set of related actions and another. For fuller discussions see *M*, pp. 132–133 in Part Three and Chapter 4.

Cut: See **transition.**

Cutaway: See **transition.**

Dailies: See **rushes.**

Deep focus: See **focus.**

Depth of field: That property of a lens that holds subjects in focus through a depth (from foreground to background) of the field of view of the lens. The technique of **deep focus** photography depends on this property. See also **focus, selective focus,** and the discussion in Chapter 4.

Dissolve: See **transition.**

Documentary: A type of film that documents a state of affairs already in existence. Although the documentary can be and frequently is a form of non-fictive narrative, it is to be distinguished from fictive narrative by its purpose, which is to appeal not to the imaginative but to the discursive faculties.

Dolly: A transport for the camera in making **moving shots;** a vehicle for the **moving camera.** The word is often used as a verb—for example, "The camera dollies in on her face." See also **tracking, traveling shot,** and **trucking.**

Double: An actor used in place of a star, usually to perform physically hazardous action.

Dub, dubbing. To dub a scene is to record the dialogue of that scene and substitute it for the original sound (usually recorded in a foreign language); dubbing is also necessary where the original recording was faulty in some way.

Editor: The technician responsible for assembling and editing **shots** and **tracks** (q.q.v.) into the finished work in its final form.

Establishing shot: This type of shot pictures the subject at a considerable distance in order to *establish* it in its environmental context and thus provide the spectator with a model of where the action takes place. The term is sometimes used interchangeably with **long shot** (q.v.), but we take it to mean the **long shot** that begins the sequence, in order to distinguish it from one that does not establish a locale.

Exposure: The quantity of light permitted to fall on raw film stock for the purpose of laying down a latent image. Various degrees of exposure are used to control the surface texture, color, and density of the film and hence the quality of what is visible on the screen. Exposure is one means (lighting and type of stock are still other means) of controlling **contrast** (q.v.).

Expressionism: A wide-ranging and influential aspect of modern art and literature. Cinematic expressionism, which is unrelated to the larger modernist movements, is represented chiefly by Wiene's *The Cabinet of Dr. Caligari* (1924) and is characterized by the use of bizarre and distorted effects, chiefly in decor (settings, costumes, makeup, and so on) —but also in camera work—for the purposes of revealing and *expressing*, directly, interior states of mind and heart. For a fuller discussion, see the chapters on *The Last Laugh* (pp. 49–75) and *M,* (pp. 104–136).

Exterior: Representation of an outdoor—as opposed to an indoor (**interior,** q.v.)—scene.

Extra: An actor hired by the day to work in crowd scenes or wherever else background populations are needed.

Eye level: When the **camera lens** is positioned at the height of the eye of a standing person, we may say that the **camera angle** is at eye level.

Fade in, fade out: As the **camera** is running we close down the aperture of the lens, thereby gradually reducing the quantity of light exposing the film stock. The visible effect of this procedure, the gradual reduction of light and detail until the image is dark, is called a fade out. A fade in is the exact reverse of the effect. There are numerous examples of **fades** in the films discussed in Part Three.

Fantasy: In the psycholgical sense, an internal image—on the conscious level—of superb vitality, ambition, possibility. For its analogous denotation as a movement of narrative fiction films, see the "Perspective" to Chapter 10.

Feature film: A film of a certain length—in the United States at least 8,100 feet (of 35mm film) or 90 minutes—long enough to constitute the *feature* presentation on a film program.

Filter: A piece of optically ground glass whose function is usually to exclude certain bands of light from the visible spectrum and thus produce certain special effects, such as high contrast, low contrast, color saturation, **soft focus,** and so on.

Flashback: The return to a point earlier in fictional time than the present tense of the film action ongoing. Sometimes it refers to the brief repetition of a piece of prior action. In *Wild Strawberries* there are numerous flashbacks.

Focal length: The distance from the optical center of a lens to the plane of principal focus. It is an important property of a **lens** (q.v.).

Focus: To adjust the **lens** so that the subject image is most perfectly resolved into a sharply defined picture; when this is done, the picture is said to be in focus.

Deep focus: See Chapter 4.

Selective focus: Within the same shot, focus can be adjusted from a subject in the foreground to one in the background (or vice versa), thus affording the **cinematographer** the use of selective focus.

Soft focus: When the perfect degree of resolution of a picture in focus is slightly reduced to produce a degree of haziness in subject detail, the picture is said to be in soft focus.

Follow shot: Denotes the **shot** in which the **camera** follows behind, moving from place to place as its subject does. Examples of this kind of shot are found in the final sequence of *L'Avventura*, as Claudia wanders through the hotel in Taormina. See also **tracking, traveling shot, trucking,** and **moving camera.**

Footage: Length of film measured in feet.

Foreground: That perpendicular picture plane closest to the **camera** lens. See also **background.**

Frame: (1) A single transparent photograph of the series that is printed consecutively along the length of cinematographic film. (2) At any one moment the contours and area of the screen image.

Dynamic frame: Sometimes used to denote the effects of masking portions of the image and then either enlarging or diminishing the size and dimensions of the screen by more masking or by filling in with more picture the masked portions. See also **masking** and **iris effect** and the uses of these in *Jules and Jim* (p. 469), *The Gold Rush* pp. 98–99), and *The Last Laugh* (p. 57).

Freeze frame: A synonym is **frozen frame:** A single frame from a shot rephotographed for a certain length and then spliced into the sequence will produce the effect of stopped or frozen action. The effect is identical with that produced when a still photograph is filmed. It is a device with many aesthetic possibilities. See especially the work of Truffaut (*Jules and Jim*).

Reframe: Used to denote slight adjustments in **panning** and **tilting** in order to recompose an original staging **composition.** (See *Grand Illusion.*)

Grain: The experience of a pebbly texture. These are really particles of silver salts held in suspension in a photographic emulsion; that they are visible may be due to a number of factors. The deliberate production of a grainy surface texture is an element of aesthetic control.

High angle: A camera position vis-à-vis the subject in which the **camera** is angled downward from the horizontal; the camera height may be just a foot or two higher than the subject height, as is usually the case in a **close-up,** or it may be hundreds of feet higher, as is the case of **establishing** a **long shot** of, say, a whole town. In *M*, Fritz Lang employs high-angle shots to such an extent that they become a visual motif. See p. 136.

Insert: A tight (or extreme) close-up, usually of an inanimate object, or sometimes a part of the body—a hand or a foot—*inserted* into a sequence for normal dramatic purposes. When, in *Wild Strawberries*, Isak looks at the watch his mother is offering to him, we cut to an insert of it.

Intercut: See **cutaway.**

Interior: Used to describe a scene taking place indoors.

Iris effect: The progressive widening and growth of a tiny circular spot in the center of a black screen until the whole picture is revealed to cover the screen is called an **iris in.** The **iris out** is the reverse: a very large circle begins to appear around the outer edges of the **frame,** and, closing down to a tiny circular spot, blacks out the screen entirely. The effect has an emphatic function: it calls the viewer's attention to whatever image it either reveals or blacks out. An uncommonly uesd effect in films nowadays, it was frequently used during the period of silent films. (See *The Gold Rush* and *The Last Laugh.*)

Jump cut: When a segment of film is removed so that a character moving toward a destination need not—now that the section is removed—traverse the distance toward his destination, we may say that the resulting transition is a jump cut. It has *jumped* across space to save time.

Lens: A transparent glass refracting medium, bounded by two surfaces, one curved and the other either flat or curved, its purpose is to concentrate or disperse light according to certain optical laws. The student of cinema should bear in mind two special properties of lenses. Those of relatively long **focal length** (q.v.) (that is, telephoto lenses), in addition to bringing distant action closer, have (1) a relatively shallow **depth of field** and (2) produce a foreshortened perspective: background and foreground seem closer toegther than when seen by the naked eye. On the other hand, wide-angle lenses have relatively short focal lengths and are used to record action over a wider **field** than is permitted by long focal length lenses. They tend to (1) have a very great depth of field and (2) elongate perspective so that foreground and background seem closer together than when seen by the naked eye. See *Il Posto*, pp. 442–443 for a discussion of how the long focal length lens is used.

Location: A real environment used for filming, as opposed to studio settings especially made for such purposes. Documentary films, needless to say, are always made on location. Fiction films or parts of them are sometimes made on location as well.

Long shot. See **shot.**

Low angle: A camera position vis-à-vis the subject in which the **camera** is angled upward from the horizontal. The height of the **camera lens** is lower than the subject and is looking up at it. This is a frequently used camera angle; it sometimes produces distortion: the subject seems to tower above the spectator.

Main title: The card containing the title of the film; sometimes used to designate titles and credits at the start of the film.

Mask, masking: The phenomena associated with the **dynamic frame** (q.v.). See the masking effect in *Jules and Jim.*

Medium shot: See **shot.**

Montage: Also called **dynamic editing.** The art of building up a sequence out of short strips or shots in such a way as to analyze space and time, synthesizing the separate shots into something more than their mere sum. A crucial element in the rhetoric of film. See Chapter 4, Part Two, for a full discussion.

Motion: See in Chapter 4, "Motion," for a full discussion.

> **Fast motion:** A synonym for **accelerated motion.** The illusion of motion taking place at a greater speed than normal. The opposite of **slow motion.**
>
> **Reverse motion:** When a shot is printed in reverse order the effect is to reverse the motion within the frame. This technique is frequently used for comic or bizarre effect. See the discussion in *Beauty and The Beast,* p. 289.
>
> **Slow motion:** The illusion of motion taking place at a slower rate than normal. The opposite of **fast** or **accelerated motion.**

Moving shot: When the **camera** is transported from place to place keeping pace with moving action. See also Chapter 4, "Motion."

Moviola: The trade name for an editing console which is capable of producing a small image of the picture track and the synchronous sound that goes with it; the value of such a console is its capacity to vary speed and reverse motion with extreme ease, thus facilitating the whole exacting process of film editing.

Negative: Raw stock, when it is exposed and developed, produces a negative image from which **positives** are produced. Occasionally, negatives are projected in order to produce **special effects** (q.v.).

Neorealism: See the "Perspective" to Chapter 17.

New Wave: A translation of the French *nouvelle vague.* For a discussion of this movement, see the "Perspective" to Chapter 18.

Nonsynchronous sound: See **sound.**

Pace: A measure of the rhythm of movement, usually applied to editing. When relatively short (or progressively shorter) strips of film are spliced together, the effect is a fast pace. The opposite procedure produces a slow pace. A synonym for **tempo.**

Pan, panning: When the camera is moved about the vertical axis, we have a pan or a panning shot.

360° pan: A **panning shot** in which the **camera** revolves a complete circle about its vertical axis. The shot of the "Steamboat Engine" girl in *Jules and Jim* is a 360° pan.

Point-of-view shot: A synonym for **subjective shot.** The second in a sequence of two shots, as follows: (1) close-up of character; (2) wider shot of what he sees.

Print: A positive piece of film. A copy of a whole film. Many prints are made for release and distribution to exhibitors. Also the usable **take** (q.v.).

Production: a synonym for a film while it is in the phase of principal photography or shooting.

> **Preproduction:** That phase of making a film in which the script is being prepared, actors engaged, shooting schedules determined, decor being designed, and all else done preparatory to entering production or the phase of principal photography.

> **Postproduction:** That phase of film making after principal photography has been concluded; during postproduction, the film is edited, sound effects and music tracks are assembled, and the completed film is brought to its release stage.

Projection: The act of running the film through a projector so that it appears on the screen. Modern sound films are run at a projection speed of 24 frames per second (fps), the same speed at which they are shot. Because silent films were shot at 16 fps, they give the illusion, when projected at 24 fps of **fast** or **accelerated motion.** (See *The Last Laugh* and *The Gold Rush.*)

Reaction shot: Usually a silent closeup of a character recording his reaction to some narrative turn of events.

Realism: For a brief discussion of this term as it is ordinarily used, see the "Perspective" to Chapter 17; for a special viewpoint on realism, see the "Perspective" to Chapter 10. Of course, in its most popular usage, realism is what we all possess in great abundance.

Rear screen projection: Projection of a film clip onto a screen from behind the screen or, in certain cases, from overhead. The purpose is usually to provide a moving background against which actors working in a studio setup can be photographed. The technique is frequently used when a moving vehicle is to be depicted and synchronous dialogue is recorded. In *Wild Strawberries* the car scenes are done with rear screen projection. This is not the case, however, with the moving car shots in *L'Avventura.*

Reduction print: A print of a narrower gauge than the original from which it has been struck; an example would be a 16mm print from an original 35mm master. Students nearly always see reduction prints in 16mm. The reduction almost always results in some loss of surface quality in the picture and clarity in the sound.

Reel: A standard size spool, or the amount of film that can be wound onto it; in 35mm film this amount is 1,000 feet, or slightly more than 11 minutes of projection time. The 16mm equivalent is 400 feet.

Rushes: The prints of takes that are made on completion of a day's shooting; these are immediately projected for the director and staff so that a close check can be made on the progress of the work. A synonym for **dailies.**

Rhythm: See Chapter 4, passim, for a full discussion of this term.

Scene: We use the term in Part Three to designate a series of actions or shots in the narrative that tend to form a single unit for reasons having to do with locale or narrative movement. Also, a piece of continuous action; a convenient designation for parts of a screenplay.

Screenplay: Synonyms are **scenario** and **shooting script.** The form in which a film story is cast so that a director can realize it on film.

Screen ratio: See **aspect ratio.**

Sequence: The major division of a film; refers to the sequential order of shots, but it also refers to scenes which together form a single phase of narrative action or continuity. See the sections in Part Three, "Analysis of Major Sequences."

Shoot: To photograph.

Short: A film whose length is less than 3,000 feet of 35mm film (roughly less than half an hour). Films longer than this, although not **feature** length, are not shorts, either; but they are seldom made except for television.

Shot: The unit out of which scenes and sequences are made; the strip of film made from a single uninterrupted running of the camera, regardless of movement by the camera or the subjects.

>   **Long shot:** A type of shot in which the subject is pictured at a considerable distance; human figures must be fully visible, from head to toe, for the shot to qualify as a long shot. See also **establishing shot.**

>   **Medium shot:** Action is pictured in this shot considerably closer than in a long shot. Human figures are seen at least from the knees up in a medium shot.

>   **Three shot:** One in which three people are pictured, usually in a medium shot or closeup.

>   **Two shot:** One in which two people are pictured, usually in a medium shot or close-up.

Slate: A synonym for **clapsticks.** A slate board, set in a wooden frame, with a piece of hinged wood at the top; the hinged portions are set with painted lines that join at an acute angle when close together. The two pieces of wood are clapped together at the start of a scene in which synchronous sound is recorded in order to permit synchronization of sound and picture tracks. The scene number is recorded on the slate itself. The whole is necessary to keep orderly control over the cinematic materials.

Soft focus: See **focus.**

Sound: Refers usually to the natural sounds indigenous to a particular scene—for example, footsteps, breathing, crowd and traffic noises, the wind, and so on. To be distinguished from dialogue and music, which are also recorded and finally mixed together onto a single **sound tract.** See the section, "Perspective," in Chapter 7.

> **Nonsynchronous sound:** The principal nonsynchronous sound is dialogue. Some purists of film criticism and theory, notably V. I. Pudovkin, have always insisted that nonsynchronous sound is the only sound appropriate to artful film works.

> **Synchronous sound:** Dialogue recorded and synchronized exactly to the lip movements of the actors who produce it.

Special effects: Any unusual effect introduced into the texture of a film, whether by means of laboratory opticals or special work on objects to be photographed during the normal course of principal photography. See pp. 239–240, for a discussion of the special effects in *Beauty and the Beast.*

Speed: Gauging motion. See **projection** and "Motion" in Chapter 4.

Staging: The manner in which the movement of actors and objects is designed into the scene or sequence; a matter of in-frame movement and positioning.

Static: Stationary; a term applied to a shot in which the camera has been locked into position; without movement.

Still: A photograph of some moment in the action or behind-the-scenes production of a film. Where the still pictures some moment in the action, the action has been especially staged for the still camerman; a still is generally not taken from the actual cinematographic picture track for technical reasons. The illustrations in Part Three are all stills.

Stop-action photography (stop-motion photography): The technique of photographing objects one frame at a time (the motion of the camera is stopped after a single frame), at regular but lengthy intervals, permitting great changes in the object being photographed. An often seen example is that of a plant or a flower; seen in stop motion photography, the growth seems phenomenal because it is instantaneous. See p. 239 for a discussion of stop-action effects in *Beauty and the Beast.*

Structural rhythm: See Chapter 4, "Motion."

Studio: A place where interior settings are built for the purposes of film making. The property of a film production company.

Subjective camera: A pattern of usage of camera angle and point of view such that a spectator experiences the visual images as primarily the subjective view of a particular character. See Chapter 4, "The Iconography of the Frame," and the discussion on pp. 72–73, *The Last Laugh.*

Subjective shot: See **point-of-view shot.**

Subtitle: The translation of foreign dialogue inserted across the bottom of the frame. The alternative to subtitles is **dubbing** (q.v.).

Surrealism: A 20th century movement in several arts which finds a heightened sense of reality in the objects of subconscious mental activity as these are directly represented. For a discussion of this movement as a film movement, see the "Perspective" to Chapter 10.

Swish pan: A panning shot (real or apparent) at very high speed; a form of transition between shots. (See *Jules* and *Jim.*)

Synchronous sound: See **sound.**

Take: A single trial run of a shot made during production. Because several trials are usually made before one or more satisfactory recordings are made, each trial is given the designation of take and a number—for example, **take ten.**

Tempo: A synonym for **pace.**

Tilt: A movement of the **camera** around its horizontal axis. The camera is tilted up or down; sometimes the expression **pan** or **panning shot** is used to designate all movements of the camera (pans and tilts) that do not involve transporting it from place to place.

Time: Students of cinema should think long and hard about this seemingly obvious concept. First, there is **objective time,** a measure of so-called objective reality. Its chronological progression in a linear and irrecoverable direction affords an index to the order (or disorder) of events. Then there is **psychological time,** which is altogether different, for it is an index to wishes and personal freedom. Both kinds of time are treated in narrative films, in a judicious mixture ordinarily; sometimes, however, films pursue the elusive psychological time to the exclusion of the objective world. Time in *Wild Strawberries,* for example, is principally of the latter variety.

Screen time is simply the time it takes the length of any film to run its course. *Narrative time* is different from screen time, in that the latter usually condenses the former. There are, however, exceptions even to this rule. (See, for example, the discussion of "Style and Approach" in *L'Avventura,* Part Three, pp. 427–429.)

In any case, objective time makes history and psychological time makes character. The student of cinema must build his filmic notions with both.

Title Cards: Cards containing printed material. These are then photographed in order to provide information to an audience that cannot be otherwise conveyed. A device of the silent screen. (See *The Gold Rush* and Truffaut's more modern use of this device in *Jules and Jim.*)

Track, tracking: A verb describing the **moving camera.** It derives from the fact that the wheeled vehicle for conveying the camera was frequently fitted into and moved along special tracks. Synonyms are **trucking, traveling,** and **moving, dollying.**

Transition: Any method of going from shot to shot. The generic name for this movement.

    Cut: The simplest transition: simply the joining of two strips of film. The value of this type of transition can range from the smooth and imperceptible to the sharpest of impact—depending on the particular pieces of film to be joined.

    Cutaway: A shot to which the major sequential shots of a scene are joined, usually as a means of relief from the concentration of cinematic material in that scene. A good example occurs in *Wild Strawberries*: as soon as the journey in the car begins, Isak and Marianne speak and are pictured in a series of close-ups and two shots; when a dramatic moment is reached, there is a cutaway to a moving shot, angled up from the road to catch the trees and sunlight overhead. The purpose is to release or relax dramatic tension.

    Match cut: A shot that *matches* in size or composition the preceding shot in the sequence. A good example would be a series of cuts featuring two people facing each other in conversation. Each cut in such a sequence would be a match cut. The value of the match cut is close association or linkage.

    Dissolve: The overlap of the end of one shot and the beginning of another in such a way that the first shot is fading out and the second is fading in. The effect is of the first shot *dissolving* into the second. The value of the dissolve is a softening; very often it connotes a lapse of time, and at other times simply a softening of mood. There are numerous examples of this discussed throughout Part Three.

    Match dissolve: Where locale or camera angle is fixed and a lapse of time is to be indicated, the match dissolve is valuably employed. See the excellent example in *Wild Strawberries*, where Isak's view of his family's old summer house is changed through a match dissolve into a place in a flashback.

    Wipe: In this form of transition, a line or margin moves across the screen, eliminating one shot and revealing the other as it trails behind the line. Artful use of the wipe is made by Kurosawa in *Rashomon*.

Voice over: A voice heard over the picture which is not the synchronous speech of a participant in the scene. It may, however, be the non-synchronous voice of such a participant. For example, in *Wild Strawberries* we hear Isak's voice in this manner and in *Jules and Jim* we hear Jim's.

Zoom: The action of a variable focal length lens. Almost always the sudden change of focal length, the movement into a close-up or out to a long shot from a close-up, has the value of dramatic impact. This type of lens is a relatively modern invention, but the effect was used with remarkable success by F. W. Murnau in *The Last Laugh*.

CHAPTER 4

The Rhetoric of Film

The student of cinema who has begun to understand the language of film must now confront the means by which this language is best employed for the artistic purposes of individual works; that is, he must confront the rhetoric of film. This is by no means, however, a closed body of knowledge; it is, rather, a constantly expanding corpus of information and principle on how language becomes expression. As each new masterwork enters the canon of cinema art, the rhetoric of this art is enriched. Sometimes new rhetorical ideas are added and sometimes old ones are seen to have fresh possibilities in them. In any case, it should be understood that the rhetoric of film is not proscriptive. Art flows from sources that are unregenerately outside the law.

It should also be understood that the rhetoric of film is very large indeed. It may seem commonplace to say so, but we think it bears repeating that the art of a particular film consists in its rhetorical employment of *all* the elements that enter into its making: actors, outdoor locations, studio interiors, natural sound, dialogue, music, camera setups, editing, staging and composition, and the iconography of the frame. However, we will, in this chapter, be concerned with discussing these elements under four main headings: (1) motion; (2) montage versus deep focus; (3) the iconography of the frame; (4) tracks: dialogue, effects, and music. Thus, we would also remind the student that these matters are also discussed—where applicable—in the chapters of Part Three, which are devoted to individual films, especially in the sections "Analysis of Major Sequences" and "Style and Approach."

Motion

Motion is clearly the most convenient—indeed, the essential—rubric under which to begin our discussion. For film is above all a temporal art, even more so than are the arts of theater, opera, dance, or music. This is so because, as Rudolph Arnheim has pointed out, the motion picture "shows changes in time . . . it looks different every moment" (from his 1934 essay, "Motion," in *Film As Art*, Berkeley and Los Angeles: 1969, p. 181). This is quite a different proposition than the different moments encountered in theatre, opera, and dance, where the possibilities for changed looks are severely limited by the fixity of the stage setting, and different also from music where, because of its very nature, "differences" are blunted by the necessity to recapitulate theme in a regular pattern. What this difference means is that cinema is inherently motile.

The experience of motion in film is induced in the spectator by three essential elements: (1) in-frame movement by subjects—characters, animals, vehicles, vegetation, and so on; (2) the effect of the moving camera; and (3) the effect of editing; the ways in which strips of film (shots) are assembled and edited into what Arnheim calls "an over-all composition of motion" (ibid., p. 182). We might add that the experience of motion is intensified by the ways in which shots, in themselves depicting various kinds of motion, are joined together to synthesize new harmonies or atonalities of movement.

Now the values associated with motion are naturally linked to life. Thus, motion tells us what is happening in a film: a car is moving along a road, a character is walking into a building. But it also defines the quality of those events: speed suggests haste, excessive speed possibly frenzy and desperation. The car careening around a corner and a man running into a building are models for easy interpretation—based on motion within the frame. The drama in deliberate motion—seen on the screen at the appropriate moment—is a commonplace of film rhetoric known to all who have ever seen, say, a Hitchcock film. The student who contrasts the movement patterns of *Jules and Jim* with those of *The Caretaker* will at once grasp this point.

The case of the moving camera is somewhat different and calls for a little more consideration. The importance of this addition to the repertoire of film rhetoric cannot be overestimated. (See "Style and Approach" for *The Last Laugh*, pp. 72–75.) The employment of the moving camera provides, in a way, a method of staging sequences that defies montage and offers an alternative to it. With a moving camera (one that moves from place to place, as distinguished from a camera that pans or tilts along its axes) we can *move*—without cutting from separate shot to separate shot—from long shot to medium shot to close-up, or even closer to an extreme close-up. The implications in this possibility are enormous and the selection by the director of one or another of these possibilities is crucial. (See the subsequent section, "Montage versus Deep Focus." To be sure, deep focus is possible with a static as well as a moving camera.) Yet the moving camera of such masters as Murnau, Hitchcock, Renoir, Welles, Ophuls, and others serves another purpose as well. (But see in this volume discussions of the moving camera as it pertains to Ophuls, Renoir, and Murnau, in Part Three.)

The moving camera is a means of linking subjects together in a thematic way. Consider, for example, that Renoir, in *Grand Illusion,* makes use of the moving camera wherever it is possible to link up captors and captured, prisoners and masters, in order to make the point that such antithetical groups have more in common with each other than conventional thinking allows. Consider the sequence in Rauffenstein's squadron mess. The lengthy opening shot of this sequence, showing Germans and Frenchmen sitting down to eat together, is a model of fluid motion and amply demonstrates that the artful use of the moving camera is able to make such linkages. (See pp. 143–144 for a fuller discussion of the scene.)

The opening shot of *The Last Laugh* accomplishes a similar linkage: the camera, descending with the moving open-cage elevator in the hotel lobby, persists in adhering to its subject, as if linking him with the flood of busy action in the foreground of the shot and thereby declaring that the Doorman is an inextricable part of the environment we are seeing.

In Max Ophuls' *La Ronde,* the moving camera serves still another function. In the episode entitled, "The Girl and the Soldier," a single moving shot embodies most of the action; it carries the action back and forth in a plane perpendicular to the direction of view of the camera and thus creates a pattern of motion—a tidal ebb and flow, so to speak—that *embodies* the flow of the narrative: first we think they *will* get together (the Whore and the Soldier) and then we think they will *not* and then they *will* and so forth.

The variable focal length or zoom lens—a modern addition to the technical repertoire—also induces the experience of motion. Like the moving camera, the zoom lens is capable of altering, by moving, the size of the shot from long to medium to close. Almost invariably, however, the zoom lens is used dramatically: movement from long shot to close-up, or vice versa, is accomplished with speed; the effect is shock or high impact. On the other hand, panning and tilting, the movement of the camera about its axes, are usually slower processes (except for the swish pan, see Chapter 1); the slow movement of a pan or a tilt up or down invariably suggests, in addition to the kind of linkages described (with relation to the moving camera), revelation. A kind of suspense is produced when a slow pan directs the spectator's eye round a setting to reveal—*what?*

On the experience of movement due to editing rhythms we could, in justice, write a book—so large is the subject and so complex are the possibilities. We will, however, limit ourselves to a discussion of the subject under the following rubric.

Montage versus Deep Focus

Montage is a term that needs defining at once. (Later, we will of course take up the question of deep focus.) In a narrow sense, a montage is an impressionistic sequence consisting of a number of shots, usually with high impact value and containing strong visual rhythms, for the purpose of bridging a time gap within a film by only briefly indicating the kinds of events that took place during the interval. We will *not* be concerned with that kind of montage. What we mean by the term is what Serge Eisenstein meant when he employed it. (See his *The Film Sense*, 1942, and *The Film Form*, 1943, passim.) That is, we are talking about the juxtaposition of two or more pieces of film (shots) in such a way that the sum total of meaning is greater than the meaning in the individual parts would lead one to believe. In Eisenstein's words, "the juxtaposition of two separate shots by splicing them together resembles not so much a simple sum of one shot plus another shot—as it does a *creation*." (*The Film Sense*, translated and edited by Jay Leyda, New York, 1942, p. 7.)

The principles of montage as set out by Eisenstein and, since his time, by many others are many; but no single set is entirely satisfactory. Let us, therefore, reiterate here a classic Eisensteinian example and then arbitrarily set out a few very clear (perhaps the only satisfactory) principles that account for the motion quality of montage. Eisenstein's example is that of the two shots, one a grave and the other a woman in mourning clothes weeping beside it. The Soviet master of the cinema points out that *woman, grave*, and *mourning clothes* are all representations: all are visually representable. What is *not* representable, however, is the spectator's inference that the woman is a widow and that the grave might be her husband's.* *Widow* is not representable—except with dialogue. In this case, therefore, it is the third thing—that which is more than the mere sum of the shots. Similarly, the hunt sequence in *The Rules of the Game* builds the same kind of logarithmic increment in meaning: first a shot of a bird flushed from a copse of birches, then a shot of a hunter swinging his rifle into position and firing; result: the hunter has killed the bird, his bullet has penetrated the animal; the animal has flown, or tried to fly, from impending death.

Let us now consider those movement principles in terms of our two examples. (1) In the case of the woman and the grave we might join relatively longish strips (shots); the result would be a relatively slow tempo or pace, in keeping with the theme of mourning, loss, time, and so on. But (2) we would—as Renoir has—join relatively brief shots in the hunt sequence, creating a fast and suspenseful tempo, in keeping with the themes of terror, chase, and death. (3) If we were to vary the length

---

* It is worth noting here that a very important property of silent film action is here brought to our attention. As Eisenstein correctly points out, the fact that the woman is a widow is an inference, but *other inferences* are possible. As he notes, by referring to a section of the Ambrose Bierce story, "The Inconsolable Widow," from the author's *Fantastic Fables*, the woman could be mourning for a lover and not a husband. In other words, it is worth bearing in mind that the rhetoric of cinema, unlike the inherent capacity of language, does not point directly to an unambiguous meaning. Meaning may, and most often does, reside in the mind of the spectator, his choice depending on the structure of his own imagination.

of the shots, joining pieces of decreasing length, we should get an even greater tempo of suspense and psychological anxiety. We should then cause the acute experience of being on the edge of our seats, so to speak, familiar to anyone who has ever watched a thriller.

A particular kind of montage, which illustrates very well this process of great motion and great inferential power, is called cross-cutting. (For a close analysis of a sequence that employs cross-cutting, see pp. 114–116 of *M*, in Part Three; in the same chapter, pp. 132–133 contain a further theoretical discussion.)

Cross-cutting is also known as parallel editing, parallel development, or shots in counterpoint, but we shall employ the term cross-cutting here to avoid confusion. In this type of montage, two separate series of actions that are nevertheless intimately related but out of touch with one another are alternately pictured on the screen. The prime example of such a procedure, seen on movie screens the world over, is the almost obligatory scene in the Western in which the hero is pursuing one course of action— frequently tracking down his opposite number—while the villain is pursuing another. The suspenseful question, as we cross-cut from one course of action to the other, is what will happen when these two come together? One interesting variant from the same genre is the case in which the heroine or some other innocent third party, who is perhaps also in some danger, is the goal prized by both hero and villain. In such a case, the cross-cutting turns the screw of the suspense created around the question: who will get there first? Because cross-cutting is so commonly employed, its enormous value may go by unappreciated. Therefore, the reader will do well to consider how this device opens up the possibilities of space-time analysis in narrative films and how unique it is to have such a device in the arts of the twentieth century.

But as central as is montage to the rhetoric of cinema, it has its limitations. And these limitations can be most readily seen when we consider montage alongside the possibilities inherent in what we will refer to as deep focus staging or full-shot photography.

Deep focus, or in-depth, photography (or shots) can be distinguished from montage by an example from the English film *Where No Vultures Fly*. It is cited by André Bazin in his essay, "The Virtues and Limitations of Montage" (in his *What Is Cinema?* essays selected and translated by Hugh Gray, Berkeley and Los Angeles, 1967, p. 49). A young couple in South Africa, having organized a game preserve, are living in the bush with their only child, a little boy. He wanders away from camp, however, and, mindless of the danger, picks up and starts to play with a little lion cub. Meanwhile, the lioness discovers it missing and starts to follow along after the little boy. Finally, the little boy having reached the camp, we are shown the parents—who now see the little boy and the lioness about to spring at the kidnapper of the cub. At this point, *after* the story has been told in a sequence of shots—in montage, in short—we are shown a full shot of what Bazin prefers to call the dramatic space: lioness, child and cub, and distraught parents.

It should be clear now what the difference is between montage and deep focus styles; it should also be fairly obvious that directors are never committed to using one or the other in their films with rigid exclusivity. The point is that each style has its values and its limitations and these are worth discussing here.

Suggesting that deep focus is suitable for certain subjects where montage is not, Bazin, in the same essay, notes that "Above all, certain situations can only be said to exist cinematographically to the extent that their spatial unity is established, especially comedy situations that are based on the relations between human beings and things." (Ibid., p. 52.) The reader need only recall the many situations in which Chaplin is to be found in relation to "things" to see how right Bazin's formulation is. In *The Gold Rush*, for example, Chaplin is involved with a giant chicken, a teetering house, a bear, a storm, a ship, and piles of snow—in his canon, the list of objects is virtually endless. Slapstick comedy, in fact, is a whole genre in need of the shot in-depth to be fully realized.

The comic action of *The Rules of the Game*, especially the farcical materials in the final sequence at the chateau, is admirably suited to deep focus stylistics and is treated that way with elegant skill by Jean Renoir. (See the discussion of that style in *The Rules of the Game*, in Part Three, pp. 201–202 and also in the chapter on *The Gold Rush*, pp. 102–103.)

But what of Bazin's example in *Where No Vultures Fly?* Bazin's point is that the full-shot treatment of the little sequence of a child in danger and the consequent parental concern is crucial. He insists that the question must revolve around whether the "episode was shot with due respect for its spatial unity. Realism here resides in the homogeneity of space." (Ibid., p. 50.) There is no question but that his point is well taken. Montage in such sequences *does* have an element of trickery about it and the spectator's belief in the reality of the dilemma may be sharply challenged by his not being shown the factors of the drama within the same frame.

We would not perhaps follow Bazin in formulating, as he has done, his analysis into a rule: " 'When the essence of a scene demands the simultaneous presence of two or more factors in the action, montage is ruled out.' " (Ibid.) But we should agree that the presence of characters and stakes—what Bazin calls factors—in the same frame are crucial stylistic choices to be made by the film director.

Such a choice has as its primary value what Bazin calls due respect for spatial unity; secondly, and perhaps in our view, more important, it has due respect for dramatic unity. Two examples from the films discussed in Part Three will make the point clear. In *Rashomon*, when the Bandit first sees the Samurai and his Wife riding the great white horse, he is asleep underneath a tree. As the couple goes past him, Kurosawa chooses a shot in depth, such that the camera must pan with his look (at the couple); it continues to hold the Bandit in the foreground of the frame and picks up the couple as they go past and recede into the background. The choice of the shot is impeccable, partly because it holds the factors in the same frame; it reinforces and actually embodies the narrative point being made at that moment by the Bandit's story of his transgression: that he needed desperately to have that woman, the Samurai's Wife. What an enormous difference there would have been in our experience of the scene had Kurosawa insisted on a series of cuts from the Bandit to the couple—regardless of how dynamic these had been!

A second example is from *The Rules of the Game*. This is a static shot, in the chateau, picturing in long shot the corridor outside the bedrooms upstairs. The guests who have gathered for the fete are bidding each other goodnight with a great display of manners and a superb charge of *élan* while servants are scurrying back and forth discharging various duties. We see the whole of it from a fixed camera position. It is a slightly high angle and we can see the whole of the action as figures come toward us and race away. The panoply of guests and servants, lovers and friends, nasty tempered old men and vacuous young women is a true picture—because they are seen in the same frame. In both cases, that of the shot from *Rashomon* and the one we are here discussing, the dramatic unity and the spatial unity go hand in hand. Better reasons for such staging there cannot be.

But staging itself, the arrangements within the frame, the choice of angle, perspective, and design—these matters are important elements of the rhetoric of film and we should now turn our attention toward them.

The Iconography of the Frame

Iconography is that branch of knowledge dealing with representational art; thus the iconography of the frame deals with matters that account for the design of all that enters the frame: staging and composition, the chosen perspective (camera angles in general, the issues revolving about "subjective camera"), lighting, texture, and visual and structural rhythms.

The first directorial choice to affect the iconography of the frame is the choice of perspective. From what point of view is the camera seeing the subject matter? In documentary films, the perspective is plainly objective; the audience is intended to be observing unvarnished reality from an entirely detached perspective. On the other hand, the subjective point of view frequently informs the fictive narrative film; yet, neither point of view is completely exclusive in this genre. Directors of the latter type of film, for the most part, itermingle objective and subjective points of view.

Nevertheless, the fictional film has a greater stake in the subjective point of view, and for this purpose a rhetorical element called subjective camera is of first importance.

As we note in our discussion of *The Last Laugh* ("Style and Approach," pp. 72–75 in Part Three), the subjective camera theme has two modalities: the subjective (or point of view) shot itself, which is simply a shot that by its placement in the sequence following a close-up of the subjective indicates to the spectator that *it* is what the subject is seeing. Robert Montgomery's *Lady in the Lake* (1946) is the only example of a whole film shot entirely by way of the subjective shot. But a great many films make use of the second modality of the technique we call subjective camera.

This second modality is employed by a director who wants to make clear to his audience that he is interested in the life of a single protagonist, or whenever there is a need to focus on a single character in a particular sequence of a film. For this purpose a whole group of technical devices make up the rhetoric of the subjective camera. There is, first, the employment of a pattern of close-ups of the subject. The employment of this kind of pattern works to establish an intense field of interest. The reader will recognize such a pattern when considering, for example, how *Wild Strawberries* manages to assure us of its field of interest by means of such a pattern.

Another device in the subjective camera technique is the skillful employment of the moving camera. For with the moving camera recording a subjective shot, the kinesthetic sensations of a subject can be pictured. In *The Last Laugh* (see Part Three, pp. 63–65), the camera moves back and forth over some distance immediately after we have seen a tuba being played and at a time when we are sure that the movement reflects the inebriated Doorman's sensations; that is, the moving camera depicts how *he* experiences the sound of the tuba. In that film, too, the swinging pan round the room (the shot which includes the drunken one in it) also depicts kinesthetic sensation. Simpler moving shots can also depict simpler subjective situations. An example is to be found in *Jules and Jim:* when the friends go to the Aegean island in search of the statue, they find it in a sculpture garden and a shot moving around the statue depicts their sensations as *they* move around it.

The whole canon of expressionistic devices is also at the disposal of the director inclined to use the subjective camera. Extreme inner states, especially dreams and fantasies, are particularly able to be depicted by expressionistic means. These means vary greatly—from the pushing of the photographic texture itself, as in the dream sequences of *Wild Strawberries* and the fantasy moments in *Beauty and the Beast* and *The Gold Rush*, to the more macabre constructionist movement in *The Last Laugh*, in which a building seems to tumble, and nature herself, in the form of wild winds, seems to be enlisted illusionistically in order to *express* the inexpressible inner consciousness of the old Doorman. Various devices for altering focus also belong to this category of devices: a simple lens adjustment can make the focus soft, but a halated effect can also be achieved by the use of diffusion lenses. In *The Last Laugh,* we see many shots in which focus is altered in order to capture the inner sense of the Doorman's altered states of perception. In *The Rules of the Game,* however (as well as in *Beauty and the Beast,* in the close-ups of Beauty), the Marquis is frequently pictured through a diffusion lens in order to give to his appearance a sense of his own self-idealization.

The selection of the angle for a particular camera setup is also important in the field of subjective camera, although it is also a crucial element in creating a particular *tone* (which is simply the suggested way the film maker wants his audience to view his subject). At this point of our discussion we think it important to urge on our readers the necessity of becoming shot conscious, for most of the shots one sees in narrative films, although they appear to be made from the so-called normal, or eye-level perspective, are in reality made from slight variants of eye level: low- or high-angle shots; and only by becoming shot conscious and training the eye can the serious student of film begin to discern these important differences.

For they are important. Camera angle determines the picturing of the appropriate scale and size of objects and persons. Low angle shots cause perspective distortion such that the camera subject appears to loom out over the spectator. High-angle shots, on the other hand, tend to make for reduction in size; diminishment becomes the message from this kind of shot.

A few examples will make apparent the importance of camera angle. In the episode of "The Young Man and the Maid" in *La Ronde,* the pattern of single shots of the Young Man is almost invariably made from a high camera angle; the pattern has the effect of reducing him in size somewhat, and thereby reflecting his reticent position vis-à-vis the surer sexual position of the Maid. On the other hand, the low angles from which the old Doorman in *The Last Laugh* is pictured in the first half of that film have the effect of enhancing his stature; we see him as relatively powerful through the medium of the chosen perspective. Finally, in *The Rules of the Game* and in *Grand Illusion*—indeed, in many of Renoir's films of the late 1930s—the camera perspective is carefully placed at eye level and at such a distance as to make very clear that we are spectators at a theatrical event. We are sitting in a theater watching a spectacle of comedy, pathos, and tragedy.

If the moving camera contributes to subjective camera rhetoric, so does the static shot, especially one as static as the freeze frame shot. In *Jules and Jim,* many examples of the freeze frame—shots of the statue, shots of Catherine at various moments: when the two men first see her, when she is performing for them on the veranda of their seaside villa—suggest the subjective points of view of Jules and Jim. That they see the statue and Catherine in frozen aspect clearly indicates that both are related in being the incorporated ideals of their psychic lives.

Before we leave the concept of subjective camera, however, we would do well to cite a shot that may make the concept clear by virtue of its being quite the opposite of the subjective in orientation. In *Il Posto*, when Domenico goes to the company's New Year's Eve party, he is seen entering the long, rectangular ballroom from a very lengthy long shot made from a camera position at one end of the room. The take lasts several minutes and depicts with aching fidelity his disappointment in the fact that the room is empty, his hesitation in walking forward, his gauche indecision over where to sit. Each detail is seen with precise clarity. And we are meant to understand that objectively these things constitute the truth about Domenico in his situation. Had Olmi elected to use the subjective camera technique, an entirely different kind of shot (or shots) would have been required—even though the meaning of the subjective sequence would invariably have been the same.

In Part Three, we discuss the films and the techniques of several especially gifted practitioners of pictorial composition (for example, Antonioni, Kurosawa, Bergman, *et al.*); and indeed artful composition enhances the iconography of the frame. Composition, a technique that films share with other plastic arts, is simply the arrangement of everything in the frame with respect to everything else. It is achieved by staging the scene —arranging the movement of the actors vis-à-vis one another—against a carefully selected background. Because things change in film from moment to moment, composition has in one sense an iron structural function: it imparts an unusually subtle but unmistakable visual strength to films. Moreover, because contours and masses and planes and volumes are all continuously moving in film, staging and composition produce especially complicated and interesting visual rhythms. For visual rhythm is an aspect of static plastic arts—such as painting and sculpture—and is thus a powerful presence in motion pictures.

By visual rhythm we mean the effect produced by the repetition of elements within a movement or unit larger than that which is repeated. Thus, it is easy to see that all kinds of mass movements within the frame —movements involving, for example, lines of people, animals, or vehicles— always produce visual rhythm of the strongest kind and that is easily recognized, too. The flagellants in *The Seventh Seal*, moving so forcefully and with so much apparent multidirectional and linear vitality, contribute importantly to the emotional effects of the film and give us a sense of its power and beauty. The bicycles traveling along the wooded roads by the seashore in *Jules and Jim* are another instance of affecting visual rhythm. (In the Truffaut sequence, moreover, the visual rhythms of graceful motion along curvilinear paths is further enhanced by the structural rhythm

in the shot selection of this sequence: just the structural rhythm of alternating long shot to medium shot to close-up to long shot again helps to
complicate and enhance the beauty of the sequence.)

The visual rhythm produced in the extraordinary final sequence of
Fritz Lang's *M* (The Trial) is another case in point. The structural
rhythm that takes us back and forth between the great massed body of
juror-criminals and the starkly solitary figure of Peter Lorre produces a
meaningful contrast between mass and line, volume and contour, and
ultimately power and helplessness and society arrayed aagainst the individual.

Visual rhythms, however, are not purely associated with large effects
such as we have discussed here. They are apparent and effective in a
special way on smaller scales. For example, visual rhythms frequently
turn our attention to patterns or designs of activity or classes of objects
which then become what we will call visual motifs. (See the full discussion on the use of visual motifs in "Style and Approach" for *M*, in Part
Three, pp. 133–134.) In *L'Avventura*, discriminating cutting and composition call our attention to the visual motif of a pair of women—Anna,
dark-haired; Claudia, light-haired—such that when the theme of Anna's replacement by Caudia needs dramatizing, the mere placement of a dark
wig on Claudia's head does the work.

In *The Rules of the Game*, Robert's collection of mechanical music
makers and figures, actually powerful symbols of his life-style and thus
potential carriers of the central theme of the film, is also made into visual
motifs by virtue of the visual rhythms in which the art objects are employed. The result of this fact is that a single shot with Robert standing
next to a mechanical organ of great beauty and delicacy is enough to reveal his whole character to us. Moreover, not just objects and people but
also forms can achieve this status. Witness the masterful use of the circle
motif in *M*, how from the opening shot of a group of children holding
hands in a circle (and children are the threatened parties in this film) the
circle is modulated so finely by means of visual rhythm that by the time
the film has ended we are aware that there is a social circle and that the
powerful prohibition against violation of that circle is at the thematic
heart of the film.

We will not discuss the important area of color film on the grounds
that the subject is just too complex for the space allotted and that the
films we have selected for study, with a single exception, are all in black
and white. (Students of Agnés Varda's *Le Bonheur* who want to investigate problems of color in films should consult Robert Gessner, *The Moving
Image* (New York, 1968) and Raymond Spottiswoode, *A Grammar of the
Film* (Berkeley and Los Angeles, 1962).

What there is to say first about the rhetoric of lighting and texture in
black and white films is that the director of photography has it within
his power, in almost every case, to present us with a pictorial surface that

displays the full range of tones in the grey scale. In addition, also with some very few exceptions, he can alter the texture; he can add grain or reduce its presence, and he can furnish as sharply resolved a surface as he likes. It is, therefore, well to bear in mind that such control is possible and has been available since early in the decade of the 1930s.

Lighting is of first importance because of its sheer power of illumination. In this role it helps us to *see*—in many cases as we have not seen before—objects and people. It is true, of course, that color film is a better medium for this purpose in that the separation of objects by differential coloring fosters better the illusion of three-dimensionality, but the lighting capacity in black and white films is not to be ignored on that score. For example, cross lighting, with the principal source of illumination striking an object at a very shallow angle, can greatly enhance our perception of certain objects, especially those whose identities depend on interesting surface textures, such as sculptures, stone walls, aging skin, and so on. The careful lighting techniques used in *The Rules of the Game* contribute to our perception of the rich materials used there—the satins, mirrors, chateau exterior (and the superbly designed floors inside)—and thus enhance the reality of the status of the Marquis and his set. The same is true of the lighting of objects in *L'Avventura,* whereas the same effects give opposite impressions when we watch the things photographed in *Grand Illusion* and *The Seventh Seal.* The crudities of medieval Sweden are displayed so sharply as to support the notion of the universal plague in that dark land.

However the frame is lit, the frame that displays the full range of gray scale values is invariably filled with visual vitality and interest. Moreover, control of these gray scale values makes many combinations available. The frame that contains high contrasts, with very deep, velvety blacks and crisp, flawless whites, will impress us with the contrasting forces in a dramatic situation. The first dream of Isak in *Wild Strawberries* is a scenic display of just such a high contrast (and high grain, low resolution) surface. The conflict in the soul of Isak is expressed here with startling dramatic impact while picturing faithfully the iconography of our dreams.

Thus, following the function of sheer illumination, the most important function of light and texture in films is to establish mood and reinforce drama and theme. The enormous range of potential in such manipulations can be indicated with reference to three kinds of lighting and texture manipulation in films discussed in Part Three.

Light in Cocteau's *Beauty and the Beast* is used in an almost painterly fashion for the purpose of distinguishing two worlds, the lavish mystery of the Beast's palace from the mundane meanness of the Merchant's house. The latter is always lit in naturalistic fashion: day is day, night is night, and nothing in the lighting ever disturbs our impression of the insistently ordinary. On the other hand, the Beast's palace is a marvel of lighting textures: the exterior, or gardens, is constantly in twilight at all hours of the day and night. The interior is always essentially dark, a texture relieved by the flickering of light from candles and mysteriously energized objects. Thus, the disparity in the two milieus, so essential to the thematic center of the film, is realized in light patterns.

A less dramatic set of tonalities is exhibited in Renoir's *Grand Illusion*. Virtually the entire film is an unrelieved (yet, magically, not monotonously) visual experience of scenes captured in the middle range of gray tones. The choice is made in accordance with a central theme of the film—that is, that war, and especially that aspect of war in which men hold others in captivity, is a dreary and undramatic experience. It is only during the truly dramatic climax of the film, the theatrical event staged to enable Maréchal and Rosenthal to escape from the fortress of Wintersborn, that Renoir's frame changes values. There we see a dramatic set of contrasts—darkness, snow, stabbing beams from searchlights—and the contrast of the two lighting textures takes on meaning.

In *Il Posto*, lighting is for the most part documentary in character, partaking of the modality known to still photographers as available light. Still, Olmi uses dramatic lighting as well; the whole central section of impressionistic sketches of the clerks is rendered in softly muted, expressive sets of shadows. These are carefully constructed to mirror the lives of the participants and are dominated by very low levels of light—darkness to match the impossibility of their drab futures.

We mentioned earlier that the primary function of lighting is to expose objects to our view. The iconography of the frame is also enhanced by the appropriate selection of these objects—especially where these are not merely single things but together are entitled to the rubric of decor: settings, including whole rooms; interior structures such as stairways, windows, doorways, and floors; schemes of decoration of these architectural members; larger units such as houses; and so forth. The selection of decor is an essential element in film making and, in cases such as *La Ronde*, *The Rules of the Game*, and *Beauty and the Beast*, decor can rise to the force and substance of character. The reader should try to imagine, if it is possible, the action of, say, *La Ronde*, and how it would seem were it played out against less elegant decor. Or, consider the elements of Christian Berard's decor in *Beauty and the Beast* (including the masterful "beast" makeup worn by Jean Marais). Can we imagine a *less* magical summons into an equally magical world?

But it is time to consider another dimension beside the visual.

Tracks: Sound and Music

Although it always seems convenient to divorce the discussion of the auditory dimension of modern films from their visual aspects, we do so with the prior understanding that we do not think these auditory aspects are actually separable from the whole. As in any analytic enterprise, however, we take this liberty for the express purpose of enlarging understanding. Moreover, in Part Three, we have our say about the great controversy over silent versus sound films—over which is the "purer" art form (see "Perspective," for *The Last Laugh,* pp. 50–53 in Part Three)—and discuss fully how one film, *M,* embodies a very wide range of the sound possibilities in film. Here we will introduce the subject in its basic rhetorical aspects.

First, it should be noticed that although the advent of the sound film was indeed revolutionary, it was not an event that "had" to happen in order to complete the naturalistic representational powers of cinema. The absence of sound in silent movies was not experienced as a violation of the realistic illusion because, as Arnheim has pointed out, "in order to get a full impression it is not necessary for it [the silent screen image] to be complete in the naturalistic sense." ("Selections Adapted from *Film,*" op. cit., p. 33). Sound then is not an element crucial to the complete registration of authentic reality. As Arnheim shrewdly suggests, it is "Only after one has known talkies [that] the lack of sound is conspicuous in a silent film." (Ibid.).

In addition, music was never altogether absent from silent films; from the start, piano accompaniment was a regular musical feature of moviegoing. Music, which we shall undertake to discuss fully in a moment, is inherent in the rhythmic nature of the medium. But human speech and natural sounds (all other sound emanations from nonhuman sources) are not. They are, instead, extrinsic elements which have been artistically fused into the modern film and they are principally used to enhance the dramatic form of the narrative film. Human speech, moreover, acts to extend the range of cinematic subjects.

To pursue the latter point: dialogue in any language makes it possible for narrative film art to deal with abstract subjects and with inner states of feeling and existence. A work like *The Seventh Seal* would not be possible without dialogue, for the Knight's inner turmoil is virtually impossible to represent visually without the precision of expression afforded by dialogue. The reader familiar with this film should recall the scene between the Knight and Death in the confessional of the small chapel in order to see that this is the case. This is the case, of course, with dialogue synchronized with the lip movements of actors. The whole range of possibilities is greatly extended by the use of nonsynchronous (asynchronous) sound. The voice-over commentary on Jim's feeling states in *Jules and Jim* is another example of how dialogue functions to extend the subject matter of cinema and, by contrasting with or reinforcing the simultaneous visual materials, contributes a kind of poetic texture to films.

Natural sound, too, is a device to enhance dramatic values, to deepen and intensify the narrative development of stories and, indeed, to make certain kinds of story development possible. (Once again the reader is referred to the "Perspective" of *M* for concrete examples.)

Natural sound has become a crucial element in any kind of dramatic development. The tinkling mechanics of Robert's dolls in *The Rules of the Game*, the thumping heartbeat in *Wild Strawberries*, the sound of the clock ticking away time and the youth of the protagonists in *Jules and Jim* (as well as the ominous ambiguity of the rocking chair, doing the same thing in the same film), and the hoot of the train whistle and the sound of the wind in *L'Avventura* are all examples of the artistic use of natural sound in dramatic development.

The case of music is equally subtle and complex—and yet in some cases more simple. Roy Huss and Norman Silverstein quote the well-known film composer Elmer Bernstein and suggest that music can be either *kinetic* or *implicit* in function (*The Film Experience: Elements of Motion Picture Art*, New York, 1968, pp. 79 ff.). That is, it can either be used to supplement the physical energy of the action, as when percussive instrumentation accompanies the Woodcutter's opening walk through the forest in *Rashomon* (*kinetic*) or, as is the case later in that same film, it can resonate along with the emotional tonality of the sequence it accompanies: the *Bolero-like*, conflicting figures that accompany the three sided conflict scenes. Music can separate two different worlds, as is the case in *Beauty and the Beast*. There music is part of the mystery of the Beast's world, whereas its absence makes contrastingly ordinary the world of the Merchant's house.

Music can psychologically energize an audience; it can accompany a character and become his or her theme in such a way as to *be* that presence when the character is dead and gone (as is the case at the end of *Jules and Jim*, when after Catherine is cremated she lingers on in her triumphant song); it can be used with words, in a song, to insinuate feeling *and* message—the possibilities are numerous.

But the possibilities among the several rhetorical aspects we have discussed in this chapter are also numerous. The reader will find many detailed analyses of rhetorical matters in Part Three and, as he reads the materials there, should enjoy seeing the films under discussion.

Part Three

*I*n *Part Three, twenty films are analyzed. Chapters 5–18 are each devoted to a single film examined in detail. In Chapter 19, only background notes and introductory statements are provided for the six films dealt with there. The order in each category is chronological.*

The rationale for this arrangement is to allow a reader to move from greater to lesser dependency on our material. Thus, for example, a class can proceed through selections from the first section before what it has learned about the principles and methods of film analysis is tested by works from the second group.

The films that we have selected are so rich in meanings and techniques that the pages we have devoted to them do not begin to exhaust their possibilties. We hope that readers will go beyond our statements. The bibliography at the end of this book can be helpful, but our goal is to encourage individual judgments and insights, not to supply them. For this reason, our interpretations especially are not inclusive; rather they are the ones we found most interesting, while recognizing that other exegeses may also be valid. Only in one area do we feel a reader will be hard put to be censorious. We repeatedly checked what is actually presented on the screen. Within the possibility of inevitable human error, if we note that there are two dissolves between three shots or there is a cut from a two-shot to a tight close-up, that is what was on our print.

Fidelity to a film per se is not as universal in books relating to cinema as might be expected. For example, the publication of film scripts during the last few years is a welcome sign of an increasing interest in cinema. Too many of them, however, are derived from shooting scripts in which last-minute changes and cuts done in an editing room are not included. When it was available, we read a script, but our analysis of a film is based completely on actual viewings. We believe that our chapters on the fourteen films are specific enough to make scripts superfluous except for the most intensive study.

Another problem is involved when a film is in a foreign language. There are usually marked differences between printed dialogue in a film script and subtitles. In keeping with our emphasis on the experience of viewing a film, we quote, unless otherwise stated, the subtitles as they appear on the prints. While referring to foreign films, we should mention that four of the films included in this book (La Ronde, L'Avventura, Il Posto, and Le Bonheur) are best known by their original titles, so we have not translated these titles into English.

The format we have used for the fourteen extensive analyses requires explanation. Although there is a consistent breakdown of each chapter into general topics, the grouping of those topics is determined by the requirements of each film. Seven of the film exegeses in the first section are prefaced by a "Perspective." Each of these commentaries deals with an aspect of cinema pertinent to the film discussion it precedes. It is intended to be solely introductory in nature; in a few pages one does not explore in depth such topics as "the silent film" and "the new wave."

The headings under which we divided each of the analyses are self-explanatory. By focusing on one aspect of a film and then another, however, we could not avoid some repetition and cross references. This is especially true of the brief summary of the story of a film that begins each analysis, but was necessary if the sections on characterization (and themes in some cases) were to be comprehensible. To facilitate an appreciation of the development of a film, "Analysis of Major Sequences" is usually subdivided into specific sequences with descriptive titles. What constitutes a sequence within a film is always debatable. We must take responsibility for the determination of sequences and the phrasing of their titles.

One limitation in our selections may disturb some readers. Only one American film, The Gold Rush, is included. This was not the result of any snobbery toward American films, but simply that the ones we would like to have studied were not available to us. We hope this disadvantage is counterbalanced by an advantage. We examine two films each by Renoir and Bergman (with an additional one by Truffaut in the second group) so that a viewer can see how a director's style is consistent beyond a single work.

Any list of significant films is open to criticism. We do not believe, however, that a critic can argue that any one of our films is not worthy of extensive and intensive study.

CHAPTER 5

The Last Laugh

[Der Letzte Mann]

Directed by F. W. M U R N A U

In Friedrich Wilhelm Murnau, the greatest film-director the Germans have ever known, cinematic composition was never a mere attempt at decorative stylization. He created the most overwhelming and poignant images in the whole German cinema.

Lotte H. Eisner, *The Haunted Screen* (Berkeley, 1969), p. 97.

CAST

THE DOORMAN	*Emil Jannings*
HIS DAUGHTER	*Maly Delschaft*
HIS SON-IN-LAW	*Max Hiller*
HIS AUNT	*Emilie Kurz*
HOTEL MANAGER	*Hans Unterkirchner*
A YOUNG GUEST	*Olaf Storm*
A CORPULENT GUEST	*Hermann Valentin*
A THIN NEIGHBOR	*Emma Wyda*
A NIGHT WATCHMAN	*Georg John*

CREDITS

DIRECTOR	*F. W. Murnau*
PRODUCER	*Erich Pommer*
ORIGINAL STORY AND SCENARIO	*Carl Mayer*
ART DIRECTOR	*Robert Herlth and Walter Roehrig*
PHOTOGRAPHY	*Karl Freund, assisted by Robert Baberske*
Ufa Production 1924	Black and white 77 minutes

Perspective: The Silent Film

There are serious students of cinema who maintain that its golden age was the era of silent films, of "pure" cinema. The basic premise of this view is that cinema is intrinsically a visual art and that the advent of sound in its tripartite manifestation of dialogue, natural sounds, and music distracts a viewer's attention from images. The effects on film makers, so the argument goes, were equally disastrous. Spoken dialogue encouraged directors, scriptwriters, and actors to depend on a line of dialogue to explain or justify an emotion or action in a scene that could more aesthetically be communicated solely by a gesture, expression, or sensitive montage.

Opponents have no difficulty in formulating a counterargument to this stance. Those who find sound films an advance rather than a retrogression in the history of cinema point out that the majority of films are narrative—that is, they tell a story involving human beings. People do communicate with each other, discuss ideas and feelings, through words. There is a dimension of human experience and relationships that simply cannot be communicated in a dramatic story through images alone. In addition, sounds other than dialogue are a vital element in certain types of experience. For example, even the most inspired cutting from one image to another cannot truly convey the degree that the boom of a cannon or rattle of a machine gun contributes to a soldier's fear. As for music, silent films were usually accomplished by a piano, the effectiveness of the background music depending on the skill and ingenuity of an individual player. Finally, the concept of pure cinema suggests a seamless continuity of images. The visual continuity of most silent films, however, was disrupted by titles.

This type of dialectic argument could be continued for pages. A more fruitful approach is the resolution offered by Rudolf Arnheim, one of the most perceptive writers on cinema aesthetics: "Sound film—at any rate real sound film—is not a verbal masterpiece supplemented by pictures, but a homogeneous creation of word and picture which cannot be split into parts that have any meaning separately." (*Film*, London, 1933, p. 213.) From this perspective, silent films and sound films are two distinct forms of a medium, each with virtues and limitations that should be judged within the context of its form.

There are other criteria for evaluating both forms of cinema that should not be ignored. No art form can be completely divorced from the social and intellectual context in which it was produced. This holds true for silent films. Before considering a silent film, we should make adjustments in our critical lenses to compensate for the type of scripts, style of acting, artistic and intellectual movements, and type of audience current during the period of silent films. Furthermore, because any film depends on mechanical equipment, we should be aware of what type of equipment was available to film makers of that time.

The Great Train Robbery (1905) was the first sustained fictive narrative. The first genuine sound film, *The Jazz Singer*, was produced in 1927. By 1930, most films had a synchronized sound track. When we speak of the age of silent films, then, we are referring to approximately two and a half decades of cinema.

During these twenty-five years many mechanical advances were made, especially in the size of cameras and the sensitivity of lenses, but there were limitations in equipment that affect what we see on a screen today. The light-sensitive emulsion on film stock in those days rested on a nitrate base. This compound is highly combustible and images imprinted on it are quickly subject to fading. Only a limited number of duplicate prints could be made from a master print. Today we transfer silent films to more stable acetate cellulose. In the process some definition is lost, so that faces and long shots with a good deal of light seem bleached. There is one advantage for us in the heightened contrast of black and white: make-up and painted backdrops seem less obtrusive. In *The Last Laugh*, Emil Jannings uses heavy make-up; however, because of a lack of shadow definition his face in close-ups appears less artificial than it might.

Camera speed in the era of silent films was 16 frames per second. Today's projectors are set for the standard 24 frames per second. This accounts for the speeded up movements we associate with silent films (there are projectors available that compensate for the difference in camera speeds). This effect is not obtrusive in *The Last Laugh*, except in long shots of many people walking quickly.

Obviously, painted backdrops are another artificiality in silent films. What is lost in verisimilitude, however, can be compensated for by bold, imaginative images. Such backdrops are the most memorable aspect of *The Cabinet of Dr. Caligari*. A viewer of *The Last Laugh* does not easily forget the repeated shot of two tenement houses with a strangely shaped supporting beam between them.

Finally, we should keep in mind that, at the earliest stages of cinema, cameras were kept stationary, angling up and down and panning right and left. The degree to which the camera itself should be moved was a matter of controversy. Eisenstein, for example, advocated as little movement of the camera itself as possible. Other directors, such as Fritz Lang and F. W. Murnau, experimented with new possibilities, even to the extent that for a scene in *Metropolis* Lang placed his camera and cameraman on a large swing. Murnau, in *The Last Laugh*, moved actor and camera together in a swinging arc to create a sense of the Doorman's inebriation. Generally, however, silent film directors did not develop the type of fluidity within a single sequence that we find in post-silent films. Instead, they depended on cutting from one shot to another with clear, even obvious transitions.

A different acting style is another aspect of silent films to which a modern viewer must adjust. At the turn of the century the predominant style on the stage was declamatory, with broad, theatrical gestures and exaggerated facial expressions. This approach, at its best, was represented by Sarah Bernhardt. Another method of acting—more restrained and realistic—began attracting attention, particularly through the efforts of the director Stanislavsky and the actress Eleonora Duse. When actors appeared before a camera and were unable to use their voices, one of their chief means of expression in the theater, they resorted to the older fashion.

The silent film style of acting is usually effective in comedy, but in serious feature films it can seem ludicrous by our present standards. This is not to say there were not great dramatic movie actors before sound. Yet, even the silent film style of Emil Jannings, George Arliss, Alla Nazimova, Lillian Gish, and Greta Garbo appears somewhat extravagant today. The best actors of the day, however, within this extravagance, attained a form of moving restraint (the epitome of this approach is Falconetti in Dreyer's *The Passion of Joan of Arc*). Later we will discuss the acting of Jannings in *The Last Laugh*, but the point we are making here becomes obvious if one compares the moment when the Doorman learns he has been demoted with the reaction of the Aunt when she sees him working in a lavatory.

Every aspect of silent films that we have thus far considered is related to style; that is, the means those participating in the making of a film had available and the methods they used to present a story. Any work of art should be an indivisible union of style and content, but for purposes of analysis, a separation of the two can be useful, provided the original unity is not lost sight of. The content of many silent films—and we mean by content not only the script itself, but the social values and attitudes presumed in the story—strikes us today as outdated, melodramatic, and naive.

One suspects that rabid enthusiasts of silent films unconsciously separate style from content, as most of us separate a libretto from music when listening to a nineteenth-century opera. What is usually lauded is an effect, an image, a moment of superb acting, a sequence of cinematic virtuosity (as the Odessa Steps in *The Battleship Potemkin* or the drunk scenes in *The Last Laugh*). Although there are exceptions, such as *The Passion of Joan of Arc*, rarely does one hear high praise for the subtlety of conflict and depth of characterization of a silent film story. It is interesting to speculate what role this focus on style in silent films played in the development of the *auteur* approach to film criticism.

Some of this limitation is inherent in the silent film form itself. Without dialogue (and titles must be brief if visual continuity is not to be lost), it is difficult to establish delicate and involved relationships between people, and there is just so much facial expressions, gestures, and symbols can communicate of the inner conflict of an individual. For example, in *The Last Laugh* we recognize the love between the Doorman and his Daughter, but the meaning and dimensions of the love remain mysterious. We are left with the stereotype of "daughter." Most characters in silent films, in fact, are two-dimensional. Even more complex figures, such as Gösta Berling and Trina and Mac in *Greed* (both films, incidentally, adapted from novels), tend to become flattened and slide into stereotypes by the restrictions of being presented solely in visual images and a few lines of printed dialogue.

The genre of silent feature films ranges from fustian melodramas to frothy comedies. However, two modes still impress us. Broad comedy does not depend on subtle characterization or complex plots; its appeal is primarily visual and immediate. There is an evergreen quality to silent film comedy that has not faded to this day. Also, we are still stirred by the epics of Griffith, Eisenstein, and Pudovkin. We are moved by the sweep and scope and style of the films, and the individual vignettes of ordinary people caught up in the drama of history. As with comedy, the epic does not make demands that the silent film cannot meet.

Of the other modes of silent films, the content of two types is of historical interest and is occasionally exciting, but today they usually seem dated and artificial. The attempts to explore the world of the unconscious of the expressionists and early surrealists lay the groundwork for such masters of the psychological film as Dreyer, Cocteau, Bunuel, Bresson, Bergman, and Antonioni. The early efforts, however, on the whole, strike us as self-consciously "arty" (for example, Lang's *Metropolis*), intellectually naive (Pabst's *The Secret of a Soul*), and too prone to compromises with an unsophisticated audience (the ending of Wiene's *The Cabinet of Dr. Caligari*). The weaknesses of silent films on proletarian life—the cinematic counterpart to literary naturalism—are of another sort. The social conditions and mores of our world have changed so greatly since the first three decades of the century that the problems of a Jeanne Ney seem unreal to us. If the main characters emerged as interesting individuals in themselves (as, to a degree, the Doorman in *The Last Laugh*), we might become involved in their lives as we do those in the finest fiction of Zola and Dreiser. Usually they do not. Once again we return to the limitations of the silent film in portraying full-dimensional characters and their inner conflicts.

We have emphasized the weakness of silent films not in order to denigrate them, but to prepare a modern viewer who has not encountered too many examples to see—both literally and emotionally—the limited but genuine artistic values to be found in this form of cinema.

Story and Characterization

The story in *The Last Laugh* is simple, almost simplistic. An elderly Doorman at a grand hotel is proud of his position and is respected, almost idolized for it, by the inhabitants of the tenement in which he lives with his Daughter and Aunt. Eventually he cannot handle heavy luggage, and so he is demoted to attendant in a lavatory. He is emotionally devastated and scorned by his family and friends. The last fourth of the film consists of a happy ending in which the Doorman inherits millions of dollars and is able to show his gratitude to the one person who was sympathetic to him in his travail.

The content of the film, then, falls into three parts: pride, defeat, and wish-fulfillment. Before analyzing, however, the major sequences that translate this tripartite content into visual images, we will discuss briefly the major and minor themes of the film.

Themes and Interpretations

The most obvious theme of *The Last Laugh* is the cruelty of Western society toward its aged, especially at that time in history before pensions and unions. But to stop at this surface level of interpretation is naive, like labeling the main theme of "The Rime of the Ancient Mariner" as a warning of the dangers of cruelty to birds.

The world of the hotel and that of the tenement are continually juxtaposed (symbolized by the most repeated static images in the film—the facades of both structures). The bustle of one is paralleled by the movement in the other. The contrast, of course, is between the appearance, manner, and style of life of the two.

The Doorman is the connection, the bridge between the upper and lower classes. He acts as a touchstone that reveals the attitudes of the one toward the other. Before defining these attitudes, however, we should be aware of the bifocal vision with which both classes see the Doorman. He is simultaneously a uniform propelled by a man fulfilling a specific role and a human being. Since the beginning of civilizations uniforms have enabled individuals to recognize what authority a person possesses. As Tolstoy points out in *War and Peace,* the naked corpse of a general is indistinguishable from that of a private. Also, uniforms simplify our relations with others, for we not only assume a uniformed person's function, but also tend to presume his income, personality, attitudes, and beliefs. In this way a uniform dehumanizes the wearer: we react to a stereotype fostered by the dress of a person rather than confront the individual himself.

At the beginning of *The Last Laugh,* the patrons of the Hotel Atlantic treat the Doorman with good-natured condescension. They know his role and appreciate his vitality. In the hotel hierarchy he holds a position of some importance (note the respect he receives from the bellhops), and the wealthy usually are shrewd enough to accept at face value degrees of authority in hierarchies that serve them. When the man can no longer function, however, he is callously demoted by the manager, the service arm of the upper class.

In the lavatory in his plain white jacket, the Doorman is treated either in a pitying, patronizing manner (first visitor) or with arrogance (second visitor). When he becomes a millionaire, he is stared at and laughed at by the diners in the restaurant. He is wearing the proper uniform (an obviously expensive suit), yet he does not act properly in it: he is gauche and breaks the rules. His uniform is a disguise, not an extension of his role. Under no circumstances will the wealthy deal with him as a human being.

There is nothing very startling in these attitudes of the upper class toward a member of the lower class. It is in revealing the other side of the coin that Murnau and Carl Mayer, his scriptwriter, are more subtle. The inhabitants of the tenement idolize (almost literally) the Doorman's uniform, a symbol of his association with wealth. It would seem that these proletarians are embedded not only in poverty but also in the groveling, worm's eye view that poverty can engender. That the Doorman's position is a relatively minor one does not diminish their awe, nor are they disturbed by the fact that he does nothing concrete to improve their lot. The Doorman is their assurance that a magic realm of money and power does exist, and this assurance makes their own existence a little more bearable.

The scorn that the Doorman's neighbors, and even his own family, pour on him when he loses his position can be accounted for to a degree by the all-too-human defect of spite, of pleasure in knowing that even the proud and mighty can fall. Yet, that scorn is so cruel and intense that other motives must be at work. The tenement dwellers feel betrayed; the Doorman's family is disgraced. The women laugh derisively not at their neighbor and friend, but at a fallen king who through his power that has failed deprives them of a living symbol of a glorious world beyond their own.

What we have been describing is a theme that could be the content of great art. *The Last Laugh* does not, however, reach this exalted level. We believe the fault lies not in any inability of Murnau to use fully the potentials of the silent film, but in the inherent limitations of that medium and the way in which the director and scriptwriter conceived the character of the Doorman.

We have already discussed in "Perspective" how difficult it was for the silent film to convey emotional complexity and conflict. Murnau and Mayer, however, did not even attempt to struggle with such difficulties. The Doorman is presented as completely of his class, even to accepting without question its values. At no point, except feebly in the manager's office, does he challenge his fate or the system that degrades him. There is a touching dignity in the way in which this basically good man endures, but there is no resistance or rebellion.

Murnau and Mayer, then, have taken as their basic theme how a ruling class, at least in Germany in the 1920s, instills in the lower class an inability even to question the right of those in power to deal with them as service units rather than as human beings. They chose to illustrate this social theme with a simple-minded, passive old man, whose only reaction to injustice is self-pity and wish-fulfilling dreams that make his passivity even more pathetic. By making the Doorman unexceptional, however, they missed the opportunity to create tragic art (which, admittedly, was not their main purpose in making the film).

It is unfair for a critic from the safety of his desk to indicate how *he* would have directed another's film. What we want to convey here is our explanation of why most viewers of *The Last Laugh* are moved to pity and outrage, but not that exhilarating purging of emotions that is the hallmark of great art.

Analysis of Major Sequences

To highlight the structure of this film our analysis will be divided into three parts listed in "Story and Characterization": pride, defeat, and wish-fulfillment.

I. Pride

The film opens with an overhead shot of the lobby of the hotel. The camera moves from above to the ground floor level. We advance swiftly across the lobby to the revolving door, and through it to the Doorman outside.

During this first sequence the camera is constantly moving; it is positioned either in the lobby facing the door and looking out or in the street revealing what is happening at the entrance. The center of our interest is the Doorman and the door, which is continually admitting and expelling people. All the agitation of camera, door, and people conveys a sense of energy and activity.

The door is the first dominant symbol of the film. It appears a number of times, including in the Doorman's dream. As a few critics have pointed out, it can be seen as a wheel of fortune. In the first section of the film, the Doorman, with obvious pride, controls it; later his replacement holds this power. We would add the contrast, consciously pointed up by Murnau, between this entrance door and the bare, less frequently used doors to the lavatory staircase.

The Doorman, at first in a raincoat and holding an umbrella, strides with pride and pleasure from door to carriages and back (Figure 5–1). When he removes his raincoat (which he allows with regal condescension to be taken by a bellhop), he is revealed in his resplendent uniform. With self-satisfaction, he looks into a pocket mirror and preens himself. Erect

Figure 5–1. *The Doorman of the Hotel Atlantic enjoys his work.* (Courtesy Janus Films.)

and tall in his splendid uniform, he is the image of a man completely happy in his job.

Then the instrument of his destruction appears in the form of two steamer trunks. At this point Murnau employs a favorite device of silent film directors—an iris or adjustable diaphragm in the camera. Iris effects (a constricting circle of light from the edges of the frame or the reverse) were used as transitions from one shot to another or to spotlight an object or person.

In this scene we see from the street perspective a carriage pull up before the hotel; the camera is high, angled down so that we notice the trunks on the roof. There is a shot of the Doorman looking up. Next a shot, from the point of view of the Doorman, revealing in a frame the roof of the cab. Darkness from the edges of the frame expands until there is only a circle of light with the luggage in the center. This technique not only makes us aware of the trunks, but also allows us to know what the Doorman is observing. Cut back to the Doorman as he takes a deep breath and moves toward the camera and the carriage. He staggers to the entrance door with a trunk on his shoulders, but he is so exhausted by the effort that he must desert his post and sit down to rest in an alcove near the door. This is noted by the Hotel Manager.

Unaware of the catastrophe that awaits him the next day, the Doorman struts through the streets at evening on his way home, conscious of an occasional admiring glance from those he passes. It is, however, as he enters the courtyard of the tenement in which he lives that we have an insight into the source of his pride in his uniform and position. Obviously, to these dirty, poorly dressed, crude-faced workers the Doorman is king. And it is as a king that he responds to their greetings and bows with a nod of the head or a quick but snappy salute. We follow him as he goes up the stairs to his apartment.

In the previous two sequences the camera was usually moving. In contrast, the next scene is static. It consists of a lengthy shot of the painted backdrop of the tenement. This vivid image (the squat, bald façade of the building is depressing, yet a dramatic effect is achieved with the strangely shaped support between two apartments, Figure 5–2) is infixed on our memory and comes to symbolize for us, with the courtyard, the gray proletarian world. This shot also serves another purpose. The lighting on the backdrop slowly fades to darkness and just as slowly returns to brightness as the lights come up. Within approximately forty seconds of screen time we have moved from evening to night to morning. This change could have been suggested by three quick shots, but Murnau in this film makes very clear visual time transitions.

The following sequence begins with the men leaving for work and the women appearing on small balconies to brush clothes and beat eiderdowns. We join one young woman (through a cut) as she enters an apartment. The scene that follows is interesting, among other reasons, because it illustrates the difficulties Murnau faced in foregoing the use of titles. The young woman cleans the room, then opens an oven and takes out cakes. There is a well-lit, long, tight close-up of her. Her feelings of quiet joy are evident in her expression, but, equally important, one notices how young she is. We see her inscribe with frosting on one of the cakes a welcome to "our wedding guests." A cut to the Doorman trimming his beard in a mirror; there is also a reflection of the woman. He watches her reflection sadly. A reverse angle shot as he leaves the mirror,

Figure 5–2. *The tenement where the Doorman and his family live.* (Courtesy Janus Films.)

goes to the cake and tastes it with approval. The following series of shots occur: he points; cut to the wedding veil; cut back to his wistful face; cut to the veil again; Doorman walks into frame and touches veil; young woman also walks into frame and rests her head on the Doorman's shoulder. The point has been made even to a dull and inattentive viewer: the young woman is the Doorman's Daughter and she is to be married that day. Of course, one line of dialogue or a title would have immediately identified the girl as the Doorman's Daughter (if we had forgotten the credits—a form of title). Less central to the story and therefore ignored is the other woman in the Doorman's family. There is no visual hint whatsoever that she is the Doorman's Aunt (she appears very young to be *his* Aunt), much less the feelings between the two except for her inordinate respect for his position.

The Daughter respectfully pats the coat before uniform and man leave. On the landing outside his apartment, the Doorman meets a group of smiling, head-bobbing neighbor women. This scene will be repeated again the next morning, only then the women's faces will swirl before the eyes of the inebriated Doorman.

The trip back to the hotel follows the same pattern in reverse, with one additional incident. In the courtyard the Doorman protects, consoles, and gives a piece of candy to a small child who has been knocked down by his playmates.

We emphasize once again that our impression of the Doorman and the other people in the film is dependent entirely on images. The characteristics of the Doorman that are established are a pride that appears too simple-minded to at any time be called arrogance; love for his Daughter; and sympathy for the rejected (that he will not receive, with one exception, when he "falls"). There is no subtlety or shading in the substance of these emotions (as opposed to the imaginative use of the camera to present the exterior of these emotions). Only in the relationship with the Daughter do we sense a moment of conflict between his happiness because she is happy and his sadness in losing her. There is, though, a dramatic value in the fact that the Daughter is marrying that day (in addition to an excuse for the drunk scene). His Daughter and his job seem to be the only things that are important in the Doorman's life. With the former already gone, the loss of the latter is even more devastating.

II. Defeat

This section of the film opens with an establishing shot of the revolving door at the entrance to the hotel. The camera is positioned on the street side of the door, so we look through the door at the Doorman approaching. (The previous shot was of the Doorman walking along the street; he must have come into the hotel by way of the servants' entrance.) He is expelled by the door. A close-up reveals his bewilderment and fear when he finds another person in his place. He is led back by a bellhop. Dissolve to black—like an exclamation mark after images of the Doorman's turbulent emotions.

A cut to a long shot of the lobby; another cut to the Doorman inside the Manager's office. We noted in the previous section how Murnau made a clear transition in time by holding a shot of the painting of the tenement. Here is another very clear transition, only of space rather than time.

In the first shot of the office the camera is outside the glass enclosure. We observe the Doorman as he receives a letter, puts down his hat, takes out his eyeglasses, and reads. When we compare this shot with the two previous scenes (walking along the street, in front of the hotel), we are reminded of an important aspect of the visual rhythm Murnau established in the film. He counterpoints his moving camera with such lengthy, static shots as this one.

The camera now moves quickly through the glass to a close-up of the Doorman, cut to the letter, then another, long close-up of the Doorman. The swift movement of the camera can be described as creating a "zoom effect." Of course, Murnau did not have a zoom lens in his camera, so he must have tracked toward the Doorman very rapidly. The glass between the camera and the subject suggests the technical difficulties silent film directors encountered and with what care and ingenuity Murnau and his cameraman prepared their shots. The camera probably was moved toward the glass, but stopped and turned off, the actor "froze," and the glass slid aside (we know *The Last Laugh* was filmed in a studio); then the camera was turned on again and continued moving to the close-up. This conjecture is supported by a momentary blur or "halo" around the head of the Doorman, which could have been produced by the slightest movement of the camera or actor between the time the camera was stopped and started again.

The close-up of the letter is the first time we see extended print on the screen. Even Murnau could not do completely without words.

The long shot of the Doorman as he reads the letter is from above. To emphasize the change in the fortunes of the Doorman there is a shift from the slight angle up in shots of him to this point to a slight camera angle down for the defeat section of the film.

The look of suffering on the Doorman's face after he has read the letter is so intense and naked that it approaches the tragic. It is a great moment in the history of silent films and the most impressive in *The Last Laugh* that does not depend (as in the drunk sequence) on the various techniques of the director. All that follows in this section are variations on the humiliation of the Doorman that never move us as much as that quintessential image of human pain.

We will not have another opportunity to consider Emil Jannings's portrayal of the Doorman. It is hard to imagine anyone who would not be impressed by Jannings's acting in *The Last Laugh*. Within the conventions of silent film acting, he is remarkably restrained. Those conventions tolerated, even encouraged, the type of eye-popping Jannings indulges in when the Doorman sees his Aunt from the entrance to the lavatory. Compare this type of facial rhetoric, though, to such acting highlights of the film as the scene in the Manager's office, the moment with his Daughter and the wedding veil, the whole drunk sequence, the scenes with the Watchman and his replacement in the lavatory. A comparison between Jannings and the other actors in the film, especially the Aunt, confirms his distinction.

It is not simply through facial expressions that Jannings communicates to us. His whole body conveys the emotional state of the Doorman. Note his erect and puffed up posture in his pride, how stooped and shrunken he is in his defeat, the way his upper torso sways slightly and his knees bend extravagantly the morning after his reveling. And those superb, always right, yet always surprising, gestures: his hand over his heart as he leaves the Manager's office; the diffident, guilty way he takes off his hat before his son-in-law on the stairs; putting a cigar in the mouth of his replacement in the lavatory, then patting the old man's jaws closed. Our respect for his impersonation of an aged man is increased when we learn Jannings was only thirty-seven at the time.

But let us return to the film itself. The Doorman pleads with the Manager. He desperately attempts to prove he is still capable of his duties by lifting a trunk in the corner of the room. He drops it and collapses, appearing even to suffer a minor stroke. A bellhop is called in to help him. When he recovers sufficiently, he is helped to his feet and stripped of his uniform like a disgraced soldier. In the process a button is ripped off. There seems to be no special significance to this loss (the button is later sewn on by the Aunt), but if the character of the Doorman were not so simple, even shallow, one would be reminded of King Lear just before he dies when he utters the line: "Pray you, undo this button." The humiliation of the Doorman is accentuated by the shabby clothes he wears under the uniform. The patched sweater and baggy trousers also remind us that the impressive uniform was only a façade, the man beneath it was a product of the tenement world (symbolized by another type of façade).

Throughout his confrontation with the Doorman, the Manager acts with callous indifference to the suffering of his employee. In keeping with his stereotyped character, yet in his one original action in the film, he washes his hands after helping the collapsed old man to a seat.

The Doorman is led away by the hotel housekeeper, but not before he has stolen the key to the closet in which his uniform is stored. Loaded with a pile of towels, shrunken and bowed, he shuffles to the lavatory which, appropriately, is at the bottom of a flight of stairs.

During these two scenes Murnau uses a couple of interesting cinematic techniques. The first is three cuts to images that represent what is in the mind of the Doorman. In none of these shots is there a distortion of reality, but in the case of the first there is a manipulation of reality. It occurs just after the Doorman has collapsed in the Manager's office. For a moment we see the new Doorman lifting a trunk with ease, yet in the rain. We know that when the Doorman came into the hotel a few minutes earlier, it was not raining; we recall that there was rain when he struggled with a trunk and thereby lost his job. The Doorman's mind has created a vision that emphasizes the fundamental difference between him and his replacement.

The other two shots are straightforward indications of what the Doorman is thinking about. After he steals the key to the Manager's closet, there is a cut to his Daughter's wedding. Finally, as he collects towels for the lavatory, we see for a moment the new Doorman blowing his whistle. The whistle is for the Doorman (as we will see in the drunk sequence) a symbol of authority, like a king's scepter. Another now exercises that power.

The second expressive cinematic device Murnau employs in these scenes is to have the stairway to the lavatory in complete darkness. First we see the Doorman and his reflection on the mirrorlike doors. Then, with his bundle of towels, he disappears into the blackness as though into a hole of death or hell. The doors close behind him with a depressing finality, and for a moment the camera lingers on the unadorned, utilitarian portal, a complete contrast to the huge revolving door he once controlled with such relish. Later the stairway will be lighted; now, however, a symbolic representation of the dark state of mind of the Doorman takes precedent over reality.

Evening comes. Once again, as with the tenement backdrop, a time transition is clearly indicated. The lighting on the front of the hotel is slowly dimmed. A cut to the wedding celebration at the Doorman's apartment. The bride comes out onto the balcony looking for her father (a movement that will be repeated by a neighbor the next evening when, having learned of the Doorman's demotion, she maliciously awaits his return). Unlike the shots in the previous two scenes, this one is not in the mind of the Doorman, but is a means of indicating what is happening at a locale some distance from where the main action of a scene is occurring.

We return to the hotel and watch the Doorman emerge from the lavatory, avoid the Night Watchman, steal his uniform, and go through the lobby past the sleeping personnel. The shots of the Night Watchman constitute another (see the previous paragraph) of those repeated or echoed patterns of action by which Murnau unifies *The Last Laugh*. In this case, we will see the Night Watchman the next evening walk down the same corridor and light his pipe at the same spot.

The Doorman leaves the hotel and slouches up a street across from it, with the uniform bundled in his arms, against a heavy wind (again reminding us of King Lear). He looks over his shoulders at the hotel. Here Murnau inserts an expressionistic shot (see "Style and Approach"). The hotel seems to be collapsing over the Doorman. A cut to him protecting himself; then he looks over his arms. We see the hotel is standing as usual. We have been given a visual insight into the intense guilt the Doorman feels for his theft. With trembling hands he puts on his uniform.

In the next scene the wedding guests rush out to greet him as he climbs the stairs. With a visible effort he straightens his hunched shoulders as they approach. The party itself is cleverly indicated by the camera fixed on the outside of the windows of the Doorman's apartment while silhouettes of the revelers move and dance.

The guests leave and the famous drunk sequence begins. We see two unsteady guests, one tall and the other short, in the courtyard; the latter is blowing a tuba. The camera is very high, angled down, as though from the balcony of the Doorman's apartment. The circumference of the frame is masked in black so there is a spotlight effect in blurred focus on the "musician" and his friend. From a close-up of the tuba's horn there is a cut to the Doorman inside his room. In response, he salutes (Figure 5–3), swings his arms, and blows his whistle to the tune of the music, greatly to the amusement of the Aunt who is leaving.

There are a series of cuts between the Doorman and the two guests below. The camera also moves back and forth in depth, as though not

Figure 5–3. *After his daughter's wedding celebration, the inebriated Door-man responds to a tuba being played in the tenement courtyard.* (Courtesy Janus Films.)

quite able to focus properly, in what can be described as a musical rhythm. Here is a rare example in silent films of synesthesia. Even if there were complete silence (no piano or the modern sound track turned off), a viewer *hears* the tuba through visual movement.

The Doorman staggers into a seat with his back to the table. He glances around, a silly grin on his face; he sees the room as out of focus and it begins swaying. Next the Doorman and the camera sweep right and left, with the room in the background flying by. We can assume that Murnau attached by some sort of platform the chair Jannings was sitting on and the camera, moving the two from side to side in the stable set of the room.

A pan of the table cluttered with party debris follows. Strangely, the Doorman is not included; in fact, this pan is a break in the aesthetic unity of the scene. It cannot be through his eyes (he is seated with his back to the table and remains so), nor does it adhere to the principle used thus far of the camera observing the Doorman yet reflecting in focus and movement the disorienting effects of his inebriation.

The transition to his dream consists of a blurred close-up of him, a cut to a very much out-of-focus close-up of the tuba horn, and back to the sleepy face of the Doorman. The face blurs further and we see for a moment, superimposed, an elongated image of the revolving door of the hotel. Then the head splits and the image of the door is held between the halves.

The "split head" is an ingenious idea. It was probably done by superimposing a strip image of the hotel on a shot of a still of Jannings's face that had been cut and separated with black in between. Rarely is a viewer, whatever the physical device used, so very aware of "entering" the mind of a character.

The two head portions black out; the camera moves swiftly toward the hotel image; fade-out to the Doorman in front of the hotel. A cut to a group of faceless bellhops struggling with a trunk. The Doorman enters the frame from the right, once again erect and proud, picks up the trunk with one hand and, to the extravagant amazement of the bellhops, carries it left out of the frame. The images that follow, in true dream fashion, are blurred, confused, and superimposed.

From the fixed lights in the background we determine that the camera has reversed itself and is now outside facing the hotel doors. The skeleton of the hotel door, shaped like a cathedral entrance, is revolving slowly. The trunk seems to float in the air. We follow the Doorman and luggage into the lobby. A panning shot of people in the lobby staring at the Doorman. In the center of the crowd he throws the trunk into the air. He salutes his audience as he waits for it to return, and catches it with one hand. Applause. This prodigy of strength is repeated again. The dream ends with a dissolve to the Doorman sleeping in his apartment.

It should be noted that, as visually effective as the sequence is, no new insights into the character of the Doorman are added, except the obvious one that he wishes that he were physically stronger and could retain his old position. The Germans have compounded a word to describe this type of dream—*Wunschtraum* (compensatory dream).

The Aunt enters, gives him coffee, and helps him to dress in his uniform. Throughout this scene there are repeated inserts of the courtyard with the men leaving for work and the women cleaning. The Aunt sews on the missing button. Some critics maintain that at that moment the Doorman is reminded of his humiliation. We find no evidence in the expression or gestures of Jannings to support this assertion. On the contrary, we see the sewing on of the button as an example of dramatic irony: the viewer is reminded of the Doorman's downfall, while he remains oblivious. Also, it is unlikely that he would act as he does in going to work or be so shocked when he sees his replacement if he recalled his situation earlier.

The Doorman is still very much under the influence of the previous night's celebration. When the Aunt comes in, he sees her face as double until he squints at her. Later, when he looks up at her on the balcony from the courtyard, her figure is blurred. He almost falls asleep a couple of times while he puts on his uniform. At the top of the stairs the faces of a group of neighbor women swirl in his mind (an echo of a meeting the previous morning). On his unsteady way to work he salutes passersby. His first view of the hotel is out of focus.

Then comes the moment of painful recollection. Camera activity in the morning sequence up to this point has been leisurely and fluid, even the distortions have been paced, like waves lapping the edge of consciousness of the sleepy Doorman. The camera now suddenly becomes agitated. A zoom effect brings a medium close-up of the new doorman before us. A cut back to the Doorman: he leans against the wall and covers his eyes; finally he moves across the street.

A cut to the railroad station where the Doorman checks his uniform. A shot of a clock increases our anxiety, for he is late. Next we see him furtively passing through the glass doors that lead to the lavatory.

In the lavatory he dons a simple white jacket and very slowly, in a stillness that is in contrast to the activity of his former station, he sets out the towels. The large mirrors over the basins make the room seem larger than it is, reinforcing the loneliness and sadness of the Doorman.

A hotel guest comes in and good-naturedly laughs at the semisomnambulism of the lavatory attendant, previously the Doorman. After cleaning up, the Doorman turns his head toward the basement window at one end of the lavatory, which reflects a grille of shadows like the bars of a jail. This window is a clear transition to a shot outside of the hotel of the Aunt carrying soup or coffee to the doorman.

Murnau inserts a touch of social criticism in the cut back to the hotel. We see patrons of the hotel languidly listening to music and feasting on elaborate, rich food prepared for them. It is quite clear what the director intended by a contrast of the pail the Aunt is carrying (as well as the bowl from which the Doorman later eats) and the culinary fare of the wealthy.

Meanwhile, an arrogant visitor to the lavatory points up how far the Doorman has fallen. The hotel patron complains to the Manager, and the latter, although we do not witness it, obviously reprimands the Doorman. There is one aspect of the scene that is subtle and effective. As the well-dressed hotel patron combs his hair and beard, we are reminded of the Doorman himself at the very beginning of the film when he primped himself in a hand mirror. The difference between the two men lies only in the wealth of the one and the social status that is derived from that wealth.

The acting of Emilie Kurz as the Aunt in these scenes is what gives silent films a bad reputation among modern viewers. Her giggling coyness as she holds out the pail to the doorman and shock when she discovers it is another man is ridiculous. She reacts to seeing the Doorman in the lavatory with a hysteria worthy of discovering his dismembered corpse. Even Jannings in the shot of him looking out from the door of the lavatory (Figure 5–4) is infected for a moment by this absurd overacting.

We see the Aunt informing the Daughter of the catastrophe. A neighbor overhears and with malevolent pleasure spreads the news. The climax of the scene is when a woman shouts across the courtyard and the camera seems to leap through space (zoom effect) to a close-up of the ear of the listener.

A contrast to this agitation is provided by a cut to the Doorman in the

FIGURE 5–4. *The Doorman, now a lavatory attendant, watches his Aunt leave after she discovers that he has been demoted.* (Courtesy Janus Films.)

lavatory. The last image we have of him in the brief scene is a famous one, often reproduced as a still (Figure 5–5). It is a long shot of the lavatory, with mirrors, basins, two bare bulbs to the left; shadows to the right. The lines of the lavatory accouterments, which fill half the frame, lead our eyes to the far wall. The large window there has bar shadows slooping to camera right. Beneath the disheartening window sits the Door-man. His head leans to the left and down, his shoulders hunch, his elbows press against his body, and his knees are tight together. In his hands he holds a bowl and spoon. The upper portion of his body is reflected in the mirror to camera left.

In watching films we tend to forget that they consist of moving *pictures* and of shots that preserve a unity of time and space. An artistic director like Murnau whenever possible composes his images, which are the building blocks of his shots, with the aesthetic consciousness and instinct of a fine still photographer. It is worth pausing now and then, if only in memory, to appreciate the art of single images.

But in a dramatic film the single image must convey simultaneous with aesthetic pleasure (often more effective because of the pleasure) insights into a character and his situation. In this case, the picture of the huddled, tight, broken figure of the Doorman in a room of shadows and glistening mirrors and marble communicates intensely to us how degraded and lonely he feels.

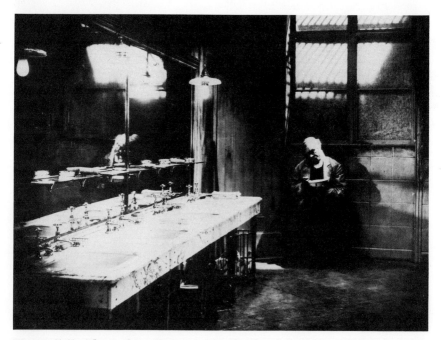

Figure 5–5. *The forlorn Doorman in the hotel lavatory.* (Courtesy Janus Films.)

The passage of time from day to night is once again indicated by changing lighting on the front of the hotel. The Doorman leaves to pick up the uniform at the railroad station. A cut to the tenement reveals that the neighbor women await his arrival with spiteful anticipation.

A large shadow against the wall within the archway leading into the courtyard of the tenement announces to us that the Doorman has returned. The German directors of the 1920s, and Murnau is no exception, were fascinated by shadows and dark silhouettes. On the positive side, such shadows in highly dramatic or group scenes (as the silhouettes of guests at the wedding celebration) can be striking; on the other hand, looming shadows at an inappropriate moment can imbue a scene with melodrama, like a tenor in an opera holding a high C when asking someone to pass the wine. We feel the shadow in the archway is an example of the latter rather than the former.

The Doorman cautiously appears, then ducks back into the archway when someone approaches. It is a false alarm: the passing man simply tips his hat. Now the Doorman more confidently walks into the courtyard.

The camera follows him, then leads him as neighbor women come out from doorways to laugh at him. We see the horror on his face and his staggering walk, as though each laugh is a blow on his back. There is a cut to an expressionistic shot of crude, cruel laughing faces—one in the center and the others rotating around that center. This shot echoes an earlier one in the morning in which the still woozy Doorman met his neighbors at the top of the stairs. Then the laughter was friendly, amused; now it is malicious, a weapon intended to bruise and lacerate emotionally. A cut to him entering the house.

He stops first at his own apartment: empty, curtains stirring in the wind, and a table void even of the remnants of the gaiety of the previous evening. He struggles up the stairs to his Daughter's apartment. After hesitating for some time, he finally pulls the bell cord. We see the consternation his arrival produces on his family on the other side of the door. The Doorman starts to walk down the stairs when the son-in-law comes out.

The movement with which the Doorman takes off his hat to his Son-in-law and the sorrowful, hurt, guilty look on his face is another example of the acting art of Jannings. It is a touching moment. The Son-in-law, on the other hand, is, in an acting sense, a true son of the Aunt. He treats the Doorman as we imagine he might an old man convicted of child molesting. Inside the apartment, with the Doorman at one end of the table and his family huddled at the other end, he finds only rejection, not an iota of sympathy beyond the hysterical tears of his Daughter. He leaves.

We return to the hotel with a transition from the front to inside where the Night Watchman repeats his movements of the previous night. A hand covers the mouth of the Watchman; it is the Doorman. He tells his story. The Watchman, also old, is compassionate and pats the Doorman on the shoulder. He returns the uniform to the Manager's office while the Doorman (with a long hold of the shot) leans against the wall in the semidarkness, like a figure about to be shot in a Goya etching.

The two go down to the lavatory. The Doorman collapses in the chair and covers his face with his hands. The Watchman takes his coat off, drops it on the shoulders of the Doorman (a poor but sincerely offered replacement for the lost uniform), and pats him on the head. A cut to a brief shot of the tenement and back to the lavatory. The Watchman leaves. Fade out.

The essential point of this sequence is the kindness of the Night Watchman, the only person in the film who is truly sympathetic to the Doorman's plight. Also, although there is hardly a need for it, the agony of the Doorman is reemphasized. Jannings's acting is broad and intemperate; for the first time his overacting is counterbalanced by the restrained performance of another actor, the Watchman.

The most striking cinematic device Murnau uses is the light on the Watchman's chest. We have already pointed out the director's fascination with lights and shadows. In these scenes Murnau has an opportunity to indulge this fascination, and he takes full advantage of it. The Watchman's chest lamp acts as a spotlight, usually framing the face of the Doorman. This is an original idea, but it might have been more effective if it had been used with more discrimination and Jannings's acting been more subdued. The use of the lamp after the first few minutes seems to make melodramatic rather than intensify our sense of the suffering of the Doorman. In cinema, as in most arts, there are times when "less is more."

III. Wish-Fulfillment

After the fade out at the end of the last section, a title appears (spoken in a modern print with sound track added) that announces: "In Real Life the Doorman Would Have Nothing to Look Forward to But Death. But the Author Took Pity on Him and Provided an Improbable Ending." Roger Manvell and Heinrich Fraenkel point out that in the original silent print the author's manuscript is seen in the typewriter and the words are typed out (*The German Cinema*, New York, 1971, p. 37).

The Doorman becomes a millionaire by the most improbable means imaginable: An American multimillionaire leaves his money to the person in whose arms he dies, and naturally he dies in the lavatory held by the Doorman. The Doorman is now wealthy enough to be a patron at the hotel.

The photography here is conventional and fluid. Social comment, however, does enter into this section of the film. The Doorman, for all his newly acquired wealth, is still an outsider among the other guests at the Atlantic Hotel: they laugh at him and the Night Watchman. Yet, the

Doorman does not care; money has freed him. The old man who went through the agonies of hell when he lost his uniform and position and was scorned by his neighbors now easily breaks the rules, especially the cardinal one of preserving a distance between the haves and have-nots. He lavishes gifts on the Night Watchman and others and brings a beggar into his carriage. Money has made him an egalitarian.

The Watchman, however, is still imbued with respect for social hierarchies. He distrusts the bellhops who try to relieve him of his packages; he starts to rise from the table, until restrained by the Doorman, when the Manager approaches. Beneath his fine but ill-fitting clothes (symbolic as well as amusing) exists the servile proletarian.

This section of *The Last Laugh* is delightful to watch. It is humorous and Jannings acts with vitality and aplomb. This last section of the film, in addition, appeals to a childlike desire in most of us to believe that all is well in the world, that virtue is rewarded and evil punished. It is difficult to imagine a viewer of the film so sophisticated and cynical that he would not be pleased, at least secretly, that the Doorman triumphs over his oppressors. The ending, then, is a form of audience wish-fulfillment.

It can also be considered, of course, as the Doorman's wish-fulfillment. In fact, this last section can be interpreted literally as the Doorman's dream. (The last shot in "Defeat" was of a tired old man at night slumped in a chair with his hands over his eyes.) It is significant that the millionaire-Doorman is not seen visiting his tenement neighbors, which surely would give him his greatest satisfaction. Even in wish-fulfilling dreams there are restrictions: a dreamer may fear challenging the reality that had hurt him the most.

Cinema critics usually explain the last third of *The Last Laugh* as a satire on the happy endings that were typical of Hollywood films in the early 1920s. (Note that it is an *American* millionaire who leaves his money to the Doorman.) Murnau and Mayer are obviously laughing at what they are doing. The means by which the doorman inherits his wealth is so ridiculous that no one for a moment can assume that the creators of the film are serious. This makes it easier for us emotionally to shift gears from semitragedy to comedy.

To remind us that films are influenced by commercial considerations—a fact cinema scholars too often forget—mention should be made that Ufa, the company that financed *The Last Laugh*, put pressure on Murnau to give his film a happy ending.

Offering rationales and explanations for the last section of the film does not confront the issue that will be most important to serious students of this film: Is this section a defect in the aesthetic unity of the film? As always in matters of taste, there can be no dogmatic answer. We can only state our opinion. Although we would regret losing the pleasure of the last third of the film, we believe these sequences blunt the emotional impact of the plight of the Doorman. This section does not flow naturally from what preceded. It is, we feel, simply like an appendix to a text, interesting enough in itself, but superfluous to the basic form and meaning of *The Last Laugh.*

Style and Approach

The two most important general features of Murnau's style in *The Last Laugh* are camera movement and use of a subjective camera. An understanding of these two techniques is necessary to an appreciation of the cinematic artistry of the film. The fact that they were used in *The Last Laugh* in 1924 is also of historical importance, for no previous film used these techniques so extensively and successfully.

Who deserves major credit for these innovations is a problem worth considering. It was Carl Mayer who wrote the original screenplay for *The Last Laugh.* There is a controversy that has lasted to the present as to what role Mayer played in the making of this film. His scripts were famous even in his own day. As Paul Rotha points out: "[Carl Mayer's] scripts were written in infinite detail, with meticulous instructions to director and cameraman. He frequently presided at the shooting and always had final say on the editing." (*The Film Till Now,* rev. ed., London, 1967, p. 713.) Karl Freund, who as cameraman was an important contributor to the making of *The Last Laugh,* attributes the basic concepts of the moving camera and the subjective camera to Mayer. (See ibid., Appendix IV, pp. 716–717.)

Although for convenience we may refer to "Murnau's *The Last Laugh,*" we should keep in mind, in all fairness, the remark of Freund: "It was out of . . . teamwork that all the innovations in *The Last Laugh* evolved." (Ibid., p. 716.)

Now to return to the techniques themselves. Camera movement and use of a subjective camera are interrelated, but we will discuss each separately.

In "Perspective" we mentioned a controversy that persisted throughout the silent film era between film makers who advocated dependence chiefly on montage rather than movement of the camera and those who experimented with camera mobility. Murnau's camera in *The Last Laugh* is very often mobile. In the very first shot of the film we see the lobby of the hotel in a descending perspective. We follow the Doorman as he moves along the streets, in the courtyard of a tenement, through the corridors of the hotel. It is as if the camera has become so fascinated with the Doorman that it is reluctant to relinquish its close relationship with him by continually shifting perspective.

Nevertheless, Murnau does not eschew conventional editing. While the Doorman is in the lavatory and the Aunt approaches the hotel, there are cuts from one to the other. Also in the intimate scene between the

Doorman and his Daughter a series of cuts between the two and the wedding veil is used. Many other instances could be cited, but it is Murnau's moving camera that excites our critical attention.

The subjective camera is used to suggest the inner feelings and point of view of a character. There are two modes of this technique. In the more limited sense, a camera is subjective when it reveals what a character actually sees; that is, the camera acts as the eyes of that character. This approach is carried to its logical conclusion in Robert Montgomery's *Lady in the Lake* (1946), a mediocre movie except for its use of the subjective camera. We see the entire film through the eyes of the narrator; in fact, the only time we actually see Philip Marlowe is when he is reflected in a mirror. Most directors, however, confine themselves to the subjective shot.

The subjective shot is a staple of cinematography and was used by Griffith and his contemporaries. An example: a close-up of the face of a subject, cut to another image, and return to the face. We are to assume that the middle image is what is seen or thought by the character.

A broader mode of the subjective camera is when the camera shows a character in the shot but still conveys his emotional state and point of view. It is this more general approach that Murnau and his collaborators developed in *The Last Laugh*. The devices the director used to make his camera subjective, in addition to the moving camera, fall into three categories: focus on a single character; techniques that had been initiated by Murnau's predecessors and were the stock in trade of any imaginative director in the 1920s; and techniques that are associated with the movement of expressionism in cinema.

Murnau does not, as did most of his contemporaries, make his camera in *The Last Laugh* omniscient, an objective outsider shifting from one character and perspective to another. As much as possible, the director focuses on the Doorman both externally and internally. Everything and everyone is subordinated to the Doorman's story, to his subjective view of what happens to him. In this sense, Murnau's *The Last Laugh* is the cinematic forefather of Bergman's *Wild Strawberries* and Fellini's *8½*.

Any gesture or expression of a character in a narrative film reveals to some degree his emotions. What we are concerned with here are techniques that particularly communicate inner emotions. The close-up is obviously one of these. Murnau has frequent close-ups of the Doorman's face; the most effective instance is when the Doorman learns in the Manager's office that he has been demoted. More dynamic cinematically is the subjective shot already discussed; it is used a number of times in *The Last Laugh*—for example, the Doorman while in the Manager's office twice envisions his replacement. The last device of this type we want to emphasize is to invest an object with symbolic overtones through discriminating cutting back and forth between the object and a person. One of the ways in which we comprehend the Doorman's feelings toward his

Daughter is when Murnau cuts to the wedding veil in the scene between the two. The coat functions similarly when the Doorman gazes at it hanging in the closet of the Manager's office just after it has been taken from him.

We have outlined the principles of expressionism on pp. 207–209 of this book. We need only mention here, then, that the essence of expressionism in literature, film, and painting is a distortion and exaggeration of reality to transmit to a viewer or audience the intense, subjective, and unconscious emotions and impressions of the artist or his characters. The first important expressionistic film, it may be recalled, was Robert Wiene's *The Cabinet of Dr. Caligari.*

Murnau was not only familiar with Wiene's *Caligari,* but the script writer for the film, Carl Mayer, also wrote the scenario for *The Last Laugh.* The most obvious example of this influence on Murnau's film is the drunk sequence, with its dream scene, moving camera, and blurred or swirling faces of the Aunt and neighbors. Two other expressionistic shots (not sequences) in the film are similar in form yet different in kind.

The Doorman's aberrant vision and dream are the result of his inebriation. No justification, however, is offered for the following two shots: When the Doorman leaves the hotel at night with his stolen uniform, he looks over his shoulder and sees the hotel falling on him. When he returns home the next night and runs into a gamut of laughing female neighbors, he has a momentary vision of whirling, jeering faces. In both cases, we are presented directly and without excuses distortions that reveal in images the subjective feelings of the Doorman.

Other techniques in the film to which a viewer should pay attention if he is interested in the style of Murnau include the following: dramatic use of light and shadows (as the dimming light or the reverse projected on the tenement and hotel to indicate the passage of time, silhouettes in the windows of the guests at the wedding celebration, and the light on the chest of the Watchman to focus attention on the face of the Doorman in the darkness of the hotel); a zoom effect before the zoom lens existed (as when one neighbor shouts across the courtyard to another); the camera peering through glass doors and then actually moving through them (our first view of the Doorman outside the hotel and later on in the Manager's office); and the use of mirror images (the Doorman looking at his Daughter in the morning or when he is in the lavatory). All of these techniques have at least been mentioned—and at times discussed—in our analysis of major sequences.

In attempting to summarize Murnau's style in *The Last Laugh,* the first word that occurs to us is *orchestration.* We intend not so much a musical analogy as the idea of a director arranging, putting together, and organizing. Murnau was not a major innovator in cinematic techniques. The subjective camera and moving camera were used by predecessors, although only haphazardly; and expressionism on the screen actually was beginning to decline in significance by 1924. What Murnau did accomplish in this film was to take many devices and approaches and unify them into a cohesive style. Single frames are often aesthetically impressive; the director's early years as a student of art stood him in good stead. Each sequence has an appropriate rhythm of its own, without jarring transitions between shots. The basic film (excluding the superfluous epilogue) has an organic development, not descending to extraneous subplots or compromises with popular taste as in, say, Lang's *Metropolis.*

Whatever criticism one may have of *The Last Laugh*, there are few viewers who would deny that the style of the film is the work not only of a craftsman but also a cinematic artist.

CHAPTER 6

The Gold Rush

Directed by CHARLES CHAPLIN

One may place "fools" in "wise situations," so that in their acts they are "wiser than they know." Children are often "wise" in this sense. It is a principle that Chaplin has built upon.

Kenneth Burke, *A Grammar of Motives* (New York, 1945), p. 18.

CAST

THE LONE PROSPECTOR	*Charles Chaplin*
BIG JIM MACKAY	*Mack Swain*
BLACK LARSEN	*Tim Murray*
GEORGIA	*Georgia Hale*
CHUM OF THE GIRL	*Betty Morissey*
JACK CAMERON	*Malcolm White*
HANK CURTIS	*Henry Bergman*

CREDITS

WRITER, DIRECTOR, AND PRODUCER	*Charles Chaplin*
ASSOCIATE DIRECTOR	*Charles Reisner*
ASSISTANT DIRECTOR	*H. d'Abbadie d'Arrast*
DIRECTOR OF PHOTOGRAPHY	*R. H. Totheroh and Jack Wilson*

1925   Black and white   85 minutes

Story, Plot, Characterization, and Themes

The plot of *The Gold Rush* centers on the adventures of a Lone Prospector (Charlie) in the Klondike during the gold rush of 1897–1898. Caught in a snowstorm, he seeks refuge in the cabin of a murderer, Black Larsen. The two are joined by Big Jim MacKay, who has been blown there from his gold mine by the storm. Larsen is forced to brave the storm, ostensibly to find help. After killing two lawmen, he stumbles on Big Jim's mine.

After the storm Big Jim returns to his cabin, but is knocked unconscious by Larsen. The murderer is destroyed in an avalanche. Big Jim awakens and, still stunned, wanders through the snow.

Meanwhile Charlie enters a town and meets a dance hall hostess, Georgia, with whom he falls in love. Big Jim also reaches the town, but has amnesia and cannot remember the location of his mine. Charlie invites Georgia to dinner on New Year's Eve. She ignores the date, yet regrets her callousness when she sees the trouble and expense Charlie went to for the occasion.

The next day, through the maliciousness of Jack Cameron, his rival for Georgia's affections, Charlie is mistakenly led to believe that the young woman loves him. At that moment Jim finds the tramp and drags him away. If Charlie shows him where the cabin is, Jim is sure that he can rediscover his "mountain of gold."

During another storm, the cabin is blown to the site of the mine. After a harrowing experience in which the two men almost go over a cliff with the cabin, they find the claim.

The partners, now multimillionaires, are on a ship going back to the States. Charlie meets Georgia on the boat and the two, presumably, will be married.

Chaplin's scenario for *The Gold Rush* obviously is hardly a creation of overwhelming inventiveness and subtlety, but it served its purpose. That purpose was as a framework wherein Charlie could create a world of his own. As in all of Chaplin's Charlie films (except perhaps for *The Kid*), our attention is attracted almost entirely to the tramp. Settings and objects have little intrinsic value; their chief importance is as props that stimulate reactions from Charlie. The same holds true for the people in the films. Because we know the tramp, we are interested in his feelings and actions. The other characters are so flat that emotions only flicker across their surfaces. Once we have identified a person by his physical appearance and labeled him as a bully or a friend or the loved one, usually we have exhausted what we will learn about that individual. There are no surprises, no hidden depths revealed; no subtleties of sensibility rise to the surface.

Without Charlie's presence, the fantastic plot and shallow characters would draw scorn rather than indulgence from us. With him in the film, trite situations are transformed into moments that can make us laugh and otherwise move us; impossible events become unbelievable because anything can happen in a world that contains the little tramp. Any discussion of story, characterization, and themes in *The Gold Rush*, therefore, must be concerned primarily with one major question: Who is Charlie?

A person seeing Charlie for the first time would immediately notice the clothes that proclaim him a tramp. A tramp is a restless traveler, a classless person with no roots; he has no past, a dubious future, and only he can make his present bearable. Because he has no status or home, he can wander into and out of people's lives without questions being asked. Whatever he feels or thinks in his relations with others, he is essentially a human catalyst, influencing the lives of others while retaining his own identity. For this reason, a changeless Charlie can appear in film after film and we do not wonder how the successful prospector could then become a circus clown.

Although a tramp may endure material deprivation, he retains one treasure—his freedom. Charlie guards this treasure as assiduously as others do their status and bank accounts. No job can more than temporarily chain him to a routine, no luxuries can seduce him into settling down, no ideology can trap him into conformity. Policemen are his most consistent enemies, for they have the power forcefully to restrict his freedom. Policemen in Charlie's world, however, are usually clumsy and stupid; he can easily outmaneuver and outwit them. The real danger to his freedom comes from within himself: he is very protective of those who are vulnerable—a child, an animal, a drunk, an attractive young woman. It is particularly the fragile, transitory loveliness of a young woman and, in his view, her defenselessness in a society of bullies and cruel men that can tempt Charlie to sacrifice his freedom. Fortunately for those of us who cherish the image of a free Charlie, the little man's success with women is in inverse proportion to his susceptibility.

The tramp pays a price for his freedom: he is the perennial outsider. Even in a crowd, such as in a dance hall in Alaska or at a party of socialites, he is alone. People cannot control him and he sees beneath their hypocrisies and defenses, their superficial values and cramped emotions. So they punish him for his freedom, which they secretly envy, and his perceptiveness, which they fear, by either ignoring him or bullying him. The wanderer, Jew or Gentile, is a convenient scapegoat.

Charlie, however, would not so endear himself to us if he were solely a mythic personification of freedom, a modern Ahasuerus. He has his own defenses, vulnerabilities, and means of surviving. With his small size and thin frame, he had to learn to be physically agile. He shows no hesitation in dodging and running from someone bent on hurting him, although his pride demands that he exact some sort of revenge. He will use any means available in his uneven battles, even a gas lamp to asphyxiate a giant criminal. Because his fists are small and weak, he depends on his feet. If a normal kick is too obvious, he uses a backward kick that does not betray itself.

Physical nimbleness cannot carry a small, frail man very far in his battles against bullies if it is not directed by an adroit mind. Charlie is unquestionably clever. In fact, his resourcefulness amounts to genius if one means by this term seeing relationships that more ordinary people could never imagine. One of the sources of delight in watching Charlie

is his ability to surprise us repeatedly. We murmur in astonishment as
he extracts himself from a tight situation or revenges himself on an opponent: "Why yes, of course, but who would have thought of that strata-
gem!"

A tramp, no matter how resourceful, finds it difficult to meet the challenges of a society that judges people by appearances and the size of
their pocketbooks. His problems are compounded if the moneyless wanderer is by nature gentle and sensitive. What he needs is a shield, "a face
to meet the faces," a "front" that will give him self-confidence, that will
proclaim his individuality, and that will serve as a pennant always flying
defiantly even in adversity. Charlie's first shield is his outfit. In an excerpt
from *Comedy Films,* by John Montgomery, that appeared in *Focus on
Chaplin* (ed. by Donald W. McCaffrey, Englewood Cliffs, N.J., 1971, p.
23), the author quotes from an interview with Chaplin in 1923. The actor-
director pinpoints the symbolic overtones of Charlie's costume: "The derby
(bowler), too small, is striving for dignity. . . . The mustache is vanity.
The tightly buttoned coat and the stick and his whole manner are a gesture toward gallantry and dash and 'front.' " Chaplin goes on to say that
the tramp is fully aware of his bluff, to the extent that he can laugh at
himself and even at times pity himself a little.

The word *dignity* in the preceding quotation is important. This dignity
combined with a grace of movement defies anyone to consider Charlie as
defeated and down and out. In panic or when knocked down, he can lose
his composure, but only for a few moments. He is like those figures for
children with weighted bases: no matter how often you push them over,
they always right themselves. We notice that the first thing Charlie does
after he recovers from being sent sprawling is to reach for his lost hat
and cane. Then, with a little shake of his body that pulls everything back
into place, he once again presents to the world his self-chosen role of a
nobleman in disguise.

Such insistent dignity would be pathetic rather than admirable if it
were not for Charlie's perfect manners. Never, especially when dealing
with women, does he fail to be a gentleman. The shy, almost effeminate
gestures, ingratiating smile, and repeated bows confound people who
never believed the adage about clothes not making the man and who
live by such clichés as that a tramp is dishonest and vulgar and at the
very bottom of the social ladder. Charlie's manners are always more gentlemanly than the "gentlemen" that surround him. This fact, intentional or
not, is one of Chaplin's most devastating comments on the hypocrisy
and coarseness that permeate many levels of twentieth-century American
society.

This is the Charlie, then, who meets a world he obviously never made,
for it is so out of tune with his nature. Dissonance—with moments of harmony—appears in his relationships with human beings, yet even more
so with inanimate objects. Almost all of the "things" he has difficulties

with are man-made. Perhaps this is because Charlie is basically a product of the city, and they constitute a major part of his milieu. Most of his films have cities as their setting. When he is a prospector in Alaska or a farmer, as in *A Dog's Life*, we sense that he is not in his natural habitat. He might have his troubles with wind and rain, snow and ice. Being a sensitive person, however, he admires the beauties of nature. Being a sensible person, he respects the self-contained indifference of the forces of nature; he knows exactly how to deal with a snowstorm—get out of it. His associations with man-made objects, though, are more complex.

Every implement we have created is predictable in that it fulfills the function for which it was created. Modern man feels most secure surrounded by tools, for in their case he can depend that there is a clearly discernible relationship between cause and effect. He also may find such consistent predictability dull and emotionally vitiating. Not all human beings, however, have subscribed to the belief that inanimate objects have no will of their own and are unresponsive to human emotions. Primitive people, children, and poets have known that a rose is not always a rose is not always a rose. With a little imagination we can almost agree with a child when he tells us that there is *really* another world in a mirror.

Charlie has the imagination necessary to invest objects with life, to make things unpredictable and function in ways never conceived of by their inventors. Perhaps it would be more accurate to call this ability a compulsion, for it seems involuntary and does not always work to his advantage. He takes apart a watch and suddenly springs become flying worms and nuts become jumping beans. He boils the sole of a shoe, and it is a Thanksgiving Day turkey. Of course, the adult in us is not deceived. And if we were exclusively rational beings we would have contempt for the ineffectual little man who cannot control objects. In each of us, however, an archaic man-child-poet is submerged beneath layers of logic. We laugh, kindly and easily, rather than sneer at Charlie's struggles with implements because although in our minds we feel superior to the child-like man, our emotions are relieved that finally an adult has demonstrated that we were right to punish by kicking it a folding chair that would not fold.

One would suppose—and thinking about Charlie encourages whimsy in us—that things would be grateful to the magician that brings them to life. Perversity, however, is obviously not confined to living creatures. There are ladders, roller skates, chairs, escalators, and stoves—to name but a few items—that one could swear derive pleasure from frustrating Charlie. André Bazin, in his brilliant essay on Charlie Chaplin (*What Is Cinema?*, 1967, Vol. 1) attributes the obstinacy of things to Charlie's awkward use of them as tools and his tendency to force objects to function in ways for which they were never intended.

Human beings do not often give solace to Charlie in his world of indifferent nature and cantankerous objects. He really does look for the best in people; however, mostly he is disappointed. *The Gold Rush* contains examples of some negative types that appear in Charlie films. First, there are the crowds. People in large groups are usually indifferent to Charlie. If individuals do notice him, they are not only repelled by the fact that he is a tramp, but also by the incongruity between their image of a tramp and Charlie's clothes, cane, and gentlemanly mien. Contempt for a social outcast is thus reinforced by suspicion of an undefinable stranger. In *The Gold Rush* a tall, bearded prospector in a dance hall watches Charlie as if he suspected the little man might steal something at any moment.

When the tramp does attract attention, it is most often as an object of ridicule. A rope Charlie the prospector ties around his waist has, unknown to him, a dog at the other end; he is finally dragged across the floor. The patrons of the dance hall laugh at him.

Charlie occasionally has a moment of triumph before a crowd, as when he knocks out Jack Cameron in *The Gold Rush*. Such incidents, however, are infrequent. Charlie, the outsider and scapegoat, can never be part of any large group. He can, in this way, preserve his freedom, individuality, and dignity, but as a consequence he must endure ridicule and loneliness.

In Chaplin's films most villains are selfish, narrow-minded, pompous individuals or crude, burly bullies. There is an example of the latter in *The Gold Rush* in the person of Jack Cameron. He is large and handsome —as a subtitle notes, a "ladies' man." He spends money freely, yet he is ruthless and cruel when he wants to be; he is definitely a bully.

The cast of characters in *The Gold Rush* includes an unusual villain. Rarely in a Chaplin film do we find such a murderous, irredeemable, dyed-in-the-wool villain as Black Larsen. On the other hand, no Chaplin film has a setting in which simple survival is so precarious, except perhaps for the slum in *Easy Street*, with an urban Black Larsen in the form of a brute giant.

Charlie usually appears astonished and disappointed that bullies and murderers exist, but the pragmatist in him rises to the surface and he is plucky and ingenious in playing David to their Goliath. There are, however, two categories of people that the tramp obviously derives satisfaction from harassing: hypocrites, especially religious ones, and the ostentatiously wealthy. Neither type appears in *The Gold Rush*. For an example of Chaplin's satire of the former, one can turn to *The Pilgrim*. Instances of Charlie deflating the rich occur in most feature length films and practically every other two- or three-reel productions. Chaplin, who was born in a London slum and eventually became a millionaire, considered satirizing the rich one of the foundations of his comedy. He maintained that people as a whole enjoy seeing the wealthy getting the worst of things, for "nine tenths of the people in the world are poor, and secretly resent the wealth of the other tenth." This is a quotation from probably the most concise statement by Chaplin on his comedy techniques, an essay entitled, "What People Laugh At," which appeared in 1918. (A lengthy excerpt is included in *Focus on Chaplin,* op. cit., pp. 48–54.)

On occasion kind and generous individuals do exist in Charlie's world. The sheriff in *The Pilgrim* immediately comes to mind. In *The Gold Rush* Hank Curtis feeds the impoverished prospector and allows the tramp to use his cabin. More typical are people who will befriend the tramp if it costs them little or they can get something from him in return. They would not consciously cheat or ridicule Charlie; on the other hand, their capacity for sacrifice is extremely limited. Such a person in *The Gold Rush* is Big Jim MacKay. He starves with Charlie until hunger gets the better of him. Then, friend or no friend, the little man begins to look appetizing. He makes the tramp a partner only when he needs him, yet he plays fair in sharing his wealth. Big Jim, Chaplin seems to be saying, is no better or worse than most of us, and only a Dr. Pangloss would argue with this premise.

We have already mentioned Charlie's idealism of women and his susceptibility to them. Georgia (Georgia Hale) in *The Gold Rush* is the first genuine romantic interest in a more than three-reel Chaplin-directed film. She sets a precedent of physical attractiveness for those who follow her: the equestrienne (Merna Kennedy) in *The Circus* (1928), the blind girl (Virginia Cherrill) in *City Lights* (1931), and the Gamin (Paulette Goddard) in *Modern Times* (1936). In most other respects she is different from the young women with whom Charlie later falls in love. She is harder, more experienced, more selfish and cruel, and more self-sufficient than the others. She has some of the sauciness of the Gamin, but none of the latter's innocence. Unlike the other three, she does not appreciate the virtues of the tramp until the very end when he is rich (or so we assume).

Charlie's feelings toward all four women, however, is consistent. His love is pure, chivalrous, self-sacrificing, and apparently sexless. He idealizes his women, and nothing they can do, even Georgia's cruelty on New Year's Eve, can diminish his constancy. Such devotion and idealism strike most modern viewers as sentimental. Chaplin encourages this sentimentality by making Charlie's women flat, unbelievable creatures. Perhaps only the Gamin in *Modern Times* reminds us of a human being. Even when there are potentials in the plot for developing a mature woman, Chaplin as scriptwriter and director blinks his eyes and turns away. One wonders if he was afraid of a rival to Charlie for our attention.

Georgia, in *The Gold Rush,* might have been an interesting character if we had learned more about her emotions and conflicts. We can understand that Chaplin making a "family film" in the 1920s would prefer not being explicit about the lovely young woman's duties as a "hostess" in a dance hall in the Klondike. He could have given us, however, at least more concrete clues as to her feelings toward the men in her life. We accept the shallowness of her relationship with Jack, for that is an unimportant subplot, of significance only because it creates a rival for Charlie. We cannot be uncritical, however, of the ambiguity—and this is too positive a word—of her attitude toward the tramp. Is she at all impressed by his manners and devotion? Is her shame for what she did on New Year's Eve more than fleeting?

This vagueness reaches a point in the epilogue where even a viewer who approaches the film as pure fantasy is embarrassed. Does Georgia finally reciprocate Charlie's love as he seems to assume? Why? Is it because of his money? Is it because she suddenly recognizes his virtues? What happened to the pert, selfish Georgia of the Monte Carlo Dance Hall? These questions are unanswerable, for she is in this sequence a shadow serving only the purposes of plot, not a substantial character.

At moments Charlie's sentimental attitude toward women can by the sheer genius of Chaplin be exalted to the level of art, as in a magnificent scene in *City Lights* in which the blind girl, sight restored, first sees the tramp. There are no such moments in *The Gold Rush,* unless we put the dream scene in this category.

In our discussion of Charlie and his world we have only touched on a basic problem: Why are his films so funny? Chaplin himself can help us reach some tentative conclusions.

The one constant in all Charlie films is that the tramp repeatedly encounters difficulties. Chaplin viewed this as "the secret of being funny." "An idea, going in one direction, meets an opposite idea suddenly. 'Ha! Ha!' you shriek." (From an excerpt in op. cit., p. 29.) The tension—and ultimate resolution—between two opposing forces is the essence of all drama, yet it is not inherently humorous. Chaplin does not develop his "secret." We can, however, if we consider the three elements involved in this opposition of forces from the point of view of comedy: who Charlie is and his goals, what opposite ideas are encountered, and how he reacts.

Charlie's character, as we have pointed out, is filled with contradictions that make us smile. Here is a tramp with the manners of a gentleman and the soul of a poet; he is frail but agile and graceful; he is shy and unassuming and idealizes women.

What happens to Charlie is often fantastic. Even so, there is always within the context of an incident a clear cause and related effect; in fact, this relationship is consistently made visually explicit. What startles us is that a cause should lead to such an unlikely effect; the law of averages is made to stand on its head. The possibility is astronomically low that a storm could blow a cabin intact to the edge of a cliff next to a lost gold mine. Yet Charlie is constantly finding himself in such improbable, potentially dangerous situations. There appears to be a fickle fate, a diety with a sense of humor that governs his destiny. At the same time there also seems to be a special providence protecting him (perhaps a combination of St. Christopher, the patron saint of travelers, and St. Nicholas, the patron saint of children). In *The Gold Rush* a bear follows him along a trail but disappears into a cave without making his presence known; Charlie escapes from the cabin just before it goes over the cliff.

How insecure is his world! This leads us to speculate as to how much of our laughter at Chaplin's humor is an expression of relief, a nervous reflex, that our own world is not so fantastic, not so filled with unexpected challenges.

Charlie reacts to a problem by first accepting the situation, no matter how improbable—he is no philosopher questioning existence. Then he is completely pragmatic in getting around a problem rather than solving it —he is no tragic hero. As André Bazin points out, the tramp shows "complete absence of obstinacy when the world appears too strong an opposition. . . . A temporary way out is enough for him. . . ." ("Charlie Chaplin," p. 145.) He can find a "way out" by means of his ingenuity, imagination, and resiliency. Perhaps here too, as with our response to Charlie's insecure world, our identification with him plays a role. We may laugh with relief that the tramp can with cleverness and luck extract himself from danger.

Another source of humor in Charlie's reactions is his desperate attempts to preserve appearances no matter what happens to him. In the essay, "What People Laugh At," from which we have already quoted, Chaplin remarks that comedy is inevitable when a "man who, having something funny happen to him, refuses to admit anything out of the way has happened, and attempts to maintain his dignity." (Op. cit., p. 48.) This is why, as Chaplin continues, Charlie is always clutching his cane or straightening his derby under the most bizarre circumstances. But our laughter is benevolent when the tramp tries to maintain his front—his dignity is so genuine and fragile. We laugh with a touch of sadistic satisfaction at pompous people who refuse to admit they have appeared ridiculous, for their dignity is artificial and self-imposed. Besides, we have confidence that Charlie will deal with his problems with fascinating imagination and no residue of bitterness, whereas most other characters in Charlie's films are predictable, stolid, and revengeful when their façade of self-respect is cracked.

When we add to these comic qualities the following: restraint ("One of the things I have to be most careful about is not to overdo a thing, or to stress too much any particular point," from "What People Laugh At," ibid., p. 53.) control (although nothing seems more spontaneous than Charlie's movements, Chaplin has repeatedly pointed out how carefully he planned even a gesture), grace, wit, and a capacity for sharp satire— then we realize how complex is the art of Chaplin's comedy.

Charlie can make us laugh, but also move us in other ways. We like the little fellow and feel protective toward him. We know that he is a complex character with his own emotions, needs, and frustrations. Periodically the laughter dies down and we have glimpses of a sensitive human being.

We cannot dismiss his problems and his resolution of these problems as merely humorous, as inconsequential as the antics of a puppy, for we are too often reminded between comic turns that we are being presented on a two-dimensional screen with a three-dimensional personality.

This noncomic dimension of Charlie presented difficulties for Chaplin. Charlie was able to endear himself to all ages and to members of all social and intellectual levels because the tramp communicated in the universal language of visual comedy in a manner that appeared spontaneous and unsophisticated (like a painting by Dubuffet, an example of art disguising art).

How was Chaplin to preserve this apparently simple tone for noncomic moments? The answer the actor-director found was to make Charlie's emotional reactions, at least on the surface, as immediate and simple as possible. This approach was most useful when the tramp was involved with women. His idealism, vulnerability, and devotion were consistent and uncomplicated. The difficulty is that this method, as we have noted, can easily slide from the touching to the sentimental.

The trait of sentimentality in Charlie may be one of the reasons why his creator disposed of him in the 1930s. One suspects that Chaplin felt restive under this restriction as well as others imposed on him by the character of the tramp. After his last Charlie film and *The Great Dictator*, in which he played a barber who still preserved some of the qualities of Charlie, Chaplin produced *Monsieur Verdoux*. Verdoux murders women for their money. He is the complete opposite of the tramp, like an alter ego of Charlie revenging himself on women.

Another reason for the disappearance of Charlie was the advent of sound. Language is the means of conveying intellectual ideas, ambiguities of emotions, and shadings of feelings in relationships. Charlie is no less complicated than Monsieur Verdoux, but he is not a thinker. Only through pantomime can he express his emotions. There is no sidetracking into the region of intellect between his feelings and actions. This is his glory and his limitation.

It must also be admitted that the individualistic, ingenuous, sentimental little tramp seems an anachronism in our complex, anguished post-World War II culture. Although fewer than four decades have past since his last appearance on the screen, Charlie seems to belong to a distant age when life was simpler and humor less bitter. We find Estragon waiting for Godot more a comic symbol of our time.

Yet Charlie lives. His films are shown repeatedly. Children still laugh at his antics, perhaps, though, with a little puzzlement and a slight air of superiority. Adults smile sadly as often as they chuckle. They wonder if they really laughed so hysterically when they first saw the film eons ago in those pretelevision years. An appreciation of Chaplin's art is greater, but the emotional involvement is less. Still, the image of Charlie will always remain with us, if only as a symbol, as long as we can admire an individual who travels the open roads alone, free, and with the confidence that he can deal with any experience that comes his way.

Analysis of Major Sequences

I. Prologue: On the Trail to the Gold Fields

This sequence, consisting of seven shots, establishes the setting of the film and introduces two major themes.

In the first shot we see a long, uneven line of men plodding through the snow. The remaining shots are of the Chilkoot Pass. Particularly during the last four years of the nineteenth century, thousands of prospectors in search of gold passed through this famous thirty-mile pass, for it led into the Klondike region of the Yukon in southeastern Alaska.

A long shot (#2) is from the base of Mt. Chilkoot, showing a camp at the bottom of the frame and a trail of men marching up the pass (Figure 6–1). Shot #3 is the same scene from the perspective of the mountain. An outcrop of rocks represents, as a title indicates, the top of the pass. Shot #4 is from a side angle as the men trudge behind the rocks. Next the prospectors, seen from a high angle, move past the rocks and toward the

Figure 6–1. *Prospectors marching up the Chilkoot Pass.* (Courtesy Janus Films.)

camera. In shot #6 the rocks are behind the men; again they walk toward
the camera, although it is a little closer to them, then out of the frame,
camera right. The last shot is a repetition of the second, suggesting a
continual stream of travelers. Between shots #1 and #2 an iris out is
used and the last shot ends with an iris in to black.

The four panoramic shots (1, 2, 3, and 7) impress us with how small
man is in this vast region of snow and rocks. We are constantly made
aware during the film that human beings are at the mercy of nature.
Prospectors can be brought to the point of starvation by a snowstorm; a
cabin can be blown miles from its original site; a sudden crevice in the
snow can destroy an individual and his sled.

Even though man, greedy for gold, fights back, only the heartiest and
most courageous or ruthless can survive. A title card identifies the Chilkoot Pass as "A Test of Man's Endurance." In shot #5 we notice a prospector with a sled on his back. In the next shot he falls down to the side
and the others callously pass him by. Every person in the film, in one
way or another, is being tested. We also learn that the adversary is not
only nature but other men and their cupidity.

II. *Two Prospectors and One Gold Strike*

We now meet two of the main characters in the film, Charlie and Big
Jim MacKay. Because Chaplin incorporates a good deal of cross-cutting
or parallel development in *The Gold Rush*, it is worthwhile illustrating
how effectively he uses this technique in this sequence. "1" below refers
to scenes in which Charlie appears; "2" to those that include Big Jim.

1. A cliff outlined against the sky. Here comes Charlie, briskly walking
and sliding along a trail on the cliff. As he passes a cave, a huge bear
comes out and follows him. It enters another cave just before Charlie
turns around. The little man stops for a moment. After an almost imperceptible shrug of his shoulders and a twirl of his cane, he continues walking.

With the very first scene involving Charlie we realize that an aura of
fantasy emanates from his world, in contrast to the realism of the first
sequence. The mountain walls are obviously papier-mâché. Our prospector wears no coat or scarf in freezing weather, only gloves, and carries
the smallest of packs on his back with a pickax sticking out. The incident
with the bear also prepares us for the improbable events that follow.

2. Close-up of a sign being knocked into the ground with "Jim Mac-
Kay" written on it. A title appears: "Big Jim's Lucky Strike." A shot of
Jim and his tent. It is strange that the title appears here rather than before
the scene in which he actually discovers gold.

1. Charlie slides down a hill of snow, then stands up and leans on his
cane. The cane sinks into the snow and he falls. Quickly recovering, as
usual, he walks out of the frame.

2. Big Jim strikes gold. His exaggerated gestures and facial expression

of joy are typical of the acting style of most of the actors, except for Charlie Chaplin himself, in the film.

1. Charlie takes a sheet of paper out of his pocket on which are drawn the points of the compass. From it he determines which direction is north. A sheet of paper serving as a compass is, naturally, ridiculous. We laugh at Charlie's misplaced confidence. What we, the audience, often do not realize is that the laugh is also on us, for in Chaplin's comedies these irrational devices often do work for Charlie.

Cut to a shot of Charlie walking into the frame and reading a sign. We assume at least some time has elapsed between the previous shot and this one. Chaplin the director is very cavalier about time. A viewer is never quite sure, unless there is a title card or the context of a scene indicates it, how much physical time supposedly has passed.

The sign Charlie reads memorializes "Jim Sourdough," who died on that spot on Friday, 1898. Charlie moves quickly away. This is the only clue in the film as to when the story is taking place. We also note how in even the smallest details Chaplin preserves a comic tone. We are amused that the day but not the month is included.

A title appears: "Then Came a Storm."

III. A Storm Brings Three Disparate Men Together

A good deal of action is condensed into the following series of shots and titles: Charlie buffeted by the storm; "A Lone Cabin," shot of cabin; "And a Lone Man," Black Larsen burning posters showing that he is wanted for murder; Charlie again in the storm with the cabin in the distance; both Big Jim and his tent blown away; Charlie outside the door of the cabin.

Nothing humorous has happened for a few minutes, so it is inevitable that when Charlie knocks on the door, snow from the roof falls on him. Larsen leaving by one door as Charlie enters by another sets a movement pattern for certain scenes in the cabin (Figure 6–2). Later Big Jim and Charlie will also play this door game. In fact, the three doors (one leads to a storage room that gives access to the outside) are the most important comic props in the cabin.

Larsen comes in, discovers Charlie chewing on a bone he has found, and orders him out. Then follows the incident of two of the doors and the wind. During this comic turn, Big Jim, so to speak, blows through, but he returns to take the bone from Charlie. The little tramp's reaction is typical of the way he deals with someone aggressive and physically larger than himself when a vital issue of chivalry or dignity is not involved: he gives in with good grace.

Larsen reappears and orders them both out at gun point. Jim and he wrestle for the weapon. Through a miracle of perverse chance, the barrel of the gun continually points at Charlie no matter where he moves. Big Jim wins the struggle. Charlie shows defiance toward Larsen—from behind the broad back of Jim.

Figure 6–2. *Charlie cautiously enters Black Larsen's cabin. (A posed photograph.)* (Courtesy Janus Films.)

The next scene is introduced by the title, "And Three Men Were Hungry." Another title, after a shot of snow and wind outside the cabin, announces that the storm has been raging for days. Three events occur: Charlie eats a candle, he mistakenly surmises that Big Jim has eaten the dog, and cards are cut to see who will brave the storm. Larsen loses and sets out, supposedly to find help.

Throughout this sequence in the cabin, we are especially conscious of how stable the camera is (no panning or tracking, only cuts) because of the "missing fourth wall" set. We are familiar with this device in the theater, where on a proscenium stage a set with three walls is presented; the fourth is invisible and through it the audience observes the play. This is what happens in the cabin in *The Gold Rush*. We never see the fourth wall, for the camera is stationed there. Often there is no cinematic movement whatsoever. In such cases all the action, as in the scene of the two doors and the wind, is in a fixed frame and at medium-shot distance. Otherwise, the camera moves forward to close-ups, two-shots, and so on, by means of cuts.

IV. Murder, Hunger, and Thievery until the End of the Storm and the End of Black Larsen

The development of this sequence depends on cross-cutting between what happens to Black Larsen in the storm and events in the cabin; it ends with the confrontation between Big Jim and Black Larsen and the death of the latter.

In the first scene Larsen accidentally encounters two lawmen. He kills them and steals their sled.

We return to the cabin. It is, as a title informs us, Thanksgiving Day. This scene and the "roll dance" later in the film are probably the most famous moments in *The Gold Rush*. Both depend on the ability of Charlie to transform ordinary things, a shoe and two rolls, into more impressive objects, a turkey and the feet of a dancer. As a viewer recalls these scenes, he realizes that a dual perspective was in operation while he watched. On the one hand, he is aware of the reality of the situation; objectively he relishes the brilliance of Chaplin's acting art. On the other hand, he is entertained and, in a way, astonished that Charlie the character appears to believe completely the illusion that he has created for himself.

This contrast between reality and illusion is pointed up in the Thanksgiving Day scene by the presence of Big Jim. In three two-shots and repeated cuts back and forth between the two men, a counterpoint is established between Jim's disgusted but dogged efforts to eat what he knows is the leather of a shoe and Charlie's chewing with gusto the heel and sole of a shoe, twirling the shoestrings on a fork as though they were spaghetti (Figure 6–3), and sucking the bones—nails—even to offering a bent nail to Jim as if it were a wishbone.

At the end Chaplin uses a technique he learned from Mack Sennett:

Figure 6–3. *A starving Charlie eats an ersatz Thanksgiving Day dinner.* (Courtesy Janus Films.)

milk a gag until just before an audience's delight begins to wane, add an extra punch, and then proceed to something else. The added punch occurs just before the scene closes. After finishing his dinner, Charlie hiccups, a satisfied expression suffuses his face, and with gentility he pats his chest. Fade to black.

Black Larsen stumbles on the claim of Big Jim. As periodically in this film, credibility is thrown to the stormy winds. The chances against Larsen coming upon the mine—in a snowstorm yet—are infinitesimal.

Meanwhile, back at the cabin . . . Big Jim is crazed with hunger, but he refuses Charlie's offer of another shoe. His subjective view of Charlie's metamorphosis into a rooster is a reversal of the previous scene in the cabin. Now Jim acts on his illusion and Charlie is the realist. The difference, of course, is that the little man's illusion helped Charlie to exist, whereas his friend's hallucination could be fatal to him.

The chase, with Charlie once again turning into a rooster and the gun and doors as important props, is hilarious. By the end of the scene, Jim is so hungry, as a title puts it, that "Chicken or No Chicken, His Friend Looks Appetizing." The two finally go to bed. (A note on one technical point in this scene. Chaplin, so very restrictive in his camera techniques, does use a superimposition each time Charlie is transformed into a rooster and back to himself.)

A brief shot of Larsen. With heavy-handed irony Chaplin shows us the villain, who has deserted the others, cooking bacon.

It is morning at the cabin. Charlie has shrewdly arranged things so that, although it looks as though his feet are at one end of the bed, he is actually facing Big Jim under the blanket with rifle in hand. Using those indispensable doors, Jim eventually gets close enough to grab the gun and struggle with his friend. A black bear interrupts, but is soon shot by Charlie. Food is now available. Charlie carefully wipes the plates and sharpens a knife.

The little man's caution when he realizes Jim is beginning to hallucinate (immediately hiding the knife and burying the gun), cleverness (arranging the bed), tenacity (in the struggle with Jim for the rifle), courage (killing the bear), and sheer luck (turning back into himself just before Jim is going to shoot him; the bear coming in during the fight)—these qualities explain how Charlie the tramp has survived in a hard world.

The storm, both literally and figuratively, is over. The two men shake hands outside of the cabin and go their separate ways.

Big Jim returns to his mine. Black Larsen, however, is there. In the ensuing fight, Jim is knocked unconscious. Larsen pulls his sled along the edge of a cliff. A title: "The North, A Law to Itself." For no apparent reason, a fissure appears in the snow and the edge of the cliff on which Larsen stands breaks off and avalanches down the mountain. So by chance or divine intervention Black Larsen is destroyed.

A final shot is the scene of Jim rising to his feet, looking bewilderedly around him, and, weaving from side to side, stumbling out of the frame.

V. Charlie Arrives in Town

Whereas the wilderness is the setting for a ruthless search for gold that leads to conflicts between man and nature and sets man against man, the town is the locale of more subtle dangers. In meeting the challenges of the land and of violence Charlie somehow comes through. Although he is physically puny, he holds his own in a masculine world in which human greed and selfishness are aboveboard, the destructive powers of nature amoral, and friendship, if pragmatic, is at least honest within its limitations.

In the town Charlie is vulnerable. Love for a woman can bring him disappointment and pain less potentially fatal yet more piercing than that of hunger. Loneliness on the frozen wastes of Alaska is disheartening; it is less oppressive, though, than loneliness in a crowd. It is in the town that Charlie's self-respect and self-sufficiency are truly tested.

This sequence opens with two shots of the town's main street. Jack Cameron, "A Ladies' Man," arrives in a sled. A cut to an attractive woman walking out of a store. The title identifies her as Georgia (so that we do not miss her significance, a rose is drawn on the title card). She refuses an invitation to ride with Jack and his girl friends.

A cut to a pawnbroker's shop and Charlie, "A Disappointed Prospector," entering it. He comes out minus his pack but with money, "The Only Gold He Made with Pick and Shovel."

The next scene is at the Monte Carlo Dance Hall. Georgia greets a man who hands her some photographs of herself. Angered by an attempt on Jack's part to take one, she flings a photograph on the floor.

Outside we see Charlie go into the dance hall. The title describes him as "The Stranger." A repeat of the long shot of the hall that opened the scene. Charlie walks in from camera right and stands, with his back to us, in the center, lower portion of the frame. The crowd surrounds him, yet ignores him. This shot and the two that follow, interrupted by one insert of Georgia, constitute a memorable few moments in *The Gold Rush*. They establish how much of an outsider Charlie is in the town. A variation of this situation, even more poignant in portraying the tramp's isolation, occurs at New Year's Eve.

After the long shot of the hall, there is a medium one of Charlie with people all around him greeting each other. Although his back is still toward us, he turns his head to left and right to look at the others.

After a cut to Georgia near the piano player there is a return to the long shot of the hall. The crowd rushes forward to dance, leaving Charlie like a piece of driftwood after the tide goes out. During the remainder of this lengthy shot, Charlie's dark figure is accentuated by its contrast to the light background and gray tones of the dancers. His back still to us, he leans on his cane, which is, in a sense, the prop of his self-respect. His right hand is on his hip. We notice that his left foot is still swathed in cloth. After a few moments he drops his right hand and pats his thigh, presumably in time with the music.

The sight of Charlie in an elegant stance is touching. He bravely preserves his dignity in his loneliness. Chaplin manages to convey to us what Charlie feels without our seeing the tramp's face. Here is the essence of pantomime—and not in the service of comedy.

A case of mistaken identity follows. Charlie thinks that Georgia is smiling a greeting at him, but it turns out that she is looking at the man standing next to him (Figure 6–4). Charlie moves to the bar and, ever resourceful, filches a drink from a waiter's tray. Georgia and a girl friend stand near him. A depressed Georgia remarks (via a title): "Guess I'm Bored. If I Could Only Meet Someone Worthwhile—I'm So Tired of This Place." She then turns and looks around. Her gaze passes right by Charlie, who is trying to look as though he had not been eavesdropping; evidently Georgia does not consider the tramp "someone worthwhile." Charlie, however, now has another reason for interest in Georgia: not only is she attractive, but she is a damsel in distress.

FIGURE 6–4. *Charlie sees Georgia for the first time at the Monte Carlo Dance Hall.* (Courtesy Janus Films.)

After Georgia walks away, Charlie notices something on the floor. A close-up shows that it is the photograph she threw down. A hand reaches into the frame and grips the photograph. Cut to Charlie standing up and putting it in his pocket. A tall, bearded man is watching the tramp with disapproval. There is no reason why Charlie should care what the man thinks, yet he does. Part of his front is not to show his vulnerability, his sentimentality. He cannot depend on the generosity of strangers, who usually resent his shabby appearance and take advantage of his small size. Instead of pocketing the photograph, he pretends to use it as a fan and walks away.

Jack comes in. He tries to persuade Georgia to have a drink with him and then to dance. Georgia repulses him, although in a provocative manner. She decides to put Jack in his place by rejecting him in favor of the least likely dance partner; she chooses Charlie. The dance begins well, with Charlie executing a number of elaborate steps, but his luck cannot hold out. His pants begin to fall and he inadvertently attaches himself to a dog. The result is that Charlie is dragged away by the dog. He has the good grace to laugh at himself. He is rewarded by Georgia with a rose.

Jack, undaunted, continues his pursuit of Georgia. He is even going to follow her into her dressing room, when Charlie blocks the way. Our intrepid hero defends the privacy of his lady against a man twice his size. Jack pushes Charlie out of the way, whereupon the little man kicks him. A kick is less effective than a punch; however, it is more devastating emotionally, for it suggests a contempt for one's opponent and an assault on his dignity.

Jack responds, after a pretense of reconciliation, by shoving Charlie's hat over his eyes. The tramp blindly swings his fist and hits a post near where Jack is standing. A cut to the top of the post shows that a large clock is dislodged by the blow. Luck this time favors Charlie—the clock falls on his opponent's head. When the tramp pulls off his hat, he sees Jack unconscious on the floor and concludes that his punch laid low the bully.

Charlie, after rubbing his fist, picks up his cane and walks away. The last image of the scene, a long shot, is of the little man walking jauntily toward the camera between two rows of awed people.

The following morning Charlie deals with the problem of his empty stomach. He once again demonstrates his ability to stay alive, only this time it is in the town rather than the wastelands. His method of duping Hank Curtis into giving him breakfast by pretending to be frozen is obvious but effective. He also has a survivor's knack and nerve to take full advantage of an opportunity. This starving tramp puts two spoons of sugar in his coffee and asks for salt for his food.

A title and a brief insert remind us of Big Jim's predicament. He has lost his memory and is still wandering in the snow.

Back to the town cabin. Charlie has ingratiated himself to Hank, who leaves the tramp as caretaker of the cabin while he and a partner make a trip to their mine.

The next scene begins with four women from the dance hall, including Georgia, frolicking in the snow near Hank's cabin. Inside, Charlie is pouring kerosene into a lamp and spills some on his cloth foot covering. Again we have an example of something seemingly inconsequential happening that will justify a comic incident later: a lighted match dropped by one of the women will ignite the kerosene-soaked foot and start a fire under her chair. Hearing sounds outside, Charlie opens the door and finds Georgia. After receiving a couple of snowballs in his face, he invites in her and her friends.

Throughout this scene Charlie is the perfect host. He is polite, gracious, and considerate of his guests' comfort. His reward is to be laughed at behind his back. While he is out getting wood, Georgia accidentally finds her photograph and the rose she gave him under his pillow. She shows the others, and they all find this evidence of devotion comical. Our suspicion of Georgia's insensitive nature is confirmed and thus we are prepared for her cruelty on New Year's Eve. It is also in keeping with her character that now that she knows of Charlie's feelings toward her, she flirts with him. It is she who suggests a dinner date for New Year's Eve, the least likely time that these dance hall hostesses would appear.

The kerosene fire breaks up the gathering. After the women have left, Charlie goes wild with joy. Georgia unexpectedly returns for her gloves, and cannot imagine what the tramp is doing. A delightful effect is achieved by the promptness with which Charlie recovers his poise: with dignity and nonchalance, amid the disarray and floating down from a pillow he has ripped in his exuberance, he hands her the gloves.

A title tells us that Charlie must beg, borrow, and shovel to prepare for the dinner. The scene of the shoveling—in which the snow is moved by Charlie from in front of one store to another and finally is piled before the jail—reminds us that Chaplin's early years were spent in English vaudeville, a source of many of the comic situations that he adapted to the film medium.

VI. New Year's Eve

Chaplin carefully organized the events that occur on New Year's Eve. The central scene is Charlie's dream. Tension and pathos are derived from a contrast between the actions of one group (Georgia, Jack, and their friends) and Charlie. The two never meet that night. A related counterpoint is between the dance hall, a setting of fraternity and warmth, and the cabin, a place of loneliness. A series of cross-cuts between the two locales, favoring Charlie at the cabin, precedes the dream; another series, with more shots devoted to Georgia and company at the dance hall and later at the cabin, follows the dream.

Shots of the crowded dance hall open the sequence; it is four minutes to eight. Cut to Charlie setting the table for his expected guests. Back to the dance hall with Georgia and Jack greeting each other and moving off, arm in arm, into the crowd.

Charlie bastes his roast and continues his preparations. He even has gifts for the women. A mule intrudes, but is driven away. Some final adjustments and Charlie is satisfied. He sits down. A cut to the clock—almost 8, the time the guests should be arriving. Charlie leans his chin on his hand and looks into space.

The next shot is of the women seated at the table. There has been no emphatic transition, such as a fade to black or an iris in or out, only a quick dissolve. For a moment one almost believes that Georgia and the others have kept their appointment, but when one remembers the last shot of the dance hall and the character of Georgia, such hopes disappear. The dream consists entirely of cuts to individual shots. In addition to group shots, there are three- and two-shots, usually including Charlie, and medium close-ups of him. The perspective is consistently from the end of the table opposite Charlie, to the right of the woman sitting there. The interior of the cabin is dark, so that all light seems to emanate from the candles on the table, pushing away reality from the dinner circle.

The women open their gifts. Georgia is particularly appreciative and gallantly Charlie kisses her hand. He rises, still holding Georgia's hand, and says, "Oh, I'm So Happy. Oh, I Can't." After sitting down, however, he announces that he will do the "Oceana Roll." He spears two rolls with forks and the dance begins.

Throughout the dance, the camera, facing Charlie and at eye level, never stirs. The lighting changes, so that Charlie's body blends into the darkness and only his face and the rolls are spotlighted. The lengthy shot is a masterpiece of pantomime. Through Chaplin's magic we see rolls but feel a dance is being performed, just as in another superb moment in *The Gold Rush* we know that Charlie is eating the sole of a shoe, but we can almost taste the turkey.

In *Cocteau on the Film*, (New York, 1954), p. 94, the French director reports that Chaplin sometimes wished that he had eliminated the "Oceana Roll" from *The Gold Rush* because so many viewers and critics praised it as the high point of the film, although it is only a picturesque interlude. One can appreciate Chaplin's point. Unlike the Thanksgiving dinner, the "Oceana Roll" is completely extraneous to plot and characterization. It is a tour de force that exists for its own sake.

At the end of the dance, applauding hands appear on the sides of the frame. Georgia declares that Charlie is wonderful, stands up, and kisses him. The emotional little man faints, and the others laugh. A dissolve to a brief shot of Charlie alone, his head on the table as he sleeps. A fade to black; time passes.

The face of a clock surrounded by darkness indicates twelve o'clock. An iris out reveals it is the clock in the dance hall. Cut to the group dancing and singing. Georgia shoots a pistol in the air. Cut to Charlie awakened by the sound. The following shots succeed each other: the dance hall; Charlie goes to the door; the dance hall; Charlie shakes his clock; and the group at the dance hall (seen from a high angle) makes a circle (visual variation for the purpose of pathos of Charlie's dinner circle) and sings "Auld Lang Syne."

The next two shots are lengthy and intended to point up a contrast. In a medium shot we see Charlie at the door of the cabin listening to the song. A cut to a medium close-up. His face is in profile. He fully realizes that he has been forgotten and is once again an outsider. He swallows. A viewer does not see tears forming in Charlie's eyes, but suspects they are there.

At the dance hall Chaplin actually uses a pan of the circle of singing people. This is the first of only two clearly discernible pans in the film (other camera movements of 5 to 10° do not qualify). Immediately Chaplin returns to his more typical techniques and there are cuts to individual faces, including a shot of Georgia and Jack singing together.

A return to Charlie, in medium close-up, who turns from the door to the camera. On his face is that unique Chaplinesque expression we have seen in other films when Charlie is rejected: compressed lips, a downward tilt of the head, eyes filled with disappointment and pain. He walks out of the frame.

At the dance hall there is a long shot at a high angle of an old man doing a frenzied dance; the circle breaks up as he is joined by others. A cut to Georgia sitting on the bar eating. She suddenly recalls the appointment with "Our Little Friend, The Tramp." The others agree to "Go Up and Have Some Fun with Him." A brief shot of Charlie putting on his hat, pulling up his collar, and leaving the cabin. Just after Jack and Georgia in their coats leave the New Year's Eve celebration, they kiss and Georgia admits that she loves him.

Cut to the inside of the dance hall. Then a shot of the outside, including a window. Charlie enters and moves to the center of the frame. The camera right half of the frame is in darkness. The upper portion of Charlie's body is silhouetted in profile against the lighted window, but his head is turned toward the window as he peers in looking for someone. His shoulders are hunched; his hands are in his pockets. We see the side of his face as he looks down and walks out of the frame, camera left. Another unforgettable shot in the film has ended.

The group arrives at the cabin. Georgia goes in first. She sees the elaborate preparations for the dinner, and she is stirred by shame. Jack follows her in. His sensitivity is as frozen as the earth of the wastelands, so his only interest is in kissing Georgia, who refuses him. When the others join them, she announces, "The Joke Has Gone Too Far, Let's Go." In the doorway, Jack forces a kiss on Georgia. She slaps him hard. The furious would-be lover slams the door behind him.

VII. New Year's Day

The next scene is in the recorder's office the following day. Big Jim wanders in; however, he cannot remember the location of his "mountain of gold." The others think he is crazy. The amnesiac realizes that if he can find the cabin, he might from there reach his mine. Outside the recorder's office, Jim passes a forlorn Charlie. The two are looking in opposite directions. This device of two people just missing each other is used at least once in practically every feature length Chaplin film.

At the dance hall that evening Georgia is on the balcony writing a letter to Jack: "I'm Sorry for What I Did Last Night. Please Forgive Me." She adds, "I Love You." Georgia sends a waiter with the note to Jack, who is below dancing.

As Jack, now sitting at a table, reads the note, there is a pan (the second of the film) to Georgia on the balcony. At the end of the pan, the young woman is in the upper left quarter of the frame. This is a decisive moment for Georgia: her relationship with Jack depends on his reaction to the letter and, although she does not know it, her future with Charlie.

Chaplin has visually established her connection with Jack by means of a pan. He now wants to focus our attention on Georgia. He does this with an iris in that ends with a circle of light enclosing her.

Jack rejects Georgia. He shows the letter to the others at his table and laughs. A shot of Georgia, so we know she has not missed his betrayal. Charlie comes in. Jack baits him, then decides to revenge himself on the tramp and the woman who slapped him by having a waiter give the letter to Charlie without telling the little man where it came from.

Charlie's response to the note is dynamic, resembling his frenetic movements after Georgia had accepted his invitation to dinner. He is conforming to one of the characteristics of his personality. Charlie is usually still when he is sad or disappointed, but moves frantically, almost hysterically, when he feels exuberant.

He runs from one person to another asking where Georgia is. Big Jim is at the bar, and is overjoyed to find the only living person who knows where the cabin is located. He guarantees to make the tramp a millionaire in less than a month. But Charlie has other things on his mind. He spots Georgia on the balcony. He climbs up to her, embraces her, and promises to "make good" just before he is dragged away by Big Jim.

The set of title cards in this scene is unusual. One considers titles as insufficient as a means of indicating emphasis beyond exclamation marks; however, the size of letters can give this type of effect. After Jim sees Charlie, the first titles present "The Cabin" in large letters; the lettering of the third title, "THE CABIN," is much larger. The same enlarged letters are used a moment later when Charlie spies Georgia and calls out her name.

The large letters on the title cards reinforce the change in the rhythm of the scene after Charlie reads Georgia's note. This event divides the action into a first portion in which a leisurely pace is maintained by both action and length of shots, and a second section in which people are moving quickly, the lettering on the title cards is enlarged, shots are brief (with hands and parts of bodies moving in and out of the frame), and cuts are dynamic, even abrupt. This careful planning of the visual rhythm of a scene within the limitations of his conservative camera techniques is characteristic of Chaplin's work as a director and one of the secrets of the success of his comedies.

VIII. A Cliffhanger

"After a Long and Tedious Journey" Charlie and Jim arrive at the cabin. Charlie carries in an impressive amount of food while his partner works on a map. Every time he passes the table, the tramp takes a swallow from a bottle of liquor; finally he collapses on the bed.

During the night a second storm occurs. "Man Proposes, but a Storm Disposes" (another of those somewhat pretentious, arch titles which

Chaplin was prone to use). The cabin spins as it is blown by the storm. We have already noted that the painted sets are crude even by the standards of the mid-1920s. The same holds true for the special effects. One could argue that it would have been incongruous to have had realistic scenery and effects in a film with such a fantastic plot. On the other hand, a cynic might assert that probably Chaplin as producer was saving money.

The storm is over; it is morning. The first shot is a hold on the cabin hanging over the edge of a cliff. The next shot is inside the cabin. Repeated cuts from interior to exterior dominate the over-all visual pattern of this scene. There is no mistaking the meaning of an increased slope of the floor inside the cabin, for usually we are immediately shown the effect on the shack as it tilts farther over the precipice. The interior point of view remains the same as it was in all the previous cabin scenes: the camera is situated where a fourth wall would be. One unusual device Chaplin uses to increase our awareness of the angle of the cabin is to lift one end (camera left) of the base line of the picture so that the cabin floor and the men lying on it slowly move toward a diagonal from one corner to the other of the rectangular screen (Figure 6–5).

The reactions of the two to this crisis are consistent with their individual personalities, and again demonstrates how the wilderness of Alaska encouraged in men an instinct for survival that took precedence over

FIGURE 6–5. *A cliffhanger: Charlie, Big Jim, and the cabin at the edge of a precipice.* (Courtesy Janus Films.)

friendship. Although each helps the other when one is sliding out the door, there are two moments of hysteria when it is every man for himself. Later, when a choice must be made, the stronger, more dominant Jim uses Charlie as a ladder. Considering the respective sizes of the men, the reverse would have been more sensible if logic had ruled.

Jim manages to scamper out of the inclined cabin. Earlier we had seen that what kept it from falling over was a rope attached to the chimney (noticeable when the cabin was spinning in the storm), the other end of which was stuck in a pile of rocks. It just happens that those rocks identify where Jim's mine is located. The big man is so ecstatic that he completely forgets his partner's danger. Gold is more important than life. Fortunately, Jim comes to his senses in time to throw a rope to Charlie. The tramp, as might be expected in a cliffhanger, makes it to solid ground a moment before the cabin falls into the precipice.

While Jim embraces his partner and dances with joy, Charlie, always the realist when it comes to danger, simply nods and faints.

IX. Epilogue: On the Sea from the Gold Fields

On the "Good Ship Success" Jim and Charlie, now multimillionaires, are returning home. They are surrounded by newspapermen, progenitors of the *papparazzi* of *La Dolce Vita*. For the first time we see Charlie in an overcoat. Early habits, however, die slowly, for the millionaire-once-tramp cannot resist the temptation to pick up the butt of a cigar on the ship deck.

In the ship cabin we discover that Charlie has not forgotten Georgia—"Everything But Georgia"; her photograph and the rose are on his night table. He wistfully looks at the picture as he changes into his "mining clothes" for the press photographer.

A cut to Georgia on the same ship, although in third class. A search is going on for a stowaway. It does not take much imagination to anticipate that through an accident Charlie will be mistaken for the stowaway. Now Georgia has a chance to redeem herself. She offers to pay the passage of the tramp so that he will not be put in irons. Thus, Charlie's faith in her is justified. If beneath her beautiful surface beats not quite a heart of gold, at least it has a vein of generous impulses.

Charlie whispers to a newspaperman that they are engaged, or that is what we deduce from the reporter's congratulations. The two go to the first class deck where a photographer asks to take their picture. They move close together and look at each other; finally Charlie kisses her. The photographer remarks, "Oh, You've Spoiled The Picture." Charlie (Chaplin the director?), with a wave of his hand, disregards the criticism.

Earlier we defended our view that this epilogue, if it does not actually "spoil the picture," does compromise the artistic integrity of *The Gold Rush*.

Style and Approach

That Chaplin as director was conservative in his cinematic techniques is a cliché of film history that is valid. We documented this conservatism in the previous section of our analysis. We indicated that in *The Gold Rush* Chaplin keeps his camera stationary. His film dynamics are supplied by cuts. There are only two genuine instances of panning and there is practically no tracking. Quick dissolves are usually reserved for transitions between scenes. One scene contains superimpositions. There are four uses of an iris, a low count for a device very popular among directors of silent films.

The basic unit of a Chaplin film is the lengthy individual shot. The frame, however, is not sacrosanct, for people often move into a frame and then out. The perspective of the camera tends to remain constant, so that a room is consistently shot from the point of view of a missing fourth wall.

Why Chaplin was so chary of using imaginative cinema techniques known in his day is difficult to understand. There are, however, two possible justifications for his approach. Camera movement could distract our attention away from Charlie. In addition, a fixed, lengthy shot allows us to observe the grace and wit of the tramp's pantomime expressed through every limb of his body as he reacts to situations that are changing each moment. Here fluency of movement is supplied by what happens in front of the camera rather than by the camera itself and editing.

Another cliché of Chaplin criticism is that his scenarios for feature length Charlie films (which the director wrote himself) were awkwardly put together. Here, again, there is a good deal of truth in this view. Chaplin had difficulty in fusing his human interest stories, especially those involving women, with the other adventures of Charlie. Ideally, one story line should grow out of and be inextricably bound with the other. This is rarely the case. In *The Gold Rush*, for example, what happens in nature (the wilderness) and what transpires in the town could make separate films. The two plot lines are related rather than interdependent.

Also each scene that makes up a story line is often loosely connected rather than articulated to the next. Chaplin was obviously more concerned with the success of individual scenes than sequences.

Finally, to go a step farther, the script for a Charlie film usually lacks the basic architectonic structure that allows a plot to develop rather than simply to happen and arranges the sequences of a film into a cohesive whole.

It is in respect to this last weakness that *The Gold Rush* is uncharacteristic. The film is based on a carefully constructed scenario; it is, in fact, the most coherent of Chaplin's film scripts. In Diagram 1 we lay bare, so to speak, the bones of the script. We can see now the circular

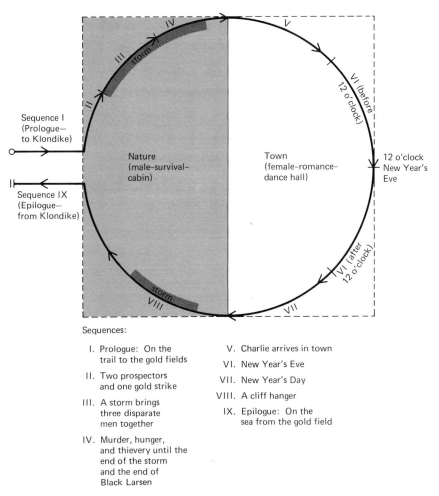

Sequence I
(Prologue—
to Klondike)

Sequence IX
(Epilogue—
from Klondike)

Nature
(male–survival–
cabin)

Town
(female–romance–
dance hall)

12 o'clock
New Year's
Eve

Sequences:

I. Prologue: On the
trail to the gold fields

II. Two prospectors
and one gold strike

III. A storm brings
three disparate
men together

IV. Murder, hunger,
and thievery until the
end of the storm
and the end of
Black Larsen

V. Charlie arrives in town

VI. New Year's Eve

VII. New Year's Day

VIII. A cliff hanger

IX. Epilogue: On the
sea from the gold field

Fig. **DIAGRAM 1.** *Schema of the script for* **The Gold Rush.**

arrangement of the plot and the division between the world of nature (in which men struggle to survive) and that of the town (where Charlie finds Georgia and romance). The cabin symbolizes the former and the dance hall the latter. The role of nature as controlling force in its own province is made clear by the two storms: one during most of sequences III and IV, and the other during sequence VIII.

What could not be included in this diagram is the effective way Chaplin uses cross-cutting: II (Charlie and Jim), III (Larsen, Charlie, and Jim), IV (Charlie, Jim, and Larsen), V (Charlie and Jim), VI (Charlie and Georgia).

That Chaplin was able to hold together so well the strands of even a bifurcated plot demonstrates that the careless over-all structure of his other scripts was not due to lack of knowledge or ability.

CHAPTER 7

M

Directed by FRITZ LANG

Forebear to judge, for we are sinners all.

Shakespeare, *King Henry VI*, Part II,
Act III, Scene 3

It is one of the many dilemmas into which mankind has maneuvered itself that here again the humane claims made for the individual are in opposition to the interests of mankind as a whole. Our sympathy with the asocial defective . . . endangers the security of the nondefective.

Konrad Lorenz, *Civilized Man's Eight Deadly Sins* (New York, 1974).

CAST

THE MURDERER, HANS BECKERT	*Peter Lorre*
INSPECTOR LOHMANN	*Otto Wernicke*
SCHRÄNKER	*Gustaf Gründgens*
MRS. BECKMANN	*Ellen Widmann*
ELSIE BECKMANN	*Inge Landgut*
CHIEF OF POLICE	*Ernst Stahl-Nackbaur*
THE MINISTER	*Franz Stein*
INSPECTOR GROEBER	*Theodor Loos*
THE BURGLAR	*Fritz Gnass*
THE SAFEBREAKER	*Fritz Odemar*
THE PICKPOCKET	*Paul Kemp*
THE CONMAN	*Theo Lingen*
THE BLIND BEGGAR	*Georg John*
THE NIGHT WATCHMAN	*Karl Platen*
THE LAWYER	*Rudolf Blümner*

CREDITS

DIRECTOR	*Fritz Lang*
SCENARIO AND DIALOGUE	*Thea von Harbou (with Paul Falkenberg)*
DIRECTOR OF PHOTOGRAPHY	*Fritz Arno Wagner*
ART DIRECTORS	*Emil Hasler and Karl Vollbrecht*
CHIEF EDITOR	*Paul Falkenberg*
Nero Film 1931	Black and white 99 minutes

Perspective: Sound in Cinema

The advent of sound in cinema caused a revolution in film making. Although in the first few years after the appearance of *The Jazz Singer,* in 1927, sound was considered primarily a novelty ("The Movies Talk!"), it soon became apparent that a significant dimension had been added to motion pictures. In the perspective that precedes our analysis of *The Last Laugh,* we discuss the advantages and disadvantages of both silent and sound films. In those pages we suggested a test by which one can judge whether a sound film is intrinsically different from a silent film: if the sound track were eliminated, the film would have to have been conceived in other ways.

In 1930 a film appeared that has become a classic not only because of its emotional intensity and striking visual techniques, but also for its historical significance. In *M,* sound was integrated with the other elements of the film to a degree previously not achieved. In the following paragraphs we will explore some of the means by which sound can be a vital component of a film, illustrating our generalizations whenever possible with examples taken from *M.*

A sound track conveys to us three basic types of sound. The most obvious is human speech. Then there are physical sounds: a glass breaking, footsteps on stairs, a train whistle (no one who has seen Hitchcock's *The Lady Vanishes* will forget the use of this sound at a climactic moment in the film), a door slamming—the list is endless. In this category belongs music played or a song sung by someone on the screen and heard on the sound track. Finally there is background music that serves, among other things, to create atmosphere, to heighten dramatic scenes or comment on them, and to facilitate transitions between sequences.

As the finest of silent motion pictures demonstrate, a film can be a work of art without sound. It is a question, however, of the degree of effectiveness and the possible expansion of the potentials of the medium. The former is especially true of human speech. We are not referring only to the ability of speech to increase the verisimilitude of a film, but also as a means of intensifying the drama of a scene. Instances of this quality in *M* include the children singing in the first shot of the film; Mrs. Beckmann calling Elsie's name (no title card could have conveyed the poignancy of her increasingly desperate and fearful cries); the Murderer's confession (the repeated phrase *"Ich kann nicht"* is etched in our memory as vividly as any image in the film).

An expansion of the potentials of the medium involves devices and scenes in a sound film that would be impossible without a synchronized sound track. Once again we turn to *M* for examples. The device of the whistled theme from *Peer Gynt* obviously could not have been used in a silent film. Of the scenes dependent on sound, one in particular is often cited by film historians to illustrate sound in cinema coming of age. It is the scene in the business office loft just before the Murderer is captured. The criminals have only five minutes to search six compartments. The camera holds on the Murderer huddled at the back of a compartment as we hear not only voices but also the noise of crashing doors and boxes being knocked over in increasing volume until the climax when a light is flashed on the Murderer. The suspense in the scene could not have been as intense without a sound track. There is also the scene in which the blind balloon seller in his union headquarters reacts first with pain to dissonant sounds on a barrel organ and then with pleasure to a melody. This evidence of his sensitivity to music makes more believable his recognition of the tune whistled by the Murderer.

The subject of sound in films becomes more complicated when we recognize the many combinations there can be of sound and images. Siegfried Kracauer, the brilliant writer on cinema history and theory, with his usual thoroughness, has categorized these combinations in *Theory of Film*, New York, 1960. We will ignore his variations and confine ourselves to a summary of the four major types of synchronization that he postulates.

Synchronization is when "the sounds and images coinciding on the screen are also synchronous in real life." (Ibid., p. 112.) Parallel synchronization occurs if speech and image carry parallel meanings, as in *M* when the camera is on the Murderer and he confesses in expressions and words his suffering before a court of criminals. We have counterpoint synchronization if the speech and image carry different but related meanings. The Murderer speaks works of innocence and defiance when he is first brought before the criminals, yet his face suggests his guilt and fears.

Asynchronization is when "sounds and images which do *not* occur simultaneously in reality are nevertheless made to coincide on the screen." (Ibid.) Here again there are two subdivisions. In counterpoint asynchronization the difference between the image and words is obvious; the relationship is more subtle and requires that we exercise our intuition to recognize it. In sequence II of *M*, a distraught mother calls out her daughter's name. As "Elsie!" is heard twice on the sound track, the screen presents a shot of an empty stairwell directly from above, followed by one of an empty basement (or loft).

In parallel asynchronization the sound is synchronized with images other than those of its source; however, speaker and images are intrinsically related. This device is used imaginatively by Lang in *M* twice to present pictorially what would otherwise be tedious recitation. The first is when the Chief of Police verbally lists the activities of the police and illustrative shots or brief scenes are flashed on the screen. The second example is when Lohmann looks through Inspector Groeber's report. A series of stills, one dissolving into the other, represents visually what Lohmann is reading. We hear on the sound track his reactions in comments or exclamations.

With synchronized sound, cinema gained not only in realism, but, even more important, added a dimension that when used creatively greatly increased the artistic potentials of film.

Story and Characterization

A child murderer has been at large for some months in a German city. The citizens are outraged and driven to semihysteria. We see a young girl, Elsie Beckmann, led away by a shadowy figure; later her body is found.

The police are stymied by a lack of clues. One procedure recently initiated is nightly raids on known hangouts of criminals.

A raid on The Crocodile is presented. We are introduced to Inspector Lohmann, chief of the Murder Squad. Across the street from the café a meeting takes place after the raid of representatives of divisions of the union of criminals. Schränker, master criminal, presides. The frenzied, indiscriminate activities of the police are endangering illegal activities. The four representatives agree with Schränker that they must attempt to capture the Murderer themselves.

Meanwhile, at a meeting city officials approve of Lohmann's plan to check on all mental patients released from asylums in the last five years.

The members of the beggars' union act as the eyes of the underworld in its search for the child killer. The police also are active. A detective searches the room of Hans Beckert, a former mental patient. While the detective is in the room, we follow Beckert, who is the Murderer, as he is frustrated in his designs on a little girl alone on a street, and we see that he struggles with his violent impulses.

In Lohmann's office, the detective gives his report. The brand of an empty packet of cigarettes found in Beckert's room is the clue the chief of the Murder Squad has sought. A second search of the suspect's room leads to conclusive proof that Beckert is the Murderer. The detective and two other plainclothes men wait for him to return.

At the same time that the police are finally having some success in their investigation, the criminals are also closing in on the Murderer. A Blind Beggar recognizes a tune being whistled in the distance as the one he heard when he sold a balloon to the man with Elsie Beckmann. He sends a colleague, Henry, after the Murderer. Henry manages to chalk an "M" on the back of the Murderer's coat, and then informs his superiors by telephone that the Murderer is being followed.

The Murderer runs from the young girl he is taking into a toy shop when he discovers the mark on his back. He evades his pursuers by disappearing into an office building. He hides in the loft, but is locked in there by a Night Watchman who is unaware of his presence.

Schränker and his associates raid the building, tie up the watchmen, and begin a thorough search. While the search is going on, the Murderer attempts to force open the lock in the loft door. Before he succeeds, however, he is located by the criminals. One of the bound watchmen manages to set off an alarm. In the moments before the police arrive, the criminals reach their victim and leave with him. The Burglar, one of the searchers inadvertently left behind, is apprehended by the police. Lohmann tricks him into revealing what has happened and where the Murderer has been taken.

In an abandoned distillery the Murderer is put on trial by members of the underworld. He is assigned a Lawyer. The Blind Beggar gives evidence. In an anguished confession the child murderer states that he cannot help murdering. The "defense Lawyer" supports his client and demands that the accused be handed over to the police.

After a moment of hesitation the "jury" of criminals divests itself of all pretense at lawfulness and moves as a mob toward the Murderer. Suddenly there is silence as everyone looks toward the cellar door. The police have arrived. A hand grips the Murderer's shoulder as a voice proclaims, "In the name of the law. . . ." Fade to black.

Even from this brief synopsis it is evident that there are four major characters in this film: the city and its citizens, Inspector Lohmann, Schränker, and Hans Beckert.

The city seems dense and solid (a cinematic illusion, for the film was a studio production). The walls, doors, arches, and pavements appear heavy and substantial, an effect accentuated by tonal contrasts of light and dark. On the other hand, this solidity is honeycombed with rooms, streets, stairways, and windows. It is as if man had not built the city but hollowed it out of stone and darkness. The camera repeatedly peers down narrow streets, corridors, and stairwells, usually from a very high angle, as though it is so confined that it must move up in order to achieve perspective.

High camera angles also make the people on the streets look small, crowded, and ineffectual. When they gather indoors, it is in confined quarters (the first café scene, at The Crocodile, the headquarters of the beggars, the trial). Faces in the crowds are individual, yet they are either flabby and tired or brutal and shifty. Only the children give an impression of freshness and innocence; however, in the first scene even they are singing about an evil man in black with his little axe. And there is little distinction between the "good citizens" and the denizens of the underworld. The same suspicion and outrage erupt in the bourgeois café as in The Crocodile; the same procedures and lines of authority appear in the meeting of the city officials and that of the criminals; the same hysteria is found in the street when an elderly man is surrounded by a mob as at the end of the trial of the Murderer.

Whatever their social level, occupation, or age the city dwellers are hemmed in, forced into an emotional symbiosis. The social organism can exist and generations succeed each other as long as everyone accepts his role in the hive. It is the outsider, prompted by irrational motives, that is the greatest threat to city dwellers, for he disrupts the equilibrium by means of which they survive and the city functions.

It is the responsibility of a branch of the law, the police department, to prevent such anarchy. This department is a microcosm of the city itself: an efficient organization that uses technology, yet depends for initiative and direction on human beings. The personification of this human element is Inspector Lohmann.

Lohmann is a cog in the machine, as we see at the meeting of officials, and relies on information supplied by his underlings. He could never have identified the Murderer without the list of former patients of asylums prepared for him and the report of the detective who examined Beckert's room. But through his intelligence and imagination he conceives of the line of investigation that eventually bears fruit; he makes the connection between the brand of cigarettes Beckert smokes and the same type of butts found at the scene of one of the murders; he tricks the Burglar into explaining what happened at the office building and confessing where the trial is taking place.

As with the other major characters in the film, he wears a disguise. The rotund, moon-faced police inspector, with his slicked-back hair and mouth puffing on a large cigar, has the appearance one associates with a prosperous bourgeois. Only his eyes—shrewd, penetrating, missing nothing—suggest his profession.

No one would mistake his profession, however, when he actually functions as a police inspector. Lohmann's attitude toward the criminals in The Crocodile is almost paternal (he addresses them as children). He can afford to be friendly, for he is completely in control of the situation. The criminals he deals with play a serious game according to certain unacknowledged rules, and Lohmann is a master player. But he is successful because he knows his quarry: their motives, weaknesses, and methods of operation. All he needs is a clue, even one as small as a circled article in a newspaper, and with the police machinery, his experience, and imagination, he can proceed from a crime to the identification of the culprit. The Murderer is at large because, as an inspector at the meeting of city officials notes, "the criminal and the victim are connected only by chance. An ingenuous impulse is the killer's only motive." With no clues that lead anywhere and such irrational behavior, Lohmann takes eight months to conceive of a procedure that will finally lead to an identification of the Murderer.

Lohmann has a professional's contempt for the interference in his business of outsiders and amateurs. This is demonstrated at the meeting when he sneers at help from the public. He is a product of the ant hill city, of Metropolis. Each group in the community has its own function and authority. This is another reason why the Murderer is so dangerous. He is subverting roles, so that citizens become avengers and criminals act as policemen and jurors.

The Inspector is not only a personification of the intelligence behind the police operations; Lohmann is also a person. He is individualized enough for us to identify with him and be interested in him as a human being. Although we are told nothing about his personal life, we can recognize the harassed public official who is irritated by the typing errors of a subordinate and grumbles about the coffee he is drinking while working overtime in his office. In one shot we see Lohmann as a fat man in shirtsleeves, with wrinkled socks and trousers unbuttoned at the waist.

As the police organization has a counterpart in the union of the underworld, so Lohmann has an alter ego in Schränker. The master criminal, with his steely eyes, black gloves and cane, and quick, calculated movements, is a sinister figure. He has committed at least three murders. Yet, as he explains in differentiating himself and his colleagues from the child murderer, he has always acted according to the rules:

SCHRÄNKER: When I run into a cop on my business, he knows the risk— and so do I. If one of us dies, okay, that's the risk one must take.

A moment later he points out, "We must make a living." The Murderer, on the other hand, is a "monster" who must be exterminated.

His horror of the Murderer is not only moral but also practical. The reputation of the corporate underworld is suffering; funds for "various projects" are running low; the operations of the organization are being disrupted by the increasing number of police raids.

As the police have used every resource available to them to track down the Murderer, so the criminals set in operation *their* machinery. It is Schränker who has the idea of using the beggars to look out for the killer, as Lohmann conceived of investigating former mental patients.

Once the Murderer is captured, Schränker is the most fervent of the criminals in preserving a semblance of order. He tells the Murderer that in his trial everything will be done "according to law." The final judgment, however, is a foregone conclusion. Schränker acts simultaneously as chief judge and prosecuting attorney. He adheres to order and procedure because they leave him with authority and work to his advantage. His goal is not justice but power and efficiency. He uses the law the way he uses people. When the Lawyer seems to be persuading the criminals, Schränker argues. He becomes silent, however, when he realizes that the mob will take control and fulfill his intention of having the Murderer executed.

The police and the underworld converge on the isolated outsider, the Murderer. Dramatically he stands between Lohmann and Schränker, a bourgeois like the former and a criminal like the latter, yet rejected by both. He shares with them, however, a physical disguise. Lohmann, as we have pointed out, does not conform to our image of an inspector of police in charge of murder cases; the ascetic looking, fastidious Schränker does not appear to be an archcriminal and murderer. Least of all does the fat, wide-eyed, apple-eating Beckert look like a child murderer. The disguises of these three are in contrast to most of the others in the film, who seem to have been typecast (indeed Lang did hire actual criminals for the trial sequence).

The background of Beckert is as little revealed as those of Lohmann and Schränker. All we learn is that he has been in an asylum, now lives in a boarding house, and has a friend named Paul who sent him a postcard. There is nothing more, not even how he earns a living. Our attention is drawn to the conflict between his drive to kill and his horror of what he does, climaxed by his outburst at the trial in the distillery. We soon realize that *M* has little to do with Hans Beckert the man, but focuses on that dangerous, pitiful Murderer that emerges from Beckert.

Themes and Interpretations

Fritz Lang has asserted that his motivation in making *M* was "to warn mothers about neglecting their children" (Marguerite Tazelar, "Fritz Lang Likes Hollywood, America and Social Themes," *New York Herald-Tribune*, Feb. 7, 1937. Quoted in Paul M. Jensen, *The Cinema of Fritz Lang*, New York, 1969). This statement makes one aware that D. H. Lawrence's adage about trusting a tale rather than the teller applies to cinema as well as fiction.

M, however, conveys far more than a cliché on parental responsibility. This is not to say that the film is void of any overt social message. It pleads persuasively that the mentally ill who commit illegal acts not be judged by the same standards as the rational criminal. We believe, however, that the most important theme in the film involves the relationship of the individual to the community. Most other themes suggested in our analysis are related to this major one.

In the preceding discussion of plot and characterization, we noted that the community is a character in *M*. Any modern community perpetuates itself through its children and sustains itself through machinery (technological and governmental) and an authority that preserves order. The essence of authority in a social organism is the acceptance by its members of limitations on the rights of the individual. A citizen must restrain his antisocial impulses when they seriously threaten order, acknowledge that laws are necessary for order, and respect those, such as the police, entrusted with preserving the law.

There are, of course, groups other than the police that maintain order. We see in *M* that the underworld of the city has become as organized as the police department, with its own hierarchy, specialists, unions, and operating methods. Theirs is a high-risk business. Life and freedom are at stake, but their endeavors may yield for them optimum financial rewards. The city does restrict the free enterprise of the criminals through the police. This system can only work, though, if there is between the police and the underworld some degree of mutual respect, recognition of ground rules (even when unstated), and not gratuitous violence. In this way each segment of the community, including that of the criminals, knows its role in the social organism and supports the community as a whole.

The greatest threat to the status quo is unbridled individualism, when a person will not or cannot accept limitations on his freedom. The Murderer is such a person in the film. Not only is he violently attacking the future of the community—its children—but also, like a disease carrier, is psychologically infecting its citizens. The symptoms of this disease are fear, suspicion of others, and loss of respect for authority. The ramifications are that individuals attack each other (as in the first café scene) and become mobs (as with the citizens in the street and the criminals in the distillery). Standard identities become blurred. The Murderer must be apprehended or the community will be destroyed. This is a fact recognized both by the conventional citizens, their chief arm of power, the police, and by the criminals.

The basic theme of *M*, then, is the need for the law to control dangerous individuals. If this film were less of a work of art than it is, we would find only an unimaginative insistence on the validity of vigorous authority. Instead, there are ambiguities. Although we are horrified by the child murders that Hans Beckert commits, we cannot help but feel a grudging sympathy for him. This is partly the result of the anguish that the Murderer endures from being subjected to inner forces he cannot suppress, carefully pointed up in Lang's direction and in Peter Lorre's superb performance. There is also the unfairness, no matter how justified, of a whole community relentlessly pursuing one person.

Siegfried Kracauer, in his famous study *From Caligari to Hitler*, Princeton, 1947, attempts to prove that pre-Hitler German films reveal a national predisposition toward authoritarianism. *M* well illustrates Kracauer's thesis. To a lesser degree, however, does the film support another theme he develops in his book: While German directors predominantly opted for authority, they were tempted by the opposite pole of freedom, even if it was associated in their minds with chaos. So Kracauer states that *The Cabinet of Dr. Caligari* "exposes the soul wavering between tyranny and chaos" (ibid., p. 74) and refers to *M* as "wavering between the notions of anarchy and authority" (ibid., p. 222).

We feel that "wavering" is too strong a word in the case of *M*. Lang has tempered his presentation of the need for authority by dealing with the Murderer as sympathetically as possible, but by making Hans Beckert a child murderer he has stacked his cinematic deck against any alternative. No sane person would argue that Beckert should have the freedom to continue to murder children. We might have misgivings, though, about a film—especially one produced in Germany in 1931 with a script by a writer who later became a staunch supporter of the Nazi regime—that has as its major theme that authority, both civil and criminal, should use every means at its disposal to protect the community by destroying or confining a destructive outsider. Too often in our century has "the law" and authority identified "the destructive outsider" in arbitrary terms that justify a prevailing ideology rather than the cause of justice. The specific case of a child murderer, however, supports the inherent logic of the plot of the film and its major theme.

Analysis of Major Sequences

I. A Children's Game

The first shot of the film is of children playing and the voice of one child singing on the sound track. The camera is very high, with just enough of an angle from the direct vertical for us to see the faces of some of the children. This is the first of a series of overhead shots conveying a sense of confinement and a diminishing of human beings, as though the camera were the eye of a deity objectively observing the activities of creatures in a maze.

The children are in a circle with one girl in the center (see circle motif, p. 133). The girl chanting a rhyme about a nasty man in black with his "little chopper" eliminates from the circle the child at whom she is pointing at the end of the song. The element of chance that determines who is "out" echoes the arbitrariness, so frustrating to the police, with which the Murderer chooses his victims.

The camera pans from the courtyard where the children are playing their ominous game up the side of the apartment to a balcony. A pregnant woman carrying a basket chides the children for chanting "that awful song." Her pregnancy suggests an investment in the future and she is concerned about the children.

The woman leaves, but the camera remains focused on the balcony.

Parental authority has gone and the children continue singing. A cut to a shot of the door to one of the apartments. The woman is ringing the doorbell. Mrs. Beckmann appears and takes the basket of laundry.

We follow Mrs. Beckmann into her kitchen and watch her in a medium close-up washing clothes. A cuckoo clock strikes; the camera pans to the clock. Church bells ring. It is 12 o'clock. Cut back to the mother as she smiles and dries her hands.

II. Elsie Beckmann

Lang uses cross-cutting throughout this sequence, except for three brief scenes at the end. To demonstrate how he applies this technique, we will now indicate the two lines of action in parallel development: the numeral "1" will refer to Elsie Beckmann on the streets and "2" will indicate Mrs. Beckmann at home.

1. A shot of the entrance to an elementary school with parents waiting. The children come out, and a pretty girl leaves the group and steps off the curb. A car blows its horn and she jumps back. A policeman halts the traffic and escorts her across.

The incident with the traffic is not a casual one. Every child in the city is exposed to dangers. We anticipate, however, standard dangers and employ figures of authority, particularly policemen, to protect our children. However, our protective barriers are not effective against a threat in disguise, such as a friendly, pudgy child molester, that can strike unexpectedly at any time.

2. A brief insert of Mrs. Beckmann setting the table.

1. The moving camera follows the girl as she walks along the street. She carries a satchel of schoolbooks attached to her back and bounces a ball with her right hand. She stops and throws the ball against a wall with a poster on it. The camera tilts up and tracks in so that we read the poster: "10,000 Marks Reward. Who is the Murderer?" For almost a year a child murderer has been at large (later we learn that eight children have been killed during the previous eight months). A shadow appears on the poster and off camera a soft voice admires the ball and asks the girl her name. She responds, also off camera, "Elsie Beckmann."

Probably the most reproduced photograph associated with *M* is of Elsie looking up and the shadow of a man silhouetted against the poster (Figure 7–1). One assumes this is a still from the film itself, but it is not. What we do see is the shadow on the poster and we hear only Elsie's voice off camera. The famous image is actually a still photograph taken on the set for publicity purposes.

2. Mrs. Beckmann is cooking. She glances up. A cut to the clock which reads 12:20. She hears sounds outside and goes to the door. A shot of two girls climbing the next flight of stairs. They tell Mrs. Beckmann that Elsie did not come with them. Cut back to the mother as she looks in the direction of the clock in the apartment; she closes the door.

Figure 7–1. *The Murderer speaks to Elsie Beckmann. (A posed photograph.)* (Courtesy Janus Films.)

1. A Blind Beggar is selling balloons in a high angle shot. The Murderer, his back to us, buys one, in the shape of a doll, for Elsie, who thanks him with a curtsy. Throughout this scene the Murderer whistles a tune: the theme of the trolls' dance from Part IV ("In the Hall of the Mountain King") of Grieg's *Peer Gynt Suite,* No. I. This theme becomes the Murderer's auditory leitmotif and, as we will see, the means by which he is captured by the underworld.

The Murderer leads Elsie away out of the frame, camera right.

2. Mrs. Beckmann is cooking lunch. She hears a bell and rushes to the door. It is a newspaper seller. With a haggard look on her face, as though

already anticipating what has happened to her daughter, Mrs. Beckmann asks the man if he has seen Elsie; of course, he has not.

After he leaves, she stands for a moment, then goes to the stairway banister and looks down. Cut to a shot of the stairwell directly from above: tiers of empty stairs from the edges of the frame to a square of emptiness at the center. The mother calls Elsie's name twice.

Mrs. Beckmann returns to her apartment and closes the door. A cut to the clock—1:15. In a long shot of the room, we see the mother open a window and again call out Elsie's name twice. The following shots succeed one another as Mrs. Beckmann calls her daughter's name with increasing desperation:

Brief repeat shot of the stairwell.

Cut to a shot of the basement of the apartment house (or it could be a loft). It is completely empty except for clothes hanging on a line. The contrast of light and shadow is dramatic, almost theatrical.

Medium close-up, slight angle down, of Elsie's place at the table, with a setting and empty chair.

1. Medium close-up from above of patches of grass and bushes on the side. Elsie's ball rolls from the bushes and stops in the center of the frame. Cut to a shot, very low angle, of the doll balloon caught in some wires, finally carried away by the wind. Fade to black.

The epilogue of this sequence consists of three brief scenes.

A shot from high above of a newspaper seller surrounded by a crowd as he announces a new child murder. Time has elapsed since the fade to black; Elsie's body has been found.

The Murderer is seated at a large window ledge. He is writing, smoking, and whistling the theme from *Peer Gynt*. His back is to the camera, angled down, which soon tracks in. Cut to what he is writing. The police have refused to take any notice of his letters, so he is writing directly to the press. "I am the child murderer and I have not yet reached the end."

The last scene of this sequence begins with a close-up of a poster. The camera slowly tracks back, again from a high angle, to reveal a crowd reading the poster. The last statement read aloud by one individual in the crowd refers to "terror in our town." The sound of the crowd and the reader mixes with the voice of a radio announcer as there is a cut to the next scene.

III. Accusations in a Cafe, a Home, and on the Street

The newscast mixes with the voice of an old man reading from a newspaper. We are in a café, with the camera hovering over a table at which sit a group of elderly, obviously well-off men. How terror has instilled distrust in even the substantial citizens of the town is demonstrated by the way accusations are recklessly made.

The next three scenes also illustrate how the child murderer has poi-

soned the body-citizenry with fear and irrationality. A search of a work-
ingman's room by the police is prompted by an anonymous letter. A man
is threatened by a mob because he speaks to a little girl. Hysteria reigns
in a crowd when the rumor is spread that an arrested pickpocket led off
a bus by a policeman is the murderer.

IV. The Machinery of the Police in Action

A Minister is talking on the telephone to the Chief of Police. The latter
reports on what action has been taken. This scene makes use of a counterpoint of sounds and image that can be labeled parallel asynchronization
(a definition is given in the "Perspective" section of this chapter).

As the Chief of Police speaks, the following shots or scenes (with occasional inserts of him and the Minister on the telephone) succeed each
other: police studying fingerprints; an official dictating a report; the
Murderer making faces in a mirror; a police station at night; detectives
searching a park; a map of the city with circles and dates on it (see circle
motif, p. 133); two shots of detectives questioning owners of shops; a
detective talking to a grocer and his wife; a scene of two witnesses arguing about their evidence; police searching a woods and other areas; police dogs at the edge of a lake; detectives checking papers at a flophouse;
papers being checked at a railroad station; a deserted street at night.

One of these images is incongruous with the others, that of the Murderer making faces (the first time we actually see his face). It is not, of
course, a direct illustration of something the Chief of Police is saying; it
does, however, sum up visually the major problem he faces. Not only does
the Murderer leave no significant clues, but he is in disguise. If the fat
rather effeminate, almost shy face of the Murderer had the distorted
menacing appearance of the image in the mirror, then he could easily be
identified. But the demonic creature dwells within the Murderer and does
not appear physically (see mirror motif, p. 133).

V. The Crocodile

After the Chief of Police notes that there are nightly raids on various
underworld hangouts, we shift to one such raid, but never return to the
Chief of Police on the telephone.

From the second shot of this sequence, a dark, wet street seen from a
very high angle, to the appearance of Inspector Lohmann in the bar,
Lang creates a number of visually exciting shots. Characteristics of these
shots include high angles, unusual perspectives (such as the platoon of
policemen seen from within a narrow alley), and an emphasis on shadows
contrasted by areas of brightly lit, effective group scenes (such as the
police marching down the street and the criminals rushing to escape,
halted at the staircase, and pushed back by the police).

There are two incidents in this sequence that set precedents repeated in one form or another in many crime films involving police raids to the present day. First, there are the ingenious, usually humorous, but inevitably unsuccessful efforts of criminals to escape the police. In this film one criminal tries to get away through a skylight, and another hides in the ladies' toilet. Secondly, the equipment and weapons confiscated by the police often are piled up. For some reason, the existence of these implements, such as a burglar's kit, usually amuses an audience. Perhaps this is so because varied and intricate instruments seem incongruous with our romantic image of the criminal as daring, self-sufficient, and in revolt against the complexities and conformity of our technological society. These tools of the trade also reinforce Lang's theme of the parallel between the underworld and the bourgeois world.

This sequence shows the attitude of the criminals toward the Murderer, how the frantic efforts of the police are disrupting the activities of the underworld, and the relationship of the police and the criminals. It is the proprietress of The Crocodile who sums up the criminals' view of the raid and the Murderer as she talks to the sergeant: "Do you know how mad everyone is about this guy. A raid every night. . . . Crooks get sort of tender when they see kids. If they catch that murderer and pig, they'd wring his neck."

Lohmann is introduced in this sequence. He is almost paternal toward the criminals. His first statement is, "Now, now, children." For their part they may taunt him and refer to "fatty Lohmann," but they obviously admire and respect his authority. Although they object to the raid, the criminals accept the Inspector examining their papers. This is standard procedure, in accordance with the "rules" of the *modus vivendi* that exists between the police and the underworld.

As the proprietress of the café watches the sergeant and a policeman leaving, there is a cut to a medium close-up of a man at a window in another setting looking through binoculars. This is a transition to the next sequence.

VI. *Two Meetings*

The four men in the room opposite the bar are evidently criminals. Their conversation reveals their two preoccupations. The way in which the police activity has interfered with the business of the underworld is once again emphasized. The manner in which they speak of Schränker indicates the awe with which they regard him. We learn that the police have been searching for him for six years and that he killed at least two policemen in London in escaping from a trap set for him. As the Safebreaker puts it: "The best man between Berlin and San Francisco."

Schränker finally appears. After chiding them for leaving the curtains open, he removes his leather overcoat and sits down. He is elegantly dressed and wears black gloves. His bowler hat is on the table and throughout the sequence he will handle his cane walking stick.

As chairman of the board he convenes with authority the meeting of officials of "our union." The four men represent the organizations within the union with voting power. The only item on the agenda is what to do about the Murderer, who is "interfering with our business" and is an "outsider."

During the scene of the opening of the conference there are various medium close-ups, two- and three-shots of the five men, and high-angle or eye-level shots of the whole group around the circular table. It is, however, Schränker who is the visual as well as emotional center of interest. There are more close-ups of him than any of the others; one shot is from behind him with the four looking at him with rapt attention; shots of the others often include in the frame his gloved hands moving back and forth across his cane.

During a speech at the end of this section of the scene, there is a cut from a medium close-up of him to a high-angle shot, the camera facing Schränker. He says, "I ask you . . ." and makes a gesture with his right hand. A cut to the Chief of Police at a meeting of officials around a long conference table. He makes the same gesture as Schränker and completes the criminal's statement: ". . . for advice."

Thus begins the second unit of cross-cutting (the first was of Mrs. Beckmann and Elsie). It consists of eleven fragments of scenes (from a single shot to many), beginning with Schränker making his gesture and ending with his shadow on the wall. Words spoken in one setting may overlap those spoken at another, but this does not happen visually— there are no superimpositions or dissolves. The gist of what is said by a criminal and a police official is also on occasion similar. The chief effect of this juxtaposing of the two meetings is to emphasize the parallel nature of the organization and operation of the officials of the police and the criminal leaders. Also we recognize the importance of leadership, for it is Lohmann and Schränker at their respective meetings who finally offer intelligent—and ultimately successful—plans for catching the child murderer.

After Lohmann's final speech there is a shot of the criminals at the table. A cut to Schränker's finger pointing, then his hand flat, fingers spread out, pressed on a map of the city. In the upper portion of the frame we see his cane and part of his hat. It is a frightening image of power over the city, especially because the hand is gloved, as though its owner has protected himself from human contacts that might make him vulnerable and less ruthless. There is a cut to the shadow of the group on the wall; Schränker's silhouette is in the center. As he announces that it is the beggars' organization that can guard the children, he rises. His shadow swells, his left hand a pounding fist, his right hand at his hip. This sihouette, with none of the humanity a photograph of the man might suggest, is a personification of power and confidence.

A cut to the beggars' headquarters.

VII. The Beggars Organized and in Operation

In the building housing the beggars' union, we first visit a cafeteria. A pan to the ceiling, dissolve to outside, then another pan to the second floor and a track in through the window bring us to an office in which the beggars are assigned areas of the city. Schränker in his leather overcoat is leaning against the wall. A cut to a room where there is a collection of secondhand goods; a barrel organ is being demonstrated. We see in a close-up the Blind Beggar who sold a balloon to the Murderer when he was with Elsie Beckmann. The blind man's sensitivity to music is revealed as he reacts with pain to noise and with pleasure to a melody. A polka played on the barrel organ is a transition to a series of scenes of the beggars in operation.

The first shot of the first scene is notable. It shows from a very high angle a beggar operating a barrel organ; he is in the camera left, lower corner of the frame. Four groups of youngsters at various spots along the edge of the frame form an uneven, broken circle (see circle motif, p. 133). Unlike the very first shot of the film, in which the children were chanting, there is no one in the center. Unknown to the youngsters, they are being guarded from the Murderer.

In the remaining scenes in this sequence, we observe beggars, including a fraudulent blind man, watching various children.

VIII. The Circle around the Murderer Constricts

From the street there is a cut to Lohmann in his office. He is going through reports from mental institutions and a file of present addresses of patients.

A cut to the Murderer coming out of a house and moving to camera left. Another man, from camera right, enters the building.

The second man is a detective, but like the beggars, he disguises himself. He tells the woman who rents Hans Beckert a room that he represents the "income tax people." The landlady, Mrs. Winkler, brings him into Beckert's room. When she leaves, he searches it. In a high overhead shot we see him examining a large oval table (see circle motif, p. 133) in search of evidence that it was used for writing the letter to the press.

A cut to a medium close-up of the Murderer buying fruit.

Back to the detective continuing his search. Among other things, he finds an empty cigarette pack. Although the detective does not realize it at the moment, this is the clue that will lead to the identification of the Murderer as Hans Beckert.

We return to the Murderer before a window display. The camera is next positioned inside the store, so that we watch the Murderer looking at the display. His head is framed by the reflection of a diamond-shaped array of knives, the points directed at him (see knife motif, p. 133). Other patterns glitter around him as this innocuous-looking, baby-faced man eats an apple with one hand and holds a bag of fruit with the other. From a subjective shot, from the point of view of the Murderer, we observe that the knives are set around a mirror (see mirror motif, p. 133). Once again we view the man from inside the window. He stops chewing and stares intently. Cut to the street perspective, so that we observe what he sees in the mirror: it is a girl leaning against a railing across the street behind him; her reflection is also framed by the knives. The effect of this image on the Murderer—seen in a lengthy close-up of him—is startling: his eyes bulge, he wipes his hand across his mouth, he sways slightly. Another cut to a shot of the image of the girl. Return to the Murderer; he seems to have difficulty breathing; his eyes close; and he sways slightly. The reflection of the girl walks out of the mirror. The Murderer in the next shot has gained control of himself, or rather something has gained control of him. His expression is sinister as he turns and watches where the girl goes. He walks out of the frame, camera left, whistling the *Peer Gynt* theme.

A brief insert of the detective in Beckert's room.

Another window display viewed from the street. The small girl we saw in the mirror is looking at the display, particularly at an arrow moving up and down and behind it a whirling spiral (see circle motif, p. 133). She continues to walk. We hear the familiar Grieg theme. The Murderer is not seen at this moment, just as he did not appear (only his shadow and his voice on the sound track) when he approached Elsie Beckmann. Suddenly the girl halts, turns, and runs to a woman who has entered, camera right, into the frame. The whistling abruptly stops. The camera pans as they walk past the Murderer, his back to the camera, in the doorway of a shop. The woman and girl turn a corner. Cut back to the Murderer as he emerges from the doorway and watches them walk away. He looks exhausted and tense as he nervously scratches his left hand clasped to his chest. Behind him, the shadow of the arrow in the window display moving up and down appears repeatedly to pierce the whirling spiral (see circle motif, p. 133).

The next shot is of the Murderer entering the terrace of a café and sitting at an outdoor table. The camera is beyond the trellis covered by ivy, so that his profile in the camera left portion of the frame is barely visible through the foliage. After he has ordered a brandy, the camera tracks in to a medium close-up. Throughout the scene the camera remains outside the foliage, as though unable or too discreet to close in on the private agony of the Murderer.

He begins to whistle the tune that obsesses him. The brandy is brought; he swallows it in one gulp, then does the same with a second glass. As he leans forward and stares into space, he puts a cigarette in his mouth, but immediately throws it down and presses his fists into his eyes as if blocking out a vision. He begins shrilly whistling or, it is not clear which, hears the whistling in his mind. Now he covers his ears with his fists.

The lights of the café come on. The Murderer starts and quickly rises.

The camera pulls back. He pays his bill. Composed, his hands in his pockets, whistling once again, he strolls out of the frame.

Through the scenes in front of the window display and the one in the café we learn of the inner conflict of the Murderer. His agony is so genuine that we cannot help but feel sympathy for him.

IX. The Murderer Is Identified

At the end of the café scene, with the Murderer walking away, there is a cut to Lohmann in his office. The detective we saw in Beckert's room is making his report. The brand of the empty cigarette pack, Ariston, strikes a responsive chord in Lohmann's memory. He calls for the file on one of the earlier murders.

Cut to the Blind Beggar with his balloons. On the sound track we hear the Murderer whistling his tune. His shadow sweeps across the body of the balloon seller. The Blind Beggar recognizes the tune as the same one that was whistled when he sold a balloon to the man with Elsie Beckmann. He sets a colleague, Henry, in pursuit.

The Murderer has captivated another young girl. Henry follows the two to a shop where the Murderer buys fruit and candy. The young man hides as they emerge from the store. The Murderer accepts an orange from the bag of fruit offered by the girl.

The melodramatic movements that follow are an obvious but effective attempt on Lang's part to frighten us. The Murderer looks anxiously up and down the street. He reaches into a trousers pocket and . . . cut to a very tight close-up of a knife in the Murderer's hand. The blade of a switchblade knife flicks out, glittering in the street light. The position of the knife in relation to the body of the Murderer gives it a sexual overtone (see knife motif, p. 133).

An insert of Henry ready to intervene.

Anticlimax: a shot of the blade being used to peel the orange.

Henry takes out a piece of chalk and draws a large "M" on his hand. We watch him walk past the Murderer, pretend to stumble on an orange peel, and press his hand on the back of the Murderer. Henry's complaint, supposedly referring to the orange peel, is ironic: "I should report you to the police. You're a public menace."

When Henry bumped into the Murderer, there was a quick cut to a close-up of the knife on the ground. When we return to a two-shot of the Murderer and the girl, we see him, evidently frightened, staring in the direction in which Henry has gone. Once again there is a close-up of the knife. The hand of the girl enters the frame and grasps it. The camera follows her as she straightens up. A medium close-up of the two as the girl hands the knife to the Murderer, whose eyes are now closed and lips parted. The girl pushes the knife toward him and says, "Uncle." He takes the knife. As he does so, the camera pans around him and we see the "M" on his back near his left shoulder.

A cut to Lohmann's office. He has confirmed his recollection that the cigarette stubs at the scene of one of the murders were Aristons. The detective suddenly realizes that perhaps the letter was written on the window sill rather than the table.

The next scene takes place in Beckert's room, where Lohmann and his assistant find all the evidence necessary to prove that Hans Beckert is the Murderer.

Cut to Schränker and the other chief criminals, who are informed by telephone that the Murderer has been "marked."

X. *The Murderer Pursued and Captured*

We return to the Murderer walking down a street with the girl. We see that the Murderer, unknown to him, is being followed.

We watch the two from inside a window display of a toy shop (Figure 7–2). Directly over the head of the Murderer are the legs of a harlequin, that master of disguises and initiator of problems. The girl points out a toy. As they are about to enter the shop, the girl remarks that there is a mark on "uncle's" shoulder. The Murderer looks into a mirror (see mirror motif, p. 133) and in a close-up we see his expression of shock and fear (Figure 7–3).

FIGURE 7–2. *The Murderer and a girl looking at a window display of a toy shop.* (Courtesy Janus Films.)

Figure 7–3. *The Murderer discovers that he is marked with a chalk "M."*
(Courtesy Janus Films.)

The girl tries to wipe off the letter, but the Murderer grips her hand
and starts to move away. A high-pitched whistle is heard. The Murderer
lets go of the girl and runs away.

A set of shots shows his desperate efforts to escape. The most effective
is an overhead one of an empty street. The Murderer rushes in first one
direction, then another, like a terrified insect in a box. Every exit is
blocked by beggars. Shrill whistles echo in the air; appropriately, whistling, the physical indication that the Mr. Hyde in him has taken command, betrays his identity and is the means used by his enemies to
organize their pursuit of him.

The Murderer rushes into the courtyard of an office building. Cuts between shots of him hiding and the beggars trying to locate him. A clock
strikes six. A crowd of office workers leaves the building.

Cut to the detectives waiting in Beckert's room. One of them says it is 6:30. We see here how Lang manipulates cinematic time as opposed to physical time. There is not necessarily a simultaneity between sets of shots in parallel development. Between the shot of the office workers leaving and the one of the detectives half an hour has elapsed, although it was only a moment on the screen.

Back to the office building as a watchman closes the grilled gates. Shots of a beggar explaining on the telephone what has happened and the criminals considering the situation. When the beggar describes the building and mentions it has a loft, there is a cut to the half-opened entrance door to the loft area. A Watchman halts before the door and then enters. He begins testing the locked doors to individual storage areas. We see the Murderer hiding in one near the end of the loft corridor. This searching of the compartments will be repeated, although with greater suspense evoked, when the criminals do the same.

The Watchman only goes halfway down the corridor, then returns to the door and leaves. The Murderer is relieved until he hears the Watchman lock the door.

A return to the criminals. Schränker insists that the police not be called, but that they capture the Murderer themselves. He has a plan.

It is 11 o'clock when a policeman walks up to the gate and rings the bell. It is Schränker in perhaps the most incongruous of the many disguises that appear in this film. He forces the watchman to unlock the gate and is followed in by a large group of criminals carrying their tools. The watchman is tortured until he reveals that there are two other watchmen on their rounds.

From this point in the film to when the Murderer is actually captured, we see the criminals searching the building with the efficiency and skill of a commando squad. During this search there are three cuts to the Murderer. In the first, he frantically tries to open the lock. In the process he snaps off the blade of his knife. His sole weapon is gone; now he is impotent. He stops in terror as he hears a watchman passing. In the second set of shots he pulls a nail from a plank of wood. Finally, he hammers on the nail with the handle of his knife. The tapping is heard by one of the criminals, who rushes off and tells his colleagues of his discovery.

We return to the Murderer attempting to use the nail to open the door. Cut to a shot of the other side of the door where the criminals are gathering. Back to the Murderer as he looks at the nail with satisfaction and is about to place it in the lock. At that moment the handle moves very slightly. The Murderer moves away from the lock in terror. Panic-stricken he switches off the light and rushes down the corridor.

The door flies open and a silhouette of Schränker and the other criminals stands out against the light. The search of the loft begins.

Meanwhile, one of the watchman manages to pull the alarm. A cut to a police station where a bell rings and a ticker-tape machine begins operating. A policeman reads the numbers and a filing cabinet is consulted. Technology has taken over.

One of the criminals informs Schränker that the alarm has been set off. The master criminal, always cool and authoritative, points out that they have five minutes left. The search continues frantically. The suspense has been cleverly heightened, for now the criminals are working against time.

Cut to the Murderer hiding at the back of one of the compartments. A faint light is supplied by a barred window behind him. The camera holds on this medium shot as on the sound track we hear Schränker, other voices, and the noise of doors being knocked down. As the sounds become louder, the Murderer shrinks farther down behind his barrier until only his hat is visible. The criminals reach the door of the compartment where the Murderer is hiding. A crashing sound, the Murderer jumps up and is spotlighted by the beams of flashlights; his expression reveals the terror and helplessness of a trapped animal. He falls back as voices cry, "Here he is. Here he is!"

The men leave the building in a rush carrying the Murderer trussed in a carpet. There is now silence, in strong contrast to the voices and agitation of the previous scenes. A shot of the deserted watchmen's office and two bound and gagged unconscious guards.

The first sound we hear is the voice of the Burglar, who is unaware that his companions have left, from the floor below coming up through a hole. Then begins the humorous scene of the Burglar climbing up into the arms of the law. There is a transition from the office building where the Burglar begins to speak to the office of Inspector Groeber where he completes the sentence.

XI. The Police Learn They Have Collaborators

Groeber is unable to persuade the Burglar to reveal what has happened. From one of the watchmen he learns that the criminals were searching for someone. Groeber is confused, and he decides to turn to Lohmann for help.

A cut to Lohmann in his office talking on the telephone to the detectives still waiting for Beckert to return. There is a shot of Lohmann from under the table: his socks hang, his pot belly is protruding, his eyes are half closed, his face is lined, a cigar smokes in his mouth—the very image of an overworked, exhausted Inspector of Police. Groeber enters and brings a report with him.

Once again we have an example of parallel asynchronization; the last time was when the Chief of Police was talking on the telephone to the Minister. Seventeen brief shots, almost stills, dissolve one into the other illustrating what Lohmann is reading. We have his comments on the sound track. Some viewers may find this series repetitious, for it shows what was already observed in the last sequence. There is, though, a possible justification. We see through the eyes of the police a ransacking of a building that is apparently without motive. We are reminded, as with the child murderer, that the machinery of the police cannot operate on a crime without discernible motive or clues—in other words, an illogical crime. In the case of the ransacking, however, the apprehended Burglar is a clue.

Lohmann immediately sets to work on the Burglar. He communicates to the prisoner the false impression (a form of disguise) that one of the watchmen has died. The possibility of a murder charge is too much for the Burglar, and he confesses.

The exchange between the two men reveals Lohmann's cleverness, but also offers Lang another opportunity for humor, the last in the film. When Lohmann suggests that one of the watchmen is dead, there is an insert of the Watchman gorging himself on sausages, sauerkraut, and beer. The Inspector's astonishment on hearing that the criminals were searching for the child murderer is delightful to see: his mouth falls open and his cigar drops; his trembling hand moves to his mouth for a cigar that is no longer there; a few moments later he douses his head in water.

As the Burglar informs Lohmann that the Murderer has been taken to an abandoned distillery, there is a cut to the façade of a factory.

XII. *The Trial of the Murderer*

After three external shots of the distillery, during which the Burglar and Lohmann's voices are heard off camera, there is a cut to the interior. Two men come down a short flight of stairs. In a few moments, they reappear, shoving the protesting Murderer up the stairs with his jacket pulled over his head. Cut to a longer flight of stairs, an iron door at the top, seen from a low angle. The Murderer is pushed from above through the open door and falls to the bottom of the stairs. As he curses the men, he pulls the jacket off his head. He turns and stares.

The next shot presents what the Murderer sees. A pan from camera left to right reveals a group of more than a hundred people crowded at one end of what must be the basement of the distillery. The two end portions of the group rise back into vaulted areas. In front of the longer center segment of the crowd, about three rows in depth, is a table consisting of three frame horses supporting planks. Seated at the center of the table is Schränker, his cane before him, the Pickpocket to his right, and the Conman and Safebreaker to his left. Thick ropes are tied to each of the end horses supporting the table planks; these ropes disappear on each side, at the lower corners, of the frame. Later we see the ropes enclose the area where the Murderer is confined during the trial. An inverse L frame, like a part of a miniature gallows, leans against the table and supports a single bulb.

During the slow pan of the jury or tribunal not an individual stirs and there is not any very sharp definition of the faces. It is even possible that the pan was of a blowup of a still photograph. The absolute stillness is broken by the Murderer's cry of "Help!"

From now until the end of the sequence there will be a struggle between two groups. On the one side is the jury of criminals: belligerent toward the Murderer from the beginning and at least twice becoming a revengeful mob. They are led by Schränker, who both restrains and encourages them.

Opposing the tribunal is the Murderer and the Lawyer. The two men at one point in the struggle seem to be eliciting sympathy for their side. They could not, however, possibly succeed in the end, if only because Schränker would not allow it. That the Murderer is not himself murdered is only because of the last-minute intervention of representatives of an authority greater than that of Schränker.

The trial proper begins with the Murderer insisting there must be some mistake. The camera tracks to a medium shot, then the Murderer moves toward the camera until there is a medium close-up as he pleads his innocence. A hand appears in the frame from camera left and moves with uncertainty near the head of the Murderer; finally it falls heavily on his shoulder. This is the first of three times during the sequence when a seemingly disembodied hand will reach out and grip the Murderer's shoulder. The Murderer cries out in fear.

The camera tracks back to a two-shot of the Blind Beggar and the Murderer, who has turned around to face him. "No mistake," the Blind Beggar says. The camera moves farther back and now we see that in the Beggar's other hand there is a balloon in the shape of a doll. It was this type of balloon, the Beggar points out, that the Murderer gave to Elsie Beckmann. At the mention of the child's name, the balloon rises to the full length of a string attached to it. A cut to a shot from above: the balloon in the foreground, the terrified Murderer staring at it, a portion of the crowd in the background (once again the crowd appears to be in a still photograph). The Murderer stumbles back, stuttering Elsie's name, until he bumps into the table. The next shot is from behind the Murderer; the staircase is still guarded by two men.

Schränker begins speaking. At the sound of his voice, the Murderer whirls around and faces the camera. A series of eight shots follows, alternating without exception back and forth between Schränker, showing photographs of murdered children (or the photographs themselves), and the Murderer biting his hand and backing up again.

The semihysterical Murderer loses all control and makes a dash for the door. In the scene that commences now, the barely repressed bloodlust of the "jury" comes to the surface and it turns into a mob that screams, curses, and encourages the men on the stairs to beat him. The Murderer is knocked down the stairs and thrown against a wooden barrier. As he protests that they have no right to do this to him, we see a woman shouting at him that he hasn't any rights and demanding that he be killed. This last cry is taken up by the mob. In one shot, from the point of view of the Murderer, we see the group screaming and gesticulating; even at a distance the hate they feel is evident in their expressions.

With a shout and a gesture Schränker quiets them and turns to speak to the Murderer. As he assures the prisoner in a sarcastic tone that he will get his rights, even to having a lawyer, the camera moves along rows of marvelously individual, attentive faces in the crowd. We recall that Lang hired actual criminals to play in this sequence.

The Murderer, crouched against the wooden barrier and snarling his contempt, looks up when for the second time a hand enters the frame and taps him on the shoulder. The camera pans up to reveal the Lawyer, who makes it clear that his "client's" life is at stake. The horrified Murderer alternately begs and demands to be turned over to the police, which provokes laughter from the criminals. Schränker will not allow this because he will plead insanity ("paragraph 51") and spend the rest of his life in an institution, escape, or be pardoned to resume his crimes. Schränker asserts with intensity that they will not permit this to happen.

In medium close-up we see the Murderer falling to his knees, covering his face with his hands, and sobbing, "I can't help it . . . I can't . . . I can't help it." After one of the criminals sneers, "The old story," the Murderer lowers his hands and begins his long and moving confession.

In every sense this is the climax of the film, its strongest scene. In the next section of this analysis we will discuss the objective approach that Lang develops in *M* and how and why that objectivity is rent in this scene. We should point out here, however, that even the Murderer's fear from the time he is labelled with an "M" to this moment at the trial is like a simple tune played in many keys without any imaginative variations. Having become accustomed to an objective approach and repeated expressions of one emotion, we are unprepared for the searing intensity of the Murderer's statement, and it is all the more moving for just that reason.

Peter Lorre has been highly praised for his acting in *M*. His confession in this scene justifies that praise. Until the final sequence he depended mostly on his face to convey the ambiguity of the Murderer: a boyish face with large eyes and fat cheeks that somehow suggests decadence, as if at any moment he might smile charmingly and whisper an obscene phrase. There are a couple of perfect gestures, such as scratching his hand when the girl he sees in the mirror escapes him. His presentation of inner conflict when we see him from within the window display and later in the café are effective within their limitations. The scene in the business office loft and at the beginning of the trial generally demonstrate how many ways an actor can express fear by widening and bulging his eyes. This is not noted solely as a criticism of Lorre. A viewer who is concentrating on the actor soon realizes how little material the script writer, Thea von Harbou, has given Lorre until his monologue. Previous to the trial, the

Murderer speaks twelve sentences, not one of which is more than four words. Only in his monologue does Lorre have the opportunity to express complex emotions.

The monologue (only key phrases are quoted here) builds up to two main climaxes. The first is reached at the sentence "They are there, always there"; the second at the end when he exclaims, "I can't go on."

The camera is a bit above eye level as, in a medium close-up, the Murderer, on his knees, drops his hands and begins. "What do you know about it? . . . You're criminals because you want to be. . . ." His voice is tense but quiet and in control. It becomes high-pitched as he says, "I can't help myself," clutches his hands to his chest, and stares ahead. "This evil thing inside me. . . ."

A cut to Schränker and a portion of the crowd as the criminal asks, "You've got to murder?" Back to the Murderer in a close-up, directly facing the camera. The agony in his voice is naked. "Always there's this terrible force inside me. . . . Always I walk the streets alone. . . . And always I am followed—soundlessly. It's me pursuing myself. I want to run —to escape from myself. But I can't. . . . Forced to run endless streets . . . pursued by ghosts . . . ghosts of mothers . . . children."

During this portion of the monologue, there are three cuts to individual criminals: an old man nodding understandingly, two staring men, and two prostitutes, one of them nervously twisting her handkerchief. After the last insert, the Murderer is seen in a medium close-up again, still facing the camera, although the angle is higher. The first climax is reached as he shouts hysterically, "They are there—always there."

"Except when—" His voice lowers, his eyes cloud over as he watches an inner vision, his lips part, his clutching hands rise toward his neck, a neck. We can almost see him being seduced into his vision of sadistic satisfaction. A moment of silence. The taut wire of emotion within him breaks: his shoulders sag and hands drop to his sides. "But I can't remember anything. . . ." Tension is quickly building up again. "Who knows what it is like to be me. . . . How I'm forced to act. . . . Don't want to . . . must. . . ." He screams: "And then—a voice screams." It is as if his own scream were an echo of what he hears. "I can't bear to hear it." His body tightens into a ball of agony and he throws himself against the wooden barrier, his fists pressed against his ears. "I can't go on," he howls. At the second and final climax of the monologue, the repeated *"Ich kann nicht"* pounds in our ears and, for most viewers, for that moment, our horror of the Murderer turns to pity.

But the cold Schränker is not moved. He stands up and insists the fact that the Murderer cannot help himself is his death sentence. First one woman behind him, and then many others shout approval. We see the agitated "jurors" behind Schränker.

The Lawyer rises to speak. Throughout this scene every shot of him will be from a slightly low angle. His defense is a simple one: No one can be punished for something for which he is not responsible. A sick man should be handed over to a doctor, not an executioner. This man must be granted the protection of the law.

His plea is constantly interrupted. The camera cuts back and forth between the Lawyer and individuals in the crowd, Schränker, or a segment of the group. Schränker repeats his previous statements about the inadequacy of "paragraph 51." Then he settles back; further manipulation of the group is unnecessary, for its own momentum is transforming it into a mob. A prostitute makes the most inflammatory speech when she reminds the other of the suffering of the mothers of the dead children.

Resolutely the Lawyer stands up to them, but the swell of hate finally breaks and the screaming, hysterical mob rises up and rushes toward the Murderer. There is a long shot that gives the impression that they must travel a great distance to reach the Murderer.

A voice and a whistle penetrate the noise: "Police . . . Hands up!" An abrupt stillness falls on the group and the immobilized criminals slowly raise their hands. Schränker is the last to do so after having looked around for a means of escape.

A cut to the Murderer as he rises, shaking his head in bewilderment. The camera tracks into a medium close-up. For the third time a hand moves into the frame and grips the Murderer's shoulder. A voice off camera intones: "In the name of the law. . . ."

The theme from *Peer Gynt* is heard as the scene fades to black. After a moment we hear Mrs. Beckmann's voice saying, "We, too, should keep a closer watch on our children." Many viewers will consider this statement anticlimatic and a clumsy effort to end the film on a moral note.

Style and Approach

Of the thirty-nine films Fritz Lang directed in Germany and the United States between 1919 and 1960, *M* is the most carefully structured and stylistically imaginative. There may be more striking scenes in *Metropolis* and more impressive shots in *Die Nibelungen* and *Der Müde Tod* (*Destiny*), but in none of Lang's German films and surely not in even the best of his generally undistinguished Hollywood movies did he so effectively fuse as in *M* what he was attempting to convey with how he conveyed it.

Lang employed a number of techniques and approaches in addition to the cogent use of sound discussed in "Perspective" to make *M* a visually and emotionally memorable film. Chief among these are the following: a clear articulation of one sequence to the next that gives a forward thrust in time to the film; effective cross-cutting; visual motifs; achieving the tone of a documentary until the last sequence; and a borrowing from cinematic expressionism of certain pictorial effects.

Lang is particularly clever in *M* in creating types of transitions from one sequence to another that are not only fluent, but also give a forward thrust in time to the development of the plot. It is as though the film built up an internal momentum that carried it inexorably to its conclusion.

In the previous section of this chapter on *M*, we indicated specifically the forms of transition from each sequence to the next. Two examples, however, will illustrate what we mean by fluency and forward thrust in time. At the end of sequence IV, the Chief of Police describes the efforts of the police, and we have shots or brief scenes of each of these activities. He mentions raids on underworld hangouts. We expect another example in the series. But we never return to the Chief of Police, and the raid on The Crocodile becomes a sequence in itself. The articulation between the two sequences is smooth, graceful, and unobtrusive, to the extent that we are unaware that a transition has occurred until minutes later.

At the end of The Crocodile sequence there is a cut to a man in another location looking through binoculars. He turns to his friends and remarks, "So it's 'The Crocodile' tonight." Again the transition from one setting to another is fluent. Now, however, the element of time has become important. In the first example one could not be sure that the raid was happening as the Chief of Police spoke. In this case, we know time has advanced.

By means of the techniques of cross-cutting a director can give a sense of simultaneity to events occurring at approximately the same time but in different settings. Cross-cutting (also called a parallel development or shots in counterpoint) has been used particularly to increase suspense (as in Griffith's pursuit or rescue sequences) or for contrast (as Russian directors used it to point up the differences between the life of the aristocrats and that of the workers).

In *M* cross-cutting for suspense can be found in both individual sequences and in a whole section of the film. Two examples of the former are shots of Mrs. Beckmann counterpointed to those related to Elsie and shots of the Murderer in the loft developed parallel to those of the criminals searching the office building. A section of the film, sequences VIII ("The Beggars Organized and in Operation") to X ("The Murderer Pursued and Captured")—from a dramatic point of view the middle portion of the film—contains repeated cross-cutting between the Murderer, the police, and the criminals. Tension builds as we watch the two groups closing in on their quarry.

Lang only incidentally suggests contrasts, as in the methods of the police and the criminals. It is in indicating just the opposite that his cross-cutting is most imaginative. The alternating shots of the meeting of the city officials and that of the criminals, with a couple of verbal bridges, establish the similarities between the ideas, approaches, and even personalities of the two groups. We continue to be aware of these parallels (and contrasts) as we observe cross-cutting between the two organizations in operation.

Another device that helps to coalesce visually the elements of the film is the visual motif. This can be defined as a shape or object that reappears a number of times in a film and assumes a symbolic significance beyond its denotative meaning. In other words, it is a visual symbol. The word *motif*, however, emphasizes repetition of the image and suggests that the director, like a composer of music, by changing the context in which the image appears and even its contours can mold and create variations in our conscious and unconscious associations with a specific image. The most significant visual motifs in *M* are the circle, the mirror, and the knife.

The opening shot of the film is of children in a circle; in the second unit of cross-cutting (sequence IV) we see a shot of a map of the city with three circles of different sizes sharing as a common center the spot where Elsie Beckmann's body was found; there is a broken circle of children around an organ grinder (sequence VII); the table in Hans Beckert's room, sequence VIII, seen from above, is oval; and in the window displays in sequence VIII there are circles and variations of circles (most prominently a diamond display of knives and a circle with a spiral design).

The circle in the film is a multifaceted symbol, but primarily it suggests either danger from the Murderer or what threatens him. He is surrounded by children and chooses one by chance as in the children's game. He is also encircled by enemies, both the police and the underworld, closing in on him. As the film progresses, the circle becomes transformed in our minds into a tightening noose.

The first appearance of the mirror motif is in the second unit of cross-cutting when we see a shot of the Murderer making faces in a mirror. As we pointed out in our analysis of sequence IV, the mirror in this case symbolizes the duality of Hans Beckert. In a mirror Beckert as Murderer is presented. In fact, every time Beckert looks in a mirror the reflection is somehow involved with the Murderer. When he observes the first window display in sequence VIII, the glass acts as a mirror and reflects an image of knives surrounding his head. These knives do not threaten the apple-eating Beckert but the Murderer within him. A moment later he sees the little girl in the mirror in the display case: the obsession of the Murderer appears almost magically. Finally, it is in a mirror that he sees the "M" on his back that labels him the Murderer.

As with the circle, the knife motif represents danger to the Murderer in one form and danger to the children in another. We mentioned previously the reflection of the knives threatening the Murderer. In the very next shot, however, the mirror in which the little girl's image appears is surrounded by these knives. It is this latter type of association that further variations of the knife motif develop.

A knife can be a murder weapon that penetrates innocent flesh. In the second window display the most striking object is a spinning circle with a spiral design and a large arrow whose shadow, from one perspective, as it moves up and down, appears to penetrate the spiral. The girl, who is soon met by her mother, is fascinated by the mechanism. We see the Murderer's own knife later when he is with another youngster just before he is branded with an "M."

Nowhere in the film is it stated that the Murderer sexually molests his victims. However, the sexual overtones of the circle-arrow window display and the position of the switchblade knife in relation to the body of the Murderer when he snaps it open in front of the second child suggest to us, if only subconsciously, that the Murderer's obsesssion is primarily sexual.

The final appearance of the knife motif occurs when the Murderer attempts to use his knife to open the door to the loft. He breaks the blade and is helpless. We notice that it is his tapping with the handle of the knife that betrays his presence and leads to his capture.

Thus far we have been dealing with specific techniques in *M*; now we will turn to two general approaches that influence the tone of the film as a whole.

Probably the most often repeated criticism of Lang as a director is his "coldness," a quality of keeping a distance between himself and the feelings of his characters. This does not mean that he is incapable of achieving dramatic intensity, but that his camera seems always detached, the objective observer, functioning intellectually rather than emotionally.

In *M*, however, this detachment works to the advantage of the film. Until the last sequence, the film appears to be almost a documentary. Documentaries can reveal with insight and passion the feelings of people, as directors from Flaherty to Frederick Wiseman have demonstrated. Generally, though, the emphasis in a documentary is on process—how things happen—rather than on the why of human emotions.

Most of *M* is devoted to describing visually how the police proceed, how the criminals operate, how a bar is raided by the police and an office building by the criminals. A few moments of the film illustrate in miniature this documentary approach: when we follow the mechanical process set in motion by a watchman pulling the alarm (sequence X).

The most poignant sequence in the film—Mrs. Beckmann waiting for Elsie—ends before the mother learns that her daughter has been killed. We never actually see the Murderer hurt a child. We learn little of the personal life of any of the characters. As we pointed out earlier, even in the café where the Murderer drinks brandy and struggles with his obsession, the camera keeps its distance behind a barrier of leaves. All of this prevents us from becoming too involved in personalities.

There are a number of reasons that could be offered to justify this encouragement of a viewer's objectivity. The major theme of the film is the need of the forces of order and authority to contain or destroy dangerous impulses toward irrationality. We must be made aware of authority in operation to recognize this theme, with just enough attention given to representative personalities—Lohmann and Schränker—to hold our interest. The same holds true, although to a lesser degree, for the forces of irrationality presented in sequence III: "Accusations in a Café, a Home, and on the Street." The source of this anarchy, the Murderer himself, must also be kept at a distance. If we saw directly the details of his violence, we might lose any incipient sympathy for him; then the argument that he should not be held responsible for his action would be less persuasive.

There is also a structural justification for Lang only hinting at the Murderer's inner conflict until near the end. Beckert's confession in the last sequence is the dramatic climax of the film. One of the reasons this scene is so intense and moving is that for the first time we penetrate to the inner world of the Murderer.

Finally, there is evidence in the script of how consciously Lang and Thea von Harbou sought to make their characters abstract. Hans Beckert, except when the police are tracing him, is never referred to except as "Murderer" (a practice we have adhered to in this analysis). Most of the characters in the film script are designated by generic names, such as Chief of Police, Burglar, Night Watchman, Prostitute. Only nine out of more than two dozen individual roles (ignoring groups of children, citizens, police, and criminals) are named.

A use of generic names is a characteristic of German expressionism. This leads us—imitating in the progress of our discussion Lang's cinematic transitions in *M* from one sequence to another—to the influence of expressionism on *M*. Elsewhere in this book (pp. 207–209) we discussed how this movement affected film makers, particularly German ones in the 1920s and 1930s, both in the content and cinematic techniques of their films. In both respects *M* is not basically an expressionistic film; however, it does borrow from the movement. The following are examples of influences on the content of the film. The reference to generic rather than proper names reflects an emphasis on types rather than individuals, on the essential rather than the personal. This was a device, especially in drama, often used by the expressionists. The city in *M* is oppressed by structures and forces that dehumanize people—a major theme of the movement. The Murderer is mentally ill, a type of character that fascinated cinematic expressionists, especially after *The Cabinet of Dr. Caligari*. On the other hand, there is little opportunity in the plot, with the exception of the monologue confession, to present the Murderer's vision of reality with the subjectivity and highly charged emotion that is a hallmark of expressionism.

We find the echoes of expressionism in *M* more in cinematic techniques than in content. As we have noted, the chief manifestation of the movement in cinematic technique was in distortions of reality, actual and symbolic, to express the emotions of characters, particularly those beneath the surface of consciousness. Also used were stylized settings, shadows and dramatic lighting, unusual camera angles and shots, reflections, and abrupt or even disorienting cuts from one shot to another. In *M* there are shadows, unusual camera angles, and reflections. Lang does not, however, apply these techniques to reveal in a specific scene the deepest levels of emotion (except for the reflection in the first storewindow display in sequence VIII), but rather to create the *atmosphere* of danger and mystery.

We have already discussed how repeated overhead shots, particularly in streets, result in an effect of claustrophobia and a sense of the dehumanization of people in a world governed by impersonal forces. Ominous shadows frequently appear in *M*. There is the Murderer's shadow when he talks to Elsie and when he is with the other girl and passes the Blind Beggar selling balloons. The police raid on The Crocodile is made more dramatic, especially at the beginning of the scene, by the presence of dark masses and shadows. At the end of the meeting of criminals in sequence VI, Schränker's shadow looms up on the wall.

The place in *M* where one might expect cinematic expressionistic techniques is in the Murderer's monologue confession. In photographing the confession, however, Lang does no more than move his camera into close-ups, high-angle shots, and cuts from shots to the right and left of the Murderer. This is not to say that expressionistic distortion could have made the scene more effective. Considering the over-all tone of the film, Lang probably made the correct choice.

We have dwelled on this topic because so many critics refer to "the expressionistic elements in *M*" without defining what they mean. Although the characteristics of the movement are debatable, in our opinion this film contains the shadow, not the substance, of cinematic expressionism.

Whatever the virtues or defects of *M*, it has transcended the age in which it was created (no mean compliment for any film—or any work of art, for that matter) and still fascinates both the general viewer and the student of the history of cinema.

CHAPTER 8

Grand Illusion

[La Grande Illusion]

Directed by JEAN RENOIR

Q: 1. *Which of the films dealing with peace, and war, do you think are most effective? What do you think is their ultimate effect on the spectator?*
   2. *What films need to be made dealing with the problems of peace and war? How can they be made? How should they?*
A: *In 1936 I made a picture named* La Grande Illusion *in which I tried to express all my deep feelings for the cause of peace. This film was very successful. Three years later the war broke out. That is the only answer I can find to your very interesting enquiry.*

Jean Renoir, Paris from *Film: Book* 2, ed. by Robert Hughes, (New York: 1962). (Quoted in Pierre Leprohon, *Jean Renoir*, trans. Brigid Elson (New York, 1971).

CAST

VON RAUFFENSTEIN	*Erich von Stroheim*
MARÉCHAL	*Jean Gabin*
DE BOELDIEU	*Pierre Fresnay*
ROSENTHAL	*Marcel Dalio*
THE ACTOR	*Julien Carette*
THE ENGINEER	*Gaston Modot*
THE TEACHER	*Jean Daste*
FRENCH SOLDIER	*Georges Peclet*
ENGLISH OFFICER	*Jacques Becker*
DEMOLDER	*Sylvain Itkine*
ELSA	*Dita Parlo*

CREDITS

DIRECTED BY	*Jean Renoir*
SCENARIO, ADAPTATION, AND DIALOGUE	*Charles Spaak and Jean Renoir*
PRODUCER	*Rélaisations d'Art Cinématographique (RAC)*
	(Frank Rollmer, Albert Pinkovitch and Alexandre)
MUSIC	*Joseph Kosma; lyrics for* Si tu veux, Marguerite . . . *by Vincent Telly and A. Valsien (as sung by Fragson)*

CREDITS (Continued)

TECHNICAL ADVISOR	*Carl Koch*
ASSISTANT DIRECTOR	*Jacques Becker*
PHOTOGRAPHED BY	*Christian Matras*
ASSISTANT PHOTOGRAPHER	*Claude Renoir*
ART DIRECTOR	*Eugène Lourié*
EDITOR	*Marguerite Huguet*

1937   Black and White   117 minutes

Story and Characterization

The plot of the film is, as we shall see, much less important than the interaction of the characters—that is, the manner of their presentation by Renoir in the context of their given situation in World War I. Nevertheless, we may briefly summarize the narrative as follows:

Boeldieu and Maréchal, two French air force officers on a reconnaisance mission, are shot down behind enemy lines by von Rauffenstein, a German squadron commander. Captured near the German airfield, they are Rauffenstein's guests for lunch, but are soon taken away by the military police to a prison camp for Allied officers. There, they befriend, among others, a French officer named Rosenthal and become involved in an attempt to tunnel out of the camp. Before this plan can be set in motion, however, the entire population of the camp is transferred.

Boeldieu and Maréchal are transferred from camp to camp and, although we do not see this series of adventures, we learn later that they have been moved from place to place because of their numerous attempts to escape.

Eventually, they are transferred (along with Demolder, another French officer) to a supposedly escape-proof prison-fortress, Wintersborn. Here they are again under the enforced hospitality of Rauffenstein, who, having been severely wounded in combat, is now fit only for this rear-echelon duty as prison camp commandant. Still intent on escape, they are reunited with Rosenthal. A plan evolves that will permit only two men to escape. Boeldieu insists that these be Maréchal and Rosenthal while he, Boeldieu, distracts the guards and gains them the time to complete their escape. The plan is carried out. Boeldieu is killed and the other two escape.

Rosenthal and Maréchal, making their way on foot to Switzerland, run into trouble when Rosenthal suffers a severe ankle sprain. They take refuge in the farmhouse of a German woman, Elsa, whose husband has been killed earlier in the war. After a brief, idyllic period with Elsa and her daughter, Lotte, during which time Maréchal and Elsa become lovers, the two men leave to rejoin their units and carry on the war. As we last seen them, they are two black specks struggling across a snowy field toward the Swiss border.

Besides Maréchal and Rosenthal, there are two other major characters, Boeldieu and Rauffenstein. The action and meaning of the film is generated by a series of contrasts involving these four. That is, we are meant to be impressed by the similarities and differences between Boeldieu and Maréchal, Boeldieu and Rauffenstein, Maréchal and Rosenthal, and perhaps even Rosenthal and Rauffenstein.

In any event, Boeldieu and Rauffenstein are members of the same class and caste. Officers and aristocrats, their similarities are repeatedly emphasized, beginning with their clothing and appurtenances of rank and station (for example, they share a predilection for monocles and white gloves and a rather impeccable taste in uniforms), continuing on to their cosmopolitan linguistic competence (both speak English, French, and German), friendly discourse with one another, and their ultimate fates: one kills the other in the so-called line of duty (about which, more later). Symbolically (as well as actually), Rauffenstein is wounded, and hence rendered *hors de combat*; similarly, Boeldieu is a prisoner and is, therefore, also removed from action.

Neither is able to exercise his aristocratic function in life—that is, both are fallen warriors. What remains for each is to enact a kind of heroic paradigm; just as Boeldieu's "performance" in playing the fife on the battlements in order to permit the escape is a grand heroic gesture, so is Rauffenstein's shooting him the same kind of theater. For Rauffenstein need not have shot Boeldieu at all. His action was *not* in the line of duty. Awareness of each man's destiny and a kind of kinship of class motivates Rauffenstein's fatal shot and the famous cutting of the geranium after Boeldieu's death is also motivated by Rauffenstein's self-consciousness; as one critic has remarked, it is Rauffenstein's not Renoir's symbol.

Boeldieu shares with Rauffenstein a deep awareness of class distinction and its place in the social order. To Rauffenstein's remark that the end of the war "will be the end of the Rauffensteins and the Boeldieus," Boeldieu answers that "perhaps there is no more need for us." Moreover, Boeldieu's awareness extends to a calm acceptance of the manner of his death: "for a man of the people, it's terrible to die in the war. For you [Rauffenstein] and me, it was a good solution."

Thus, in the dramatic action, Renoir isolates these two; except when they have scenes together, each is depicted as alone within his milieu. Rauffenstein lives in lonely splendor in the converted chapel of the castle and not even an aide-de-camp disturbs his dignified solitude. Boeldieu, on the other hand, must live with the other prisoners; but he takes no part in their enterprises—except for the tunneling plan in the first prison camp. In contrast to Rosenthal, who is a lively participant in the camp theatrical—sewing costumes, acting—Boeldieu is signally aloof from such activities. Nor can Boeldieu's lonely status be disturbed by considerations such as affection; he is quite prepared to escape through the tunnel while Maréchal, his comrade, is in solitary confinement. Only Rosenthal feels enough sense of community to be disturbed by that.

The world inhabited by Boeldieu and Rauffenstein is etched even more finely by contrast to Maréchal and Rosenthal. The former is a worker, casual in everything, unashamed of either his ignorance ("what's it mean," he says to the engineer who is washing his feet, "the ordinance survey?") or his unabashed patriotism (it is he who leads the prisoners in "The Marseillaise" when a brief Allied victory is announced during the camp theatrical). Unlike Boeldieu, moreover, he is quite plainly emotional. Although Boeldieu effectively prevents Maréchal's being direct in expressing himself, Maréchal's feelings are directly visible in the glove-washing scene. On the other hand, Boeldieu's feelings are deeply hidden.

By contrast with the formal discourse of Boeldieu and Rauffenstein, we have the explosive outbursts of anger between Rosenthal and Maréchal during their walking escape. Their emotional relations are a model of community, good fellowship, and easy commerce. Explosion ventilates anger and they are soon on good terms again.

The vivid emotional colors of these two are also consonant with Rosenthal's conviviality. His role as provider at the table of his prison comrades expresses perfectly his instinctive good nature. Although he confesses to "showing off" with his gourmet provisions, it is not a deeply ingrained or well-dramatized motive. Rosenthal's vitality has a more natural source: he is a good-natured nouveau riche devoted to communal relations.

The presentation of these four is at the heart of the film and the meaning of this presentation is at once simple and complex.

Themes and Interpretations

Grand Illusion is, of course, a war film. On that simple level its theme is pacifism. Indeed, it would be difficult to think of a war film which does not have pacifism for a theme. From *All Quiet on the Western Front* to *Forbidden Games* and *Paths of Glory*, the war film has cried out against the horrors of its subject matter. But these films have dramatized their themes with reference to combat and the way that combat perverts into brutality even the most decent of human impulses (even *Forbidden Games* cannot resist indulging in its brilliant opening sequence, which depicts the helplessness of a civilian population when confronted by war machines). The trouble with most war films is their inevitable tendency to glorify man's adaptability even to such monstrous circumstances; war films invariably depict war heroes. And on a scale of pacifist sentiment such productions rank low.

What distinguishes *Grand Illusion* from the typical specimen of the genre is its steadfast refusal to take part in a generic ritual. There are no combat scenes in *Grand Illusion*. Even at the risk of violating an important temporal transition (from the opening to the following sequence: the time between Maréchal's and Boeldieu's take-off on their photography mission and their capture by Rauffenstein), Renoir does not show us a combat scene. The shooting down of Maréchal and Boeldieu must be imagined, and even Rauffenstein takes off his flying suit quickly. Moreover, Boeldieu's final fife-playing scene—an opportunity to do so—is not pictured as violent combat but rather more as a performance, a stylized encounter between members of a heroic caste.

Renoir goes further away from the war film genre by insisting that war is an illusion. It is an illusion because it has no basis in the relations of men. Rauffenstein the German is depicted as having no quarrel with Boeldieu the Frenchman; in fact, they are closer to one another in *real* ideology than Boeldieu and Maréchal who wear the same uniform. (White gloves are the real uniform they wear.) Even on the level of the minor characters, Renoir constantly insists on the common humanity of Frenchman and German. For example, by the time the prisoners leave their first camp, Arthur, the German adjutant who is their immediate commandant, displays a wry affection for his charges. So, too, does the old guard who comforts Maréchal in his solitary cell.

Over and beyond this lack of differences between men of different nationalities, Renoir poses something positive: the real sense of community that men of real differences and temperament (a Maréchal in company with a Rosenthal) can achieve. Their escape together provides an opportunity to add a woman and a child to this thematic strand, so that simple humanity (the washing of feet, tending cows, celebrating Christmas, and the pleasures of air and simple food) can be contrasted with the harsh forms we saw in the confinement of the prison camp.

It is true, to be sure, that (as in *The Rules of the Game* and in other Renoir films) one notices a certain regret over the passing of an aristocratic order; Boeldieu *does* die a beautiful death: it is pictured romantically. (See Fig. 8-4) But what one comes away with from *Grand Illusion* is not nostalgia. Of course we do not know what will happen to Rosenthal and Maréchal as they pick their way across the snow-covered frontier. And it is an illusion to suppose that Maréchal will, just because he says he will, return to Elsa after the war. (Renoir is gentle, it is true; but he is too tough-minded to sell us *that* sentimental bill of goods.) However, it is also an illusion to speak at all of a national frontier, and thus it is no casual piece of dramaturgy that Rosenthal and Maréchal cannot be sure of its exact location. Yet, we do not leave *Grand Illusion* without a sense that values have been counterposed against each other (and that in such a juxtaposition lies our major thematic strand): war and form and rigidity and death against friendship, openness, community, love and,—yes, even plain food—and possibility, albeit a tenuous and perhaps tragic one.

Analysis of Major Sequences

I. From Freedom to Rauffenstein's Luncheon and Beyond

Fade in on a close-up of a record player, a World War I era gramophone, with its big, curving horn. Now the camera pans up to Maréchal, who is hunched over the machine, singing along with it. Our first glimpse of the pilot is a revealing one: his kepi is askew, and because his uniform coat is unbuttoned, we notice that he is wearing a rough black turtleneck. Maréchal notices someone going by behind him and moves toward the man, a soldier. Camera moves to follow and record their brief dialogue. Maréchal has a date with Josephine and wants a lift to town. As he turns out of frame to return to the gramophone, we push into the door to notice the entrance of another officer. Now we are aware of being in an officers' mess; we can see several of them sitting at table, a bar staffed by an enlisted man, posters, and the like.

Captain Ringis, the officer who has just entered, is looking for someone and spots Maréchal immediately. Camera leads him over to where Maréchal is again back at the gramophone. Ringis says that someone from the general staff is there to see Maréchal. As for Maréchal, though Ringis has come at a bad time, he thinks that Josephine will just have to wait. Maréchal's whole attitude is casual, easy, resigned. As Ringis and Maréchal move off toward Ringis's office, we pan over to the bar and tilt down to read the motto posted there: "Squadron M.F. 902. Alcohol kills slowly! But who's in a hurry?"

Cut to a close-up of Boeldieu just as he inserts his monocle, the better to examine the enlarged aerial photograph in his hand. With his stiffly military bearing, featuring an impeccably tailored coat, an officer's baton, and a pair of dark gloves, he is an exact contrast to Maréchal. Now on a wider shot, Ringis and Maréchal enter. As he is introduced, Maréchal throws his smartest military salute at Boeldieu, he recognizes a real military man when he sees one.

Boeldieu is worried about one of the details in the photograph he is holding. It has been taken by Maréchal's copilot, who is now on leave. There is a grey smudge on the photograph which Boeldieu points out below the road. But Ringis thinks the road is a canal and Maréchal chimes in with the opinion that it is a railway. This exasperates Boeldieu into making a coolly ironic remark about the French photographic services, which Maréchal only shrugs off. He suggests the poor resolution resulted from the foggy weather they had the day the photograph was taken. But Boeldieu insists on another flight to resolve the enigma of that landscape feature. Ringis phones to order a plane; Maréchal goes off to get ready: he will be the pilot. Ringis asks Boeldieu if he would prefer overalls or a goatskin, but the fastidious staff officer rejects both: "Overalls smell badly" and "goatskins shed hairs."

The scene, in its economy, sharply (although casually, undramatically) etches the characters of both Maréchal and Boeldieu. It does so by contrasting Maréchal's dress and his casual attitude toward his appointment with Josephine with Boeldieu's dress and *his* attitude toward clearing up the matter of the smudge (as well as his fastidious response to the choice of flying suits). It should also be borne in mind that the smudge is the unheroic motive for this mission, as a result of which both men lose their freedom and Boeldieu his life. In fact, the smudge gathers symbolic overtones as the film proceeds; it becomes, in retrospect, a kind of offensive blemish on the white glove perfectionism of both Rauffenstein and Boeldieu.

From the last shot in Ringis' office, featuring Boeldieu as he remarked on the flying suits, we dissolve quickly to the doorway of Rauffenstein's squadron's officers' mess. Rauffenstein, wearing his flying suit, enters quickly and, after unbuckling his gear, pauses at the bar. There he downs a glass of schnappes and is joined by his orderly and a slowly gathering group of fellow officers. The orderly is sent to look for the occupants of the plane he has just shot down. "If they are officers," Rauffenstein says, "invite them over for lunch."

Now, at Rauffenstein's suggestion, the officers toast Rauffenstein's second kill and, as the shot widens, we see that this German establishment is very much like its French counterpart, Next Rauffenstein suggests, in a rather commanding way, that one of his officers (Fessler) concoct for the impending luncheon one of his "famous 'fruit punches'." As the officers drink and Rauffenstein is helped out of more of his flying gear, Fessler begins to give his list of fruit punch ingredients to the barman and we pan along the bar and search the walls until we end on several photographs of women, World War I German pinups. The women are gracefully out of the *fin de siècle*, however, and though we can only see them for a moment, the effect, with Fessler's voice over saying, "A can of pineapple, three lemons, and some sugar," is to impress on us a mood of conviviality and grace. And the effect is enhanced by the Strauss waltzes playing on the gramophone. Fade out. Fade in on the same doorway to the squadron mess.

The door opens to admit a German officer who first announces and then ushers in Maréchal and Boeldieu. The latter looks about as he did before the flight: impeccable; but Maréchal is clearly the worse for wear. His kepi is gone, and his arm, wounded, is in a sling.

It is worth reminding the reader at this point that, as we pointed out earlier, Renoir has here foregone the opportunity to show an exciting aerial dogfight. He simply refuses to glorify war.

Now we see the second of Renoir's beautifully designed fluid master shots. (The first of these was the one that opened the film; the student of Renoir should compare these.) We have been on a medium long shot of the mess, facing the door, as Maréchal and Boeldieu were ushered in.

In this same shot, Rauffenstein, with heel-clicking correctness salutes and introduces himself to his two prisoners, "Very honored to have French guests," showing a very subtle difference in manner to each. He knows at once, by instinct, that Maréchal is not a professional officer.

Boeldieu and Maréchal reply in kind. Camera pulls slowly back now as Rauffenstein leads his guests toward table, seating Boeldieu on his right and Maréchal on his left. In the same movement, an orderly rushes deftly to take Boeldieu's coat. The shot takes perhaps a minute all together and ends by revealing the whole table full of officers seated formally for lunch and the orderlies waiting on them. The effect of the fluid moving shot is to bind together all its elements, characters, and environment, into a single cohesive whole.

Rauffenstein, who has used German-accented but impeccable French to introduce himself, continues to use French as we now see him discoursing with Boeldieu in a two shot. He recalls the name "Boeldieu." He remembers a "Count de Boeldieu," and his guest acknowledges the Count to be his cousin, a military attache stationed in Berlin before the war. The thing they now have in common causes Rauffenstein to switch to English. "He was a mervelous rider," he comments, to which Boeldieu replies, "Yes. In the good old days. . ."

Camera now pans slowly from left to right as we hear the beginning of dialogue between Maréchal and the officer seated beside him. Camera halts on a two shot of the pair. The German officer, also speaking French, notices Maréchal not eating. When he finds that the Frenchman's arm prevents his cutting his meat, the German immediately does it for him.

It is a classically balanced little encounter; it matches exactly the exchange we have just seen between Boeldieu and Rauffenstein. Now, when Maréchal comments on the German's command of the French language, the German answers that he acquired the facility while working at a factory in Lyon. Maréchal reacts with pleased excitement, for he, too, he says worked there; Thus he, too, is a mechanic. They look together off camera.

At this moment, the good fellowship of the luncheon is interrupted. We cut to the rear door of the mess to see a German enlisted man enter with a large wreath. We read the printed ribbon: it is a tribute from the German squadron to a French pilot shot down in flames some time earlier. Rauffenstein rises stiffly to apologize for the "coincidence." He signals to the barman who stops the record on the gramophone.

Form and ceremony have intruded, perhaps a bit heavy-handedly, but effectively nevertheless. After a brief silence, during which the officers rise and stand to attention, the music resumes and the officers resume conversing together. But another interruption occurs. A military policeman comes to take Boeldieu and Maréchal away.

II. The First Prison Camp: A New World

The transition to the arrival here of Maréchal and Boeldieu is a series of shots taken from the interior of a moving train. They represent the prisoner's point of view and suggest the limited glimpses of the outside world that are afforded to incarcerated men. One overriding value of Renoir's film is freedom and at this stage it is denied the travelers.

At the camp, a German noncommissioned officer, whom the Allied prisoners affectionately call Arthur, reads to the newly arrived prisoners the camp regulations (Figure 8-1). Then they are searched and assigned quarters. During this interval, we see also the system of food package distribution. Renoir uses these casually staged scenes to compare and contrast prisoners and their jailers (for example, in showing the guards at a meal, juxtaposed with the French receiving their food packages: the similarities and differences are significant), and Maréchal and Boeldieu (while the former is comically "sorry" he has no valuables for the German guards to steal, Boeldieu insists on deference from these guards as they conduct their search, under threat of reporting them to their commanding officer). At the same time, we are introduced to Rosenthal as he receives one of his typical gourmet packages. In general, the atmosphere is not strained; there is a mood of casual, good-natured relations between prisoners and guards and within each group as well.

Figure 8–1. *Boeldieu and Maréchal arrive at the first prison camp.* (Courtesy Janus Films.)

Maréchal and Boeldieu are eventually assigned to quarters they are to share with Rosenthal, an Actor, an Engineer, and a Teacher. Here Rosenthal provides his bounty.

ROSENTHAL'S MEAL

Renoir uses this sequence to sharply characterize each of the men by placing each solidly within his social class. The meal is the appropriate vehicle for this placement and the scene begins with a two-shot of Maréchal and the Actor, who is holding out a piece of burning paper from which Maréchal lights his cigarette; they are about to converse a bit. Naturally, the Actor wants to know if Maréchal has ever seen his act, and just as naturally Maréchal disclaims interest in the theater. Bicycle racing is his meat, and as he names a series of his favorite riders, the shot widens and the camera pans around the room to pick up the others as they move toward the table. The Engineer is standing near Boeldieu when Rosenthal, at the table, unpacks his food. Boeldieu is astonished at the riches being displayed, and, deciding that such stuff is available to buy, declares that he will purchase from the canteen a "comfortable sort of arm chair, playing cards, some books and English cigarettes." Now Rosenthal's orderly puts the last napkin in place on the table and Rosenthal is finally ready to seat his "guests."

We should contrast the informality of his manner with the formal manners of Rauffenstein at the meal in his squadron officers' mess; both hosts, we see, are eager to please their guests, but their styles are very different—Rauffenstein seeming much more secure in his reticence than Rosenthal in his ebullience.

Rosenthal announces the menu. It is spectacular: pâté, cold chicken, pickled fish, and brandy. The Teacher declares it to be the best meal he's ever eaten; and he's quite sincere. It even passes muster with Boeldieu, which is no small compliment. Boeldieu's appreciation pleases Rosenthal, who wishes very much to have Boeldieu's approval. What does not please Boeldieu is a vulgar joke told by the Actor, and the aristocratic staff officer does not hesitate to tell him so. Surreptitiously, as if in reply, the Actor picks up Boeldieu's monocle and, in a kind of comic revenge, mimics Boeldieu's upper-crust manner.

As the scene ends, Rosenthal, in a flush of pride over having been the good provider, tells Boeldieu that the brandy was sent to him by a barman at Fouquet's. Their common experience of this rather elegant restaurant and sidewalk café, located on the corner of the Champs Elysee and Avenue George V, encourages Rosenthal to ask more about Paris. "How was it?" he inquires, as if the two shared membership in a social set. Boeldieu's answer is perfectly in character: "Maxim's was crowded."

Mention of the two upper-class restaurants, Fouquet's and Maxim's, is enough to touch off a revealing set of responses by Maréchal and the Teacher. The latter has simply never heard of these places; on the other hand, Maréchal knows but rejects them both. He would rather go to a small bistro with a good cheap wine list. The Teacher, he insists, is missing nothing by his ignorance of Maxim's. Now the Actor, who has been silent since Boeldieu's put down over the vulgar joke, seizes on the Teacher's rather pedantic dullness and begins to mimic what he had said earlier—that is, that when he was in Paris he ate at his brother-in-law's ("it's cheaper"). Hoping that this joke at someone else's expense will please Boeldieu, who is no longer the subject of his mimicry, he slaps him on the back. But Boeldeu's reaction is stiffly disapproving. He looks contemptuously at the Actor through his monocle. They are far apart.

The visual style of the scene also contrasts with the fluid moving shots of the Rauffenstein luncheon. Here we see the scene in a series of cuts, static two-shots, close-ups, and full shots of the table. It has the effect of analyzing time and space—as do all such shooting and editing methods— and of separating its subjects. This is in keeping with the general purpose of the scene: to separate the characters into social and characterological groups.

During an episode in which Maréchal's feet are washed by the Engineer (Maréchal's arm wound prevents his managing his personal hygiene), he learns of the escape plot, a tunneling enterprise (Figure 8-2). The Engineer, who was silent during the meal, wants to be assured of Boeldieu's good will before revealing this plan. Obviously, Boeldieu's mere

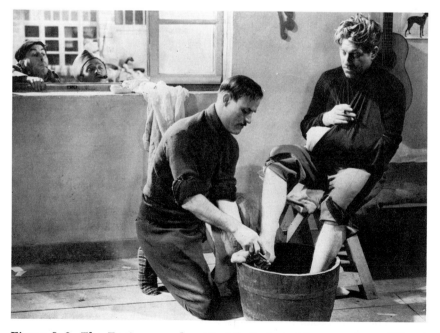

Figure 8–2. *The Engineer washes Maréchal's feet.* (**Courtesy Janus Films.**)

appearance is enough to suggest a large gulf between himself and the others.

That night, the Actor takes his turn in the tunnel and nearly suffocates. At the same time, as the Teacher learns when he is sent to the courtyard to investigate a commotion out there, another prisoner, attempting an escape, is killed by the guards. The next day, as the barracks mates are disposing of tunnel dirt in the prisoners' vegetable garden, they are informed that the costumes have arrived and they rush off with great excitement to see them.

THEATER

For the prisoners have been planning a camp theatrical. And here we may suggest that the theater and its symbolism constitute a leading motif in all of Renoir's work. Here it is used on a number of levels to suggest a complex set of interlaced ideas: for one thing, the camp theatrical signifies not just the vitality of bored prisoners but also their yearning for freedom. Here, art takes on a modern metaphorical connotation. Moreover, the show expresses their solidarity with one another, and, as they say, their confidence in the eventual triumph of their cause. But it also identifies obliquely but touchingly one of the greatest deprivations suffered by men at war: their separation from women.

As the barracks mates go off toward the recreation hall to examine the costumes, Maréchal and Boeldieu remain behind. Maréchal, with some irony, asks Boeldieu if he is going off to play his favorite game of solitaire, Boeldieu acknowledges that Maréchal's guess is correct and adds, apropos the camp theatrical, "My competence in theatrical matters is dubious . . . I am a realist." The irony in this remark becomes apparent only later on, when Boeldieu arranges a piece of theater that enables Rosenthal and Maréchal to escape.

But the scene in the recreation hall opens with a panning shot. We see the English prisoners on stage in a chorus line rehearsing and singing "Tipperary," while in other parts of the hall smaller scenes are being rehearsed and scenery is being built. The panning shot ends on the German guard, Arthur, who, as Rosenthal and the others watch him, is examining the contents of a costume crate. Once again, Renoir's fluid master shot embraces and connects Allied prisoners and their captors.

Arthur reaches into the crate and rummages about for contraband, but all he can come up with is a corset. He leaves and the men cheerily bid him goodbye.

Then they bend to their work with enthusiasm and begin to dig excitedly into the crate. Rosenthal emerges with a satin evening gown. Immediately he holds it up against himself, closing his eyes as he does so. "You have to handle stuff like this with delicacy . . . and with closed eyes." The others look at the dress with some intensity. They are astonished at the length; the dress ends just above the knee. Maréchal wants to see someone wearing the dress. A relatively clean-shaven soldier, Maissonneuve, is selected.

As they wait for him to change into the dress, Maréchal and the Actor twit the Teacher—who is obviously ill at ease with all the talk about women's styles. "They're wearing their hair short, too," says Maréchal. "That's like going to bed with a boy," retorts the Actor. In the right side of the frame, we see the Teacher get even more worried at this exchange. Now Rosenthal takes a pair of women's shoes from the trunk. Smiling, he says he had forgotten how small they were.

The Actor and the Engineer together bring out a pair of stockings. The Teacher touches them in awe. Another soldier gapes at still another pair of black stockings, and then all the men fall silent as they turn to look at something. A gentle pan away from the group reveals Maissonneuve dressed as a woman.

Along with the gown, he wears high heels and a blonde wig; his lips are painted, too, and although the affect is not entirely transformational, the observers are deeply impressed, each filled with his own fantasies (Figure 8-3). Maréchal finally breaks the silence by forcing a laugh and remarking to Massonneuve that it's funny, "he looks like a real girl." Again silence takes over. The camera pans a row of faces staring in the same direction in absolute silence and ends on Maissonneuve, the

Figure 8–3. *Maissonneuve as a woman.* (Courtesy Janus Films.)

object of the men's attention. Aware of this attention he cannot help but respond as he imagines they wish him too: he makes a few coy feminine gestures. Fade out.

In an annex of this recreation hall, which Rosenthal and his friends have converted into a sewing workshop, they are at work making and pressing costumes for the show. The scene starts with a closeup of a German guard at the door as he is closing it, leaving the men alone. Next we see the Actor, wearing a funny hat and ironing costumes. Then we cut to the other side of the room where a window looks out on the prison courtyard. On either side of the window are Maréchal and Boeldieu. They alone are not engaged in sewing or pressing. Maréchal simply looks on with wry amusement while Boeldieu is watching a squad of German recruits drilling in the courtyard. We see Boeldieu in close-up as he remarks on what he sees: "On one side children who play like soldiers [the recruits], and on the other soldiers who play like children." There is no response. Instead, the conversation turns toward "home" and "escape" and particularly the motives for the latter wish. The Actor is bored and wants to escape for the fun of it; the Engineer is, as he says, "contrary" and simply wants to fight again because now he is unable to. Maréchal, on the other hand, merely wants to be like everyone else. "I hate stagnating here while others are risking their lives." Rosenthal has a patriotic motive: to protect his family's newly developed ecnomic and social status. Boeldieu, in contrast to everyone else, declares that "a prison camp is to escape from." It is a reflex action for him.

Boeldieu appeals to Rosenthal to confirm the logic of his motive, calling Rosenthal a "sportsman" who would understand his desire. The Actor, however, denies that Rosenthal can be a sportsman because he was "born in Jerusalem" (that is, he is a Jew). This provokes Rosenthal to offer some of his background. His origins as the scion of a newly wealthy banking family are then revealed and are contrasted with the Teacher's amusing story of how *he* got into the service—he cured his stomach trouble as his doctor had recommended. His brother, by contrast, suffering from the same ailment, had continued to aggravate his condition and was declared medically unfit to serve.

Suddenly a military band starts up in the courtyard: we can hear the sounds of drums, fifes, and brass. The sounds of the marching conscripts join the band music. Boeldieu turns to look out of the window.

From outside, we see the window and Boeldieu standing looking out at the spectacle. Immediately, he is joined by the others, who form a kind of circular tableau as they arrange themselves to get a good view of what's happening. The camera pans in close-up from face to face as they react. Boeldieu declares that he hates fifes. The Teacher says that the music is certainly stirring, but Maréchal corrects him. It is not the music, he says, but the "thud of marching feet," not an abstract symbol but the concrete sound of real men massed in a single purpose. The men are solemn. Suddenly, Rosenthal notices something burning. It is his iron, which has burned through a costume. With a kind of jolly indifference, he makes light of it and the others join in his gaiety. The noise summons a sentry who enters to check what's going on. The sentry, seeing the dancing Actor, taps his forehead gravely, as if indicating that the actor is insane. Fade out.

In this little scene, too, Renoir wanted to dramatize the separateness of the men from each other, deepening their individual characters, and to show at the same time Boeldieu's special isolation from the rest. For only he can think of no real motive for getting out of the camp; he wants to escape only because the camp is *there*: "what is the purpose of a golf course? To play golf. A tennis court? To play tennis. Well, a prison camp is there to escape from."

Similarly, only he claims to be untouched by the martial air of the marching bands below the window; "I hate fifes," he says, coldly, ironically reminding us of the role that a fife will play in his death.

In contrast to Boeldieu, the others have a variety of reasons for wanting to escape and tell of a whole range of circumstances by which they were inducted into the army; their responses range from the wildly comic (the Teacher's story of himself and his twin marks him as a fool—and Renoir confirms this by having a clown's ruff slipped over his neck toward the end) to the utterly modern patriotic (Rosenthal is defending his country to protect his family's wealth).

Following the sewing scene, we see a shot, at night, of a poster against a brick wall in the prison courtyard. It reads that Douaumont has been captured. The church bells in a nearby town start pealing and camera pans to a lighted window through which we can see German officers in their mess celebrating this victory of German arms by singing, drinking, and playing the guitar. In the same shot, one of these officers emerges from a door beside the window and starts moving across the courtyard. Camera follows him to include a group of French prisoners framed inside a window as they look out at the action. The officer leaves the frame and we move in slightly—still in the same shot—to see our barracks mates from the previous scene. This framing provides a visual link to the previous scene in which we had a similar piece of iconography.

A brief conversation ensues, in which Maréchal dispels the doubt voiced by the Actor and the Teacher about puting on their camp theatrical in the face of this French defeat at Douaumont. He wants to put on the show "more than ever," he says defiantly, and suggests also that they invite the camp commandant and his officers. Boeldieu congratulates him on his spirited attitude.

Renoir's moving camera has been used here to provide a visual link between winners and losers. The same fluid visual style is put to work in the next scene, during the prisoners' show, when Maréchal charges out onto the stage to interrupt.

Before he does, however, we see one of Renoir's favorite kinds of sequence, an actual performance. This time it begins with a vulgar Paris music hall number sung by the Actor wearing a baggy full-dress suit. Despite the fact that his rendition is not very good, the Frenchmen in the audience are appreciative. The German guests sit indifferently through this number and only when the girls' number is on—the bewigged and costumed prisoners in feminine costumes kicking and dancing about the stage—do they join in the general applause. This number is the hit of the show: the audience enjoys the Actor's low clowning with the girls and his antics with a toy car. But here Maréchal, standing in the wings with Rosenthal, takes a newspaper from his friend's hands, struck with his motive to interrupt the show.

He charges out onto the stage, yelling for the orchestra to stop and announces that Douaumont has been recaptured. For a moment there is complete silence, then the whole audience rises. There is a cut to one of the players, a "woman" standing near the orchestra. As soon as the orchestra strikes up the "Marseillaise," the player pulls off his wig, stands stiffly at attention and leads the entire audience in singing the anthem. Camera begins to pan—away from the player—and completes a slow, circular movement, including the entire hall, watching the German officers as they take a hurried leave, and finally coming to rest for a moment where it began: on the player beside the orchestra. From there we pan to the audience and watch as they continue to sing.

Maréchal has insisted on the primacy of reality over the theatrical illusion; his gesture is large, unthinking, spontaneous. It lands him in solitary confinement where, through the bars of his cell, we are able to learn of still more news from the outside world: the ironic announcement that Douaumont has fallen to the Germans once more. In terms of the theatrical metaphor, this piece of theater staged by Maréchal has for its counterpart the theatrical staged by Boeldieu at Wintersborn. There, as we know, the results are somewhat better but also more costly.

Maréchal's stay in solitary is brief. When he gets out, he joins the others, who are on the verge of using the completed tunnel, just as the entire camp population is to be transferred.

III. Wintersborn: The Last Escape

The transition between the first prison camp and the arrival here of Maréchal and Boeldieu consists of a series of shots from the interior of a moving train—like the transition from Rauffenstein's mess to the first prison camp, with this difference: here there are more dissolves, featuring a number of large signs identifying several different camps. The effect suggests the passage of time. Their transfer to Wintersborn is motivated by the numerous escape attempts they have made while confined in the other camps.

REUNION WITH RAUFFENSTEIN

We see the last camp sign immediately after a long shot of the forbidding castle-fortress of Wintersborn. It is a crag of monolithic stone battlements and redouts and we are meant to be impressed by its seeming impregnability. Now we cut to a huge wooden crucifix. Then camera pans down to its base to show an altar. Here we see a framed portrait of Kaiser Wilhelm II.

Now in closeup camera starts a slow pan around this room to observe the personal possessions of von Rauffenstein. We can tell by what we have just seen, as well as by the stained glass windows and the Gothic architecture, that this room was once a chapel. Now we see the window with the potted geranium, a pair of binoculars, some daggers. Resting on the top of a small table is a champagne bucket with a bottle in it, a copy of Casanova's *Memoirs* with a pistol lying on it, and a framed portrait of a young woman. The pan ends on a shot of the commandant's orderly blowing into a pair of white gloves in order to spread the fingers.

After complying with Rauffenstein's order to open a window (spoken off-screen), the orderly reports that there are only two pairs of white gloves remaining. To this, Rauffenstein replies, "Well, try to make them last till the end of the war." The orderly serves coffee and, finally, presents the commandant with a dossier to read. Rauffenstein inserts his monocle and begins to read; the prisoners arrive.

Rauffenstein's demeanor to this point in the sequence—his shout to open the window because "it stinks" in the room, his complaint about the bad coffee—is a model of dissatisfaction and Stroheim's acting conveys the message with precision: a warrior has fallen on idle days.

From the outer room, where we see Maréchal, Boeldieu, and a third prisoner, Lt. Demolder, we can also see through the door into Rauffenstein's quarters. While his orderly fusses over him and tidies his uniform, the commandant sprays himself with scent from an atomizer. Then, picking up his saber and the prisoners' dossier, he comes toward us in white-gloved elegance. And now we can see more clearly the effect of his wound and of the chin brace he wears. It gives an altogether startling stiffness to his carriage, at once military and pathetically askew. (The brace was von Stroheim's idea and Renoir loved it; its effectiveness is stunning, the touch of genius.)

Speaking again in French, Rauffenstein's greetings to Maréchal and Boeldieu is as correct, as chivalric, and thus quite as ingratiating as it had been at their first encounter many months previously; moreover, Rauffenstein has not forgotten the difference between Boeldieu and the other two men: he shakes hands with Boeldieu but not with his fellow officers.

Then he sits while his prisoners stand at their ease in front of his huge oak desk.

As he speaks we learn that the prisoners have attempted a number of escapes in their previous confinements and have been sent here to Wintersborn as a consequence. Even though Rauffenstein admires and respects their patriotism, they must understand that "nobody escapes from this fortress." In fact, he says, "so that there will be no cause for complaints of German barbarism, I've decided to apply French regulations." After issuing to each a copy of these regulations, he asks politely if he may escort them on a tour. They acquiesce—just as politely.

The iconography of this sequence is dominated by the deliberate appearance of certain objects of strong symbolic value. For example, the binoculars, saber, and white gloves all suggest the contemporary World War I military officer caste, as does the portrait of Kaiser Wilhelm II (Rauffenstein's commander and also a symbol of the commandant's devotion to duty, order, and loyalty). The champagne bucket, Rauffenstein's atomizer, the portrait of the young woman, and the copy of Casanova's memoirs add the note of aristocracy and chivalry already suggested by the setting—a chapel in a castle. The setting also evokes the air of holy knighthood. And all this is appropriate to Rauffenstein's anachronistic world.

The tour through Wintersborn is filled with images of cold stone; stairways, tunnels, and arches predominate. It is also Rauffenstein's opportunity to point out those features that make it escape proof. No doubt part of Rauffenstein's motive in making this tour is politeness; he has a vested interest in showing especially gallant behavior to his prisoners. But, in part, his wound must also be a factor. Rendered *hors de combat*, he must be eager to demonstrate that his power is still alive. To this mood of the tour, Boeldieu reacts with lighthearted witticisms. When Rauffenstein points out his Maxim guns, Boeldieu replies with a joke about the restaurant, Maxim's. So that by the time the tour is ended—at the prisoners' billets—a kind of challenge has been made to Boeldieu and at least the beginning of a reply to it is dimly discernible.

REUNION WITH ROSENTHAL

Rauffenstein regrets being unable to provide Boeldieu with separate quarters, but at least he has billeted him (and Maréchal) with Rosenthal. As the German NCO reports Rauffenstein's reasoning, "He said you'll be fed better this way." This NCO, unlike his counterpart at the first prison camp, does not have to be reprimanded by Boeldieu for the manner in which he searches the prisoners. He is a model of respect, and we might attribute this, too, to the influence of Rauffenstein. Nevertheless, Maréchal explodes with anger when he is searched. In addition to sharing with Rosenthal, they also share a billet with Demolder, a professor of Greek, a locksmith, and a Senegalese black.

As the Senegalese sits hunched over his drawing, Rosenthal and Maréchal talk. They are pleased to see each other, but not overly demonstrative; it is as if their meeting were pleasantly inevitable. As they exchange stories about their amorous adventures, Maréchal notes that "Nice people usually give you the clap." This provokes Boeldieu's observation on the distribution of diseases by class. "But," he notes, "that, along with so much else, is becoming democratic." Boeldieu is playing patience, as usual, and now Demolder comes to the same table and prepares to set out his Pindar texts (he is translating the Greek poet). But he is getting in the way of Boeldieu's game and is coldly reminded of the transgression. Demolder makes a diffident apology and offers as his excuse that "Pindar has always been so badly translated." Boeldieu's ironic reply borders on the contemptuous, and Maréchal, wondering what the fuss is about, asks in his usual way, "Who is this Pindar?" This angers Demolder into a passionate defense of his translation: "You can joke. For me Pindar's more important than anything . . . you, me, the war. He's the greatest Greek poet."

Renoir shows both Demolder, in this scene, and the Teacher, in the first prison camp, to be fools—comic butts of casual laughter—and it might seem that he is thus expressing an anti-intellectual bias. But this does not seem to us to be the case; both the Teacher and Demolder *are* fools, the latter in his excessive love of translating Pindar and the Teacher because he seems to have no such passion. Both are extremists and are treated accordingly.

At this point, Renoir juxtaposes scenes between Maréchal and Rosenthal on the one hand and Rauffenstein and Boeldieu on the other. The purpose is a deeper dramatization of their complex interrelationships.

First, we see Maréchal and Rosenthal as they look over Rosenthal's surreptitiously acquired map. Rosenthal is quite enthusiastic, even though his escape plan, requiring a two-hundred mile walk spread out over fifteen nights with very little food for sustenance, is dangerous. Maréchal's response is negative: "You know you're as batty with your map as that guy with his Pindar." But Rosenthal is not as crazy as Demolder; for his madness is in the service of freedom and current reality as Demolder's obsession is not.

The Senegalese now interrupts the two plotters with his finished picture, "Justice hunting down Crime," but they pay little attention to it. Like Demolder's, it is an abstract activity and has little to do with present reality.

As this point, the Germans make one of their periodic searches of the barracks, looking for evidence of an escape attempt. Boeldieu's quick thinking saves the rope they have been knotting by hand: he shoves it out a window and lets it hang down into the rain gutter. At the end of this scene, as the German soldiers are about to search Boeldieu's effects, Rauffenstein appears and orders them to bypass the French officer: "Give me your word you've nothing here against regulations." Boeldieu does so, but he wonders why his word should be sufficient and not those of Rosenthal and Maréchal. In a close-up of Rauffenstein, we *see* why: "The word of a Rosenthal," he asks, "or a Maréchal?" They are simply not of the appropriate class or caste.

This is given final reinforcement in the scene between Rauffenstein and Boeldieu in the former's quarters that follows on the search scene. This scene begins with reminiscences of Boeldieu's cousin, the Berlin military attaché whom Rauffenstein had mentioned in his squadron's mess when he had first met Boeldieu. What he admires most is Boeldieu's (the cousin's) horsemanship; it is the admiration of one knight errant for the skills of another. The remainder of their discussion touches directly on important themes of the film: in response to Boeldieu's query, Rauffenstein says that he has invited Boeldieu rather than the others to his quarters because he, Boeldieu, is a member of his, Rauffenstein's, class: a career officer in national service. Rosenthal and Maréchal may be good soldiers but they are not officers; they are merely "a gift of the French revolution"—rabble. And although Boeldieu seems wryly resigned to the fact that "Neither you or I can stop the march of time," Rauffenstein acknowledges that the end of the war will be "the end of the Rauffensteins and Boeldieus" and finds it "a pity." Nevertheless, Rauffenstein, although no botanist, lavishes tender care on his geranium in a place where only ivy and nettles grow naturally.

In contrast to this scene is the next bit of a scene—again between Maréchal and Rosenthal—to which we cut from the grandeur of Rauffenstein's quarters and his and Boeldieu's sentiments.

Maréchal and Rosenthal, sitting in their barracks, are glad to be escaping together. Although they acknowledge that Boeldieu is a "great guy," both agree that in a "jam" he would always be "de Boeldieu," whereas they would be simply a "couple of jerks." They are, in a word, pals, but neither of them can relate properly to Boeldieu.

Boeldieu has sensed the quality of the relationship between Rosenthal and Maréchal and, despite their genuine opposition to his plan, decides that the best possibility for escape lies in only two men making the attempt. Rosenthal and Maréchal will make the attempt while Boeldieu creates the necessary diversion.

UNBRIDGEABLE GAP: BOELDIEU AND MARÉCHAL

In a two shot featuring Maréchal and Boeldieu on either side of a caged squirrel, the latter outlines the escape plan. Maréchal is overcome with emotion at Boeldieu's willingness to be the decoy—though Boeldieu has insisted, in this scene and previously, that there is nothing personal in his decision—and attempts to express his feelings. But he admits to

Boeldieu that he is too embarrassed to speak. It is important to note that Boeldieu never divulges the plan for his final theatrics, and Maréchal will leave Wintersborn ignorant of his companion's fate.

A few days after the decision has been made, Maréchal approaches Boeldieu, finding him alone in their quarters, to try once more to tell him of his appreciation and admiration. Boeldieu bends over a basin, washing his white gloves. Maréchal goes to stand in front of him, embarrassed and not knowing how to begin. But Boeldieu will not let him begin. "Pour me some water to rinse my gloves." Maréchal complies and then tries to begin again. This time Boeldieu cuts him off by getting right to the point; he is not doing anything "for you personally." That "eliminates any sentimentality." Maréchal tries to answer and starts to say, "Still, there are times"—but again, Boeldieu won't have it. "Let's skip it, shall we?" And, having finished squeezing out his washed gloves, goes to hang them on the line to dry. Maréchal wants to know if Boeldieu will wear the gloves during the distraction. Yes. Maréchal shakes his head. If he were in Boeldieu's place, it would never occur to him to do such a thing. "Matter of taste," is Boeldieu's reply, but Maréchal goes on to note that Boeldieu "can't do anything like everyone else." He has known Boeldieu for eighteen months and the latter still uses the polite form *vous* in addressing him. Boeldieu replies that he also uses the polite *you* for his wife and mother. What more can they say to one another? The scene ends as Boeldieu offers Maréchal a cigarette. He declines. "English tobacco hurts my throat. In short, gloves, tobacco, everything separates us." Fade out.

Boeldieu's motive in doing what he does is beautifully realized in Renoir's subtle film. For one thing, Boeldieu has recently spoken with Rauffenstein and that discussion has convinced him that Rauffenstein is correct, that his and Rauffenstein's day is over. Moreover, Boeldieu has seen Maréchal and Rosenthal together over a long period of time and knows that he is an anachronism in their world; as Maréchal put it, "everything, really . . . comes between us." Not being able to experience community with these "pals," wanting still to follow out his own destiny and function according to his own "taste," Boeldieu's choice is inevitable.

Boeldieu's Performance

For the first time in the film, we have a sustained piece of montage, employed by the director to build up the excitement and drama of, first, the revolt of the fife-playing prisoners, then the Germans' attempts to stop it, and finally the locating and shooting of Boeldieu on the ramparts as Maréchal and Rosenthal make good their escape down the walls of Wintersborn.

After the fifes have been taken away and the well-rehearsed prisoners have once again begun to make a racket with such improvised instruments as pots and tubs, a general roll call is ordered to be held in the courtyard.

In their quarters, Rosenthal and Maréchal make ready to go and Boeldieu prepares for his great moment. Demolder is delighted with his diversionary role—he has been happily hitting the inside of a big basin with a big spoon—I understand my students' rowdiness now," he says, as he leaves. It will be a similar kind of experience for Boeldieu, who remains behind in the room—the others having gone to line up for roll call. Maréchal is the last to leave and their farewell is unsentimental, quite unlike, as we shall see, his farewell to Rosenthal at the end of the film. "Be seeing you," says Maréchal, and they shake hands. Maréchal goes. Boeldieu buttons up his gloves and smiles as he walks toward camera, and we cut to the courtyard.

In the blackness and cold of the courtyard, the roll call is taken after Rauffenstein arrives. At the critical moment, when Boeldieu fails to answer the call, we cut to the surprised face of Rauffenstein and then hear the tune on the flute, the *"Petit Navire,"* that Boeldieu is playing and that later will be sung by Rosenthal and Maréchal on the mountain road at *their* moment of critical communion. Now camera pans from Rauffenstein to locate the source of the music; the little panning movement effectively links the two principal players in the unfolding drama: spotlights come on and search upward, too, climbing stairs, going up, up, ever higher, like theatrical spots reaching for a star player at the top of a music hall set of steps. Like the star that he is now, Boeldieu steps into the circle of light. With perfect calm and control, he plays his song, slowly, melodically. Rauffenstein tries hard, looking up, to understand this absurd behavior.

Meanwhile, Rosenthal and Maréchal make good their escape from the fortress and light out for the woods.

Back in the courtyard, the rifles of the sentries are aimed skyward as Boeldieu, stopping now and then to play his tune, consulting his watch now and then (to make sure that his comrades have had enough time to go over the wall), climbs higher and higher. As he goes, he is spurred on by the mounting crescendo of music. An officer gives the order to fire, but Boeldieu ducks and is not hit. After this first volley, however, Rauffenstein stretches out his arm in a gesture halting the firing and walks to the center of the courtyard for a better view of his prisoner on high. Now both are center stage and their aristocratic duel, their single destiny is set in motion as they begin to converse in English. The dialogue is personal, clubby—as if each understood the hidden meaning of the other's coded words; "Are you insane?" "I am perfectly sane." "You understand . . . I shall have to shoot . . . I dread it, but . . . man to man . . ." "Damn nice of you, Rauffenstein, but it's impossible." It is as if each were following some unspoken set of rules that demanded the end that now comes: Rauffenstein fires; Boeldieu, first glancing at his watch, falls, mortally wounded. Only then does Rauffenstein receive the news that Boeldieu's act was a diversion and that two prisoners have escaped.

Thus, it is natural that Boeldieu's death scene should take place in Rauffenstein's quarters. These two are related as one: each is a knight of a vanishing order. Boeldieu's death marks the end of Rauffenstein as well.

Yet, Rauffenstein's surviving pain dictates the shape of the actual death scene. It begins close up on the extreme unction box held by a military chaplain. When camera tracks back to reveal the scene, we see that Boeldieu is laid out in Rauffenstein's quarters and that a nurse is also in attendance. Rauffenstein enters as the priest is leaving and Rauffenstein is waiting to help him on with his cape; the action is registered in a panning shot from Boeldieu's bed to the door, another of those linking pans that Renoir employs with such skilled unobtrusiveness.

As the priest leaves, a German officer enters and reports to Rauffenstein on the progress of the search for the prisoners. Rauffenstein acknowledges the report, the officer leaves, and he walks to the bed, where the nurse gives way, making room for him. Then camera tracks forward and catches them in a medium two-shot (Fig. 8-4)

Rauffenstein asks forgiveness, but Boeldieu insists that he did his duty and, although the stomach wound is quite painful (Rauffenstein: "I

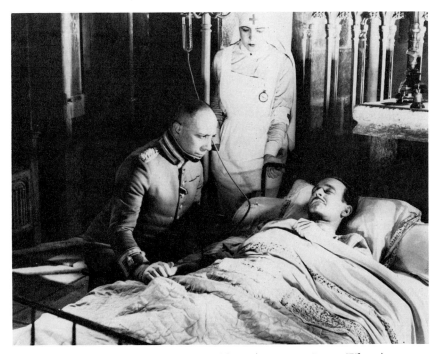

Figure 8–4. *The death of Boeldieu.* (Courtesy Janus Films.)

aimed at your leg . . . ."), Rauffenstein musn't blame himself for he, Boeldieu, was more than one hundred and fifty yards away, in bad light, and was running besides. Rauffenstein insists, however, on his own clumsiness. But Boeldieu reminds him that of the two of them Rauffenstein is worse off: "It's not I who's to be pitied. I'll be done for soon, but you . . . you're not finished yet." Rauffenstein acknowledges that he has missed his "good solution" to his anachronistic, "useless existence." It motivates him to rise and go to his whiskey chest and bolt down a brandy. In the interim, Boeldieu dies.

Rauffenstein does the duty of closing Boeldieu's eyes; then, after a moment, he goes to the window. For a long time he watches the thick snowflakes falling on a grey world. Then he looks at the geranium on the sill. He takes scissors and cuts the only flower in the fortress. Winter is intensified.

IV. Freedom

In this same winter, the German countryside is seen in a long shot. In the background, coming toward us along a dirt road, a peasant, heavily bundled up against the cold, leads a horse. Pan from this scene off the road to where Rosenthal and Maréchal huddle in a ditch, both dressed in ill-fitting, mud-spattered civilian clothes and both stubble-bearded.

They are a bit snappish with one another—Maréchal scolds Rosenthal for thinking the peasant with the horse is a man and not a woman—and cold and tired. Rosenthal prudently wants to wait for nightfall, but Maréchal insists on moving out then and there in order to fight the cold with brisk movement. He moves out of the ditch and out of the frame. Rosenthal sighs and starts to follow, but it is a painful business; he slips getting out of the ditch and we can see that his leg is game.

Now from a reverse angle—camera low to the ground and angled up— we see them full figure as Rosenthal tries to catch up. In the background are snowy mountains and the nearby foliage is stark and bare; they are alone in a hostile environment and have nothing but each other. Maréchal offers a lump of sugar to his companion; Rosenthal takes it eagerly, but he is alarmed over their dwindling supply. Maréchal adds that they haven't covered much ground considering how much they've eaten. He declines to take any; he's had his share. Besides, he wants Rosenthal to hold the cache from now on, so that he "won't be tempted." As they begin to walk away from camera, Maréchal points up ahead and declares that they will skirt around the town whose spires are now just barely visible in the distance. Rosenthal limps after him. The foot is very painful.

Dissolve to another part of the countryside. This is mountainous country that is also covered with large patches of snow and ice. Pan down to a gully where we see the two Frenchmen asleep, huddled together for warmth. The image captures their situation precisely: as we said, they are alone in a hostile environment and have only each other.

Maréchal wakes up and is immediately on his feet and eager to continue the walk. Rosenthal struggles to his feet and follows, but it is clear that his foot is worse, for we see that he must now hobble along with the aid of a cane cut from a tree branch.

Dissolve again to a steep mountain road. Rosenthal is in worse shape. He is five yards behind Maréchal and is now hopping with his good leg in order to spare the bad one. Maréchal is annoyed at their slow pace and, unable to help himself, he blows up at Rosenthal. Rosenthal shouts back and their exchange rises in crescendo; we learn that their food has run out. Finally, Rosenthal urges Maréchal to "beat it." The latter agrees, bringing the reply from Rosenthal that he is "so happy" he "could sing."

The shot widens as Maréchal leaves the frame; then we push in close as Rosenthal, in his exhaustion, sinks down onto a large boulder by the side of the road. Frustrated and full of rage, Rosenthal starts to sing; a closeup: he continues to sing. Defiantly showing that his spirit is still alive, his singing is a brave and touching gesture: "He was a little boat/he was a little boat/ who had never, never, never navigated,/who had never, never navigated." It is, of course, the same song that Boeldieu had played on his fife.

Now we cut to Maréchal, already quite a distance away. Camera leads him as, turning his head and hearing Rosenthal, he first hums then sings another stanza of the same song: "At the end of five or six weeks/at the end of five or six weeks/we ran, ran, ran out of provisions/we ran, ran, ran out of provisions." Now, suddenly, Rosenthal's voice is no longer heard. Maréchal strains to hear, slows his pace, cocks his read in the opposite direction to his walk.

Cut back to Rosenthal, sitting on the rock, dejected, defeated, his head sagging in complete physical and spiritual exhaustion. Stilled by this emotion, and staring at the earth, he does not notice the fold of Maréchal's coat enter the frame beside him. Camera pulls back and the shot widens to include both men; Rosenthal, now a beaten man, looks up to see Maréchal. With a simple, rough-hewn gesture, the latter reaches his arm around Rosenthal and lifts him up. "Come on, let's go." And they move off together, the crisis ended, friends again.

This emotional (indeed, nearly sentimental) scene is meant to contrast sharply with the carefully orchestrated dialogues of Rauffenstein and Boeldieu and the aborted, tongue-tied, one-sided ones Maréchal has had with Boeldieu—especially the one in which Boeldieu was unable to receive Maréchal's warm gratitude for his sacrifice. In fact, this encounter bears out exactly what Maréchal had said to Rosenthal regarding *their* friendship during such a "bad time." It is the opposite of what would have happened had "de Boeldieu" been a participant. The kind of storm these two weather on a freezing mountain road is a symbol of their intimacy and community—a value Renoir is at pains to espouse.

Following this scene is their meeting with Elsa in her barn.

Elsa needs nothing but the fact of the men's exhaustion and fear to make her decision to take them in. Nothing that actually happens in the scene—except possibly the anguished innocence in Rosenthal's outburst ("Call the police! I can't take another step!")—accounts for her trusting these unkempt strangers. It is a pure gesture of instinctive trust. Elsa, reaching out as she does, redeems Renoir's belief in the latent possibilities of freedom. Nor should we think of this belief as either sentimental or naive. The simplicity of setting, acting, and script will not allow such an interpretation and the overtones of a manger scene reinforce the prohibition. Renoir's genius here is to have let such a moment simply happen.

After Elsa's acceptance, they move into her kitchen where food is provided: a piece of bread and a mug of milk, food that contrasts sharply with the elegant food available to these men while in captivity.

Elsa cautions them to keep silent because her little girl, Lotte, is asleep. Then she prepares a basin of warm water with which to treat Rosenthal's foot and provides Maréchal with bread and milk. At this point, Elsa's friendship is tested: a squad of German troops passes the house and the squad leader knocks on the window to ask directions in the dark night. Calmly, Elsa opens the window, answers their questions, and sends them on their way. During her conversation with the German *feldwebel*, however, Maréchal and Rosenthal have tensely moved toward the door, preparing for sudden flight if necessary. They relax when they see her fasten the shutters. Rosenthal returns painfully to his seat, Maréchal to his food. Elsa kneels at Rosenthal's feet and begins to remove his boot. It hurts. He cries out. "Careful," she says, "my child's asleep." Fade out.

We learn a good deal from Elsa's behavior during this scene: from her nurturing of Rosenthal, her providing Maréchal with food, her caring about her sleeping child, her whole attitude toward the two strange men. We learn a good deal about the values of community and concern. And the special image conveying this mood is Elsa kneeling at Rosenthal's feet; it confers a sense of Biblical hospitality on Elsa's house, and we recall a similar image from the camp: the Engineer kneeling and washing Maréchal's feet.

Next morning Elsa's suffering is revealed through the expressive visual symbols of the photographs and the empty table. Elsa points out to the two men a row of photographs on the wall: "My husband was killed at Verdun." Her finger moves to the next photograph and the shot widens slightly to include some of her profile—linking her to the tragedy she so soberly describes. "My husband and my brothers, killed at Liege, Charleroi, Tannenberg . . . our greatest victories!" She moves to join the seated Rosenthal and shot widens even more. "And now the table is too big." She motions toward the table and camera pans there. Lotte, a five year old girl, sits alone at the long table finishing a piece of bread and butter. In the background a cross hangs on a white-washed wall. Chairs are turned upside down on the tabletop, as in a restaurant after closing. The little girl, isolated at one end, makes a poignant image. We remember crowded, food-laden tables from the beginning sequences of the film and the importance Renoir attaches to them as symbols and concrete facts of human community and we understand the harshness he wishes to convey in this appallingly empty picture.

Again Renoir presses home, but gently, the theme of false barriers—illusions great and small—in a scene between Maréchal and the cow in the barn. It follows immediately the image of Lotte at the empty table. The action consists of Maréchal filling the trough with hay and urging the animal to eat; while it does, he speaks to it, resting his hand on the cow with just the right amount of familiar ease. As he speaks camera pushes in for a closer angle on him. Here is the dialogue in its entirety, which, together with the simplicity of the visual setting, makes the point:

MARÉCHAL: Don't be afraid. It's only me. You don't care if a Frenchman tends you, do you? You smell like my grandfather's cows. It's a good smell. You're from Wurtemberg and I'm from Paris. But we're friends anyway, eh? You're a poor cow and I'm a poor soldier. We each do our best, eh?

He slaps the cow on the rump and leaves the stable. For a moment, we hold on the scene, and we watch as the cow turns toward the departed Maréchal and moos.

Outside, we look over Maréchal's shoulder and see the whole expanse of the valley, as he, too, looks outward from the farm. Up to this point, we have been virtually isolated within the scrubbed confines of Elsa's farmhouse world. Now we see the rest of the proximal universe and what Renoir permits us to see jibes beautifully with what we have already seen: a pastoral world removed from harsh illusions. And, as if to kinetically make the point, Maréchal yawns and stretches and moves off toward the farmhouse. In another shot we see him pause for just a moment beside the chopping block. As he passes, a burst of energy activates him: freedom takes hold, amiable and aimless, and he sinks the axe into the block. The thud reverberates in our minds.

What we have so far described of this sequence takes place in just a few scenes. Yet, in this brief interlude with Elsa, Renoir has built up a picture of a life quietly ravished by a war that seems very far away. The spare simplicity of the clean-scrubbed farmhouse, the rustic sweetness of barn and cow, Elsa's goodness and simplicity of manner (something in her face and in Dita Parlo's face suggests a type of the suffering Marian figure), the exhaustion, hunger, and need of the two Frenchmen, the innocent little girl at the empty table, the memorial photographs of Elsa's male relations—all these represent a collation of images from which emanates a complex system of irony about illusory war and real human relations. The world of Elsa's farmhouse, although different from the world of prison, controverts nothing we learned there; it only makes those lessons stand out more sharply. Elsa's world dramatizes Renoir's contention that "The Frenchmen in this film are good Frenchmen and the Germans good Germans. . . ." (Quoted in Georges Sadoul, *Dictionary of Films*, translated, edited, and updated by Peter Morris, Los Angeles, 1972, s. v. *La Grande Illusion*, p. 134b.)

At Christmas time, the men prepare a surprise for Lotte. It is a miniature reproduction of the scene in the manger made of cardboard and wood and peopled by Biblical figures carved from potatoes. Although Maréchal thinks it shoddy, Elsa is greatly moved by the fact that they have done it at all, for they have had to improvise everything. Lotte, too, is delighted and we see it in a softly striking tableau: a shot past the burning candles that includes the shining faces of child and adults, all moved by a common mood of joy and content.

Now Elsa and Maréchal take Lotte off to bed, but the mood is still one suffused with uncommon goodwill and feeling. After the child has been put to sleep, the three adults gather around the manger. Elsa thanks them. There is an awkward, embarrassed silence, as if each were aware that families (as they seem to have become) need not undergo such strained moments. But only the recognition that one thing more is needed to seal their identities causes this tension.

Elsa says goodnight. They murmur to each other. And now in a familiar pattern of Renoir iconography, featuring doors and rooms as symbolic objects, Elsa and Maréchal will come together. Maréchal says good night to Rosenthal and goes to his room. Restless, he walks about, camera following; he eats an apple; then he notices through the door into the dining room that Elsa is still in that room, standing beside the Christmas display. Surprised to see her—because he had entered his own room from Rosenthal's and had not thought he would see her—he walks very slowly toward her, out of his room and into the dining room. Camera stays reticently in his room, observing the action with great discretion at a modest distance. She raises her face and he takes her in his arms as the music swells.

Juxtaposed with this culminating development is an image of a snowy vista. It is morning. The Frenchmen must leave. The irony of this scene following on the last is strong. Maréchal's newly established closeness to Elsa complicates his having to leave; he cannot bring himself to tell her. Rosenthal must do it. Maréchal tries to comfort the weeping Elsa by assuring her that he will return after the war and take her and Lotte to live with him in France. However comforting, it is still another illusion, and our last view of the farmhouse features little Lotte. Elsa removes three plates and once again Lotte sits alone at the long table.

The mountainous landscape is covered with snow as we pan across it and then tilt down to see Maréchal and Rosenthal hiding among pine trees at the edge of a deep meadow (Figure 8-5). Maréchal wonders where the Swiss border is located: "You're sure that's Switzerland over there?" Rosenthal consults his map. He is sure. To Maréchal, however, it is still a mystery because "It all looks alike. Frontiers are an invention of man." But Rosenthal has faith that there is a man-made frontier up ahead even though "nature doesn't give a hoot." Rosenthal reminds Maréchal that they will have to resume fighting once they have returned to France. Maréchal's reply to this is vehement: "We've got to end this stinking war . . . maybe it'll be the last." To which Rosenthal answers, "You've still got illusions." Then, after deciding on what to do in case they should run into a German patrol, the two friends embrace affectionately and start across the snowy meadow.

Cut to another mountain, flanking the meadow on the other side, as a German patrol descends, following a set of tracks. Suddenly, one of the soldiers looks across the meadow. Noticing Maréchal and Rosenthal, he alerts the others and they begin to fire. But at last their sergeant turns to one of the soldiers. "Don't shoot. They're in Switzerland." It is the final gesture of decency from one poor soldier to another. Camera pans across toward the meadow; then we cut to the final shot: the two insignificant specks crawling blackly across the white snow.

Figure 8–5. *Maréchal and Rosenthal at the Swiss border.* (**Courtesy Janus Films.**)

Style and Approach

The most prominent characteristic of the style of *Grand Illusion* is its reticence. (And this of course is not so different from the style of Renoir's other films. See, for example, our comments on *The Rules of the Game*, p. 201ff.) It is a style that does not call attention to itself and is likely to go unremarked upon by a student, especially one who is enraptured by his first meeting with the films of this master. When asked to discuss Renoir's style, such a student's response is likely to be, "But there *is* no style!"

But of course there is, and we can observe its dimensions under the following convenient rubrics.

Camera

First, there is the sparing use of odd camera angles. Renoir's camera sees most frequently from modest eye level, and he does not use camera perspective to create effects, as do, say, Welles or Hitchcock.

Even more important, however, are Renoir's use of the moving camera and his deployment of depth of field. Two examples of each will be enough to make clear how importantly each figures as an element of the cinematographic style here. First, the moving camera: a rich example is in the moving shot at the luncheon at von Rauffenstein's squadron mess (see pp. 143–144).

This moving shot records a series of actions: A formal introduction of Boeldieu and Maréchal and the elegant taking of their coats, as would be due members of the same caste (military officers)—the reader will remember that von Rauffenstein's invitation to the Frenchmen had *depended* on their being officers; the ushering of the guests to table; the seating of the whole group; and the beginning of the service by orderlies. In other words, the visual effect imitates the subject by linking invitation and meal, officer and officer, and relating the role of orderly to officer; in other words, it describes the arbitrary divisions of society by linking its effects.

A second example is the moving shot after the poster announces the German capture of Douaumont (see p. 151). The shot links losers and winners as if to suggest that there are not very many differences between them; and, indeed, events prove that the designations (losers and winners) are only temporarily valid, for the French recapture the town almost immediately.

An example of the use of depth of field occurs in the prisoner's quarters at Wintersborn. As Boeldieu, Maréchal, and Rosenthal plot to escape in the background, Demolder, in the foreground, quietly and obliviously translates Pindar. The richness of the irony in this staging matches its compelling realism. Our second example similarly allows the audience to see more: the staging of the prelude to Rosenthal's meal in the first prison camp (see p. 146). Camera moves from group to group in the room, starting with the Actor and Maréchal and ending with Rosenthal and his orderly. Renoir has explained this stylistic preference, saying that "The longer I continue in my profession the more I am induced to stage scenes in depth." (From "Souvenirs," *Le Point*, No. 18, Dec. 1938. Quoted in Leprohon, op. cit., p. 200). Renoir's motive seems to be the revelatory power of this mode.

TEXTURE AND LIGHT

Renoir has noted that "reality is in fact magical. It takes a lot of patience and work and good will to find it." (*Cahiers du Cinéma*, No. 78, Christmas 1957; quoted in ibid., p. 168.) And indeed, he has employed all these qualities to produce, for example, the magically real texture of what we see on the screen. The style of the film inheres also in the subtle use of the whole middle range of gray scale tones, especially at the appropriate dramatic moments. For example, we are virtually bathed in middle range gray tones, without a trace of sparkling whites or deep blacks, until the one place where such dramatic tonality would express the action best. We refer to the escape from Wintersborn, especially the theater of Boeldieu's diversion. In that sequence, rocks, snow, Boeldieu's uniform, especially his gloves, and the beams of the interior of the castle all become elements in the showy drama (and in the pattern of light that we see). This is all the more remarkable when we consider that we do not seem similarly impressed by the final sequence at the border, featuring elements that would also normally make for a black-and-white dominated tonality (that is, the snowy meadow, the black pines, and so on).

SOUND AND MUSIC

Unlike some film makers working in the neorealist tradition, Renoir does not attempt to recreate an environment through the use of natural sound. Instead, natural sound is used to solve artistic problems, where it can, and thus to generate meaning. One example in the scene at the first prison camp when the prisoners are in the costume room preparing for the camp theatrical will make the point. Here the sound of the German recruits, drilling on the parade ground beneath the window, is artfully used to make the point that both sound and music have inevitable physiological effects on listeners, and that war is likely to be one of those effects when the correct, conventional combination is heard.

Renoir's use of music is not so much sentimental as it is plain and emphatic. Just as he used Mozart and other eighteenth-century composers to underscore the anachronistic world of the Count in *The Rules of the Game*, so here he uses equally programmatic scoring to achieve a plain and unmistakable audience response. The martial music we hear behind the titles is an exception in the sense that its effect is intended to be ironic: *Grand Illusion* is not a war film in the usual sense. However, else-where in the film, as when we hear the Strauss waltzes in Rauffenstein's squadron mess or listen to the singing of the "Marseillaise" at the camp theatrical, we are cued to respond in unambiguous ways. It is a use of music derived from a theatrical talent, a wish to create effects, to suggest without adornment the verve and emotionality inherent in human inter-action.

ACTING

One is greatly struck, when reading over the recorded utterances of Jean Renoir, by his recognition of the collaborative nature of his medium, but the collaborators with whom he seems to have had the greatest rap-port are the actors. And this accounts for the marvelous performances we see in Renoir's films, generally. It is not less true in *Grand Illusion*.

What we must notice first, we think, is the naturalness of the acting; not a gesture seems out of character, whether it is the gestures of the aristocrats—von Stroheim and Fresnay—or the middle-class or working-class figures, Dalio and Gabin. Moreover, Stroheim's flexibility within his rigid characterization is remarkable. For his range is extraordinary—and quite essential. We need to see, within that disdainful, overly-bred Prussian mask the rich play of other colors that Stroheim gives us: charm, a sweet sincerity, and a real registration of a whole range of anguished responses. Without this depth and control over an emotional range we would merely have had a villain to root against and this would have been very very far from what Renoir wanted and from what makes the film the complex experience it is. Gabin's "rightness" in his role also deserves comment—for other reasons. Gabin, too, elicits our broad sympathy, but alongside the delicacy of Stroheim he seems monochromatic. Neverthe-less, the acting style is such that the word *naturalness* describes it prop-erly.

IMAGERY

By imagery, we mean a recurring, detailed picture, usually of a con-crete and sensuous nature, to which, by virtue of its repetition or an especially powerful charge of cinematic energy inhering in it, there accrue complex associations and meanings. In Renoir, imagery is usually associated with community in some way, and we think that a brief dis-cussion of two of these will make this clear.

The taking of food is an especially meaningful and beautifully staged image in Renoir's films, especially in *Grand Illusion*. The film begins in a place where men meet to take food and proceeds immediately to the elegant luncheon at Rauffenstein's squadron mess where we discover that these so-called enemies are not necessarily that at all. The discovery is an essential element in the meal they take together; the sacrament of food makes it possible. Later, at the meal sponsored by Rosenthal at the first prison camp, we see that the work of community goes on very fruit-fully at table; what human beings have in common and what they do not is quickly learned at communal meals. Of course, multiple ironies are generated by the contrast between these meals and the kinds of food Maréchal and Rosenthal eat at Elsa's, as well as by the modulated image we see there that stays longest in the mind: the long table, emptied by war, at which a lone child sits in deprivation.

The second strain of imagery is the theatrical. (See the discussion of this imagery by Leo Braudy in *Jean Renoir: The World of his Films,* Garden City, N.Y., 1972, Chap. III.) The two great theatrical events in the film are the camp theatrical and Boeldieu's performance on the battle-ments with his fife. In both, the central issue is freedom for Rosenthal and Maréchal in the case of Boeldieu's performance, and metaphorical freedom in the camp theatrical. In both cases creativity is the spur and the emblem of a deeper kind of freedom. For Renoir the theater is no mere comforting illusion. It is, perhaps, a great and sustaining one, a myth of power and choice where none exists otherwise.

The image-making artistry of Jean Renoir is all the more remarkable in that it serves no ultimately illusionistic purposes. Although the possi-bilities for community and convivial social relations are uncertain in *Grand Illusion,* we are never falsely persuaded by the art of this film maker that there is more than that much. In his hands, we are at least delighted that there is at least so much.

CHAPTER 9

The Rules of the Game

[La Regle du Jeu]

Directed by JEAN RENOIR

CAST

THE MARQUIS, ROBERT DE LA CHESNAYE	*Marcel Dalio*
CHRISTINE	*Nora Grégor*
ANDRÉ JURIEU	*Roland Toutain*
OCTAVE	*Jean Renoir*
GENEVIÈVE	*Mila Parely*
CHARLOTTE	*Odette Talazac*
THE GENERAL	*Pierre Magnier*
SAINT-AUBIN	*Pierre Nay*
LA BRUYÈRE	*Richard Francoeur*
MME. DE LA BRUYÈRE	*Claire Gérard*
JACKIE (CHRISTINE'S NIECE)	*Anne Mayen*
THE HOMOSEXUAL	*Roger Forster*
THE SOUTH AMERICAN	*Nicholas Amato*
BERTHELIN	*M. Corteggiani*
LISETTE	*Paulette Dubost*
SCHUMACHER, THE GAMEKEEPER	*Gaston Modot*
MARCEAU, THE POACHER	*Julien Carette*
CORNEILLE, THE BUTLER	*Eddy Debray*
THE CHEF	*Léon Larive*
THE KITCHEN SERVANT	*Celéstin*
THE SERVING GIRL	*Jenny Helia*
THE ENGLISH SERVANT	*Henri Cartier-Bresson*

CREDITS

DIRECTED BY	*Jean Renoir*
SCENARIO AND DIALOGUE	*Jean Renoir, in collaboration with Karl Koch and Camille François*
ASSISTANT DIRECTORS	*André Zwoboda and Henri Cartier-Bresson*

CREDITS (Continued)

Music Arranged and Directed by	*Roger Désormières*
Director of Photography	*Jean Bachelet*
Decor	*Eugène Lourié*
Editor	*Marguerite Houlet-Renoir*
Reconstituted Version Produced by	Les Grands Films Classiques (*Paris*); *Jean Gaborit and Jacques Durand*

1939 Black and white 113 minutes

Story and Characterization

The complicated story of the film begins at night at Le Bourget Airport outside Paris where André Jurieu, a dashing young pilot, has just completed a heroic and record-breaking transatlantic solo flight. He is bitterly disappointed that his lady love, Christine, the wife of the Marquis Robert de la Chesnaye, has not come to greet him and join the celebration attending his arrival; and he expresses this sentiment over a national radio hook-up. He had undertaken this exploit for Christine's sake, but instead of Christine, only his friend Octave is there to greet him.

Meanwhile, the radio broadcast is heard by a number of Parisians who belong to the social set dominated by the Marquis, a wealthy aristocrat who is addicted to his collection of mechanical birds and music makers, objets d'art that reflect his need for stability, order, and an unemotional façade. He too hears the broadcast—as does Christine—and he is so moved by his wife's seeming fidelity to their marriage (as reflected in her failure to meet Jurieu at Le Bourget) that he decides to break off his relations with his mistress, Geneviève.

Nevertheless, when the Marquis organizes a hunting party at his country home, La Colinière, he invites Geneviève, and is persuaded by Octave, an old friend of Christine's who also loves her, to invite the distraught André Jurieu as well. Thus is generated a love-intrigue plot at this level of society.

At La Colonière, another love-intrigue plot is generated when Robert impulsively hires Marceau, a poacher, as a member of the household staff; Marceau begins to make overtures to Christine's maid, Lisette, incurring the angry jealousy of her husband, Schumacher. Schumacher is the head gamekeeper on the estate.

After a superbly organized hunt, the two plots gather momentum. There is an elaborate fete, featuring theatrical entertainment and dancing, and Schumacher's anger explodes. He goes after Marceau with a gun. Meanwhile, André declares his undying love for Christine and asks her to go away with him, but she, confused by the way the love game is played, declares her love for Octave. At the conclusion, Octave gallantly gives way to André and sends him out to the greenhouse to be with Christine. Wearing Octave's coat he rushes out to the greenhouse. There, Christine is wearing Lisette's coat. Thus it appears to the angry Schumacher that Octave is making love to his wife and he shoots André to death. Robert takes over and calmly assures everyone that an accident has taken place and that all will be well.

While Jean Renoir was still working on the scenario for *The Rules of the Game,* he was asked what it would be and he answered, "An exact description of the *bourgeois* of our time" (from "The Birth of *Rules of the Game,*" reprinted in *Rules of the Game,* a film by Jean Renoir, translated by John McGrath and Maureen Teitelbaum, New York, 1970, p. 6). Yet, it is clear that he must have changed his mind at some point, for the film clearly focuses on aristocratic society and the milieu of its servants. Robert (the Marquis de la Chesnaye), Christine, Octave, André, Geneviève, the General, Saint-Aubin, and La Bruyère all represent an aristocracy with no visible means of support and enough leisure time to spend two weeks in mid-November hunting at La Colonière.

Renoir is here clearly interested in levels of society; thus, the film also dramatizes the life of the servants, to whose estate, indeed, the still lower classes aspire. Witness, for example, Marceau's ambition to become a servant; in the end, when he is fired by Robert, he is misty-eyed and grateful that Robert had done him the unforgettable kindness of sponsoring this ambition.) This is because all levels of society, Renoir seems to be saying, aspire toward a condition where rules prevail. In Marceau's case, movement into the servant class satisfies the aspiration.

At the highest level of the social hierarchy, nobody has an occupation; but there the rules are in greatest force. This fact is embodied in the character of the Marquis. Robert de la Chesnaye is an artistocrat par excellence. His occupation is to provide an occupation for himself and the other members of his set; but he has one preoccupation: caring for a large collection of mechanical singing birds and musical instruments. With these he seems obsessed. So gratified is he by the unfailing regularity with which the birds and organs perform their functions that we become aware of the contrast between these perfect artifacts and imperfect humanity: their music is sweet but human emotions are bound sometimes to be discordant. Thus, the mechanical instruments become symbols, signifying for us the decorum and order, the perfect "rules" by which the life of this social class is made into an acceptable series of "games." If it is doubted that the world he inhabits is as orderly and structured as this would suggest, one need only look carefully at Renoir's picture of Robert. Surely the arched eyebrows, the carefully correct clothing, the impeccable formal manners, and the languid air he affects are also artifacts and contribute to the stability so important to his life.

The principal method of characterization in any dramatic film is of course the interaction of characters. We learn about a character by what he does. But perhaps as important here is another, less conventional method of characterization, one which we may call imagistic. It is a thoroughly cinematic method and it consists of arranging a striking re-velatory image, a moment on screen when each character is most wholly *seen* as himself. In each, the iconography of the frame is arranged with special care and exactness, the acting is rather more completely informed by the particular fictional verve of the character, and certain symbolic objects are employed with unusual felicity. Thus, Robert's moment comes at the climax of the fete, when he presents his gorgeous mechanical or-gan. We see a close-up of the bejeweled wonder of the machine itself and pan to see the look of indescribable joy that comes over Dalio's face when the brittle music begins. In the mechanical marvel of shiny and useless surfaces, in the artificiality and control apparent when it works at his command, is the triumph of a life so designed that it has warded off pain. (See pp. 195–196.)

For Christine, on the other hand, such a moment comes twice. The first is with Octave, during a scene in the bedroom of her townhouse. Octave has just given her an important lesson, explaining the rule of friendship between the sexes (and alluding specifically to André and Christine). She repeats what she has learned: "In Paris, one does not have the right to be nice to a man without. . . ." Octave has suggested that she cor-rect her error by inviting André to the hunt. When she demurs, Octave starts to leave. She stops him, throws him down on the bed and starts to be very nice to him. Too nice. She has not learned her lesson well. Later, she will almost convince Octave that she loves him and is ready to run off with him. In the lushness of her bedroom, among the satins, the crystal chandeliers, and the boudoir mirrors, Christine reveals herself to be the image of a painfully innocent aristocrat.

The same image forces itself on our attention when she holds André's hand in the foyer of the chateau and delivers her charmingly naive speech.

The excuse for Christine is that she is a foreigner and she is not yet familiar with the rules; she has only been a member of the group for three short years, which coincide with the duration of her marriage to Robert and with the beginning of his affair with Geneviève. Yet Christine tries to adapt. After the hunt, where she has seen through the telescope her husband embracing Geneviève, she makes an effort to assimilate herself into society. The touching scene in the bedroom between the two women dramatize this effort. There, she acts a role utterly foreign to her: the sophisticated wife. She is willing to discuss with her husband's mis-tress Robert's habit of smoking in bed and carries on with Geneviève in a brittle and knowing tone. (Ironically, it is she who prevents Robert's reformation: Geneviève had planned to leave the chateau and end her affair with Robert, but, convinced by Christine's artificial good will, she stays on.)

However, Christine's ultimate fate reinforces Renoir's theme. For during the hubub of the fete, Christine's complete disorientation is revealed. In the space of fifteen minutes of screen time, she flirts aggressively with Saint-Aubin, succumbs to André's interruption of *that* tryst by declaring her love for *him*, then changes her mind and insists she *really* loves Octave, with whom she agrees to run away at once! But for her, too, the rules of the game are too strong. Her innocence has not stood her in good stead in this milieu, for as Renoir said, "it is much more complicated than that" ("The Birth of *Rules of the Game*," op. cit., p. 7), and when we last see her she has come so far toward membership in the group that she is comforting the hysterical Jackie and admonishing her to control herself because "people are watching."

The passionate rule-breaking André—the romantic hero who is ready to forego everything for love—also succumbs to the rules. We are at first led to believe that André is a true outsider, that he has no use for the rules of this society. So inflamed is he at the prospect of not seeing Christine that even Octave, the most reasonable man in the cast of characters, cannot control him. After the car accident, when Octave reminds him that there are such things as rules, he rages almost out of control; he cares nothing for rules. Octave is impressed; he arranges an invitation to the hunt for André.

But André must die for his impulsiveness. At La Colonière we discover—in one of the film's most brilliant comic moments—that André is as much a member of the society as Robert. When at last Christine declares her love for him, the moment he has been waiting for all along, all he can do is ask for a little time in which to "talk things over" with Robert. (Later, we discover—and this is even funnier—that he wanted Christine to spend a month in the country with his mother while he continued to explore the situation with Robert.) Nevertheless, André has gone too far; he has made a public spectacle of himself and Christine; he has moped and mooned away his time at La Colonière (even threatening Octave with his departure the same night that they arrive); he strikes Saint-Aubin for flirting with Christine and makes a mockery of Saint-Aubin's intention of challenging him to a duel; but, perhaps worst of all, he allows his romantic passion to reassert itself. Octave was right when he told Christine that André was the type of romantic hero that could fly the Atlantic but not cross a street safely. At the fatal moment, he allows himself to be sent out into the adventurous night and is shot.

Octave is the "confidant of all the others, the hero in spite of himself" (according to Renoir, who goes on to explain why he played the role: "So I could be more inside the film. And because for a part as special as that of Octave . . . I could not see who could play the part with more docility than myself"). (Ibid., p. 9) Taking his name, perhaps, from Doña Anna's suitor in Mozart's *Don Giovanni*, Octave is nowhere revealed to us with more impact than on the night of the fete. The musician and artist manqué, he reenacts a glorious moment in the life of a conductor. It is a piece of gossamer magic, stylish and delicate, but it is all the more touching because Octave is also a realist and breaks off the enactment before the baton can fall. Octave is like Christine in possessing a large measure of real sincerity and unlike her in having a perceptive view of the social world he inhabits by invitation. Thus, he is sensible. Yet, he is also a type of André, and he is susceptible to romantic impulses. Thus when Christine turns to him in the darkness of the little greenhouse and asks him to kiss her "like a lover," he is swept away. Yet, as we should expect from having seen his performance on the terrace, he is perhaps more deeply the realist; he gives way to Lisette's argument and accepts his place in the world. Reason saves his life.

Octave acts as one of the bridges to those who enact the subplot: the servants. In his casual, playfully erotic attentions to Lisette, he is a shadowy representative of that eighteenth-century master who has designs on the coquettish servant girl.

The servants in *The Rules of the Game* enact a comic drama below stairs that parallels the goings-on upstairs. There, too, we see a disturbing triangle: Schumacher-Lisette-Marceau. But the servants, the film seems to say, are not quite as well in control of themselves as their masters. Whatever the emotional temper upstairs, there is always a rule to clamp down on a passion. Not so with the servants, however. Even though their intrigues generate the broadest of the farcical materials on the night of the fete, they too provide the tragedy, and one of them, Schumacher, offers us his blatant tears. The tragedy of servants, Renoir seems to say, is that they have too little by way of social rules.

Lisette is the other part of the bridge between upstairs and downstairs. It is she who is closest to Christine. She, in fact, is Christine's only *friend;* for Octave is right about friendship betwen the sexes: there can be none. Lisette, moreover, is a model for Christine, in that she is more deeply inculcated with the values of the society than is her mistress. She understands instinctively the flirtation rule below stairs; thus, she is willing to engage in a playful kind of flirtatious banter with Marceau and know what it means—exactly. This is in contrast to Christine, who needs to be told by Octave and still does not understand a similar rule upstairs.

Lisette's mastery of rules is seen in the moment when Marceau first appears at the dining table (see p. 189). There she carefully lays out the rules for his behavior toward her. On the other hand, Schumacher's entrance into that same scene a few moments earlier had made it clear that he was quite outside any discussion of rules. He refuses to take part when asked, because he does not belong to the milieu; to all questions of decorum, the foreign-named Gamekeeper might repeat his key piece of dialogue: "How could I know?" For Schumacher has, perhaps, the most authentic (and certainly the most visible) passion in the film. By its persistent understatement, his love for his wife impresses us with its sincerity and its seriousness. Blunt, plain-spoken, angry at Marceau's free-wheeling style, Schumacher is only concerned to be close to Lisette. Thwarted first by the employment of his wife in the Paris townhouse while he himself is occupied in Sologne, Schumacher is pushed to the edge by Marceau's comic attentions to his wife and finally unhinged by the mistaken notion that Octave is also pursuing her. His epiphany comes after his dismissal, when Marceau encounters him and we see the unashamed tears stream down his cheeks.

Marceau, on the other hand, aspires not toward love but status; as he tells Robert at their first meeting, it is the uniform of the servant that dazzles him. That badge of status fires his ambition. Marceau is, like Octave, something of a realist, and perhaps that is why they make their final appearances in the film together.

Nevertheless, the parallels between the lives of the servants and those of the masters are sharply made. Corneille, the marvelous stiff-postured major-domo, addresses the more menial servants at the chateau as "my friend," just as Robert does. The epigrammatic wit of the servants also matches that of the masters:

ROBERT: Corneille! Corneille! Stop this farce!
CORNEILLE: Which one, Monsieur le Marquis?

The actions of the former, their essential manners, are copies of those of their masters. Thus, when Robert and André stop physically assaulting one another over Christine, they come together in casual cameraderie, just as do Marceau and Schumacher when they stop fighting over a woman. In addition, the standards of the servants are perhaps higher in some respects—but are certainly not below—the standards of the masters. The Chef's tale of Robert's rejection of the spoiled potato salad confirms this.

The narrative constantly reveals these characters as they obey, test, manifest, and sometimes try to violate the rules. And always the cardinal rule is subtly in force: thou shalt not hurt another; for to do so is to make another aware of emotions that cannot tolerably be made public. For these people, death must be kept in the dark. The light of the game provides cover.

Themes and Interpretations

So frequently have we alluded to the major theme of the film (in the preceding section of this chapter) that it is virtually redundant to discuss it further. Nevertheless, in the interest of clarity, it should be said that we can read of that theme in Renoir's own words: "I want to show that every game has its rules. He who breaks them loses the game." (Ibid., p. 6.) Thus, André and Schumacher both lose the game, the latter without ever having tried to learn the rules and the former despite the impulse and the effort to conform.

Yet, there is more, as is always the case with such complex and finely wrought art as this. For Renoir has also noted that "the group [the aristocracy] is impure" (ibid., p. 13), and in his film he has delineated the nature of the impurity. It is, of course, that the rules of this particular game are built with a deadly quantity of hypocrisy and the unconscious savor of death, the warding off of which is the whole purpose of the rules. Although as Renoir has said, "it was a light picture . . . and [I thought] the big problems were so well hidden that the audience wouldn't be hurt in their feelings" (ibid.), the lightness of the film did not entirely cover up the "big problems" dramatized there. Renoir got a "big surprise and a bad one" (ibid., p. 14).

This is because the artist Renoir worked deeper veins than he realized. *The Rules of the Game* dramatizes the absolute rigidity of class structure in the France that existed between Munich and the beginning of World War II, just a few weeks after the film's premiere in July of 1939. The Marquis' set is seen to be very much wrapped up in a life that permits luxurious excesses, handsome living arrangements, elaborate leisure activities, personal liberty to the extent of indulgence in erotic charades —and worse. Schumacher, an honest man, is seen to be caught up in a bitter tragedy because his wife has assumed the mores of the Marquis' class. Indeed, the entire servant class is depicted as even more snobbish than their masters. Ultimately, the aristocracy portrayed here gets away with murder; that is the essential dramatization of its impurity.

Nevertheless, Renoir's satire never shows a dislike for the class at which he is aiming. That is a remarkable property of his vision. He likes Robert and "the others were good people, I loved them. . . . I wish I could live in such a society—that would be wonderful." (Ibid., p. 13.) In *Grand Illusion*, Renoir mourned for a lost chivalric order; here, although he does not mourn, he dramatizes his affection for a way of life that he criticizes deeply. That he was able to maintain these impulses in equilibrium is a tribute to and a sure sign of his artistry. Let us examine that art more closely.

Analysis of Major Sequences

I. The Hero and the Aristocracy

Fade in on a medium close-up of a radio engineer operating a portable console. Pan down to a spool of cable; as a technician unwinds it, we pan along its length to where a woman radio announcer broadcasts into a microphone and moves, simultaneously, toward the action: it is the landing at Le Bourget Airport after a record-breaking twenty-three hour transatlantic solo flight. As she says, she is fighting her way through a "howling mob," and the flight can be compared to "Lindbergh's."

Now the mob breaks past her. Cut to a sliver of a white monoplane, circa 1939, as it touches down in the darkness. Then cut back to the crowd, surging past the announcer and breaking through a cordon of police to get to their hero. What seems like a series of shots is actually one: it pictures the crowds, the police, the announcer, and, finally, the plane as it taxies toward camera.

Now we are close to the plane's cockpit. Willing hands pull back the cowling and assist the occupant up and out; but we do not get a good look at him: bodies block our view and a popping flashbulb blinds us. At last, he is on the ground. A representative of the government greets him: "The minister" regrets that he could not attend personally. In the finest tradition of modern romantic (and tough-guy) heroes, Jurieu replies, "The plane deserves the credit," and then he spots his old friend: "Octave! Good old Octave!"

Now we are on a tight two-shot of Octave and André and can see the contrast between their respective appearances. André, in his flying helmet, young and dashing, is the picture of a hero; Octave, at least ten years older and wearing lumpy, quite ordinary clothing, seems just the opposite and his reply to his friend confirms it: "The hell with the flight! I'm glad to see you!" It is the perfect part for Renoir the director, permitting him to act out the convivial humanism that is a hallmark of his films. In this, at this moment of the film, the character he plays seems removed from Jurieu.

This shot registers the balance of the exchange between the friends and the intrusion of the radio announcer asking for a statement from André.

He asks Octave "Is she here?" and Octave answers in the negative. Immediately, André is jolted into anger and disappointment. He has made the flight for her sake. The least she could have done is to greet his landing. The announcer moves between the men: the flyer must have something to say. Cut to a close-up of André as he takes the microphone and begins to speak. It is the first time we have seen him so large on the screen and it finds him disappointed, the typical mood state of the romantic in that the romantic is essentially seeking an ideal that cannot be realized. André blurts out his feelings, as the announcer watches in amazement. He ends with, "She has let me down."

Cut to a shot of the back of a radio, showing its exposed inner works. Camera rises to reveal that we are in Christine's bedroom. Lisette, her maid, kneels at her feet, presumably to adjust the hem of her gown. Both women are in the background looking toward camera, listening, as the announcer, who has taken over the microphone from André, tries to cover up the hero's faux pas by alluding to André's exhaustion. The rigors of the flight have made him irresponsible. Lisette rises. Christine comes toward the radio and into a medium close-up. Her hand goes to the control switch.

Back at the airport, the engineer describes the plane in which André flew. Cut to a tracking shot, as the camera leads Octave and André. The former is scolding the pilot for his ill-tempered outburst. He doesn't deserve Christine, so wretched has his behavior been.

Back in Christine's bedroom, she is asking Lisette how long the maid has been married. We are on a medium shot of Christine's dressing table, and we see her enter the frame from the right as Lisette enters from the left. Christine sits and attends to her makeup as Lisette stands camera left. From this angle, however, Lisette is also reflected in the mirror and appears in the right-hand portion of the frame as well; Christine is, therefore, pictured between two images of Lisette and that is the appropriate way to image the scene, since the dramatic burden of their encounter is the dominance of maid over mistress. Lisette, we see from this scene, will be a teacher to Christine, who does not understand very well the rules of the social game.

Their exchange of dialogue has to do with the rules concerning women and their lovers; Christine questions Lisette closely on her "sweethearts" (of whom, she claims, Octave is one—an important piece of foreshadowing, vital to the tragic end of the film): do they kiss her? How far do they go? (Figure 9–1.)

Lisette is even Christine's teacher when it comes to the proper lipstick for evening wear; she tries to withhold the one that Christine prefers, evidently, in Lisette's mind, the wrong one. The scene ends with matching close-ups at the door to the bedroom, as Christine, elegantly gowned and wrapped in an even more elegant white fur coat, is about to leave. "What about friendship?" (with a man), she asks. Lisette's answer, "I'll believe it when I see it," leaves no doubt that she thinks it impossible.

Christine leaves her bedroom and goes out into the elegant corridor of the townhouse; across the richly carpeted floor, a maid drags a reluctant dog, a pampered household pet. Another servant scurries by in the background; the impression is of the richest luxury. Christine asks for her husband and is directed by the maid to Robert's study.

Cut to the study. Camera angled on the door as Christine enters. The radio is on. A voice is describing the end of the coverage from Le Bourget. Pan right to see Robert, a smallish man who nevertheless possesses stature; he is dressed in a formal suit, white tie, and as he sees his wife enter he shuts the radio and goes toward her: "We are late, my dear." "Yes," she says, "As usual."

Looking at the top of a table that is between them, she notices an elaborate mechanical doll, a black woman with a turban. She wonders

Figure 9–1. *Lisette and Christine discuss love, friendship, and marriage.* (Courtesy Janus Films.)

if it is new. It is an eighteenth-century doll, he replies, and it works perfectly. He turns on the mechanism. The tinkling music begins. Cut to a close-up of the doll. It is the first of several such objects we will see in the film and is a crucial symbol of the social order being depicted here.

Cut to a medium close-up of Christine, who says that she prefers it to the radio. This seemingly harmless expression is actually a holophrastic utterance, introducing between them the whole subject of Christine's relations with André. Robert comes right to the point; he is surprised that Christine had not given André what he wanted, which he interprets as sexual relations, and which he mockingly chides André for having equated with "love." "Men are so naive," he says. All through his speech on this subject, he has been toying with the doll, shutting the mechanism, adjusting it, and then lifting it and placing it on a shelf along with some others. It is significant action to underscore the discussion of his wife's putative lover, for he is discussing a regulated manner of dealing with those who mistake congress for passion and the doll is an emblem of the social order that lives by such rules.

To Christine, however, what her husband has said indicates that he *knows* she has been faithful to him. She is immensely happy and does a little dancing twirl to indicate this. She is relieved that she need no longer "lie" about André. Robert thinks she exaggerates about how much of a "lie" it was, and he ushers her out the door.

On the other side, Corneille, the ever-attentive Butler, makes a magical appearance with Robert's muffler and coat. From the discreet distance of a long shot, well back in the hall so that the three subjects are more than full figure in the frame, we see Robert putting on his outer garments, assisted by the butler. As he does, he asks Christine if she thinks that *he* lies to her, and when she answers that she trusts him completely, he excuses himself for a moment. Camera pans with her as she starts down the regal marble staircase.

And we cut to a close-up of Robert dialing on the telephone in his study. He needs to speak to his mistress.

He arranges to see Geneviève the next day because this revelation of his wife's fidelity has shaken him. Jurieu's declaration has entered his life to create a shock wave; together with his wife's assertion that she trusts him, it has undermined his confidence in one of the rules of his existence. After he speaks with Geneviève, we see her in company with several members of their "set," and gather from their conversation that Christine is a foreigner, from Vienna, and is perhaps for that reason living outside the rules.

The next morning Robert confronts Geneviève with the demand that they break off their relationship. Geneviève resists, declaring that in order to "be worthy of " his wife, as he has said he wished to be, it is not necessary for them to break with one another: Christine could forgive the fact of their liaison but not the hidden character of their relations, which have been going on since Robert married her. Geneviève does not know if she loves Robert or not but of one thing she is certain: she could not stand the pain of their separation. Robert responds at once: he would not think of hurting her, and he ends the scene by suggesting they go to lunch.

André is driving a car and his passenger is Octave. André is grim, Octave frightened. A moment later there is an accident; the car goes off the road, and there is an angry exchange between the friends. We learn that Octave has known Christine a long time and that he loves her, in his way, and feels responsible for her, because, as others have already said, she is a foreigner here and in need of protection. André wildly protests his love for her, but Octave is at first not impressed, principally because André has broken the rules; instead of acting like a proper hero at Le Bourget, he broke the rules by speaking of Christine. Although he loves her, he must understand that she is a society woman, a woman who lives by rules. But André keeps insisting that he loves her and is better for her than Robert, who plays with toys, is a liar and a snob. "But at least he's got his feet on the ground," answers Octave. Nevertheless, André persists. "If I don't see her again—I'll die," and this argument gets to Octave. Calmed down now, he assures André that he will arrange for André to see her again.

The Raisonneur

Fade in on the landing of the townhouse of the Marquis as Octave jauntily takes the last two steps on the marble stairs. Lisette is right behind him. Now cut to another angle: we are looking out of the doorway of Christine's bedroom. Octave and Lisette come toward us, exchanging greetings. Both sides of the frame are darkened by the vertical boundaries of the doorway; our attention is on the full figures we see in the center portion of the frame. Octave and Lisette also exchange warm embraces; they are on terms of intimacy that can only exist between those who share class affiliations. For Octave, despite what we will soon see as his intimacy with the Marquis and Christine, is not quite an aristocrat; neither is he a member of the servant class, but something in between, a mediator, an analog of the mediator so often encountered in classical French theatre. Thus, the iconography of the frame of this shot seems to mirror Octave's function, namely, to cross thresholds.

For a few moments they stand there and speak. Lisette knows by his looks ("awful") that something is wrong and she also knows what it is: "that aviator," because of whom Madame "can't sleep." Octave asks her to trust him. He will take care of it. They start toward camera and the doorway, where Lisette is met by a footman bearing Christine's breakfast tray. She takes it and enters, going past camera, while Octave is stopped by a hail from Robert who now appears in the background; he, to, can see by Octave's appearance that there is "trouble," but he is carrying one of his mechanical birds and is concentrating on that. He knows Octave wants to see his wife, but he wants only to say hello to her himself and both men walk toward camera to enter Christine's quarters. As they reach us, Octave notices the bird and asks what it is. A warbler, he is told; to which he remarks that it is moth eaten. "Yes," Robert replies, "but it sings every twenty seconds."

The reliability of the mechanical toy is most important to the Marquis —more important than its appearance. Throughout the remainder of his appearance in this scene he will be toying with the bird, trying to adjust the mechanism, and at the end it will sing.

Inside the doorway of her suite of rooms, Christine greets Octave, the third person in this brief interval of a scene, with a reference to how bad he looks. It is a mark of aristocratic, orderly competence to be able to interpret appearances; thus Lisette, Robert, and Christine all recognize

Octave's distress. Nevertheless, Christine greets him also with a warm embrace; this is followed by a request from Robert, "May I?" And he proceeds to bend over her hand and kiss her fingers. The gesture is formal, correct, and not without affection—but entirely in contrast to Octave's bear hug.

Lisette draws the blinds and, as the Marquis sees her, he mentions that he has heard from her husband. Christine is curious about it and he tells her the contents of the letter: Schumacher is unhappy at La Colonière without his wife, and wants her to join him there. A close-up of Lisette at the blind registers her answer: "Leave madame? I'd rather divorce!" The Marquis is amused: "Stop dramatizing things," but he continues to play with his bird and joins Christine and Octave near her bed where she has gone to eat her breakfast. But Octave is impatient to speak to Christine, and Robert, picking up his cue, starts to leave. We pan with him as he activates the music and we hear the bird sing. "See," he says, "every twenty seconds," and he goes. Lisette asks Octave if he wants to have some breakfast, but he declines; this confirms for her that he must be out of sorts, and she turns on her heel and goes.

Now Christine pulls Octave down beside her. A two-shot records their dialogue. Octave, in a somber mood, says he wants to talk about André and his recent "suicide" attempt in the car. Christine at first refuses to believe it happened, but when she is finally convinced she wants to know if it was her fault. Octave says it was partly her fault and that while apologizing would be going "too far," she might atone for her bad behavior by inviting André to La Colonière. Christine has broken an important rule which she herself formulates as, "In Paris, one does not have the right to be nice to a man, without. . . ." The case is different with Octave, he reminds her, because he is like a member of her family; he grew up with her, was a kind of a son to her father.

Christine resists agreeing to invite André, which prompts Octave to stand up and start to leave. A two-shot captures his rising; he comes toward camera, meaning to leave. But she comes after him, and, when he insists that he will not come to La Colonière—he will remain to comfort his friend André—she relents. She calls him a ninny and shoves him back down on the bed. In a medium shot, looking down on them, we see her kiss and hug him. Mockingly, she agrees to invite André, because she doesn't want to be regarded as the one who caused the disintegration of a public hero. Octave is so overjoyed that he calls her an angel in her native language, "*Du bist ein engel!*"

Octave is a shrewd student of manners. After recovering his appetite and ordering Lisette to fetch him a big breakfast, he goes to see Robert in order to have *him* extend André the invitation. His scene with Robert reveals that he knows about Robert's difficulty with Geneviève, but he can only jokingly offer to marry her and get her off Robert's hands. He has no real solution to Robert's problems; as he says in this scene, "everybody has reasons." At the end of the scene, Robert agrees to the invitation, and Octave, happy again, chases Lisette around the table in Robert's study.

II. The Servants and the Aristocracy

At La Colonière, Robert's magnificent estate in the Sologne, the plot moves to introduce among the servants a love intrigue that parallels the one operating among the masters. The idea is introduced in the first scene at La Colonière. It begins with a fade in on a long shot looking out over a lovely pond, bordered by barren but slender wintry trees. In the distant background, two automobiles make their way as camera pans with them. Now we cut to a shot just inside the main gate of the estate and watch the cars come through; we pan with them to reveal the long driveway leading up to the chateau.

In front of the chateau, the Marquis' car comes to a halt. Several servants are drawn up at the foot of the stairs awaiting the Marquis' party. Schumacher is first to go to the door when the car stops, removing his cap before opening the door from which the Marquis steps. The first thing on his mind is his wife and he immediately asks Robert what he has decided. But Robert refuses to decide. If Lisette wishes to change jobs, he says, that is her decision to make and not his. Before Christine and Robert can enter the chateau both are accosted by an old retainer, a caretaker, who reports that he has completed certain chores attendant on their arrival. To this, Robert responds by ordering the old man to tell Corneille, the butler whom we see hovering in the background. But Christine responds to the old man by asking after the health of his wife.

Christine and Robert enter the chateau and Corneille receives the report of the old man. They go off. Now Schumacher gives Lisette a hasty embrace and she hurries off into the chateau with her husband following after her.

The complex of hierarchical relationships we have just seen is worth commenting on, for they are crucial to Renoir's interests in showing social relations. Schumacher's application to his master is a piece of feudalism and Robert rightly refuses to accept suzerainty over his employee's marital relations. What is important is that Schumacher is willing that he should have it. Furthermore, the attitude of the old man is virtually of the same character; he is eliciting from his masters paternal concern for his family, as if that were his right and as if it were the proper relation between master and servant. Naturally, this function lies with the lady of the manor and Christine is aware of her duty. Finally, Robert's referring the old man to Corneille and Corneille's executing his duty in questioning the old man are examples of the prevailing respect for order and duty along rigidly proscribed lines.

MARCEAU

In one sense Marceau is the ironic counterpart of André. Both belong to what Renoir has described as "my old problem: what would happen to the stranger who wants to belong to a milieu which is not his. And, of course, the problem of how the Poacher is going to be admitted to the servant milieu" (from Renoir's Celebrity Lecture at the London Film Festival, November 19, 1967, reprinted as "A Certain Grace," in ibid.).

Marceau is introduced immediately after the visiting party arrives. The Marquis goes on an inspection tour of his estate accompanied by Schumacher. There he makes it clear to the Gamekeeper that he is not satisfied with Schumacher's progress in ridding the fields of their rabbit population. Schumacher suggests that a fence around the property could keep them out but Robert will have none of that. He wants, as he says, neither the rabbits nor the fence and the rest is up to the Gamekeeper. It is a typical aristocratic wish, arbitrary and absolute, and it is expressed in utter confidence that it will be gratified.

The Gamekeeper and his assistants, making their rounds, flush out Marceau as he is emptying one of his illegally placed rabbit snares. They are escorting him off the property when Robert sees them and asks what is happening. Something disorderly in Marceau's character, his adventurous and piratical nature, touches Robert who, underneath his orderly surface, must have impulses similar to those of the Poacher. Robert entertains the idea of hiring Marceau to do what Schumacher and his staff have not: rid the estate of the rabbits, but Marceau has other aspirations. He wants to enter the service of the Marquis by joining the household staff of the chateau. He has always wished to be a servant. The uniform is its attractive feature because it would confer on him the status for which he has always yearned. As the scene ends, Robert is smiling to himself, agreeing, we suspect, to do just as Marceau wishes.

We should note that all through this scene there is considerable hostility between Marceau and Schumacher. It appears to be the natural kind of animosity between members of the lower classes when one party enjoys the advantage of greater respectability than the other. We should also note that the situation between them is the ironic reverse of that which exists between André and Robert; *they* are (until the climax of their rivalry for Christine) all politeness and good manners.

In a pouring rain, Geneviève arrives, smartly decked out in a leopard skin coat and matching hat; she greets some other guests, who have arrived earlier, and we see that the topic of their conversation—diet, hairdressing, Geneviève's mistaking young Jackie's academic pursuit of pre-Colombian art for studies in Chinese, how long the rain will keep up—reflect the essential shallowness of the social relations in the chateau. Christine, a thoughtful hostess, goes below stairs with Mme. la Bruyère in tow to inform the kitchen help of the special dietary needs of her guests, and we see that even these are trivial. (Mme. la Bruyère can only eat "coarse salt"—as if the size of the grain were significant.)

The Arrival of André: Christine's Speech

We are looking out the door of the main entrance of La Colonière and we see, in the same pouring rain, André being escorted up the stairs by Corneille, who is shielding him with an umbrella. André wears a dashing trench coat and stops at the entrance to turn back toward the car and ask Octave what he is looking for. Cut to a two-shot of Christine and Mme. la Bruyére coming into the main hallway from the kitchen. Mme. asks who is standing in the doorway and Christine identifies André for her. Camera moves to reframe the scene, coming to rest looking over Christine's shoulder as, in the background, Octave enters to join André just inside the door. It is a striking image to see these protagonists facing each other across the tiled floor of the chateau foyer. Christine, After a second, rushes across to greet them. Now we cut to a reverse angle as Octave enters the frame, his back to us, to catch and embrace Christine. Camera pans with her as, after greeting Octave, she moves to offer André her hand. He kisses it. Her greeting is perfectly correct: "How kind of you to come!" The noise of the other guests in the hall grows agitatedly louder as they become aware of the hero in their midst.

Now we cut to another angle and see Robert scurry in from a doorway in the background. He grasps André's hand warmly. A series of guests come at him now: Geneviève ("Didn't you fly here? Oh I must kiss you!"), Mme. la Bruyère ("You must visit our factory"), the General ("You're a real man, Jurieu. The race is dying out"), and others ("May I kiss you, too," they ask, after Geneviève has had the first chance).

Cut to a close-up of Christine. "And may I," she asks, "I think I have the right to . . ." and goes to him. Camera pans with her as she goes to kiss him. "Does he play pinochle," someone asks, and camera pans left to allow the couple to go out of the frame and then moves in to a tight two-shot of the General and Saint-Aubin. Saint-Aubin says, "It's all in the family," and leers suggestively at his companion.

The General: What do you mean?
Saint-Aubin: Jurieu and Christine!
The General: What do you care? We came here to shoot, dammit, not to write our memoirs!

The gossip continues. We cut to a tight two-shot of the Homosexual leaning over Charlotte's shoulder: "Well," he asks, "Have they or haven't they?" Charlotte's answer is a model of wry disbelief in the Homosexual's naiveté: "They have," she says to him, the look on her face conveying her boredom with the Homosexual's ignorance.

Now begins the counterpart to André's airport speech—that is, now begins Christine's little public speech. We cut to a close-up of her with André in the background. As the scene proceeds, camera reframes to a two-shot of this pair with Robert in the background between them. Some slight movement of the others around Robert is also discernible, making it clear that a circle of listeners is forming to hear Christine's speech (Figure 9–2).

What she says is that she and André have been in pursuit of that "rare thing," friendship; that they have spent many hours together and that, having heard his plans for the flight, she feels as if she had served a "purpose." As she finishes, she drops André's hand, which she had charmingly taken in her own as she began to speak. And the end is a signal for congratulations. The group is charmed by her little performance; her niece embraces her, Octave does the same, and Robert decides that this is the time to dedicate a party, the fete, in honor of Jurieu. (That the party would have been held in any case is confirmed for us by one of the guests who, still not aware of the *occasion* for it—even after Robert's announcement—suggests that they can make it a charity event.) The shot widens to include the whole group, then pans along with Robert who is shaking hands and implicating everyone in the party plans.

The sequence delineates Robert's milieu with special clarity and force; as we have said, it is a group without an occupation, one which seizes on any occasion to design away their lives. The speech Christine has made

Figure 9–2. *Robert greets his guests just before Christine's little speech.* (Courtesy Janus Films.)

meets with their approval and she is congratulated, not for any special honesty of utterance—although that was surely her motive (that is, to dispel doubts, to counter the gossip we saw just before the speech)—but because she has behaved with special style and grace. She has, in fact, supplied André with what he missed at Le Bourget, acknowledgment that she appreciates his gesture in flying the Atlantic for her sake. But she is not aware of these things. However, Renoir is, and he has staged the scene with that knowledge. The camera has moved to unite the participants and the editing has effected their reconciliation.

LIFE BELOW STAIRS

The transition between the previous sequence and this one is that the same subject—Christine and André—is being discussed by the Serving Girl and the Chauffeur as the camera pans them across the kitchen toward the table where the servants are eating. The Serving Girl acknowledges that André is good-looking and expresses some sympathy for Robert. However, when the Chauffeur informs her that Christine has seated André at her right during a meal the Serving Girl immediately pronounces judgment: "She's wrong! Those things just aren't done!" For, as we shall see, the life below stairs is as rigidly bound by rules as life above stairs, and perhaps even more so.

Now we cut to a shot of Lisette at the head of the servants' table—Christine's counterpart here. Clearly, she is the "hostess." And we see her offer asparagus to someone on her left. His answer is that he never eats canned food, which is deficient in vitamins. We cut to a two-shot: two chefs are preparing a meal; one of them declares that Mme. la Bruyère will eat what everyone eats, for though he accepts diets he does not accede to "fads." Back at the table, the Serving Girl thinks that Robert "has gone too far" with Jurieu, presumably in allowing him to visit here, but someone counters what she says by remarking that "shocking people is half the fun." Corneille, when asked his opinion of the matter, prefers to say nothing. He is reminded that he once worked for the Comte de Vaudois and that the countess had had a lover (the implication being that he must have gossiped about *her* affairs; this he denies, only to be reminded by Lisette that at the countess' age, eighty-five, that would be natural and that the countess cannot be compared to Christine. The Chauffeur brings up the count's nationality, French, and then remarks that the Marquis had a grandfather named Rosenthal. (This of course expresses some of the servants' latent anti-Semitism; the name Rosenthal playfully alludes, also, to the fact that the actor who plays the Marquis, Marcel Dalio, also played Rosenthal in Renoir's *Grand Illusion*.)

The Chauffeur, noticing that Schumacher has just started to come down the stairs, asserts that no doubt Schumacher would agree with him. But Schumacher does not know what the Chauffeur is talking about; it is a reply that certifies the Gamekeeper as no member of the class. His being an outsider to a world of strict rules is important in that his position leads to the final tragedy.

Now the Chef takes up the "Jewish" question and makes an important distinction. He had worked for a Jewish nobleman, but that was not why he had quit his service; the Baron d'Epinay had, quite simply, eaten like a pig. *That* was why he quit.

Schumacher interrupts the Chef's tale to ask if Lisette will be long, but she is not interested in him at this moment and says that Christine will probably need her.

The Chef continues. The Marquis had scolded him the week before on account of the potato salad. The Marquis may be a foreigner, says the Chef, but he knew that the potato salad had been improperly prepared; it had not been made by pouring white wine over the still boiling hot potatoes. Anyone who can tell that difference, the Chef concludes, is an aristocrat!

Camera pans and reframes now to watch as Schumacher leaving and Marceau entering pass each other on the stairs. The former Poacher seeks out and is interviewed at the table by Corneille, who determines his qualifications and assigns him to shine shoes. (Marceau replies, resourcefully, "When it comes to clothes, I'm a specialist.") Marceau bends to ask if this is where he may eat; then camera pans him toward the head of the table where a chair on Lisette's right has just become vacant. She asks his name and he tells her. "And what is your name, Miss?" She corrects him. "Mrs.," she says, and identifies herself as Schumacher's wife. He is about to leave on hearing this, imagining himself to be as hostile a figure for her as he is for her husband, but she motions to him to sit. Thus, he, like André, winds up to the right of the hostess at table. At this moment, he is André's downstairs counterpart.

As he begins to eat, we cut to a shot of him over Lisette's shoulder, so that we can watch his sly and insinuating look—directed flirtatiously, lecherously, at Lisette, who returns it almost in kind. Over this shot, the other servants at table are heard continuing their chatter: they hope the Gamekeeper is good enough to bag a healthy supply of pheasant; they will eat anything but rabbit; the Marquis' car is splendid.

Later that night, on the eve of the hunt, guests, hosts, and servants are pictured in the corridor onto which give the bedrooms of the chateau. They are excited over the prospects before them, not only of the hunt but of their general interactions, and Renoir stages the brief scene with a rich variety of movement, showing people and ideas flowing smoothly from one to another, in pairs and singly. In the last part of the scene, we catch four telling vignettes, featuring, in order, Robert and Christine (Robert is pleased with his wife because her little public speech did not in any way embarrass him); Christine and Lisette (Lisette announces that Marceau has joined the staff and Christine warns her about her husband); Lisette and Octave (a flirtation); and Octave and André (the latter is full of anxiety). It is a miniature rondo that dramatizes the cohesiveness of the societies depicted.

THE HUNT

In the hunt sequence, we are shown the very realistic killing of the rabbits and game birds and the very stylized relations between the members of the hunting party. A clue to the concealment function of all such rituals as the hunting ritual is found in a pair of matching encounters between Saint-Aubin and La Bruyère. One of these begins the sequence and the other comes after the killing of the animals. In the first, La Bruyère apologizes to Saint-Aubin for having shot at a pheasant that he thinks was not really his to shoot at—according to the rules of this particular game. He insists it belongs to his companion, who, in turn insists just the opposite. Underlying emotions never get to the surface as exquisite good manners govern behavior. Even Renoir's staging emphasizes how ritual politeness is linked to the whole hunting ritual. A low-angle camera sees the pair approaching; against the lovely November skies of the Sologne district, the figures get larger in the frame as they speak, emphasizing their importance and the importance of the discussion (Figure 9–3). Then, as their interchange ends, with La Bruyère gracefully accepting the bird, camera pans left with them, giving us a wider shot to reveal the whole group of hunters—just as Robert again strikes the ritual note: "I've kept blind number seven for you, General."

In their second encounter, however, all of their good manners fall away. This time, as Saint-Aubin sends one of the beaters to retrieve his fallen pheasant, La Bruyère enters the frame to insist that this time the bird is his. But Saint-Aubin will have none of it; now he reveals how he really felt last time there was a question: that La Bruyère was nothing but a poacher and that he had held his tongue, held back how he felt.

The death of the animals, which is a metaphor for the underlying pain of real emotion, is presented in the most realistic terms and is pictured for us following the exact, formal structure of the hunt. The beaters, in long, white-coated lines, track through the wooded thicket whacking their sticks against the trees, flushing the game. Schumacher follows and guides them, blows his horn, and is answered. On the other side of the thicket, the hunters wait in their blinds. There is a contrast between the moving shots that register the game and the beaters and the static shots that depict the hunters. Each hunter is seen in his separate cover with a gun bearer discreetly in the background; each is seen from a low angle and thus isolated against the sky, to emphasize his stature at this moment of life and death.

As they fire at the game, we see the awful recoil of their rifles. These are no simple-minded Hollywood shoot-outs where the guns might as well be toys. The recoil of the weapons pounding against the shoulders of the

Figure 9–3. *The General and Saint-Aubin: The hunt sequence begins.* (Courtesy Janus Films.)

hunters is fierce—and real. Similarly, the montage sequence of animals running and being hit, flying and dropping out of the sky as they are torn by patterns of shotgun pellets—this is real. The final shot in this little sequence, the little rabbit quivering to stillness, is a symbol of the entire hunt. It foreshadows the death of André and the *Danse Macabre* which precedes it.

Juxtaposed against this "death scene" are the relations among the members of the hunting party. First there are the outsiders: Schumacher, although nominally the major-domo of the hunt, is identified as an outsider when we see him hesitate over part of the ritual. (Robert must remind him that the bag is to be displayed at the chateau. (Then there is André whom we see, first, displaying to Octave his "suffering." Octave reminds him that he will "get over it." We also see André breaking another rule when he tells Jackie that he does not love her. André's status as outsider is further confirmed by the beaters, who compare his shooting to that of the Marquis and find it inferior.

Octave, of course, is a special case, neither an insider nor an outsider. We never see him with a gun and his most characteristic moment in the hunt is familiar: he wrestles with Christine for the telescope.

Christine, also an outsider, does not like to hunt. Her dislike elicits from Robert a promise that the following year they will forego the hunt in favor of a ski party. Thus, Christine gets hold of the telescope and inadvertently sees Geneviève and Robert in their "final" embrace. The sight of her husband and his mistress ends the sequence and marks the movement of the plot toward the final human tragedy (that is, the death of André).

But Robert and Geneviève's encounter marks the central, orthodox, emotional plane of the hunt sequence. Here, concealment is the order of the day. Geneviève wants to end their affair and Robert is willing, but Geneviève also insists on a little illusion, a last, passionate embrace in which she can blot out the reality of her lover's love for his wife. Nevertheless, he is willing to take part in the illusion and preserve surface reality. He will not say goodbye; only *au revoir*.

Of the other insiders, we have spoken of two (Saint-Aubin and La Bruyère) and of how they broke a rule; but this is perhaps offset by the story told by another insider, the General: his gruesome story of how "Georges" shot himself to death is perfectly in keeping with the ceremonious commitments of an insider.

The next morning, there is a bedroom scene between Geneviève and Christine in which Christine is seen making the effort to change into a game player. She persuades Geneviève to stay for the fete, and when Geneviève asks if Christine likes André, she says that the flyer is "too sincere . . . sincere men are dull."

That same morning, Marceau begins his serious flirtation with Lisette and is caught by Schumacher, who threatens to shoot him if he catches him at it again. The farcical aspect of the sequence here mingles with the tragic. We are preparing for the denouement embodied in the fete.

III. The Fete: A Farcical Dance of Death
The form of the last third of the film follows closely the ebb and flow of a wild party, shot through with staged entertainment and unstaged entertainment of another order—farcical encounters intermingled with elements of tragedy. To help the reader follow the analysis, the following

outline is presented (the analysis that follows the outline will refer to the numbers here):

1. End of the Tyrolean dance on stage. Christine disappears with Saint-Aubin. Marceau teases and flirts with Lisette.
2. The *"Danse Macabre."* Marceau runs from Schumacher. André looks for Christine.
3. Geneviève tries to persuade Robert to run away with her. He says he must first consult Christine.
4. Marceau and Robert speak of women. Robert can learn from the poacher.
5. André discovers Saint-Aubin with Christine and they fight.
6. Dance of the Barbers (men with beards). Robert presents his mechanical organ.
7. Schumacher discovers Marceau in the kitchen and pursues him.
8. Robert surprises Christine with André. They fight.
9. Octave takes Christine outside and finds that she has declared her love to André.
10. Shots fired by Schumacher interrupt the fight of André and Robert.
11. Schumacher fires on Marceau, who is in the middle of the guests; they think it is an act to attract their attention.
12. Robert and André take the drunken Geneviève upstairs to bed.
13. Schumacher is finally subdued.
14. The guests go upstairs to bed.
15. Robert dismisses both Marceau and Schumacher.
16. Robert gives up Christine to André.
17. Marceau and Schumacher confide in one another.
18. Octave takes Christine out to the grounds. Lisette lends her mistress her cape.
19. Schumacher takes Christine for Lisette and wants to kill Octave.
20. Octave returns to the chateau to get his coat but instead lends it to André and sends him to Christine in the greenhouse.
21. Schumacher kills André.
22. Marceau announces the death.
23. Christine returns to the chateau. Robert informs the guests that there has been an accident.

1–4. Renoir's camera work in the beginning portion of the fete prepares us for the dizzying pace of the evening's mad antics. The camera is constantly on the move and people are continuously in movement in the frame. Coupled with the gyrating movement of a single theatrical spotlight—the only source of illumination in some of these scenes—the camera work establishes the mood of this final sequence. It prepares us for the sudden coming together of the servant-antagonists, the bizarre intensity of feeling among the participants in the aristocratic love triangle, and the pell-mell farcical atmosphere. We are wonderfully disoriented by this portion of the sequence.

The "Dance of Death" is the crucial symbolic picture here; it is as eerie as the image which begins it—that is, the shot that shows the piano playing itself (and then pans up to a blackened stage, whose curtains then part to reveal the phosphorescent bones of the skeletal dancers). It prepares us for the tragic thread soon to be woven into the satiric and comic tapestry of the film. The dancers spread out into the audience. Part of their act is to try to frighten the guests, who respond with what seems like real fear. Their reactions here are in sharp contrast to the way they respond later on, when they are unable to discern the seriousness in Schumacher's murderous pursuit of Marceau.

Marceau enlists Robert's help in eluding Schumacher, and they talk as Robert ties his tie (Figure 9–4). Marceau has something to teach his master. Although both admit to getting into "trouble" over women, Robert cannot bear to hurt them. Marceau, however, has an established technique, a ritual form for dealing with the pain they cause. In this respect, Marceau is more a member of the aristocracy than Robert.

5–6. The camera position during these scenes is that of the theatrical spectator; and this is appropriate for the farce it depicts. This part of the sequence begins in the main entrance hall. André, looking for Christine, runs into Schumacher, who is looking for Marceau. André accosts the gamekeeper who assures the flyer that he cannot help him. Then Schu-

Figure 9–4. *Robert and Marceau: Two worldly men.* (Courtesy Janus Films.)

macher hears something from the gun room and turns around. Noticing that Lisette, who had been in the hallway a moment before, has disappeared, he rushes to the door of the gun room and tears it open, as André races to join him. The camera stays at a distance to catch the action, as if it were being played out on stage. When Schumacher satisfies himself that Lisette is not inside the gun room, he walks off. André, noticing that Christine and Saint-Aubin *are* in the room, enters, but *he* is stopped and wrestled with, by Jackie who is asking where André is! The single shot captures a brilliant piece of farce comedy.

We cut inside to the gun room where Christine stands with Saint-Aubin. André advances toward the couple; Jackie appears in the doorway and advances farther into the room as the scene progresses. André's attitude is, surprisingly, that of the outraged husband, asking if Christine were aware that he had been looking for her, and "demanding" an "explanation." The farce heats up. André slaps Saint-Aubin. The latter demands satisfaction; he will send his seconds to André. André kicks him in the rump. Jackie struggles to restrain Saint-Aubin as Christine does the same with André, but it is no use. The men begin to fight and their bout moves them back out to the hall.

In a long shot in the hall, we see Saint-Aubin attempt to get away from André by running up the stairs. As André follows him, the ever-efficient Corneille enters the frame and walks to the foot of the stairs where Jackie and Christine also watch. Corneille stands there patiently until André knocks Saint-Aubin down. Then, after André and Christine have returned to the gun room, Jackie faints from the excitement. Corneille, however, is perfectly alert; he coolly snaps his fingers to summon his footmen. They matter-of-factly dispose of the bodies: Saint-Aubin, prostrate on the landing, and Jackie, prostrate at the foot of the stairs.

Inside the gun room, André, his back to the door, asks Christine why she did not come to the airport. In a long shot from the door, keeping a discreet distance, the camera catches her full figure as she says, "Because I love you!" After a beat, they come together. He is overjoyd. She is radiant. They will go away, she says. When, he asks. Now, she says. The farce heats up again. But wait, he says, "I must tell Robert . . . there are still rules!" The tables have turned. Foreshadowed by his surprising husbandly conduct at the beginning of the scene, André's conduct is now no longer that of the hero-outsider-romantic. Suddenly, even he is following rules.

On his word, "rules," we cut to the stage. Four bearded dancers are just finishing the Barber's Dance. It ends to rounds of applause. They retire behind the curtain and return almost immediately, beardless this time, pushing Robert to center stage in front of them. There is a high-angle shot of the stage recording this entrance and a low-angle shot from the audience as Robert announces the next attraction. It is "the climax of my career as a collector." Modestly, he says he thinks the audience will like it. He gestures. The curtains part. Triumphantly, he points to an enormous mechanical music maker, so tall it towers over his head. Again he gestures, and the music maker lights up. He is wildly excited and struts over to stand next to the machine, his handkerchief in his hand. Now we cut to a close-up of a detail: at the top, surrounded by light, a delicately sketched female nude. Now another cut: to a close-up of another detail, one of the mechanical dolls that moves with the music now issuing forth. Pan slowly past a row of such figures until camera comes to rest on a close-up of Robert, a kind of ecstatic nervousness evident on his face.

This is his characteristic moment. (See pp. 173–175.) He is one with his proudest possession. Nothing touches him more deeply. As Renoir has said, "it is the shot in front of the mechanical organ which provides the clearest explanation of the character of la Chesnaye." (From "Interview in Sologne," reprinted in ibid., p. 12.)

7–16. This portion of the sequence details the action from Schumacher's discovery of Marceau with Lisette in the kitchen through the end of the chase, Robert and André's fight, the departure of the guests, and Schumacher's and Marceau's dismissal. The action is frantic, farcical, and fragmentary.

Just before he discovers Marceau, Schumacher informs Lisette (as she eats an apple, the image of the temptress) that they will quit together the next day and leave for a new life in Alsace. This development parallels and contrasts with Geneviève's wish to leave with Robert and Christine's wish to go off, first with André and then with Octave. Also part of the intricate series of parallels in the action is Robert's discovery of Christine and André in an intimate situation. Here Robert, like André when he had caught Christine with Saint-Aubin, throws the first punch. His explosive behavior suggests that the fete has been a holiday, a time of release, when all tendencies are reversed. André has become a husband, Robert a hero—but temporarily in both cases.

The farce reaches its climax here when Schumacher catches Marceau among the dancing guests and fires away at him; the guests think it another act, an excessive part of the planned entertainment. Schumacher is finally subdued (by a nifty piece of footwork on the part of Corneille) and some of the guests depart from the chateau, while others go up to bed as if nothing had happened. Robert dismisses the pair of unruly servants and he and André, now united by a common, gentlemanly plight, discuss Christine. As Robert helps his rival into his jacket, brushing away lint from the shoulders—André then returns the favor—he coolly agrees to surrender Christine to him; he is glad that André is a member of the class. The coming together of these two parallels the coming together of Marceau and Schumacher after they are dismissed and emphasizes and dramatically prepares for the temporary alliance of Christine and Octave.

Earlier in this part of the sequence, Octave had his revelatory moment. It is worth discussing.

We are in the chateau, looking at an empty frame—a pair of French doors—when Octave enters, followed by Christine. He is remembering an occasion when both had witnessed her father, a musician, conducting some sort of royal or command performance. The gist of the recollection is that the father had performed with cool distinction under difficult circumstances, and now Octave is acting out that triumph in the retelling.

Finally, at the appropriate moment, as he recalls the conductor's "entrance," Octave opens the French doors to the night and acts out the passage of the conductor across the stage. This entails his going out onto a long stone terrace that runs the width of one side of the chateau. Christine, an appreciative audience, leans against the jamb, enjoying Octave. On the terrace, Octave stops and recalls how the king himself had applauded. Christine laughs. He continues to walk toward the imaginary podium.

Now we cut to the second shot in this scene, a long shot from the garden, facing square onto the terrace and including a flight of steps leading down into the garden. Octave halts at the top of the steps, bows to us—in this position the camera is the audience—and takes up the imaginary baton. Then he turns to the chateau—the imaginary orchestra—and raises the baton.

We cut to a low-angle shot, much closer to Octave, and we see him from behind; he cannot bring himself to lower the baton and start the "orchestra" playing. Defeated, weary, he comes toward camera and sinks down onto the steps. Christine rushes to his side, sits down beside him, consoling, but he cannot bear the gesture of sympathy. He jerks his arms away and rises.

The scene is over; and so is Octave's revelatory moment. Unable to conduct, unable, literally, to "take the stage," he is forever in the wings, unable to take his life into his own hands. As he will tell us later in so many words, he is dependent, a parasite, living off the generosity of friends. A failed artist, all he can do is admire art and artistry, record by remembering its glories. His own emotions kept in check, he serves to soothe the unkempt emotions of his friends. The visual image reveals it all.

17–23. The fete is over and the night has become still. In the garden of the chateau is a quiet pool and the only sounds of the night are the frogs croaking on the banks. Lisette, having refused to leave with her husband as he had requested when Robert dismissed him, goes out to the garden to seek her mistress, to find out if she is still in her good graces. There she finds Christine with Octave, quite willing to forgive and forget all (Figure 9–5). Christine reminds Lisette that women are not responsible for the madness of men. But she is somewhat dismayed that Lisette had

Figure 9–5. *Christine and Octave in the moonlight.* (Courtesy Janus Films.)

known all along of Robert's affair with Geneviève. However, Lisette's explanation, that she had not wanted to hurt her mistress, satisfies Christine and the three-year lie that she had lived is further ameliorated in her mind by Octave's explanation of the lies in public life. He argues that if the government, the press, and the cinema constantly deal in lies, the individual is entitled to do so too. Lisette gives Christine her hooded cloak to protect her from the cold (the cloak was a gift from Schumacher) and Christine and Octave wander off into the night.

Later, they stop on a little bridge and we see that Octave is depressed over his sense of himself as a failure. Earlier, back on the steps of the podium, he says, he had almost believed in his own possibilities, but now he realizes it is all a dream. He is not in "contact with an audience" but a mere parasite.

Marceau emerges from the darkness, carrying his suitcase, ready to leave the estate. We track in front of him, leading him, until he sees something in the left-hand part of the frame—as we do—and stops. It is Schumacher, leaning dejectedly against a tree. We track in closer as Marceau moves toward the Gamekeeper. Cut to another, closer, angle on the two. There is a glint of wetness on Schumacher's face. "You're a mess?" Marceau asks. Cut over Marceau's shoulder onto another, even closer

angle of Schumacher. Now we can see clearly that he is crying unasham-
edly, tears rolling down his cheeks. A series of cuts back and forth. Neither
has seen Lisette. Schumacher's reply to whether he has seen Lisette is
almost pathetic, a touchingly high-pitched squeak of a "No." But Marceau
knows that she is with madame, for as he shrewdly and painfully advises
his companion, "she is married to madame, not to you." And that is the
truth of this moment. It reveals the deeper strata of Schumacher's character: he is devastated but unashamed of the emotions the devastation calls
forth. The devastation is caused by the fact that it has at last been said:
his wife thinks more of her status as a lady's maid in a great household
than she does of their closeness as man and wife. Schumacher's is, thus,
the most open revelation of feeling that we see in the film.

The two men sit on a rock, side by side, and discuss their plans. Marceau will return to the life of a poacher, but this time with a difference.
He will acquire a game dealer's license so that at long last he can have
respectability. In his terms, this means safety from harassment by the
gendarmes. But Schumacher is as unmovable as the rock on which he sits.
He intends to "hang around here" until he gets his wife back.

From here, the action moves swiftly toward an end. The strolling Octave
and Christine pass by the rock where the servants have been sitting and
Christine is mistaken for Lisette. Marceau and Schumacher follow the
pair to the "little greenhouse." There, Christine, in the symbolic setting
signifying nurture, shifts her affections to Octave. ("You're all right . . .
you just need someone to care for you.") Seeing this, Schumacher drags
Marceau with him as he goes to fetch a rifle. ("You still have your pistol?
Let him have it!" says Marceau. "I fired all my bullets at you," replies
Schumacher. "Tough luck.") Then Octave and Christine agree to go off
together and Octave rushes to the chateau to get Christine's coat.

As Octave runs toward the chateau, André and Robert are strolling on
the main floor having a last cigarette before bed. They agree that Christine is probably with Octave but that Octave can be trusted. "He's a good
guy." And Robert declares that although he has really come to the point
of not believing in anything, he is beginning to believe in friendship.

Now Octave enters and asks Lisette for Christine's coat. Lisette
shrewdly guesses without being told why he wants it and begins to argue
with him the foolishness of what he is about to do. Judging her adversary
well, Lisette persuades him that he is too old and too poor to take proper
care of Christine; in short, he is playing the role of the romantic outsider.
As he stands with his head down, overcome by the truth of her analysis,
André enters—like a shadow. Impulsively, Octave turns to him and tells
him that Christine is waiting outside for *him*. It takes very little to persuade André, who is overjoyed to react with the same impulsivity. Wearing Octave's coat and carrying Christine's, he rushes out to the greenhouse, where he is shot dead by Schumacher's rifle. (After André leaves

Lisette and Octave, Robert joins them. Lisette begins to weep. "Stop that," Robert orders sharply. "You don't see me crying!" But he acknowledges that he is suffering nonetheless.)

Marceau brings the news. And the reactions of those receiving it are uniformly unexcited, as if the tragedy had been in the offing all along and each of them had known of it. Robert and Jackie both rush out to get to Christine; and only Octave bothers asking who fired the shot. But he only asks later, when he is once again out on the terrace where he had reenacted the concert, and only after Marceau, to comfort him, has declared of André's death, "I can swear to you he didn't feel it. It [the shot] caught him squarely and then he rolled over like a rabbit."

Octave is stunned. He asks plaintively why Lisette had not "permitted" him to go out to Christine rather than André. "What can I do with my life now?" He asks her to tell Christine that he has gone. She will understand. Then he kisses her goodby and goes off with Marceau. He is going to Paris, he tells the Poacher, and yes, perhaps the two of them *will* meet again: "Anything is possible."

Now the strength of the Marquis' rules asserts itself. Everyone is caught up in those rules. A group returns from the greenhouse, with Robert firmly in command: "I've posted a guard at the greenhouse." When Jackie starts to break down, she is flanked by Lisette and Christine. "Pull yourself together," says Lisette. "A girl with your education should show courage." "People are watching you," her aunt, Christine, reminds her.

As, indeed, they are. A number of guests, wearing pajamas and dressing gowns, have gathered at the foot of the terrace steps. The royal party must ascend in full view of them; which it does, with great dignity. Lisette ushers Jackie through the French doors while Christine pauses in the doorway. Robert bends at the waist to kiss her hand and reminds her that she must be exhausted and needs to sleep. The doors close after Christine.

Robert comes forward, and, assuming the position that Octave had been unable to, addresses the assemblage. A "regrettable accident" has occurred. Schumacher fired his rifle at what he thought was a poacher. André Jurieu was a "victim of fate." We cut to a close-up of Robert as he continues. "We shall leave tomorrow, in mourning for our friend . . . a true gentleman who succeeded too well in making us forget he was famous." He turns toward the chateau. "It is a chilly night and you may catch cold. I advise you to go inside." With which he starts to open the French doors; but Corneille is there—everything is in its place again—to complete the job. The inside of the chateau beckons invitingly. Robert flaps his arms from his sides in a shrugging gesture. Everything appropriate has been said.

We cut to Saint-Aubin and the General. The former has just now swung toward the General with a heavily ironic remark: "A new definition of the word 'accident.'" The General, however, sets things to rights: "No, not at all. La Chesnaye has class—and believe me, his race is dying out." They leave the frame to move inside the chateau. We are left looking at shadows moving through the light. FIN.

Style and Approach

"What pushed me to make *Rules of the Game* was an ambition to treat a subject which would allow me to use the exterior forms of a French comedy of the eighteenth century. I was also a little bit influenced by Musset, but my ambition was to find a certain elegance, a certain grace, a certain rhythm which is typical of the eighteenth century, French or English." (From Renoir's Celebrity Lecture at the London Film Festival, November 19, 1967, reprinted as "A Certain Grace," in ibid., p. 13.)

Thus, Renoir's style owes its first influence to the classical French theater (particularly, as he says, to Musset, but also to Marivaux and Beaumarchais, whose lyrics, from act 4, scene 10 of *Marriage of Figaro*, appear on the second title card). The "exterior forms" of eighteenth-century French comedy are certainly present: the love intrigues, especially, with cases of mistaken identity and farcical repercussions; the characters (a philandering nobleman, a maid who is her mistress' confidante, a raisonneur); and the gaiety of aristocratic entertainment (the play within the play, so to speak, the fete) at a noble residence (the chateau). Moreover, although Renoir's work does not overtly allude to conditions in French society, as, for example, Beaumarchais's *Marriage of Figaro* does, his film is equally critical of it and is a remarkable parallel, on the eve of the great war, to the work of Beaumarchais on the eve of the French Revolution.

"A certain elegance, a certain grace, a certain rhythm" are thus, together, the central stylistic motif of the film. Renoir achieves this through (1) the work of the camera and the method of staging scenes; (2) the choice of decor and location; (3) the organization and concept of the two milieus—servants and masters; (4) and the characterizations, especially of Christine and Robert.

In terms of camera work and staging, Renoir was using deep focus, as André Bazin points out, long before Orson Welles made it famous in *Citizen Kane*. (See Bazin, *What Is Cinema?* Essays selected and translated by Hugh Gray, Berkeley and Los Angeles, 1967, p. 34.) In *The Rules of the Game*, it is the dominant style of the camera work, with the exception of the hunt sequence, in which montage is responsible for the effects. Renoir's camera not only records the shot in depth, but also moves with fluid elegance and accepts the in-frame movement of characters. This method of staging has the effect of encompassing the action within a singular, smooth, and rhythmic embrace: it is a visual gesture that links together the members of the respective levels of society and thus conveys meaning. It also contributes to the graceful elegance that strikes us as we watch.

The organization and concept of the servants and masters: the balance and variety in choosing characters; the matching of triangles and Octave as the link between the two worlds; and the rich variety of striking minor characters (Mme. La Bruyère, the Chef, Corneille), all of whom work harmoniously within a smooth-working context of manners, gives us a sense of what we mean by our central stylistic motif.

The decor cannot be too highly praised for its effect. It is not simply beautiful; it is absolutely correct, from the marvelous feathered hats that Geneviève and Christine wear during the hunt to the patterned floors both upstairs and downstairs in the chateau. The decor is always imbued with taste and correctness—within the context of the groups being portrayed.

Camera work and decor combine to produce much of our style: in addition to the in-depth shot, Renoir uses the full shot more consistently than he does the close-up. Thus, the camera is frequently positioned to simply *show* us (and thus have impressed on our consciousness) the environment of these wealthy people. We recall shots looking down the bedroom corridor in both the chateau and the Paris townhouse; shots that shows us Geneviève's tasteful apartment; Christine's bedroom, and so on.

These elements join with the characterizations of Robert and Christine to produce the effect we are discussing. (See "Story and Characterization" for a fuller discussion of the two protagonists.)

Renoir has frequently alluded to "the joy of work, of making something" (from an interview in *Cinema 67*, No. 117, June, 1967, reprinted in *Jean Renoir*, op. cit., p. 165). That this mood controls his work as a film director is confirmed again and again by actors who have worked in his films. But it is also, and more importantly, confirmed by the evidence of the films themselves. It is perhaps this sense of joy and release that ultimately informs his films and gives them their special ambiance. And, perhaps, we should conclude our discussion of *The Rules of the Game* by suggesting that its style, its distinctiveness as a work of art, is the sheer verve, the sparkle it reflects from the mind and heart of its maker.

Beauty and the Beast

[La Belle et la Bête]

Directed by JEAN COCTEAU

And this gave the creature such strength,

it grew a horn out of its brow. One horn.
To a virgin it came hither white—
and was in the silver-mirror and in her.

FROM *Sonnets to Orpheus*, Part II, 4
by Rainer Maria Rilke,
trans. M. D. Herter Norton,
New York, 1942

CAST

AVENANT, THE BEAST, THE PRINCE	*Jean Marais*
BEAUTY	*Josette Day*
FÉLICIE	*Nane Germon*
ADÉLAIDE	*Mila Parely*
LUDOVIC	*Michel Auclair*
THE MERCHANT	*Marcel André*

CREDITS

DIRECTOR	*Jean Cocteau*
PRODUCER	*André Paulvé*
SCENARIO	*Jean Cocteau*
TECHNICAL ADVISER	*René Clément*
DIRECTOR OF PHOTOGRAPHY	*Henri Alekan*
COSTUMES AND SETS	*Christian Bérard*
MAKE-UP	*Arakelian*
MUSIC	*Georges Auric*
EDITOR	*Claude Ibéria*

1946   Black and white   90 minutes

Perspectives: Realism versus Fantasy, Expressionism, and Surrealism in Cinema

It is a cliché of cinema history that at the very beginning of that history two individuals, in the contrasting types of films that they created, initiated two main approaches to film making that have existed to our time. Louis Lumière not only invented the Cinématographe with his brother August, but also directed, in 1895, a number of influential films with his camera-projector. His goal was to record "life as it is," and his primitive documentaries were devoted to such subjects as workers leaving a factory, a child eating breakfast, and a wall being demolished.

A contemporary of Lumière was Georges Méliès who, between 1896 and 1913, produced literally hundreds of films. Although the subjects of his films were varied, including one on the Dreyfus case, he is noted primarily for his use of illusions. A magician in his youth, Méliès realized not only the value of specially designed studio sets, but also the potential of the camera to create illusions by using such techniques as superimposition, double exposure, and stop-action photography. Although his camera was stationary and he did not conceive of the variety of shots, cuts, and transitions developed later, he established that the motion picture camera could, as well as record "life as it is," project a world beyond everyday reality.

We have come to label Lumière's approach as realism and that of Méliès as fantasy. Neither of these terms, especially the latter, can be defined precisely; however, they are useful to indicate the attitude in a specific film of the director and his associates toward the kind of reality they will represent on the screen. We will first consider realism.

In the "Perspective" preceeding our analysis of Olmi's *Il Posto*, we will discuss realism as a method of representation, a philosophical and political attitude, and a circumscribed subject matter. Here we will confine ourselves to the first area and explore further some fundamental principles.

Realism in cinema, as well as in the other arts, is usually defined as a fidelity to actuality or verisimilitude ("the quality of appearing to be true or real; likelihood"). Two questions immediately come to mind: What is *actuality*? How does the camera record it?

All of us to one degree or another live during our waking hours in a world that we believe is dominated by cause and effect. This is particularly so in our view of our physical world. We are less sure about emotional causes and effects, no matter what behaviorist psychologists maintain, yet we do assume that if a person grinds his teeth and makes a fist, he is angry. Most of us, however, accept the existence of chance and the unknown. It is possible, although very unlikely, that a bottle with a note in it dropped into the Pacific Ocean from a beach on Hawaii will be picked up by the individual to whom it is addressed as he walks along a beach in California. Most of us do not believe that a human being can touch lead and instantly change it into gold; however, no one can state with absolute certainty that tomorrow such a person will not appear. Probability, then, is a matter of averages, and belief is a confidence in what experience has taught us as confirmed by those averages.

On the other hand, we all have experiences, as in dreams and hallucinations, during which the law of averages is suspended. Furthermore, the way an individual's senses apprehend reality, especially the visual, is influenced by his state of mind. Distortions occur not only in dreams and hallucinations and during drunkenness, but also, although to a lesser degree, when a person is experiencing emotional tension. A frightened individual actually *sees* a figure lurking in the shadows, whereas if he were in a calmer state, he would recognize that no such threat exists.

The realistic approach in cinema does not deny the existence of far-fetched or distorted sense perceptions; it simply restricts the former and generally ignores the latter. Realism focuses on the familiar and the likely. Discernible causes of manifested effects are emphasized, particularly the influences of environment on an individual's feelings and actions. The world of realism is one we recognize as real, actual, and probable when we are awake and clearly seeing what is happening to ourselves and others.

In a realistic film the camera attempts to be as objective as possible within the conditions imposed by the medium itself. Our qualification requires an explanation. Earlier we referred to Lumière's concept of the camera as primarily a recorder of the real world as registered by our senses. From this view the camera is like an unblinking eye staring at images of the phenomenal world outside itself, and it generally functioned in just this way at the very beginning of cinema. As soon, however, as the camera moved left and right, up and down, and in and out, the situation changed radically. Camera movement involves choice (you cannot have simultaneously without splitting the screen a long shot and close-up of a person), and choice means that what the viewer sees on the screen is determined by the director and his associates. Their basic material will be limited to what is before the camera, but the content and rhythms of the final print will reflect their own intellectual and emotional decisions. A film, since the beginning of this century, has not been a record of reality, but a recreation of reality dependent on a human vision (individual or group). It is for this reason that a film can be a work of art. Few writers have explored this fundamental principle of cinema with greater insight than Rudolph Arnheim in his *Film As Art*, Berkeley, 1960.

When we refer to realism in cinema as objective, we intend within the medium's attempt at what aestheticians call "mimesis"—an *imitation* of reality. More specifically, in terms of techniques, the camera avoids subjective shots: showing on the screen what a character sees, with possible distortions and disorientation. An environment is often presented in detail. Illusions are shunned. There is a preference for lengthy shots and a stable camera.

Although we have indicated some aspects of realism in cinema, we must emphatically state that they are not offered as unequivocal criteria for determining whether or not a film is realistic. We must always keep in mind that the term is imprecise, a means of focusing our attention on tendencies rather than on absolute characteristics. A realistic film may violate one or more of the tenets of an abstract concept called realism. A director might even include what are clearly sequences of fantasy in a film that we categorize as realistic.

In the end, all we can say with some confidence is that a realistic film creates the total impression that it avoids the improbable, the unknown, the subjective, and the illusional. It emphasizes logical causes and effects and the influence of environment; it predominately preserves the objectivity of the camera.

Fantasy, on the other hand, has as its *raison d'être* an acceptance of the improbable and the unknown. In fantasy, agents of the devil can assume human shape (as in Marcel Carné's *The Devil's Envoys*); a child can have magical powers (Vittorio DeSica's *Miracle in Milan*); a beast can be a prince enchanted by evil fairies (Jean Cocteau's *Beauty and the Beast*); and a dead RAF pilot can be tried by a court in heaven (Powell and Pressburger's *A Stairway to Heaven*).

There is no attempt in a fantasy film to trick us into believing that a farfetched situation actually occurs. There is always the possibility that the devil's agents and evil fairies exist, but this is not usually the basis on which we approach a fantasy. What a viewer should give, however (in the phrase Coleridge used in *Biographia Literaria* when discussing the supernatural in poetry), is "that willing suspension of disbelief for the moment . . . ."

We are not to assume that fantasy is completely divorced from reality; on the contrary, at its best it is grounded in human nature and does not take undue advantage of the improbable to solve human problems. At times the supernatural in a fantasy may be ambiguous; for example, what is presented on the screen could be the hallucinations of an individual, as in *A Stairway to Heaven*.

The advantage of fantasy is that it is not confined by fidelity to actuality and can raid for material the provinces of heaven and hell, the past and the future. On rare occasions, as with Murnau's *Nosferatu*, Wasznsky's *The Dybbuk*, and Cocteau's *Beauty and the Beast*, a film fantasy can incorporate into itself the dimension of the mythic, so that on the screen are manifested projections of our unconscious fears, hopes, and conflicts. More often it affords us glimpses of what might have been and what could be (the latter now called science fiction films, from Lang's *Metrop-*

olis to Kubrick's *2001: A Space Odyssey*). Fantasy can also offer its creators opportunities for social satire, as in *Miracle in Milan*.

As a realistic film may include fantasy sequences, especially in the form of dreams, so a fantasy may have aspects that are realistic. (*Miracle in Milan* is an example.) The determining factor, again, is the total effect of a specific film.

In the tradition of Méliès, directors of fantasies usually make extensive use of illusions. In the "Style and Approach" section of our essay on *Beauty and the Beast* we indicate in some detail how Cocteau created the illusions that appear in the film. They are divided into two types: those obtained by manipulating properties and those possible only by means of a camera. Whether the rhythm of a film is agitated and rapid (brief shots, many angle changes, and abrupt cuts) or stately (lengthy shots, stable perspectives, and numerous dissolves) depends more on the style of the director than his intention to produce a fantasy.

A fantasy film does not necessarily encourage subjective shots and scenes. It depends on the point of view. Most film fantasies are from beginning to end from the point of view of the audience watching what is happening in the fantastic world within the film. The situation is different, however, if the fantasy is primarily experienced by an individual character. Here the form of transition is important. In *A Stairway to Heaven* we are never sure if what is presented on the screen are improbable events that supposedly take place or the pilot's hallucinations. In the movie *The Secret Life of Walter Mitty* (directed by Norman Z. McLeod), the transitions make clear that the fantasies that constitute most of the film are Mitty's daydreams.

Fantasy and realism, as we indicated in "Interpreting a Film," can be considered film genres (if one has no objection to definitions that act as intellectual Procrustean beds). That the two are opposed in the way they view reality is obvious. Now we will turn to two cinematic movements that are generally antirealistic, but that on many principles also differ from fantasy.

Expressionism and surrealism share one premise: inner experiences can be presented directly to an audience. Because these experiences are usually illogical, improbable, and distortions of our waking, everyday reality, they cannot be presented in realistic terms. Both movements, in fact, originated as rebellions against what their advocates felt were the restrictions of realism. Expressionism and surrealism are sometimes described as subdivisions of fantasy, but they deviate from this genre in a significant way. Fantasy moves outside of the human psyche to explain its improbabilities and illusions. In addition, artists who were members of the two movements developed techniques usually not found in fantasy.

Expressionism and surrealism also are at variance with each other in certain tenets and techniques; however, these will become evident as we

consider each movement in turn. A summary of the history of expressionism as a movement in art can be found in most encyclopedias, so we will
only note that it had its origin in the German theater at the beginning
of the twentieth century and found inspiration for its theories in the
works of Freud and Marx and for its practice in the drama of Strindberg
and the painting of Van Gogh. Few of the Western arts—particularly
theater, fiction, painting, sculpture, and cinema—were not affected by the
concepts of expressionism during the first three decades of this century.
The movement continues to influence the arts to the present, although
in a more individual and less organized fashion than during its heyday.

Its themes include the need for freedom from oppressive bourgeois
values, condemnation of the destructive pressures of mass society, the
important role the artist can play in revitalizing our society, and the
validity of insights into human nature that can come from abnormal
states of mind, particularly insanity.

Cinema explored these themes in films by such German directors as
Robert Wiene, F. W. Murnau, Fritz Lang, and Paul Leni. Enthusiasm
for expressionistic cinema lasted less than a decade, from the end of
World War I to the mid-1920s. One principle of a type of representation
of reality and a number of cinematic techniques developed by expressionists, however, were to influence film makers well beyond this period
of time.

We have already suggested the expressionists' revolutionary stance
toward representation of a type of reality (in referring to inner experiences presented directly to an audience). The camera becomes, in the
fullest sense of the term, subjective. This can be done in two ways. The
camera can take the place of the eyes of a character and present directly
what he sees during periods of intense emotion or abnormal states of
mind. The inevitable sense distortions, mystery, and improbabilities are
preserved intact. The second method is more indirect. We do not see
through the eyes of a character, but the director creates a reality on the
screen that is appropriate to and reflects the feelings of the character.

The devices the expressionists developed to express subjective emotions encompassed distortion through special effects (for example, superimposition, slow-motion and stop-action photography, and cheat shots),
shadows and dramatic lighting, unusual camera angles, abrupt transitions
from one shot to another, stylized sets, and exaggerated acting styles.

There are few films that make use of all these devices from beginning
to end. The closest is Robert Wiene's *The Cabinet of Dr. Caligari*. And
even in this work the opening and closing scenes are realistic. Most directors, and this was so increasingly after the 1920s, limited themselves to
expressionistic sequences in their films. An example of such a film discussed in this volume is Murnau's *The Last Laugh*. The techniques of
expressionism can also be used for purposes other than those originally
intended by the expressionists. We deal with this point in our remarks on

"Style and Approach" in Lang's *M*. In our opinion much of the paraphernalia of expressionism is evident in this film, but not the principle that we
consider the touchstone of the movement: the atmosphere of mystery
and danger that is intrinsically a reflection of the intense emotions of the
characters.

Surrealism has been a far less significant movement in cinema. It shares
with expressionism, as we have noted, a rejection of realism and an intention to present directly on the screen manifestations of the unconscious. It differs, however, in its uncompromising distance from waking
reality and its dependence on the disorientation of dreams rather than
the controlled distortion and atmosphere of expressionism. A surrealistic
film usually remains from start to finish in its self-contained dream
sphere. Such a film may be meticulously accurate in details, as in a painting by Salvador Dali or Max Ernst. Yet, what actually happens is utterly
improbable by the standards of logical consciousness. There is no "plot"
in a surrealistic film, only a series of images that are connected by associations unrelated to the logical world and coherent only in terms of
the dynamics of the dream world.

Leaving a surrealistic film may be like awakening from a dream, but
its creators are not entirely uncalculating. Somehow a satire of our most
cherished institutions, beliefs, and attitudes is indirectly conveyed to us.
The sheer visual beauty of many surrealistic films is also a reward for our
bewilderment and the uneasy feeling that we are being presented with
truths about our innermost needs and desires that we would rather ignore.

It is inevitable considering the demands that surrealistic films make on
audiences that few of them have been produced and those few have been
popular only among the most ardent film buffs. During three years, 1928
to 1930, the major classics of the movement appeared: Germaine Dulac's
Seashell and the Clergyman (1928), Salvador Dali's and Luis Buñuel's
The Andalusian Dog (1929) and their *The Age of Gold* (1930), and Jean
Cocteau's *Blood of a Poet* (1930). These films demonstrated the freedom
possible in the medium to directors who followed. Only Buñuel, however,
remained faithful to many of the principles of the movement and still
attained the status of a major director.

Cinematic realism and forms of antirealism are not mutually exclusive;
they reflect and call to our attention, through the sensibilities of filmmakers, the many interdependent realities we experience in the process
of existing.

Story and Characterization

In the opening scenes of Jean Cocteau's *Beauty and the Beast* we are
introduced to Beauty, a gentle, lovely young woman who does the house-
work in her father's villa; Félicie and Adélaide, her selfish, domineering

older sisters; Ludovic, her self-indulgent brother; Avenant, companion of Ludovic, who is in love with Beauty; and the Merchant, a widower, once wealthy but now barely able to support his family.

The Merchant learns that one of his ships, though lost, has returned to port. When he reaches town, however, he is informed that his creditors have appropriated his profits. He is forced to return home on a stormy night. He loses his way in a forest and takes refuge in a seemingly empty palace that is obviously enchanted. In the morning as he leaves he remembers a promise to Beauty that he would bring her a rose. When he picks one in the palace garden, a beast appears—half man, half lion—and demands his life or that of one of his daughters.

Beauty insists on going in her father's place. The Beast is kind to her, and each night asks her to marry him. Although she repeatedly refuses, she comes to sympathize with and feel warmth toward the creature. By means of a magic mirror, she discovers that her father is sick with grief at her absence. She begs that she be allowed to visit him. The Beast reluctantly agrees if she will pledge to return in a week's time. To prove his love, he entrusts her with a gold key to the pavilion of Diana, where his wealth is stored. She is magically transported to her father's house.

At home, Beauty's jealous sisters induce her to remain longer than a week. Meanwhile, Avenant has persuaded Ludovic to join him in an attempt to destroy the Beast and steal his treasure. They leave on the horse Magnificent. The mirror reveals to Beauty that the Beast is very ill; she returns to the palace. He is indeed dying. She realizes then the depth of her feeling for him and encourages him to live for her sake. But he dies. While she is with the Beast, Avenant and Ludovic break into the pavilion of Diana. A guardian statue kills Avenant. His body turns into that of the Beast.

At the moment Avenant is killed, the Beast disappears and a handsome prince appears in his place. He explains that through the spell of evil fairies, he was to remain in the shape of a monster until a pure woman gave him a look of love. The two leave for the Prince's kingdom, where, we assume, they will live happily ever after.

The setting of the film is late seventeenth-century France. Cocteau chose this age because, as he tells us in his book on the making of *Beauty and the Beast, Diary of a Film, New York,* 1950, the idea of directing a version of the tale came to him as he was looking at Gustave Doré's illustrations for the story, and the nineteenth-century artist created seventeenth-century settings and costumes.

The best known version of the story of Beauty and the Beast is by Mme. Leprince de Beaumont (1711–1780). Her text, in fact, is an appendix to *Diary of a Film.* The differences between this account and the director's own scenario suggest that Cocteau was attempting more, even though he denied it, than a straightforward cinematic rendering of a fairy tale.

Many of these differences can be explained by the need of a script writer to simplify the plot: in the earlier version the Merchant has three sons and three daughters; Beauty has a number of suitors; the Merchant is permitted by the Beast to take home a chest of gold; the sisters marry; the Merchant takes Beauty to the Beast; a ring rather than a glove is the means of magical transportation; a good fairy helps Beauty; and the sisters are turned into statues at the end.

More important are Cocteau's major innovations: the character of Avenant, the pavilion of Diana, the transformation of Avenant into the Beast at the end, and the inner conflict of the Beast between the animal and human sides of his nature. Conjectures as to why the script writer-director introduced these elements into the story will be offered after a few paragraphs on characterization.

Only three characters in the film—Beauty, Avenant, and the Beast—are more than two dimensional. The Merchant strikes us as fairly simple-minded, and neither a coward nor a particularly courageous man. On the other hand, his indulgence and passivity toward his children are, at the least, unusual. Although he obviously loves Beauty, he allows his older daughters to be overbearing and cruel toward her. He makes no attempt to restrain their arrogance and selfishness. When his son is responsible for the furniture of the house being carted away by a usurer, he simply says, "Ludovic, you did this!" His only real passion is his need and dependency on Beauty. When she leaves his home, he takes to his bed and languishes. One does not need to have read Freud to recognize that this extravagant feeling of an elderly widower for his beautiful daughter is unhealthy.

The sisters are consistently narcissistic, greedy, and malicious. Only once, when Ludovic leaves with Avenant to kill the Beast, does one of them, Adélaide, think of someone other than herself. This moment of uncharacteristic concern for her brother's safety quickly passes. The sisters are surprising in only one respect: they are physically attractive, unlike the ugly older sisters of classic fairy tales. The contrast between physical beauty and internal ugliness and the reverse is, however, a major theme of the film.

Ludovic is the typical dissolute son of an overindulgent father. He seems to be capable of only occasional twinges of guilt that others must pay for his pleasures. Like his father, he is basically a passive person, taking the line of least resistance—as when dealing with the usurer—and a follower if confronted by a stronger individual, such as Avenant. When his ego is bruised or his comfort threatened, he reacts in small, spiteful ways, as when he nudges Avenant's arm during the archery match at the opening of the film, when he responds to his sisters, or when he denounces his best friend as an adventurer who wants to marry his sister for her money. His only redeeming virtue presented in the film is his genuine feeling for Beauty. Even here, however, he has neither the courage nor strength of will truly to defend his youngest sister against the harassment of Félicie and Adélaide.

One's first impression is that Beauty's virtuous nature contains not the smallest rent, not even one patched over. She has courage, as is evident throughout her stay with the Beast. She has physical beauty and grace, dignity of bearing, an inexhaustible store of kindness, and enough wit to see beneath the monstrous exterior of the Beast to his intrinsic goodness.

On the other hand, Beauty's tendency toward emotional passivity finally conveys a pallid personality. Her willingness to subordinate her pleasures and wishes to those of others borders on the masochistic. Although the men in the film seem to find her an ideal daughter and sister and potentially an ideal lover and wife, her submissiveness would hardly endear her to a loyal chapter of the Women's Liberation movement.

Cocteau emphasizes this amorphous quality of the young woman by continually photographing close-ups of her in soft focus. He restricts Josette Day, the actress who played Beauty, to four unambiguous expressions—blankness, sadness, fear, and happiness. Beauty's lack of facial animation reflects her uncomplex character and her function in the film as an archetype of female virtue and virginity in a mythic tale rather than a flesh and blood woman dealing with the realities of her role in a man's world.

Avenant is another dissolute young man, but unlike Ludovic he has manliness and courage. His virility does make him impatient with Beauty. He attempts to force himself on the young woman rather than persuade her to accept him. In this he is in direct contrast to the Beast, who, innately the chivalrous gentleman, never, even though she is in his power, makes claims on Beauty. He wins her love rather than demands it.

Yet, the two men are in subtle ways connected, are played by the same actor, Jean Marais, and at the end exchange places. Possible explanations of why this is so and further explorations of the characters can best be attempted within the perspective of specific interpretations of the film as a whole.

Themes and Interpretations

Although Jean Cocteau willingly talked and wrote about *Beauty and the Beast* (see pp. 234–242), he was surprisingly silent on one aspect of the film: what ideas, emotions, and symbolic meanings he was attempting to convey. His defense of his reticence in interpreting the film was that *Beauty and the Beast* is solely a cinematic rendering of a fairy tale with self-contained images of beauty and mystery. This is the main point of his statement that appears immediately after the credits, summed up in the sentence: "I ask of you a little . . . childlike simplicity."

One way of experiencing this film, then, is to take the director at his word and enjoy its aura of beauty and mystery without reaching after fact and reason. Yet, most viewers feel uncomfortable with this restriction because Cocteau used so many potent symbols whose significance reverberate in our subconscious and arouse our curiosity by introducing a new character, Avenant, and relating him so closely to the Beast.

Many themes are evident and interpretations possible once one delves beneath the glittering surface of *Beauty and the Beast*. We shall confine our comments, however, to three approaches that we label the illusionistic, the humanistic, and the psychoanalytic. It may be superfluous to do so, because we have reiterated this caution so often in this book, but again we insist that the three interpretations, different though they may be, are not mutually exclusive. That we can view *Beauty and the Beast* in the light of at least three different perspectives proves how multi-faceted a film it is.

The contrast between reality and illusion is definitely a theme of Cocteau's film. The most obvious manifestation of this contrast is between the realism that pervades the Merchant's house and the illusions present in the Beast's palace. In the Merchant's house human beings polish floors and wash clothes, the sun rises and sets, objects remain inanimate, and money is a problem. We note that there is no background music, except when Beauty is thinking or talking about the Beast. On the other hand, in the Beast's palace invisible servants do the work and time is suspended. Inanimate objects are alive; even the stones in the paths seem to breathe. Music is heard more often than words are spoken.

The director underscores this separation of the house and the palace by limiting cross-cutting to a bare minimum: while Beauty is at the palace, there is only one scene that takes place at the house; during the stay with her father, there is one cut to the Beast.

Cocteau is too subtle, however, to perpetrate in this film without qualifications such a neat, artificial dichotomy. When we watch Beauty in one dwelling, the other seems distant, unreal. We might expect this impression when she is at home, but the feeling also grows on us while she is in the palace. Perhaps this is what Cocteau had in mind when he insisted in *Diary of a Film* that he wanted the Beast and his palace to be "fantastic yet 'real'."

The symbol of this shifting prospect on illusion and reality is the magic mirror. In the palace Beauty learns of her father's illness through an *image* in the mirror. Later she is informed at home that the Beast is dying through an *image* in the mirror. It is as if there were two worlds on either side of the mirror, neither one more substantial than the other, yet each is the inverse of the other. When Beauty is ready to return to her father, the Beast remarks that when it is night in his world, it is morning in hers.

Another form of inversion that relates the two settings is the disunity between physical appearance and emotional nature. The Beast is horrifying externally, yet, although he must struggle with his animal instincts, he is basically virtuous in character and gracious in manner. In contrast, the people we see in the Merchant's house are all physically attractive. The sisters, however, are cruel and crude, the Merchant is selfish in his dependency on Beauty, and Ludovic and Avenant are wastrels. Only in the case of Beauty is there harmony between her appearance and nature. For this reason she can function in the two worlds.

Appearance, then, is an illusion in both realms, even though Beauty is exempt from this rule. At the end of the film the conflict between external and internal is resolved when the Beast is transformed into the Prince and Avenant's body becomes that of the Beast.

Beauty's name is descriptive as well as given. In this respect, too, she fits into both settings, for each has its own type of beauty. The palace is a place of extravagant and immediately impressive beauty. The rooms and hallways are spacious. The architectural decorations and furniture are baroque in style, with convoluted lines and details that lead to aesthetic surprises and delights. Sculptures and objets d'art are everywhere. The costumes and jewelry worn by Beauty and the Beast are rich and elegant. This wondrous beauty is enhanced by preternatural mystery.

On the other hand, the Merchant's villa possesses a mundane beauty in its uncluttered rooms, functional furniture, and bare floors. Straight lines and sharp angles, even sheets hanging from lines move us with their qualities of balance, simplicity, and repose. What is lacking is that ultimate glow, magic, and Dionysian freedom that is more readily found in illusion than reality.

As one considers the contrasting characteristics of the two settings, it is natural to speculate if the Merchant's house is intended to represent waking reality and the palace to be analogous to the dream world. The justification for such a view is evident if a reader goes back over our discussion of reality and illusion in *Beauty and the Beast* and substitutes the word *dream* for *illusion*. Cocteau's lifelong commitment to surrealism also supports this position. The statement of the director, previously quoted, that he wanted to make the palace "fantastic yet 'real'" is not a rejection of surrealism but an expression of his individual approach to the movement. Wallace Fowlie sums up the essence of Cocteau's surrealistic method in the theater and film:

The pure surrealist method would be the direct narration of [dream] experiences as they come to us in free association. Cocteau takes this method one step farther, or leads it to its necessary conclusion, by imposing on the confessional dream world a very deliberate and calculated form. . . . Myths come to life over and over when an artistic work has enough formal solidity to contain them.

(*Age of Surrealism,* New York, 1950 p. 136.)

One final twist of perspective is possible within this interpretation. If one can say of so protean an artist as Cocteau that there is one theme that dominates his work, it would have to be that the poet (in the sense that Shelley used the term—an imaginative creator in any medium) transforms everyday reality "into something rich and strange." The illusion the poet creates is closer to the truths of our unconscious, where the essence of ourselves resides, than ordinary experience would allow us to discover unaided.

Our attention shifts, then, from the contrast of illusion and reality *in Beauty and the Beast* to the illusion of the film *itself*. Any meanings or interpretations a viewer may attach to specific scenes or characters are of secondary importance. What is primary is his immediate experience in toto of a poet's rendering his own vision in cinematic terms. This vision draws on the concreteness of reality and the mystery and beauty of dreams and myths, but the combination of the two worlds results in a unique creation—an illusion of the highest order, a work of art.

A less esoteric and ingenious approach to *Beauty and the Beast* is the humanistic, in which an analysis focuses on the characters, their relationships, and their values.

Because we have anticipated a good deal of this approach in earlier sections of this essay, we will consider here only one set of significant relationships: those between Beauty and the three men in her life—her father, Avenant, and the Beast. Each woos her in his own way. The father takes advantage of his daughter's sense of responsibility and of her need to be needed. He does nothing for her in return for her love: he allows her to be a servant in the house and be dominated by her sisters. His love is basically selfish.

Avenant unquestionably loves and wants Beauty. His wooing, however, lacks grace and respect. He is impetuous and demanding. He is also self-indulgent; otherwise, he would have proven earlier, when not seeing a rival in the Beast, that her love was more important than his life of dissipation. Avenant's physical attractiveness is to his advantage; he looks like a prince. But beneath his striking appearance is an egocentric, domineering male.

The Beast, for all his physical ugliness, has the character of a courtly prince. The adjective *courtly* is intended here to convey more than a description of manners. In his brief discussion of *Beauty and the Beast* in *Classics of the Foreign Film*, New York, 1962, p. 171, Parker Tyler makes the following statement: "Courtliness is very much a part of the 'fable' of *Beauty and the Beast*; it is, in fact, the essence of its symbolism." The critic does not expand on this idea; however, we believe that it can be related to the tradition of courtly love.

This tradition is a philosophy of love that originated in France in approximately the twelfth century and spread to other countries during the

Middle Ages and Renaissance. Although at its earliest stage courtly love included elements of the illicit (many advocates even held that love was incompatible with marriage) and sensual, it soon became infused with a Platonic idealism. The lover is in agony and confusion until his lady accepts him. At that moment he becomes transformed into a potential hero inspired by his lady. In its ideal form courtly love rejected sexual intercourse as an impediment to the purity, even sanctity, of this special relationship between a man and woman.

The Beast in everything he does and says personifies the courtly lover. His external ugliness and animal instincts symbolize forces that work against courtly love, but he is able to remain true to the character of a prince in spirit as well as name.

When Beauty chooses the Beast over Avenant and her father, she has decided in favor of virtue and the courtly ideal. She has followed her intuition rather than what her eyes see. In the end she is rewarded for her perceptiveness by being given the best of two worlds—a husband who both externally and internally is a prince.

In this humanistic approach to *Beauty and the Beast* the provocative symbols and actions in the film that suggest the major characters may be driven by unconscious, primarily sexual, motivations are ignored. It is to Freudian psychoanalysis that we now turn to explore our final interpretation of the film.

As far back as the early eighteenth century a few writers, such as Giambattista Vico, maintained that fairy tales and myths are not simply stories for children and meaningless fantasies of primitive peoples, but contain in disguised forms significant insights into man's view of himself and his society. In the late nineteenth century and after, this proposition was documented by anthropologists, particularly E. B. Tylor, Andrew Lang, and, in greatest detail and most comprehensively, J. G. Frazer in *The Golden Bough*. It was Sigmund Freud, however, who drew attention to how often fairy tales and myths include symbolic expressions of the sexual drives of human beings. The most popular, yet not oversimplified, presentation of this aspect of Freud's premises and methods can be found in Erich Fromm's *The Forgotten Language: An Introduction to the Understanding of Dreams, Fairy Tales, and Myths*, New York, 1951.

We will begin our Freudian interpretation of *Beauty and the Beast* by first summarizing how psychoanalysts have viewed the tale itself, and then turn to Cocteau's cinematic version. The following summary is derived from two articles: J. Barchelon, "*Beauty and the Beast*: From Myth to Fairy Tale," *Psychoanalysis and Psychoanalytic Review*, 46, No. 4, 1959, pp. 19–29; and Thomas Mintz, "The Meaning of the Rose in *Beauty and the Beast*," *Psychoanalytic Review*, 56, No. 4, 1969–1970, pp. 615–620.

From a psychoanalytic perspective, the rose is the central symbol of the story. It represents female sexuality, particularly newly blossoming sexual desires. More specifically, Beauty has unconsciously become aware of her sexual potency. The Merchant, sensing her flowering sexuality, incestuously desires his daughter but feels guilty about his desire. When Beauty asks her father for a rose, she wants him, as Mintz puts it, "to respond to her sexual desires, or perhaps she merely wishes to let him know that she is growing up." (Ibid., p. 617.)

The Merchant's plucking of the rose is a substitute for sexual intercourse with his daughter. The Beast represents simultaneously the animal part of the father and the virility of other men; the latter role makes the monster a competitor who condemns the Merchant to death if he will not release his daughter.

Beauty's willingness to die for her father suggests that she shares to some degree his forbidden wish and accepts punishment for it.

The Beast is good to her, but she refuses to marry him (have intercourse with him) because she is revolted by his ugliness (his masculine sexual drive). She finds an excuse to return to the less overt threat of her father. She is eventually forced, however, to make a choice. The kindness and virtue of the Beast have won her love, so that she can at least tolerate the animal portion of his nature (she can attach herself to a man even though he retains the virility that frightens her). An instinctive desire to grow emotionally also influences her decision. In leaving her father for the Beast, she is rejecting an essentially sterile relationship of the past for one in the future that will enable her to become a mature woman.

When she declares her love for the Beast, he is transformed into a handsome prince. To once again quote Mintz: "Love transforms what is ugly, such as a penis, sexuality, animal passions, into what is beautiful." (Ibid., p. 618.)

We have only outlined how Freudian psychoanalysts, or at least two of them, interpret the tale. We have included, however, sufficient evidence that the story of "Beauty and the Beast" can be viewed as a disguised representation of the psychic conflicts a young woman endures as she passes from an Electra fixation to an acceptance of a sexual drive in the male and herself.

Cocteau has not indicated anywhere that we can discover to what degree he was influenced by psychoanalysis while conceiving and creating *Beauty and the Beast*. We do know that he was well acquainted with the writings of Freud and his followers and incorporated many of their ideas in his fiction and films. (*The Blood of the Poet* is a veritable treasure-trove for Freudians.) However, whether consciously or not, Cocteau, in his cinematic version of "Beauty and the Beast," includes every component necessary to a Freudian interpretation. Furthermore, he actually adds variations that reinforce, although with his own special emphasis, such an interpretation.

Cocteau leaves unchanged the ambiguous relationship between father and daughter, but by adding the character of Avenant he complicates Beauty's choice. The young man is vigorous and aggressive in his attempts to bring to the surface Beauty's sexual nature: the very first time we see him alone with the young woman, he tries to kiss her. There is a suggestion of violence in his character: he strikes both Ludovic and Félicie. The Beast, on the other hand, is ashamed of manifestations of his sensual instincts and struggles against them. Not once does he attempt to force himself physically on Beauty. He plays "the waiting game." He depends on kindness and courtesy to draw the fearful girl to him.

It is in the last third of the film that Cocteau symbolically emphasizes the differences between Avenant and the Beast and makes a judgment on their contrasting methods of wooing Beauty.

In the Beast's garden is the pavilion of Diana, a structure that looks like an oversized jewel casket. Although the Beast has a golden key to the building, neither he nor Beauty may enter. He tells the young woman that his "true riches lie locked in that pavilion."

It does not take a professional knowledge of Freudian psychology to recognize that the pavilion is a womb symbol (enclosed areas, such as caves and houses, are archetypal female symbols). A treasure in a container, particularly a jewel box, usually represents virginity in the forgotten language of the unconscious. A virgin in the sexual sense is "cold." Hence, there is snow falling in the pavilion. It also fits this context that Diana, goddess of chastity, should protect the treasure.

The Beast appreciates the power of magic or romance and does not attempt to penetrate the pavilion. On the other hand, Avenant is a nonbeliever (in a conversation with Ludovic, he denies the existence of magic). He storms the structure and breaks in. As the Merchant's plucking of the rose is a displaced wish-fulfillment of sexual intercourse with his daughter, so Avenant's violent entrance is symbolic of raping Beauty. In punishment for this desecration, he is killed by Diana. The treasure (virginity) reached by such brutal means becomes dead branches and leaves. Avenant is also transformed into the Beast, so that the bestial nature hidden beneath his handsome exterior is revealed.

When the Beast gives Beauty the key to the pavilion, he is putting in her hands the choice of her role as a woman. He also gives her the three remaining secrets of his power (in additon to the rose and the key): the magic mirror of truth, the glove, and the horse Magnificent. The last two are traditional symbols of masculine sexual potency. In other words, the Beast surrenders to her all his power over her so that she can freely decide which man to accept. She makes a choice when she returns to the dying monster.

The Prince with whom Beauty is finally rewarded combines the virility and attractiveness of Avenant with the consideration and courtliness of the lord of the palace. In leaving with him, we understand that she is entrusting to the Prince without fear the key to her pavilion of Diana.

Analysis of Major Sequences

We believe that the structure of *Beauty and the Beast* will be clearer if we organize our discussion under headings indicating sections of the film rather than individual sequences.

I. The Merchant's Family and His Meeting with the Beast

The opening shot is a brief one of the window of the Merchant's house; we hear two female voices complaining about Beauty.

A cut to Ludovic, the brother, and Avenant, his close friend, shooting arrows at a target set against the house. When it is Avenant's turn, the spiteful Ludovic, angered by the poor result of his own shot, knocks against his companion's arm.

The arrow enters the house through the window and almost hits a dog. We see Félicie and Adélaide dressing themselves in rich apparel with the aid of Beauty, who is wearing very plain clothes. The two older sisters exchange insults with their brother.

Félicie and Adélaide leave to visit the duchess. They must rouse four servants to carry them in sedan chairs. The verbal battle with their brother continues.

Our interest in the scene focuses on Avenant. It seems an unlikely coincidence that our first view of the young man is of him shooting a potentially dangerous arrow and that he is finally killed by an arrow. It is also significant that we do not see his face until the next scene.

That scene opens with a mirror image of Beauty on a polished floor. She is kneeling, washing the floor with the arrow still in it. Avenant's hand moves into the frame and pulls out the arrow. She looks up at him, then he kneels beside her (Fig. 10–1).

We have already noted that the magic mirror that later appears in the story is capable of revealing truths beneath conventional surfaces in the Merchant's house (as when the sisters look into it). The image on the polished floor anticipates this quality of the mirror. The arrow suggests danger to both Beauty and Avenant. We finally see the latter's face because in the context of the story his identity and reality exist only in relation to Beauty.

After they both rise, there is a lengthy two-shot followed by alternate close-ups, during which Avenant tries to persuade Beauty to marry him. She insists that she must stay with her father. She will make this declaration twice more—to her father and the Beast. The frustrated Avenant attempts to kiss her.

Ludovic enters and reacts to seeing them together with a statement that must have been repeated through the centuries since the first time a dissolute young man had a virtuous sister: "I'm proud I'm a rotter, but

FIGURE 10–1. *At the Merchant's house: Avenant kneels beside Beauty. (Courtesy Janus Films.)*

I won't allow [my sister] to marry one." When Ludovic orders his friend out of the house, Avenant knocks him down.

The altercation is interrupted by the sound of a door opening; in a high shot from the top of the stairs we see the Merchant entering with friends. After the three young people join the Merchant and his company sitting at a table, he announces that one of his ships has reached port and he may be able to recoup his losses. Ludovic unfairly accuses Avenant of proposing marriage to Beauty because he knew of the good fortune. The reaction of the father when he hears of the marriage offer is immediate. He grasps Beauty's hand and says with an expression of consternation: "Are you leaving me?" Beauty reassures him that she will never leave him. The Merchant's face brightens with relief and pleasure. This is the first indication of the widower's selfish and proprietary feelings toward Beauty.

The sisters enter and act with their usual social gaucherie. The Merchant seems almost proud of their arrogance, commenting with affection that "they're devils." In this scene the Merchant as father is hardly a model of dignity and authority.

Two brief scenes follow. In the first the Merchant leaves for town. The sisters demand extravagent gifts; Beauty asks only for a rose. Then we see Ludovic borrowing from a money lender with the furniture of his father's house as security.

In town the Merchant learns in a lawyer's office that his creditors have appropriated his profits. He does not have even the money for a room, so he must travel back through the forest on a foggy night.

As the Merchant mounts his horse and begins his trip home, we hear music on the sound track for the first time; it is ominous and dramatic. Almost as if to remind us of the semirealism that has characterized the film to this point and that now is to give way to fantasy, there is a shot of poor people, including a crippled child, on the street as the Merchant rides by.

The scene of the journey through the forest is shot predominantly from a very high angle, indicating the fear and vulnerability of the traveler. The music, dark shadows, fog, and occasional thunder and lightning reinforce this atmosphere of threatening forces. Cocteau organizes his shots quite efficiently; a few moments of film suggest hours in the forest. The camera does not move: either the Merchant and horse cross in front of the camera and out of the frame or the two are followed by means of a pan. The transitions to the first and second forest shots are dissolves, thereafter cuts.

In the first two shots, the Merchant is riding his horse; in the next one, he dismounts; in the following four he leads the horse. In the seventh shot in this series, we see the merchant in one-quarter profile with the horse behind him, camera left. The branches in the background separate and a palace appears a few yards away. The Merchant hesitates, then leads his horse through the parted branches; he turns around and watches as they close. Throughout the shot, the camera remains stationary.

In the next shot the Merchant and his horse have not moved but we see them from the side. The camera now moves with the Merchant as he comes to an open stable door; tracks in a bit on his back as the door closes of its own accord after the horse has entered; and pans to follow the Merchant as he runs up a broad marble staircase shouting, "Is anyone there?" He continues running until he moves out of the upper camera right corner of the frame. The camera holds on the empty staircase. After staring at the stones of the stairs for even a few moments, we almost feel that they are stirring. Here is a clever device Cocteau frequently uses in the palace for investing inanimate objects with a supernatural "aliveness."

We next see the Merchant before the door of the palace. He leans back and looks up. His shadow rises huge against the entrance, another ominous touch. The door opens magically. The Merchant shouts once more and then enters. The music that we have heard since the journey began abruptly stops.

For the following shot the camera is positioned inside the hall facing the doors. There is just enough light to see that the Merchant has entered. The camera angle is high, on a level with the wall candelabra above the Merchant's head. The first candlestick flickers on. The camera pans along the wall to the Merchant's right, as each of the remaining five sets of candles in turn blossom into flame. Each candelabrum has a human arm as a wall bracket.

At the end of the pan the camera holds as the Merchant moves into the frame. He looks over his left shoulder. The camera completes a 180° pan. We then see two candelabra light themselves (they are on the wall to the left of the Merchant). The hand holding the candelabrum closest to the camera releases it and points. The candleholder is suspended in air. The second hand repeats the action. We notice, however, a momentary hesitation before pointing. Either the arm is a novice at levitating a candelabrum or the actor on the other side of the black screen was afraid that the candleholder would sway on its wires and weaken the illusion. In any case, for a few seconds human indecisiveness enters the scene and a slight false note is struck in this orchestration of magical effects. It is surprising that Cocteau, such a perfectionist, retained even this small visual dissonance.

A cut to the blazing fireplace; a table and two chairs are in the foreground. The Merchant backs into the frame from camera right. He turns with a start and looks up as the clock over the fireplace chimes eleven times (the dial is too far away to read). One would expect it to be midnight, the bewitching hour—and it is. Even the clock is influenced by the atmosphere of the Beast's palace where reality with few exceptions is greatly or slightly askew. In a later scene when we are informed of the time (at 7 o'clock the Beast joins Beauty at dinner), the clock will strike one less than the appropriate chimes.

As the clock sounds, the camera tracks in toward the Merchant, at the same time moving, camera left, around him. He is almost facing the camera when he turns, calls again, and places his hat and gloves on the table. The camera continues to move left, only stopping when the chair at the head of the table is included in the frame. The Merchant can now sit down in the chair without the need for a cut.

The music begins again, but a chorus is added, intoning, without words, a shimmering, mysterious melody. The music will continue until the end of the scene. From the Merchant there is a cut to a marble bust of a young man that surmounts the decorative post of the fireplace. As the music heightens, the white face comes alive; the eyes, pinpointed by light, and the head itself turn in the direction of the Merchant. A pan, camera right, to the bust on the other side of the fireplace and the process is repeated, only now smoke issues from the mouth. Whereas the self-opening and closing doors and the living hands holding the candelabra are evidence of magic permeating the palace, the human busts indicate that the Merchant is being observed.

We return to the Merchant seated at the table. In contrast to the previous lengthy shots, there is now a series of brief shots. This change of rhythm is appropriate because for the first time since the Merchant entered the palace there is agitated action. The Merchant leans forward to reach for wine; behind the crystal bottle is another arm in the center of the table with the hand holding a candelabrum. A brief subjective shot, from the point of view of the Merchant, of the hand releasing the candlestick and moving toward the wine bottle. Cut to the Merchant as he jumps back against the chair so quickly that his long hair flares out from his head. The camera tracks in a little and holds on him and his look of consternation. Three shots follow of the disembodied arm as it slowly pours the wine and then again grasps the candelabrum. The last of these shots includes the Merchant (Figure 10–2). In the only touch of humor in this scene, he lifts the edge of the tablecloth and peers under the table. The camera stays on the Merchant as he looks around, and it moves up as he stands. He turns around and we see past him one side of the hall illuminated by the candelabra. The camera pans down to his hand as he picks up the glass of wine, then holds as he sits down again and drinks. Fade to black.

Thus far in this sequence there has been no suggestion that the Mer-

FIGURE 10–2. *At the Beast's palace: The Merchant recovers after being served wine by a disembodied arm. (Courtesy Janus Films.)*

chant is in any danger. He has been mystified and observed, but in no way threatened. This situation, however, changes in the very beginning of the next scene.

Fade from black to a shot of one of the living busts as it opens its eyes and looks toward the Merchant. A cut to the table candelabrum. Its candles are burned low and in the background we see that the fire in the fireplace is out. A long period of time obviously has passed since the last scene. The camera pans from the candelabrum to the second bust and from a high angle down to the Merchant asleep in the chair with the sunlight on him. We are lulled into a sense of peace and security.

There is a cut to the left hand of the Merchant resting on the end of the arm of the chair. The calm is broken, startling us and the sleeping man, by the roar of a beast. The Merchant's hand leaps away from the chair arm like a frightened creature, and we see that the hand covered the carved head of a lion. This is a very effective, intensely dramatic shot. It conveys to us visually that, after all, the Merchant is exposed to danger in this palace of serving hands and observing eyes.

We see the Merchant rise. He puts on his gloves and picks up his hat. An insert of one of the watching busts on the fireplace. The stationary camera pans, following the Merchant as he walks quickly into the hallway, then holds as he moves in wisps of fog to the entrance door. The wall candelabra go out in turn as he passes by.

The next scene begins with the Merchant outside; the door slams shut behind him. The music begins again and increases in volume. The Merchant walks along a path, then a rampart lined with figures of seated lions and large vases silhouetted against a gray sky. He reaches the garden of the palace. He stumbles on a deer with its throat ripped away. The association is inevitable between this evidence of bestial violence and the roar that awakened the Merchant. He takes a couple of steps farther along the garden path.

A close-up of a single rose appears on the screen. Suddenly it assumes a preternatural glow. The violins in the background music produce luminous tones. Cut to a shot from behind the Merchant as he picks the rose.

The encounter between the Beast and the Merchant that follows is the dramatic climax of this series of scenes at the palace. This conflict is pointed up by cuts, alternating with a single exception from one to the other. The dangerous predicament of the Merchant is emphasized by generally photographing him from a high angle, whereas shots of the Beast are at eye level or from a low angle. The music stops at the appearance of the lord of the palace and is not heard again until the Merchant leaves.

Just after the Merchant picks the rose, there is the sound of a roar and a wind that pushes the terrified man away from the rose bush. The first shot of the monster is a medium one of his whole figure that establishes for us that he has the head of a beast and the body of a man. The camera tracks in to a medium close-up, from the waist to the top of the head. The shot confirms how frightening is his lion head, but we are not close enough, as on occasion when he is with Beauty, to perceive the humanity in his eyes. We note his rich apparel and his aristocratic stance—left hand supporting his right elbow.

The Beast growls that he loves his roses more than anything in the world. Later he tells Beauty that they are one of the five secrets of his power. The penalty for the theft of a rose is death.

The Merchant stammers his excuses on his knees, the wind coming from the direction of the Beast still blowing strong. As the Beast says that the Merchant must die, there is a cut from the latter to a shot of the body of the deer at the feet of the Beast (this is the only exception to the alternate-shot series), then a pan back to the Merchant.

In the next shot the Beast seems to weaken enough to allow the Merchant to substitute one of his daughters for himself. We learn at the end of the film, however, that the spell on the Beast could only be broken by the love of a pure woman. He is far more interested in drawing a woman to the palace than killing a man.

Over the shoulder of the Beast we see and hear the Merchant objecting. In the following shot the Beast imperiously silences him and has him swear to return in three days if one of his daughters does not appear in his place.

The last two shots in the scene, now that, in a sense, the conflict between the two is resolved, are lengthy ones. After the Beast explains about using the horse Magnificent, he disappears behind the same bushes from whence he first came. The camera holds as the Merchant grips his hat, runs down the long path, and turns a corner.

The background music begins again as we see a shot similar to the first one of the palace. Only now, the Merchant on Magnificent rides directly toward the camera and passes out of the frame. The camera holds its position as the Beast comes from behind a tree. Branches close in front of the camera. The Beast separates them and looks through. Fade to black.

The Merchant has just finished telling his family and Avenant of his adventure. Avenant wishes to kill the beast; the sisters worry about themselves; Ludovic is passive, as usual; and Beauty insists on going in her father's place, for she would rather be devoured by a monster than die of the grief of losing her father. A quarrel breaks out and the distraught Merchant is helped to his bed. Fade to black.

II. Beauty at the Beast's Palace

Beauty secretly leaves her father's house by a side door. She enters the stable, mounts Magnificent, whispers the magic words, and the horse carries her away.

We have observed the father on a similar trip, so Cocteau can condense the passage through the forest and the arrival at the palace. The director encourages the dreamlike quality of the journey by repeating the settings and camera angles of the father's trip and by means of dissolves (a type of transition that he has used rarely to this point). The music also helps. When Beauty leaves the house, there is soft background music. From the moment Magnificent gallops from the stable to Beauty's entrance into the hall of the palace, we hear a stirring theme reminiscent of Wagner's "The Ride of the Valkyries." The forest trip ends with a fade to black.

The next shot is from within the hall of the palace as the door opens and Beauty enters (Figure 10–3). The music is now ethereal. The camera tracks back as Beauty runs down the hallway with its candelabra lit; she catches up with the camera and passes out of frame, right. She is photographed in slow motion. With her long black cloak and graceful movements she is a dream vision who also seems to be dreaming.

A cut to a shot from the fireplace side of the table, set as when the Merchant arrived. Beauty is seen in profile, still moving in slow motion, The camera moves with her as she climbs the stairs, then holds as she reaches the last steps and glides away from the camera.

At the top of the staircase is a doorway blocked by two arms, each one holding a candelabrum. Beauty stops, then sweeps her body—still in slow motion, her cloak swirling—to the camera left side of the doorway. It is a ballerina's movement, one of ineffable grace, but exaggerated, appropriate

FIGURE 10–3. *Beauty enters the Beast's palace for the first time.* (*Courtesy Janus Films.*)

only to a dancer on a stage. This is perhaps the very reason Cocteau included it: another unrealistic element that contributes to the fantasy of the scene.

A cut to a shot of an upstairs hallway. The camera is at the opposite end from where Beauty enters; it remains stationary as she progresses down the corridor. On camera right are windows with white curtains billowing in the wind. On the other side of the gallery are high doors. The chorus joins the background music to intone its song without words. Beauty floats toward the camera without moving her feet. This shot is one of the three or four most exquisite in *Beauty and the Beast.*

Beauty comes so close to the camera that her head disappears over the top of the frame and her body blacks out the shot. A cut to behind her as she approaches a door. The candelabra on either side come closer together and the door informs Beauty that it is the entrance to her room; it opens itself. We see Beauty enter from inside the room. The camera begins to pan, then there is an abrupt cut to a bust similar to those on the posts of the fireplace, with its eyes open. We observe more of this rich and strange boudoir as Beauty runs to the window and then returns to sit despondently on a chair before a table and mirror. The camera tracks in as the mirror says, "I am your mirror, Beauty," and she stares at it. A cut to the mirror, on whose surface the Merchant's face emerges; he is breathing heavily and his eyes are closed. Back to Beauty from a side view as she turns her head. Swift pan to what she sees: a fur blanket magically sweeps to the side of the bed. Pan back to Beauty. Her eyes widen in fear and she runs from the room.

So ends Beauty's entrance into the Beast's palace.

Next we see Beauty leave the palace and walk quickly down the entrance staircase. The Beast appears and asks where she is going. At her first sight of him, Beauty faints. Cocteau chose to photograph the next shot—the Beast kneeling beside the girl, lifting her up, and carrying her up the stairs—through a barred window and from a slightly high angle. This suggests that both are imprisoned: she by the Beast and he by powers that force him to remain a beast.

He carries the unconscious young woman through the palace to the door of Beauty's room. As the two enter, Cocteau, in three shots, transforms Beauty's cloak and simple dress into an elegant gown. After the Beast lays her down on the bed, and the music increases in volume, there is a magnificent tight close-up of the Beast's head. Beauty awakens and cries out again. The Beast backs away, afraid that she has seen in his eyes too soon his need of her. He promises to appear before her only at dinner.

In the following seven scenes in the palace (separated by fades to and from black) that precede Beauty's return to her father, she comes to appreciate the Beast's essential nobility and capacity for love and respect. She also slowly recognizes—and even more important, learns to accept— the animal portion of his nature. Her attitude does not develop directly from negative to positive, but rather grows first in one direction and then another. In this dreamlike, timeless world the scenes, as pieces for a collage, only form a discernible pattern when all have been combined. To facilitate a viewer's recollection of these scenes, we will number them here.

1. Beauty is at dinner in the great hall. The clock dial shows 7 o'clock, when the Beast said he would appear, but only six bells chime. This confirms our suspicion that the Merchant entered the palace at 12 o'clock, even though the clock sounded only eleven times. Another attempt on Cocteau's part to confuse our time sense also occurs in this scene. When we see the clock dial again, it reads 7:15, yet only two minutes of film time have elapsed.

For all her obvious fear, Beauty is gentle and understanding with the Beast (Figure 10–4). When he says that his heart is kind, even though he is a monster, she responds that there are men whose ugliness is all within. Before he leaves, the Beast tells her that every evening he will ask her the same question: Will she be his wife? Beauty's negative response is quite emphatic.

2. Beauty is exploring the hallways when she hears the roar of a wild beast and the death cries of an animal. She hides behind a statue. The Beast, with streaks of fog clinging to him, comes down the corridor where Beauty is standing. His hands are smoking. We are reminded of Cocteau's written statement, which appeared on the screen just after the credits, that a child believes "the hands of a human beast will smoke when he slays a victim." There is a memorable medium close-up of the Beast as he looks at his smoking left hand. The position of his head and, most of all, his staring eyes convey his anguish and self-revulsion.

He wanders to Beauty's room and, in the magic mirror, he sees that she is in the hall behind the statue. Beauty soon enters. With a spirit that she has not demonstrated before, she demands to know why he is in her room. A necklace forms in his hand. This is not enough of an excuse for Beauty and she regally orders him to leave.

3. In the garden Beauty happens upon the Beast on his hands and knees lapping water from a pond. He does not notice her, and she withdraws.

4. Beauty joins the Beast on the ramparts of the palace. He is splendidly dressed and offers his hand with princely grace. She admits that she has come to look forward to his appearances at dinner, but still refuses to be more than a friend to him. The first portion of the scene is shot from a low angle, giving stature to the two as they are outlined against the sky and walk past the dark lion figures.

We might almost forget the animalism of the Beast, emphasized in the last two scenes, but we—and Beauty—must be convinced that this aspect of him is as intrinsic as his kindness and courtesy.

As Beauty is talking to him, there is a medium close-up of the Beast. His eyes narrow, his nose twitches, and his ears move forward—he turns

Figure 10–4. *The Beast talks to Beauty while she eats dinner.* (*Courtesy Janus Films.*)

his head to the side. Cut to a brief shot of a deer running through the woods. Beauty asks him if he is listening. Back to the Beast: he is gazing past Beauty and takes a step away from her. One senses his inner struggle as he says, "Forgive me." Beauty realizes what has happened. The Beast murmurs, "It's nothing," and puts his hands to his forehead. After a moment he offers his hand to her. The camera tracks back, and there is a lovely, high-angle shot as the two walk with dignity and grace down a flight of stairs toward the camera and out of the frame. The music, slow and stately, contributes to this atmosphere of aristocratic manners and élan.

Cut to the two in the garden near the pond. The Beast again puts his fingers to his head; he remarks that he is thirsty. Beauty takes water in her cupped hands and offers it to him. On his knees he laps it up. In another of those wonderful close-ups, the eyes pathetically human, he asks if she minds. "No, I like it," she replies, her face in a soft-focus close-up. This is the first positive act on the part of Beauty that shows her growing affection for her captor. This gesture of solicitude and warmth is the more genuine because it occurs so soon after she recognizes how strong are the animal instincts of the Beast.

5. Beauty paces up and down before the fireplace observed by the eyes of one of the busts. We see from the clock that it is 7:30. A pan from the clock to the mirror above, where there is a reflection of the Beast as he walks into the room. After a brief dialogue, Beauty falls to her knees and begs the Beast to allow her to visit her father. He insists that she rise and he now kneels beside her. As she promises to return, Beauty gently scratches the Beast's mane. Somewhat resentfully he says, "You speak to me as an animal." "But you are," she replies. He asks that she walk with him as he considers her proposal.

Cut to an enclosed part of the garden. In response to the Beast's question, Beauty admits that someone has proposed marriage, that he is handsome, and that she refused the offer because she could not leave her father. When Avenant's name is mentioned, the Beast reacts violently, shown in a strikingly dynamic and fluent shot. He hunches over, almost on all fours, runs to an archway, leaps into space, lands on the ground, and disappears in the distance. Beauty enters into the frame and calls after his retreating figure.

6. While lying in bed, Beauty hears a sound. She rises and opens the door of her room. Suspense is maintained by our seeing first the effect on Beauty before being presented with what she sees. In a high-angle shot she staggers back, a look of dismay on her face, the roar of a beast reverberating on the sound track. A cut to a close-up of the Beast; we are shocked by his tossing head, smoking body, and mane stained with blood.

To his abject plea to be forgiven for being a beast, Beauty once again (as when she found him in her room) reacts with stately dignity. Her head held high, disgust flaring out her nostrils, she exclaims, "Aren't you ashamed?" She throws a large veil to him. "Clean yourself and go to bed."

He clutches the veil to his chest, then shouts that she must quickly close the door, for he cannot bear her looking at him that way. He moves back into the shadows and only his eyes gleam white in the blackness. He frightens Beauty, so that she puts her hand to her face, backs up, and closes the door.

This is the last scene in the film in which the Beast's animality will reveal itself. The point has been made that it exists and that he is struggling with his impulses. Beauty has come to understand the violence within him, and acts to restrain it by shaming him.

(There is a break in this series of events at the Beast's palace as we return for one scene to the Merchant's house. The usurer is collecting the furniture, leaving only the bed on which the Merchant lies ill.)

7. Back to the Beast's palace. Beauty lies prostrate on her bed; she knows her father is dying and insists that she must go to him. The Beast, standing at the foot of the bed, relents, but extracts a promise that she will return in a week.

He leads her on to the balcony of her room, points to the pavilion of Diana, and explains that it contains his true riches. The subjective shot of the pavilion (as Beauty sees it) is from a very high angle, so that it looks small, like a jewel casket or doll house. The Beast then speaks of the five secrets of his power: a rose, the magic mirror, a golden key to the pavilion, his horse, and his glove. Beauty has already received the rose; she now is being given the key and glove; later the Beast will send to her his horse and the mirror. The possible symbolic meanings of these objects have been discussed earlier in "Themes and Interpretations."

The Beast makes clear that he is placing his power in her hands to prove his trust, especially because all will be hers if he should die. He insists that he will die if she does not return in a week's time. With the words, "Remember your promise," he leaves the room.

By means of the Beast's glove, Beauty is magically transported from the palace to her father's villa.

III. Beauty Comes Home

The Merchant revives at the sight of his daughter. In their conversation, Beauty confesses her feelings of sympathy and pity for her captor, and she declares, "The monster is good." Music is heard as she speaks of the Beast.

The famous sheet scene follows. The white bedsheets on clotheslines function at the beginning and end of the scene as curtains, in the latter case somewhat ironically as Avenant smiles and almost looks directly at the camera as he drops a sheet he has been holding up and follows the others. Within the scene the sheets are surfaces of white at various levels of depth on a two-dimensional screen; they frame actors within a shot (for example, Avenant chopping wood), or they are props around which the actors are artistically arranged (as when the young people, only their heads visible above and to one side of a sheet, first see Beauty in the distance and mistake her for a lady from court). One is reminded of the way Japanese film directors use screens in interior scenes in a similar manner. A major difference, of course, is that the decorated screens are works of art in themselves, whereas Cocteau has taken bedsheets, one of the most mundane of household objects, and transformed them into planes of abstract beauty.

The sheets are not essential to the action of the plot; the scene could have occurred in another setting. Perhaps this is why Cocteau, eight years after *Beauty and the Beast* appeared, declared this scene too picturesque, an example of beautiful photography for its own sake (*Cocteau on the Film*, New York, 1954, p. 94). There is definitely a self-conscious artistry evident that is out of keeping with the tone already established for the setting of the Merchant's house.

Beauty is welcomed by her brother and Avenant, but her rich attire arouses the jealousy of her sisters. In speaking to the two young men, she mentions that she possesses the key to the Beast's treasure.

Plots begin immediately. Avenant cannot stand the thought of Beauty returning to the palace and the possibility of treasure attracts him. He insists to Ludovic that he does not believe in magic, so the Beast will have no power over him. Meanwhile, the two sisters, feigning tearful sorrow (with the help of onions) at the prospect of losing Beauty, entreat her to remain longer than a week. Félicie steals the key to the pavilion of Diana and eventually gives it to Avenant. The two young men will leave as soon as they can find a way to reach the palace.

Beauty is back to serving the others at dinner and to being insulted by her sisters. Avenant tries to persuade her to leave with him. He promises to reform and go to work. He insists that the Beast has forgotten her; however, Beauty only shakes her head with tears in her eyes. There is music once again on the sound track.

A shot of the Beast pacing up and down in Beauty's palace room. His despair is evident in all his gestures, contradicting Avenant's assertion.

The sisters, Ludovic, and Avenant are in the stable when Magnificent arrives carrying the magic mirror. The young men mount him and leave. Adélaide for the first time shows a touch of humanity as she worries about her brother and Avenant. This concern is not shared by Félicie. In turn each looks into the mirror: Adélaide's reflection is that of a repulsive hag; Félicie sees a monkey dressed as she is. Neither admits to the other what the mirror revealed to her.

The two deliver the mirror to Beauty, who is dressed in one of her palace gowns, with a lie as to where it came from. After the sisters leave, she gently and lovingly presses it to her cheek. Beauty lies down on her bed with the mirror on a table beside it. Cocteau brilliantly arranges the scene, which could have been simply one of Beauty looking into the mirror and cuts from her to the mirror and back. Instead, he positions the camera so that we see Beauty lying in bed and over her right shoulder her reflection in the mirror—a striking composition. She moves forward a little; her reflection disappears and the face of the Beast appears. He is obviously very ill.

Quickly Beauty puts on the glove, leans back in bed, and vanishes. In a moment she is in her room in the palace, but she remembers that she does not have the golden key. She returns to her father's house and searches desperately for it. The plight of the Beast is more important. For the second time she leans back in her bed at home. As she does so, the mirror shatters. An instant later the bed is empty.

IV. Beauty Returns to the Beast

Beauty runs from her palace room, down the stairs, and outside to the gardens. She repeatedly calls out in anguished tones, "My Beast!" The camera is generally stationary, depending primarily on panning and cuts to create a sense of Beauty's desperate search.

She discovers the Beast lying at the edge of the pond where she first saw him drinking. The camera tracks in as Beauty attempts to lift his head. During the tracking we see a couple of swans pecking viciously at the hand of their fallen master. "I am the monster, Beast. You must live!" Beauty exclaims. In a close-up the Beast only whispers, "Too late."

Cut to Avenant and Ludovic at the pavilion of Diana. The latter is more interested in getting at the treasure than killing the Beast. The keyhole in the door glows mysteriously as the golden key is brought near it. Fearing a trap, they decide to break in through the glass skylight. Avenant leading the way, the two climb up to the roof. They see below a glittering treasure surrounding a statue. Avenant identifies the statue as Diana.

We return to the dying Beast. Beauty encourages him to fight death. He replies in a tight close-up that he could do so if he were a man, but poor beasts can only prove their love by giving up their lives. His eyes close slowly and he dies.

The cross-cutting continues between Beauty and the Beast at the pond and Avenant and Ludovic at the pavilion. Avenant breaks in the glass and, holding on to Ludovic's hands, his back to the statue, lets himself down. Cut to the statue with snow drifting down on it. Slowly it turns in the direction of Avenant and fixes an arrow to a stringless bow.

A series of quick cuts accelerates the visual movement. The arrow enters the back of Avenant. Three subjective shots seen from the point of view of Ludovic follow: Avenant's face and then his hands are transformed into those of the Beast; finally, the crumpled body of the Beast-Avenant lies on the floor of the pavilion.

At the pond a miraculous metamorphosis occurs: the dead Beast comes alive as a handsome prince. His erect form swings straight up from the ground before a startled Beauty. The Prince explains that because his parents did not believe in magic, they were punished through him. He could only be saved by a look of love, for love can make man a beast and beautify ugliness. Beauty soon gets over her ambiguous feelings about the fact that the Prince looks so much like Avenant, and accepts him. He will now take her through the air to his kingdom, where she will be queen; her father will be there and her sisters will carry her train.

During this scene there have been two inserts. The first is a shot of the smoking glove of the beast near the pond. The second is of the body of the Beast-Avenant, also smoking, in the pavilion, the snow falling on him, the treasure now a heap of dead leaves and branches.

In a field where the Prince brings Beauty, he kisses her hand and puts an arm around her. In a long shot we see the two rise into the air. Against a background of clouds, they whirl and fly away. The last shot of the film is of the billowing clouds, a suitable closing curtain for a fairy tale.

Style and Approach

We are all aware that the making of a film requires the talents of many artists and technicians. The director is the most important figure, for he must orchestrate the efforts of the individuals involved and establish a consistent style that results in, hopefully, a seamless unity of form and content. With most films we can hazard only tentative generalizations about the contribution of each major member of a film-making team and the intellectual principles and intuitive insights that guided a director in the multitude of decisions he must make in the stages of preproduction, production, and postproduction. *Beauty and the Beast* is an exception. We have a good deal of information about the creation of the film because Cocteau published, in 1950, *Diary of a Film*, an account of the year (August 1945 to June 1946) he devoted to directing *Beauty and the Beast*. In addition, he refers to the film a number of times in a series of interviews with André Fraigneau which appeared under the title *Cocteau on the Film*, New York, 1954.

These statements give us an opportunity to discuss those chief elements and techniques of the film that influenced Cocteau's general style and approach: costumes, music, lighting, dialogue, acting, use of the camera, and cinematic illusions. Whenever possible we will quote from Cocteau's *Diary of a Film*.

Cocteau rightly pays high tribute to the decor and costumes of Christian Bérard:

His costumes with their elegance, power, and sumptuous simplicity play just as big a part as the dialogue; they reinforce the slightest gesture, and the artists find them comfortable. (Ibid., pp. 34–35.)

This statement applies, with one exception, only to the costumes worn by the Beast, the Prince, and Beauty at the palace, for the Merchant's family and Avenant are clothed in practical if graceful apparel. The exception is the first scene in the film when the two sisters are dressed with some elegance, although hardly sumptuously, as they prepare for their visit to court. Later, Cocteau confirms this distinction between palace and house with the remark: "apart from Beauty when she's dressed as the Princess, none of the women wear jewelry." (Ibid., p. 53.)

In commenting on the costumes, the director makes a passing complaint with which surely every viewer of the film would agree: "What a pity it is that France cannot afford the luxury of colour films." (Ibid., p. 35.) (He was writing in 1945; World War II had just ended and France's film industry was working under the most stringent conditions.) There are films that demand a dimension they are lacking. Dreyer's *The Passion of Joan of Arc*, for example, is like a mute person desperately wishing to speak. Similarly, *Beauty and the Beast* seems incomplete without color. To an enthusiast of the film the following observation by Cocteau is distressing: "The arrival of Beauty at the wash-house, wearing her grand sky-blue dress, surrounded by black chickens, was an absolute miracle." (Ibid., p. 35.)

We have noted more than once the lack of background music when the setting is the Merchant's villa, except when the horse Magnificent carries someone to the palace or Beauty arrives home and speaks of the Beast. In these cases, music clings like perfume to anyone or anything associated with the world of the Beast. Music also reinforces the mystery of the palace. It ranges from being an almost imperceptible auditory aura to being an indispensable contributor to the dramatic intensity of a scene. At climactic moments a chorus sings a melody without words, as though at those times the characters are closest to the spirits that dwell in the palace and can hear them. Without the choral background, experiencing the memorable scene in which Beauty, after arriving at the palace, floats through the hallway on the upper floor would be like tasting an exquisite wine without being allowed to inhale its bouquet and to contemplate its color.

Anyone attempting to describe in words a musical work usually finds himself resorting to verbal images that draw a smile of pity rather than approval from a reader. Cocteau, however, is more successful than most when in one poetic sentence he sums up Georges Auric's score for *Beauty and the Beast*. After insisting that the music impregnates and consummates the film, he writes: "The Beast enchants us till we sleep and this music is the dream within our sleep." (Ibid., p. 194.)

Lighting is another means by which the mystery of the palace and the realism of the house are underlined. As Cocteau points out, the exterior of the palace or "Beast's Park" is in perpetual twilight, no matter what the time. Within the palace a conflict of darkness and light from candles and fireplace creates a fluid pattern of shadows. At times a fog seeps through the corridors and staircases, reminding us of the smoke from the Beast's fingers. Some objects, such as the statues, glow with an inner light. Beauty's room is always well lit, but even that illumination has an unnatural evenness and coldness of tone, as though the light were frozen within the four walls.

In contrast, the Merchant's villa appears to be naturally lit. At daytime there is sunlight and the expected deep shadows, as in the sheet scene. At night the lighting also offers no surprises. Here is a world we recognize, with nothing of the preternatural about it.

The dialogue in the film is spare and simple. Only the Beast and Avenant have speeches of any length. Most of the time the characters speak one-sentence lines. The lines themselves are straightforward, contain practically no imagery, and usually devoid of adjectives and adverbs.

This degree of brevity and simplicity is not found in Cocteau's other scripts. For example, those for *Orpheus* and *The Eternal Return* are approximately twice as long as that for *Beauty and the Beast*, even though the running time of the latter is four minutes more than *Orpheus* and ten minutes less than *The Eternal Return*. Cocteau's scenarios are always more enigmatic in content and visual imagery than they are elaborate in language, except for *The Blood of the Poet*. However, *Beauty and the Beast* possesses the most unadorned speeches of all his films.

The restraint in the dialogue is echoed in the style of acting Cocteau imposed on his actors:

One could treat the film in an entirely different way . . . but instinctively I am after a more simple approach. . . . The other method wouldn't suit the short lines that I have given the characters . . . they need movements stripped of unnecessary gesticulation and clutter. (Ibid., p. 53.)

We pointed out earlier that essentially Beauty is a figure in a fable, less a character than an archetypal image of beauty and virtue. Probably this is what Cocteau had in mind as he repeatedly mentions in his diary that he encouraged Josette Day to express herself more in movement than in speech or facial expressions. Mlle. Day was once a dancer, and it shows. The director remarks, in *Cocteau on Film* (p. 75), that the background of his main actress enabled him to film the arrival of Beauty at the palace in slow motion: "Now it is very dangerous to use slow motion for a person who is running. Every fault of movement is revealed."

Even though Beauty is graceful at all times, it is in the palace that her movements edge toward the artificiality and intensified beauty of dance. This is most obvious in her arrival at the palace, especially that exaggerated sweep of her body just before she enters the hallway on the upper floor. There are also her stately, stylized gestures as she walks with the Beast, such as when she places her uplifted hand on his fist as though beginning a minuet.

The most intense emotions in the film are reserved for the Beast. His fantastic make-up, however, restricts his facial expressions to his eyes. As with Beauty, he uses his body to advantage. We note his elegant stance when he accosts the Merchant, the flourish of his gestures as he walks or stands with Beauty, his athletic vigor when he jumps from the window after Beauty has told him about Avenant; he is not even awkward as he runs on all fours or laps up water from a pond. He combines the natural grace of an animal with the refined movements of an aristocrat. Compare the way the Beast walks with the almost stamping stride of Avenant; for instance, when the latter moves from the Merchant's stable to the horse Magnificent. The fact that the two characters are played by the same actor, Jean Marais, makes us realize how consciously the two roles were individualized by the director and the actor.

The settings, costumes, music, script, and actors were, so to speak, the raw material that Cocteau molded into an aesthetic unity with his camera. The visual illusions he created for the film have given many viewers the impression that Cocteau uses his camera with a technical virtuosity, often for its own sake, that one associates with Orson Welles or Luis Buñuel. Actually, Cocteau's cinematic style is closer to that of Jean Renoir. He favors lengthy shots, a generally stable camera, and clear transitions from one shot to another.

Anyone who doubts that Cocteau's style in *Beauty and the Beast* is basically simple should turn back to those pages in "Analysis of Major Sequences" in which we detailed camera technique. Take, for example, the scene from the moment Beauty first enters the palace to when she flees from her room (pp. 226–227). This takes three and a half minutes, yet there are only nine shots. The camera tracks in or out during two of these shots and pans in three. Only in one shot does the director use a moving camera beyond tracking.

Surely Cocteau could not have been more straightforward in the directing of this series of shots. This not to say that he is an unsophisticated director. In his other films, he is far more experimental, including in *Orpheus,* for instance, a 360° pan. In *Beauty and the Beast* he consciously attempted to keep his camera technique as uncomplicated as possible, as these quotations from the diary confirm:

In a spirit of instinctive contradiction I am avoiding all camera movement, which is so much in fashion that the experts think it is indispensable.

This film must prove that it's possible to avoid camera movement and keep to a fixed frame.

I suppose it's because I'm trying to keep the camera fixed and the shots simple, that makes Bérard say my angles are flat. (Ibid., pp. 27, 50, 64.)

We think of *Beauty and the Beast* as filled with surprises and mysteries. This effect is primarily because of the illusions created in the film. These illusions can be divided into two types: those that depend on stage props and those that would be impossible without a camera.

The first category includes the living statues and the arms holding the candelabra. Doors controlled by wires open and close magically. By means of a platform on wheels pulled by a rope, Beauty seems to float through the upper story hallway when she first arrives at the palace. The Beast, after hearing the name of Avenant, leaps from a window of the palace with the hidden aid of a springboard. Wind, fog, and the smoking fingers of the Beast could have been presented in the theater as well as on the screen.

The fabulous make-up created by Arakelian for the Beast belongs with this group of theatrical devices (Figure 10–5). Jean Marais did not wear a mask, but make-up that was applied layer by layer. It took three hours each time simply to prepare Marais' head. The actor's dedication is un-

FIGURE 10–5. *Head of the Beast (Courtesy Janus Films.)*

questionable, for the glue constricted his circulation, he sometimes had to keep his make-up on for fifteen hours at a stretch, and he could only take liquid sustenance through a straw. The psychological effect of the Beast's appearance on the actor is interesting. Cocteau notes:

Marais is visibly distressed by his make-up. He's revolted by his own appearance. And trying to control his feelings he has about him a quiet tension, which shows through his normal interpertation of the role. (Ibid., p. 71.)

Most of the illusions created by Cocteau for *Beauty and the Beast* depend on certain mechanical devices of which only a motion picture camera is capable: slow and reverse motion, superimposition, and stop-action photography. Also essentially cinematic are special effects editing and cheat shots.

Slow motion is used not only for the scene in which Beauty arrives at the castle, but also in some cases in which reverse motion is necessary. A couple of examples of a combination of the two types of motion occur at the end of the film. In the first, the Beast turns into the Prince and rises from the ground: "a shot of him falling backwards which we'll project by reversing in slow motion so that it will look as though he rises in a single bound with the grace of another world." (Ibid., p. 178.) A few moments later the Prince and Beauty appear to fly into the sky. The illusion was achieved by having Marais and a stand-in for Josette Day jump backward from a twelve-foot high stage to the ground; this movement was shot in slow motion from the top of the platform and projected in reverse. Reverse motion also accounts for the candles in the candelabra seeming to burst into flames spontaneously.

Superimposition made possible the change of Avenant into the Beast after the former is killed by Diana: "Marais as Avenant and Diot [a stand-in] as the Beast had each to stay absolutely motionless, one each side of a glass and superimpose their reflections one on another." (Ibid., p. 173.)

In stop-action photography the camera and actors are stopped during a shot, changes are made in the scene, and then the camera and actors continue; the result can be an effect of magical transformation. An example in *Beauty and the Beast,* with the help of superimposition, is Beauty's instantaneous transfer from the palace to her father's villa and back again. Some of the mirror shots also appear to depend on this technique.

Special-effects editing attains the same results as stop-action photography but does so through editing together separate shots rather than working within a single shot. When the Beast carries Beauty into her room, her apparel changes as they cross the threshold. Cocteau obviously first photographed Beauty in her simple dress and cloak from outside the door and then repeated the action with Beauty wearing a magnificent gown, but during the repeat the camera was positioned in the room facing the door. Eventually he intercut the two shots. There is also the scene in which the two sisters look in turn into the magic mirror and one sees a hag and the other a monkey. Separate shots were done of Mila Parely (Adélaide) made up as an ugly old woman in the frame of the mirror without glass and a black backdrop and then of a monkey in the same setting. The two shots were finally edited into the scene so that it appears that the sisters are seeing these images as reflections.

In a cheat shot part of a background is excluded so that the viewer does not see how an effect has been achieved, such as when an actor seems to fall from a great height but is actually caught by a hidden net a few feet below. In each case in *Beauty and the Beast* in which a candelabrum hangs in air, the camera angle and lighting were arranged so that we do not perceive the black wire supports. A cheat shot also is used when the Beast watches a deer and his ears twitch. The camera excludes from view a person behind Jean Marais animating the ears with a forked twig.

We have quoted from *Diary of a Film* to help us understand the whys and hows of the film. There is also material in this book, however, that does not necessarily increase our appreciation of the work of art we see on the screen, but will be of interest to anyone who wants to learn about the process of film making. The first type of information consists of Cocteau's views on improvisation versus rigid planning. The second concerns the difficulties encountered in shooting the film.

Near the end of the book we find this sentence: "The film evidently is the very opposite to improvisation, it opposes an unscaleable wall to anarchy." (Ibid., p. 191.) Yet, at the beginning of the volume the author writes: "Too much care, no doors open to chance, and poetry, which is difficult enough to trap, will certainly be frightened away. Whereas a little improvisation makes it come a bit nearer." (Ibid., p. 150.)

These two statements are not irreconcilable when one learns of Cocteau's method of film making. Before film production even begins, he has planned every shot. In his mind is an image of every illusion that he hopes to create. In actual production, though, problems come up to which he must adjust. The ideal yields to the reality of a shooting schedule, a sick actress, an effect that is too expensive and must be eliminated, a shot or even a whole scene that simply does not come off. Most important, the director and his colleagues must be open to the unexpected, the unforeseen, the visual poetry that arises spontaneously.

Particularly striking are three instances that Cocteau mentions in his book of accidents or unplanned events that were incorporated into the film and enhanced it. When the scene in which the Beast is dying by the edge of a pond was being photographed, the crew attempted to prevent the swans, angered by collars that had been put around their necks, from pecking at Jean Marais. Cocteau, however, recognized that the sight of the swans attacking their sick and powerless master "added a terrible pathos to the scene." (Ibid., p. 173.) In the scene in which the Merchant awakens in the palace, only in the actual shooting did the director notice the actor's hand on the end of the arm of the chair carved in the shape of a lion's head. Cocteau perceived that by a close-up he could suggest that the hand woke up at the beast's roar and ran away. (Ibid., pp. 156–157.) In one of the earliest scenes in the film, the two sisters go to their sedan chairs and find chickens in them. This had been carefully prepared. It was a surprise, however, when Félicie sat down and two ducks came out in single file from beneath her skirt. This delightful touch was left in; the only problem was preventing the crew from bursting into laughter. (Ibid., p. 48.)

At the opposite pole from "discovered" images is the rejection of film footage or even scenes. Sometimes Cocteau notes that an effect did not photograph properly and there was no opportunity to redo it. More often material was eliminated because it did not fit into the over-all rhythm of a sequence. We are often not given a specific reason. For instance, he describes a comic scene in which Ludovic and Avenant lock the Merchant in a cupboard (Ibid., p. 133). In the printed script (Cocteau, *Three Screenplays*, New York, 1972) there is another scene involving the two young men in which they steal from and knock down the usurer. Neither incident appears in the final print, and we are not told why. Cocteau is more specific about a long panning shot of Beauty's room: it was suppressed because it was "redundant." (Ibid., p. 190.)

One may not always agree with Cocteau's decisions. We believe, for example, that the shots of Beauty's room are too abrupt and that a long pan would have preserved the slow rhythm that was established before and continued after.

The difficulties encountered in making *Beauty and the Beast* are delineated in great detail in *Diary of a Film*. Any film, dependent as it is on so many individuals and under the pressure of schedules and limited financing, faces problems in being produced. Surely, though, few distinguished films were created under more adverse conditions than *Beauty and the Beast*.

First of all, Cocteau endured a number of illnesses that read like a list of the afflictions of Job. During the nine months of shooting, Cocteau suffered at one time or another, and often simultaneously, from boils, toothaches, impetigo, inflammations of the eyes and hands, tracheitis, lymphangitis, and jaundice. As if this were not enough, the actress Mila Parely (Adélaide) fell off the horse Aramis (Magnificent) and was hospitalized; during almost the entire time she was involved in the film she ran high fevers and was generally ill and nervous. Jean Marais developed a carbuncle on his thigh and contracted a cold that lasted for months.

This film was made almost immediately after the end of World War II. Film stock was poor and difficult to obtain. Processing laboratories were understaffed and disorganized, so that negatives came back scratched.

The electric current was undependable, which meant that on a set or on location lighting was unavailable for hours and, even worse, at any time film footage could be lost in the laboratory if the current went off at the wrong time. In addition to these unusual problems, there were the typical ones of periods of inclement weather, props that did not work, and the inevitable human errors.

It is a miracle that a final print was ever produced, but a miracle for which one is grateful. Whatever shortcomings the film may have, few others in the history of cinema have conveyed so vividly to the screen an aura of beauty and mystery. In this respect, *Beauty and the Beast* ranks with the best works of Jean Vigo, Jean Renoir, Akira Kurosawa, and Marcel Carné.

CHAPTER 11

Rashomon

Directed by AKIRA KUROSAWA

Japanese are terribly critical of Japanese films, so it is not too surprising that a foreigner should have been responsible for my film's being sent to Venice. It was the same with Japanese woodcuts—it was the foreigners who first appreciated them. We Japanese think too little of our own things. Actually, Rashomon *wasn't all that good, I don't think. Yet, when people have said to me that its reception was just a stroke of luck, a fluke, I have answered by saying that they only say these things because the film is, after all, Japanese, and then I wonder: Why do we all think so little of our own things? Why don't we stand up for our films? What are we so afraid of?*

> Akira Kurosawa (Quoted in Donald Richie, *The Films of Akira Kurosawa,*
> Los Angeles and Berkeley, 1970, p. 80.)

. . . the Western and the Japanese live side by side in my mind naturally, with the least sense of conflict.

> Akira Kurosawa (Quoted in "Kurosawa and his Work," by Akira Iwasaki,
> trans. John Bester, reprinted in *Focus on Rashomon,* ed. by Donald Richie,
> Englewood Cliffs, N.J., 1972, p. 22.)

CAST

TAJOMARU, THE BANDIT	*Toshiro Mifune*
TAKEHIRO, THE SAMURAI-HUSBAND	*Masayuki Mori*
MASAGO, THE WIFE	*Machiko Kyo*
THE WOODCUTTER	*Takashi Shimura*
THE PRIEST	*Minoru Chiaki*
THE COMMONER	*Kichijiro Ueda*
THE POLICE AGENT	*Daisuke Kato*
THE MEDIUM	*Fumiko Homma*

CREDITS

DIRECTOR	*Akira Kurosawa*
SCREENPLAY	*Shinobu Hashimoto and Akira Kurosawa, after two short stories by Ryunosuke Akutagawa*
PRODUCER	*Jingo Minoru*
DIRECTOR OF PHOTOGRAPHY	*Kazuo Miyagawa*
ART DIRECTOR	*So Matsuyama*

243

CREDITS (Continued)

LIGHTING   *Kenichi Okamoto*
MUSIC   *Fumio Hayasaka*

        1950   Black and white   88 minutes

Perspective: National Cinema

Rashomon interests us first and foremost because it is a masterwork of
cinema art. Beyond that, however, it has considerable historical significance, for this film was by itself responsible for the introduction to the
world of a whole national genre called Japanese films. (This it accomplished by winning the Grand Prize at the Venice Film Festival of 1951,
after which it was purchased for distribution in Europe and the United
States.) After the success of *Rashomon*, we began to see a steady stream
of beautiful and satisfying Japanese films. Our experience of films was
enriched by the addition.

The experience raises several questions: What is a *national genre?* In
what ways will a definition of the term help us to analyze a specific
film? Just what is Japanese about *Rashomon?*

Now it is a commonplace to say that virtually all the industrial nations
of the world (and some not so heavily industrial) have by now developed their own national cinemas. Like any other cultural mode of expression, cinema traditions embody the exact and distinctive identity of
peoples and nations. The Japanese cinema is no exception. Thus, it is
worthwhile to consider its special nature on the grounds that the Japanese
culture, like other Asian cultures, is farther removed from our own than,
say, the traditions of Western Europe. We are simply (and still, alas) on
one end of the dichotomy of East and West.

Yet it would take a volume or more to discuss the particular character
of Japanese cinema; so our essay in this direction will of necessity be
brief and perhaps somewhat simplified. (To appreciate this fact, see, for
example, *The Japanese Film*, by Joseph L. Anderson and Donald Richie,
New York, 1960; and *Japanese Movies*, by Donald Richie, New York,
1961. The account that follows is based largely on these works.)

There is, in Japan, a real lust for classifying films. There are literally
dozens of classifications of film types and even subdivisions of these. One
of the largest and most popular, however, is the *jidai-geki,* or period
film. To this group, *Rashomon* nominally belongs (although as we will
see, Kurosawa is far from having deliberately chosen to work in a specific
genre). These may have either a medieval setting or refer back a mere
hundred years or so. They are usually saturated with gruesome concat-
enations of violent action—sword play is virtually obligatory—and, al-

though there may be many variations of plot and resolution, certain Japanese values are consistent in them.

For example, there is nearly always a dramatization of the conflict between duty and emotional inclination. In the working out of this conflict, Anderson and Richie emphasize that in any event the action is "usually compelled by forces outside the characters involved, because the governing philosophy (of the films) is that an individual's ability to influence his future is almost nonexistent . . . the course of action is usually compelled by fate." (Op. cit., p. 316)

Now the very concept of duty in a Japanese cultural context must include the duty toward one's personal honor, a state of grace inexorably bound up with one's obligations to class, caste, and institution. Invariably, these considerations have emphatic importance in not only this but other Japanese genres as well. Needless to say, there is a tendency in Japanese films for the action to depict a triumph of duty, honor, and obligation; the social good comes out on top.

In every Japanese genre, moreover, values and attitudes—regardless of how close they *might* seem to those of the West—are essentially antithetical to Western ideas and assumptions. For example, one of the ideas permeating Western culture in the last seventy-five years has been the notion of reality having multiple dimensions, the idea of the mask and the face; it is surely a coin of our cultural currency that objective reality is only *part* of the story, that subjective truth must be counted into the equation. The corollary of this concept is that of unique personal identity. If subjectivity counts, each such sum is individual and unique.

By contrast, Eastern philosophy—its root assumption—is at an opposite pole. "The Eastern assumption," Donald Richie notes, "is that reality lies on the surface and that things are real, to this extent, all the way through . . . the mask *is* the face" (Richie, *Focus on Rashomon,* op. cit., p. 2.) The corollary to this is that Western ideas of "personality" are unknown.

As we proceed to analyze the film, we will be struck again and again by ways in which *Rashomon transcends* and subverts (while at the same time embodying!) its Japanese generic class and its identity as a *Japanese* film.

What is left to say is that certain specific elements of Japanese techniques and visual (cinematic) motifs—belonging to the Japanese national genre—are also displayed in *Rashomon.*

Japanese film makers are in the habit of using haikulike images in their films. (The practice sometimes sounds suspiciously like associative montage, a technique developed and used by Eisenstein, among others, in which two disparate images are juxtaposed in order to invest the first with the attributes of the second.)

Kurosawa used a little haiku image in *Yojimbo* (1961): to indicate the hero's (Mifune's) recovery from a savage beating by the boss' underlings.

Kurosawa first focuses on a close-up of a leaf as it is caught in the wind; as he pans with it, a knife impales the leaf on the wood floor of a cottage near a stream. The shot widens to include Mifune and the self-satisfied look on his face. Thus we can see that he had thrown the knife, and we can also see that he is now so adept at knife throwing that his recovery—his hand is now fast enough to contend with nature (the leaf and the wind)—has been signaled in a flash by the image. In *Rashomon,* there is a continuous manipulation of sun breaking through the crowns of thickly growing trees and shots of the forest floor showing the patterns created by the same sun—all in the service of haikulike revelation.

In fact, nature itself as context and personification is very commonly depicted in Japanese films. (To be sure these uses are not unknown in the West, but the frequency with which they are used in Japan is worth noting.) Of the symbolic use of rain, for example, Anderson and Richie say that "it rains frequently in Japan and perhaps more frequently in Japanese pictures. . . . a scene in the rain is almost obligatory. . . . a sure sign that a film is Japanese." (Op. cit., p. 325)

Finally, we suspect that a unique part of the tradition of early Japanese silent cinema may have something to do with a central aspect of *Rashomon.* We refer to the Japanese *benshi.* The *benshi* was a highly prestigious and vital part of a silent screen performance. He "explained" the film, supplying information that in other countries was offered through title cards. From the beginning, the role of the *benshi* expanded to include interpretation. An unfailingly curious people, the Japanese were eager to know everything about the film they were watching. (Indeed, this interest and curiosity extended to the projection equipment; one exhibitor, catering to this taste, put the projectionist and the screen onstage. Thus, the audience was restricted to a rather oblique angle view of the screen, but they were more than satisfied by the splendid view they had of the magic lantern itself.)

Thus, the role of the *benshi* became so important that they were frequently paid more than the movie stars, and the craft at one time attracted some of the best of the stage actors in Japanese theater. Moreover, after a time, film producers began to distribute explanatory scripts along with prints of their films and the *benshi* became thereby artistic contributors to the work on screen by often filling in continuity (saving producers the money required to insert explanatory visuals). Indeed, it is ironic to note that *Rashomon* was at first so puzzling to Japanese audiences that for a little while the tradition was revived and *benshi* were hired to explain this puzzling work.

To us it seems that the tradition of the *benshi* is alive in the narrative drive of *Rashomon.* The film literally turns on the idea of knowledge and explanation from a certain source—the Woodcutter. The role of the audience demanding to know is in a way assumed by the Commoner.

But what of these sources? What drives them to know and to tell? And what of their stories?

Story and Characterization

The film revolves around an incident of rape, theft, and possible homicide perpetrated by the Bandit on the Samurai and his Wife. The "facts" of the case are narrated by a Woodcutter and a Buddhist Priest to a third party, a Commoner, as he is designated in the script, but perhaps better described in our terms as a drifter. These three have taken shelter from the rain under a ruined gate (known as the Rashomon) to the medieval Japanese city of Kyoto. It is a time of famine and ruinously destructive little civil wars and thus a time when the rules of human conduct are only lightly in force.

Although there seem to be four individual accounts of this single incident—the genius of the film lies partly in creating this plausible illusion—all four versions are actually filtered through either the Woodcutter or the Priest. When three of the versions (Bandit, Wife, Husband) turn out to be contradictory in vital respects, the Woodcutter is forced (by the sheer power of the narration he has given and heard?) to revise his story and to admit that he had observed more than he had at first been willing to admit. His version adds to the store of contradictions.

When he has finished his final narration, the cry of an infant is heard. The Commoner finds it and proceeds to strip off its clothing. While the Priest shelters the child in his arms, the Woodcutter attacks the Commoner's ruthless lack of feeling. The Commoner defends himself with his cynicism and then forces the Woodcutter to admit his own avarice in having stolen the dagger belonging to the Samurai. Stung by his own admission, the Woodcutter reaches out for the child, but the Priest recoils—mistrusting now the Woodcutter's intentions. But the Woodcutter wants only to adopt the baby and make it a member of his larger family. The Priest is satisfied (his faith in men is restored) and, as the rain ends and the sunlight begins to shine down on the gate, the Woodcutter goes off with the child tenderly cradled in his arms.

Even without thinking very much we can see that this narrative pattern is an exquisite design that strikes the very bell note of contemporaneity: the relativity of truth, the subjective coloring of the nature of reality, violence, shock, outrage, and the moral landscape of these things—all speak powerfully to a modern consciousness. In addition, it is richly suited to cinematic representation insofar as the various versions of the central incident spring from the imaged experience (be it what they have *seen* or merely *imagined*) of the narrators; what *they see*, in any case, is what they know; and what they tell is what *we see*.

Much space could be given over to analyzing the subtle intricacies of this narrative pattern, but we will limit ourselves to the following observations.

1. What we will call the frame story or the framing action—that is, the action that takes place at the gate while the rain is pouring down—is a late addition to Kurosawa's original idea (adapted from the Ryunosuke Akutagawa story, which is merely the testimony of the witnesses, or, in other words, the unencumbered narration of the four versions). Kurosawa tells us that the original production company, when approached to back the film, did not understand the material and this motivated him to add the framing action. So that the framing action would seem to be superfluous—and even so astute a critic as Parker Tyler would agree. But we cannot believe it, for the framing action seems to us crucial to Kurosawa's film.

For one thing, the three participants in the framing action represent a spectrum of moral interests. The Priest, who is desperate to believe (and finally does believe) in the goodness of all men, is at one end, while the Commoner, a persistent (if wise and sometimes insightful) cynic, is at the other; the Woodcutter is somewhere in between. Of the three, the Commoner is most firmly entrenched in his position. Both the Priest and the Woodcutter are shaky in theirs. It is this uncertainty shared by the two narrators that generates the telling of the tales. Without it, the *raison d'être* for the telling would be absent.

Moreover, it seems clear that whatever other meanings the film generates, the idea of renewal through participation in a complex recounting of experience is one of them. The renewal is clear in the symbolic resonance of the infant restored to a set of parents and hope springing up anew in the breast of the Priest. Without the framing action, both the tension of the narration (its generating force) and the moral dimension of its meaning would be seriously diminished.

2. Although there is a clear mystery presented by the doubly refracting narration (what is the truth of the Samurai's death? Did he die by sword or dagger? Who did it? Where did the Wife really go afterward?), *Rashomon* is not essentially a mystery film. Nothing in the film, no set of subtly placed clues and no pattern of character strengths and weaknesses can finally answer these questions. (For a review of all the evidence, see Donald Richie, *The Films of Akira Kurosawa*, Berkeley and Los Angeles, 1970, pp. 70 ff.)

For Kurosawa does not intend us to "solve" a whodunit. Nor are we to judge which of the participants is telling *the* truth. The mystery here is rather of another order, the mystery of existence itself, as Parker Tyler has pointed out (in his brilliant essay, "*Rashomon* As Modern Art," reprinted in his *The Three Faces of Film*, New York, 1960.)

3. Again as Tyler has pointed out, the viewer notices that the initial facts of the Bandit's attack, his tricking of the Samurai (and the Samurai's

greed in succumbing), and the rape of the Wife are not contested by any of the participants. Certain facts are indisputable: the human condition is marked by the here and now of rape and violence *and* the violent ambiguity of sexual experience. Neither the Wife nor the Husband disputes the Wife's reflexive participation in the rape she has at first fought to forestall.

We can consider the characters in two groups of three—the participants in the incident, and the moral participants in the narration. Of the former group, caste and role determine their motives and the shape of their narrative reconstructions. The Wife, by her own account, has behaved in the manner prescribed for her by her status. As the Wife of a Samurai, she has resisted—and spiritedly, at that: we need only recall that the Bandit was attracted by this quality in her—the rape, cannot remember (so unthinkable would it be) any offer to go off with the Bandit, and understood plainly the shame and dishonor accruing to her Husband on account of *her* dishonor. She is willing—perhaps even eager—to die rather than suffer the opprobrium of her Husband.

The Husband, too, is bound by the imperatives of his caste. Dishonor is visited on him by his ignominious defeat at the hands of the Bandit. His only possible response is suicide. (We should note that the suicide is not a ceremonial hara-kiri; the swift downward thrust of the dagger resembles nothing so much as an act of high emotion.) Thus, *his* recounting of events depicts the suicide. But it also includes salt rubbed in the wounds caused by the rape; according to his version, his Wife was ready to run off with the Bandit, making it a condition that the Bandit kill him beforehand. The base conduct of his Wife, in his view, shocked even his adversary so that he, the Bandit, would have been willing to kill the woman, should the Samurai have given the word. What is not in character for the Samurai—what seems to stand outside his rules of Samurai behavior—is his initial response to the Bandit. For the Bandit had appealed to his greed in order to get him to follow him into the woods.

As for the Bandit, he is of course the most interesting character of the three because he alone has had the freedom of action to initiate events. In his persona is acted out the classic conflict of the *jidai-geki* genre of Japanese films—that is, the conflict between passion and obligation. Because he is a Bandit, however, the decision is easily made on behalf of passion. And the animality of the Bandit, so ferociously embodied in Toshiro Mifune's portrayal, is the physical symbol of the runaway instinct. It is an incitement that goes far beyond the formalities of caste and class and reaches down to the bedrock of human behavior—a cataclysmic burst of human possibility.

All the narrators agree to this aspect of his character, although in his own recounting of events, while not denying his sweaty, bug-slapping, demonic nature, he nevertheless emphasizes evidence of his heroic stature.

Indeed, there is more than a little in his version to indicate his envy of the Samurai's status. For example, the Bandit is careful to insist that he bested the Samurai in a fair fight and he praises him for having been able to cross swords with the Bandit twenty-three times, noting that nobody else had been able to get past twenty. This bit of information serves to raise the Bandit to the level of the warrior caste because it shows him to have beaten one of them in fair combat.

What the narratives of all three have in common is the urge to enhance the self-image of the teller by a positive report of how each responded to the cataclysm of the Bandit's attack. In terms of the traditional Japanese conflict that we have discussed, each victim is eager to show himself to be the epitome of whatever dutiful virtues attach to his station and rank. They hope to overcome the triumph of passion by insisting on the stead-fastness and recuperative powers of duty and obligation. The Wife, for example, shows herself to be both a dutiful wife (she fights off the at-tacker with all her strength) and a dutiful *Samurai's* wife (she under-stands, first, even before her shock has worn off, that her Husband has been dishonored by the attack on her own person). The Husband depicts himself as a model of the honor and deportment bound to be exhibited by a member of his caste: he remains unreconciled with his Wife (be-cause she has failed to kill herself to make amends for her disgrace) and calmly commits hara-kiri himself (although we should note again that there is little in his performance of the formality such a ritual requires). Similarly, the Bandit colors himself as romantic, heroic, and liberated. Although he is realist enough to acknowledge his criminal vocation and his seedy man-ners, he is nevertheless proud of being the *famous* Bandit Tajomaru. Moreover, he depicts himself as sensitive and aesthetic (by virtue of the qualities in the Wife he claims most to admire, that is, "she was an angel" and "I admired her spirit"), chivalric (in his fight with the Samurai), a splendid horseman (witness how he turns on the Police Agent at the sug-gestion that *he* could have fallen from the horse), and above all, some-body who gets what he wants in this life.

Even the Woodcutter partakes of this modality. He, too, by indirec-tion, enhances his self-image by diminishing the stature of others; for his account of the trio in action is devastating to all their viewpoints; by his lights, the Wife is a shrew and both men are sniveling, henpecked cowards. By exposing their "lies," he puts into perspective his own (or *did* he steal the dagger?).

Themes and Interpretations

Parker Tyler, in his previously cited essay on the film, suggests that *Rashomon* deserves the status of a major artifact of modern art because it shares certain root affinities with the art of the exemplar of modernity,

Pablo Picasso. Tyler suggests that the character of the film is *multiform*—that its multiple perspectives on time are analogous to the multiple spatial perspectives of futurist painting and, especially, of such specimens of modern art as Picasso's *Guernica* and *Girl Before Mirror*. (To this one could add, of course, Duchamp's *Nude Descending a Staircase*.) The multiciplicity in both dimensions analyzes a single reality into its component, dialectic, resonant, competing, antagonistic parts. The reality is one though the perspectives be divided.

We agree with Tyler. *Rashomon*'s main theme is just that: reality is a complex of multiple perspectives, some of which conflict with each other but none of which, despite the appearance of contradiction, cancel each other out. Rather, they vibrate together in a kind of atonal harmony.

As this idea is dramatized in *Rashomon*, it generates further thematic implications—namely, that the perspective developed and narrated by each of the characters is in some sense an attempt at the restoration of morality. Here, as Tyler has pointed out, the initial incident—the attack and the rape—had the effect of wiping out all civilized standards, all morality, and the reconstruction of events by each participant-observer is a necessary piece of work in the restoration of civilization (another word for a complex of moral structures). Without this restoration, the film sems to say, civilization cannot proceed.

Not to be overlooked in an analysis of themes is the one mentioned earlier (see Story and Characterization, pp. 247–250)—namely, that the complex recounting of experience is a powerful agent of change and renewal. The effect of the narrative recounting in *Rashomon* can be seen clearly on the Woodcutter. From a state of agitated uncertainty in the beginning he moves, through the ritual of probing narratives, to a state of relative peace. In this final state, he is willing to accept not only his own imperfection but also (we must surmise) the imperfections of the Bandit, the Samurai and his Wife, and he can sustain his own faith with an act of charity. Thus, Kurosawa seems to make out a case for the moral efficacy of art.

Analysis of Major Sequences

1. The Beginning: The Woodcutter's Stories

After the title sequence, which consists of ten shots of the half-ruined Rashomon gate from various angles (the final one of which brings our eyes to rest on a massive pillar), we see a long shot, from a very low angle, of the gate. It is pouring down rain. The Priest and the Woodcutter sit silently within, staring off into space. This is followed by a medium shot of the same scene: we see the two from a higher angle and watch them in parallel profile as the Woodcutter speaks: "I can't understand it. I just can't." The Priest raises his head vacantly in response, then turns away again. When the Commoner arrives, he stands a little apart from the other two; and it is only the repeated thoughts of the Woodcutter that motivate him to join them. We see, then, a medium two-shot of the Commoner and the Woodcutter and then a three-shot. The composition of this three-shot is worth noting. On this graphic design, Kurosawa will wring miracles of subtly-textured triangular compositions, frequently played off against two-shots of various combinations of three people. One piece of the structural iron in his film is this extraordinary consistency of compositional elegance.

The Commoner's questions ("What's up? What's worrying you?") are answered by his two companions. The Priest says that despite his personal experience of war, famine, robbery, and various other atrocities, it is the "queerest" thing he has ever heard. For the Woodcutter, "it" is something simply inexplicable. The Priest's moral comparisons are too much for the Commoner. He moves away and begins to tear some loose boards from the gate in order to start a fire.

But the Woodcutter is agitated to the breaking point. He *must* speak. He moves to the Commoner and squats beside his fire. At the apex of the composition triangle is the Priest, sitting in the background. The Commoner agrees to hear the story the Woodcutter wants to tell. But "Take your time," he tells him, "this rain won't stop for some time."

There is a cut to a high-angle shot of the signboard identifying the ruined gate. The rain pours down. Camera tilts to reveal the three figures below, small in the frame. There is a cut to a tight close-up of the Wood-cutter; his eyes are opened wide as if he were caught up in some kind of mesmeric emotion. He begins his recollection.

This first sequence at the gate effectively sets the stage for the first flashback. The Commoner tearing boards loose from the partly ruined structure is an effective piece of characterization and the rain has now affected us with its symbolic value: it is as if something needed to be washed away, needed cleansing. The agitation of the Woodcutter and the solemn emotion of the Priest impel our interest in what the Wood-cutter must tell.

The Woodcutter describes his walk through the woods; how he came upon the Wife's and the Samurai's hats, an amulet case, and, finally the corpse of the Samurai; how he had run off in horror and gone straight to the police.

From the opening shot of the walk through the woods to the point where he halts, having seen the woman's hat on a tree branch, there are sixteen shots forming a superb vignette. The shots are virtually all mov-ing shots. That is, the camera itself moves, or, when it does not, it pans with the moving subject. Intercut are close-ups, medium shots, and a series of point-of-view shots looking up through the network of tree branches to observe dazzling patterns of sunlight filtering into the forest. Moreover, the shots are intercut in such a way as to confuse our orientation. The passage of the Woodcutter begins by showing his movement to be left to right across the frame; but this is altered. We track with him, following his back; he moves right to left; we track in front, leading him with the camera. We see him once towering above us as, from a very low angle, he crosses a log bridge across a small gully. All this time, a musical accompaniment is heard; it is a highly rhythmical woodwind orchestration and we hear it frequently in the film to enhance and underscore various moments of physical and emotional movement.

The effect of the walk through the woods is to impress on us a sense of profound mystery; we anticipate a great deal; we are lost; only stark and vibrant sunlight can guide us—to what? The second shot of the sequence, tracking after the Woodcutter in a shot holding the glinting axhead very close, adds an ominous note—a trill of terror.

These sunlight images have all the condensed power of haiku.

After the Woodcutter has seen the corpse, he runs through the woods (tossing away his axe) and there is a wipe (in the same direction as his run) to reveal him kneeling in the prison courtyard facing the magistrate of police.

This camera setup is one we will continue to see as each witness makes his appearance, and it is an ingenious solution to an obvious problem, as well as an artistic one. For by this means Kurosawa obviates the necessity of showing us the magistrate (who, it should be added, is also absent from the Akutagawa story). Moreover, the staging of the shot—the way the characters appear to be directing their stories to us—seems to ask the audience to judge the reliability of the various testimony. (However, if we look closely at the direction in which each witness looks, we notice their gazes are directed slightly higher than eye level, perhaps above and beyond us, hence beyond judgment itself.) We may also note the principal element in the graphic design of the frame: the horizontal line across the width of the frame provided by the wall of the courtyard in the background. It seems to weight the testimony delivered against it with a kind of leveling—as if the narratives were all to be given equal weight.

The shot of the Woodcutter in the courtyard is replaced by a wipe with a matching shot of the Priest. Now the figure of the Woodcutter is seen squatting in the right background, a witness to a witness. (Later, we will see *both* Priest and Woodcutter sitting in the background witness position. This serves to establish that they had indeed heard all the reports. Moreover, at one stage of the proceedings—when the Husband-medium reports that he had felt the dagger being withdrawn from his chest—it functions dramatically; for at that time, the Woodcutter reacts visibly to this report and we understand, with effective ambiguity, that it might have been the Woodcutter who removed the blade.) The Priest merely reports that several days earlier he had seen the Samurai and his Wife. We see this, economically rendered in a single, fluidly designed shot, and

FIGURE 11–1. *The Bandit falls into the hands of the police. (Courtesy Janus Films.)*

we notice a brief exchange of looks between the Samurai on foot and his Wife on the horse: the Samurai glances at her, smiling and proud, the picture of a proud and happy warrior.

Another wipe fills the frame with the Bandit, whose arms are firmly tied behind him, and the Police Agent who captured him. Obviously proud of the arrest he has made, the agent describes the capture in terms that the Bandit does not like (Figure 11–1). He did not fall from the horse, the Bandit retorts; he, the great Tajomaru, is a horseman of superb skills. To underline the point, there is a magnificent cut away to a distant horizon, very low across the frame, with a great and angry sky above. There, in dramatic silhouette, the Bandit rides his thunderous horse across the frame; one can hear the dramatic hooves, the flying musical accompaniment. Moreover, the Bandit goes on, *he must be believed* in this matter; for he is quite prepared to confess that *he had indeed killed the Samurai*—had bested him in fair combat. Because he is aware that he will be punished by execution for this there is no reason for him to lie. His testimony is truthful. So begins the first of the testimonies that are designed by each participant to enhance his self-image and to assure his auditors of his high moral stature.

The Bandit recalls his meeting with his victims.

We see the top of a hugely gnarled and fat-trunked tree. (We will not harp on the many phallic images present in the film, but the reader should be aware that this central incident is essentially a phallic attack and that such images are subtly but unmistakably present.) Camera tilts down the trunk and reveals the Bandit using as a pillow the base of another, nearby, tree sleeping off the heat of the afternoon. A tinkling music begins: high-pitched, delicate bells, disturbed by the wind into music. It signals the approach of the Samurai and his lady. In a closer, medium shot of the Bandit, camera dollies closer to him, then pans around, holding him in the foreground, as the pair approach. The camera movement here *links* the couple to the lone figure with visual precision.

A following shot of the traveling pair is followed by a close-up of the Bandit. He slaps at flies. He opens his eyes to glance at them. Her veil is closed. Nothing to see. The Samurai sees the sleeping figure, hesitates. For an exchange of two shots, they both stare—trying to assess one another. The Bandit scratches his leg, closes his eyes as if to sleep. The Samurai decides to move on. We see him start to go—although he moves toward us, toward camera.

Then comes the breeze. The Bandit had cited the importance of this breeze in the courtyard: "Suddenly I felt a cool breeze on my face. Yes, or else he wouldn't have been killed by me." Now he feels it in his hair. He opens his eyes and looks. What he sees is a shot that begins on her dainty feet as they trail over one side of the horse. Then camera tilts up to see that the same breeze has pushed aside her veil. Here is the beautiful Machiko Kyo. Back to the Bandit: his eyes are wide.

Again there is a tantalizing glimpse of Machiko Kyo, and the Bandit shifts his position. A medium shot from behind him catches in a panning movement the horse and couple moving past the sprawling figure; he arches his body to gaze after them. Now we see him alone: he decides something, then pulls closer to him the sword that has been resting between his legs.

Thus, "fate," he seems to say, through the agency of the wind that disturbed his sleep and offered him a glimpse of some ineffable beauty, has compelled his action.

The visual strength and elegance of this piece of film narrative is hard to overpraise. With just a few basic shots, some static shots of both parties to the rape, and some vital moving and panning shots linking them together graphically, Kurosawa has motivated the course of his film's inciting action. Using music, the stillness of the forest, the sunlight, tree shadows, actors—in short, the basic environment of the narrative—Kurosawa builds a crystal clear sequence. It is also worth noting the Bandit's choices in the telling of his tale; for example, he makes much of the wind; it is as if he were laying his behavior at the doorstep of fate. This is to generalize his motive for attack and to say that once having *glimpsed* the prize, he, *like anybody else,* had to have it. If the wind had visited any other full-blooded male, the story would have been essentially the same. Moreover, he is careful, up to this point, to assure us that he had no wish to kill the Husband. As he says after the rape, he is glad that he was able to accomplish his task without having to kill the Samurai. The story puts him in a class with all men.

Tajomaru runs after the couple. Leaping a brook, dropping down a steep slope, his journey accompanied by chase music, he catches up to them. The Samurai is at first suspicious, but soon surrenders to the Bandit's tale of buried swords and mirrors—available cheaply (Figure 11–2). He accompanies the Bandit into the woods where the latter jumps him, ties him up, and then races back—gleefully, demonically—to the Wife, whom he drags back through the woods to the tree where her Husband is tied.

There, in a kind of devilish, yet amazingly graceful ballet, he leaps at the spirited Wife; she resists, her arms flailing the white sleeves of her robe in futile swirls of antagonism. The Bandit is overjoyed; he likes it. Despite the gleaming dagger with which she attempts to ward him off, she has no chance (Figure 11–3). He catches her in his arms.

During this chase, we have cut back once to the Bandit testifying in the courtyard and heard his confession that "She stared at me in a childish manner—horrified" and that "her look made me envious of him—mad at him" [at the Samurai]. Now with the Wife in his arms, he has his wish. She claws at his face, but he struggles his head close and presses his lips to her mouth. There is a cut to the sky again—the motif of the sun blinding us as it arcs across the crowns of the great trees. They are close together, kissing, in a two shot; we notice her eyes fearfully, yet erotically, wide open. The sun shoots through the trees. Back and forth, through several closer and reverse angles, affording us clearer views of her one visible eye, we see the prolonged kiss, the echoing sun, and finally, an insert of her hand, in which is still clutched the useless dagger. Slowly her fingers open. The dagger falls straight and quivers its point into the ground. Now, from behind, close on Tajomaru's glistening back, we see her arms snake up and around his shoulders. She joins in the embrace (Figure 11–4).

A shock cut. We are back at the prison courtyard and hearing the hyena cackle of the Bandit enjoying his retrospective triumph. It is as if, for him, and for his auditors, a law of human nature has been confirmed; he cannot help but exult in such success.

Back in the forest, as he is preparing to move off and leave the assaulted couple, the Wife flings herself at his feet. "One of you must die," she screams (Figure 11–5). The shame and the disgrace would be insupportable if she had to go on living with the knowledge that *both* the Bandit

Figure 11–2. *The Bandit's tale traps the Samurai. (Courtesy Janus Films.)*

and her Husband knew of her shame-wounded state. The Bandit gives in. He cuts the Samurai's bonds and they fight. The fight is difficult, but fair, and in the end the Bandit kills the Samurai. The latter had fallen back into a thicket and become entangled there. The coup de grace is a savage sword thrust through the body. We are shown a low-angle medium shot of the execution site and we recognize the framing arms of two nearly vertical branches. This is where the Woodcutter found the body.

FIGURE 11–3. *The Bandit and the Wife: Resistance.* (*Courtesy Janus Films.*)

After the shot of the killing of the Samurai, we cut back to the prison courtyard. Tajomaru declares that he needed to kill the Samurai "honestly" and did so. The camera pulls back to reveal the Police Agent at his side and the Woodcutter and the Priest in the right background. Then he concludes his story by telling of his disposing of the Samurai's sword for drinking money and the stealing of the horse. As for the woman, she was gone. But, he declares, "she was a woman after all . . . her temper fascinated me." Finally, in answer to the unheard question of the official to whom he is speaking, he acknowledges that he had simply forgotten the dagger, which had seemed to him to be an expensive item. It was a great mistake, he says, and roars with laughter.

At the gate, the Commoner disbelieves a small part of the Bandit's story: the Commoner has heard of this Tajomaru and it would be typical of him to have killed her. But the Priest says that she too turned up at the police station; for the police had found her at some temple where she had gone to take refuge. The agitated Woodcutter interjects that both her story and the Bandit's story are lies. As he tears loose more of the wooden railings to add to the fire, the Commoner answers that "men can't speak the truth. They're mortals. Often [they] won't speak the truth even to themselves." The Priest goes a step farther and attributes the deception to their essential weakness. "That's why they have to tell lies." But the woman's story was quite different from the Bandit's. Camera holds him in close-up as he prepares to narrate her story.

II. *The Wife's Story*

In the courtyard, the Wife is sprawled across three quarters of the frame in a posture of anguish; she is in tears as she begins to speak over the quiet strains of the main theme music. This accompaniment continues virtually uninterrupted throughout her story.

After "having taken advantage" of her, she begins, the Bandit had told her who he was, the famous Tajomaru, and had then "sneered" at her Husband. Her Husband, she implies, was all she could think of. Blindly, she raised herself from the ground and ran toward him, intending perhaps to loosen the ropes against which she says he struggled, only to find them getting tighter the more he strained.

We see this movement in a long shot from behind her, with her Husband in the background. As she nears him, the Bandit pushes her to the ground and goes past her to her Husband. He takes the sword and starts to leave, but not before we have been shown a medium shot of his "sneering" gesture. As he does this, we hear the Wife's sobs and then see Tajomaru laugh, point at the husband, and then walk off into the woods.

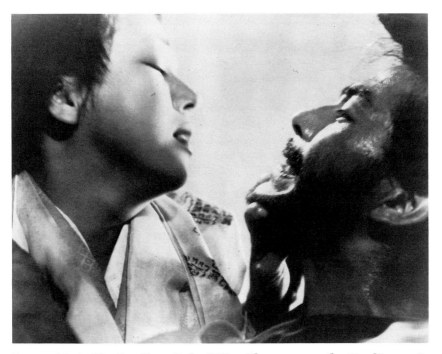

FIGURE 11–4. *The Bandit and the Wife: The rape—as the Bandit sees it. (Courtesy Janus Films.)*

FIGURE 11–5. *The Wife exposes her sense of shame. (Courtesy Janus Films.)*

We then see a series of three shots, each one larger than the preceding one: they show the Wife lying weeping on the ground near her Husband. This is followed by a close-up as she raises her head to look broken-heartedly at the helpless man. In profile, we see him staring at the ground. A matching close-up of her: she starts to rise; a full figure from behind the Wife as she rises and runs toward him: she throws herself at his rigid body.

So far, Kurosawa's selection of shots has been calculated to merely narrate a sequence of events as economically as possible; they are designed to simply analyze the action by breaking up the full playing space.

Now we see some fresh cinematic art in the following shot selection: continuing from the full shot of the Wife's run to the Husband, there is a cut to an over-the-shoulder shot of the Wife. In her narration, she has indicated that her attention was directed at her Husband, *his* suffering as a result of what had taken place in front of his eyes and the final insult of the departing sneer from the Bandit. Thus, Kurosawa shows us, first, *her* face past his shoulder; *her* face registers by reacting to what is on his face. *That* we see next, in a matching over-the-shoulder shot. And the timing, for which Kurosawa (who always acts as his own film editor) is justly famous, is superb. The shot featuring her is held for twenty-one seconds, whereas the one featuring him is held for only three seconds. For we only need a glance at his face to confirm what we know of it from having seen *her* reaction to it for the longer space of time. Next, as if to release the tension built up here, Kurosawa cuts back to the court-yard.

Here the angle on the woman is slightly wider, to include our ubiquitous, witnessing Woodcutter and Priest in the background again. She describes the look on his face: "In his eyes I noticed no anger, not even sorrow, but a cold, steady gleam, scornful of me."

We are back in the woods, back now on the same over-the-shoulder shot featuring the Wife. Without taking her eyes from him, she pulls herself back, away from him a little; she weaves from side to side. She begs him to stop staring at her like that. Anything would be preferable to the ac-cusation of his look. Even death. Camera weaves with her as she speaks and here it seems clear that the camera is at least partly a subjective camera, reflecting the Wife's interior state. She sinks to the ground at this point, her hands covering her face, protecting herself from the wound-ing hatred of his look.

Suddenly, she starts, looks around, and starts to rise. In a beautiful long shot of the two figures, we see the dagger in the foreground, still sticking point down in the earth. She rises to her feet, comes toward camera and removes the knife from the ground; then she goes back to her Husband and cuts his bonds.

From over his shoulder we see her extend the dagger toward him. "Kill me, please," she shrieks. Camera dollies in to her face, then pans around to feature her Husband from over *her* shoulder. The shot recapitulates the visual motif of over-the-shoulder shots we saw a moment earlier—but with a difference: this time, Kurosawa uses a moving camera to indicate what binds them now, the knife and the Wife's wish for punishment at her Husband's hands.

Now we see her in close-up as she looks imploringly, rises, and starts to back away. A medium shot follows: the camera moves toward her as she backs away. "Don't—oh don't—don't!" She starts her hands toward her face again and we see she still has the knife. She will, through the eight shots remaining in her story, be followed by the camera as she alternately retreats from and moves toward him. And these movements are intercut with static shots of her unmoving (because *unmoved*) Husband. The final shot moves with her in close-up as she goes toward her Husband with the knife raised at the level of her chin. Finally she lunges out of frame toward him.

But back in the courtyard, in the next shot, she tells us that at that crucial moment, she fainted. When she opened her eyes, she saw the dagger in her Husband's chest. Here she begins to weep again and continues with the denouement: not having known what to do, she had run through the forest (although she cannot exactly remember having done so) until she reached a small pond at the foot of a hill. We see a brief intercut of the setting she describes as she concludes that she had thrown herself into the pond in order to kill herself but had failed. "What should a poor helpless woman like me do?"

Again at the gate, the Commoner admits to being "mixed up" (Figure 11–6). Women have that effect, he says. But the Priest has more to say. He wants to report the Husband's story. Dead men tell no lies, he says— at least he "can't believe that men are so sinful." But even if they did it would not bother the Commoner. "After all," he says, "who's honest nowadays? Though some believe they are, men want to forget the things they don't like. So they make up stories. That's easier." Grinning, he bites into a piece of fruit and leans back to hear the dead man's story.

III. The Husband's Story

The dead man tells his story through the agency of a woman, a Medium whose body he inhabits in order to offer his version. The Priest narrates what he saw: the Medium performed a rite of seance and suddenly began to speak in the voice of the dead Samurai. Her performance, marked by the use of a bell, a burning censer, and her own frenzied movements, takes place in a high wind; together with the sound of a drum, the auditory effect is eery.

From a long shot, we see the Medium move toward camera, which waits a beat then dollies in toward her. The Husband's voice announces that he is in "darkness" now and he utters a "curse upon those who threw me into this inferno." Then the Medium falls to the ground and begins to writhe. The camera follows these movements, constantly panning with her jerking body. Suddenly, she sits bolt upright and camera moves in to an extreme close-up as she begins: "After attacking my Wife, the

FIGURE 11–6. *From the framing story: The Priest, the Commoner, the Woodcutter. (Courtesy Janus Films.)*

Bandit began to console her." Abruptly the music stops. We are in the woods.

The Bandit and the Wife are squatting on the ground, the Bandit hunched over her, in a consoling posture. Camera pulls back to reveal the Husband, bound to the tree, now in the foreground of the compositional triangle. The Husband's voice describes how the Bandit is working to persuade the Wife to go off with him, because he, the Bandit, actually loves her very much. Now the Husband turns his head toward the couple. We cut to a dreamy, soft close-up of the Wife as she looks up at the Bandit, listening to his persuasions. Accompanying this shot, the Husband's voice takes note of her look. This is followed by a cut to a medium shot of the Medium back in the courtyard, a haggard face, twisted at the mouth, whose voice (the Husband's) says: "Never had her face looked so radiant in all our married life." The irony and bitterness of the commentary are underscored by a cut back to the Husband in the woods—a close-up revealing this bitterness. It is too much to bear; he closes his eyes. He recounts how the Wife asked the bandit to take her away with him and followed this request with "I can't marry you if he [the Husband] is alive." It is for this act of treachery, he says, that he is now "in darkness."

As the Wife urges the Bandit to "kill him," she is seen in a medium two-shot with the Bandit, and as she does so, she starts to edge behind his back (Figure 11–7). Repeating rhythmically, mindlessly, the phrase, "kill him," she is next seen in a masterful close-up. This is what the *Husband* sees: in the foreground, in the bottom of the frame, her sinewy nailed fingers, clutching the sweating hump of the Bandit's shoulder, which itself curves away most of the Wife's face, leaving only a pair of piercingly inflamed eyes, staring askew at her Husband. This is followed by a matching close-up of Tajomaru, who jerks her around to shoot her a look of contempt with his eyes; it is enough to back her off. Clearly, his response is outraged contempt.

In long shot, we see the rest of his response: he flings her away from

FIGURE 11–7. *The Wife pleads with the Bandit. (Courtesy Janus Films.)*

him. She falls down to the ground, sprawled out, a crumpled heap, rejected. The Bandit places his foot on her carcass, so to speak—a satisfied, triumphant hunter. He offers to kill her. The triangular composition catches all three in the frame from a low angle. The camera then dollies around to show the Samurai in profile. Off screen we hear his voice: "I almost forgave the Bandit for these words." Again from the low-angle perspective we see Tajomaru release her from under his foot and stride toward the Samurai for a decision. As he does so, she rises quickly to her feet and runs off into the forest. The Bandit sees and pursues, the camera panning to follow them as both disappear into the woods.

The Samurai is left alone. "Hours later," as he tells it, the Bandit returned to report that he could not find her and to cut the Samurai loose before going off for good. Thus, alone, the Samurai plunges the dagger into his own breast.

The Husband's story reflects with great force and clarity his status as a Samurai and outraged Husband. Moreover, he goes further in his indictment of his Wife: for it is her willingness to run off with the Bandit, provided Tajomaru agrees to first kill the husband, that has thrown him "into darkness"—presumably the hell reserved for those whose honor is especially stained. But the Husband gives away his passionate bitterness too: for he does not commit the ceremonial self-destruction of hara-kiri; his suicide, romanticized to be sure by the beautiful shadows in the long shot that pictures it, is sudden, swift, and emotional.

The section dealing with the Husband's story ends with a close-up of the Medium in the courtyard. The composition involves the Woodcutter, sitting in the right background. Therefore, when the Medium speaks and tells us that "someone seemed to approach quietly. . . . Who could it be? . . . someone's hand grasped the dagger and drew it out"—we have been given a visual clue to whom that someone might have been.

The rain continues to pour down on Rashomon gate, and now as we return there we see the Woodcutter's agitation in a kind of moving counterpart to the falling drops. He paces restlessly across our field of view and camera pans with him. Suddenly, he stops. The Medium's last words have been too much for him to take. Her (the Husband's) words are untrue. There was no dagger there. The Samurai had been killed by a sword. Shrewdly, the Commoner guesses from this that the Woodcutter knows all. Why didn't he tell the police? Because "I didn't want to be involved," he answers. The Commoner seems to understand that because of his lie to the police he wants to talk about it now; the point seems to be that a story *will* be told regardless of the teller's reluctance to tell it at any one moment. Moreover, says the Commoner, "now you may talk"—perhaps on the same account. The exchange between the Commoner and the Woodcutter has been registered for us in successive two-shots, in which the urging, questioning, commentating Commoner is caught over the shoulder of the Woodcutter, creeping up on him, insinuating into his very skull.

Now the Woodcutter agrees to say more, although the Priest has said he cannot bear more horror.

The Commoner starts him going. "How much do you know?"

IV. The Woodcutter's Revised Version

The Woodcutter speaks: "He was down on his knees begging her forgiveness." And we see the scene in the woods from a medium shot, a low angle. From this point to the conclusion of the Woodcutter's version there is hardly a note of music on the sound track; it is an absence worth noting, because it seems to signal a kind of purity in the Woodcutter's tale, an absence of embellishment or emotional color given to the scenes he describes.

And indeed, Tajomaru, the great, the splendid, the (in his own eyes) heroic Bandit seems to be begging. He speaks almost without pause and the burden of what he says is familiar: "I am begging you. I'll do anything to please you," he declares fervently, "please marry me, I am in love." We hear him announce a whole catalogue of bourgeois modalities he would be willing to adopt if only she would say the word. Yet, it is a violent begging on Mifune's part; when she does not respond, he threatens to kill her in fact. And we see the desperation in him by means of two cuts to closer angles. Finally, she rises into a close-up, her eyes wet with tears. "How could I? I am a woman," she says, meaning, how could I answer a question like that? And quickly she gets to her knees and with the camera panning after her crawls to where the dagger is stuck in the ground. She goes toward and then past Tajomaru, who falls spinning to the ground in alarm, then she goes to her Husband and cuts his bonds. Then she backs away and, sobbing, sinks to the ground.

We see the three of them in this position from behind Tajomaru. The composition clarifies the alignment of ambiguous forces. The Bandit understands that she wishes the men to decide whether she will marry him by fighting to the death.

But the Samurai will have none of this. He refuses to fight for her. He thinks her a "shameless whore" and wonders why she doesn't commit suicide. He would, in fact, *give* her to the Bandit; the loss of his horse would cause him greater regret. The Wife is thunderstruck; she cannot believe it. Kurosawa captures her amazement, her look toward the Bandit for *his* response (a look that both pleads and demands), and the Bandit's decision—all this in a masterpiece of wordless, pictorial cinema. From a profile of the Wife looking at the Husband we see her other profile as she turns to look at the Bandit. Then a medium shot captures her and the Bandit. The latter looks at the Samurai. In a medium shot, with the Samurai in the foreground, the men look at one another. The Samurai looks at his Wife and the Bandit. The close-ups follow: pleading woman, frowning Bandit. The pictures say it all: the Bandit is disgusted and will have none of her.

The Bandit starts to walk away from the scene, warning the abjectly weeping Wife not to follow him. The Samurai adds insult to her injury; he tells her that nobody will be taken in by her weeping. This rouses a twinge of sympathy in the Bandit; the Samurai must desist because women are naturally weak and cannot help their crying.

At the word weakness, the Wife comes alive. She begins to spit a stream of insult and invective at the two men. As they stand frozen in their tracks, she lets loose her contempt for them both. The burden of her argument is that they are both weaklings, that neither of them has the courage to be a "real man"—whom alone a woman can truly love—and thus the object of a real woman's raging passion. If either of them had any virility, she goes on, they would challenge the other at once. Only by the "sword" can they settle the question of weakness and strength. Her goading has its effect.

The fight is a parody of the heroic encounter that the Bandit, according to the Woodcutter, reported to the police. The men are anything but anxious to fight; they are, in fact, terrified. There is a great deal of comedy in their slipping and sliding over the terrain, the swords coming loose from both their grips, their fear of each other every time they accidentally touch. The outcome of the fight could have gone either way, and the victor dramatizes this fact for us by showing us how utterly debilitated he is at the end. For a long time after the fatal sword thrust, he sits on the ground beside the Wife, stupefied with exhaustion. After a moment, he begins to make overtures to her, but she scampers away: she will have nothing to do with him and eventually escapes into the forest. Once again he sits on the ground, his breath coming in great gulps. Finally, he rises, starts away from the scene, and then, realizing he is moving toward the body of the dead Samurai, reverses his direction and limps away into the dark forest. He is barely able to carry away his loot: the Samurai's sword.

Thus, the Woodcutter's version does what it is calculated to do vis-à-vis *his* character: like the other versions, it has the effect of enhancing his own self-image because it denigrates the stories told by the others. The three participants, heroic in their own eyes by virtue of caste or status, claim to have lived up to the letter of their special roles and duties; they have satisfied expectations about their own behavior. But the Woodcutter's claim, by virtue of his having countermanded *their* claims, is that he cannot seem so bad by comparison.

V. Renewal at the Gate

A very brief shot opens this final sequence: it is virtually a still life and a design. An immense diagonal bar almost obliterates the upper half of the frame. Beneath it, on the left, sits the Priest, looking across to the right side where the Commoner, rising, is also laughing at the conclusion of the Woodcutter's story. The Woodcutter sits opposite him, his back to us.

The Commoner is skeptical, but clearly he has enjoyed the story-telling interlude. The Woodcutter is somewhat indignant that the Commoner does not believe in *his* version. "I don't tell lies. I'm not lying I tell you." The Priest is aghast at their conflict: "If men don't trust one another—" the conclusion is clear, although unspoken. The Commoner agrees, but the Priest refuses to believe it. Well, the Commoner goes on, "Which one of these stories do you believe?" Before the Priest can reply, the Woodcutter interjects: "It makes no sense. I can't understand it. They don't make any sense." But the Commoner urges him not to worry: "Men are reasonable." And as he starts to toss some of his burning embers from the fire out into the rain, a baby's cry is heard.

The three men try to locate the source of the crying. The Commoner gets there first. When the Priest and the Woodcutter join him, they find him kneeling by an infant's blanket stripping off the baby's clothes. At once the Priest picks up the infant while the Woodcutter goes up and pushes the Commoner, demanding an explanation. The Woodcutter is disgusted by this latest "horror," but the Commoner defends himself with a series of shrewdly cynical thrusts: if it hadn't been him, somebody else would have stolen the clothing; on a scale of evil, he, the Commoner, is far better than the parents who abandoned the child so pitilessly. The Woodcutter counters by pointing to an amulet the parents left with the child, for good luck; to him the amulet is an emblem of their anguish in abandoning the child. To this last appeal, the appeal to human sympathy, the Commoner is totally unresponsive: selfishness, he says, is the necessary attitude if one wants to go on living.

This enrages the Woodcutter; in a fury, he accuses the Commoner of being one with the selfish Bandit and Samurai and leaps at his adversary's throat. Here, they struggle out into the rain. The Commoner strikes the most telling blow, however, by pointing out to the Woodcutter that his story hadn't fooled *him*. The Woodcutter slumps guiltily into a defeated posture: the Commoner pushes him back into the shelter of the gate, against a wall near where the Priest is huddling with the baby. He accuses him of having stolen the dagger: "A thief calling others thieves!" The Woodcutter's head is bowed. The Commoner slaps him and laughs in triumph: "Anything [else you want] to say?" he sneers, and then, still laughing, he leaves.

From a short distance away from the gate, we see the Commoner come out into the rain; in the background, the Priest and the Woodcutter are listlessly leaning against the wall, sheltered.

A quick dissolve to a closer shot from another angle is followed by a similarly brief dissolve to still another two-shot. A third dissolve leaves us on a tight two-shot of the two men. The sequence of dissolves has been beautifully calculated in length and angle to achieve two things: it has encompassed the passage of time and it has captured the somber mood of the two men.

The baby cries. Now we are back on the long shot, from outside the gate, only now the rain seems to have stopped; only occasional drips of water fall from the eaves of the gate and slosh onto the stone steps. The Priest steps forward a few paces. The Woodcutter follows: he approaches the Priest and moves to take the baby away from him. The Priest resists violently: "Stop it! [are you] trying to strip it?"

We are on a low-angle two-shot with the Priest in the foreground and the Woodcutter behind, looking smaller as the Priest, looking larger, actually looms up in the picture (which is the intention of the particular choice of angle: the Priest's size relative to the Woodcutter's is meant to match his ostensible moral stature). The Woodcutter is shocked and looks humiliated, as he silently shakes his head. "I've six kids of my own," he says, "another won't make it much harder, will it?" From a reverse angle, we see the Priest apologize for misunderstanding; but the Woodcutter acknowledges his own suspicions about the behavior of others. "I'm ashamed of myself." The Priest says he is grateful. The Woodcutter's willingness to adopt the child has restored the Priest's faith in man.

Now in a full-figure shot of both men, the Woodcutter bows. The Priest hands over the child. We hear the faint stirrings of music, clearly traditional Japanese music. From farther away, we see them bow to each other again and see the Woodcutter turn to go. From behind both men, as the Woodcutter leaves the gate, we see the clearing sky. The Priest watches the Woodcutter as he goes. He walks toward a great square opening in the gate. It is brilliantly lit.

From a reverse angle, we watch the Woodcutter come toward camera, the baby gently cradled in his arms; in the background the Priest is small against the sky, still watching. The music reaches up. The Woodcutter reaches the backtracking camera and goes out of frame. We cut to the signboard.

Style and Approach

Kurosawa has made the following remarks on the style of *Rashomon* to his foremost interpreter, Donald Richie: "I like silent pictures and I always have. They are often so much more beautiful than sound pictures are. Perhaps they had to be. At any rate, I wanted to restore some of this beauty. I thought of it, I remember, in this way: one of the techniques of modern art is simplification, and that I must therefore simplify this film." (*The Films of Akira Kurosawa*, op. cit., p. 79a.) The notion of simplicity, then, ought to be the starting point for any discussion of style in *Rashomon*. The film shines with it.

That this film eschews dialogue wherever possible is very much in the manner of the silent films. Some sequences are played out with virtually no words spoken while large chunks of others depend entirely on visual story-telling. Nor is this forced on the viewer. As an example, we cite the Wife's story; except for her words imploring her husband to kill her, the whole of the drama is conveyed pictorially. This is also the case with a large portion of the Samurai's story.

Another remarkable manifestation of simplicity is the fact that there are essentially three locales in which the action takes place. When this is compared to virtually any film that comes to mind, the difference is astonishing. The compact power of the film derives in part from the mesmeric (almost ritualized) manner of the repeated returns to one or the other of these locales. Kurosawa's drama must (and does) make up for the lack of visual excitement available to the director who *can* switch locales as many as forty or fifty times.

In terms of camera technique, there is also exhibited an artful simplicity. Kurosawa is a master of montage—when a sequence or a scene might be enhanced by dynamic cutting, such as in the opening walk of the Woodcutter through the forest where a variety of impressions are directed at us by means of a cutting analysis of space and time. When the scene calls for separation of characters the director is again masterful in employing montage techniques; as one example, consider the scene in the Woodcutter's revised version (see pp. 266–267) where the Husband's refusal to fight for the Wife elicits a decision from Tajomaru. The intercutting here not only builds suspense (a classic function of montage), but also defines characters, their separateness, and their interrelations.

There is also great reliance on depth-of-field photography: there is a dazzling assortment of carefully worked out camera moves, panning shots (many on the end of moving camera shots), and in-depth compositions. Each of these is calculated to a direct purpose: either to link together characters and action or to dramatize decisions and events. Recall, if you will, the subtle moving and panning shot when the Wife (during her story) backs away from the Husband and camera follows her and then pans behind her, refusing to lose sight of her and gathering the Husband into the image in the same movement.

This characteristic of the camera technique is also employed in the service of the masterly composition we see here. We have remarked about this aspect of Kurosawa's technique here and there in the "Analysis of Major Sequences" (pp. 251–269), so we need not pursue it further.

That Kurosawa is his own editor is not surprising. His sure instinct for timing the length of shots and for the delicate matching of shots is by now well known to viewers of such of his films as *Ikiru* (1952), *Seven*

Samurai (1954), *Yojimbo* (1961), and *Sanjuro* (1962). Among the 420 shots listed in the transcript of the film there are numerous instances of this particular skill. (See *Rashomon: A Film By Akira Kurosawa*, translated by Donald Richie, consulting editor, New York, 1969.) For example, we recall especially the matching close-ups of the Bandit and the Wife when he decides she's not worth fighting for; the over-the-shoulder shots at the gate featuring the Priest and the Woodcutter as the baby's fate is being decided; and many more.

In European film criticism the simplicity of Kurosawa's style would be referred to, for example, as "pure" cinema. This is because the style makes itself felt in a direct, physical way. Kurosawa's films manifest this sensuality always—and nowhere do they do so as much as in *Rashomon*.

CHAPTER 12

La Ronde

Directed by MAX OPHULS

I want to make films from the inside. If you want to see something else, go to the Musée Grevin [the Wax Museum].

Max Ophuls

CAST

NARRATOR	*Anton Walbrook*
THE WHORE	*Simone Signoret*
THE SOLDIER	*Serge Reggiani*
THE MAID	*Simone Simon*
THE YOUNG MAN	*Daniel Gelin*
THE MARRIED WOMAN	*Danielle Darrieux*
THE HUSBAND	*Fernand Gravey*
THE SHOPGIRL	*Odete Joyeux*
THE POET	*Jean-Louis Barrault*
THE ACTRESS	*Isa Miranda*
THE COUNT	*Gerard Phillipe*

CREDITS

DIRECTOR	*Max Ophuls*
SCREENPLAY	*Jacques Natanson and Max Ophuls,*
	based on the play Reigen *by Arthur Schnitzler*
PRODUCER	*Sacha Gordine*
DIRECTOR OF PHOTOGRAPHY	*Christian Matras*
ART DIRECTORS	*Jean d'Eaubonne and Marpaux, M. Frederik*
COSTUMES	*Georges Annenkov*
MUSIC	*Oscar Strauss and Joe Hajos*
EDITORS	*Leonide Azar and S. Rondeau*

1950   Black and white   97 minutes

Perspective on Style

Max Ophuls, who was born in Germany in 1902, spent a lifetime working in the theater and the cinema. From 1919 to 1932 he worked in the theater, principally as an actor and producer; from 1930 until his death in 1957, two years after finishing his last film, *Lola Montes,* he directed twenty-three films in four countries (including four in Hollywood, the best known of which is *Letter From an Unknown Woman,* starring Joan Fontaine and Louis Jourdan). But his reputation rests largely on the last four films he made in France: *La Ronde* (1950), *Le Plaisir* (1952), *Madame de . . .* (1953), and *Lola Montes* (the only one he made in color, an international extravaganza whose first finished version ran some 140 minutes).

These four films have a great deal in common. They are all evocations of the baroque stylishness of the early 1900s in certain parts of Europe; each revolves about themes of the precariousness of love and happiness, seduction, shattered ideals, and a bittersweet dream world; each finds its characters and/or narrative style being forcefully manipulated into balanced modalities; for each the director assembled the same group of co-workers (film editor, scenarist, cameraman, art director); and each presents dazzling technique, images of beautiful women, and dazzlingly and charming, if empty, men.

Critical opinions on Ophuls are divided into two sharply contrasting camps. For example, Roy Armes, in his fine history of French cinema declares that Ophuls is "virtually a test case of one's approach to the cinema. For those whose concern is purely visual and whose ideal is an abstract symphony of images, Ophuls has the status of one of the very great directors. For spectators and critics who demand in addition to the images the sort of human insight and moral depth that a play or a novel can give, he is merely a minor master, a maker of exquisite but rather empty films." (*The French Cinema Since 1946: Volume One, The Great Tradition,* 2nd enlarged ed., London and New Jersey, 1970, pp. 62–63.) In any case, Armes concedes that "he is an artist of considerable sensitivity and possessor of an incredible technical command of his chosen medium." (Ibid., p. 63.) Nevertheless, Armes chooses to side with those who demand what a "play or novel can give." Of *Lola Montes,* he says, "what is lacking is depth: the whole tour de force is dazzling but ultimately quite remarkably hollow" (ibid., p. 62); of *La Ronde,* "only in the eyes of the most fervent admirers of Ophuls does this lighthearted work contain a tragic demonstration of the futility of man's quest for pleasure." (Ibid., p. 58.)

Countering this view, François Truffaut and Jacques Rivette have declared that Ophuls "was as subtle as he was thought ponderous, as profound as he was thought superficial, as pure as he was thought vulgar.

He was considered old-fashioned, out-of-date, antiquated though he dealt with eternal themes: passion without love, pleasure without love, love without reciprocation. Luxury and insouciance only provided a framework for this savage painter." (Quoted in Georges Sadoul, *Dictionary of Film Makers,* translated, edited, and updated by Peter Morris, Los Angeles and Berkeley, 1972, p. 189b.)

What all critics agree on, however, is that Max Ophuls's cinema was stylish. And it is to this idea that we must address ourselves before analyzing *La Ronde* in detail. For it seems to us that we cannot appreciate Ophuls unless we come to grips with this very difficult idea. Unless we understand *La Ronde* we cannot take sides in the critical debate.

What is there in the work of Ophuls that evokes the responses clustering around the idea of *style?* For one thing there is the period in which the works are set: *fin de siècle* Europe (most notably Vienna). There is a distinctive uniformity in the decorated environment of this period; it is a period that is sharply aware of its taste (which Ruskin assured it was a matter of strict morality) and it exercised that taste in its architecture, interior decoration, clothing, furniture, and other *objets d'art.* Late Victorian striving after visual beauty took the form of a flamboyant and breath-taking use of line and contour and interlaced patterns of relief in sculptured ornamentation—in short, it took the form of the rococo. The energy and vigor in the designed quality of rococo, an appelation first given to the style prevalent in early eighteenth-century France but much imitated afterward, should not blind us to its airier qualities. Rococo is spacious and graceful and suitable for the dance; it celebrates its surfaces.

Such a style is filled with certainty; it *knows* what it likes and it practices what it knows. Thus, we are also likely to find associated with decor of such certain substance, personal manners (or social graces, as it might have been called in the early Victorian period). Manners are also much in evidence in Ophuls's work. By this we mean that whatever is distinctive to an individual in his personal manner of dress, discourse, interpersonal relations, and physical deportment.

These seem to us to be the principal elements in Ophuls's work that call forth the designation stylish.

But let us go back to the previous paragraph in which we speak of distinctive personal manner. Isn't individuality in manner what we mean by character? Should we then have to say that character denotes style? Indeed it does. The problem is that while we use style in ordinary discourse to denote just such a relationship, we do not use that other terribly vague word *stylish* unless the style—the character, the manner—shows forth with some emphasis, some urgency—much as a rococo panel shows its fretted design in high relief. To the degree that Victorian taste is discernible, that is the degree to which character—personal preference, another word for taste—shows itself.

As Wylie Sypher has said of the rococo, it "is an essentially urban art. . . . an art of the middle class that has not yet been entirely hemmed in by the metropolis. It is quite literally urbane. . . . The city has not yet become a prison; and the middle class has not yet been deprived of tradition by a machine age. Hence, the note of taste and politeness in rococo." But, he adds, "Rococo is a sign of an interim social condition." (*Rococo to Cubism in Art and Literature*, New York, 1960, p. 28.)

Style and stylishness, then (at least in this discussion), can be thought of as regular human attributes. We suggest, further, that stylishness is in fact analogous to a psychological defense mechanism in that it maintains an economically functioning balance between contending impulses. On the one hand is the assertion of what one likes—taste—and on the other, surely, what one does not. Wherever style is at such a height of visibility as to summon our aesthetic, or indeed our emotional, contemplation, we may be sure we are in an age in which a hidden impulse is asserting itself against a prevailing equilibrium. As the manifestation of style develops toward a clear aestheticism, the status quo is being heavily challenged and the "interim social condition" is about to be replaced.

As we shall see, this is exactly the situation in *La Ronde*.

Themes and Characterization

(We depart here from our practice of summarizing the story: each episode is separately summarized in "Analysis of Sequences.")

Arthur Schnitzler's *Reigen,* the play from which the scenario of *La Ronde* was produced, interested Ophuls precisely because of the shape of its narrative: a set of ten connected episodes in which a character from one appears prominently in the succeding one until the final story in which a character from the ninth connects with one from the first to form the tenth, thus completing a circle. Students of *Le Plaisir, Madame de,* and *Lola Montes* will see at once that the Schnitzler play afforded Ophuls the opportunity to practice a stylish transformation on it.

The richest change Ophuls rang on Schnitzler's play was the creation of the Anton Walbrook character, a Narrator, a master of ceremonies (like the Ringmaster in *Lola Montes*), a *meneur de jeu,* a representative of the maker of the film. But there are perhaps three main functions for this character and in each he speaks for us, for the audience. First and foremost, Walbrook narrates the stories and thus makes it possible for us to give way to our voyeuristic impulses (an impulse, we might add, operating virtually every time we go to the movies); as he says to us, in so many words, "I am the personification of your desires." Thus, we do not identify with him in the sense of taking part in his *action* but in his unrivaled opportunities (and ours) to *see*. Similarly, he acts out our conventional censorship standards, as when, just at the moment when an action is proceeding in such a way that we would soon *see* lovemaking, the Narrator is shown wrapped in loops of 35mm film, making the appropriate "cut" with an enormous pair of scissors.

Secondly, by *acting* various roles in the episodes, the Narrator literally *acts* on behalf of our wish to see the action; he furthers the action for us. Then by maintaining his *distance* from the action, on the other hand, by remaining an ironic observer, he helps Ophuls to poise truth against the illusions represented by the players in the episodes. In so doing—and by the remembered impact of the opening sequence, in which he asks whether we are in Vienna or in a film studio—he mediates for us the distance between illusion and reality; by so doing he tells us we are merely enjoying a game, thus separating us from the illusion-ridden characters in the episode.

For the characters are filled with compound illusions: that love is constant; that the pleasures of sex are really the passions of love; that there is a rite of seduction in which the innocent fall and the experienced triumph; that, and this is perhaps the most damaging of all, the lover's experience of the "other" is unique to each lover.

Thus, the Housemaid, the Wife, and the Husband, at least, share the latter illusion, whereas to varying degrees the other characters participate in similar kinds of illusions. What we are struck by in each case, however, is the way that the most experienced of these lovers (or the most innocent, for that matter) are surprised by their erotic adventures: the Young Man is almost as surprised when the Wife succumbs as he is eager that she shall do so; the elegant and experienced Count is equally overwhelmed by the Actress' willingness; and the Soldier is astonished at the erotic needs of a Whore. The surprise is shared to some extent by all of the participants. And this is because of Ophuls's major theme: we are all amateurs in the game of love; that regardless of the universal and eternal nature of love, sex, passion, pleasure and seduction, we are still surprised by their vagaries.

The 1950s (when the film was made) perhaps heralded the sexual revolution of the 1960s and 1970s, and surely the hidden impulse, the contending impulse we spoke of earlier (see pp. 273–275), is no doubt the more open sexual style of our age. A concomitant of our more liberated impulses is surely the notion that love is cruel sometimes and doubtless sex is too. That notion seems to be at the bottom of our more liberated impulses, and here, in the first and last episodes, framing the film as it were, are dramatizations of this cruelty. We can see it in the real cruelty of the Soldier toward the Whore and in the impotence of the Count with this same woman.

Character and theme are interrelated then by a kind of dialectic of experience in which wish and expectation seldom meet and where experience cannot guarantee immunity from pain. This is the message and these the colors of our "savage painter."

Analysis of Major Sequences

The opening shot of the film is pure Max Ophuls. It sets the tone of the cinematic style and of the stylishness of what we are about to see. We fade in on Anton Walbrook's back, full figure in the right-hand portion of the frame, as he walks away from us cutting right to left in a diagonal and ascends some steps to what looks to us like a fog-shrouded stage in the left-hand portion of the frame; to our right is a handsome bridge over a river (presumably the Danube, because this is Vienna), and beyond it, in the right background, is a gauzy, nighttime skyline. The camera moves with Walbrook, continuing to run without a cut for the next four minutes.

As he walks across the stage, he speaks.

NARRATOR: *La Ronde*. Who am I? The author? The announcer? A passer-by? I am you. [And now he turns and walks back the other way, camera still panning with him.] In fact, any one of you. I am the personification of your desire—of your desire to know everything. People always know only one side of reality. And why? Because they see only one side of things. But I—I see every aspect. I see from every side. *La Ronde*. That allows me to be everywhere at the same time. Everywhere.

Now he has stopped pacing back and forth across the stage and has come down the left side of it and started along a street. As he executes this movement, he asks, "But where are we?" And we see in the foreground as he walks a studio movie camera on a tripod and a microphone boom. "In a studio?" he asks. "Oh, in Vienna," he answers himself.

Here he comes to a clothes rack and exchanges his belted camel's hair trench coat for an evening cape and top hat (to complete his full dress evening suit, for under the trench-coat he had been wearing all but the cape).

Superbly attired at last, he spouts an epigram: "I adore the past. It is so much more restful than the present and so much more reliable than the future." It is *almost* worthy of Oscar Wilde, but certainly a manifestation of high style in discourse.

Now he continues along a Viennese street. The light has been changing subtly. Now it is clearly a sunbright day. He sets the stage for us—he tells us that it's spring and that the fragrance in the air is a sure indication of a love story. But first we must have a waltz. So that Voila! He reaches a carousel, which he mounts, and, going to the center, begins to operate the mechanism. And we hear now for the first time the famous Oscar Strauss waltz that we will not fail to be humming after the film has ended. This is the introduction of the theme of love as a rondo. He sings the first chorus to us and as the merry-go-round turns (remember: we are still on the one single shot!), Simone Signoret (the Whore) appears.

Again the light changes on his cue, as, deflecting her attempt to pick him up, he assigns her a special corner to work for the "fading" part of the day. "Soldiers again," she complains. "There are always soldiers," he says wisely. "The sixth is yours." Resigned, she moves out of frame to take her place. We move in slightly on our master of ceremonies and he gives us the title of the episode: "The Girl and the Soldier."

There are a number of things to notice beside the superbly managed single shot that opens the film, the visual metaphor of linkage that articulates the patterns of the film narrative. Ophuls also makes several other visual suggestions. For one thing, if we look carefully at the stage as he crosses we notice that the painted backdrop is a virtual copy of the (real?) background that we see on the right side of the frame. Moreover, as he descends from the stage and asks where we are, we see the equipment of a film studio, a microphone boom, lights, and so on. Both artifacts are intended to suggest that the line between reality and illusion, the natural and the artificial, is not easily discerned, and so adumbrate a major theme of the film. In addition, we are urged by his verbal introduction to use this interlocutor to both enter into and stay detached from the action we will see. It is a rich ambiguity that Ophuls has designed into this character.

The meeting of the Soldier and the Whore is also managed with a sure economical camera technique. It takes just two shots to enact the scene, a static long shot, and a magnificent, very lengthy, tracking two-shot that follows the couple back and forth across the setting like a wave, suggesting the way the tides of this sexual advance alternately get thrown back and forth as the dramatic vicissitudes occur. The scene is also, as we have noted, one of the cruelest episodes (Figure 12–1). The Soldier is quite indifferent to the Whore, who nevertheless offers him sex under the virtually impossible conditions on which he insists. The sound of the bugle in the barracks, played by our *régisseur* who is now wearing a bugler's uniform, brings the Soldier back and provides a transition to the next episode.

This is facilitated by the *régisseur:* Walbrook calls after the Soldier urging him not to be late and (presumably) so to draw a punishment tour of duty, because "I want you to go out on Saturday!" The episode, entitled, "The Maid and the Soldier," again features the Soldier—this time as he is paired with the Maid, Simone Simon. He is, essentially, in a lustful frame of mind as he leaves the dance with her to seek out a trysting place in a fairyland park (Figure 12–2). This was also his frame of mind in

FIGURE 12–1. *The Soldier and the Whore: Negotiations.* (*Courtesy Janus Films.*)

the previous episode and now he repeats the action: he leaves the Maid right after they have had their sexual encounter and runs back into the dance palace to chase after a blonde.

Thus begins the paradigm of the successive action; the Soldier who had learned from his previous encounter with the Whore that he could "love and run," so to speak, now uses what he has learned to deal with the new partner. He treats the Maid as he treated the Whore (Figure 12–3).

Alone outside, the Maid, naively (although in some way sadly, for she has experienced something of the Soldier's shallow purposes) waits for him to conclude his business because he has promised to see her home, is approached by the *régisseur*. He takes her arm and escorts her, "through time and space," to the next "round" of this filmic waltz: that is, to her encounter with the Young Man. In this action by the Narrator, one sees a sympathetic gesture. The Narrator is not entirely without feelings; for the first time we see the possibility that he is mere conduit for the audience, no mere vehicle through which we identify. But Ophuls is not con-

FIGURE 12–2. *The Soldier and the Maid: Deep in the park.* (*Courtesy Janus Films.*)

sistent in employing this facet of the Narrator's character. For example, even though he allows the Narrator to show a certain cold indifference to the Husband's problems in his scene at the restaurant with the Shopgirl—the Husband, acting in that scene like a perfectly pompous ass, deserves such treatment—Ophuls does not at other times permit his Narrator to take emotional sides in the drama.

"The Young Man and the Maid" carries out the paradigm. Here we have, in the Young Man, a character quite at the opposite end of the spectrum from the Soldier; where the latter knew what he wanted and went after it (all too brutally), the Young Man is confused about his sexual urges. He wants the Maid but cannot bring himself to express the desire. She, on the other hand, having learned from the Soldier what men want, is able to facilitate the Young Man's expressing it. In this episode, the Narrator's action parallels this motif: he sits outside the apartment and wards off the Language Teacher, whose 5 o'clock appointment would interfere with the tryst beween the young couple.

The experience of the Young Man in this episode has the effect of increasing his confidence; the Maid's facilitating his ability to express his desires has turned him into a confident seducer. Thus, he is able to go after "bigger game"—the Married Woman. The Narrator, now acting the role of the hansom cab driver, also and again facilitates the encounter by driving Madame to the apartment the Young Man has rented. It is

FIGURE 12–3. *The Soldier and the Maid: Gallantry in action.* (*Courtesy Janus Films.*)

an opulent apartment, indeed, and the environment the seducer has arranged helps to sway her at a moment of indecision (Figure 12–4); for she is not quite so confident of what she should do as he is of what he can do. Perhaps even more decisive is the confident gesture of the Young Man: as the Wife sits in the foyer, close to the door, wavering in her indecisiveness, the Young Man (not too calmly, but enough) goes into the kitchen for a glass of champagne; as he struggles with the bottle, she struggles with her conscience. And even though he thinks, when he comes

FIGURE 12–4. *The Wife and the Young Man: A form of worship.* (*Courtesy Janus Films.*)

from the kitchen, that she has gone, she has not. After their lovemaking, he is struck with a kind of wonder at the enormity of what he has accomplished—so much so that he is inclined to discuss it with the Wife in terms of his profoundly cosmic love for her. It is a transcendent notion, he insists. But this is not the whole truth, for he also alludes to Stendahl's *On Love* (the chapter called "Failures"), a sure indication that love in this case is more of a game and less of a transforming sacrament. The point gets reinforced later. After he has seen her to the carriage he turns toward his apartment, kicks his heels in the air, and—almost hugging himself for joy—gestures to us his pleasure in the conquest, not the cosmos. The paradigmatic action here, the transforming experience that is carried to the next episode, is richly ironic; it is the Wife's somewhat ironic, detached attitude toward the youthful seriousness of her lover. This is no more than her ability to place this entire episode of her life into appropriate perspective—something that the Young Man cannot easily do (even though his detachment is already beginning by the time the episode comes to a close).

"The Husband and the Wife" is worth our careful, critical attention. It is a model of Ophuls's work throughout the film.

It takes place entirely (and appropriately) in the bedroom they share and neither (also appropriately) moves from his own bed at any time. The first shot is a very slow moving shot pushing into the bedroom from behind the headboards of their respective beds. In the background, we see the clock that will play a prominent part in symbolizing the undercurrent of the scene.

It recapitulates the "time" motif of the previous episode, in which the Wife was constantly worried about the time. Time enters the picture when age and solidly familial arrangements dominate the love scene.

Still in terms of the first shot, we note the stylish decor at once—it is the major item in our visual experience, occupying us on a level of consciousness just slightly below the presence of the people in the frame. Here it is most prominent in the ornateness of design in the head- and footboards of their identical beds. The design features elegant curves, fretted wood, and raised patterns; later, during the very next shot, in fact, we will see from the reverse angle that the bed setup is very close to being another proscenium arch, a theatrical setting, for the beds are framed in a high rectangle and the light coming down from on high as it does suggests spotlights focused from a tormentor strip in a theater.

From this second shot, after the cut, camera tilts down to frame the couple between the legs of an animal. A swinging pendulum indicates that the animal is in fact, an ornate clock. Then we push in very slowly (matching the opening tracking shot; the scene is dominated by such balanced harmonies of design in camera work) and hear them begin the scene.

There is something unusual about their situations this evening; the Husband notices first. What *he* does causes her to ask him what's the matter. He remarks on how lovely she is and then introduces the theme of change: "You were young. Now you are in full bloom." To her, this can only mean that "business is going well."

But he is working, as he says ("husbands have worries; their minds aren't always free"), and, hearing this, she decides to go to sleep. But this worries him. Now we cut to a new angle: a low-angle two-shot, from his side of the bed (again, we will see a matching shot from her side). "Do you remember Venice," he asks; whereupon we cut to a close-up of her from her side (naturally) and hear him complete the sentence "on our wedding trip?" (We will not see a matching close-up of *him*, however; the absence is a subtle way of indicating that the scene is *hers*.)

Her answer doesn't satisfy him (that is, her saying "Yes. It was lovely."). Now he must pursue the matter, for clearly he thinks she is disappointed that he has not made love to her this evening. He explains that sexuality is a function of "rhythmical cycles," periods of "calm" ("when one lives like friends") that alternate with "less calm ones." The delivery of Fernand Gravey is important here: it is tentative, insecure, reasonable—ultimately defensive. In short, we do not quite believe this explanation; he is not charged with the sexuality with which he would like to be charged.

His explanation is neat, circular, and unconvincing. If there were no periods of calm, there would be no *other* periods. She agrees that his explanation is *clear,* but *he* cannot quite accept that she is satisfied. He drinks a little water; he decides to assert his superior experience—just declare it—as if to assure her that the character of their respective roles gives authority and force to what he has been saying. "Marriage is . . . marriage is the disconcerting mystery. You young women of good families come to us ignorant and pure" (as if now he has been speaking for *all* husbands). "You haven't lived and cannot know. But we know—but at what price? One could be disgusted with love if one knew the woman of our first time; but there's no choice."

Of course, this last assertion has piqued her interest. She wants to know about these "women." He is alarmed that she should evince such an interest; surely she must be the confidante of some friend who is having an affair. The anxiety thus aroused, touching as it does on both their concerns, is matched by the pace and style of the editing: now we are in a pattern of intercuts of single close-ups—back and forth.

The climax of his anxiety is marked as he flips on his bed light. We are on a two-shot, from her side of the beds, she in the foreground, he in the background. He cannot bear the idea that she *might* some day be in contact with a woman of small virtue (that is, a married woman having an affair). The reason she might be prey to such a person is that "women of doubtful reputation seek the company of honest women in a kind of nostalgia for virtue." Pleased with himself for thinking of that particular phrasing, he smiles. "That's something very deep."

He admits to having had such an affair—once. But the woman is dead. The Wife is horrified, the more so because he places such young deaths in a moral category. "Are you sure," she asks, "they *all* die young?" "It's a fact," he replies, "there *is* justice." Now she is even more horrified; "Did you love her?" she asks. "One doesn't love those women." She is wiped out; she leans back on her pillow, her breath gone.

We cut now from the two-shot to another, a high-angle full shot from the front of the room, looking down on the beds. The light pours from overhead. Each puts out his bed lamp again. The shot widens and pulls back to include the animal clock in the center foreground. She wants to know what time it is. "What difference can it make," he answers. "We have our whole lives before us." "How reassuring," she purrs, ironically. He asks for her hand.

As she gives it to him, we cut to a low-angle shot from behind their beds: we can see between the beds as their hands move across the space and clasp each other. Now camera raises up and starts back. We are in the same shot as the one with which the scene began—this time pulling back instead of pushing in. The scene is over.

The time motif, which we have seen objectified in the image of that dominant foreground clock, is a central element in this episode, for it suggests the innocence-experience polarity so central to the whole film. Yet, although the scene implies that the Husband is the experienced one, it does not confirm this. In the Wife's ironical "How reassuring" lies the meaning that her innocence itself has been an illusion and that she too has all the time in the world—and *has* had it all along.

The Wife's timidity in the face of her Husband's pompous moralism has served to solidify his own conception of his role in the sexual game. He is licensed to have an affair. Ironically, his Wife's disappointment in him has also stirred him to go out and again seek the kind of sexual experience that he had ostensibly garnered long ago in order to fulfill his function as an experienced lover. He has been a failure and now he tries to regenerate that sexual prowess in his new affair.

"The Husband and the . . ." as the episode is titled depicts the "affair" as it is abortively begun. But by means of the Narrator, who here acts the role of the restaurant maitre d' in as suave and knowing a manner as one could wish, the Husband's real gaucherie is again exposed; of course, the Shopgirl's expertise in such matters also contributes to our picture of the suave lover defeated by his lack of polish. Ophuls seems to be saying that at least one party to these illicit liaisons must be innocent, and indeed the dramatic vitality of the scenes suffers when one of them is not. For the Shopgirl's experience, coupled with the already exposed innocence of the Husband (exposed in the previous scene), flattens this episode and robs it of its dramatic energy. Nothing really "happens" here.

Another problem is revealed in the next episode. "The Shopgirl and the Poet." Despite the flamboyance of Jean-Louis Barrault in acting the Poet, the character has already decided on what the Shopgirl will and will not do. There is not enough energy devoted to getting what he wants. As a result, this episode too is not up to the level of the earlier ones.

"The Poet and the Actress" is a brief and vivid little episode in which

Ophuls introduces also his single note of pathos. This is rung when the Shopgirl, who has been advised to do so by the Poet, shows up in the wintry street outside the stage door of the theater where the Actress is starring in the Poet's play. It is a sentimental little moment and a jarring note in an otherwise rigorously well-orchestrated sequence of moods.

The episode is much like a vaudeville blackout skit, but then the form is admirably suited to the material, which dramatizes the extremes of the artificial life-styles of both the Actress and the Poet. Only these two could understand the highly stylized forms of discourse in which each engages.

"The Count and the Actress" seems almost as if Ophuls were hurrying through the end of his film; again, there is a dramatic pattern of innocence versus experience, but like the episode involving the Poet and the Shopgirl, this one is robbed of its possibilities by the Actress' too great self-assurance; she knows too well what the Count will and will not do and his compliance with her wishes is less dramatic than documentary.

The final episode brings us back to the Whore and marks the dark current beneath the surface lightness of the whole film. The Count's impotence, expressed as it is to the Whore, who was victimized at the outset of the film, is a moving piece of sobriety (Figure 12–5). It counters the exuberance of much of the film and underscores what really preoccupies the archstylist Max Ophuls.

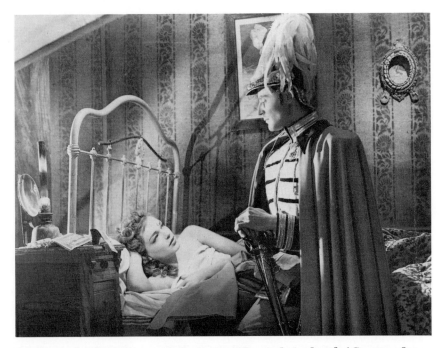

FIGURE 12–5. *The Whore and the Count: The circle is closed.* (*Courtesy Janus Films.*)

Style and Approach

Five discrete elements of *La Ronde* seem to us to embody its special stylistic dimension. As we stated in "Perspective," there is, first and foremost, decor (concretely, decor is the sum total of the physical objects selected for us to see). There is also the use of the camera; the articulation of episode to episode; the employment of the Narrator (about whom we have already spoken; see pp. 275–276); and the witty and ironic tone some of the characters employ with one another, a tone that impresses us with the character's special kind of self-consciousness. A discussion of these elements follows.

DECOR

What remains to be said about this element is to remind the reader that Ophuls learned his trade in the theater. There, unlike the case in, say, the documentary cinema, every part of the visible environment is *made;* in the theater there *is* no *vue vérité* to match *cinéma vérité*. Of course, it is equally true that all film makers working outside the tradition of *cinéma vérité* photograph action against selected backgrounds and that in that sense their environments are also made. We suggest, however, that decor as artifice is especially prominent in Ophuls's work and accounts for the cohesive identity of his style. Let us explore several examples.

First, a setting—the park where the Soldier takes the Housemaid in order to make love to her. This is no ordinary manicured and civilized piece of city garden. Viewers of *La Ronde* can observe that it is, first, a park built on a gentle slope, so that as the couple gets deeper and deeper into it, they seem to rise. Metaphorically the effect suggests that these lovers are moving toward some uplifted goal, their erotic encounter, their highlight, their apex—only to prepare us for the girl's being dashed to earth by the dispatch with which the Soldier is prepared to abandon her when they return to the lower ground of the dance pavillion. Moreover, the sinuously winding paths of this fake garden of Eden are extraordinarily twisted and convoluted. As the lovers make their way along its winding course they seem thereby to be getting lost (an effect that is enhanced by the way the setting is lighted; as they go deeper and deeper into the shrubbery, the darkness and light alternately close in and retreat); this is another metaphorical effect of the strictly designed, artfully constructed character of this setting.

And virtually all the settings have this look of dramatic purpose about them; they all seem brittle to us for their having been constructed for this one dramatic purpose.

The same point holds for other aspects of the decor. The full dress clothing of the Narrator, for example, is only more formally romantic than the outfit he exchanged it for, his adventurer's trench coat. Other clothing serves similar purposes. The Whore is not dressed in an especially whorish fashion; one cannot imagine from her clothing alone that she sells sex; and this is precisely the intended effect. For, indeed, she is dramatically a woman with needs, an ordinary woman; hence, her ordinary clothing. In another case, the utterly virile clothing of the Count stirs our imaginative grasp of his seeming magnificent authority. This prepares us for his ironic downfall, first at the hands of the Actress, who has much more authority than he has, and then in his encounter with the Whore, where his impotence deflates his stature.

So much, in fact, does Ophuls want us to be aware of the physical world of his films that he actually incorporates that world into the basic repertory of his camera style.

CAMERA

Let us take an example of camera style from one episode. There is a lengthy tracking shot into the apartment, the lover's hideaway, arranged by the Young Man for himself and the Wife. As the camera moves, we cannot help but notice that it deliberately interposes between itself and the subjects it is framing many decorated structural pieces of the apartment—for example, columns, wall inserts and so on. In the same episode, a few moments later, when we are in the bedroom after the couple has made love, the camera, static this time, persists in this same kind of interposition. This time, we are aware of curtains, gauzy materials between us and the subject of the shot. The idea in both cases is to force our attention on to the environment and to make us consider the people and the physical world in one act of visual perception.

Another aspect of camera technique is its determination to provide us with a smooth and seamless visual experience. Thus, the moving camera of *La Ronde* ingeniously gathers together action, subjects, and environment in one graceful visual curve. We have already alluded to the way this is done in the superb opening shot of the film, as well as to the lengthy tracking two-shot of the first episode. And there are many other examples.

The same motive, of giving to the film its look of a seamless length of images, accounts for the smooth articulation of one episode to another. Consider the transition from the first to the second: it is accomplished through the bugle notes the Soldier hears and to which he responds; then, when we are inside the barracks, we find that the bugler is our old friend the Narrator. The transition is unbroken. Similarly unbroken is the next transition, from the second to the third episodes; here it is accomplished again by the Narrator. It is he who persuades the Housemaid to leave the pavillion and accompany him, and it is he who takes her through a gradually dissolving background, in which the environmental changes are made without shocks, to the home of the Young Man where she will be employed and where she will play out the next episode. Again, the transition is flawless.

TONE

The witty and ironic tone we spoke of is consistent throughout the film, except in the last few episodes where the structure, as we noted, tends to lose energy; along with vitality, the dialogue is also a casualty of this failure. Nevertheless, the reader will recognize the tone at once from this exchange:

SOLDIER: Ah, Fraulein, you're the nicest, softest one of the whole bunch!
HOUSEMAID: You tried all of them?

Even in the mouth of such a seeming innocent as the Housemaid, Ophuls and Natanson place dialogue of that kind. Similarly, there is this exchange between the Wife and the Husband:

HUSBAND: You were young [not ugly, then]; now you are in full bloom.
WIFE: Business is going well.

We could offer a dozen more of these examples, but the point would be the same: the wit and irony in the tone of these dialogues serve to underscore the self-consciousness of the characters, who are richly aware of what they are doing and where they stand in the battle of the sexes. The tone is also important in establishing firmly the comic perspective of the film, for its ultimate impulse is to suggest the round of life, the never-ending, reconciling cycle of love, sex, and sensuality. The reader must take these elements into account. He must align the music, laughter, and gaiety with the dark colors he sees here and take sides in the critical debate—so armed.

Is *La Ronde* so shallow as some critics have said?

CHAPTER 13

The Seventh Seal

[Det Sjunde Inseglet]

Directed by I N G M A R   B E R G M A N

I can't help thinking that I am working with an instrument so refined that with it, it would be possible to illuminate the human soul with an infinitely more vivid light, to unmask it even more brutally and to annex to our field of knowledge new domains of reality.

Ingmar Bergman, "What Is 'Film Making'?" *Film Makers on Film Making,* ed. by Harry M. Geduld, Bloomington, Ind., 1967.

CAST

JÖNS, THE SQUIRE	Gunnar Björnstrand
DEATH	Bengt Ekerot
JOF	Nils Poppe
ANTONIUS BLOCK, THE KNIGHT	Max von Sydow
MIA	Bibi Andersson
LISA	Inga Gill
TYAN, THE WITCH	Maud Hansson
KARIN, THE KNIGHT'S WIFE	Inga Landré
THE GIRL	Gunnel Lindblom
RAVAL	Bertil Anderberg
THE MONK	Anders Ek
PLOG, THE SMITH	Åke Fridell
THE CHURCH PAINTER	Gunnar Olsson
SKAT	Erik Strandmark
THE MERCHANT	Benkt-Åke Benktsson
WOMAN AT THE INN	Gudrun Brost
LEADER OF THE SOLDIERS	Ulf Johansson
THE YOUNG MONK	Lars Lind

CREDITS

DIRECTOR	Ingmar Bergman
PRODUCER	Allan Ekelund

CREDITS (Continued)

SCENARIO .... *Ingmar Bergman*
DIRECTOR OF PHOTOGRAPHY .... *Gunnar Fischer*
SETS .... *P. A. Lundgren*
MUSIC .... *Erik Nordgren*
EDITOR .... *Lennart Wallén*

Svensk Film   1956   Black and white   96 minutes

Story, Characterization, and Themes

Following the credits, a background statement appears on the screen:

It is the middle of the fourteenth century. Antonius Block and his squire after long years as crusaders in the Holy Land have at last returned to their native Sweden. A land ravished by the Black Plague.

Death comes for the Knight on a desolate shore. The specter is persuaded, however, to play a game of chess. Antonius may live as long as the game continues.

The Knight and his Squire (Jöns) ride inland and encounter their first evidence of the plague—a decaying corpse. They pass a wagon where a juggler (Jof), his wife (Mia), their child (Mikael), and the actor-director of the company (Skat) are asleep. Jof, after he has awakened and left the wagon, has a vision of the Virgin Mary and Child.

The two crusaders have arrived at a church. While Jöns talks to a painter who is depicting on the walls of the porch of the church scenes from the plague, the Knight enters the chapel. He confesses to a monk whose face is hidden his religious doubts, his search for manifest evidence of God's existence, and his desire to perform a significant act before he dies. He also describes the strategy of his chess game with Death. The monk turns out to be his opponent. When Antonius and Jöns leave the church, they find soldiers guarding a young girl (Tyan) who is accused of being a witch and is to be burned at the stake.

Knight and Squire next stop at a deserted village for water. Jöns meets and threatens a renegade priest (Raval), who is robbing corpses. The Girl whom the Squire saves from being raped by Raval agrees to become his housekeeper.

The actors are performing before an inn, with the Knight, the Squire, and the Girl in the audience. Skat goes off with Lisa, the wife of the smith (Plog). Jof and Mia's singing is interrupted by a procession of penitents and a monk's sermon.

Later Jof is bullied by Raval in the dining room of the inn, but is saved by Jöns, who brands the renegade priest. Meanwhile, near the inn the Knight enters into a conversation with Mia. Jof, bruised and frightened, arrives and is solaced by his wife. The three sit down to a repast of strawberries and milk; they are joined by Jöns and the girl. Antonius is deeply moved by the peacefulness of the moment and with new confidence continues his game of chess with Death.

Before the Knight and his company, which now includes Jof and the juggler's family, leave the inn and enter the forest, Plog, who is searching for his errant wife, attaches himself to Jöns. In the forest, they meet Skat and Lisa. To escape the burly smith, the actor pretends to commit suicide, but after the others have left, he is actually taken away by Death. The specter appears again as the group witnesses the burning of Tyan. While they are in the forest, Raval comes to them infected with the plague and dies in agony.

Soon after the death of Raval, the Knight loses his game with Death; however, he is able to divert the specter while Jof, Mia, and their child escape. During a storm that arises, the juggler and his family hide in their wagon.

The Knight and the remainder of the group (Jöns, the Girl, Plog, and Lisa) reach his castle and find Antonius's wife (Karin) awaiting him. During dinner Death appears.

In the epilogue, Jof and Mia emerge from the wagon at the edge of a shore. Jof has a vision of his friends dancing in a line led by Death. He and his family move along the shore in the light of a clear dawn.

Bergman has cast this tale in a very difficult form: a story with mythic overtones permeated with realistic details. The spine of the mythic dimension is a quest. The Knight is in search of a manifest God, As is typical in such a mythic pattern, his journey is simultaneously a physical one and a spiritual one into his own psyche.

To the events of his physical journey, Antonius Block is chiefly passive. He seems indifferent to the people who join and leave his company. He is not seen on the screen when Jöns meets the Girl, the smith asks to accompany the group, Lisa returns to her husband, and Raval dies. Even after the procession of penitents has passed, he makes no comment. The reason for this passivity is obvious: he is so preoccupied with his inner journey that human beings, nature, and art mean little to him. The exceptions to his indifference to reality (meetings with Tyan and Jof's family, the arrival of Death at his castle) are directly related to his quest. The Knight is, therefore, isolated from his fellow man and imprisoned in his dreams and fantasies. He realizes this himself, for he admits to Death in the church that only his search for God is important to him.

Antonius has not always been a selfish seeker after certainty. We are given three glimpses of another type of person. When he speaks of his wife to Mia, we envision a man in love, laughing and happy. Earlier Jöns meets Raval in the deserted village and recalls why his master and he went on the crusade. He implies that the Knight was so fervent in his religious belief and so concerned about righting the world's wrongs that, inspired by Raval's sermons, he left his home and remained away for ten years to fight the infidels. Near the end of the film Karin sees in her husband's tired face the traces of the boy who left her.

The Knight traveled into the world and lost his faith in God and man. In the first sequence, we watch Antonius attempt to pray and realize that for him it is an empty gesture. Then comes the moment for him, later described by the Knight in the church, when a human being can no longer avoid facing the question of what his existence and existence itself means. Death arrives, but Antonius Block is granted a reprieve. Between the appearance of Death and the actual death of the Knight how much time elapses? Is it but a matter of seconds and all the adventures of the film a dream, or the half an hour noted in St. John's *Revelation,* or the hour and a half of viewing time, or the twenty-four hours of cinematic time? In a sense, this question of time is irrelevant, for in the world of the spiritual or the unconscious physical time is suspended; the experiences of the Knight could have occurred in a moment or many hours. All we can be sure of is that a power beyond or within him allows him to embark on his quest.

We have no trouble in identifying Sir Antonius Block as an archetypal figure of the intellectual in search of God. He has lost innocent, unquestioning faith, yet life and death are meaningless to him without faith. He cannot accept an absurd universe, and so he wrestles with shadows and begs them to declare that they are God. The evidence of God that will convince him is more ambiguous than the fact of the quest itself. As an intellectual (a chess player), he does not trust his feelings. Like a fourteenth-century Job, he insists that God reveal Himself, that He speak a word.

It is in sequence IV, when the Knight and Death talk together in the church, that the evidence of God's existence Antonius will accept is enunciated. First, he speaks of "knowledge," then a little later of using his life for one "significant act." We wonder what the relationship is between the existence of God and that significant act, and what he means by the latter.

There is a possible explanation, although we may be attempting to cover up what could be a weakness in the philosophical foundation of the film. If the universe is absurd—beginning and ending in purposeless accident that is governed as long as it exists by physical laws of cause and effect—then no deed can be meaningful, if one means by this phrase an action that convinces the doer that there is some purpose in existence. (It is worth noting that "significant act" is the translation of the Swedish that appears in the subtitles of the film, whereas in the script published by Simon and Schuster, the phrase appears as "meaningful act.") The logic of the Knight might be that if he can perform an act that he considers meaningful, then the universe is not entirely absurd, some power beyond the physical is controlling our lives. This seems rather an equivocal proof of God's existence, depending as it does on individual evaluation. The Knight, however, is desperate and strains to hear even in the slightest sound what he can identify as the authentic voice of God. In any case, as we will see, Antonius does not accept finally his significant deed as the evidence he seeks.

It is in sequence IX that the Knight is next at center stage. We know his conflict; now we observe the first possibility of a direction toward resolution. He speaks to Mia and meets Jof and Mikael. He is greatly moved by the experience. For the first time since his quest began that morning, he has encountered human love, simplicity, and faith. Still, his rhapsodizing about a sign and a great content seems rather extravagant. On the other hand, he is, as we just noted, desperate for signs. His reaction may be similar to that of a man who has been on a desert for days without anything to drink and when rescued honestly praises the bouquet and flavor of a glass of water. Perhaps the best way to approach the sequence is to consider it as symbolic as the milk and strawberries.

Anyone who has viewed Bergman's *Wild Strawberries* and *The Virgin Spring* will recognize that strawberries are a personal symbol for the director of guiltlessness and goodness. There is another parallel between *The Seventh Seal* and other Bergman films, particularly *Wild Strawberries* (discussed in the next chapter of this book). In the latter film, the two Saras and Marianne point Isak Borg toward psychic salvation. It is, as in the later film, a woman in *The Seventh Seal* who helps a despairing man when no one else can.

Antonius, then, recognizes Jof and his family as of great value: an oasis of goodness and innocence in a desert of selfishness and guilt. When he leaves them at the end of sequence IX to continue his game, he concludes from a seemingly casual remark made by Death that they are threatened. It is in the forest that this veiled danger seems to become real.

Two sequences later, after the death of Raval, the Knight is losing his game of chess. He is also being defeated because he has not so far gained anything from his reprieve. At that very moment an opportunity presents itself. From the point of view of the Knight, in some inexplicable way, Jof is aware of the presence of Death; as objective viewers, we see that the juggler has a vision that prompts him to attempt to escape. The Knight decides to help. Although Death remarks that nothing and no one escapes him, Antonius obviously feels that by appearing accidently to knock over the chessmen, he gives Jof and his family a chance to flee.

The Knight has performed his significant act and now should be truly content. Yet he continues to question Death just before the specter leaves. In the castle at Antonius's last moment, he cries to God for mercy. As we point out in our analysis of this penultimate sequence, he is asking God to reveal Himself before it is too late. As far as we know, the silence is not broken. The Knight has failed in his quest and in the end, with the others, he dances to the tune of Death.

We are once again confronted with the possibility that the philosophical underpinnings of *The Seventh Seal* are shaky. The Knight informs Death that he wishes for a reprieve in order to perform a significant act, yet when he does so, it seems to make no difference to him. If we have faith in Bergman as a script writer and director, we begin to question whether the Knight's quest is other than appears on the surface. Antonius maintains that life is absurd unless God manifests Himself to the human intellect. Is it possible that this premise is wrong? Could it be that in the context of the film God reveals his presence by the very existence of love in the world, and one of the forms of love is when a person without thought of his own advantage, out of sheer altruism, acts for others? From this perspective, what Antonius does for Jof and his family is a significant act, a meaningful act, an act of love, a revelation of God.

The Knight thus has failed in his quest only in terms of the conditions he has set; actually, although he does not recognize it, he has succeeded. He is almost completely selfish until he helps Jof, Mia, and Mikael. The basic problem of the Knight is not that God does not reveal Himself, but that Antonius is so confined by his intellect. He is so preoccupied with crying and whispering his questions that he cannot hear the still, small voice of God and cannot realize that in his case the Almighty has been merciful.

If we consider the film objectively, we may not only be critical of the Knight's spiritual blindness, but also of the script. The significant act of Antonius would have been more meaningful if it had involved more of a sacrifice on his part. He is only one move away from defeat when he knocks over the chessmen. By his act, he personally loses nothing. Would it not have been more dramatic, although admittedly more obvious, for Antonius to have lost some advantage in time or position by his gesture. Of course, one of the pleasures of criticism is hindsight; it avoids the problems of implementing a supposed improvement in a work of art.

Antonius Block is the chief character in the film, but not the only one of interest. Each person, however, is related to the Knight's quest, for the search for God—or more generally, the search for meaning in life and, therefore, of death—is a touchstone that reveals how each individual reacts to his circumambient universe. The ways of the other characters are principally in contrast to the way the Knight has chosen to deal with a problem that every human being must confront in one way or another, to one degree or another.

The Squire Jöns seems to have found an answer: there is no God and the universe is absurd. His commitment is to life and the pleasures of the senses. Because he does not doubt and question, he is a man of action. He deals with Raval in the deserted village and at the inn as efficiently as we are sure he could, if he wished, dispatch the soldiers that guard Tyan.

An earthy Sancho Panza to his master, a spiritual Don Quixote, he is a pragmatist.

On the other hand, Jöns is neither stupid nor selfish. As he tells Plog, he is an educated man, and reveals it in his wit and verbal facility. He sees through hypocrisy, conceit, and the necessary pretenses that govern such a relationship as that of the smith and Lisa. His intelligence prevents him from being arrogant and self-centered. He can even laugh at himself, as when he denies Plog's assertion that he believes his own nonsense. This very intelligence, however, combined with another quality —compassion—makes him vulnerable. He is not a happy man, for he is aware of the differences between what is and what should be and he feels the suffering of his fellow creatures. At the church, he is appalled at what the plague does to people physically and emotionally, he helps the Girl in the village and defends Jof in the inn, he must turn away from Tyan burning at the stake and makes no pretense that he is indifferent to the agony of the dying Raval.

As the vision of the Knight is restricted by his intellect, so the Squire has limitations. His cynicism prevents him from admitting to the existence of anything beyond the physical world; he cannot enter the church but only go as far as its porch. There is no evidence that he appreciates the special qualities of Jof and Mia. Although he obviously admires Antonius, he is unsympathetic to the Knight's prodding and searching, and feels compelled to disabuse his master of any illusions. After the procession of the penitents, at the burning of Tyan, at the appearance of Death at the castle, Jöns acts as a one-man chorus in a play by Euripides arguing with the main protagonist.

The chief justification for the view of a number of critics that *The Seventh Seal* is an existentialist film lies in the character of Jöns. The fourteenth-century Squire would have no trouble understanding a philosophy which advocates that existence precedes essence, that the human condition is absurd, that man is free to create his own values, and that the man of good faith must engage in actions for which he accepts responsibility. The Squire's last words in the film might serve as an epigraph for any book on existentialism: "Yes, [I accept death], but under protest." It is thus understandable that many viewers identify more easily with Jöns than Antonius Block and consider him the true hero of the film.

As is appropriate to a clown of God, Jof is less complex than the Knight and his Squire. One can easily imagine him reincarnated a couple of centuries later as Barnaby, our Lady's juggler, described in the story by Anatole France. His innocence is real and his faith complete. He is not, however, a plastic saint. He sings bawdy songs (as well as composes sacred ones), is hardly a personification of courage in the inn, and steals Raval's bracelet, then allows his wife to believe that he bought it for her.

Jof is taken advantage of by Skat and bullied by Raval. Perhaps in compensation for being put upon by other human beings, he has been granted the gift of visions. In our analysis of the last sequence of the film, we discuss the validity of his visions. Whether they are genuine or not, he does have insight into the danger of death accompanying the Knight, and in his final, cosmic fantasy, confused and inexplicable though his identification of the dancing figures may be, he senses the power of Death to cleanse his victims of suffering.

It is, however, the juggler's first vision that reveals most clearly his role in the philosophical substratum of the film. Once again, we have dealt in greater detail with this point in our analysis of the scene. Both visually and through the background music Bergman conveys to us that Jof's feelings for the Virgin and for his wife are two forms of the same impulse. In other words, he does not distinguish in his reactions, as in the case of the Knight, between the divine and the human; both are permeated by a love that sustains and exhilarates him.

Yet, Jof, too, has his limitations. Although he does entertain people and compose songs, manifestations of his goodness and what he gains from the perceptions of his inner vision are basically confined to himself and his family. Unlike Jöns, the compassionate man of action, he makes no attempt to help his fellow man. In horror, but without stirring or comment, he watches the procession of penitents, the burning of Tyan, and the death of Raval.

An ideal person, the complete human being, would be one who possesses a combination of the virtues of Antonius Block, Jöns, and Jof. Unfortunately, on this earth such an ideal rarely appears. We are fragmented and incomplete, and we need to recognize and respect the strengths of others to compensate for our own weaknesses. And this may be just the point Bergman is making in his characterizations of the three major figures in the film.

Mia comes closer to the ideal of a woman than the three as individuals to that of an exemplary man. We are referring, however, to a masculine ideal that a modern feminist would not be likely to endorse. Mia is lovely and sensual with an innate dignity and graciousness that is especially revealed in her conversation with the Knight. She is clear-headed and practical, so that she is skeptical about Jof's visions. Yet her love for her husband is so deep and secure that she can verbalize it without embarrassment. She even mocks him gently, for example, when he pretentiously points out to the Knight his responsibilities as director of the company after Skat has disappeared. Although Mia may question her husband, she fundamentally respects his visions and submits to his decisions. This submissiveness extends to life itself. She does not question (as the Knight), protest (as Jöns), or go beyond the immediate and the real (as Jof). Existence is simply to be accepted and enjoyed. To the Knight she says that things are nearly always nice for her, one day is like another, and she cannot understand why people torture themselves. We sense that as long as she has her son and husband, food and shelter, she will be happy.

This contented creature, however, can serve a very positive function for men. She solaces their wounded bodies and spirits; she represents the eternal feminine, the great mother figure, the "anima." As we noted earlier, this type of woman appears frequently in Bergman's films. In sequence IX, Mia tends her husband after he has been battered at the inn and revives him. Even more important in the context of the film, she encourages the Knight to speak of past happiness and by example, comment, and her very presence leads him out of his self-centeredness to an awareness of love in the world that will enable him to perform his significant act.

Bergman took a risk in making Jof, Mia, and Mikael such an apparent reflection of the Holy Family (at least he did not name the child Immanuel). We are not offended, however, by this obvious association because husband and wife in their own rights are fallible, real individuals. Still, we do sometimes feel uneasy about the way the director manipulates the family to serve the purposes of the symbolic meaning of the film.

The minor characters in *The Seventh Seal* are straightforward and unambiguous, with one exception that we will consider in a moment. Plog the smith is dim-witted, crude, and clumsy. His love for his wife and desire to have her back is more pitiful than admirable. He does, however, at one moment earn our respect when he faces Death in the castle with unassuming dignity. Lisa, his wife, is a selfish wanton. One can understand her sensual needs and desertion of Plog, whose flaccid nature encourges such cruelty, but it is difficult to be indulgent toward a woman who urges her husband to kill a lover who has disappointed her. Skat, actor and ineffectual lover, is a comic character even at the moment of his death.

Raval is definitely not a comic figure. He is so evil and cowardly that he is almost unbelievable. Yet, we are drawn to imagine what led him from being a priest recruiting for a crusade to his present state, and we cannot help but feel pity for the man in agony dying from the plague. Tyan is also a victim of the plague, but it is her own delusions and the fears of her age that destroy her rather than *Pasteurella bacilli.*

We can add to a betrayed husband, a trollop, a conceited actor, a villain, and a hysterical girl the following: a cynical painter, a group of guilt-ridden flagellants led by a sadistic monk, soldiers who are willing to burn a young girl for pay, and diners at an inn that are insensitive and cruel. This is hardly a cast of characters to encourage an optimistic view of human nature.

The plague in the film is obviously, as in Albert Camus's novel *The Plague*, not simply a disease, but a personification of the destructive forces inherent in the human condition. As such, it is a test of the inner strength and values of individuals. The conclusion we can draw from *The Seventh Seal* is that Bergman's view of the majority of human beings, at least at the time he created the film, was predominantly negative.

In contrast, but not counterbalancing this motley crew, whose qualities range from the best of ineffectualness to the worst of evil, are the four major characters and two others (the faithful dog by his dead master is not a character, but is more admirable than most of the human beings in the film). Karin, the Knight's wife, is a true lady of a castle in bearing, self-possession, dignity, and courage. We assume that she has directed the activities of the castle herself for ten years. Although a plague is raging, she remains at home in the center of danger awaiting her husband's return. When Death appears, it is she who moves to the front of the group and courteously welcomes him. Even when she sees her husband for the first time in a decade, Karin preserves her reserve. We sense that this reserve is not evidence of a cold woman, but rather of a passionate one in control of herself. She says that she sees in the Knight's eyes the boy who left on a crusade. We see in the small smile, affectionate look, and gesture with which she touches her husband's cheek, a momentary vision of the Knight's description of her to Mia as a maiden in love filling the castle with laughter and song.

The other significant woman in the film is the exception we referred to earlier to straightforward and unambiguous minor characters. We know nothing about the background of the Girl who may be mute that Jöns finds in the deserted village. Until the penultimate sequence, we find expressed in her handsome face only fear (as the procession of penitents passes and during the trip through the forest) and compassion (at the deaths of Tyan and Raval). Yet, she seems to be sensitive to the nuances of what is happening around her. At the picnic of milk and strawberries in front of the actors' wagon, she stares at Mia and the knight as they talk.

It is in sequence XII that her sensitivity is fully revealed. From the moment that the knight and his friends enter the castle, there are more close-ups of her than any of the others. Her eyes move restlessly along the hallways and rooms of the castle as though she were searching for someone the others could not see. She is the first to see Death; she delivers the last words (the only time she speaks) of the film before the epilogue; and her face is the last on the screen in the scene.

We have speculated in our analysis of this sequence on what Bergman might be trying to convey through the Girl (never given a proper name in the credits or the film). She appears to welcome Death and the sentence she speaks associates her with Jesus before he died on the cross. In addition, she is not among those described by Jof as dancing with Death. All this suggests that her life has been one of suffering and death is a release. We feel, however, that in the case of the Girl Bergman has teased us intellectually and promised more visually than he has delivered emotionally. She remains an enigma for us. There is nothing wrong with enigmatic characters in a film except when they are clearly intended to carry a meaning and are too unsubstantial to bear the burden.

Death, as with the others, is a character in the film, but also a specter and a force. How can we speak of motivation in a figure who is beyond freedom or compulsion? He does at moments reveal echoes of human qualities. He seems intrigued by the challenge of the chess game. He jokes with Skat as he cuts down the tree. He seems to sympathize with the suffering of the Knight as he listens to him in the chapel. He seems to enjoy deflating the contentment of Antonius at their third meeting with a question about Jof and his family. "Seems"—we cannot avoid this qualifier when referring to the intentions of Death.

The main problem concerning Death is whether he is to any degree a free agent or is completely controlled by an omniscient and omnipotent deity that has already planned every move of the game of life. Evidence for the latter view includes Death's own statement that there are no secrets and he knows nothing, although he is infuriatingly ambiguous in everything he states and we share the Knight's sense of frustration. We wonder why Jof and his family are allowed to live, for nothing and no one escapes Death. Or were they never threatened? Death has only insinuated that they were in danger. Perhaps they were not destined to die at this time. In that case, Antonius gained nothing for them by his ruse. Perhaps everything that happens to the Knight during his journey was staged (it is possible that the entire film is a dream), so that Antonius is allowed, although he does not recognize it, to find salavation by an act of love.

On the other hand, if Death is not a free agent, why does he trick the Knight into revealing his strategy? Or is it possible that Death is a natural force, a manifestation of the rhythms of nature that has no purpose beyond regeneration of itself? As we will point out in "Analysis of Major Sequences," one of the most repeated visual motifs in the film is the passing of man and his works while nature persists.

Antonius Block, directly and obliquely, wrestles with these questions and suppositions. He finds only silence. But we, also, the viewers of *The Seventh Seal*, confront the same enigmas and contraditions and find that Bergman, the creator of the film, is also silent. In essence, this is the major criticism that has been leveled against the film. We can better focus on this often-repeated objection if we first recognize a major structural device in the film that profoundly influences what meanings are conveyed to us.

Contrast so permeates this film that it becomes a theme. Types of contrast, manifested in the elements of the narrative, the visual, and the auditory include the following: illusion versus reality, nature versus man, skepticism versus faith, emotions versus intellect, courage versus coward-ice, selfishness versus compassion, and lust versus love. Bergman, thus, has made use of a multiform dialectic in the Hegelian sense (thesis–antithesis–synthesis). The problem is whether or not he has presented the first two stages of a dialectic without achieving the third. In other words, has he simply presented opposing ideas and emotions that be-wilder us rather than lead us to new insights into man's relationships with himself and "the Other"? Each viewer must answer this question for himself. We feel that in the end the director has not synthesized his numerous dichotomies.

In defense of Bergman, we should take into account that he may never have intended to give us answers but only to pose questions. We may be expecting too much from an hour and a half motion picture. A film is not a philosophical treatise but an emotional and intellectual experience. Few viewers would deny that *The Seventh Seal* moves and provokes us and reinforces our faith that cinema molded by an artist can do more than solely stimulate our ocular and auditory nerves. That we expect so much from the film and are tempted to consider how it might have been made more coherent and meaningful is a compliment that any director should receive with pride.

Analysis of Major Sequences

I. Prologue: Death and the Knight

After a background statement appears on the screen, the first image of the film is a cloud-covered sky; a brightness filters through from the camera left side of the frame. There is a crescendo of music on the sound track. A giant dark bird appears floating in air. It is a disquieting creature, suggesting a harbinger of doom. The next image, shrouded in silence, is equally ominous: a promontory of black rock. On the sound track we hear a voice read *The Revelation of St. John the Divine* 8:1–2: "And when the Lamb had opened the seventh seal, there was silence in heaven about the space of half an hour. And the seven angels who had the seven trumpets prepared themselves to sound."

The significance of the seventh seal is that it is the last one, the climax of the Apocalypse, when the world ends and man is judged. After the seventh angel pours out the seventh vial of the wrath of God upon the earth, "It is done." (16:17) and "men blasphemed God because of the plague of hail; for the plague thereof was exceeding great." (16:21) When the seventh angel sounds his trumpet—and the following phrase is particularly pertinent to the major theme of the film—"The mystery of God shall be finished." (10:7) Another passage in *Revelation* may ex-plain the presence of the bird in the opening moments of *The Seventh*

Seal. Just before the final slaying of the unjust, the fouls that fly in the midst of heaven are invited to "the supper of the great God," where they shall feast on the slaughtered. (19:17–18)

The Apocalypse is a catastrophe only for evil ones and the doomed. The King of Kings on a white horse will destroy the former in battle and judge the latter. Then God will bring heaven to pass, the earth and sea will be no more, and tears, death, sorrow, crying, and pain will be "former things." (21:1, 4)

So Bergman's brief quotation at the opening of *The Seventh Seal* reverberates with overtones that anticipate the symbolic meaning of the plague, the anguish of the doomed Knight and his friends, and the hope personified by Jof and his family.

From the forces of heaven and earth, we turn to the living. A very high-angle shot shows two horses at the edge of water on a desolate beach. Cut to the Knight, Antonius Block, lying on his back staring into space, a chessboard near him. There is the sound of lapping water on the sound track. The following shots succeed each other: the Squire, Jöns, asleep on the ground; the horses and the sea; the Knight again in a medium close-up; the water; back to the Squire. A visual pattern is thus established of a contrast between the transitory world of the living and the eternal one of the sea.

The Knight walks into the sea and washes his face. In a long shot we see him returning to the beach. He drops to his knees and prays—or seems to. The expression on his face in a medium close-up indicates that either prayer offered little solace or he is unable honestly to pray. He rises and walks toward the camera, which then pans to the chessboard.

A superimposition of the chessboard on the sea; in a moment the former disappears and only the waves are left. If we did not get the point of the earlier contrast of shots between the living and the sea, it is made clear now. The game of chess was created by man; both the pieces and the moves are, as has often been noted, a microcosm of human existence. But man plays his games against the background of the everlasting rhythms of nature—which may be the physical face of God. The individual, mankind itself, may vanish, yet those rhythms, like the ebb and flow of the waves, will remain.

There need be no transition from the sea to Death, for both are manifestations of the same demiurge. The shot of materialized Death, immediately after the image of the sea, is made more dramatic by sudden silence. He is framed by rocks to his right, water to his left, and the sky above him. His body from the neck down is a column of black, not even his hands are visible. His head is covered by a black hood. His face is even whiter than the sky above him. He has no eyebrows, only the suggestions of features, except for eyes as black as his cloak.

The Knight, packing his knapsack, looks up. There is little surprise or fear in his expression, for he has known for some time that Death has walked by his side. During their dialogue, there is a series of seventeen cuts, with one exception (from a long shot to a close-up of the specter), back and forth between Death and the Knight.

Antonius proposes a game of chess. Death accepts the challenge. They sink to their knees before the chessboard. The Knight sets the stakes: he may live as long as the game continues; he will be released if he wins. Of course, Antonius knows the inevitable end, but the game is a gambit for time. We have not learned yet the reason that he desires a reprieve from death.

The sea is in the background, so that it almost seems as if the chessboard is floating on water. The Knight holds out both his fists (Figure 13–1); Death chooses the left one, which contains a black pawn. The Knight exclaims, "Black for you!" Death smiles at Antonius's surprise and remarks that it is an appropriate color for himself. This is not an unimportant incident. According to the rules of chess, white has the first move and the opportunity of dominating the opening game. By choosing black (can there really be chance in a contest with Death?) the specter is indicating that he will not use his supernatural powers to win, although later we will puzzle over his tricking the Knight into revealing his strategy. Antonius will be able to exert his free will and make his own choices,

FIGURE 13–1. *Death and the Knight play chess.* (*Courtesy Janus Films.*)

even seem to be controlling his destiny. Death will bide his time and respond to the Knight's moves; yet he is completely confident of victory.

The board is turned around and the game begins. Once again there is a superimposition. The sky is projected over the players. They disappear and only an image of the sky remains. For the last time in the sequence the transitory nature of individual human affairs is emphasized.

II. First Stage of the Journey

The Knight saddles his horse, and he and the Squire leave the shore. In a series of four shots we see the beginning of the journey and hear dramatic music on the sound track. First there is a medium long shot as they move inland, then three long shots, from a very high angle—a bird's-eye view—as the two ride from the shore and between large cliffs. There is a cut to shot #1, dissolve to shots #2 and 3, and a cut to shot #4.

Dissolve to a shot of them, the Squire riding behind the Knight, silhouetted against the horizon, the land occupying two thirds of the lower portion of the frame. We see and hear Jöns sing a cynical song, obviously hoping to irritate his master but being unsuccessful. Soon he describes what he has heard of such evil omens as graves opening and four suns in the heavens. The Knight continues to ignore him. They stop beside what appears to be a man lying with his dog sitting patiently near him. When Jöns grips his shoulder to ask directions, the figure turns out to be a rotting corpse. The faithfulness of the dog now touches us; in retrospect we will admire that dog even more as we find that death encourages man's selfishness and inconstancy.

As the two continue riding, the Knight asks if the man gave directions. Jöns remarks that he said nothing yet was most eloquent. The Knight understands and looks at him gloomily.

A dissolve to a shot of the travelers passing a tree where a wagon and horses are camped.

III. The Players and Jof's Vision

Inside the wagon Jof, Mia, their son Mikael, and Skat are sleeping. Jof awakens, then crawls over the others and goes outside. He does a couple of exercises, drinks some water, and talks to the horse.

He sits on a branch and begins juggling apples; his back is to the camera. Suddenly he stops. A luminous musical theme is heard. The camera slowly tracks in toward Jof as he turns around and a smile appears on his face. The camera continues to move in to a medium close-up. Cut to a long shot of a field in which the Virgin, with a crown on her head and in a long gown, holds the hands of the Child as he tentatively walks; she looks toward the camera. Back to the medium close-up of Jof, who rubs his eyes, then stares with a questioning look. Obviously, the vision has disappeared. We do not return to the field; instead, the juggler jumps up, runs to the wagon, and climbs in.

When we discuss the last scene of the film, in which Jof again sees phantasmic figures, we will consider whether he experiences genuine visions or the images are products of his active imagination. We note now, however, that although we can barely make out the face of the Virgin, she does seem to resemble Mia.

Inside the wagon Jof wakes up his wife and describes what he has seen. Mia is indulgent but skeptical. She has been through this before, and reminds her husband of a "supernatural" event that he arranged himself. He admits to that one deception, yet stoutly defends the validity of his other visions. Skat, the third member of the company of players, complains about being awakened and goes back to sleep.

The scene in the wagon is one lengthy shot (more than two minutes). The camera moves only once: a track in to a fairly tight two-shot when Jof describes the Virgin, and then a return to its original position when he defends his vision.

Outside, Jof and Mia play with their son. They discuss Mikael's future. His father hopes that he will be a great acrobat or even a juggler who can do the impossible trick of making a ball stand still in air. Mia exclaims that the trick is impossible. Jof smiles, looks toward his son, and remarks, "Yes, for us, but not for him." Here is the most explicit of the symbolic associations of the three with the Holy Family: the given names of the couple, their innocence and love, the visionary gift of Jof, and the parallel between the Virgin and Child and Mia and Mikael.

Mia leans against a tree and closes her eyes as Jof sings a song in praise of Christ that he has just composed. The song is part of one of the many contrasts (between hope and despair, goodness and evil, faith and cynicism) that constitute a major structuring technique of the film. Jof sings of great joy in heaven. Jöns's songs are very different. In the beginning of sequence II, he opens a lyric with a reference to God above, but ends with Satan here below. He offers another cynical song in sequence V about man as the victim of the villain fate.

While Mia, an inattentive listener to her husband's singing, snuggles close to Jof, Skat comes out of the wagon holding a death mask in one hand. He complains at having to act the unprofitable role of Death so that the priests can frighten people during the pestilence. His only concern is if the women will like him in his costume. Skat loftily informs Jof that because he is such a fool, he is going to play the Soul of Man. Before climbing back into the wagon, the actor hangs the skull on a post. There is a hold on a medium close-up of it.

What follows is in contrast to the death mask and everything it represents, as well as an echo of an earlier event in the sequence. Jof is balancing apples just as before he saw the Virgin and Child. We hear the same musical theme as was played during that vision. Mia, in a quiet voice, asks her husband to sit still and listen, then whispers that she loves him. He slowly turns to her and on his face is a look that expresses how very deeply he reciprocates her tenderness. Suddenly we understand that his feelings for his wife are interfused with his feelings for the Virgin. For Jof, love for a human being and love of the divine are not separate but interrelated, two sides of a single coin of adoration, delight, and dedication.

IV. *The Knight and the Squire at a Church*

We see from a high angle Antonius and Jöns dismounting before a gateway; a church, camera left, is set back from the road. The Knight walks toward the small church, followed a few minutes later by the Squire. Significantly, Jöns never enters the chapel but remains on the covered church porch.

A painter on a scaffold is creating a mural on a porch wall. He explains to Jöns that it depicts scenes from the plague. By means of pans and close-ups three portions of the painting are presented, each one anticipating, in reverse order, a scene or sequence forthcoming in the film: the Dance of Death (the last scene of the film), a man dying of the plague (Raval's death), and flagellants (the procession of the penitents).

His verbal description of the spiritual as well as physical effects of the plague are as horrifying as his mural. Jöns puts on a brave front, but he is evidently frightened and, to the amusement of the artist, asks for a drink.

We leave the two just within the church entrance engrossed in the plague itself and join the Knight inside the church wrestling with the more profound problems of the meaning, rather than the manifestations, of death.

A long shot of the chapel from behind the Knight as he walks toward the altar surmounted by a life-sized wooden sculpture of Christ on the crucifix. In the next shot the camera is high and opposite Antonius, as though from the perspective of the face of Christ. A ray of light is behind the Knight; as he looks up there is an expression on his face of inquiry, even challenge. We then see the upper half of the Christ figure from a low angle, Antonius's point of view. The distorted, suffering face of Christ, looking away from the camera, is spotlighted, with darkness behind it. Back to the high-angle shot of the Knight. Not a word has been spoken or an expressive gesture made, yet through dynamic cutting we feel the struggle between a doubting human being and the most significant symbol of the Christian religion.

The Knight moves his eyes to his left, then turns his head. Cut to a shot of an iron grille set into the wall for confessions. On the other side of the grille is a small room with a crucifix on the wall; a monk is there who turns away so that his cowl hides his face. Return to the Knight, still seen from a high angle. He walks to the grille, places one hand against the wall next to it, leans forward, and says, "I want to confess as best I can, but my heart is a void." In a medium close-up of him (the camera on his right side), his face is in profile, eyes looking straight ahead. "The void is a mirror. I see my face." He places his head on his hand. "My indifference to man has shut me out. I live now in a world of ghosts, . . ." The shot continues, but now the camera slowly tracks in ". . . a prisoner in my dreams." We hear a voice say, "Yet you do not want to die." The Knight lifts up his head and turns toward the camera, his face looking in the direction of the large crucifix. "Yes, I do." Between his hand and unlifted head we see behind him through the grille the face of Death framed by a cowl. Death asks, "What are you waiting for?" The Knight replies, his face still turned from the grille, "Knowledge."

With this word, the lengthy shot ends, and there is a cut to the crucifix. It is presented from the same low angle as before, but the perspective has changed; now Christ's head is facing the camera, as though looking directly at the Knight (we assume this is a subjective shot from Antonius's point of view). We hear Death say, "You want a guarantee?"

Back to the Knight. "Call it what you will." He leans forward out of the frame. Cut to him kneeling, the placement of the camera still unchanged. "It is so hard to conceive God with one's senses. Why must he hide in a mist of invisible miracles?" The Knight is in the center of the frame. In the upper corner, camera left, is a portion of the grille itself; on the right is a shadow of the grille. From this point in the scene until Death reveals himself, the shadow of the grille, reminding us of prison bars, will either be above the Knight or on his face. As he noted earlier, he is imprisoned in his dreams. He is also imprisoned in a network of questions. After he kneels, he asks a series of nine questions.

"How are we to believe the believers when we don't believe ourselves?" The Knight lifts his head and turns again in the direction of the crucifix. And again there is a cut to Christ on the cross. A hold on the crucified Christ as we hear Antonius continue: "What will become of those of us who want to believe but cannot?" Return to the Knight. "And what of those who neither will nor can believe? Why cannot I kill God within me?" The camera tracks in and pans up, so that we see clearly the figure of Death behind the grille. "Why does He go on living in a painful, humiliating way? I want to tear him out of my heart."

The view of Death is a visual transition to the next shot—from inside the confession chamber. Death stares almost directly at the camera, his face white against the darkness of the cowl. His expression seems impassive; he barely moves his lips as he speaks. Yet we sense in those dark eyes and the frown lines between them an awareness of the burden of his responsibility and a sympathy for the anguish of his victims.

To Death's left is a portion of the iron screen. Behind the grille, a little lower, is the long face of the Knight marked with the shadow of the grille; one of his hands grips the iron. In the dialogue that follows, the camera will remain stationary in this lengthy two-shot (two minutes) and the two figures will move only slightly. Our attention is focused entirely on what is said (Figure 13–2).

The Knight wants knowledge, not faith or suppositions; he wants God to speak to him. Yet God is silent. Death comments that perhaps there is no one there. Antonius exclaims: "Then life is a senseless horror. No man can live with death and know all is meaningless." Most people do not think about death or the meaning of life, Death observes, until their last moment of existence. This statement leads the Knight to reflect: "I see. We must make an idol of our fear and call it God."

Antonius describes his game of chess with Death and explains why he sought a reprieve:

KNIGHT: My whole life has been a meaningless search. I say this without bitterness or self-reproach. It is the same for all. But I wish to use my life for one significant act.

Death encourages the Knight to reveal his strategy in the game.

This scene is crucial: it explains—or at least attempts to—the motives of the Knight and his basic problem of a silent God (discussed in the previous section of this analysis). In sum, Antonius Block finds life meaningless unless he can be convinced by his senses and mind that God exists; he must perform a significant act before he dies or even hope is impossible.

FIGURE 13–2. *The Knight confesses his anguish over a silent God to a monk* (*Death in disguise*). (*Courtesy Janus Films.*)

As soon as the Knight discloses his strategy, the visual dynamics begin again. There is a cut to the other side of the grille, behind Antonius. It is a low-angle shot, so that we see past the Knight's head and shoulders the figure of Death loom up as he rises and declares, "I shall remember that." Antonius also stands up and the camera tracks in to a close-up of the Knight's head, his hand on the grille, and beyond, the face of Death. We return to Antonius's face in a reverse angle shot. A third of the frame, camera left, is occupied by the black cowl Death is wearing; in the rest of the frame is the Knight's outraged face through the grille as he exclaims, "Traitor. You have tricked me!" and declares that he will still find a way.

The last of this series of four shots of alternating camera positions from Death's side of the grille to behind the Knight is from over Antonius's right shoulder. Death sets the inn as the place where the game will continue; he leaves. The Knight turns away from the grille, his back almost completely filling the screen.

In the next shot, a medium close-up, Antonius faces the camera. One hand still holds the iron screen, as though the encounter with Death had imprisoned it there, but the other hand is free. Part of his figure is in a shaft of light from a source above him. Antonius looks at his right hand and says, "The blood is pulsing in my veins." He looks toward the light: "The sun is still at the zenith . . ." He returns to staring at his hand. ". . . and I, Antonius Block, am playing chess with Death."

There is pride in the Knight's voice and his expression as he speaks with a smile. The warrior feels the exhilaration of his last battle—to be fought in his soul rather than on a field of war—as he stands with one half of his body in the sunlight of life and the other half in the shadow of death. Bergman allows the image and words to convey the dramatic intensity of the moment; there is no cut to a low-angle shot, no rhetorical gesture, no musical crescendo. The director simply cuts to the next scene.

Jöns and the painter obviously have freely partaken of the contents of a cask. The Squire drunkenly informs his companion that his master and he endured the horrors of the Crusade for ten years. He sums up his feelings in a sentence: "Our crusade was so stupid that only an idealist could have thought it out." As he talks, he is painting on a piece of wood. A cut to it allows us to see that Jöns has created a self-portrait. It is in the same style as the painter's mural and the backdrops for the stage on which the players act in a later sequence. The camera returns to Jöns and tracks in. The cynical fellow supplements his visual self-caricature with a verbal one. The statement is revealing:

JöNS: Here's Squire Jöns. He grins at Death, chuckles at the Lord, laughs at himself and smiles at the girls. His world exists only for himself. Absurd to all, even to himself. Meaningless in heaven, indifferent in hell.

The Knight enters as his Squire is speaking. He looks at the caricature. Without a word of comment, he shoves Jöns with his hand to indicate that they are leaving, and walks away. The Squire makes an impudent, disrespectful face at his master, the same one he had when riding behind the Knight in sequence II, but he rises and follows.

Outside the church, the two find soldiers and a monk putting a girl, Tyan, in the stocks and smearing a stinking paste around her. A soldier explains that the girl is a witch who has had intercourse with the devil and will be burned the next morning. The paste is to keep the Evil One away from them. The Knight stares at her and throws away Jöns's self-portrait. Her hair has been cropped, which emphasizes how young she is; she seems at the moment to be in a cataleptic state. Antonius, who has confessed a few minutes earlier that he is indifferent to his fellow creatures, can only ask her if she has seen the devil. When he meets her again, we learn why he is interested. The monk interrupts and remarks that she is believed to have caused the plague.

The final image of this sequence is a very effective one. After the two men have left by the gate through which they entered, there is a cut to a long shot from the gateway of Tyan with a soldier next to her, his sturdy legs spread apart. The girl's shrieks emanate from the sound track. Antonius and Jöns leading their horses pass directly in front of the camera, blocking out the shot for a moment. Finally there is a dissolve to the next scene.

V. A Deserted Village

Antonius and Jöns on horseback are seen in a setting similar to that in sequence II. Jöns sings a depressing song about evil in the world. The Knight quiets his Squire by giving him something to eat.

Dissolve to a long shot of a village. A feeling of threatening, unseen forces is conveyed by the background music and camera perspectives. High- and low-angle shots are used. In some the camera is located as though the two travelers are being observed by many eyes. Other shots are subjective, as the Squire sees portions of the seemingly deserted village.

Jöns gets off his horse and leaves the Knight behind; he is carrying a water sack. Eventually he enters one of the huts. At a sound he hides behind a door. We see a man enter the room and take a ring and bracelet from the body of a woman. The robber turns; the Girl is in the doorway. He admits that he steals from the dead as he pulls the young woman into the room and looks at her with cruel, lustful eyes. He pushes the door shut.

Jöns is there. He recognizes the thief as Raval, a priest who ten years earlier through his preaching had persuaded Antonius Block to join the Crusade. The Squire remarks that now he understands those ten years:

"We were too well-off, too satisfied. The Lord wanted to chasten our pride." He shoves Raval against a wall, then knocks him down and puts a knife against his throat. He will not kill Raval, however, because he is not bloodthirsty. Yet he warns the renegade priest that he will brand him if they meet again. Jöns and the Girl leave.

In one lengthy long shot Jöns washes his face at a well and introduces himself to the Girl. When he tries to kiss her, she resists. He stops struggling with her and nonchalantly comments that he could have raped her, but that he is tired of "that kind of love." He begins to walk away. He stops, looks back, asks if she would like to be his housekeeper, for he has hope that his wife has died, and finally walks out of the frame.

The young woman, who has not spoken a word and seems mute, is seen alone in a high-angle, long shot as she looks after him and then follows.

VI. The Players in the Yard of Embarrassment Inn

Jof, Mia, and Skat have set up a stage before an inn. Bergman's film script (*Four Screenplays of Ingmar Bergman*, New York, 1960) informs us that it is called "Embarrassment Inn"; there is no indication in the film of its name.

There are cuts in the first half of the sequence between what is being performed on stage and the audience. First, a pan shows us the people watching. The next two shots of the audience include a buxom blonde, whom we later learn is Lisa, the wife of the smith, Plog, the huge man behind her with a hammer on his shoulder.

The performance consists of songs, dances, and pantomime. Appropriately, Skat plays the role of the seducer; his costume and flute suggest a satyr. What the three players offer is bawdy entertainment, a contrast to the art of the painter at the church (Figure 13–3).

After Skat leaves the stage, the setting of the remainder of the sequence, with the exception of the last shot, is an area in front of the wagon. We hear on the sound track, however, Jof and Mia singing. Once again Bergman uses a contrast, only this time for satirical purposes and between a song and a visual scene (counterpoint asynchronization).

The seduction by Lisa of the very susceptible Skat is presented without words, but the lines of the surrealistic song slyly comment on the farcical ritual—it is humorous because it is so obvious and exaggerated—that the amorous man and woman go through before satisfying their mutual needs. When Lisa leans over to spread a tablecloth on the ground and outlines ample buttocks beneath her skirt, we hear on the sound track the line: "The Black One squats on the shore." Just after the actor follows Lisa behind a bush, Jof sings: "The sow lays eggs," and a chicken comes out from under the bush.

After Skat and Lisa disappear, we return to Jof and Mia on stage. In a

FIGURE 13–3. *Jof, Mia, and Skat give a performance in the yard of Embarrass-ment Inn. (Courtesy Janus Films.)*

few minutes another sound—a chantlike, rhythmic wailing—competes with their blithe song. The two stop and the camera moves in to a medium close-up of both of them, fear and wonder revealed on their faces.

The contrast between the two types of music epitomizes the differences between the reactions of two groups to the plague. First there are people enjoying a theatrical production, forgetting their dread and horror, laughing at a world gone insane, and thumbing their noses at the devil. Then comes the fearful flagellants making, to paraphrase Bergman, an idol of guilt and calling it God. The two spectacles flow one into the other; however, we will deal with them as separate sequences.

VII. The Procession of the Penitents

This sequence is less significant than others in developing the major themes of this film. Not that the subject matter is trivial. The power of guilt to corrode man's dignity and obscure his common sense is dealt with often in modern art, whether it be in the fiction of Kafka or in a painting by Francis Bacon. Still, it is the effects rather than the meaning that has made this sequence probably the most famous in *The Seventh*

Seal. The procession of the penitents is a visual tour de force, comparable to hearing a virtuoso playing a difficult Liszt piano piece.

To do full justice to the techniques of this sequence would require a cutting continuity and at least a dozen pages of analysis. Unfortunately, we have to limit ourselves to indicating only the most important principles and devices.

This sequence dramatically consists of three parts: the arrival of the penitents, the monk's exhortation, and the departure of the penitents. As with the players' stage presentation, the onlookers are drawn into the action by frequent cuts to them. In the beginning this is done through panning; later, as during the monk's sermon, it is accomplished through shots of groups or individuals. The latter includes glimpses of the Knight, Squire, and Girl (together or separately) and of Jof and Mia, always together). The horror and fear that the procession arouses in the people in the village is evident in their expressions and actions (people fall to their knees, make the sign of the cross, or shrink back).

The procession itself assaults our senses through a carefully devised combination of visual motifs, chanting and words on the sound track, obscuring fog and dust, and camera dynamics. In the first part we are introduced to certain objects and people that the camera presents more than once from various perspectives. Among the objects are an immense cross dragged along, its very bareness making it all the more oppressive, like a weighty, blanket accusation; a smaller cross with the suffering Christ figure attached to it, upright, identical to the one the Knight confronted in the church; a miniature church carried on a litter, probably the receptacle for a saint's relics; and a skull held high. The penitents themselves include black-robed monks; people crawling or staggering as they are whipped or flagellate themselves, their clothes ripped, eyes bulging, faces grimacing, some heads encircled with thorns; and cripples painfully dragging themselves through the dust (Figure 13–4).

These objects and people are seen again in the third part of the sequence. The middle portion is devoted to the preacher. He rises up into the frame like a demon from hell. Behind him in juxtaposition is the cross with the Christ figure on it propped up against the stage with its gay background and Jof and Mia in costume. He wears a tight-fitting hood that frames his face, but is open at his throat. From his neck hangs a cross. The monk's coarse features, with thick lips, suggest a repentant sensualist whose pleasure now is chastising the sensuality of others. With fanatical, sadistic satisfaction he verbally flagellates his audience; one can almost see the spittle spray from his mouth as he jerks his head from side to side.

His message is "God is punishing us." He makes no mention of repentance or hope through death. His purpose seems solely to drop a burden of shame and guilt on each of his listeners. Cleverly he intersperses his generalizations with humiliating references to individuals in his audience. As he does so, there is a cut to his victim; the first of these intercuts is of the Knight and his friends as the monk screams, "Which of you will Death strike first?"

While the monk delivers his harangue, only his words come from the sound track. Before and after we hear a dolorous chanting mixed with moans and cries. Occasionally, there is a shriek combining suffering and ecstasy, as though a climax had been reached by a person being raped.

The first shot of the procession is of two monks carrying censers emitting swirls of smoke. Throughout the first and third parts of the sequence, portions or entire shots are enveloped in smoke and dust. At times it seems as if these tortured marchers are materializing out of some hellish fog. This anticipates their disappearance in the last shot of the end of the procession.

We are conscious that the camera is stationary during the monk's sermon, with intercuts of members of the audience. Our impression is that parts one and three, on the other hand, consist of many brief shots from different perspectives, for Bergman has created a sense of movement and agitation. Actually, the camera is not moved a great deal. The first shot of the procession is a lengthy one in which the penitents stagger toward the camera and then in columns pass out of the frame to left and right.

FIGURE 13–4. *Procession of the penitents.* (*Courtesy Janus Films.*)

After a cut to the Knight and his friends and a pan of the villagers, we return to a stationary camera with the flagellants again moving to right and left. Finally, only one column proceeds out of the camera right side of the frame. The following shots, which precede the appearance of the preacher, are of varying lengths and perspectives.

In the third part, the device of columns moving toward and on either side of the camera is repeated.

Bergman shifts his camera angles quite frequently. The shots in part one, however, are predominately from a low angle, encouraging our shock and awe at the spectacle. The monk delivering his sermon is shot at eye level. At the beginning of part three, there is a very high angle shot, almost a direct vertical, of the preacher kneeling beside one of the crosses (Figure 13–5). In the last part the angles are mainly high, consistent with the disgust most viewers will feel toward this display of emotional and physical self-laceration and self-contempt.

The final shot of the procession is a masterful one. From a very high angle we see the line of penitents moving diagonally across the screen from the lower camera left corner of the frame to the upper right corner. This is a lengthy shot during which the camera does not move. We can make out first the immense cross and then the smaller one. The smoke thickens around the upper half of the procession, so that it seems as if the flagellants are disappearing into the fog (it is possible that there is an imperceptible dissolve here between two shots). Finally, four robed figures, clouds of smoke around them, are all we can see at the end of the column. Suddenly the two disappear as there is a cut to exactly the same scene. An image of the earth with no one treading on it remains for a few moments. Not for the first time in this film does Bergman remind us visually that the follies and glories of man pass but nature remains.

A brief scene follows. Jöns the cynic characterizes to Antonius what he has seen as "drivel" and refers to "the ghost stories about God the Father, Jesus Christ and the Holy Ghost." Plog the smith introduces himself to Jöns and inquires after his errant wife.

VIII. Jof in the Inn

In the last sequence Bergman forcefully shakes our confidence in the generosity and sensibleness of human beings in times of stress. Now he will relentlessly drive home his point before allowing us a gleam of hope.

In a series of shots we hear and see customers in the Embarrassment Inn speak of the plague and anticipate the Judgment Day. Jof is at one of the tables as Raval tries unsuccessfully to sell him the bracelet we saw the thief take from the body in the deserted village. Plog, still looking for his wife, joins them. The malicious Raval persuades the not very bright smith that Jof is implicated in the disappearance of Lisa.

The actor finds his situation becoming uncomfortable and tries to leave, but Raval stops him with a knife. As the knife is driven into the table

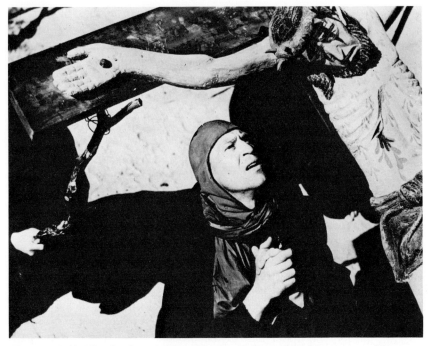

FIGURE 13–5. *The leader of the penitents at the end of his sermon. (Courtesy Janus Films.)*

between Jof's fingers, the chatter and bustle in the inn suddenly stop. Jof looks around for help. There is not a shadow of sympathy on the hard, heavy faces watching him.

Raval orders him to stand on his head and then to imitate a bear. The renegade priest grips a torch and waves it at the terrified Jof. Laughter erupts in the inn; the open-mouthed faces relish the free entertainment. Jof stands on the table. First we see only his legs dancing. The diners pound their tankards on the tables in a rhythmic beat. Cut to the upper part of Jof's body. Cut to the diners pounding their tankards; back to Jof; to the people; back to Jof; to the people; Jof; the people; Jof, his face glistening with sweat, his mouth gasping for air—pounding, pounding, pounding.

Jof collapses and falls from the table. Water is thrown on him. As he lifts himself from the floor, he spies the bracelet. He grabs it and runs from the room. Raval starts to follow, but is stopped by Jöns, who entered a moment earlier. The Squire shoving back the bully, reminds him of their last meeting. With a slash of his knife, Jöns cuts Raval's face and brands him a thief.

IX. *An Idyllic Moment—Wild Strawberries and Milk*

It is evening. The Knight studies his chessboard. Cut to Mia playing with Mikael. Antonius and Mia strike up a conversation. He sits on the grass with her before the wagon; they talk of Jof, Skat's desertion of his partners, and the child (whom, Mia says with a smile, might become a knight). Antonius confesses that he is unhappy, and the young woman wonders why people torture themselves as often as they can.

Jof bursts upon the scene. Mia solaces his wounded body and ego in a lengthy two-shot of almost a minute and a half. He gives her the bracelet without telling her how he obtained it. After he picks up his son, he is introduced by Mia to the Knight. Antonius suggests that the three join him and his company through the forest. Mia brings out the only food they have—wild strawberries and fresh milk.

Jöns and the Girl arrive and are welcomed. Mia is quite content, for things are nearly always nice for her: "One day is like another." Jof gets his lyre and begins to play and hum quietly. We notice behind him the death mask Skat wore earlier in the film, but it does not seem menacing. We sense that for these five adults a moment of contentment has arrived when "peace comes dropping slow."

In a medium three-shot Mia talks to Antonius with Jof behind them. She asks if he has no one of his own. For the first and last time in the film, he speaks of when he was young, in love, and not gripped by doubts. He says of his wife and himself: "We were newly married. We played and laughed . . . the house was full of life." Significantly, Mia asks if he will have some strawberries, but he refuses. The shadows gather around him again. "To believe is to suffer. It is like loving someone in the dark who never answers."

He seems to reflect, balancing light against dark. He comes to a decision or arrives at an insight. "I shall remember this hour of peace." The camera tracks back, so that others are included in the shot. ". . . I shall remember our words." A medium close-up of Antonius as he holds the bowl of milk in his hands. "And shall bear this memory between my hands as carefully as a bowl of fresh milk." He drinks from the bowl. "And this will be a sign and a great content." Cut again to a shot of them all in a triangular arrangement—the Knight and Squire at each end of the base, Jof at the pinnacle, and the women on either side between the men.

As we discussed in the previous section of our analysis, this is a major climax in the film. It is the only moment of peace the Knight has had since his return to Sweden, and because of his contact with Jof and Mia he is able to perform "a significant act." Like a famous predecessor on a quest, he has said, "Moment linger on! You are so fair!" Yet, unlike Faust, Antonius Block does not find salvation.

The Knight rises out of the frame. Some distance from the wagon, Death joins him and the chessboard magically appears. The music rises dramatically. The two face each other across the board; in the far background are Jof and his family. The Knight is smiling; he even seems, as Death remarks, rather content. Suddenly Death asks with seeming casualness if he is escorting the juggler and his wife through the forest.

The smile disappears from the Knight's face; it is Death's turn to look satisfied. A cut to Jof and his family.

X. Trip through the Forest I: The Deaths of Skat and Tyan

In front of the inn the company prepares to leave late in the day. Plog comes over to Jöns and the two have a conversation about women summed up in the Squire's statement: "Yes, it's hell with women and hell without them." The smith asks to accompany the group.

The Knight and his friends have not gone very far into the forest when they meet Skat and Lisa. The smith's wife is already disillusioned with her new lover, and when the two men exchange insults, she sides with her husband, even to suggesting that he kill the actor. Skat escapes for the moment by staging a suicide with a collapsible dagger. Everyone is aware of the deception except Plog and Lisa.

When the others have left, Skat sits up. He is pleased with his performance, and seeks safety for the night in a tree. We have already caught two glimpses of Death near Skat, so we are not surprised when the specter begins sawing down the actor's refuge. (Death cutting down a tree with a man in it is, incidentally, a popular icon that appears in medieval illuminated manuscripts and paintings.) During alternate shots from the perspective of Skat above and Death below, the two have a witty, if on the actor's part also desperate, dialogue. A shot of the base of the tree as the upper portion crashes to the ground. There is a hold on the stump of the tree, neither Death nor Skat in view. A squirrel hops on the stump. Here is another variation on a theme with which we are now familiar: man passes, nature abides.

The caravan has now entered deep into the forest. Bergman successfully conveys a sense of a lurking threat rather than of overt danger. There is no wind and the moon is out. Yet we are uneasy as the music becomes mysterious and the dark branches of trees, like a net over the forest, break up the moonlight. The train of travelers, seen from various angles, slowly moves against the resisting darkness. They stop. We see their frightened faces as they comment in hushed tones on how silent it is. Mia says, "I don't like the moon tonight."

Abruptly, the background music increases in volume and, as if the danger had materialized, something comes toward them. It is the soldiers bringing Tyan to the stake. The two groups are on the same path and the soldiers follow the Knight and his company. They finally reach a clearing in the forest where there is a platform and skulls on the ground.

As during the procession of the penitents, Bergman pays attention to such realistic details as the soldiers knocking together the ladder on which the girl is to be burned. The heart of the scene, however, is the dialogue between the Knight and Tyan and then between the Knight and his Squire.

Antonius dismounts and kneels next to the cage in which the girl is bound. Their conversation is shot from two perspectives: over the Knight's shoulder, featuring Tyan (slightly low angle); medium close-ups of Antonius's face. There are nine cuts from his point of view to hers. Then the camera tracks back and the Knight whirls around. Six more alternate shots of the two follow before the series ends. In each shot the Knight or Tyan is seen through the bars of the cage. We are reminded of the grille in the church behind which the Knight spoke to Death. Both Tyan and Antonius are caged, the one physically and by her hallucinations and the other by his quest.

The Knight explains to Tyan that he wants to ask the devil about God, for "surely he knows." The girl maintains in her small, childish voice that the devil is everywhere. When she suggests that he look in her eyes, all Antonius sees is fear. She says the devil is behind the Knight. When he whirls around, no one is there. Tyan insists that she *knows* the devil, although she evades the question of how.

A soldier interrupts their dialogue. Antonius is referred to the monk when he asks why the girl's hands have been broken. With the guards there has been an omnipresent black-robed figure at the edge of the group. Naturally, he turns out to be Death. He asks the Knight, "Will you never stop asking?" "No, never," replies Antonius. "But you get no answer" are Death's final words in this scene.

Tyan is tied to the ladder. Jöns stands next to the Knight. The Squire considers killing the soldiers, but the girl is nearly dead already. Flames blaze up behind them. Jöns gives Tyan water; the Knight forces between her lips something that "will still the pain." He presses her eyes closed as though she were dead. This is the first act of kindness by Antonius that we have observed, unless one includes his invitation to guide Jof and his family through the forest. Whatever he may feel, he has been physically passive to what is happening to others.

The soldiers lift the ladder into the bonfire. Jöns moves forward, but his master restrains him. The two disagree as to what Tyan feels during her last moments. Jöns argues that she sees only emptiness. The Knight, grim faced, insists, "It cannot be." Jöns, the bold one, the cynical one, cannot stand the sight of "that poor child," and he walks away.

There is a low-angle shot of Tyan, the smoke rising up before her face as she looks down. Then we see the Knight from a very high angle as he mounts his horse and rides away. As the camera, still at a high angle, pans to follow Jof's wagon, also leaving, Tyan comes into view. She collapses. The camera tracks in on her still form. Fade to black.

XI. Trip through the Forest II: The Death of Raval and the End of the Game of Chess

The Knight and his friends have camped in the forest. It is nearly dawn and an inexplicable dread oppresses them. The Knight is before his chessboard. Mia, with her husband nearby, sings quietly to Mikael the song Jof composed and that we heard earlier in the film. The other two couples are together discussing a sense they all have that something is going to happen.

A cry of pain slashes the quiet. It is Raval dying from the plague. He begs for water, but Jöns insists that he stay on the other side of a tree. Raval cries that he is afraid of death and asks for pity and consolation. The Girl grabs a water bag and moves forward. Jöns holds her back. The camera tracks in to a two-shot of them as he says, "It is useless." Raval finally falls to the ground. Back to Jöns and the Girl listening to the dying man's screams. The Squire, too, is moved by the agony of a fellow crea-ture, but he is always the pragmatist. "It is useless," he repeats, "utterly useless. Do you hear, I am consoling you." It is noteworthy that we do not see the Knight. He is too wrapped up in his quest to be concerned with the suffering of others. The contrast between the Knight and his Squire is implied rather than, as at the burning of Tyan, explicit.

The actual death of Raval and the meaning of that death are presented imaginatively. In a long shot we see him in a clearing in the center of the frame. On the edges of the frame and in the background are trees and rocks. A final cry and he dies. The camera does not move; the body lies there. Slowly the light changes; time is passing. Sunlight finally filters through the trees. It is now a peaceful scene. The body in shadows is as still as the rocks near it. A living, suffering human being is gone and the forest begins the process of absorbing his remains.

We join the Knight at the chessboard in sunlight. The camera tracks back and we see Death on the other side of the board. The Knight loses his queen.

There is a cut to Jof. The camera moves in to a close-up of his fearful, astonished face. A long shot from a high angle follows: the Knight play-ing with Death; it is a subjective shot of what Jof sees. Back to the juggler as he wakes up Mia and describes his vision. Although as usual she is skeptical, she basically trusts him and accepts his decision that they must flee.

Antonius sees what the couple is doing. He asks Death, "Nothing escapes you?" His opponent replies, "Nothing escapes me. No one escapes me." Another look toward Mia and the Knight has reached a decision. He pulls up his cloak and appears accidentally to knock over the chess pieces. Death, however, remembers the positions and begins resetting the pieces. The Knight looks past him. Cut to what Antonius sees: the wagon is leaving.

Death informs the Knight that he will be mated in one move; the game is over. With a knowing smile, he asks, "Did you gain by the delay?" "Yes," says the Knight. "I am glad. When next we meet the hour will strike for you and your friends."

Death rises, and the following exchange occurs. At each statement there is a close-up of the speaker, then a cut to the other person.

KNIGHT: And you will reveal your secrets?
DEATH: I have no secrets.
KNIGHT: So you know nothing?
DEATH: Nothing.

The Knight has performed what he considers a significant act. Now he is ready to die. But still he seeks and questions (we recall his exchange with Death at the burning of Tyan). And Death either will not or cannot answer him.

As Death says "Nothing," the camera tracks in to a very tight close-up. This shot dissolves slowly into one of the wagon rushing through the forest.

The wagon bearing Jof and his family is in the middle of a storm. Music appropriate to a storm accompanies images of branches bending in the wind and rain, lightening flashing, and the horse struggling to pull the swaying wagon. Two shots of Jof and Mia are inserted. In the first Jof tries to reassure his thoroughly frightened wife, but she is convinced something is following them. In the second shot, Jof stops the horse and insists that they go inside the wagon. They huddle together with a blanket over them. In terror Jof whispers, "The Angel of Death is rushing past. And he is very big."

Bergman balances the opening shot of the scene with a similar one at the end. The shot of the two dissolves into one of the Knight. It may be too neat an interpretation, but it is possible that the director is suggesting that Death pursues the family, whereas the Knight saves them.

XII. Death Comes to the Knight's Castle

After the shot of Jof and Mia disappears, we see the Knight arriving at his castle. The storm is here too. Antonius and his four companions cross the drawbridge and enter the castle proper. He finally leads them into a large hall. The last person to enter is the Girl. There is a hold on her in a close-up, the first of a series during this sequence. In fact, the camera focuses on her more often than on any other person.

The meeting of Antonius and his wife, Karin, after ten years, is quiet. The restrain is more moving in its sadness than any jubilant greeting might have been in its joy. A shot of the Knight, then one of Karin next to the fireplace are followed by two in which each in turn moves into a close-up.

There is a medium shot at eye level of them coming together. Karin stands facing her husband in the foreground. His companions are lined up in the background. This lovely shot conveys both emotionally and visually formality and balance, dignity and gracefulness. Now we move closer to them. There is a series of alternating reverse-angle shots, first over the shoulder of Antonius showing a medium close-up of his wife, then over Karin's shoulder showing Antonius. They both have changed, Karin observes, but she sees somewhere in her husband's face and eyes, hidden and frightened, the boy who left years ago. The Knight says that he is tired. She reaches up and touches his cheek as she remarks sadly, "I can see that." He puts his hand over hers in the only gesture of intimacy that will appear between them. Almost as if afraid of that intimacy, he turns and introduces his friends. Karin, a knight's lady, with great dignity, invites them to dinner.

The Knight knows the end is near, but his wife senses it. Their meeting is a farewell. They both appear very tired and unwilling to give in to intense emotions that might weaken the self-respect and courage that sustains them.

They are at dinner and Karin is reading from Chapter 8 of *Revelation.* The scene opens with a close-up of the Girl. "And when he had opened the seventh seal . . . ." The camera tracks back, then there is a dissolve to a shot of all of them at the table quietly eating and passing dishes. They are in the following order from camera left to right: Karin, Antonius, Jöns, the Girl, Plog, Lisa. "And the seven angels which had the seven trumpets . . . ."

A sound is heard. Jöns rises and leaves. "The first angel sounded . . ." A close-up of the Girl. ". . . hail and fire mingled with blood . . ." She looks over her shoulder. The camera angles up and passes her face to a light entering through a window hollowed in the wall; a torch hangs on the wall. ". . . and all green grass was burned up . . ." The camera tracks toward that window. Has something invisible entered through it? Is it a symbol of freedom and escape? Is the light salvation? The mystery remains; there are no answers, only speculations.

Cut to the Knight and his wife seen from a fairly high angle. ". . . a great mountain burning with fire . . . ." The camera tracks back and pans to include the Girl. A two-shot of Plog and Lisa follows. Jöns returns in a low-angle shot. "No one," he says and sits down with a grim expression.

There is a return to the Knight and Karin. "And the third angel sounded . . . ." The camera tracks back until all six are visible. The Girl is looking at and slightly above the camera. She is the first to see. "And the name of the star is Wormwood." In turn, the Knight, Karin, Jöns, Plog, and Lisa look toward the camera. The Girl rises. A very brief shot of Death in the doorway. A close-up of the Girl; she steps forward. The camera continues to track back. All have risen and also moved forward (Karin comes up from behind them).

First there is a four-shot: Karin (camera left), Antonius, the Girl, and Jöns. All continue to look directly at the camera. The Knight greets the "noble lord." His wife says, "I am Karin, the Knight's wife, and I bid you welcome in our house." The camera pans to Plog and Lisa. The smith, with unexpected dignity, introduces himself and his wife.

There is a pan back to the four-shot. The Knight falls to his knees.

First he covers his face with his hands, then he clasps his hands in prayer; his face is now in profile. He cries to God to have mercy on them. Some critics consider this a sign of weakness on the part of the Knight. We disagree. He is not, we feel, asking for mercy from Death, but for a sign that God exists. His quest is unfulfilled. This is the last chance for an answer to his question, a last moment that can give meaning to his life and thus his death. "God, who are somewhere, who must be somewhere, have mercy on us!"

For the last time Jöns argues with his master. His expression is fierce and his tone bitter as he says, ". . . there's no one to listen to your lament. You are reflected in your own indifference." He asserts the only reality he accepts—the existence of life. "But feel to the very end the triumph of being alive." Karin commands, "Quiet, please!" The medieval existentialist insists on one more sentence: "Yes, but under protest."

The Girl falls to her knees. The camera follows her and tracks in to a tight close-up. Struggling to speak, she finally says, "It is finished." She smiles and closes her eyes. The agony that was her life is over, so she can echo the last words of Jesus on the cross (according to St. John's Gospel). Karin, Plog, and Lisa accept death; Jöns protests; the Knight struggles to make death meaningful. Only the Girl welcomes Death. Perhaps this is why in this sequence her face is featured and she was the first to be aware of the arrival of Death. She seeks neither God nor life; Death for her is not a horror but salvation.

XIII. Epilogue: The Dance of Death

A dissolve from the Girl's face to that of Mia looking up. She is holding Mikael. The camera tracks back to include Jof. They sit up in the wagon; there is light on their faces.

Next we are outside the wagon. They climb down and look around. They are on a cliff at the edge of the sea with a clear sky above. Jof moves over to the horse, then stops and stares. He cries: "I see them, Mia. Over there against the stormy sky. They are all there. The smith and Lisa, the Knight, Raval, Jöns, and Skat . . ." Dissolve to what he sees: a magnificent shot of Death leading six people in a dance (camera right to left). They are black silhouettes against a clouded sky (Figure 13–6). We hear Jof's voice describing the dance. There is a slow dissolve from this shot to a close-up of Jof's face with a momentary superimposition. His final words are ones of hope: "a solemn dance toward the dark lands, while the rain cleans their cheeks from the salt of their bitter tears."

How Jof identifies the dancers raises a number of questions and causes us to doubt the validity of his visions. Why does he include Skat in the line of dancers? Jof does not know that his friend had died. Why is Karin not mentioned? Why leave out the Girl?

To complicate matters further, the shot in the film does contain seven figures, yet two of them seem to be women. Our identification of them

FIGURE 13–6. *Death leading six people in a dance toward the dark lands.* (*Courtesy Janus Films.*)

would be as follows (camera left to right): Death, Antonius, Karin, Jöns, Plog, Lisa, and Skat. The Girl and Raval do not seem to be there; Skat is recognizable because he is playing a lyre and is lagging at the end. One conjecture is that Raval is not worthy of this company and the Girl, because she welcomed Death, has either not died or has not been forced to dance.

Another possibility is that Jof's visions are products of his fervent imagination or what he sees is only an inaccurate picture of what he feels intuitively. He has not met the Knight's wife, so he mistakes her for Raval. Perhaps he does not include the Girl because unconsciously he associates her with Mia and cannot bear the thought of her death even in a dream. And in the realm of "perhaps" is where we will have to leave this enigma.

After the medium close-up of Jof and his last statement, there is a cut to Mia and Mikael. She remarks, "You with your visions!" A cut to in front of the wagon as Jof leads the horse and Mikael forward. The stationary camera pans as they go by. There is lute music on the sound track. The wagon recedes into the distance.

The film opened with a Knight meeting Death on a sea strand. It ends with a family moving along the edge of the sea toward life.

Style and Approach

Viewers preoccupied with the evasive and provocative subject matter of Ingmar Bergman's major films have often not recognized that in his use of cinematic techniques he is one of the most imaginative directors of our time. Although his style may not have the obvious experimental tone of works by Orson Welles, Luis Buñuel, Jean-Luc Godard, and Stanley Kubrick, in his own way he has been as innovative as these directors. During a period of apprenticeship in which he directed nineteen films, culminating in *Smiles of a Summer Night* (1955), his approach, as he has admitted, was eclectic. With *The Seventh Seal* he emerged as a mature and significant director. In the two decades that have followed, he has explored means of presenting in cinematic terms the relation between dreams and reality (*Wild Strawberries*); myth (*The Virgin Spring*); insanity (*Through a Glass Darkly*); the counterpoint of sound and silence (*The Silence*); the lengthy close-up and monologue as objective correlatives for inner turmoil (*Persona*); color as a reflection of psychic states (*Cries and Whispers*); and many other themes. If one can speak of so protean a director as Bergman having a main thrust in his style and approach, it might seem to be to move the camera closer and closer to a character, even, in a sense, to enter into his or her psyche without losing control and objectivity, as often happens in the case of expressionistic and surrealistic film makers.

Bergman's achievements cannot be separated from the special advantages that he has enjoyed in Sweden. He has had producers, especially Allan Ekelund, who have supported financially his self-expression without excessive regard for commercial viability. In Gunnar Fischer and Sven Nykvist he found cameramen of exceptional talent and responsiveness to his needs. The actors and actresses he gathered together form an almost unique repertory film group. He has encouraged and received magnificent performances from Gunnar Björnstrand, Ingrid Thulin, Max von Sydow, Bibi Andersson, Harriet Andersson, Gunnel Lindblom, and Liv Ullmann.

Although Bergman has employed other writers (as in *The Virgin Spring*), usually he has written his own scenarios. The scripts that have been translated into English and published in the United States offer problems. Bergman had ambitions in his youth of being a playwright, and his critics maintain that his own scripts are often more literary than cinematic. It is true that as a writer of dialogue he does include on occasion abstract language that works counter to rather than in support of the visual images, and he can strain for poetic literary effects that become self-conscious and even pretentious. It is, naturally, unfair to be critical of the language in Bergman's scripts without knowing Swedish, but it is Swedish critics who have been harshest in their judgments of the director's literary contribution to his films. (See, for example, Harry Schein's essay, "Bergman, the Poet," included in *Focus on "The Seventh Seal,"* Englewood, New Jersey, 1972).

This is not to say that Bergman is incapable of fusing words and language into an aesthetic unity. The scene, for instance, in *Winter Light* between Tomas and Märta in the schoolroom is, in our opinion, beyond criticism. What we are suggesting is that Bergman's dialogue can be a weakness in his films.

Another difficulty with the director's printed scripts is his intention to have them function as literary works as well as shooting scripts. His descriptions of what is happening and comments on the feelings of the characters can conflict with what a reader imagines and what he as a viewer actually sees on the screen. Even more unfortunate is the fact that there are not only significant differences between script and print in what is said, but even in the order of sequences. In *The Seventh Seal,* for example, the burning of Tyan occurs in the script before the meeting of the Knight's company with Skat and Lisa, whereas these scenes are in reverse order on the screen.

These background comments are necessary if we want to see Bergman's style and approach in *The Seventh Seal* in perspective. In the first section of this chapter we described the film as "a story with mythic overtones permeated with realistic details." Bergman is relentless in his attempt to present an age realistically. This applies not only to costumes and settings, but also to the smallest detail of action. When a man slaps at a fly on his face, and then takes his hand away, we see the stain of the squashed bug on his cheek. The same realism is apparent on a larger scale, in what can be seen as a parallel situation to the sudden death of a fly, when we watch and hear a man dying of the plague.

The mythic dimension must have offered difficulties to the director. Bergman could have presented Death with expressionistic distortion, as Fritz Lang did in *Destiny* (*Der Müde Tod*). Instead, Death and Jof's visions are as real to us as they are to the Knight and the juggler. This becomes characteristic of Bergman, for he will use the same approach for the dreams in *Wild Strawberries*; the transformation of Alma into Elisabet in *Persona*; and the resurrection in *Cries and Whispers*.

The director is equally restrained considering his subject matter in his use of the camera. We have already analyzed Bergman's cinematic techniques in the sequence of the procession of the penitents. We suggested in those pages that although he used various camera angles and shots of different duration, the impression of frenetic camera movement is more illusion than actuality. He can speed up the rhythm of his scenes (as when Jof dances on the table of the inn) or slow it down (as in the scene between the Knight and Death in the chapel). The point we are making is that Bergman is in complete control of his cinematic techniques. We might not always approve of the way he applies them, but we rarely feel that he is using impressive devices to distract our attention from his own uncertainty as to how to achieve the effects he desires.

One special device that appears in *The Seventh Seal* is superimposition (see sequence I) or dissolves from one shot to another that are so gradual that they are almost superimpositions (the opening and closing shots of sequence XI). This technique is used especially for contrast. In the first section of this chapter, we discussed contrast as a theme and in the second section repeatedly pointed out visual examples. Contrast, on both levels, as interdependent as two sides of a coin, is so fundamental to this film that an exhaustive study of this theme-technique would encompass practically all aspects of *The Seventh Seal*.

We have already discussed the weaknesses in Bergman's dialogue and the difficulties with the published script. There are two other elements of the film we would like to mention. The acting is superb. In a film that needs all the help it can get to be convincing, Bergman was fortunate that his performers were so capable. Even the minor actors are believable, but the most memorable performances are offered by Bengt Ekerot in the difficult role of Death, Gunnar Björnstrand as Jöns, Max von Sydow as Antonius, and Nils Poppe as Jof.

We cannot render the same praise to Erik Nordgren's score for the background music. In our opinion, it is fustian and full of clichés. Some of the scenes in the forest border on the visually melodramatic, and therefore it is especially disturbing that the composer chose to batter our sensibilities with sledgehammer chords. One is particularly grateful, after being subjected to such musical bombast, for the picnic scene and the last scene of the film in which only a lute is heard on the sound track.

There is a question pertinent to this film that illustrates what seems to be the *idée fixe* of hostile Bergman critics: Is the subject matter of a film such as *The Seventh Seal* intrinsically uncinematic? This may seem a strange question to ask about a film that contains the procession of penitents sequence, but one can understand what these critics are focusing on.

Let us consider from this point of view the scene in the church when the Knight talks to Death. Previously we were given few clues as to what is disturbing Antonius. The most suggestive visual image is his kneeling to pray in sequence I. To appreciate the Knight's dilemma, he must tell us that he seeks a manifest God; if there is no Almighty, then the universe is absurd; and that he wishes to perform a significant deed before he dies. How could a film maker possibly present such abstract ideas in visual terms? The answer, of course, is that he cannot. It is the conclusion many critics draw from this fact that is suspect.

Since the early 1930s, sound has been an integral part of cinema. As we have pointed out in the "Perspective" sections in this book, "The Silent Film" and "Sound in Film," the dimension of sound, especially dialogue, increased the potentials of cinema. Naturally, a thirty-minute philosophical discussion between two people is inappropriate to a film because this mode of expression can be dealt with more efficiently in other media, such as print. This is why film adaptations of novels and plays that are too faithful to their originals are so often failures. There is, however, nothing intrinsically uncinematic about a lengthy monologue or dialogue. The relevant questions are whether or not such a scene itself is visually dynamic and if elsewhere in the film the ramifications of the ideas are presented in ways that are unique to the cinema medium.

In *The Seventh Seal* Bergman meets our first criterion. He uses dynamic montage in the scene in the chapel, such as cutting from the face of Antonius to Christ on the cross and back. However, the most crucial section of the scene is a lengthy shot of approximately two minutes in which the two actors barely move. In future films the director increasingly uses such lengthy, static shots, but always in a context that justifies their presence. In our judgment he also effectively presents the ramifications of the ideas in cinematic terms. There are few scenes in the film, including the conversations between Death and the Knight and between Antonius and Mia, that are visually unexciting.

Yet, we also agree with those critics who do not find *The Seventh Seal* entirely successful. We feel that the director attempts to encompass too much in an hour and a half, and the metaphysical ideas in the film are often fragmented and inconsistent. It is not that the subject matter is uncinematic. Bergman simply has not spent enough time on the intellectual foundations of his film, so that some concepts sag badly and the retaining walls of logic in a number of scenes show a network of crevices and cracks.

If *The Seventh Seal*, or other Bergman films, is marred by experiments that failed and visions that are unrealized, it is because Bergman is continually testing the potentials of cinematic art. This quality, the ability to create scenes and sequences and even films that are completely successful, and the possession of a unique style and approach are the hallmarks of a great director.

CHAPTER 14

Wild Strawberries

[Smuktronstället]

Directed by INGMAR BERGMAN

I want very much to tell, to talk about, the wholeness inside every human being. It's a strange thing that every human being has a sort of dignity or wholeness in him, and out of that develops relationships to other human beings, tensions, misunderstandings, tenderness, coming in contact, touching and being touched, the cutting off of contact and what happens then. That's what is fascinating.

> Ingmar Bergman. Quoted in John Simon, *Ingmar Bergman Directs.*
> New York, 1972, pp. 29–30.

CAST

ISAK BORG	*Victor Sjöström*
SARA	*Bibi Andersson*
MARIANNE	*Igrid Thulin*
EVALD	*Gunnar Björnstrand*
AGDA	*Jullan Kindahl*
ANDERS	*Folke Sundquist*
VIKTOR	*Björn Bjelvenstam*
ISAK'S MOTHER	*Naima Wifstrand*
MRS. ALMAN	*Gunnel Broström*
KARIN	*Gertrud Fridh*
ALMAN	*Gunnar Sjöberg*
AKERMAN	*Max von Sydow*
UNCLE ARON	*Yngve Nordwald*
SIGFRID	*Per Sjöstrand*
SIGBRITT	*Gio Petré*
CHARLOTTA	*Gunnel Lindblom*
ANNA	*Eva Norée*
TWINS	*Lena Bergman, Monica Ehrling*

CREDITS

DIRECTOR	*Ingmar Bergman*
PRODUCER	*Allan Ekelund*

CREDITS (Continued)

SCENARIO		*Ingmar Bergman*
DIRECTOR OF PHOTOGRAPHY		*Gunnar Fischer*
ART DIRECTOR		*Gittan Gustafsson*
COSTUMES		*Millie Ström*
MUSIC		*Erik Nordgren*
EDITOR		*Oscar Rosander*

Svensk Film   1957   Black and white   90 minutes

Story

In the prologue before the credits we are introduced to Isak Borg, a retired doctor of seventy-eight, as he writes notes about himself and what happened to him on a day in June. What follows in the film is his account of that day.

After a disturbing dream, Isak rises early in the morning. He decides, to the chagrin of his housekeeper Agda, that instead of flying to Lund, where he is to receive an honorary degree from the university, he will drive by car. Marianne, his daughter-in-law, who is estranged from his son Evald, asks to accompany him.

After they have driven for a while, he stops the car to visit a cottage where as a young man he spent summers with his parents, brothers and sisters, and assorted family and guests. While his daughter-in-law is swimming in the nearby lake, he has a daydream or hallucination in which he recalls a particular summer day and especially a young woman, Sara, whom he had loved and hoped to marry. His vision is interrupted by another girl, also named Sara, who asks if she and two young men accompanying her can ride with him to Lund.

A little while later the five almost have a serious accident with another car. The Almans, the couple in the other car, ask to be driven to the nearest gas station, but they are so candid and vitriolic in expressing their antagonism toward each other that Marianne insists that they leave.

Their next stop is at a gas station. The attendant (Akerman) and his wife recognize Isak and recall with warmth and gratitude when he was their local physician. Isak reminisces about his years as a country doctor while the five are eating lunch at an inn.

Isak and Marianne leave the others for a while to visit his ninety-six-year-old mother.

The five depart from the inn with Marianne driving. Isak falls asleep and has a long and harrowing dream. When he awakens, the three young people have left the car to gather flowers. Isak and Marianne discuss why she has left her husband.

They finally arrive at Lund and go to the home of Marianne and Evald. In an elaborate ceremony, Isak receives an honorary degree. At that time he decides to recall and write down everything that has happened that day.

Isak is too tired to attend the banquet and prepares for bed in his son's house. He apologizes to his housekeeper for his brusque manner in the morning. Just as he is going to lie down, he is serenaded by the three youngsters. He bids them farewell from his balcony. Evald and Marianne return home for a few minutes. Isak talks to his son and says goodnight to his daughter-in-law. It appears that the estranged couple will be reconciled.

Isak has a final dream, one that leaves him contented.

This story synopsis only indicates a sequence of events. It tells us little about the character and inner world of Isak Borg, which is the basic subject of the film. Bergman's exploration of his subject is oblique, replete with symbols and subtle overtones; it is complicated further by shifts between reality and dreams, past and present. It is unquestionably a difficult film to examine critically.

We feel that *Wild Strawberries* offers us an opportunity to demonstrate the value of a careful sequence analysis of a film. For this reason, this chapter is different in format from the others in our volume: it consists only of a sequence-by-sequence analysis. In three dozen or so pages we cannot, of course, be exhaustive in our comments, but we can be more detailed than if we used our standard approach.

In Chapter 2 of Part One we discussed how an interpretation from an appropriate perspective can illuminate the characterization, themes, and symbols of a film. In those pages *Wild Strawberries* is referred to as an example of the insights that can be gained within a psychoanalytic framework; in this case, the approach is primarily Jungian. A reader might find it useful to review those paragraphs before proceeding to the following "Analysis of Sequences."

Analysis of Sequences

Quotations are transcriptions of subtitles except where they are documented as having appeared in *Wild Strawberries: A Film by Ingmar Bergman*, translated by Lars Malmström and David Kushner. Modern Film Scripts, New York, 1960.

I. Prologue
The film opens with a medium shot of Isak Borg, back to the camera, writing at a desk. Through a voice-over we learn what this seventy-eight-year-old man is writing and thinking. His statements convey a realization on his part that he has been a rigid, lonely old man, who has protected

himself from emotions by a dedication to science and an attitude of *noli me tangere.*

As he speaks of his family, there is a cut from him to photographs of his son Evald, daughter-in-law Marianne, the couple together, his ninety-six-year-old mother, and his dead wife Karin.

The housekeeper calls Isak to dinner. As he leaves the room, he pauses before a chessboard, lifts his hand as though to move a piece, but walks away without touching the board. This gesture reinforces our impression of him as a man of indecision and passivity.

Just before he leaves the room, Isak makes a statement. In the script the translation is that he is writing "a true account of the events, dreams and thoughts which befell me on a certain day." (Ibid., p. 24.) The film that follows the credits, then, is a cinematic presentation of Isak's "account." Everything that happens is filtered through his consciousness. That consciousness will be communicated to us by two Isaks: one the man we observe undergoing experiences during a single day; the other our guide and commentator, who will address us through voice-over.

Of course the prologue follows in time the film itself. However, the last English subtitle of this sequence for the film distributed in the United States reads as follows: "My name is Isak Borg and I am seventy-eight. Tomorrow I shall receive an honorary degree at Lund Cathedral after fifty years as a doctor." "Tomorrow"! Not only is the translation inaccurate, but if the prologue were antecedent to the film, there would be no justification for Isak writing about himself. Also, why does he remark as he receives his degree that he has decided "to recollect and write down everything that had happened"?

Credits Follow.

II. Dream One: Shadow and Death

The credits fade to black. Then there is a cut to Isak sleeping; he is frowning. (The last shot of the film is similar in camera angle and lighting, only at that time Isak is smiling.)

In a voice-over Isak tells us that he had a weird dream. During his early morning walk he lost his way and found himself in empty streets lined with ruined houses. As he is speaking, there is a cut to Isak walking. He turns to his right and continues down a street. The street contains a sign and one lamp post. From the voice-over to the sound of the heartbeat later there is complete silence. The street is deserted—no people or cars. There is a high contrast of light and shadow, so that contours are slightly blurred, but the over-all effect is of an unreal starkness. All this conveys to us a feeling of uneasiness and eeriness.

Isak stops under the advertisement and looks up. A cut to a watch-maker-optometrist's sign of a pair of giant eyeglasses with staring eyes surmounted by a large clock. However, the dial of the clock is blank and the eyeglasses smashed, with one eye bleeding or dissolving. We see Isak take out his pocket watch; a close-up reveals that it also has lost its hands.

In the world of dreams and the unconscious there is no temporal time, as there is none in death. It is through eyes that we perceive the world around us, but there are different kinds of perception. A person may see physically yet be blind emotionally, and the reverse is also possible. This irony is central to the development of Sophocles' *Oedipus Rex*. Tiresias is blind physically but sees with an inner light; Oedipus only "sees the light" after he has blinded himself. In our time the surrealist film makers, such as Buñuel and Dali in *Un Chien Andalou* and Cocteau in *The Blood of a Poet*, have used this idea as a theme in their work. The visual symbol of a bleeding eye suggests to us Isak's emotional blindness.

Isak is shocked and frightened. The sound of a heartbeat breaks the silence. He moves to the building and leans against it, his figure, in a medium close-up, darkened by the shadow of the sign. A cut to a view of Isak from across the street as he continues walking, in silence again, except for his echoing footsteps, the camera moving parallel to him. He passes the lamppost, hesitates, turns, and retraces his steps. When he stops, there is a cut to a close-up of him in profile against a black background; he turns his head. A shot shows what he sees, another narrow, empty street. Back to Isak as he moves in the opposite direction. A cut to a second subjective shot: someone in a black coat and hat, his back to Isak, stands next to the lamppost. A close-up of Isak as he takes a step. A jump cut so that next we see him a few feet behind the man.

When Isak touches the figure, it turns around; its face has only crude suggestions of features, like those of an embryo. In a moment, it falls to the ground and dissolves, leaving a pile of clothes and a dark liquid oozing out of where the head should be. Bells begin tolling. There is little need to explicate this image. The figure is Isak himself, or at least his emotional self—featureless and without substance.

A bewildered Isak moves past the pile of clothes. At the corner he stops and looks down the street to his right. A cut to an old-fashioned, horse-drawn hearse proceeding up that street toward Isak. In the next shot the camera is positioned where Isak stood at the beginning of the dream. We see again the street with the sign (the clothes have disappeared), only now Isak is at the far end as the hearse passes him. It moves down the street until one of its wheels is caught on the lamppost. The lamp, unlit but which could be a source of light, is knocked loose from its post. Through a series of dynamic cuts and sounds, we feel the carriage grind against the lamppost and the effort of the frenzied horses to free themselves. We see Isak in the background. The wheel comes loose. Through a low-angle shot from under the hearse, we observe the wheel first looming over Isak, then crashing into the wall as he dodges out of its way.

As with eyes, the wheel has a long symbolic history. C. G. Jung particularly has investigated this history (for example, see references in his volume *Aion*). The wheel is mainly a symbol of an individual life; horoscopes, for instance, are in the shape of wheels. It is also associated with birth or rebirth, as in a turn of the wheel of fortune. Isak's wheel of life is attached to death and—a main theme of this dream—threatens to destroy him. There is, however, the possibility of rebirth, of the crashing of the old wheel.

Isak watches as the hearse sways, emitting sounds like those of a cradle. A coffin bursts out of the carriage; the horses pull the hearse away; the church bells stop tolling. The struggle between Isak and the corpse, who turns out to be Isak himself in a frock coat, personifies the conflict of the two opposing forces symbolized in the scene. The negative force in Isak tries to pull him toward death. In the category of death symbols are the handless clock, the bleeding eye, the dissolving man, the hearse, the wheel that threatens him, and the corpse. Yet Isak, or at least a force within him, resists the power of the corpse. Forces of life renewal are suggested by the lamppost, the wheel shattered, and the cradle sounds of the rocking carriage.

There is no resolution here of these opposing forces of life and death. They are equally available to the psyche of Isak. In the remainder of this film we follow Isak Borg as he encourages the positive forces in him by coming to understand and to confront the negative ones that have ruled his life.

From the moment the corpse's hand appears there is humming, pulsating background music that reaches a climax at the end of the sequence. Significantly, the last image of the dream is the face of the corpse filling the screen. A cut to Isak awakening with a start.

III. Preparations for the Journey

When Isak wakes up at 3 o'clock in the morning, he comes to a decision: he will travel by car to Lund rather than by airplane. It is the beginning of summer in Sweden, so there is light out.

The exchange between Isak and Agda, his housekeeper, reveals the crotchety, set ways of two old people who depend on each other emotionally but only within the shallow limits of a master-servant relationship. If Isak is to gain psychic health, he must accept change and greater intimacy with human beings. His decision to travel by car, thus breaking a set plan, is a step in the right direction, but he is not ready yet for the more difficult goal of intimacy. At the end of the film, he does reach out to Agda. In the morning, however, he reacts to her by alternately bullying her and appealing to her maternal instincts, such as during his ineptitude when packing his suitcase. He ends by thinking that he can buy a reconciliation ("I'll calm the old girl down with a present.").

One passage—as Isak mumbles to himself in his bedroom—reveals the mixture of maturity and childishness in his temperament. He is intelligent enough not to be awed by becoming a Jubilee Doctor ("honorary idiot"), but is childishly defensive about his amiable nature ("I wouldn't hurt a fly").

We briefly meet Marianne. Obviously, there is a tension between Isak and her.

The significance of the sequence is conveyed primarily through dialogue and expressions in close-ups; the photography is conventional.

IV. The Journey Begins

We see Isak's car leaving Stockholm. Although there are cuts to the road below, trees and sky above, and the car itself, this scene focuses on the dialogue between Isak and Marianne: nothing is to distract us from what is being said. The scene is kept visually dynamic through a variety of conventional shots of two people in the front seat of an automobile, primarily medium close-ups with reverse angles from one side of the car to the other.

What we had suspected from the previous sequences about the limitations of Isak's personality are confirmed by his exchange with his daughter-in-law. We learn that Isak, although well off, has allowed his son to struggle to pay back a loan that enabled Evald to complete his medical studies, for "a promise is a promise." Marianne fires a verbal shot that shakes the walls of egocentricity behind which Isak hides when she says that Evald hates his father, rather than, as Isak sees it, understands and respects him. She also tells her father-in-law that when she arrived he insisted that he was not to be drawn into her marital difficulties and had "no respect for mental suffering." Significantly, Isak does not remember these cruel remarks. His habit of repressing the truth about himself has molded him into, as Marianne puts it, an old egotist, "hard as nails," and completely inconsiderate.

This scene is a negative one in terms of Isak's psyche, revealing to us the dimensions and ramifications of his problems. A positive counterforce is now set in motion when Isak mentions his dream. Marianne is not interested, but the fact that he refers to it shows that it is on his mind.

We move away from the two and see a long shot of the car as it turns off the main road. The script tells us that Isak suddenly had an 'impulse' (ibid., p. 33) to see the summer house. Impulses are the most direct expression of the unconscious. Whatever force in Isak's unconscious created his dream and prompted him to change his mind about traveling by airplane expresses itself in an impulse that leads him to the next step in his inner journey.

The car moves briefly along a country road and then is seen behind some trees. Isak and Marianne get out and in a long shot we observe them going down a path. They pass a ladder leaning against a hut (it appears in Isak's second dream). Finally they pause next to a tree in a Y shape; the tree appears a number of times and identifies for us the location of the strawberry patch. As the two talk, we see the deserted summer house in the background. Isak associates the house with childhood and youth, for his family spent every summer there for the first twenty years of his life. Marianne leaves to swim in the lake.

Isak searches for the strawberry patch and finds it; there is a tilt down to his hand touching the leaves (Figure 14–1). Following is a series of cuts back and forth between Isak and the summer house. Then a medium long shot of the house dissolves slowly into a match shot, only now the house is evidently occupied, for, although no one is seen, there are the voices and sounds of life, including someone singing. Through another series of dissolves we see trees, clouds, and strawberry blossoms. A musical theme, featuring violins, which we have heard faintly since the two arrived, now becomes louder.

Throughout the film the transitions from reality to illusion and back again are indicated by Bergman by dissolves (obviously more appropriate to such transitions than are cuts) with two exceptions. In the first dream (characterized by abrupt, unexpected changes) there is a cut from the sleeping Isak to him on the street; a cut brings us back to Isak awakening. There is a cut from Isak in the daydream sequence to the modern Sara in a tree (her insistent voice draws him back to the present). In the second and third dreams, however, both of which are located at the summer house, there are dissolves from Isak into the dreams and returning

FIGURE 14–1. *Isak discovers the strawberry patch.* (*Courtesy Janus Films.*)

to reality. Previous to the daydream sequence there is even an anticipation of the transition. In the car the dialogue between Isak and Marianne is edited entirely with cuts. From the moment Isak decides to go to the summer house, there is a dissolve, one cut, and two more dissolves. After the metamorphosis of the house through a match dissolve, there is one close-up, followed by four dissolves.

V. Daydream Sequence

It is not clear whether this sequence is actually a dream, a memory hallucination, or a daydream. It differs from the three dreams (clearly indicated as such): there is no evidence visually or in the voice-over that Isak falls asleep; he is a passive observer throughout the sequence; it is more coherent and "logical" than the dreams. On the other hand, it is not truly a memory. Isak is not literally remembering events and people, but creating them just as much as in the actual dreams. We learn just before the luncheon scene that young Isak is out fishing with his father, so that everything that happens in the sequence is a creation of that unconscious force within him that is revealing the truth to him. Daydream, then, seems the most appropriate label.

The last dissolve is to Sara picking strawberries, then a cut to Isak watching her. She is oblivious to his presence, even though he speaks to her. Sigfrid, Isak's older brother by a year, appears.

In their exchange we learn that Sara and Isak are "secretly" engaged to be married. Contrary to what she says, Sara is evidently attracted to the virile, experienced Sigfrid. After their kiss, to which Sara responds, the girl throws herself down on the ground, knocking over the basket of strawberries, and cries. She is angry and feels guilty (or "nearly" so). She also notices a spot on her dress.

The wild strawberries not only provide the title to this film but also are its central symbol. The transition to the daydream sequence occurs just after Isak finds the strawberry patch. The second dream begins with a dissolve from birds to a basket of wild strawberries. In the third dream, at the end of the film, Isak is near the patch and the first thing Sara remarks is that there are no wild strawberries left. The strawberries in one aspect, then, are Proustian *petites Madeleines:* the associative means by which memories are evoked. When there are no longer any strawberries left, the last dream occurs and the film ends.

We see the strawberries, however, in two forms: on the bush, being picked, or being eaten; a basket of them spilled. We first meet the young Sara, innocent and in pure white, picking strawberries. This is how Isak remembers her; this is how he would like to remember his past, symbolized by the strawberries, as pure and innocent. But we see in her encounter with Sigfrid that Sara is tainted with the sins of passion and betrayal. After being kissed by Sigfrid, she knocks over the basket of strawberries; her white dress is stained.

The second dream, however, is predominately negative in terms of Isak's psyche: he sees Sara intimate with Sigfrid, he is put on trial, he observes his wife betraying him. This dream begins not with an image of the patch, but of a spilled basket of strawberries—a symbol of betrayal, of stained innocence.

In the daydream sequence Sara and Sigfrid pick up the strawberries and a gong sounds. A series of cuts show various occupants of the house responding to the lunch bell, including Sigbritt, one of Isak's sisters, placing her baby in a bassinet in the arbor (we will later see more of the baby and its crib). One of the sisters calls for Isak, but the old Isak cannot respond. The twins announce that the young man is fishing with his father.

Isak enters the house and watches the group at table from the doorway (Figure 14–2). In the scene that follows, Isak, as in the first scene of Sara and Sigfrid, is not shown and is solely an observer.

Everyone is dressed in white before a white tablecloth and dishes; in fact, a shimmering, almost spectral white permeates the scene. We learned in the prologue that the nine brothers and sisters of Isak, present at lunch, have died; so too, we assume, have the aunt and Uncle Aron; only Sara will survive. We notice that neither Isak nor his mother and father are present.

Even with a domineering and fastidious aunt presiding at the table, the

FIGURE 14–2. *In a daydream Isak observes Sara and his family at lunch in the summer house. (Courtesy Janus Films.)*

scene generally is one of warmth and charm. Prayers are said—tradition and authority reign. This dimension of innocence and unity reaches its climax as the group (minus Charlotta and Sara) sings around the piano, with the deaf, sentimental, and not very bright uncle (whose name day it is and who received the strawberries as a gift from Sara) listening through his ear trumpet.

Yet, even here Isak is not allowed to cherish a vision of a familial Eden. The serpent of discord that had appeared in the previous scene once again rears its head. The twins are its *modus operandi*. They are strange Gemini: they speak in unison, perhaps significantly are the only children who wear glasses, and seem to see and to know everything. They have observed Sara and Sigfrid. If they had not announced this fact, peace would have reigned.

Sara, furious and guilt-ridden, runs from the room past Isak and sits down on the stairs to weep; Charlotta, another of Isak's sisters, follows her. While the old Isak listens (his reactions are revealed by cuts from a two-shot of Sara and Charlotta to two close-ups of Isak), Sara talks about the young Isak. She praises him for his refinement, morality, and sensitiveness. But we also learn that he likes to kiss only in the dark and talks about sinfulness and the afterlife. Sara somehow feels older than Isak; also Sigfrid is "so naughty and exciting."

Such prissiness and preoccupation with guilt is unusual in a young man of twenty. Isak's problems started early. In addition, the attitudes of the young Isak seem more appropriate to someone who will become a minister rather than a scientist. We will return to this quality in Isak's nature in discussing a later sequence.

After the group sings, Sara runs out of the house to meet Isak's father and disappears. Isak follows and wanders to the strawberry patch. The circle of daydreaming is completed and Isak returns to reality.

VI. A Contemporary Sara

A young woman's voice brings Isak back to reality (a cut rather than a dissolve). We are introduced to a contemporary Sara. We notice that the first shot of her is as she sits in the forked tree above the strawberry patch, the spot where in the daydream and two dreams Isak always first meets the older Sara. Also the younger Sara almost immediately approves of Isak telling the truth and points out that her father owns the summer house.

It is highly improbable that it is a coincidence that the young woman has the same name as Isak's childhood sweetheart and that both roles are played by the same actress. The second Sara is how we imagine Sara would be if she had been born fifty-eight years later. Sara would still be a virgin, but more honest in her statements and less capable of guilt. Almost three generations have passed, yet the ideal that both Saras represent is still in force.

Even more important is the role of the two Saras as spiritual guides, as personifications of the creative forces within Isak that lead to his rebirth. The original Sara obviously functions in this way when she speaks directly to Isak in the second and third dreams. The second Sara is more subtle in her influence. Her very presence—her youth, vitality, sympathy, innocence, and warmth—are a constant reminder to Isak of what he has rejected in himself. Also the second Sara is capable of reconciling the conflicts between the minister and the doctor, the spirit and the mind (see sequence VIII).

Almost all of the scene in the car is shot from the point of view of the camera outside the windshield. Isak is driving; Marianne sits next to him. In the back seat, on either side of Sara, are Anders and Viktor, her two companions. Throughout the scene there is a look of gentle wistfulness on Isak's face, especially when he tells Sara that she reminds him of his first love. We learn that the original Sara married Sigfrid, had six children, and is now seventy-five years old.

VII. The Almans

From the moment we meet the Almans to the time they are ordered out of the car by Marianne, discord and hate poison the air. The savagery of their attacks on each other first astonishes us, then prompts us to feelings of contempt. But Bergman also encourages us through close-ups and other visual effects to temper our contempt with pity. The genuine hurt each one feels from the verbal slashes of the other is nakedly revealed in their faces, although a slap is necessary to wipe away the defensive smirk continually on Alman's features. The last time we see the couple is a long shot held for a long time as, small in the distance, they watch the car leave and then slowly walk in the same direction.

We are told nothing of the background of the Almans that would explain their vitriolic antagonism. There is no mention of children. Alman notes that his wife has her hysteria and he his Catholicism. She sees disease (that is, cancer) where it does not exist. He mentions that he is able to endure because of his Catholicism. Most of us find this statement enigmatic, but Isak understands. At the end of the second dream Alman comments that he does not know anything about mercy. Through Isak's insight (Alman is a figure in *his* dream), we better comprehend the man's spiritual vision, or rather his lack of it. Catholicism without mercy is a consciousness of sin without salvation, suffering without hope, guilt without redemption. Alman's Catholicism justifies to himself his suffering, but cannot lead him beyond an earthly inferno. It is appropriate that he is Isak's guide through the hell of the second dream.

Although the causes of the Almans's antagonism may be ambiguous in the film, the results are not. They suffer and cannot establish a relationship beyond the negative one of needing each other's company. It is a chain of masochism and sadism, each link articulated to the other in a circle of perversity.

Most of this sequence is, like the previous one, shot through the windshield of the car, with cuts to other angles. However, now Marianne is driving. During the acerb exchange between the Almans, we see the three young people, especially Sara, observing them with wide-eyed wonder, disgust, and embarrassment. By contrast they constitute a silent reproach of innocence and vitality to the cruelty and sterility of the couple.

The medium close-up windshield shots include Marianne in the frame. And it is she who talks to Sten Alman and reacts most strongly to what is happening.

We know that Marianne is having trouble with her own marriage, yet the revulsion she feels toward what is happening behind her suggests that she would never imitate the Almans in her relationship with Evald. If we assume, however, that the Almans are introduced as a warning to Marianne, we are underestimating Bergman's subtlety and are forgetting that everything that happens in *Wild Strawberries* is directly related to Isak.

During the altercation between the Almans in the car, there is a quick cut to Isak—a medium close-up. He is looking sadly out the window, seemingly divorced from the others. We learn later in the film, however, that he was very much aware of what was happening. He tells Marianne that Alman and his wife reminded him of his own marriage. Bergman has encouraged us through his editing to focus on the effect of the couple on the others in the car, whereas the emotional center of the scene, the main reason the Almans are introduced, is to remind Isak, to force him to confront the failure of his own marriage.

VIII. *The Akermans and a Lunch by the Sea*

The sequence consists of two scenes that appear to be distinct, but are related by their emphasis on positive aspects of Isak's past and temperament.

After the disturbing experience with the Almans, the group stops at a gas station. It is in the area in which Isak first began his medical practice and where he resided for fifteen years. Akerman, the attendant, is lavish in his praise of Isak as a country doctor. He balances for us our dominant impression of a fussy, selfish, egocentric old man and a priggish, self-conscious young man. Evidently, at one time Isak had been an exceptionally devoted and beloved doctor.

Akerman's wife is pregnant, and the couple decide to name their child after Isak. Later we learn that Marianne is also pregnant. But there is a great difference between the proud Akerman and Evald, the emotional as well as physical son of Isak, who does not want a child. Another baby,

Sigbritt's, is mentioned in the daydream sequence and will appear again in the second dream in Sara's arms. Children, the relation of parents and their offspring, and the emotional inheritance adults pass on to youth constitute an important theme in *Wild Strawberries*.

In this scene, as throughout the film, Bergman uses the technique of contrasting positive and negative examples. The heritage of three generations of self-destructive Borgs is contrasted to that which will be passed on to their children by Eva Akerman (with the innocence, "generous smile," and shyness we imagine in a preserpent Eve) and Akerman (who has roots in the town and "hasn't forgotten"). She is described in the script as being like "a big strawberry in her red dress." (Ibid., p. 55.)

One other statement by Akerman contrasts him to Isak. He mentions that "there are things that can't be paid back." We recall how Isak, in the third sequence, intends to ease his conscience about Agda by buying her a present and how he has dealt with his son's debt. He has allowed money to be a substitute for love, not primarily for material gain but as a way of avoiding emotional involvement.

Still another contrast is presented in this scene: between that time in Isak's past when he was in contact with human beings in a useful and immediate way and his present vacuous and selfish existence. Isak wonders if he should have remained a country doctor. It is significant that Isak himself says this, for it is the first time that he admits aloud that something might be lacking in his life.

The next scene shows the five finishing lunch. There has been a dissolve from the car leaving the gas station to a high-angle shot of a clear sky and a lake, then a tilt down (from the same high angle) to reveal the group at a table on a terrace. The sound of laughter is heard and the young people are looking attentively at Isak. In a voice-over Isak tells us that, feeling very lively, he related with great success stories about his years as a country doctor.

We see Isak at his best: witty, intelligent, warm. In this scene, as in the previous one, we are made aware that Isak definitely possesses positive qualities.

The setting of the scene is appropriately idyllic. The sky is clear; a calm lake is in the background. In Bergman's nature symbology, water is generally associated with salvation. The summer house is by a lake; Isak, as we will see, looks at his parents across a pond. A clear sky without a wind suggests calm. It is clear in the daydream sequence and in the last dream; storm clouds and a high wind darken the second dream when Isak descends into a personal inferno; and in the sequence when Isak and Marianne visit his mother, the sky is overcast and thunder threatens.

That the five have just finished eating and are drinking together is another positive element in the scene. Eating and drinking are usually a form of communion in Bergman's films.

Isak sits with his back to the sea (he is not ready for salvation until his last dream), but we are conscious of the setting and the table as Bergman cuts from one member of the group to the other. The shots are all medium in range except for two close-ups of Isak, reminding us that even in this unified group, he should be the center of our attention.

In the discussion at lunch Anders is revealed as a believer in God who will become a minister; Viktor is a disbeliever, a rationalist who will be a doctor. When we recall that the description Sara gives of Isak in the day-dream sequence suggests a young man who will be a minister and that Isak is now a doctor, the professions that Anders and Viktor have chosen are too neat to be a coincidence. It would seem that as the second Sara is an embodiment of the original Sara, Anders and Viktor are projections of Isak's own duality.

It is Isak who quotes, to the accompaniment of a violin in the background, with the help of Marianne and Anders, a religious poem. The poem describes a search for God that starts at dawn and continues during twilight. There can be little doubt that Isak is talking about his own twilight, the end of his life. When Viktor asks Isak if he is religious, the old man ignores the question. Whether one considers God as a personal deity, a vitalistic spirit, or a creative unconscious, we sense that Isak, as the poem suggests, has not found Him. The Anders in him is incomplete, unfulfilled.

So, too, is the second half of his bipartite alter ego. The limitations of a rationalistic doctor (as we discover in the second dream), the Viktor in Isak, has led him to his present sterility.

What is needed is a halfway position between "A" (Anders) and "V" (Viktor), a reconciliation of extremes. The means are at hand for Isak. It is Sara, through the love each young man feels for her, who is able to keep in balance the antagonistic convictions of the two. Perhaps there is a Sara within Isak himself that can reconcile the opposing forces in his psyche of the rational or intellectual and the religious or intuitive.

The discussion of the poem Isak recited has made everyone pensive or, as Sara puts it, "solemn." Isak rises and announces that he is going to visit his mother, who lives nearby, and will return for them. Marianne asks to accompany him. This tentative drawing together of the two is the last of the positive elements of the sequence.

IX. Isak's Mother

This sequence and the next three constitute the trial of Isak.

Appropriately, the sky has become overcast and thunder is heard in the distance as Isak and Marianne walk up the path leading to the entrance of a house. The house is old and worn, but it has a certain dignity. The trees surrounding it are like dark walls.

The two are let into a room by a nurse. There is a medium shot of Isak as he walks into the room, then one of Marianne, but with a momentary hold on the latter. She will say little in the scene with the mother, yet

Bergman repeatedly cuts to medium close-ups of her, as though to emphasize that Marianne is observing intensely what is happening. Later we learn that she reacts with fear and revulsion to what she sees.

The room in which the mother sits at a desk is large and richly furnished, with paintings on the walls; she is obviously well-off. The room has a heavy, oppressive quality about it; the mother stands out like a cold specter with her white hair, very pale face and hands, and white shawl.

After greeting her son, Mrs. Borg mistakes Marianne for the dead Karin, Isak's wife. She does not want to talk to Karin because her daughter-in-law "has done us too much harm."

Mrs. Borg believes, incorrectly, that Evald and Marianne already have a child. She then muses that she had ten children (all dead except Isak) and has twenty grandchildren and fifteen great-grandchildren. She mentioned a moment before that the house she lives in belonged to her own mother. At ninety-six this woman has contact, if only in her mind, with five generations. This theme of the continuity of the generations will be important in a later scene when Marianne discusses with Isak her relationship with Evald.

We wonder, though, what the texture and quality of that continuity is, what emotional heritage this mother has passed on to her children and grandchildren. The central symbol of this heritage is a box of children's toys. The box functions in a way similar to that of the wild strawberries: each toy reverberates with associations of the past, for each child who owned the toys has died; none of them belonged to the living Isak. Sigbritt's doll is one of the playthings. When we first see it, there is a clap of thunder. The doll is passed by the mother to Marianne, who holds it in her hands until the end of the sequence.

The last object in this box of *momenti mori* is one that means little to the mother beyond its intrinsic value, but everything to Isak. It is a gold watch that once belonged to Isak's father, and Mrs. Borg wants to give it to Sigbritt's son, who as a baby was present in the daydream sequence and will be in Isak's second dream. The theme of continuity of the generations is thus reinforced; however, more significant is the fact that the watch (in a black box) has no hands. We and Isak immediately recall his first dream of death and frustration. The importance of this association is underlined by a series of cuts: camera moving into a close-up of the watch, cut to a close-up of the frowning face of Isak, back to the watch (the camera moving in to a very tight close-up), return to Isak. Meanwhile, during these cuts a drumbeat like a heartbeat increases in sound, then fades away. Once again, as in the car sequence with the Almans, Bergman subtly, through a few moments of film, has pointed up that the meaning of a sequence is really directly related to Isak. Our focus of attention was on the mother. Now we apprehend that the mother herself and all she says is informing us of the destructive forces that were at work in Isak's childhood and youth and that have been passed on to his son.

Evald is the only grandchild who visits Mrs. Borg. It would have been too obvious for him to have received the watch of death; in a sense, as we learn later from Marianne, he already has. Sigbritt's son symbolizes all the generations of Borgs who have received a heritage of spiritual vacuity.

Mrs. Borg denies the past; she calls the objects in the box "rubbish." We asssume that Isak had the same attitude before his day of revelations, or surely he would have confronted earlier the emptiness of his life. There are other indications of how much the son is like the mother. Both have physically survived in a family favored by death. Both use money as a substitute for affection: the mother sends presents every year to her generations of children, and she is convinced that they are waiting for her to die for the inheritance; the son employs money as a weapon against his own son and would buy with a present the good will of his house-keeper. The mother lives isolated with a nurse in a house that reflects her personality; the son is cared for by a housekeeper and works alone in a study (although at least he has a dog). The personality resemblances between the two, which we sense intuitively as well as observe, come into focus for us in a two-shot. As Isak says goodby, for a moment the faces of the two staring at each other in profile fill the screen. The connection be-tween them on many levels is made palpably real for us in an image that visually summarizes all that has come before.

During the scene practically every shot of the mother has been a high-angle one or a tilt down to her. Bergman has applied one of the most fundamental of the principles of cinema dynamics: a camera angled down on a subject diminishes or belittles that individual, suggesting an inade-quacy or degree of powerlessness in the subject. In contrast, the shots of Marianne inserted in the scene are either from a low angle or on eye level. Shots of Isak, the man between two women and two worlds, are at eye level.

There are few viewers who will not feel a distaste for the mother. Mari-anne sums her up later with sharp accuracy as "ice-cold." Mrs. Borg her-self remarks that she has felt cold as long as she can remember. The low blood pressure that Dr. Borg diagnoses is for us symbolic of her emotional nature as well as a physical ailment.

In the four sequences that constitute a journey through hell, this first one is a warning of the future. If Isak does not change, he will become a masculine replica of his mother.

The last shot in this sequence is of Marianne putting down the doll from the box. Once again thunder is heard. The doll originally belonged to Sigbritt. In the daydream sequence and penultimate dream the original Sara holds Sigbritt's baby son. Here, then, is an association of Marianne with Sara. This connection is enforced later when we learn that Marianne is pregnant and like Sara is a positive force working to break the grip of spiritual death on the Borg family.

X. The Center Does Not Hold: Sara's Failure

The two scenes that make up this sequence are brief, but the first at least is of greater importance symbolically than its length might suggest.

The previous dissolve is followed by a shot of an unhappy Sara standing near the car. She explains that Anders and Viktor have been discussing violently the question of the existence of God since Isak and Marianne left. They escalated a metaphysical argument from the verbal level to the overtly physical. The two young men, caught up in their passions, which they call principles, ignore the reconciler, Sara.

Sara has been the center balancing the two opposing temperaments of Anders and Viktor, but even she can fail. There is a lesson here for Isak, although he may not recognize it intellectually. The last sequence demonstrated the power of destructive forces; this one indicates the limitations of positive ones.

Marianne has effected an uneasy truce between the young men. They continue the trip with Marianne driving.

A high-angle shot of the sea and overcast sky. Once again, like a signal of danger, thunder is heard. Cut to the road seen through the windshield. It has begun raining and the wipers are operating. Anders's guitar is heard in the background. A sullen silence seems to have permeated the car; we sense that something is about to happen. The camera tracks in to a close-up of Isak as his eyes close, and we hear him in a voice-over. He is going to relate his dream. His introductory statement is worth quoting:

ISAK: I dozed off but was haunted by vivid and humiliating dreams. There was something overpowering in these dream images that bored relentlessly into my mind.

As he finishes speaking, there is a dissolve from the close-up of Isak in the car with eyes closed.

XI. Dream Two: The Trial

The dream begins with a long shot of a flock of birds wheeling in a darkened and wind-swept sky: their shrieks are heard on the sound track. A dissolve to the same birds flying through the branches of trees that look like ineffectual nets. Dissolve to an overturned basket of strawberries. Dissolve to Sara, Isak sitting across from her. The atmosphere is chilling, preparing us for the disquieting events that are to follow. The birds especially seem to be harbingers of danger.

Sara is serious and her voice is low as for the first time she speaks directly to Isak. We realize that Isak will not be primarly an observer as in the daydream sequence but an active participant as in the first dream. She insists on showing Isak how he looks, and holds up a mirror before him. In the film itself we do not see where the mirror comes from, but it is revealing to read in the script that it was hidden under the strawberry basket (ibid., p. 68).

The face Isak and we see in Sara's mirror is, as she points out, old and worried, almost cringing from its own image. Isak should be facing the mirror image of his soul, but, as Sara comments, he can't bear to hear the truth; for all his knowledge he does not really know anything, and he does not understand her ("We don't speak the same language"). He is not yet ready to face his inner self, and must endure further forays into his unconscious before he can.

The exchange between the two is in the form of a visual dialectic: a series of fourteen shots in an insistent rhythm that moves, without exception, from one to the other. First there are eight reverse-angle shots of them both, favoring Sara, then Isak. The remaining six shots are types of close-ups: Sara, Isak, Sara, Isak, Sara, Isak. There is finally a two-shot as Sara rises. Bergman has brilliantly made us *see* the struggle between them. The scene is further enriched by the fact that in so many of the shots of Sara we see the image of Isak in the mirror, as though three people are present: Sara, the resisting persona of Isak, and Isak's true self.

Sara appears to speak in sibylic terms when she says that she has been "too considerate." Yet, her remark makes sense if we see her as responsible for his dreams and daydream, a form of directress of his psychic dramas. The tears that form in her eyes would then be out of sympathy for the painful experience he must still undergo before his shell of emotional uninvolvement and self-justification—already cracked—is finally shattered.

The past is the key, for it is as real and potent as the present. So Sara speaks not only to the aged Isak, as we have seen, but also to the young Isak as, without transition, she remarks that she has her whole life before her and is going to marry Sigfrid.

Sara stands up and leaves Isak. The moving camera follows her as she runs through the forest to a cradle. We hear ominous background music, the wind, birds screeching, a baby crying. There is a medium long shot of Sara bending over the cradle. The image is composed of stark white (Sara, the cradle, the lake, the sky) and black (the ground, small trees, and in the center a huge tree with a divided trunk and two heavy branches spread to the right and left, like a threatening evil spirit with outspread arms).

Sara comforts Sigbritt's son in a medium close-up, the camera angled up slightly: It should not be afraid of wind, birds, and sea, for, as she repeats more than once, she is with it, is holding it. We sense that she is speaking not only to a baby but also to Isak himself and future generations of Borgs. The camera follows Sara as she runs to the summer house holding the child; a man is waiting at the door.

The birds again. Then a shot of the cradle and background. Isak walks into the frame and stands next to the cradle. A cut to a medium close-up of Isak as he turns to look either toward the lake or to where Sara has gone, we cannot be sure which. From the moment he comes into the frame, the shrieking of the birds increases in volume and we hear drum-beats in the heightened background music (once again a use of what could be called Isak's heartbeat leitmotif). From the close-up, the camera tilts up to the dark, thick branch that hangs over his head; the shot is held for a moment as heavy-toned horns dominate the music, which is now diminishing. Thus, the trial to which Sara has sent Isak begins with a crib—a symbol of life and the future—but one that is surrounded by a threatening atmosphere. We are reminded of a similarly ambiguous situation at the end of the first dream when the coffin containing the corpse of Isak rocked in the hearse like a cradle.

A dissolve to Isak walking toward the summer house, the camera track-ing with him. A piano is being played. Isak looks in one lighted window, then moves camera left to the terrace door. We see him in a medium close-up, in profile, staring through the glass panes. A cut to what he sees. The scene is very romantic: Sara in evening dress playing the piano and Sigfrid, facing the camera, standing beside her. He leans forward to kiss her. One is reminded of a popular perfume advertisement of a violinist in a similar position kissing his female accompanist. And as Sara stops play-ing, violin music is heard. The two move to a table with candles and sparkling wine goblets on it.

We assume this is the way Isak imagines the fulfillment of his brother's relationship with Sara. This might have been his had he not lost his be-loved. As with the daydream sequence, the aged Isak is creating an illu-sion of the past. And, as with that sequence, discord creeps into the idyllic.

The camera moves back as the lights in the room go out. Clouds in moonlight are reflected on the opaque glass. A cut to a moon rising be-hind the trees. The scene is not romantic. The violin music has stopped. The moon seems cold, and we retain dark associations with those claw-like branches of trees.

Isak looks up, a medium close-up of his pained expression bright in the moonlight. He turns back to the terrace door and leans against it, obvi-ously in anguish. With his left hand, he bangs against the door, while he lifts his right hand and presses it firmly against one of the posts of the doorframe where there is a nail sticking out from the wood. He quickly withdraws his hand. A pan to his palm in the moonlight. There is a small gash from the nail.

A nail wound on a palm leads to an inevitable association. Yet, Isak is no Christ figure. He will soon be emotionally crucified, however. A cruci-fixion without Christ is like Catholicism without mercy. And sure enough, the door opens to reveal Alman. This sinister figure bows his head and with a gesture invites Isak in.

The two enter the room, now completely empty, and then pass through a hallway where there are coat hangers and a staircase to the left. We rec-ognize it from the daydream sequence. It was on the staircase that Sara and Charlotta talked. The empty room, earlier occupied by Sara and Sig-frid, is where the luncheon of the daydream took place. The door that Alman now unlocks and through which he and Isak pass should lead to a porch and an entrance to the summer house. Instead, there is a narrow corridor, illuminated by wall lights, down which the two walk. Near the end of the hall, camera right, Alman unlocks another door and enters. There is a medium close-up of Isak in profile as he looks through the open door, then he also enters.

The next shot of Isak is from within the room as he turns to his left. A cut to an amphitheater. On the tiers of seats sit ten people; Sara, Viktor, and Anders are in the front row. This portion of the room looks like a medical lecture hall. In fact, the script informs us that Isak recognizes the room as that in which he held his polyclinical lectures and examina-tions. Only now he will be the examined rather than the examiner, and the people on the benches look more like a jury than students.

The camera angle is from the point of view of the "jury," at medium distance. Alman is at a desk, facing the camera, a blackboard behind him. Isak sits on the same level, to camera right, most of his back to the camera.

Alman, who will conduct the examination in a very matter-of-fact tone, asks Isak for his examination book, and receives it. The examination itself consists of three tests. In myth this is the usual number of challenges that the hero must meet. Only in this case, our "hero" fails all three.

First, he is told to look through a microscope. All he and we see (in extreme close-up) is Isak's own eye staring back. We recall the eyes in the first dream. Once again the contrast is spiritual sight or in-sight versus seeing only surface reality. A microscope discloses what is not visible on the surface. A spiritual microscope, which this one symbolizes, should re-veal the inner being of Isak. Instead he only sees a reflection of the in-strument by which he perceives the material world; he cannot penetrate beneath his external self, his own ego.

Isak next is asked to interpret some lines of text on the blackboard. He cannot. Intellectually the text is gibberish, and it is only intellectually that Isak can "understand." At the beginning of this sequence Sara said that she and Isak don't speak the same language. To put the point Sara is making in hackneyed terms, the heart (spirit, soul, psyche, inner self) has a language of its own, and Isak has not yet learned it.

The translation Alman offers is that "A doctor's first duty is to ask for forgiveness." Later he adds that Isak is moreover accused of guilt. The two statements, of course, are related. But why, we ask, should he feel guilt, whom has he hurt that he should ask forgiveness? Most obviously—and this is confirmed in the next sequence of the film—Evald and, through him, Marianne. In a few moments, we will learn that his chief accuser is Karin, his wife. More subtle than in the case of his son are his feelings of guilt about his relationship with his wife.

Another perspective, however, is possible. We have considered those outside of Isak. Yet, it is Sara, a projection of his inner being, who brought about the trial, and it is Alman, another projection, who conducts it. The fundamental accuser of Isak, we can conjecture, is Isak himself. Those powers within him that created his dreams and daydream consider that his ultimate crime is his betrayal of himself, of the creative forces within him, not what he has done to others.

From the beginning of the examination and during the two tests both the camera and two men are predominantly fixed. There was some movement when the microscope was involved; the camera angle does shift, using the traditional practice for indicating dominance: although both are sitting on the same level, Alman is photographed from a low angle and Isak from a high angle. Generally, however, movement in this portion of the scene involves a consistent alternating of a shot of Alman and then of Isak (at one point fourteen in succession). As in the exchange between Sara and Isak at the start of this sequence, Bergman, by means of successive shots of Isak and Alman, creates visually a sense of tension and conflict between the two men.

The third of Isak's tests is to diagnose what is wrong with a patient that we recognize as Berit Alman. Isak declares that she is dead; however, Mrs. Alman sits up and laughs. Once again the distinction between physical life and spiritual life is underscored. Dr. Borg can apprehend life only in the context of his rationalistic vision. It is appropriate that Berit should be the patient. Even this tortured, self-destructive woman has an inner vitality Isak cannot recognize. One could put this insufficiency also in the past tense, for, as we have seen, Isak associates Berit Alman with his wife Karin, as he does Alman with himself. This last test will lead to Isak facing the chief source of his guilt about his relations with those closest to him: his rigid refusal to admit the emotional needs of his wife.

This portion of Isak's trial is over. At one point, after not remembering a doctor's first duty, Isak laughed nervously and looked to the jurors (a cut to them including Isak in the foreground). Their unresponsiveness revealed their condemnation, and Isak turned slowly and fearfully back to Alman. After the failure with Berit, the verdict is inevitable—incompetence. Even though the trial takes the form of an examination of a doctor, of course it is Isak the man who is in the dock. A seemingly chance remark by Alman after Isak tries to drink a glass of water sums up the reasons for Dr. Borg's "incompetence." Isak says defensively that he has a bad heart. Alman observes there is nothing concerning his heart in his dossier. Figuratively, Isak has been heartless.

Alman informs Isak that his wife has accused him of callousness, selfishness, and ruthlessness—in short, heartlessness. He is to be confronted by his wife. Alman remarks, almost casually, that Isak has no choice. The dream, no matter what the price in pain, will lead him inexorably through the labyrinth of his guilt feelings. Now we can appreciate what Sara meant when she said that she had been too considerate in the past. The implication that now she will be implacable for his sake is being fulfilled.

The two men leave the auditorium. There is a medium close-up of their dark reflections drifting across the shimmering water of a pond. As the camera pans up, we realize that they are in a forest. The foreboding music, which began when they left the auditorium and will continue until a cut to the clearing, contains Isak's heartbeat leitmotif.

As water and a clear sky are associated with salvation in Bergman's cinematic symbology, so the forest represents in many of his films the fearful, threatening aspects of the unconscious. On one level Alman and Isak are entering the woods surrounding the summer house. On the psychological level, however, Isak is penetrating into a dark area of his memory and imagination where intense feelings of guilt and frustration reside.

The men halt next to a hut near an empty clearing. During the rest of the scene Isak will stare out at the clearing looking through a burned ladder leaning against the hut (a ladder down to hell rather than a Jacob's ladder to heaven). Isak and Marianne passed this hut and ladder as they left the car and first approached the summer house. Alman is behind Isak, camera right.

A cut to the clearing. When we return to Isak and Alman, a woman's laughter is heard, like Berit Alman's laugh a few minutes earlier. Another long shot of the clearing, only now a man and woman enter. The "rape" scene that follows is enacted in silence except for her laughter and the natural sounds of movement and contact. Rape is not an accurate term for what transpires: although the woman struggles, even violently, she obviously tempts and arouses the man. It is as if she deliberately arranges to be brutally assaulted.

The scene is photographed to emphasize the crudity of the experience, with medium close-up shots and cuts back and forth between the man and the woman. Seven times during the scene between the two there is a cut to Isak, suffering evident in his expression.

During one of these cuts—after a long shot of the clearing with the man and woman copulating on the ground—Alman identifies the woman as Karin, Isak's wife, who has been dead for thirty years. He adds the startling statement: "Tuesday, May 1, 1917, you stood exactly here and heard and saw what that man and woman said and did."

Are we to take this as a literal truth? Did Isak actually observe his wife being raped and do nothing? Perhaps Alman's statement, as with the daydream sequence, should be taken as figurative: Isak created the scene in his mind after Karin had related what happened. We do not learn from the film which alternative is true. In a sense, it makes little difference; there is only a question of the form and degree of guilt on Isak's part. One would prefer to believe that he was not so cowardly or passive as to watch such a scene and not act. On the other hand, if Karin's prophecy is correct, his reactions after the fact are equally reprehensible.

The crux of the scene is Karin's monologue (Figure 14–3). She main-

FIGURE 14–3. *Karin as she appears in Isak's second dream.* (*Courtesy Janus Films.*)

tains that when she returns home and tells Isak about the assault, he will pity her, forgive her, and take the blame on himself. She does not view these reactions as Christian compassion and Christlike self-abnegation, but indifference and emotional coldness. She feels that her husband simply does not care enough about her to be shocked and hurt by what has occurred. It is even likely that she provoked the rape in order to goad Isak into a response—any response beyond what she calls his sickening hypocrisy.

The man and woman leave the clearing, going in opposite directions. A cut to Isak and Alman. Isak is not passive now; his despair and anguish are etched on his face. Alman, in his cool, measured tone, points out that "They are gone, all are gone. Removed by an operation, Professor. A surgical masterpiece. No pain, no bleeding." John Simon has succinctly and, we feel, accurately interpreted these sentences. In a letter to *The New York Times*, Nov. 6, 1960, Sec. 2, Simon rejected the suggestion by Bosley Crowther that Isak had demanded—and perhaps even performed —an abortion on his unfaithful wife. Here is Simon's paraphrase of what Alman is saying:

They are all gone: your wife, her lover, you yourself as you were then. First you talked it out very wisely and dispassionately, then you put it out of your mind, then your wife died. It has all been removed most effectively by the scalpel of your selfish unconcern—by the surgery of time and death and your uncaring egoism.

And the penalty for such egocentricity is, Alman declares, loneliness. When Isak asks if there is no mercy, Alman replies that he doesn't know. There is no mercy or grace (the translation in the script) for Isak if the word is defined as an unmerited gift from God, but if the term can be conceived of as a power instilled by God in man by means of which he can, through his own efforts, achieve salvation, then grace exists. In the latter case, for Isak the personification of grace is Sara, *his* Beatrice, as Alman is his dark Virgil.

After the exchange between Alman and Isak, the camera slowly moves in to a close-up of the latter. From the word "loneliness" the sound of violins playing the summer house theme, which had been barely audible earlier, increases in volume. A crescendo is reached during a very slow dissolve to Isak asleep in the car.

XII. *Marianne and Evald*

When Isak awakens, he discovers that the car has stopped. It is drizzling. Marianne sits next to him smoking. The youngsters are outside picking flowers.

Isak almost immediately refers to his dream, then makes a statement that reveals how far he has gone toward self-knowledge: "As if I must tell myself something I won't listen to when I'm awake." And that something? "That I'm dead, although I'm alive."

Marianne starts at Isak's statement about death-in-life. She informs him that Evald had said the very same thing. She asks if she can tell him about what has happened between her and Evald. He replies that he would be grateful if she did. Once again we realize the two have come closer together.

This scene begins (after the transition close-up of Isak) with a lengthy two-shot of Marianne and Isak. A series of nine medium close-ups of each, alternating without exception from one to the other, occurs before the flashback. Unlike a similar series between Isak and Alman in the previous sequence, there is no angling of the camera up or down. Nor is there a mirror image adding tension as in the exchange between Sara and Isak in the beginning of the last sequence. The old man and his daughter-in-law are apart, each one's attitude is different, but also they are now connected.

The transition to the flashback is not achieved with a dissolve, as when Isak enters and returns from a dream or a daydream, but with a tracking into a tight close-up of Marianne as she describes how she arranged to talk to her husband, then a cut to a medium close-up of Evald in the car, and finally a pulling back to show Marianne sitting next to him. It is too obvious not to notice that the two-shot of Marianne and Evald corresponds to one a few minutes earlier of Marianne and Isak. What Marianne has said about the similarity between Isak and his son is thus reinforced visually.

The flashback is the film's only break in being consistently from Isak's point of view. This is necessary because for the first time we move outside of Isak's own world to a living reality of others. Bergman might have begun the transition with a close-up of Isak rather than Marianne. In this case, we would have been seeing through Isak's eyes what Marianne is relating. But this is one time we do not want Isak's subjective interpretation of reality, perhaps influenced by his feelings of guilt. Marianne is a witness whose account of the debiliating effects of Isak's life-denial on his son can be trusted.

After Marianne tells her husband that she is pregnant and insists she will have the child, Evald leaves the car and, with the rain soaking his face and hair, stands beside a dead tree. Marianne joins him. Their relationship at the moment is obviously—perhaps too obviously—symbolized by the dead tree.

Evald expands on his nihilism and disgust with life. He even recognizes the source of his despair—having been an unwanted child in a hellish marriage.

The camera moves little during this scene, which consists of only thirteen shots. Nothing is to distract our attention from the faces of the people, especially Evald, and what they are saying. The flashback ends with a close-up of Evald and a cut to a close-up of Marianne. Aesthetically rounding out the scene is a repetition of a device that began it: the camera tracks back from the close-up of Marianne to reveal Isak, as it had from the close-up of Evald to reveal Marianne.

Marianne explains why she has exposed to Isak her conflict with Evald. She was repulsed by the coldness of Mrs. Borg, "more forbidding than death"; Isak has admitted that his existence is a living death; Evald is continuing the death-oriented tradition. "All along the line there's nothing but cold, and death and loneliness. It must end somewhere."

This statement weaves into a coherent pattern the strands of the theme of parents and children: Isak and his parents, Isak and his son, Sigbritt's child, the unborn children of the Akermans and Marianne and Evald. The major theme of *Wild Strawberries* seems to be the inner conflict of Isak, yet the psychic salvation of a seventy-eight-year-old man is only the flat, two-dimensional surface of the film. What gives it depth, in dimension and significance, is the macrotheme, to coin a phrase, of how the nay-saying tradition of three generations of Borgs can be ended. Isak is coming to realize that his encounter with the negative forces within himself is a struggle not only on behalf of himself but of his grandchildren and future generations of Borgs.

The inner force that is attempting to direct Isak toward personal rebirth we have seen as personified in the two Saras. What we have suspected up to this point in the film is now confirmed: Marianne is another symbolic manifestation of the creative life force. She thus has a dual role in the film, as does each of the Saras, of being both an individual person and a symbol. Evald says of Marianne in the flashback that her need is to live and create life. What better definition can there be for the life force, *élan vital,* the creative unconscious, *Erdgeist.* That this force should be personified in the female is in keeping with a tradition of myth and literature that includes Cybele, the Virgin Mary, Dante's Beatrice, and Joyce's Molly. Mention of the Virgin, intercessor with God for lost souls, in this context leads us to suspect that Marianne's name was not chosen casually.

Marianne brings up the Almans, and Isak comments that they reminded him of his own marriage. That must not happen to Evald and herself, Marianne declares, and insists, like a charm against a curse, that they love each other.

The youngsters interrupt to present Isak with a bouquet of flowers they have picked in honor of his being a Jubilee Doctor. Sara makes a pretty speech, with a vein of irony in it, in which she refers to Isak as a wise and venerable old man who knows all about life. He is somewhat embarrassed, and says, as he fingers his watch, that they must continue their journey.

When speaking to Marianne about Evald, Isak had asked if he could help. There seems to be nothing that can be done, yet the sequence does not end on a note of helplessness. In the last shot, a brief one, the camera tracks into a medium close-up of Isak. The background suddenly blacks out so only Isak's face is illuminated, and the violin music associated with the summer house is heard. As he continues to hold the watch in his hands, the expression on his face is one of determination rather than despair.

A cut to a shot of Lund Cathedral, and the next sequence begins.

XIII. End of the Physical Journey and the Festivities

The five arrive at Evald and Marianne's house. They are greeted by Agda, who has traveled by plane. She immediately and efficiently organizes things. She is still resentful toward Isak.

In the foyer of the house Evald appears in evening clothes. He is obviously tense and nervous. After responding to his son's greeting, the first thing Isak says is, "As you see, I brought Marianne with me." Whatever his intention at the beginning of the journey, he is now a bridge between them.

They go to the second floor. While Agda is unpacking Isak's suitcase in the guest room, Isak is listening to a conversation between Evald and

Marianne. Through the half-open door of Isak's bedroom we see the two in a medium long shot. One senses the emotion beneath words that are polite and seemingly casual. The door is closed.

The investiture of the honorary degree is all pomp and ceremony. We see Isak in the parade and on the dais in the cathedral (Figure 14–4). There are cuts to Evald in a top hat walking with the faculty, Sara and her young men in the crowd outside, and Agda and Marianne seated in the cathedral. After having probed Isak's personal life for well over an hour, it is restful to sit back for a few minutes and see him as the external world does: a successful man of honor and dignity.

One statement he makes to himself while on the dais, however, pulls us out of our relaxed state for a moment. He recalls the events of the day and decides "to write down what had happened. In these jumbled events I seem to discern an extraordinary logic." Here is another confirmation, if any were needed, that the prologue to the film takes place after what we observe occurring on Saturday, June 1st.

XIV. End of the Psychic Journey

Isak has come to face himself honestly. He recognizes that through his selfishness, cowardice, and feelings of guilt he has built defensive barriers

FIGURE 14–4. *Isak receives an honorary degree in Lund Cathedral.* (*Courtesy Janus Films.*)

around his ego. Not to make use of this self-knowledge, however, would be like merely climbing to the top of his barricade and looking down. Admitting that one is psychically dead is the first necessary step toward rebirth. To go no farther, though, results in a still birth. Isak must at least breach his defences and attempt to reach out to others.

In this sequence Isak makes an effort, with varying degrees of success, to come to terms with the most important forces on his life.

A dissolve transfers us in time from the festivities to Isak preparing for bed. The first shot of the scene is a close-up of Agda's hand holding some tablets and Isak's hand taking them. They are sleeping pills. A cut to a medium two-shot of the two. The camera is straightforward in recording the remainder of the scene.

As Agda helps him, Isak feels contrite for his argument with her in the morning and wants to make up with her, although now there is no mention of buying her forgiveness with a present. He apologizes. Agda's response is one of the few touches of humor in the film: she asks if he is sick. After a few moments Agda relents enough to thank him, almost shyly, for his apology. Encouraged, Isak suggests that they have known each other long enough to drop their formality and to address each other by their given names. She refuses. What will people think? She must guard her reputation, insists this woman in her seventies. "It's all right between us as it is."

Agda's ordered, correct world cannot stand the challenge of change. We suspect that until her death this good, obstinate woman, who as far as we know has never married, will wear emotional halters.

Isak has not been very successful in his first attempt to revitalize his relationships with those closest to him. But he has learned that the reborn man does not return to a reborn world. Momentous though it may be for him to offer his hand, he is still dealing with human beings who may not avidly clasp it.

After Agda leaves, Isak prepares to lie down, but stops as he hears something and smiles. By means of a pan we follow him from the bed to the terrace door. A cut from the camera behind him to in front of him as he walks onto a balcony. A very high angle shot, from Isak's point of view, shows us Sara, Viktor, and Anders below in the garden; we hear part of their serenade.

The three have come to say goodby. The young men move toward the entrance to the garden, but Sara has a personal message for Isak. She says to the seventy-eight-year-old man looking wistfully down at her: "It's you I really love, you know. Today, tomorrow, always." No matter how seriously she means her words, it is a touching, intimate statement that would have embarrassed the former Isak. Now, however, in a medium close-up of him, the last shot in the scene, he murmurs to himself with a sad expression: "Let me hear from you sometime."

The youths have gone but Isak no longer needs them. They, especially the second Sara, have served their purpose of reminding him when he needed reminding of vitality, innocence, and honesty. He has won their respect and love. More important, he has opened himself to them and will miss them when they are gone. We sense that if he lives long enough, Isak will now have no difficulty in establishing a genuine, honest relationship with his grandchild.

A dissolve from Isak on the balcony to him asleep. He awakens, and from a cut to a shot of the door ajar, we see that Marianne and Evald have returned. Isak calls out and his son appears at the door.

Two almost identical shots of Evald at the door and Isak in bed alternate four times as the two talk. This device and their conversation underscore how separate the two are. Evald explains that they have returned so that Marianne can change her shoes and then they will go to the dance. He asks perfunctorily about his father's health.

If this conversation had occurred a day earlier, the scene would have ended with Evald closing the door behind him. There is a difference now, however, in Isak's personality. He asks his son to sit down with him for a moment. A surprised Evald does so. The exchange that follows, in contrast to the one a moment before, is photographed in a lengthy medium two-shot. Even though Evald turns his head away as his father attempts to become more intimate, the two are closer than we imagine they have been for years.

In stumbling phrases, as though he were speaking a foreign language, Isak asks what is going to happen between his son and daughter-in-law. Evald reluctantly answers that he has asked Marianne to stay with him, even on her terms. The question of the child has not been resolved but having seen how determined Marianne is, we are fairly sure there will be no abortion.

Isak formally, clumsily brings up the loan of money. Obviously, he would like to cancel the debt. But Evald misunderstands and in a frigid tone insists his father will get the money.

Marianne comes and sits down on the bed. There is a held shot of the two in profile, quite close, as they speak. Marianne's dress is a shimmering white. Her face is in a deep shadow; her hand on Isak's cheek. The old man smiles warmly as he gazes at her (Figure 14–5).

After kissing him good night, Marianne leaves. Cut to a high angle, medium close-up of Isak falling asleep. As he speaks in a voice-over, the camera slowly tracks to a tighter close-up, as though trying to penetrate to the mind of the almost sleeping man.

Isak informs us that whenever he is restless or sad, he tries to recall memories of his childhood to calm down. A dissolve to a long shot of the summer house with the family, still in specter white, marching out of the front door. Sara detaches herself from the group and runs toward the

FIGURE 14–5. *Marianne bids Isak goodnight as Evald watches.* (*Courtesy Janus Films.*)

camera. She smiles a greeting and remarks that there are no wild strawberries left (see p. 337 of this analysis). Her next statement introduces the main theme of this dream scene: "Auntie wants you to look for your Papa." A cut to Isak under the tree that locates the strawberry patch for us. He replies that he has already searched for his father, but can't find him or his mother. A return to Sara who, in her last words in the film, promises: "Come, I'll help you." She walks out of the frame, camera right. In the next shot, she walks into the frame, camera left, and stands next to Isak. They both look in the same direction.

There is an insert from a high angle of the family preparing the boat for sailing and the twins pushing one of the boys into the water. This is our last glimpse of the selected memories Isak clings to of the healthy, happy family of his youth. A cut returns us to Isak and Sara watching the scene, then walking out of the frame.

In two dissolves (the first since the summer house appeared at the very beginning of the dream), we watch Sara leading a smiling Isak through a meadow; then we see the two, hand in hand, at the edge of rocks, with tall trees against a clear sky. The angle is quite low, as it will remain for the two other shots with that background. The angle up of the camera adds to our sense of Isak's triumph.

As they walk through the meadow, we hear birds singing and a theme played on a harp. The chirping of the birds will continue until the end of the scene. The harp will sound periodically at points in the remaining portion of the film, like a musical italicizing of emotional peaks in the scene. The last time will be when we return to Isak in bed.

Sara points. A cut to a long shot of Isak's father fishing and his mother knitting. They are sitting on a rocky outcrop into the lake, an inlet of water separating them from where Isak stands. A very long fishing pole propped at the father's feet leads our eyes up into the distant horizon, bright sky and white clouds, then back to the water. The image has the tone of a French impressionist painting, although it is more sharply defined and black and white, a Monet or Sisley rather than a Renoir.

The parents turn and wave in the direction of the camera. A cut to Sara and Isak, then Sara leaves. Isak stands looking downward, his hands hanging, straight and strong as the trees behind him. Back to the parents as we first saw them. Again we see Isak, and the camera moves slowly in from a medium close-up to a tight one. The face that fills the screen, tilted slightly to camera left, is memorable. That wistful, tired face sums up for many of us the meaning of old age: a looking back, knowing the past cannot be changed and that there is little of the future left, pensively contemplating with resignation that soon death will wipe away forever the memories, bright and dark, that exist in one human mind for the brief span of a lifetime.

A slow, reluctant dissolve to Isak in bed. A gentle, contented smile appears on his face as he stirs and settles himself for sleep again with a sigh. Fade to black.

Wild Strawberries ends with Isak at relative peace with himself, the climax of two sequences in which we have observed him coming to terms with his new self-knowledge and attempting to make use of it to reach out to others. The degree of his success can be judged from two perspectives.

First of all, there are his relationships with those closest to him. He has established genuine contact with Marianne and the young people, those who accompanied him on his journey. He has come closer to Agda and Evald, but basically they have rejected his efforts at creating a new intimacy. Loneliness cannot miraculously be dispersed by two tentative efforts to reach others.

Isak cannot cancel in a few moments a life of selfishness. He must continue to pay the penalty of loneliness that Alman declared, only now the interest is not so high and he is no longer emotionally bankrupt.

The most important reward Isak has received for surviving his psychic journey is his relationship with himself. If the last shots of the film are prophetic, Isak has reached "clarity and reconciliation." The phrase in quotation marks is from a memorial tribute by Bergman to Victor Sjöström, the actor who played Isak. He continues in describing the final two shots of *Wild Strawberries:*

'His face shone with secretive light, as if reflected from another reality. His features became suddenly mild, almost effete. His look was open, smiling, tender.

'It was like a miracle.

'Then complete stillness—peace and clarity of soul. Never before or since have I experienced a face so noble and liberated.' (Ibid., p. 14.)

We doubt if Isak will any longer be haunted by nightmares. He has finally reconciled himself to the image of his father, who, on one level, symbolizes his living past as his mother personifies a dead present. In coming to terms with his father (to whom, significantly, he has not referred once until this last sequence), he is coming to terms with his own role as a father. Here is the culmination of what we have described earlier as the macrotheme of this film: the emotional heritage that parents pass on to their children.

Still, as in the case of Isak's relations with others, Bergman offers no facile, final solution to the travails of Isak Borg. We recall the Prologue. We saw there an old man uncertain and still questioning. A psychically reborn human being does not find his inner life transformed by a moment of "clarity and reconciliation." He must build on that foundation stone, even though there will be failures and setbacks.

In the script of *Wild Strawberries* (ibid., p. 95) there is a shot at the very end that was eliminated from the final version of the film. After his parents have waved to him from across the inlet of water, Isak looks up at the lake. He sees the old yacht with his family and Sara abroad. If this shot had been included, our final view of Sara would not have been her leaving Isak at the water's edge, but of her on the lake lifting up Sigbritt's little boy.

One can understand why Bergman deleted this shot: it would have detracted from the dynamic drive of the last moments of the film when we never cut from the face of Isak. Still, we might have liked intellectually to have this final emphasis on a major theme of the film.

We leave Isak with his smile of contentment. Anyone who has followed his experiences for ninety minutes with emotional and intellectual antennae vibrantly alert will share—for at least that moment—his "peace and clarity of soul" and smile in response.

CHAPTER 15

Ashes and Diamonds

[Popiol i Diamant]

Directed by ANDRZEJ WAJDA

Hearts with one purpose alone
Through summer and winter seem
Enchanted to a stone
To trouble the living stream.
. . .
Minute by minute they live:
The stone's in the midst of all.

FROM "Easter, 1916" by W. B. Yeats.

CAST

MACIEK	*Zbigniew Cybulski*
KRYSTYNA	*Erwa Krzyzewska*
SZCZUKA	*Waclaw Zastrzezynski*
ANDRZEJ	*Adam Pawlikowski*
DREWNOWSKI	*Bogumil Kobiela*
PORTER	*Jan Cierierski*
PIENIAZEK	*Stanislaw Milski*
SLOMKA	*Zbigniew Skowronski*
KOTOWICZ	*Arthur Mlodnicki*
MRS. STANIEWICZ	*Halina Kwiatkowska*
WAGA	*Ignacy Machowski*
STEFKA	*Barbara Krafft*
SWIECKI	*Aleksander Sewruk*

CREDITS

DIRECTOR	*Andrzej Wajda*
SCENARIO	*Jerzy Andrzejewski and Andrzej Wajda,* *based on the novel by Jerzy Andrzejewski*
DIRECTOR OF PHOTOGRAPHY	*Jerzy Wojcik*

CREDITS (Continued)

ART DIRECTOR	*Roman Mann*
MUSIC	*Jan Krenz*
CHIEF EDITOR	*Halina Nawrocka*
Film Unit KADR 1958 Black and white 105 minutes	

Plot, Characterizations, and Themes

The setting of *Ashes and Diamonds* is a provincial Polish town the day World War II ends. There is still, however, a civil war going on between a rebellious rightist group and the ruling supporters of communism.

Two members of the rightest movement—Andrzej, a lieutenant, and Maciek, a young man of twenty-four—attempt to assassinate Szczuka, the new district party secretary, and Podgorski, his assistant, on a country road. They kill the wrong men.

At the Monopol Hotel in town, Andrzej and Maciek learn that they have made a mistake. Andrzej discusses the situation with his superior, Major Waga. The lieutenant expresses his doubts about a movement that is responsible for the death of innocent people and sets Pole against Pole, but is too disciplined a soldier to disobey Waga's order that Szczuka must be eliminated. Meanwhile, Maciek has arranged to have a room in the hotel next to the one occupied by the district secretary.

Celebrations of the end of the war are going on throughout the town. One such event is the mayor's banquet, which is being arranged by Drewnowski, the mayor's secretary and secretly a member of the rightist group. In the barroom of the hotel Andrzej and Maciek reminisce about their years as fighters in the Resistance against the Germans. They both question their present activities, but see no way other than to continue the fight. Maciek accepts the assignment of killing Szczuka. He engages in a flirtation with the blond barmaid, Krystyna, and invites her to his room.

We learn about other people in the film. Szczuka, a dedicated Communist who is convinced that his party can save Poland, lost his wife during the war; his son Marek has been brought up by his sister-in-law, Mrs. Staniewicz. The Staniewiczs, an upper-class family, are fervently opposed to the present regime. In a conversation with his sister-in-law, Szczuka learns that his son has been missing for almost a year.

Drenowski turns out to be an opportunist who is overjoyed to learn that the mayor has been appointed minister of health, and he is hopeful that he will accompany his employer to Warsaw. He becomes drunk, however, with a disreputable newspaper editor, Pieniazek, and disgraces himself at the mayor's banquet. He loses his position.

During the evening Maciek and Krystyna fall in love. The young man wants to discontinue his terrorist activities. Andrzej is unsympathetic, yet finally agrees to take on the assignment of killing Szczuka. Maciek, although torn between duty and love, accepts his responsibility.

The district secretary learns after the banquet that his son is a member of a guerrilla unit and is being held by the security police. On the way to the police he is killed by Maciek. The young man has no choice but to leave Krystyna.

Although he watches Andrzej waiting for him with a truck, he does not join his friend. Drewnowski, who is rejected by Andrzej, calls after Maciek. In running away from the former mayor's secretary, Maciek encounters some soldiers and is wounded. At the hotel a last dance, a polonaise, is organized by Kotowicz, the master of ceremonies of the evening's entertainment. The final scene is of Maciek dying in a garbage dump.

Ashes and Diamonds is usually correctly categorized as a political film; that is, the lives of most of the major characters are influenced by their political beliefs. This is not to say that the individuals in the film are two-dimensional characters who exist solely to express political views, but rather that the most important figures we encounter would be different people living different lives if they were not politically committed. Nor does Wajda propagandize for one party. Although he obviously supports the Communist People's Republic of Poland, he does justice to the arguments of the opposition. His primary interest is in how politics and the pursuit of power mold the emotions and actions of the human beings involved, especially those trapped in conflicts of idealism and pragmatism, love and duty, hope and cynicism.

Wadja had to experiment with two earlier films before he reached the maturity, in approach to his subject and cinematic techniques, of *Ashes and Diamonds. A Generation* (1954), his first feature film, deals with Resistance fighters in Warsaw during the German occupation. Although it contains some brilliant scenes, the propaganda in favor of the leftist groups as opposed to the rightist Nationalists is blatant and the love story contrived. *Kanal* (1956) describes the activities of other bands of Polish Resistance fighters. The scenes in the Warsaw sewers are memorable, but the film lacks narrative focus and the characters tend to be stereotypes instead of individuals. *Ashes and Diamonds* appeared in 1958. It demonstrates a unity, control, balance, and subtlety of characterization lacking in the previous works.

The three films are often referred to as a trilogy. This designation has been applied by critics and was not the original intention of the director. There is no character that appears in more than one film and the setting is not consistent. What they do share is that the main figures are or have been Resistance fighters against the Germans. There is also a subtheme in the first two films of the internecine conflicts between the right and left wings of the Resistance movement; this becomes the principle subject matter of *Ashes and Diamonds*.

The situation in Poland during and immediately after World War II was similar to that in other countries, such as Yugoslavia and Czechoslovakia, which became Russian satellites. Members of all political parties drew together in an alliance to resist the Nazi invaders. Individual guerrilla units, however, were in most cases controlled either by pro-Communists, whose leaders often were trained in Russia, or anti-Communists, who usually drew their leaders from the aristocracy and middle class. Even before the official capitulation of Germany, the uneasy alliance dissolved and supporters of the policies of the left fought against those of the right. After the victory of the Communists, the more recalcitrant of the opposition were executed during the Stalinist purges of the late 1940s and early 1950s. In Poland advocates of a parliamentary, capitalistic system were known as the Home Army or Nationalists.

In *Ashes and Diamonds* every major character, with the exception of Krystyna, is either pro-Communist or a Nationalist. Each side, though, includes both dedicated men who are convinced that they are battling for a better Poland and selfish opportunists. Wajda and his co-script writer Jerzy Andrzejewski (from whose novel the film is derived) are fairly even-handed in presenting both types within each group, yet they do tip the scale in favor of the Communists.

The idealists Szczuka and Podgorski are set against Andrzej and Maciek. Major Wrona has his counterpart in Major Waga. Mrs. Staniewicz and her friends are as interested in personal gain as Mayor Swiecki. The opportunist Drewnowski is as contemptible as the drunken Pieniazek.

To concern ourselves solely, however, with the place of each person in a political spectrum and abstract moral hierarchy is to ignore the human vitality communicated by the film. To do justice to the characterizations in *Ashes and Diamonds* we must recognize, as mentioned earlier, that the individuals in the film are not only politically committed, but are also human beings striving to survive physically and emotionally; haunted by the past, unsure in the present, fearful of the future; and seeking the satisfactions of love, friendship, and self-respect.

Wajda obviously intended the hero of the film to be Szczuka, the district party secretary. He has dedicated his life to the Communist party: he fought first in the Spanish Civil War, then with a guerrilla unit against the Nazis, and he has spent years in Russia. He is now devoting himself completely to implementing the programs of the People's Republic of Poland. Even his enemies, such as Major Waga, respect him.

He is not, however, a bureaucrat like Major Swiecki, who seems more interested in position than purpose. In sequence VIII, Szczuka speaks to Podgorski with passion of the misery, pain, and suffering in Poland. We realize that he would sacrifice anyone's life, including his own, to his ideal of a just country. He says as much to the workers on the roadside in sequence II. As usual with a determined man of his type, he is optimistic that his cause will prevail. He says to Podgorski, "There'll be good times again."

Szczuka's dedication and faith in the future do not blind him to the price Poland and leaders like himself must pay to create a brave new world. As with practically everyone else in the film, he deplores that Pole must kill Pole. He conveys to the workers the guilt he feels that men were killed in his place. He understands the doubts and disillusionment of Podgorski and Wrona; however, he attempts to instill hope in them.

To the burdens of leadership are added his worries about his son. The fact that Marek is a member of a Nationalist military unit not only illustrates how civil war can turn members of the same family against each other, but in addition humanizes Szczuka for us. The committed political leader is also a concerned father. When he learns that Marek is in danger, everything else, including his own safety, is driven from his mind. It is ironic and poignant that he should be killed by a young man only a little older than his own son. This point is underlined by the similarity between the name of the man who kills him, Maciek, and that of his son, Marek. The embrace that he would have given his own son is instead received by his assassin.

Podgorski needs to be sustained and given direction by the stronger Szczuka. Bewildered by what is happening in his country now that the war has ended, he looks back with nostalgia to times when issues and enemies were unambiguous. It is he who comes to Szczuka's room to recall the "good old days" and toast dead comrades. His superior sympathizes with him, yet will only allow him a few moments of escape to the past before bringing him back to the problems of the present. The scene that opens with Podgorski carrying in the phonograph player and wine ends with an image of the shells of the bullets that killed the two men.

Andrzej is dramatically the counterpart in the Home Army of Szczuka. He is as dedicated and self-disciplined as the district secretary. He too must direct his assistant and insist on looking at the present rather than to the past. He also deplores his countrymen killing each other. The significant difference is that whereas Szczuka draws on his faith in his party, himself, and the future, Andrzej is emotionally and ideologically bankrupt. All he has left is his duty to his superiors and the dubious consolation that there is no viable path open to him except the one he is following.

In his conversation with Waga he reveals that his conscience is stricken by the fact that two innocent men have been killed and he cannot understand why Szczuka must be eliminated. He is uncertain of his enemies and the justice of his cause. Just before he leaves Maciek for the last time, the young man, lacerated by inner conflicts, asks his friend if *he* thinks what they are doing is right. Andrzej refuses to answer the question; he says only, "Me? That is not important."

The thin, unsmiling, taut Andrzej seems to have consumed all excessive physical and emotional weight in his efforts to control himself and still the questions in his mind. We learn that Szczuka had a wife who died and a son that he is seeking. We know nothing about Andrzej's past except that he joined the Resistance in 1940. He obviously feels affection for Maciek, yet it is demonstrated only by a phrase here and there and a concern for the young man's survival. In the conflict between duty and friendship, however, the former is more important to him. Waga reminds him that a soldier does not question his superior officer. Andrzej applies this same principle when Maciek considers not carrying out his order to kill Szczuka. Love is no reason for what Andrzej views as desertion, even though in the end he is willing to take Maciek's place. When the young man appeals to his "only friend," Andrzej replies, "Cut out the sob stuff."

The predominant feeling of many viewers toward Andrzej may be one of waste. Here is an intelligent, efficient, sensitive, dedicated man who kills and, we have no doubt, will be killed because he has chained himself to an ideal that is slowly sinking beneath the waves of change. More than any other person in the film he is "enchanted to a stone." Although we may censure a man who refuses to be vulnerable to human emotions and connections, we cannot help but feel pity for an individual trapped in a situation that will probably cost him his life. We may even admire the courage, dignity, and self-control with which he faces the end of himself and his values.

It is Maciek and his generation that are the true victims of the civil war in Poland. We can conjecture what Maciek's life has been like. At an early age he was taught to devote himself to killing Nazis. The Resistance took the place of his parents and family, who died or escaped from the country. There was no time for the bittersweet confusion of adolescence and the thrill of rebellion against authority as he hid from the Germans, often in the sewers of Warsaw (the reason, he tells Krystyna, that he wears dark glasses). His own life and those of his fellow fighters depended on each comrade's exclusive commitment to duty and the acceptance of orders. The future was confined to another day of survival and the ultimate dream was defeat of the Nazis.

With the approach of the end of the war, however, the Resistance broke up into two warring factions. Perhaps Maciek could have simply laid down his arms. But what was he to return to, when there was no love or family awaiting him? His only close friend was his superior officer. It was easier to stay with a group that would continue to direct his life. As for political principles, he had not had the opportunity to calmly and objectively evaluate conflicting views, so he adopted the ones of those, like Andrzej, whom he respected. It was terrible to kill fellow Poles, but once having made his choice, he would, trained soldier that he was, continue unquestioningly to obey orders.

What we have offered here is only speculation on Maciek's past before

May 1945; however, it is derived from his own remarks and a pattern that appears repeatedly in postwar Polish fiction and the films of such directors as Wajda, Andrzej Munk, and Jerzy Kawalerowicz.

When we first meet Maciek, he impresses us as a self-confident, nonchalant young man who, as he tells Andrzej, does not take things too seriously and tries to have a good time. We soon begin to sense, however, his loneliness—there is no one waiting for him. He has already, as in the case of Podgorski, mythicized the "wonderful times" during the Resistance. In the bar with Andrzej before the burning glasses of liquor, he recalls years of danger, confraternity, and purposefulness. Now, he declares with a desperate laugh, all the two of them are good for is to die.

Maciek's maturation as a human being and disintegration as a calculating killer is chiefly the result of his falling in love with Krystyna. When he allows himself to think about it, prompted by his feelings for the young woman, he realizes that he is tired of killing and hiding and loneliness. For the first time he has a purpose for existing other than being a fighter. He decides to turn his back on the past. We wonder, though, considering his situation and his character, whether he is being realistic and honest with himself.

In the meeting in the lavatory with Andrzej, Maciek confronts his conflict between duty to those who have been his family for years and love of a woman and the new life she represents. Although Andrzej's suggestion that he is a deserter wounds him acutely, Maciek holds firm to his decision not to murder again. At the very last moment, however, he promises to go through with his assignment. Perhaps he is shamed by the thought of Andrzej taking his place. Perhaps handing over his gun, the symbol of his role as fighter, drives home the full meaning of what he is doing. Most likely he simply does not have the courage finally to turn away from his friend and the only way of life that he has known.

Maciek's vacillation in the lavatory now becomes characteristic of him. He hesitates before following Szczuka; he throws his gun away after the murder; he stops to watch Andrzej leave; he runs from Drewnowski; he panics when he encounters the soldiers. Each of these actions—and we cannot imagine the earlier Maciek doing any of them—leads him closer to his death.

Wajda demonstrates that he appreciates the distinction between propaganda and art when he makes Maciek politically naive. A more doctrinaire director from a Communist country would have had the young man engage in debates with himself and with others over abstract political issues between the Communists and the Nationalists (as, to a degree, occurs in Wajda's own earlier films). Instead, Maciek acts rather than thinks where politics are concerned. In this way his conflict is more immediate and universal than if his wish to leave the Home Army had been grounded in ideas rather than intense feelings.

On the other hand, the director is not completely successful in defining and making concrete to us the change in his main character. In the last section of this analysis, we will discuss whether or not Maciek precipitously falling in love with Krystyna is believable. Wajda often depends on the impressive acting skill of Cybulski and symbols to reveal Maciek's inner conflicts instead of on imaginative dialogue and clearly motivated actions. Too often we observe the young man's hestitations rather than understand them.

Krystyna is the only important figure in the film who seems completely apolitical, yet she too is paying for growing up under the stress of a half a decade of German occupation. She tells Maciek that she lost her father in Dachau and her mother during the Rising. Now she will protect herself emotionally and hide her vulnerability behind the façade of a worldly woman who chooses her pleasures. The first thing she says to Maciek after she enters his room is that she could not fall in love with him and so he cannot complicate her life.

In bed with him, she resists her deepening feelings for him. She does not want to be hurt; she does not want to have something "to get over." Maciek is also cautious, but more open to, even seeking, love.

In the church Krystyna against her will begins to hope that perhaps Maciek can "change things" and they can make a life together. From the beginning she has sensed that the handsome, charming young man flirting with her was in danger. She even admits that is why she came to him. She is suggesting that she gave into the instincts of a generous woman to offer her body to a threatened man who can find courage and forgetfulness in arms that grip him tightly. There was also the desire to satisfy her own needs, but, she seems to have told herself, her own emotions would remain inviolate. Now, persuaded by a Maciek who speaks of love, she has changed the "no" with which she defended herself to a "perhaps."

The lines by Norwid on the tombstone are from a political poem; however, they also can be interpreted in terms of love. Krystyna is afraid of being a blazing torch. And as things turn out for her, she was right to be cautious. Her expression when she says goodby to Maciek is of one who is suffering and bitter. Probably she is resolving never again to give in to hope. That morning Maciek or Andrzej or a political situation murders one man physically, but also another human being emotionally.

Whereas the five individuals we have discussed arouse to one degree or another our sympathy and understanding, Drewnowski evokes only disdain. He is obviously a coward, blatantly an opportunist. He richly deserves his downfall and even the beating Andrzej gives him. On the other hand, he is so hungry for a comfortable life, so selfish and self-protective, there is the temptation to view him with the same indulgence we might a greedy child. And we are grateful to him for supplying comic relief in an otherwise somber film.

The minor characters in the film are generally two-dimensional, so that we can sum up each one in a few phrases. Pieniazek, the newspaper editor, acts like a soused Mephistopheles leading Drewnowski to the loss of his security, which is the soul of the mayor's secretary. Our last image of him on a toilet seat clutching a bottle is an appropriate one. The complacent Mayor Swiecki is the very image of a bureaucrat on the way up. Slomka, the headwaiter, scrapes and bows in public as he mentally calculates where he can "make a bit," but he is vulgar and callous in private. Major Waga from the sanctuary of his room insists there will be no compromises with the enemy and orders that men be killed. Major Wrona is a conscientious chief of security, yet he reveals a basic humanity: he shows indulgence toward Pieniazek at the banquet and immediately notifies his friend Szczuka that Marek is in jail. Mrs. Staniewicz and her friends possess all the qualities one associates with arrogant, self-serving aristocrats. Kotowicz, one of her friends, is an ambiguous character to whom we will return in a moment.

There are also "the people"—patient and enduring. The workers at the roadside question what is happening to their country, but are dependable. The man behind the plow struggles with the rocky earth. The watchman at the chapel is outraged that the dead should be disturbed. The porter at the hotel is kindly toward Maciek. Mrs. Jurgeluska, the lavatory attendant, lives by God's will, yet understands human nature. ("First the speeches, then they'll come running.")

Wajda has assembled a large cast of characters and had them come in contact with each other in one way or another during a period of approximately twelve hours. But to what purpose? He is obviously sympathetic toward Szczuka and his party. But *Ashes and Diamonds*, as we have demonstrated, is not propaganda for the People's Republic of Poland. From a political perspective a clue to a main theme of the film is the repeated statements from both sides of the civil war that it is deplorable that Pole killed Pole. The unity of Poland is necessary, but Wajda is not naive about the difficulties that must be overcome to achieve that goal. He presents such unity symbolically rather than actually.

Throughout the film, murder, hate, and fear separate members of the Communist party and supporters of the Home Army. Only at the very end do some of them join in a dance together—the Communist Mayor Swiecki and his friends, the anti-Communist Mrs. Staniewicz and her friends, and even the apolitical Krystyna. The dance, a polonaise, by its very name represents Poland. The expressionistic quality of this scene is described in the next section of this analysis.

The organizer and director of the dance is Kotowicz, who also pretentiously proclaims universal concord. He is a strange choice for such a role. Although a friend of the aristocratic Mrs. Staniewicz, he appears to be working for the hotel as supervisor of entertainment. He is impressive physically, yet so essentially a poseur, he is even a bit ridiculous. Does the very ambiguity of his position in society especially qualify him to unify others? Or could he represent a sly comment by Wajda on the leaders of the People's Republic? In any case, something of a magician, something of a charlatan, he leads the group into the sunlight of a new future.

Ashes and Diamonds, however, has more universal themes than the political situation in Poland after World War II. Like William Butler Yeats in his poem "Easter 1916," Wajda is exploring what happens to people and the price they pay for political commitment, no matter to what party they belong. The best examples are Szczuka and Andrzej. The former is confident of his ideals, but pays for them with the lives of others, the loss of his son, and eventually his own life. Andrzej no longer believes in the rightness of the actions of his party; still he continues to support it, becoming in the process cynical and cruel.

Preoccupation with political ideology and the uses of power are confined in this film to the older characters. The young people personify the tragedy of a generation whose home life and other emotional supports, such as the land and church, have been vitiated by war. Neither Krystyna nor Maciek has any family left; Marek is brought up by his aunt. They are primarily children of towns and cities (Maciek considers himself a Warsawvian), so the land, represented by the man behind the plow, means little to them. A religion that advocates peace and brotherly love is alien to youth brought up to kill. This is symbolized by the closed door of the chapel at the beginning of the film and the inverted crucifix in the ruins of a church. There is still love between a man and woman, yet even it cannot flower in the cold winds of civil war.

These are fairly obvious themes in the film. One dimension of Maciek's predicament is more subtle and perhaps more meaningful because it transcends Poland and World War II; it is a problem faced by the youth of every generation. Maciek is enamored of the role he plays as the heroic fighter in disguise. The dark glasses he wears and the mess cup he carries are the physical evidence of the persona he cultivates. His swagger, confidence, and aura of imminent danger draw a woman like Krystyna to him. When he machine-guns the man at the door of the chapel, he does so with such passion that Andrzej must stop him from losing control.

Krystyna is tempting him not only from his comrades but also from a way of life of freedom, excitement, and violence. He is lonely and is having doubts about what he is doing, so, as we see in the barroom, his own personal golden age was when he fought for the Resistance movement. The cynical Andrzej knows that the young man's rhapsody on the war is only a cut above the sentimental nonsense of the song "The Red Poppies of Monte Cassino." It is significant that Maciek in the lavatory impulsively rejects the possibility of love and peace when he is required to give up his revolver, the one piece of concrete proof that he is a fighter.

In the last third of the film Maciek is forced to confront, without glory, the ramifications of his murderous activities. First, he is shocked by the two corpses in the chapel. Later, Szczuka refuses to die at a comfortable distance from his killer. He stumbles forward and finally falls into the arms of Maciek. This close contact with his victim horrifies the young man and he throws away the gun that he had refused to give to Andrzej.

Maciek cannot learn from the agonizing way he dies on a garbage heap, but we can. Wajda himself (though he saw little action) was a member of the Resistance movement at sixteen. He understands and presents in the film how young men can glorify the heroic fighter, who is like a torch burning for freedom. The last images of *Ashes and Diamonds*, however, are the true face of violent death—and the glow is of ashes, not diamonds.

Analysis of Major Sequences

I. Murder of Two Innocent Men

This sequence opens and closes with two traditional symbols of unity in Poland: the church and the land. The main episode illustrates the disunity that is disrupting the country. Another contrast is between innocence—represented by the little girl with flowers and the two men mistakenly killed—and the violence of murder.

The first shot is of a chapel dome with its cross. Branches of trees on both sides of the frame lean toward the chapel. There is a slow pan down the front of the chapel to two men lying on the grass a short distance from the entrance. A slim, sharp-featured man, Andrzej, is leaning on his elbows and looking tensely ahead. To the right of him, stretched out with his eyes closed, is Maciek: stocky, good-looking, and younger than his companion.

In the upper third of the frame where the entrance to the chapel is visible, a small girl goes to the door and tries it. Andrzej nervously jerks his head in the direction of the sound, then, in answer to a question from Maciek, says that the man's name is Szczuka, Secretary of the District Workers Party. The girl hears them and walks over. Only the lower half of her body appears before she kneels down; there are flowers in one hand. She politely asks that they open the door for her. Both men smile at her. Andrzej rises out of the frame; four legs move away. The camera holds for a moment on Maciek.

This has been one lengthy shot. The scene is peaceful. The only sounds are those of a bird and the voices. There is no hint of why the men are there.

From a slightly high angle we see Andrzej grasp the handle of the door; it is locked. He lifts the girl so that she can put the flowers before a religious figure in a niche above the lintel. He is gentle—a kindly man helping a child.

He turns his head to his right. Cut to a man in a hat and raincoat, Drewnowski, who whistles impatiently. That shrill signal initiates a drastic change in the tone and rhythm of the scene; now people will move quickly and violence will erupt; the shots will be brief and the transitions abrupt.

Andrzej quickly puts the girl down, tells her to leave, and shouts to Maciek. The young man leisurely pulls his sun glasses down over his eyes and rolls over, revealing two submachine guns. He angrily brushes ants off them. Andrzej again insists the girl leave as Maciek comes up and hands him one of the guns. They pass Drewnowski, who is gesticulating excitedly.

A low-angle shot of the two men standing at the top of a slope. Maciek runs down, the camera moving with him, to the other side of the road. He stands there with his gun ready. We hear the sound of a car; Maciek opens fire. The car careens off the road, up the slope toward the church, and someone drops out. Andrzej machine-guns the driver.

At Andrzej's sharp command, Drewnowski searches the pockets of the driver for documents. Cut to Maciek on the other side of the car approaching the man lying on the ground. Suddenly the man jumps to his feet and dashes out of the frame; with a curse Maciek reloads his gun. Cut to the man desperately running past the front of the chapel, camera right to left. He stops when he sees Andrzej around the corner. He rushes back to the chapel door and slams on it with his hand, Maciek fires at him.

The shots that follow constitute the climax of the sequence. Depending on a viewer's taste, he will consider the scene strikingly dramatic or artificial. Wajda might be suggesting that violence invades even the sanctity of the church, a peaceful haven, or, critically, that the church is closed to a desperate man until he is dying. The latter interpretation seems more likely when we discover that the scene anticipates one in which Maciek encounters the corpses of the men he has helped kill in another chapel just after he and his girl friend had been talking in front of a large crucifix hung upside down.

The man begins to slide down as the bullets tear into his back and set his coat on fire. The chapel door opens (have stray bullets hit the lock?) and there is a brief shot beyond the falling man of a statue on an altar in shadows. Cut to Maciek, with the camera facing him; his teeth are clenched as he presses the trigger of his blazing machine gun until Andrzej stops him. The next perspective is from inside the chapel. From a low angle we see the murdered man fall to the floor and out of the base of the frame. The camera remains stationary, so that Maciek and Andrzej are visible looking down at the body. Drewnowski joins them for a moment, tips his hat quickly, and scurries away.

In the killing of the man, Wadja has manipulated cinematic time for dramatic effect. In terms of physical time, it is impossible for there to be a shot of Maciek firing between the moment the man begins and finally does fall to the floor. The second of these three shots is simultaneous with the last one, only the point of view is different.

A long shot of a tree-lined path with the chapel in the background. Drewnowski runs frantically down the path toward the camera. The other two catch up with him, quickly take apart their guns, and shove them into a bag. Drewnowski hurries away, camera left, holding the bag and dropping his hat. Maciek, carrying the lost hat, and Andrzej casually walk out of the frame.

The last shot of the sequence is of rocky ground that fills three quarters of the frame from the base up. At the top edge of the ground two horses are silhouetted against the sky. In this lengthy shot the horses move forward and a man behind a plow appears. Boleslaw Sulik points out in his introduction to the film script (*The Wajda Trilogy*, New York, 1973) that the scene represents a well-known painting by Chelmonski, an impressionist who specialized in Polish landscapes. An educated Pole, then, would associate the shot with the peaceful and productive value of the land and natural man struggling with the earth. As noted earlier, this image and the opening one of the church enclose, as visual parentheses, an instance of internecine struggle in which Pole kills Pole.

II. Szczuka Encourages the Workers

Szczuka, the new district secretary, arrives on the scene with his assistant, Podgorski. The two men are compared throughout the film to Andrzej and Maciek. The four share a common background in resisting the Nazis, but now are at opposite ends of the political spectrum within Poland.

Szczuka and Podgorski realize what has happened and that the bullets were intended for them. As they are talking, a group of workers on bicycles stop and gather along the edge of the road. An elderly worker is the first to speak; he asks the district secretary how long they will have to watch their people being killed. Soon, however, a young man assumes the role of their spokesman.

The district secretary, seen from a low angle, paces up and down before the group as he responds to their questions. His remarks are the only overt propaganda for the People's Republic of Poland that Wajda includes. Szczuka exhorts the workers to have courage, that the fight for the kind of country they want has just begun, and that they must get on with their work. The spokesman reduces these abstractions to a human level when he asks, referring to one of the murdered men, "But what are we to tell his wife?" A close-up of Szczuka shows that he is not indifferent ("It's painful for me to speak"), but the preservation of the state is more important than the lives of individuals. He turns away.

III. A Celebration in the Street

Bells are ringing as the camera pans from a loudspeaker with a church in the background to a street. The Germans have unconditionally surrendered. It is May 8, 1945.

There is a series of four shots in which we see alternately Drewnowski searching in the crowd and then Andrzej and Maciek. From the two men's conversation we learn that Drewnowski is the secretary to the mayor of the town and that he is the source of Drewnowski's information. Neither approves of "working for both sides" and, although the secretary can be useful, they are contemptuous of him.

In the last of the four shots, the two are looking at an outdoor showing of a newsreel of people in Warsaw celebrating the end of the war and Soviet tanks in Berlin. Drewnowski joins them and is given the hat that he lost. As he hands over the bag containing the guns, he mentions that he is in charge of the mayor's banquet at the hotel that night. He also declares that he will continue to supply information, but refuses to be personally involved again in killing. Andrzej's disdain for the man seems to have reached a point of physical revulsion as he abruptly says to Maciek that they must leave.

IV. The Assassins Discover Their Mistake and Another Attempt Must Be Made

The main, although not exclusive, setting of the remainder of the film is the Monopol Hotel. Wajda skillfully uses parallel development to indicate simultaneous events in the lobby, bar, banquet room, dining room, and rooms above. The general time span, however, is from early evening to dawn of the next day. So well are the episodes that occur during these hours fused together that our breakdown into sequences is somewhat arbitrary.

Drewnowski enters the lobby of the hotel and meets Kotowicz, a strange figure who seems to know everyone. The mayor's secretary goes through the banquet room and down a corridor behind the room. He passes Andrzej and Maciek, who are washing their hands, but makes no sign of recognition. He is greeted by Slonka, the headwaiter, and shown the preparations for the celebration dinner.

Maciek and Andrzej are now in the bar. The former immediately notices the attractive blonde serving drinks. The two men stand at the bar and order vodka. When the girl attempts to pour his drink, Maciek plays a game of suddenly moving his glass away. Although she tries not to show it, she is obviously intrigued, and even the stolid Andrzej smiles for a moment. A drunken little man, Pieniazek, who will play an important role later, calls, "Miss Krystyna."

Andrzej disapproves of his young friend's attentions toward Krystyna, pays the bill, and walks away. Maciek continues his flirtation (at one point they agree that they both like violets, which develops into a symbol of their relationship) until Andrzej calls him. Krystyna watches him go.

As they leave the bar, the virile Maciek notices two women, "almost like Warsaw girls," and wishes that it were not necessary to leave. The dialogue that follows is referred to later:

ANDRZEJ: Stay. Nobody's waiting for you.
MACIEK: That's why there is no sense in staying.

This is the first indication that Maciek is lonely and not quite the independent, nonchalant young man who murders for his cause that he appears to be.

Andrzej enters a telephone booth in the lobby while Maciek waits outside.

A portrait of a military officer on a horse. Cut to a woman playing solitaire. It is Mrs. Staniewicz, whom we will meet again. She answers the telephone holding in her hand a sword the servant was polishing (rather an obvious indication that she belongs to the military upper class). She unplugs the phone and carries it down the hall to Major Waga.

Back to Andrzej still in the booth; in the background we see Maciek next to the reception desk reading a newspaper. Szczuka and Polgorski enter and ask for the key to the district secretary's room. When Maciek hears the name Szczuka, he flings down the newspaper and walks out of the frame.

Next we see Maciek knocking on the telephone booth and gesturing. An insert of Waga learning that the assassination has failed and ordering Andrzej to come to his room. Return to the two men coming out of the telephone booth. Maciek walks over and stands near Szczuka. As Andrzej goes by, he tells the young man that he will soon meet him in the bar.

Szczuka asks whether the Staniewicz family has moved, then pockets a slip on which the Porter has written their telephone number. We recognize the name as that of the woman who first answered Andrzej's call. There is no hint as to why the district secretary of the Communist party should be interested in a family of military aristocrats.

When he puts a cigarette in his mouth, a light is offered to him by Maciek. This is the first of two occasions when the young man lights his intended victim's cigarette. It is also the first time Maciek actually stands face to face with Szczuka. The camera holds from its position behind the reception desk as the party secretary slowly, using his cane, walks up the stairs to his room.

Maciek talks to the Porter, encourages the elderly man's memories of Warsaw, and receives a room next door to Szczuka's.

More than once we will observe assassin and victim in adjoining rooms. Within the privacy of four walls each will confront challenges to the validity of his way of life. Repeatedly, however, each one will hear sounds in the other room that penetrate the wall that separates them.

In a fairly low-angle shot Szczuka paces up and down his room drinking tea. He looks at the paper containing the Staniewicz telephone number, but finally does not make the call. He hears a sound next door.

It is Maciek. After looking around, he goes to the window and takes off his sweater without removing his dark glasses. He stops and stares. A zoom shot to a window across the way reveals what he sees. A woman is weeping bitterly. Slonka, the headwaiter, enters. A cut to Maciek as he leans forward. Back to the woman and Slonka.

Once again, as with the murdered man in the chapel, Wajda distorts reality. The cinemographic dynamics at this point suggest that the views of the room through the window are subjective shots from Maciek's point of view. Even though on the sound track every word of the dialogue is clear, it is unlikely that he could hear what is said across a courtyard.

The woman, Stefka, we learn, is the "fiancée" of Stasiek, the younger of the two murdered men. Slonka's sympathy is momentary, then he gives her a pair of silk stockings and puts his hand under her dress.

Maciek pulls down his blinds. He takes out his gun and removes the shell case. We wonder what the effect of what he has witnessed is on him. Does he really understand what has happened? Wajda gives us no clue, except that Maciek does stare for a few moments in the direction of the window.

A shot of Szczuka pacing up and down his room.

We join Andrzej and Florian Waga. The supposedly imperturbable Andrzej does have doubts: Innocent people died needlessly; must Szczuka be killed? The fanatical major has ready answers: "No compromises." This is the only way to a free Poland. Andrzej wipes his face with his hand. Waga cleverly concludes a defense of the Nationalists's policy with a statement that applies directly to his lieutenant. "There is only one way for people like you. To fight. That's all you can do. All other ways are closed to you. Except prison." We realize now how desperate is the situation of Andrzej and Maciek. Later when the younger man dreams of leaving behind his past, we know he is deluding himself—and we sense that he knows it too.

When Waga mentions the "man who has been giving us some trouble," there is an insert of Szczuka still pacing his room.

We learn from the major that the new district secretary is an educated and skillful Communist who spent several years in Russia. Waga divulges that the members of Captain Wilk's detachment, a Home Army guerrila band, have been captured or killed. The significance of this fact becomes clear later. Waga's final statement leaves Andrzej no choice but to continue the struggle: Captain Wilk has been killed.

V. A Man Searches for His Son while Evening Celebrations and a Love Affair Begin

Mrs. Staniewicz is entertaining her friends, Kotowicz among them. These aristocrats—one is a count and Mrs. Staniewicz's husband is a colonel (he is absent, but when his name is mentioned, there is a pan to the portrait that appeared in the previous scene in this room)—are arranging to leave Poland, yet they expect to return in a year, for the "West will strike like lightning."

The colonel's wife is called away. The visitor is Szczuka. Their conversation is held in the hallway near Waga's room. The scene consists primarily of alternate reverse-angle shots.

Szczuka begins cordially enough, but Mrs. Staniewicz, who we discover is his sister-in-law, is curt and antagonistic. She does not invite him in. We hear that Szczuka's wife died in 1941 while he was away and that the Staniewiczs brought up his son, Marek. The district secretary was aware of his in-laws' political views and had written that his son should stay with friends. Catherine Staniewicz, however, had insisted on taking charge of her nephew. When he became sixteen, a year ago, the boy left her and she has had no news of him since. The disappointed father grimly concludes as he leaves, "If he's alive, sooner or later he'll be my son again."

As Mrs. Staniewicz turns to return to her friends, Waga opens his door. After a moment the major lets out Andrzej. A minor irony of the film is the way Szczuka's path repeatedly crosses that of the two men who are ordered to kill him.

At the Monopol Hotel bar Maciek continues his pursuit of Krystyna until Andrzej comes in and the two retreat to a corner of the room. They exchange information. Maciek is told that the assassination must take place and Andrzej learns the location of his companion's room.

Maciek keeps an eye on Krystyna. He reacts with particular antagonism against Kotowicz talking to the young woman. In the conversation between the dapper man in evening clothes and Krystyna, it is suggested that Kotowicz is in some way in charge of the entertainment for the night. It is not clear whether he is an employee of the hotel.

After Mrs. Staniewicz and her two friends are seated at a table in the dining room by Slonka, Kotowicz appears on a platform before a small orchestra and introduces Miss Hanka Lewicka. She sings "The Red Poppies of Monte Cassino." Boleslaw Sulik notes that the song, commemorating a heroic battle of the Polish Second Corps, was very popular in Poland after the war (it is an anachronism to have it sung in May 1945); it is a sentimental presentation of the martial spirit of World War II. As such, it is a contrast to the reality of the battles against the Germans evoked in the next scene.

Everyone in the barroom, except Maciek and Andrzej, has moved into the dining room to hear Miss Lewicka. A waiter has left a tray of drinks on a long counter beside the wall opposite the bar. Both men rise. Andrzej leans against the counter at the end near their table, while Maciek walks to the drinks and smells them. He smiles and calls to his friend, "You remember? Our drinks at Ginger's." "No, I don't." There is a cut from the end of the counter where Maciek is to a lengthy shot from Andrzej's end (approximately a minute and a half). The young man brings two glasses and puts one under Andrzej's nose. Still no response. He ducks his head angrily and returns to the tray. After a moment, he picks up a glass and slides it down the counter to Andrzej. He does this with seven drinks. Then he joins his friend, strikes a match, and begins to light the liquor in each glass. Andrzej raises his eyebrows and calls a name as each drink catches fire: "Haneczka, Wilga . . . ." He prevents Maciek from igniting the last two and offers one of the unlit glasses to his comrade. "We two are alive."

The glasses with flames in them resemble the small, round candles in glass containers that are lit in churches to commemorate the dead. This secular ceremony is for those in the two men's Resistance squad killed fighting the Germans. It motivates remarks by Andrzej and Maciek on the past that help us to understand them. Some critics, however, have found the incident, particularly the sliding of the glasses down the counter, melodramatic.

Before Maciek drinks, he leans against the counter and laughs wildly—there is a forced, almost despairing tone in his laughter. A cut to another shot, with the camera facing Andrzej, as Maciek, back to the counter and the camera, shouts: "Those were wonderful times, Andrzej!" Then they had so many real comrades and life was better. The cynical, perhaps wiser Andrzej is skeptical, but admits that during the war they knew what they wanted and what was expected of them. We recall his conversation with Waga.

The young man, obviously moved and excited, whirls around and faces his friend. "That we should die. That hasn't changed. We can always do that." The morose Andrzej does not think that dying is much. He looks doubtful when Maciek asserts there is nothing else but to try to have a good time. Still, he lifts his glass, salutes his friend, and drinks.

During this dialogue the sentimental song is heard in the background proclaiming the glory and the honor of the war that has just ended. Two veterans of that war look back with a certain nostalgia, yet in the end the taste of victory is bitter. The war is not finished for them. They must continue to kill, while doubting as they never did before why they must kill, facing enemies who are their own countrymen. Later in the film Wajda will counterpoint this scene with one in which Szczuka and Podgorski also reminisce about past battles and find the present civil war a horror. The district secretary, however, will be the most hopeful of the four.

After a shot of Hanka Lewicka completing her song, we return to the two men. Only one of the glasses still has a flame, then it, too, goes out. People, including Krystyna, return to the barroom. Andrzej moves to a window to escape the noise; Maciek follows him.

The shot of the two of them at the window, at eye level, is another lengthy one. Ignoring one interruption (when Maciek looks over his shoulder at Krystyna and there is a brief shot of her), it is more than two minutes long. Most of the time Andrzej is staring into space toward his left; Maciek, smoking, either looks out the window, at his companion, or down. In the background is a blurred view of the people at the bar.

The older man says that Waga does not want him involved in the assassination, so it is up to Maciek. He is leaving in the morning at 4:30 to take Wilk's place. After a glance at the girl, Maciek remarks, "You said . . . that no one is waiting for me. That's true. Will you take me with you?" Andrzej agrees.

After Andrzej leaves, Maciek remains at the window. There is a subjective shot of what he sees: tanks and a poster of Stalin on a wall to one side. We have not had an opportunity before to mention that tanks and soldiers in the streets have become a visual motif. We see them when Drewnowski first arrives at the hotel, when Waga looks out of the window of his room, now from Maciek's point of view, later when the young man and Krystyna walk in the rain, and at the very end of the film. We are thus reminded that even though the war has ended, the equipment and soldiers of battle still haunt the town.

Maciek next appears at the corner of the bar. He reaches for the violets, but Krystyna snatches them away. He manages, even though the young woman is busy serving others, to invite her to his room. She holds up her end of the flirtation; however, she neither agrees to nor rejects his proposition. Before he leaves, Maciek sniffs the violets, symbol in this film of love, as earlier he had smelled the drinks that led to memories of war.

Wajda effectively conveys the bustle in the barroom, yet he is able to isolate the two by means of cuts from one to the other. There is, in fact, in this scene a series of thirty-three uninterrupted, alternate shots from various angles of Maciek and Krystyna after an initial two-shot of them.

We return to the bar again after Maciek leaves. The drunken newspaper editor Pieniazek is looking for someone to pay his bill. He finds a dupe in Drewnowski. At first the mayor's secretary is reluctant to have anything to do with him, but Pieniazek shrewdly baits his hook with a bit of information: the mayor is going to Warsaw to become minister of health. Drewnowski is caught. His only question is whether he will be taken along. He envisions a bright future as he takes his first drink.

Cut to Mayor Swiecki arriving and being greeted by Slonka. The headwaiter is very impressed when he hears of Swiecki's appointment. The mayor asks for his secretary.

Back to Pieniazek and Drewnowski, with the latter already bleary-eyed. What the secretary wants is "everything" and "lots of money," for he has "been on relief long enough." Pieniazek encourages the fantasy as he orders more double vodkas.

The conversation between the two men in the barroom is presented in two lengthy shots (interrupted by an insert of the arrival of the mayor). In the first, they are a few steps from the bar. At one point Pieniazek moves from Drewnowski's left, in front of the secretary, to his right. This device of a person moving from one side of the individual to whom he is talking to the other, in the process passing in front of the camera, is used by Wajda a number of times in the film (another example occurs in the next scene). Also, other people pass in front of the camera twice in this shot, conveying the feeling of a crowd.

In the second lengthy shot the two men are leaning against the bar. Drewnowski is staring off into space, toward his left. We are reminded of Andrzej in an earlier scene. This is obviously an intentional contrast, reinforced visually, between two soldiers plotting murder and escape in what they consider the service of their country and the machinations of the opportunists Pieniazek and Drewnowski.

VI. Maciek and Krystyna in Love

Maciek is alone in his room cleaning his gun. There is a knock on the door. He drops a cartridge as he hides the gun. It is Krystyna. After a brief exchange of words inside the door, she walks to the table and chair at the other end of the room. Maciek surreptitiously searches for the cartridge until he finds it. Now he can fully turn his attention to his visitor; on his knees, he rests his head on her lap.

During the conversation we learn that neither has a family in Poland. Krystyna is defensive (she came because she could never fall in love with him) and insists that she will not allow any entangling relationship in her life. Maciek is also wary, but confesses that he was not sure that she would come.

In the beginning of the scene there is an interesting example of how a camera angle and cutting can affect our sense of cinematic time. When Maciek is on the floor looking for the cartridge, the camera is at floor level, angled up. As the young man rises and walks to the door, the camera holds. It seems to take Maciek quite a time to reach the other end of the room. When Krystyna, the camera at eye level, leaves the door, she walks out of the frame. A cut to her at the table. Our apprehension is that the time it took her to move from the door to the table was a quarter of the time that expired for Maciek to go from the table to the door.

At the end of the two-shot at the door, Krystyna steps between Maciek and the camera, a favorite device of Wajda's that we commented on earlier. (An attentive viewer will notice a bit of carelessness on the part of the props assistant. When Maciek goes to the door, the chair is in *front* of the table. Krystyna sits down on a chair, the only one at this end of the room, to the *side* of the table.)

In the barroom Pieniazek, having wheedled an invitation to the banquet from the drunken Drewnowski, drags the secretary away. There is an insert of the mayor remarking that he is taking Drewnowski with him to Warsaw. We return to the two drinking companions weaving their way down the corridor past the lavatory and then bursting into the banquet room. Swiecki is furious with his secretary and at the presence of "this scoundrel" Pieniazek. Szczuka arrives with Wrona, the head of the

FIGURE 15–1. *Krystyna and Maciek together in his hotel room.* (*Courtesy Janus Films.*)

security police. We gather from their remarks that they know each other.

Drewnowski and Pieniazek are disruptive forces at the celebration, but they finally sit down. The mayor begins his speech.

Cut to the headwaiter Slonka talking to Mrs. Jurgeluszka, the aged lavatory attendant. The woman hearing the shouts from the banquet room wonders if a birthday or anniversary is being celebrated. Slonka remarks, "No, it's all because of Poland."

We return to Maciek and Krystyna. The scene consists entirely of close-ups of the two (with the exception of the end of the last shot), either tight ones of their faces or of their heads and naked shoulders (Figure 15–1). There is the gray light of a darkened room. The transitions between the three shots that make up the scene are dissolves. Within the soft focus shots the camera pans from the two together to one or the other or the reverse.

Their sexual experience has evidently been mutually gratifying. More important, their attitudes toward each other have changed. Krystyna finds her lover quite different now than before. She resists giving in to her emotions because Maciek will be leaving soon, but he is less cautious. She inquires about a noise. There is a two-shot favoring Maciek's full face as he closes his eyes and replies, "I think our neighbor is back." As he is reminded of Szczuka and the problem the man is to him, Maciek turns again to Krystyna. He pulls her to him and the camera pans, following his hand as it moves down along her back.

Andrzej comes looking for his friend. He eventually stands outside Maciek's door and hears a snatch of conversation within the room. Maciek is suggesting that he and Krystyna spend the next day together. Andrzej does not knock on the door as he had intended. Instead, with a worried expression he goes down to the barroom.

Wrona, the security chief, questions captured members of Captain Wilk's detachment. He slaps a defiant young man.

We do not realize until later why it is appropriate that the next shot should be of Szczuka. He is watching the dancers in the dining room from the foot of the stairs in the lobby. Cut to Maciek and Krystyna at the top of the stairs.. As the young man begins walking down, he looks around and suddenly stiffens. The two lovers part.

Szczuka walks up the stairs past Maciek. He stops and asks the young man in dark glasses for a light for his cigarette. This is the second time assassin and victim have faced each other; the next meeting will be fatal for the district secretary. After Szczuka leaves, Maciek takes a step after him, but stops and leans heavily against the banister. Krystyna comes to him and asks what is wrong. He pleads that they stay together for half an hour longer.

VII. *The Lovers in the Ruins of a Church*

Maciek and Krystyna dance together for a few minutes in the lobby and then go outside. It is drizzling. With Maciek's jacket as protection, they walk past troops and military vehicles. The rain comes down with greater force and they seek shelter in the ruins of a church.

This sequence in the church is the dramatic climax of the film. The conflict within Maciek between duty and love is expressed in words and visual symbols. A patriotic poem and a crucifix represent the two poles. Yet, Wajda makes the symbols ambiguous. Both are in a setting of ruins that suggests Poland at the end of World War II. The poem speaks not only of glory but also of death and the possibility that the quest for freedom may leave in ashes what one holds most dear. The cross with the suffering Christ is hanging upside down. As the civil war in Poland is not a simple matter of good against evil, so the conflict between duty and love is fraught with complexities and confusions.

The sequence consists primarily of three scenes: the reading of the inscription, the dialogue in front of the crucifix, and events in the chapel. In the first scene the camera pans as they run along a wall that leads them from the entrance of the church farther into the ruins. After Krystyna returns Maciek's jacket to him, she moves closer to an inscription. More than a dozen shots follow, with cuts from one to the other. The ones of Krystyna are over her shoulder as she reads the inscription on the tombstone embedded in the wall and traces the blurred letters with her finger. Occasionally, especially near the end of her reading, she looks toward her companion.

Maciek puts on his jacket and lights a cigarette as he listens. Finally, he recites the last lines of the poem himself. As he does so, he is leaning against a low arch, smoking, his shoulders hunched, with his left hand across his chest and his head down. His voice vibrates with feeling.

These are the lines from the poem by Norwid as translated by the author of the subtitles:

> So often are you as a blazing torch
> With flames of burning hemp falling about you.
> Flaming, you know not if flames freedom brings or death,
> Consuming all that you most cherish.
> Or if cinders only will be left and want, chaos and tempest shall engulf.
> Or will the cinders hold the glory of a starlight diamond,
> The morning star of lasting triumph.

It is inexplicable why the individual who supplied the subtitles did not use the word *ashes* instead of "cinders," and thus have it correspond to the English translation of the title of the film.

FIGURE 15–2. *Krystyna and Maciek in the ruins of a church. (Courtesy Janus Films.)*

The poem vividly sets forth the two possible ends for those who commit themselves to the freedom of their country (although, as noted in the previous section of our analysis, the lines could also be interpreted as part of a love poem). Maciek has been following this path of freedom. One senses, however, that he has a vision of his own end, and he sees ashes rather than a lasting triumph. When Krystyna asks, "And where are we?" he replies, "You are a diamond," with no reference to himself.

He moves quickly along a wall, then looks back at Krystyna. She walks into the frame, in front of the camera, and to the other side, so that finally we see her and Maciek. This is the first two-shot of them since they found the inscription, but they still are apart. He wants to tell her something.

The next shot is a very impressive one. The camera, at a high angle, pans down a large cross hanging upside down (it has fallen and is held by ropes) until the crossbar, part of it broken off, is a third from the top of the frame. The inverted head and shoulders of Christ in agony face the camera, with a halo, like slivers of spears, penetrating the head.

From the background the couple come forward in the fog to either side of the swaying crucifix (Maciek to camera right). During this shot they continue to move toward the camera, but still are separated by the head of Christ (Figure 15–2).

Maciek would like to lead a different life. When he says that he cannot completely explain, Krystyna replies that she understands. We never discover how much she has surmised; however, she must have guessed that Maciek is involved in a dangerous activity. He continues by saying that he has thought of nothing but survival; however, now he would like to lead a normal life and perhaps to return to school. The dialogue deals with regret and confusion, hope and needs. Between the two young people, however, like a warning, is an image of the prophet of love crucified by human beings, whose symbol has been inverted by war.

The shot ends with Maciek moving away and the camera panning with him. He stops and says that he wishes he had known yesterday what he knows at present. Krystyna's comment on this statement reveals a sensitivity and self-understanding that we had not earlier suspected in the young woman: "I wouldn't have come to you then." With a rueful laugh he observes that until that evening he did not appreciate what love was. So finally Maciek speaks of "love." This word has hovered in the air between them, but out of fear and self-defense each had avoided uttering it.

When Maciek mentions love, there is a cut to Krystyna as she takes a step toward him and stumbles. The heel of her shoe has come loose. He comes to her, promises to fix it, takes the shoe, and leaves her.

The camera follows him as he enters a lighted room; a man in a chair is sleeping outside. In a high-angle shot we see the doorway, which Krystyna leans against. In front of Maciek is an altar with a statue on it and candles; behind him is a portion of a white sheet covering some-

FIGURE 15–3. *In a chapel Maciek happens upon the bodies of the two men that he helped to murder. (Courtesy Janus Films.)*

thing. A cut to a medium close-up of the young man, from the same perspective, although at eye level, as he finds a bell with which he hammers on the heel.

The watchman, awakened by the noise, comes in. There is a series of four shots alternating between the watchman and Krystyna at the doorway and Maciek in front of the altar. When the watchman upbraids them for not respecting the dead, there is a final cut to the young man. The camera, however, has now changed position, so that it is facing the altar, thus preparing for the climax of the scene. Maciek has leaned forward and is out of the frame. He rises up and turns around toward the camera. We hear the watchman speaking off camera of "two men who are dead today." Maciek lifts up the sheet and looks. He takes a deep breath, hunches his shoulders, and stares directly at the camera, then throws the sheet to the side (Figure 15–3). The camera pans down to the bodies. Krystyna screams. There is a hold on the corpses for a moment.

If Maciek in his preoccupation with Krystyna minimized the burden of the past that he carries and his present responsibilities, he is made fully aware again of his situation by the bodies of the men he helped murder.

VIII. Maciek Comes to a Decision while Szczuka Finds His Son

Szczuka is standing before the window in his hotel room. Podgorski comes in with an ancient phonograph player, wine, and glasses. He winds up the player and we hear a Spanish marching song.

We mentioned earlier that this scene is in counterpoint to the one in which Andrzej and Maciek reminisce about the war. The parallel is emphasized by Szczuka not recalling where he had last heard the song, just as Andrzej at first did not respond to Maciek's prodding. There is also martial music in the background on both occasions. Finally, Podgorski uses a phrase almost identical to one uttered by Maciek: "They were good times."

The memories of Szczuka and Podgorski go back to the Spanish Civil War, but all four men are confused and unhappy about the present conflict. There is, however, a difference in the two leaders' attitudes toward the future. The cynical Andrzej realizes that his side will be defeated; he continues the fight only because there is nothing else he can do and the discipline of a soldier is ingrained in him. Szczuka also recognizes that there is misery, pain, and suffering in the country. He scorns selfish, pragmatic Poles, symbolized for him at the moment by the sounds of celebrating coming from below and for us by the conversation between Drewnowski and Pieniazek. On the other hand, the district secretary is confident that his party can ameliorate the situation, and he believes that "there will be good times now too."

Podgorski shows his superior the empty cartridges found at the scene of the murders. The two men finish their glasses of wine and Podgorski departs. Szczuka sits down and sets up the cartridges on end. Those shells remind us of the killings and of the danger threatening the district secretary.

In the next scene Maciek and Krystyna return to the hotel and stand before a back entrance. He tells her that perhaps he can "change things." He kisses her passionately and she leaves.

He has taken the violets from her. As he stands there lost in thought, a white horse moves close to him and sniffs the flowers. (We associate this gesture with Maciek. Could the animal represent the pale horse of death?)

He walks into the corridor behind the banquet room and is startled at seeing Andrzej at the other end of the hallway. He tries to hide by going into the lavatory, but his friend has seen him.

Maciek is still holding the violets when Andrzej finds him. The young man wants to talk "seriously." Andrzej first checks the toilet cubicles. When he opens one door, there is a shot of Pieniazek collapsed on a toilet seat, snoring, and clutching a bottle against his chest.

The conversation begins with a shot of Maciek, then continues during a lengthy two-shot, with Andrzej in the foreground. The young man is evidently agitated as he tries to convince his superior officer and friend that he is not a coward, but "I simply can't go on killing, hiding. I want to live. You must understand." Andrzej may inwardly sympathize with

his friend's dilemma, but it is as an officer in the Home Army that he refuses to relieve Maciek of his assignment to kill Szczuka. His face tense
and unyielding, Andrzej insists that falling in love is Maciek's own business; however, his personal life cannot interfere with the goals of the
movement. "Don't forget you were—and are—one of us. And that means
something." Both men look toward the door of the lavatory as we hear
loud shouting and singing.

From this point until the end of *Ashes and Diamonds* there are chiefly
brief scenes and shots with a good deal of cross-cutting. The tempo is
thus increased as we witness the disintegration of the fortunes of most of
the principles. Only a dreamlike polonaise near the conclusion of the
film suggests a symbolic unity.

From the lavatory we return to the banquet room. Drewnowski's eyes
focus on a fire extinguisher. He pulls it from the wall and, pretending it is
a machine gun, begins to spray people.

An insert of Andrzej and Maciek in the lavatory.

Drewnowski is now on the table pointing the extinguisher at everyone
in sight. He pulls the tablecloth to the floor before he is dragged away.

Another two-shot of Andrzej and Maciek, only now they are closer
together, both looking in the same direction.

Drewnowski is thrown down the stairs of the lavatory with a promise
that his career is over. He crawls up the stairs and goes by the female
attendant. Next we see him in the courtyard, stumbling into the rain and
flinging visiting cards in the air.

Back to the lavatory. Andrzej throws away his cigarette and holds out
his hand for Maciek's gun. The young man slowly takes out his pistol,
then abruptly pulls it back. "I'll do it myself," he announces. Outside of
his relationship with Krystyna, this is Maciek's first impulsive act. He is
unsure of himself.

Andrzej warns him not to be reckless and reminds him of the departure
at 4:30. Maciek states that he will not leave with his friend. The older
man frowns, and after saying goodby walks out of the frame.

Maciek, who has been leaning his head against a toilet door, still holding the gun, lifts his head and calls out. The camera pans with him as he
swiftly moves in the direction of the stairs and calls in a loud voice, "Do
you believe in what you're doing?" "That's of no importance" is Andrzej's
reply, summing up in a brief sentence the tragedy of a political activist
who has lost his ideals but feels he must still obey his superiors. He leaves.
The camera holds on Maciek as he puts the gun inside his shirt and then
anxiously rubs his face with his hand (as Andrzej did when he expressed
doubts to *his* superior officer).

As Andrzej leaves the hotel, he is surrounded by a group of children
selling bunches of flowers. He gives them some change. He takes a few
steps before he realizes that he has accepted a bouquet. The flowers are,

of course, violets. Andrzej sniffs them for a moment, then throws the flowers into a garbage can.

Back to Maciek, who straightens his back and runs up the stairs. After a moment Kotowicz enters the lavatory.

Szczuka is in his room. A lieutenant enters and delivers a message from Major Wrona. The chief of security has discovered that one of the captured members of Wilk's group is Marek, the son of Szczuka. A car is coming to pick up the district secretary. After the messenger leaves, Szczuka stares intently into space as he grips the bedstead.

An insert of Wrona with Marek.

A shot of Szczuka as he wearily rises and puts on his jacket.

IX. The Murder of Szczuka

Maciek enters the lobby of the hotel just in time to hear the lieutenant tell the porter that a car is coming for the district secretary. The young man goes to a chair under the stairs and sits there. The Porter closes the door to the dining room and turns off an overhead light.

Soon we hear Szczuka walking down the stairs, his cane accentuating his steps. We see his feet on the stairs, as well as Maciek's face behind the ironwork steps. Cut to a very high-angle shot of the lobby, with Szczuka pacing up and down. Barely visible on camera right is the figure of Maciek. There follows a medium close-up of each man.

An insert of Marek and Wrona.

Back to the lobby. The restless Szczuka comes to a decision. He goes through the hotel door.

Maciek comes out from under the stairs. After having a drink with the porter, he casually mentions that he is taking a walk before he leaves. Next we see him pacing up and down in front of the hotel. His eyes are on the street down which we assume Szczuka has gone. In the foreground we notice the garbage can in which Andrzej threw the violets. Maciek is still undecided. Suddenly he runs out of the frame in the direction in which he was looking.

A moving camera accompanies Szczuka in a medium close-up as he quickly walks. Cut to Maciek, who is striding in the same direction but in front of his victim. He opens his shirt and takes out his gun. He whirls around and moves toward Szczuka (his back is now to the camera). The district secretary stops; for an instant the two stare at each other, then Maciek fires.

Cut to behind Szczuka from an angle that includes Maciek as he continues to fire. Four brief medium close-ups follow, showing us in alternation the face of each man: Szczuka looks frightened and in pain, but even more, bewildered; Maciek's face is strained, as though it takes every bit of his strength repeatedly to pull the trigger. The fifth shot in the series is of Szczuka staggering toward the camera. Cut to behind the dying man.

His arms are open as though to embrace his murderer. Maciek retreats a few steps, yet the man keeps coming. Finally he falls into the young man's arms. Maciek holds him as the camera tracks in. Cut to a low-angle two-shot, the dead Szczuka still being held up by Maciek. A flare rises in the sky just above the murderer's head. He looks up at the sky. The camera holds as fireworks explode in the sky, their lights flickering on the two men. Finally, Maciek drops the body, throws the gun away, and runs.

A shot from outside a window in the hotel. A group of people—some, such as Mrs. Staniewicz, we recognize—are watching the display of fireworks, which is reflected on the glass of the window.

Cut to the flares. The camera pans down to the body of Szczuka near a pool of water. Abruptly the pyrotechnics end. The camera holds on Szczuka in darkness except for a shaft of light illuminating the upper portion of his body.

Maciek is in his room. In a lengthy shot we see him vigorously washing, then he pulls up the blinds and sunlight floods the room. He throws his things into his bag and finishes dressing.

The murder of Szczuka is conveyed in brilliant images. The sight of the dying man collapsing into the arms of his murderer only seven years older than his own son is moving. Yet Wajda cannot leave well enough alone. At least in our opinion the display of fireworks at the moment of the district secretary's death is melodramatic, a straining for effect unworthy of a director of Wajda's ability.

X. A Polonaise and the Death of Maciek

In the hotel weary waiters are cleaning up in the banquet and dining rooms and members of the orchestra are packing away their instruments. In the bar, however, the reveling continues. Kotowicz comes out and imperiously demands that the tired players offer one more dance—a classic polonaise (A-Major by Oginski). Other people come out from the bar. We recognize the singer, Mayor Swiecki, Mrs. Staniewicz, and others we have seen during the evening. Kotowicz, in his grand manner, begins to organize the dance.

The barroom is now empty except for Krystyna. Maciek comes in. The two stand on either side of a column. He tells her that he must leave; he could not change things.

Insert of the dancers lined up.

Maciek reaches over for Krystyna's hand, but she turns away, her whole body stiff with pain and disappointment. "Don't say any more. Go!" Maciek bows his head and walks away.

We return to Kotowicz as he continues to arrange the guests. Maciek passes through the dining room. The goal of the master of ceremonies, he announces grandiosely with arms outstretched, is "a gigantic procession," "a national pageant." To this end, he proclaims "universal concord" (Figure 15–4). The dancers begin moving in a circle.

FIGURE 15–4. *Kotowicz proclaims "universal concord." (Courtesy Janus Films.)*

Maciek is in the lobby of the hotel bidding the porter goodby. He walks quickly down one street and then another. In the distance is a railway viaduct and we hear a faraway train whistle. Is he going to meet that train? It is at least a symbol of escape. He pauses for a few moments. This is another instance of his indecisiveness. Finally, he walks to a scaffolding. In the far background a train goes over the viaduct.

There is a subjective shot of what he sees. In an open area Andrzej stands next to a truck. Drewnowski comes up and tries to climb aboard. Andrzej stops him, takes a briefcase out of his hand, knocks him down, and repeatedly kicks him. "You only came because you got the sack." As we have seen, Andrzej always had contempt for Drewnowski. One also suspects that he is disturbed because Maciek has not appeared and is venting his feelings on a man that he considers cowardly and selfish. An insert of Maciek still watching.

The truck leaves. The moaning Drewnowski struggles to his feet. A shot of Maciek ducking behind the scaffolding. It is too late. Drewnowski has seen him and hurries toward him calling his name.

Maciek runs down the street away from Drewnowski. A view of the wall of the viaduct with soldiers lounging against it. Maciek, looking over his shoulder, is walking quickly through a tunnel in the bridge and collides with one of the soldiers. He reaches for his gun, but he had thrown it away after killing Szczuka. In panic he runs away.

Once again an impulsive action has betrayed him. The cool, self-disciplined killer we saw at the beginning of the film has been weakened by love and doubts to an uncertain, hesitant individual who can no longer depend on the instincts he developed as an underground fighter. Surely he could have brazened out his encounter with the troops. Instead he runs, the one action that would galvanize the soldiers into action.

Drewnowski's voice mixes with those of the soldiers, who, convinced that Maciek has a gun, shout that they will fire if he does not halt. After the shots ring out, Maciek staggers and falls, yet rises and stumbles forward until he disappears among lines of drying laundry.

We observe the soldiers searching among the laundry, then moving off. The camera holds on a sheet as a hand comes around and across the white surface. When the hand stops, a dark stain spreads. Maciek comes from behind the sheet, looks at his hand drenched with blood, and smells it. (He inhales death rather than the odor of violets or a drink, although the three in this film are symbolically related.) He sinks down, leaning against a post. An insert of soldiers still searching. In a medium close-up, his mouth twisting with pain, Maciek tries to rise.

We are back with the dancers. Kotowicz persuades Krystyna to join the group.

A moving camera shot of Maciek coughing violently, staggering along a wall, trying to support himself with his hands.

The dancers once again. The camera holds as each of the couples, arranged in a circle, passes in front of it. The circle of people, under the direction of Kotowicz, becomes a procession that moves toward the door of the room bright with sunlight. The camera pans and holds again as the last couple in the dance enters the light.

There is a surrealistic quality to the scene. Everything seems to slow down. The music is out of tune, like a phonograph record running down. The eyes of the dancers are glazed, their faces unsmiling. Their movements are not quite slow motion, but tired, dreamlike, almost involuntary.

Wajda has created striking effects for this dance to a polonaise. A viewer's emotions, rather than his intellect, are stirred, so that it is difficult, as with the best of symbolic cinematic scenes, to interpret what is seen in rational terms. We sense a dance of life, but to music that is distinctly Polish, suggesting political overtones. It is Kotowicz who directs the dancers (see a discussion of him in the previous section of this analysis). He declares universal concord and forces people of different political persuasions, even the apolitical Krystyna, to dance together to patriotic music. In the end only his will seems to hold them together. Although they are tired, even stupefied, he is able to drive them into the light, into a new day.

A political interpretation of this dance is supported by the next shot.

FIGURE 15–5. *The dying Maciek staggers across a garbage dump. (Courtesy Janus Films.)*

The Porter goes to the corner of the lobby and unfurls the Polish flag. Then he marches out through the front door of the hotel.

Someday there may be concord in Poland, but meanwhile there are the victims of civil war.

Maciek is coughing and groaning as he alternately stumbles and crawls across a garbage dump (Figure 15–5). The camera moves with him until there is a cut to a flock of dark birds wheeling in the sky. Back to a high-angle shot of Maciek falling to his knees, tearing at the refuse and pulling it to him. He draws up his body into a fetal position; his hands are over his face as he cries and moans. His limbs tremble convulsively. Finally, he stirs less and less, and then is still. We hear a few bars of the polonaise, again out of tune, as there is a fade to black.

Style and Approach

Few viewers of *Ashes and Diamonds* would deny that Andrzej Wajda, as its director and co-script writer, demonstrates a number of admirable qualities. He unifies an intricate plot with many characters covering a brief period of time by the effective use of cross-cutting. He knows just how to focus attention on individuals among many people without caus-ing us to lose our awareness that these characters are part of a crowd or large group. He has a sure instinct for when to have his camera remain stationary, when to confine himself to lengthy shots, and when to support the climax of a scene with brief shots, quick transitions, and unusual angles. In fact, the visual rhythms of the film are masterful.

More difficult to characterize is his ability to convey the atmosphere of a small town. Hundreds of details accumulate to make the setting completely convincing. This verisimilitude is reinforced by the wonderful, appropriate faces of even minor characters and the performances he elicits from his actors. Particularly brilliant is the acting of Zbigniew Cybulski as Maciek and Bogumil Kobiela as Drewnowski.

The political situation in Poland at the end of the war was complex and often abstract. However, Wajda presents the issues through characters and, even though he favors one side, he gives representatives of the two conflicting parties opportunities to justify their views.

We have noted throughout our analysis how often scenes of visual and character counterpoint appear in the film. Two examples immediately come to mind. There is the two-shot of Andrzej and Maciek at the window of the bar talking about the future and later another two-shot (in two parts) of Pieniazek and Drewnowski drinking together and also talking about the future. Another instance of two similar situations separated by time is Andrzej and Maciek reminiscing about their past war activities and Szczuka and Podgorski doing the same in the district secretary's room. This device—when as in the case of Wajda it is used with some subtlety and without obvious plot manipulation—helps to unify a film and to develop in the minds of viewers parallels between characters who would otherwise appear diverse.

Now we proceed to aspects of the film for which praise must be qualified. Wajda has often described himself and been described as a romantic. In cinema, as in the other arts, this term is so amorphous as to be almost meaningless, yet it does suggest an approach that can help us to understand qualities in the film that many viewers find objectionable. A romantic, no matter how debatable his other characteristics, definitely does not prize restraint. And Wajda in certain scenes in *Ashes and Diamonds* is unrestrained in his efforts to surprise and overwhelm his audience.

In sequence IX, fireworks suddenly erupt as Szczuka dies. This is perhaps the most flagrant example of an effect that attempts to be dramatic but that we find embarrassingly strained and fustian. Then there are the violets that represent the love between Maciek and Krystyna. One cannot object to the symbol itself, although it could have been handled with more discretion. What disturbs us is the ponderous obviousness with which the symbol is used in one scene. In sequence VIII, Andrzej emerges from the hotel after persuading Maciek to complete his assignment, and thus in effect condemning him to death. The cynical lieutenant of the Home Army then throws a bunch of violets he has just bought into a garbage can.

Other instances are closer to the borderline between heightened drama and visual and symbolic bombast. Inevitably the exact location of that borderline is a matter of taste. Are those who criticize the scene in the bar when Maciek lights the glasses of liquor too fastidious? Admittedly, the sliding of the glasses down the counter is uncomfortably reminiscent of a Western. Is the murder in sequence I, in which the victim falls into the chapel, too obviously manipulated? Would the agonized death of Maciek have been twice as moving if it had been half as lengthy?

No one would gainsay Wajda's right to use unrealistic and mannered effects to attempt to enrich specific scenes. It is a question of how successful a viewer considers each instance. In our opinion, at least in two sections of the film, the director felicitously fuses together all cinematic and narrative elements and preserves simultaneously—without giving an impression of intellectual superimposition—the perspectives of realism and symbolism. The two sections are the scenes in the ruins of a church and the dance at the end of the film.

There is another area in which we consider that Wajda can be faulted. Maciek's doubts about his mission, as we have pointed out, do not depend exclusively on his falling in love with Krystyna. This experience, however, is a paramount influence on him. In view of the characters of the two young people, we question the credibility of their so quickly (after a couple of hours in a room together) surrendering their defenses. Perhaps we are insufficiently "romantic," but we feel that the director has required us to take on faith rather than evidence a relationship that is crucial to the development of the plot.

There are all too few distinguished "political films" in the history of cinema. Wajda's "trilogy" cannot be compared to its advantage to the works of the great Russian directors. Surely, however, *Ashes and Diamonds* should be added to that small list of memorable narrative films that center on the influence of politics on human beings and includes Sagan's *Madchen in Uniform*, Rossellini's *Open City*, Pontecorvo's *The Battle of Algiers*, Costa-Gavras's *Z*, and Bertolucci's *The Conformist*.

CHAPTER 16

L'Avventura

[The Adventure]

Directed by MICHELANGELO ANTONIONI

Thus I have rid myself of much unnecessary technical baggage, eliminating all the logical narrative transitions, all those connective links between sequences where one sequence served as a springboard for the one that followed.

The reason I did this was because it seemed to me—and of this I am firmly convinced—that cinema today should be tied to the truth rather than logic. . . . The rhythm of life is not made up of one steady beat; it is, instead, a rhythm that is sometimes fast, sometimes slow; it remains motionless for a while, then at the next moment it starts spinning around. There are times when it appears almost static, there are other times when it moves with tremendous speed. . . . I think that through these pauses, through this attempt to adhere to a definite reality—spiritual, internal, and even moral—there springs forth what today is more and more coming to be known as modern cinema, that is, a cinema which is not so much concerned with externals as it is with those forces that move us to act in a certain way and not in another. Because the important thing is this: that our acts, our gestures, our words are nothing more than the consequences of our own personal situation in relation to the world around us.

Michelangelo Antonioni, from "A Talk with Michelangelo Antonioni on His Work." L'Avventura, a film by Michelangelo Antonioni, from the filmscript by Michelangelo Antonioni, with Elio Bartolini and Tonino Guerra. George Amberg, Consulting Ed., New York, 1969.

CAST

CLAUDIA	*Monica Vitti*
SANDRO	*Gabriele Ferzetti*
ANNA	*Lea Massari*
JULIA	*Dominique Blanchar*
ANNA'S FATHER	*Renzo Ricci*
CORRADO	*James Addams*
RAIMONDO	*Lelio Luttazzi*
PATRIZIA	*Esmeralda Ruspoli*
GOFFREDO	*Giovanni Petrucci*
GLORIA PERKINS	*Dorothy De Polioli*

CREDITS

DIRECTOR   *Michelangelo Antonioni*
PRODUCER   *Cino Del Duca, presented by Robert and Raymond Hakim*
SCREENPLAY   *Michelangelo Antonioni with Elio Bartolini*
                                                              and Tonino Guerra

DIRECTOR OF PHOTOGRAPHY   *Aldo Scavarda*
ART DIRECTOR   *Pierro Poletto, CSC*
COSTUMES   *Adriana Berselli*
EDITOR   *Eraldo da Roma*
MUSIC   *Giovanni Fusco*

    1960   Black and white   145 minutes

Story and Characterization

There is nothing obscure about the narrative pattern of *L'Avventura*. It is easy to follow the train of events. Following a sequence in which we are introduced to Anna, Sandro, and Claudia, we see a group of bored Italian aristocrats disembark from their yacht onto the deserted and forbidding island of Liscia Bianca (white fishbone). After some desultory wandering and a few enigmatic incidents (which are, although seemingly trivial, highly charged with emotion), they discover that one of their number (Anna) is missing. A long and fruitless search ensues, led by Anna's lover (Sandro) and her best friend (Claudia).

Up to this point, Anna has been the protagonist of the film, and we suppose that Claudia and Sandro will play strong supporting roles. But now the group loses interest in any further search and drifts off to continue their pursuit of distraction (while they seek shelter from an impending storm), leaving the mystery of Anna's disappearance to Claudia and Sandro. Now these two become the central characters in the film. They wander off through Sicily to look for her, spurred on by a vague set of clues to Anna's whereabouts. Ultimately they betray the object of their search by becoming lovers and eventually rejoin the members of their social set at a hotel in Taormina. There, after an episode in which Sandro betrays Claudia with the American whore, Gloria Perkins, the film ends in a dawn scene of compassionate ambiguity.

So much for the bare outline, which is clear enough. What perplexes and perhaps even exasperates some audiences is the unresolved mystery of Anna's disappearance. Asked what happened to Anna, Antonioni himself replied, "I don't know. Someone told me that she committed suicide, but I don't believe it." (Quoted in Ian Cameron and Robin Wood, *Antonioni*, New York, 1969, p. 9a.) We may conclude from this, therefore, that Antonioni does not care. Nor should we. For Anna's literal disappearance is a metaphorical expression. It suggests that friends and lovers are bound to each other by the loosest of ties and that they are ultimately replaceable. Anna's disappearance, then, is Antonioni's dramatization of what he regards as a fact of emotional life.

Nevertheless, Antonioni may have miscalculated here. The sequences on the island involving the disappearance and the subsequent search are very long and persuade us by their length (hence by their aesthetic weight—the large proportion of the film that they take up) that we are watching the generic screen mystery. And so powerful is its psychological impact, so well does it do its work of arousing expectations, that the audience is invariably set up for a resolution. When it fails to come, we are, perhaps, frustrated enough to be distracted from the real issues of the film. And these are not easy. "When I finished *L'Avventura*," Antonioni said, "I was forced to reflect on what it meant." (Quoted in "But Eros Is Sick," George Amberg, in *L'Avventura*, op. cit., p. 250.)

Before we follow Antonioni's example, we should turn to the characters through whose interaction (or, as we will see, lack of it) *L'Avventura's* meaning is generated.

The central character is Claudia, because in the course of the film she undergoes changes, whereas Anna and Sandro do not. The fact is important, for Antonioni insists (not only here but in virtually all of his films) that the environment is influential in shaping behavior. Thus, Anna and Sandro represent the fixed environment, whereas Claudia is affected by it. And thus Claudia is pictured as coming from a different strata of society than the one to which Sandro and Anna belong. But Antonioni's dramatic methods are not conventional and he does not provide us with a conventional exposition. Facts about characters' lives are revealed naturally, or not at all, and we have to work hard to piece together what we must grasp in order to know a character. An example is this fact of Claudia's class affiliation.

Claudia's entrance is our first clue to her status. The staging does not emphasize her arrival; it is hardly noted: she merely slips into the frame (see pp. 403–404 in "Analysis of Major Sequences"). Next, when Anna and Claudia get out of the car in front of Sandro's palazzo, Anna perversely suggests that she does not want to go on the trip. Claudia's response is good-natured, but it also reveals that she is disappointed; she is not used to yachting trips and had been looking forward to it. Indeed, when we see her on the yacht she seems to be enjoying herself. In fact, she is the only one who does. Claudia is also puzzled, on the yacht, by Anna's shark "joke." She is not used to flamboyant and impulsive behavior such as Anna has exhibited in causing the commotion about the sighting of a shark. And Anna, to distract her, insists, with that same impulsivity, that Claudia accept one of her old blouses. Anna's condescension toward Claudia and Claudia's strikingly different behavior suggest that Claudia is a member of a lower social class than Anna and her friends. Late in

FIGURE 16–1. *The storm: Claudia and Corrado.* (*Courtesy Janus Films.*)

the final sequence, almost casually, we hear Claudia say that her upbring-ing had been "very poor," but by that time we have had to guess as much.

Claudia's attitude toward Anna's disappearance also marks her as dif-ferent from the others. She alone seems worried about her friend. By contrast, Sandro's first reaction to the disappearance is irritation: he re-marks that Anna is "full of ideas" and has engaged in another prank, like her joke about the shark. But Claudia feels *responsible* for the loss, and she insists on remaining on the island to continue the search. This in-sistence evokes Sandro's antagonism: he thinks she will be "in the way." Antonioni underscores the difference in their attitudes by showing us the growing conflict between them, culminating in the open conflict in the fisherman's hut. Here, as elsewhere, their antagonism is conveyed by a formal device of Antonioni's films: he places her in the frame so that she avoids looking at him.

But Claudia's ethical depth and human sympathies show forth even more the next morning (Figure 16–1). She apologizes to Sandro for her behavior of the previous evening. It is, however, a gesture that is lost on Sandro.

The growth of her feelings for Sandro and the fact that she ultimately becomes his mistress are not without inner conflict. For her there is always a series of spontaneous, *appropriate*, emotional responses accom-panying each stage of her drift toward Sandro. She suffers shame, humili-ation and doubt about Sandro's fidelity; and she experiences joy and exaltation when their closeness seems to her to be more genuine. Antonioni does not make things easy for us; in Claudia's replacing Anna there is no simple equation.

Anna, for example, seems to have experienced nothing like joy in her relations with Sandro. The dark-haired Anna, compared to the light-haired Claudia, is the neurotic representative of her social milieu. Her inconsolable character is revealed to us in the scene in Sandro's apartment (see pp. 404–408 in "Analysis of Major Sequences"), in her impulsiveness aboard the yacht (leaping off the stern as the boat moves through the water at full speed and then crying "shark"; giving her blouse to Claudia), and in her final disappearance. The picture of Anna's alienation is also made clear at the beginning of the film, in the scene with her father. Neither family, nor friends, nor lover are any consolation to her. In fact, as she tells both Claudia and Sandro, she prefers to be absent from her lover rather than to be close to him; she speaks of a month of separation—even a year. The two books she carries on the yacht trip, Fitzgerald's *Tender Is the Night* and the Bible, characterize her situation by allusion: the Fitzgerald novel detailing a love affair whose strength is sapped by self-pity and the Bible structuring a solidity of which she can only dream. Anna is trapped within the prison of herself.

Sandro, too, is trapped by a deadened capacity to behave spontaneously. He is concerned only with his own compensatory neurotic wishes. Thus, he reacts to Anna's restlessness when we first see him in the film by supposing that she wants to look him over. And later, on the island, the morning after his fight with Claudia in the fisherman's shack, he wants to know, first, whether and how Anna spoke of *him*. In fact, his response to Anna's disappearance is to direct his erotic impulses toward Claudia, as if Anna's disappearance represented a greater loss to him than to Anna. For Sandro is essentially insensitive to the feelings of others. This is painfully dramatized in his last scene on the island, just prior to Anna's disappearance. When she complains that she can no longer "feel" him, he construes the word literally and asks her if she had not "felt" him the previous day, when they had made love.

Insensitive as he is to others, he is also unable to make contact with himself. For example, there is his professional life. We do not learn until very late in the film that Sandro has been trained as an architect but has instead become a kind of a useful middleman in building and construction deals. (He is very good at "estimates," but ironically enough he is very bad at estimating either human needs or moral scales.) This information comes from him as—on the church roof, in the bell tower—his bitterness falls away momentarily and his suppressed aspirations rise to the surface. The delay in revealing this has its analogue in a common psychological truth: that there is a natural reluctance in communicating matters over which we are in conflict.

That Sandro is not in close touch with this matter is dramatized earlier in terms of certain aspects of his personal environment. Take his apartment. Antonioni's screenplay describes the building as a "small, but quite fashionable, palazzo." (Ibid., p. 13.) The visual image of the exterior is indeed of an ancient, worn-down elegance. But the decor in Sandro's apartment is no match for either the screenplay description or the exterior shot. The apartment, in fact, is more or less a shambles. The disjunction expresses a fact of Sandro's disordered life and is a metaphor for his lack of contact with his deepest impulses.

Sandro's characteristic reaction is erotic. It is this that Antonioni has called "a symptom of the emotional sickness of our time. . . . man is uneasy, something is bothering him. And whenever something bothers him, man reacts, but he reacts badly, only on erotic impulse, and he is unhappy. The tragedy in *L'Avventura* stems directly from an impulse of this type." (From "A Talk with Michelangelo Antonioni on His Work," ibid., p. 222.)

Yet, the equality of Antonioni's sympathy for Sandro is evident when we consider that, in plainest language, Sandro is on the make for his fiancée's best friend. However, the bare case never affects us as the language might suggest. This is because Antonioni pictures him as sincere, in his way; he really believes that he is in the grip of a growing affection for Claudia, that he has no control over its natural rhythm. But it is as much a reflex as his automatically assuming the same position in his love-making with both women. He prefers to be on the bottom. A revealing image of Sandro is presented on the yacht as it speeds over the Mediterranean morning. As Anna emerges from the cabin, having just arisen, Sandro moves to greet her in characteristic fashion. He nestles his head comfortably on her breast, a baby and his mother.

Thus, we are not invited to make easy moral judgments. "I'm not a moralist," Antonioni declares. "My film is neither a denunciation nor a sermon." (Ibid.). Yet, Antonioni *is* a critic of society.

Antonioni is interested in the typical behavior of the characters who people society. And his criticism is most explicitly felt and his dramatic method most clearly seen in how these characters function in the film.

As we noted earlier, Antonioni insists that the environment is important in shaping the behavior of his major characters. And it is the group of aristocratic characters who constitute the environment against which the human drama of Claudia-Sandro-Anna is acted out. To understand why we have used the term "bored aristocracy" to describe this group, let us hear about boredom:

Boredom: an unpleasurable state of mind combining an intense need for activity with a lack of purpose. In boredom, excitation is experienced, but its aim has been forgotten. The environment may be shunned in an effort to relieve the excitation through fantasy. More likely, however, the environment is sought in the hope that relief will come through some chance encounter with a purpose similar to the one forgotten. Bored persons pass from situation to situation like someone who has misplaced a valuable possession and inquires incessantly for its whereabouts. But the discovery of purpose has the disadvantage of responsibility. Hence, the environment is enlisted not for gratification—unknown aims cannot be gratified—but for continued diversion and distraction. (Donald M. Kaplan and Armand Schwerner, *The Domesday Dictionary*, ed. by Louise J. Kaplan, New York, 1963, p. 45.)

By these lights, Corrado and Julia, Patrizia and Raimondo, and the Montaltos are all seeking distraction, are all liable to give in to erotic impulses. An example is the case of Raimondo and his ludicrous skin diving. When Patrizia asks him if he likes it, his answer is that he does not but that he has nothing else to do. Later, we see him interrupt Patrizia's puzzle work. The puzzles amuse her, the only thing that does, as she says, besides her dog. Thus, Raimondo's fondling of her breast is a related piece of frozen and mechanical behavior. In a world bereft of purpose and values, sexuality ceases to be joyous and becomes instead a refuge, indulged in on anomic impulse, ultimately unsatisfying.

Thus, the tortured marriage of Julia and Corrado, the joyless sexuality of Raimondo and Patrizia, the pointless lust of Goffredo Montalto, and the equally spurious sexual encounters witnessed by Claudia in the train and in the Noto town square—all these and more—constitute the society and the crucial environment for our protagonists.

Themes and Interpretations

The blind reactions of the major characters in the film suggest that the major theme is the absence of human communication, or, to use a term of great cogency and precision coined by the noted child psychologist, René Spitz, the *derailment of dialogue*. (See Spitz's "The Derailment of Dialogue: Stimulus Overload, Action Cycles and the Completion Gradient," *Journal of the American Psychoanalytic Association*, Vol. 12 [October 1964], 752–775.) If we might entertain so broad a diagnosis as is implied in Antonioni's reference to the "emotional sickness of our time," we would name it precisely as a lack of real dialogue between human beings, a loss of contact and feeling for the wholeness of one another.

This condition is dramatized explicitly throughout the film. From the opening sequence, in which Anna and her father cannot reach each other, to the final scene beside the ruined church, in which only a wordless and quite ambiguous gesture passes between Sandro and Claudia, the trouble is seen to be the isolation of people from each other and their alienation from their best interests in love and work. "If anything," Antonioni has said, in mitigation of this state of affairs, "what they finally arrive at is a sense of pity for each other . . . they communicate only through this mutual sense of pity; they do not speak to one another." ("A Talk," in *L'Avventura*, op. cit., pp. 222, 224.)

Although Antonioni disclaims the status of a moralist, his film is also concerned with corruption, with a lack of moral values. This corruption is especially evident in spurious sexuality (Gloria Perkins, the celebrity as superstar whore; the newly married but already philandering druggist; and so on), but also by Anna's father, his loss of authority; by the relentless pursuit of business by Ettore; by the endless, tiny failures we see in the institution of marriage as it is manifest in the marriage of Julia and Corrado and the hardly noticeable one of Ettore and Patrizia.

The theme of art and architecture is also important. From the opening scene in which Anna's father and the workman mourn the loss of old architectural monuments, to the final scene beside the bombed-out Church of San Domenico, it is clear that the old architecture is a symbol of beauty and joy. Thus, the characters' relations to it generate a thematic value. And thus Claudia's positive attitude toward art is a measure of her grace. Sandro, too, is impressed with the unique Italian treasures we see, but he has compromised himself vis-à-vis architecture and art; he has corrupted it: his home, the palazzo, is a shambles and his profession is a demeaning one. Art, Antonioni seems to be saying, is also lost to this valueless world (just as real painting is lost to Goffredo, whose real interest is in seducing his models). Even the new architecture—pictured in one of the new Cassa del Mezzogiorno towns near Caltanisetta, through which Claudia and Sandro drive before reaching Noto—even that is pictured as empty, as devoid of people as people are devoid of *its* joyousness.

There is more to be seen in *L'Avventura*; let us examine it in detail.

Analysis of Major Sequences

I. The Beginning

The first shot of this sequence opens the film. We fade in on an establishing long shot, showing a stately villa on the left and a hedge bordering a driveway on the right. Down this driveway is our camera angle: at about eye level. Anna walks through the arch in the background and comes toward camera. Part way up the drive, the camera begins to lead her, tracking back as she walks. She stops, settling into a close-up, having heard her father's voice; then she looks off in the direction from which the sound is coming.

We cut to a full shot of Anna's father. He is talking to a workman; both lament the situation visually displayed for us in the background; first, fields and stretches of gravel, then cheap new residential buildings, and finally an elegant Quattrocento dome—the type of architecture being replaced. The workman leaves; Anna's father turns and notices his daughter. Alone in the frame for a moment he seems forlorn. Then Anna joins him and their exchange begins. We learn now that another change, besides the architectural, is taking place in the order of things: Anna's father, a retired diplomat (who was a professional teller of lies and now is in a mood to speak truth), has no influence over his daughter. Indeed, he is barred from telling the truth:

ANNA: What truth?
FATHER: You know what I mean . . . .
ANNA: Then why insist.

A combination of deep focus and matching medium close-ups has been used to present the scene until this point, and now, as Anna moves to kiss her father goodby, camera moves with her. Thus, our attention is focused on her and on the moving camera. It would be easy to miss the entrance of Claudia, who appears in this shot, swinging her purse, in the background of the upper right-hand portion of the frame. In fact, few audiences notice this. And the effect is intentional. Claudia's appearance is as mysterious, in its way, as Anna's disappearance will seem later on, and is meant to match it.

Nor does her appearance cause much of a stir. Anna is preoccupied with her father, who wants to discuss Sandro:

FATHER: That man will never marry you, my dear.
ANNA: No. I'm the one who keeps saying no.
FATHER (resignedly): It's all the same . . . .

The last shot of the sequence is angled from behind the two women, as Anna's father walks to the villa gate. As he exits the frame, camera moves to carry the women to the car, where Anna urges the chauffeur to hurry them along to Sandro's.

Thus, the opening sequences dramatizes in visual style and in visual content—as well as in dramatic action and dialogue—the inaccessibility of one human being to another, the degradation of the man-made landscape, the malaise in Anna, and one more element of future importance, Anna's condescending attitude toward Claudia. We have also seen in the framing a characteristic element of the visual style of this film: the absence of communication is expressed in the staging, in which the characters rarely look at one another, even when they are together in the same frame.

Not only is the father barred from speaking the truth, but, as the exchange with Anna confirms, he had not expected so much contact with his daughter as has resulted from her coming to say goodby to him. Values have clearly eroded here; standards are gone, and authority has no force.

AT SANDRO'S PLACE
A high-angle long shot looks down on the square in which is situated

Sandro's palazzo apartment. From this angle, the sky is excluded, so that the over-all tonal range is medium gray. But Antonioni, a close student of Eisenstein's black and white pictorial esthetic, enhances his frame to cover the full range of the gray scale. Thus, there is a white roadster parked in the square and, as the car bearing Claudia and Anna turns in to park, three nuns in black habits make their way across the frame. Attention to the vitality and sparkle of the pictorial surface is a hallmark of Antonioni's black and white films and is especially noticeable here in *L'Avventura*.

The women get out of the car and Anna perversely starts to move off toward a bar on the far side of the square. It is our first indication of the kinds of impulsiveness that dominate these characters. Claudia is confused. Anna had not seen Sandro for a month. They had *rushed* to get here—and now? Claudia resigns herself to not going on a yacht trip, and her manner of expressing it reveals something about her character. Anna's condescension toward Claudia in the previous sequence, when added to this new detail, suggests that Claudia is from a different, lower, social class than Anna.

Anna does not go to the bar but remains standing indecisively by the car, explaining her confused feelings about Sandro. Separation from him seems good because it guarantees her privacy, but it is also unsatisfactory. On the other hand, being close to the other means "everything's right there" and there is a necessity to communicate and to maintain intimacy—and that, she suggests, she cannot do.

As Anna concludes, she decides she wants to go back. But the potential move back to her father's villa is interrupted by Sandro, whose voice is heard calling her name.

In a long shot of the façade of the palazzo we see Sandro standing on a small balcony. He calls to her that he will be right down. In a medium shot of Anna and Claudia, we see, however, that a new impulse grips Anna and, touching Claudia's arm, she walks rapidly toward the entrance of the palazzo.

Cut to a shot from a camera position inside this entrance, looking out onto the square. Anna comes toward us and through the door. She goes upstairs toward Sandro's apartment. Later on in this sequence, the same shot from the same angle will recur—only this time with Claudia in the background. She will not enter, but will rather come to the door with some urgent curiosity about what is on the other side. But she will hesitate to come through. Thus, the shot is a visual motif that recurs throughout the film: Claudia will be seen through doorways, on one side or another, as if to suggest her precarious position on either side of some significant threshold.

As Anna reaches the top of the stairs that end in Sandro's apartment, he is coming around a corner, about to descend those same stairs. Literally, they run into each other. It is not the tender coming together of

FIGURE 16–2. *First confrontation of Sandro and Anna: Sandro's apartment.* (*Courtesy Janus Films.*)

lovers, but rather a blind and accidental impact. Impulsively, he kisses her. They part, and she stares at him intently. Walking to the center of the room, she stares at him again; then she turns away again and, after dropping her purse on a table, goes to the balcony window (where Sandro had stood when calling down to her in the square). She turns her back on the bright white sunlight and stares at him again (Figure 16–2), a long moment of intense contemplation that unsettles him and arouses a characteristic response.

He puts down his suitcase and strikes a pose. "Do you prefer me in profile?" he asks. But Anna merely looks at him, without amusement. It is too much for him to bear. "What's wrong with you?" he asks, and moves toward her, as if she must be deranged to make him suffer as he has in this silence.

Sandro's self-absorption is matched by Anna's attention to her own needs. Still not answering, she circles slowly around him, watching carefully to see what his reaction will be as she unbuttons her dress. He reminds her that Claudia is waiting downstairs, but Anna replies "Let her wait," and moves off toward the bedroom. Cut to the bedroom, a shot through the grillwork of Sandro's bed: Anna enters and removes her dress. Sandro enters the room as she finishes and moves to embrace her.

Cut to another shot, this one looking past the embracing couple and out another window onto the courtyard below, where we see Claudia pacing, head down. As if he, too, had seen this sight, Sandro detaches himself from the embrace and goes toward the window.

There is a shot of the bed as Anna drops down into frame, waiting for Sandro.

At the window, Sandro closes the drapes, as Claudia, down below, looks up just in time to see what he has done. Sandro, in another shot, walks back to the bed, but we can still see Claudia through a crack in the drapes.

In bed together, Anna and Sandro speak. He asks her how she is and she replies that she is awful. His "Why?" only sets her off repeating a string of mocking, mimicking "whys" in response, which ends in a little mock physical attack on him. She is irritated by his obtuseness and her own inability to speak plainly and say what is on her mind. The moment ends in a fiercely passionate embrace.

Meanwhile, downstairs, Claudia has entered an art gallery, where she casually encounters first an American couple commenting affectedly on one of the paintings on exhibition, and then a couple of workmen making rather more authentic remarks; the latter amuse her, but, however fleetingly she pauses to look at a painting, we can see that her own attitude toward art is respectful, positive.

The whole issue is important in the film, and Claudia's attitude contrasts with our picture of the rather beat-up palazzo in which Sandro lives. This fact takes on added significance later when we learn that Sandro is an architect; it also connects up to a brief moment in the police station. That building, too, was once an aristocratic villa. Sandro stops as he is leaving to look at an ornately decorated wall on which the head of a man is carved in relief. A policeman observes "He's the one who built the villa," and Sandro replies, "He's turning over in his grave." Antonioni will rely on our powers of recollection to collate in our minds this scene and several others: the scene on the church roof, in which it is made clear that Italy's glorious architecture is a thing of joy; the opening of the film, in which the passing of this beauty is noted and mourned; Sandro's palazzo; Claudia's attitude toward art; and the contrast between the beauty of the Montaltos's villa and its occupants (along with a similar contrast observable in the hotel in Taormina). All of these elements suggest the passing of an order and the fateful effect the disintegrating impulse has on the human characters living through the epoch.

When Claudia emerges from the art gallery, she steps out onto a balcony several floors below the window of Sandro's bedroom. We are shown the drapes flapping in the breeze that blows through this window, and then we see Claudia look up to see it herself. On her face is a look of some curiosity, some understanding.

Technically, the next shot in the sequence ought to feature merely this window, seen from the outside, from Claudia's point of view. But instead Antonioni cuts inside to an empty frame, which is soon filled by Anna rising from—yet still sustaining—her passionate embrace of Sandro. The effect of this shot selection is to at once continue the action of the sequence (Anna and Sandro's love-making) while indicating that Claudia's vision from the balcony is psychological: when she looks up she sees what her mind knows (not what her eye sees) is going on.

What Claudia sees is Anna on top, the aggressor in the embrace, eyes open as she literally mashes her mouth against Sandro's. It is an eroticism that is detached, mechanical, and chronic.

Walking back inside the gallery, Claudia is featured in a medium close-up from a very low camera angle (close to the floor in fact). She pauses in the frame and we can see the ceiling toward which she now looks, as if assuring herself that she has correctly guessed what is detaining Anna and Sandro. Upstairs, the love-making of the pair continues in the same vein.

Then, from inside the hallway of Sandro's palazzo, we see Claudia tentatively approach the door. She pauses for a look inside. Then, discreetly, she simply closes the door. The final shot in the sequence is a dissolve to Sandro's white roadster, taking all three toward the yacht.

II. The Island

As we noted earlier, the sequence that begins on the yacht and ends when Sandro departs for the police station is very long. We will, therefore, avoid analyzing the whole of it. However, before we begin to examine certain crucial portions of it, a few general remarks are in order.

First, the whole of the film can be roughly divided into four parts, of which this sequence is the second. The others are the one we have just concluded, the journey of Claudia and Sandro through Sicily, and their return to the San Domenico Palace Hotel in Taormina. On the island, in this sequence, we see the yachting party exposed to the elements, so to speak, and to the lot of man: a social crisis.

Antonioni has said that he chose the milieu of the aristocracy for this film because he did not want to introduce the struggle for wages, so large a part of the life of the working class; it would have been a distraction. By isolating these aristocrats in this barren natural environment he has achieved his aim. For they are here made naked. Here we are aware, for example, that they are truly disconnected from themselves and from nature. For their distractions are greatly visible here. In the beginning of the sequence, as the yacht speeds over the water, we see a symbol of this: the newspaper blown off the deck and scattering onto the water. Here, too, we will see Raimondo's scuba diving, Patrizia's puzzles, and, during the search for Anna, Raimondo's dropping (and smashing to pieces) of an ancient vase brought up by one of the divers.

One more observation can be made here. The gathering storm is an important iconographic element. Because the storm is approaching, for example, the yachting party wants to depart, to break off the search for Anna and seek shelter in a mainland port. Moreover, the storm, as it gathers momentum, parallels in a general way the instability of the characters' lives and in a particular way the growing antagonism between Claudia and Sandro. It is further used to make an assertion about Claudia, for it is she alone who braves the storm. The picture of her in the rain calling out her friend's name, however futilely, indicates an ethical dimension in her that is absent from the others.

A. ISOLATION

The sense of the characters' isolation from one another is sharply dramatized by Anna's inexplicable disappearance, but it is further underscored on the island by the way in which Antonioni pictures the search. For example, he repeatedly shows us establishing shots of waves crashing onto the inhospitably rocky shore, throwing up huge spumes of water, followed by slow pans that reveal one or another of the searchers picking his way across the treacherous rocks. The miracle of these shots is that as they do their work they also add immensely to the visual elegance of the film, to the sparkling vitality of Antonioni's pictorial surface. Perhaps the most telling of these visual images begins in the fisherman's hut when Claudia, after waking up on the morning after the disappearance, goes to her purse to remove the blouse she will wear. It is the one that Anna had given to her on the yacht. There is a cut to a close shot of the blouse in Claudia's hands; then the camera tilts up slowly to hold on a close-up of her saddened expression. This is followed by a long shot of the sea crashing against the rocky shore, from where the camera pans up a hillside (matching the tilt up from the blouse to Claudia's face) to feature Sandro, as he looks out over the sea. Thus, Sandro is linked to Claudia, but he is visually and actually isolated from her by the blouse (a ghostly presence of Anna) and the natural elements of sea and sky.

Even where two characters are seen in the search, this sense of isolation and, indeed, of mutual exacerbation of differences, is underscored. Consider, for example, the following vignette during the search.

We see a medium close-up, a waist shot of Corrado as he examines a conch shell. Casually, he lets it fall from his hands and exits the frame. This shot is followed by a long shot, showing Julia in full figure some distance away. She at first looks around aimlessly, then turns toward camera and squints—as if she were trying to recognize who it is she sees in the distance. When we cut at that moment to a medium shot from behind Corrado, the shot includes someone in the far distance whom we *think* is Julia. Now Corrado starts moving to his left; we pan with him to see that the figure in the distance *is* Julia, and that having recognized him now, she is walking toward him to make contact. However, when *he* sees it is *she*, he starts to walk away from her—but not before he has

FIGURE 16–3. *Four-cornered alienation: Raimondo, Julia, Corrado, Patrizia.* (*Courtesy Janus Films.*)

paused long enough to show us the sardonic glee on his face. The final shot of this vignette shows Julia, in medium close-up. She is large enough on the screen for us to see *her* realization that Corrado has deliberately and even cheerfully avoided her.

The picture of mutual torture between these two has been carefully building since we first saw them on the yacht. It is meant as another of the many environmental influences to which our leading characters are subject. To such a social context, we may say, our protagonists must succumb.

A single medium shot during the search is important in depicting how Antonioni's staging embodies his theme (Figure 16–3). It comes just after the first fruitless round of searching. Bunched in the right foreground are Julia, Patrizia, Raimondo, and Corrado. In a moment, Sandro will appear in the left background of the frame and Patrizia and Raimondo will turn to him to hear his conclusion about their dilemma:

SANDRO: Let's try to be practical. The best thing would be . . .

but for now, they are as if frozen in the frame. Each is as "cold, bored, and indifferent" as the script suggests they are, and each is looking in a different direction while resting against a barren outcrop of rock. The light is gray; Julia wears a black sweater and Corrado is dressed in white. The frame thus offers the full tonal range of values on the gray scale, but the environment by itself also reflects these values and presses forward to reveal these people: they are as separate from each other and as inhospitable as the rocky coast is to them. None can bring himself to join another in common sympathy for their missing comrade. Only Claudia is exempt from this cold group portrait; she is elsewhere on the island—still searching.

It is a memorable picture, and its outstanding feature—the way the characters avoid each other's faces—will, as we noted earlier, recur throughout the film.

B. A NEW BEGINNING

The scenes on the island are constructed without sustaining length. For the most part we see only fragments, brief encounters, telling little vignettes. The exceptions are the scenes between Anna and Sandro just before Anna disappears and between Claudia and Sandro on the morning after.

The later begins with a shot described previously (the panning shot up the hillside to Sandro looking out over the sea). Sandro now climbs higher along the rocky face, of the hill. The wind howls keenly; his hands are stuffed into his pockets. He stops, sits for a moment, and then turns: Claudia is coming across the rocks.

SANDRO: Are you feeling better?
CLAUDIA: Forgive me for last night.

It is a rare moment in this milieu: an apology is hard to come by. Yet Sandro seems untouched by it.

SANDRO: Are you very close to Anna?

Camera pans with him as he moves toward her.

CLAUDIA: Very.
SANDRO: Didn't she ever speak to you about me?

Claudia's answer is a model of tact and decency: "Only rarely—but always very tenderly." Sandro wonders why his affection and that of Claudia and Anna's father had meant so little to the missing woman. To this, Claudia once again replies in a finer vein; she accepts the whole burden, speculates on how *she* might have avoided it all. Now, as the sound of the wind dies to a whisper, a boat's motor is heard faintly.

They look around to see where the sound is coming from. A long shot pans around slowly; there is nothing. A close-up of both shows them searching, watching intently, but they see nothing.

Another long shot pans across rocks and picks up Claudia searching again; Sandro moves into close-up in this frame, watching Claudia.

Now the old fisherman appears in a long shot. As Sandro moves to question him, Claudia watches.

Sandro's mood has been darkened, perhaps by Claudia's steadfast emotional responses. He grabs the old man roughly by the shirt—without provocation—and begins to question him about the boat and about his being awake at that early hour. Disgustedly, he gives up and starts to move away, his anger submerged but his emotional state uncalmed.

From behind Claudia, we see him move toward her; having witnessed his encounter with the fisherman, she senses his mood and moves away from him. A trilling sound of the mournful music of woodwinds begins.

Claudia has now found a rain pool and bends over it to wash her face. In the background, Sandro appears climbing toward her; he sits and watches as she dries herself. Then she starts at seeing him there. For a moment they stare at each other, then she starts to climb past him.

But she loses her footing as she goes past him, and on this pretext he clasps her arm and smiles. She looks at him intently, trying to catch the drift of his intention.

Although she has now regained her balance, he continues to hold her wrist; she pulls her hand away. She looks at him resentfully, as she moves off; he starts to follow after her. The sequence ends as the police patrol boat approaches in the distance. We see it from behind them, as they stand on shore looking out and watching it come nearer.

C. The End of the Search

The boats that Sandro and Claudia saw approaching the island have discharged a group of police especially equipped to conduct a search. They begin a laborious and ultimately fruitless scrutiny of the rocky crevices along the shore and even put divers down to search the bottom. We see them begin, watched by Julia and Corrado; these two stand next to an officer on a cliff. He looks down and communicates by shouting to a man at the end of a rope sling, looking in the crevices. The searcher can find nothing. We are on a profile shot of the three onlookers at the top of the cliff. Anxiously, they bend forward to look down.

We cut to a high-angle shot. It is another part of the island, and we see Claudia, standing in a deep, black crevasse, looking hard. The transition from the previous shot has suggested the relationship between Claudia and Anna. The cliff watchers hoped to see some sign of Anna; Antonioni shows us—from the same angle of expectation—Claudia.

Now we see a medium shot of Sandro, arriving at a rocky ledge just above Claudia. He sees her, but hesitates about approaching. We cut back to her; she is clear about the matter and immediately moves off in a direction opposite to where he is standing. We pan with her, the shot widening. Patrizia, holding her lap dog, picks her way across the rocks toward shore. Another angle as Claudia prepares to sit down and join Patrizia; Sandro, in the background, moves off. Cut to another angle. We are watching over Patrizia's shoulder as she watches a diver getting ready to go down. She says over her shoulder: "I hope they're not the ones who find her," addressing the remark to Claudia. In a medium shot of Claudia, we see her break down and sob. Patrizia enters the frame, summoned by the tears and the sobbing sounds. But she can say nothing and she can do nothing for the bereaved young woman. It is a picture of noncommunication. Suddenly, we hear Sandro's eager voice: "Listen, Patrizia . . ." Immediately, Claudia hears it too and springs to her feet and turns sharply away from Patrizia, into camera, so that we have her in close-up, as Sandro and a police officer pick their way down to this spot. Claudia is hurriedly dabbing at her face with a handkerchief, trying to pull herself together. We cut to a close-up of Sandro and hear him say that the current might have swept Anna to another island nearby and that the police are sending a man there. The shot holds on him as he sits. Now he looks, and, noticing something about the way the two women are standing in relationship to one another, a puzzled look comes over his face.

Now we see what he has seen: a lovely structure of composition, a medium two-shot, featuring Patrizia in the right foreground looking at us and Claudia, her back to us, in the left background. We cut now to a triangle, the three of them, seen from in front of Claudia, so that her face is now full to camera and Patrizia's is turned. Sandro asks if Patrizia would mind if Raimondo goes with the police. "Should I mind?" Patrizia asks, from the two-shot of herself and Claudia. Claudia whirls round: "What if you went with him [the policeman]?" And we cut back to the three-shot. Dejected, Sandro agrees that it would be better if he went. Claudia exits the frame. A moment later Sandro does the same. Patrizia moves to follow Claudia and we pan with her. She sits in front of where Claudia leans against an outcrop of rock. Sandro, she observes to Claudia, is overwhelmingly calm—implying that he is not as concerned as he should be over Anna's disappearance; but Claudia replies quickly in his defense that Sandro had not slept at all the night before.

The little fragment is most revealing. It began with Sandro's coming upon Claudia and her immediate departure, to avoid contact; clearly, she was behaving guiltily. This was followed by Claudia's breakdown, her sobbing—which she abruptly broke off at Sandro's approach, as if she had not wanted him to see her in an overwrought condition. Then, when Sandro had wanted to send Raimondo to the other island, Claudia had turned on him, urging him to evidence more concern, and, finally, when Patrizia remarked on Sandro's calmness, she reversed herself—defending Sandro's apparent lack of concern with evidence of his genuine emotional response. As we have noted, Antonioni is interested in these nuances and contradictions of behavior and this is one of the reasons why his method is so attractive to him and why we are kept so long watching developments on the island.

Anna's father arrives to join the search, but he does nothing. When Claudia presents him with Anna's effects, he is pleased to note the Bible among them. It is, to him, a sign that things cannot be too bad; for a Bible reader believes in God and, presumably, would obey God's prohibition against suicide. He is willing to leave things in God's hands, but Sandro is not. News arrives that the crew of a suspicious boat has been picked up in Milazzo for questioning and Sandro proposes to go there.

Anna's father is once again seen as a helpless bystander in the drama of the generations; he is barred not only from telling the truth but from pursuing it. Even though he insists to Sandro that he is the "closest relative" and he is therefore "needed," he does nothing. The last we see of him he is summoning imperiously his boat, bound for we know not where.

Sandro boards the yacht to retrieve his suitcase, for the yachting party intends to pursue its schedule as if nothing had happened and go on to their next stop, the villa of the Princess Montalto. On the yacht, he is once more thrown into close contact with Claudia. They confront each other going in opposite directions through a narrow hatch and Sandro simply leans toward her and kisses her. Her hand clutches at his in conflicted agony. She breaks off and throws him a look further signifying their deepening entanglement and goes off. Sandro also leaves. Claudia announces that she intends to search all the neighboring islands. As the sequence ends, we see from a high-angle long shot three boats bobbing in the water a few feet from the rocky short. Fade out.

The Island sequence runs a total of slightly more than fifty-three minutes, from the first shot of the yacht speeding across the water to the final fadeout on the three boats anchored offshore. Together with the first sequence, a total of more than an hour of the film's two hours and twenty-five minutes has elapsed. The length of the Island sequence thus seems to us excessive. (See "Story and Characterization" for a further discussion of this issue.)

III. Sicily

So far we have been watching a drama of private corruption pervading a society of limited definition. From now on, Antonioni widens the focus, so that we are witnessing public corruption, as it exists in social institutions and as it pervades other than the aristocratic levels of society. Antonioni's net is flung far and wide and ensnares in his drama the whole of modern Italian society.

This is first demonstrated in the police station in Messina, where the crew of the "suspicious" boat is proven to be suspicious indeed, although not as had been hoped. They know nothing of Anna's disappearance; they have been engaged in smuggling. Even though Antonioni does not make clear the exact nature of their operations, he hints plainly that they are not only smugglers but that their captors, the police, are not above expropriating the smugglers' contraband cargo of cigarettes for their own use. The motif of corruption is subtly and graphically expressed in the little vignette in the station to which we have previously alluded (see p. 407)—that is, when Sandro remarks of the baroque palazzo now being used as a police station that its owner would turn over in his grave if he knew to what use his splendid building was being put. (This is, of course, an important moment in that it affords insight into Sandro, who is himself displaying the insight about architecture, culture, and corruption that is still not enough to alter his own life.)

At the station, Sandro inquires about the reporter who had written a newspaper story about Anna's disappearance and finds out from another officer that Claudia has been let off at the local railroad station.

A. THE TRAIN

The train sequence details the further development of relations between Claudia and Sandro and suggests as it does that theirs is not a special situation conditioned and motivated by their particular social milieu. Another level of society is implicated in the kind of drama being enacted by Claudia and Sandro.

In the bare waiting room of the station, Claudia sits on a white leatherette bench. Idly, she clutches a newspaper in her hand. She notices it. She reads it. It is the same story that Sandro had seen. Now Sandro appears in the doorway, coming to a stomping halt in his excitement. He goes to stand beside her. If she is going to the Montaltos's he wants to go with her. But she wants to know if he has seen the newspaper story; the newspaper is starting its own investigation. Sandro sits beside her. His response is more dutiful than enthusiastic: "Yes. I thought I'd go there." His body slumps; he stares at the floor, in this two-shot from his side of the bench. Claudia's face turns sober, determined. "Don't hesitate," she tells him. But this motivates his "What about us? When do we see each other?" And Claudia's response to this, Monica Vitti's superbly controlled yet ambiguous bodily response, is exactly right: it moves Sandro's advances the rest of the way and forces their inevitable coming together. It is a response that says yes and no at the same time, that appears always to be on the verge of articulating but never does. There is a slight shake of her head here—so that later on, as we will see, she can recall her reaction here as unmistakably clear, a clear "no." But, of course, Sandro is right to press on given this response.

Now, matching the considerable length of Claudia's wordless response, we cut to a shot over her shoulder looking down on Sandro, and watch as he stares at her, trying to fathom what she has communicated; we pan with him as he rises and walks away from her. He hears the train arriving, turns toward Claudia. We cut to a long shot and see Claudia, sitting calmly on the bench. "I know it's difficult," she begins; she is calm now because she has already given him her signal, although she is satisfied that her answer has been proper. She does not know she has given him a "yes . . . but don't make things more complicated." She rises, moves toward camera, picks up her bag and moves toward Sandro, camera panning with her. She stops when she reaches Sandro. "Above all, don't look so tragic . . . and don't wait for the train to leave." Still wordless, still thinking, Sandro moves away from her, camera panning with him; he turns his body completely around as he moves, never taking his eyes from her. He stops at the door through which he came into the waiting room. His face a mask of cruel uncertainty, he stares at her. We cut to a medium shot of her. Behind her is the only adornment in the waiting room, a poster advertising "Summer in Sicily." She turns her back and starts out, toward the train, but stops at the door and turns to face him. "I beg you," she says, completing her last utterance. She might as well have said "I love you."

We are out on the platform. The train is grinding to a halt. Claudia emerges from the waiting room and comes toward us. We pan with her as she steps aboard. Her attitude and wish is made apparent as she drops her bag inside and turns again toward us, looking back wistfully toward the waiting room, half expecting Sandro to emerge. The train moves out; Claudia moves out of frame.

In the waiting room, Sandro is at the door. In the background the train is passing; he hesitates, caught in a fierce conflict. He looks down the track after the train has slowly pulled by. He runs after it. We watch as the train gets smaller and see him hoist himself aboard.

In Claudia's compartment, we see her stow her bag in the rack and sit with her head back against the seat. The countryside flashes by. Suddenly, she turns toward the aisle door of the compartment. It is Sandro. From here on, the structure of the railway compartment will determine the character of Antonioni's shot selection (this scene was shot on location): matching single close-ups record the encounter. We see Sandro alone at the door.

We cut to a close-up of Claudia. "Now what do we say to each other? It's your turn to talk!" She is silent for a moment. Then: "I don't want you to go with me. How can I make that clear?" She thinks she has made it clear—back in the waiting room. But then, again, here is Sandro. Claudia at this point is not being insincere; she has simply deluded herself. No doubt her inner experience is quite convincing.

Sandro insists that he is no longer "resisting," while Claudia insists just as firmly that things will end "that way"—that is, with both of them forced (by what moral code?) to resist so they may as well do so now. "If Anna were here," says Sandro, "I'd understand you, but she's not." As he notes her shocked look, he explains that he is not being cynical but only practical. That is the way "things are." But to Claudia they are not. She cannot imagine things that way. She still imagines Anna alive. Her innocence emerges touchingly. "I'm not used to it," not used to the kind of replaceable part she is in the process of becoming. She asks for help but Sandro's answer is that they must remain together. She rises hysterically; Sandro must get off at the next stop and leave her in peace. She bolts from the room.

We cut to a shot from the moving train, now passing close to the shore line; we see the rushing waters go past and are immediately reminded of Anna and the island. As the surf pounds ashore, camera pans and comes to rest inside the train, in the aisle, where Claudia is leaning her head against the wall, exhausted by her ordeal. A conversation begins off screen. It is a young couple.

He is a young member of the working class; she is a servant girl. What is clear is the quality of the young man's interest and the gradually relaxing resistance of the young woman. She is very attractive; he is relentless in pursuit and woos her with a combination of an expert evaluation of her values and the tactical manipulation of material wealth, in this case a small portable radio. Claudia watches with interest and then amusement. Sandro joins her and they laugh together, ironically, for the sexual urge of the young man is as empty as, later on, Sandro's own neurotic sexuality will reveal itself to be.

Then Claudia becomes uncomfortable. Who knows? Perhaps she senses the irony of the little scene and of her own situation vis-à-vis Sandro. She breaks away from Sandro, goes to the open window in the aisle and puts her head out to the wind. When she puts her head back in, Sandro attacks again. "It will be too late . . .," he breaks off. Now is their moment and it must be seized. She wants him to promise he won't try to find her, an empty request because he knows where she is going. She breaks away again and goes to her compartment. There she waits in a kind of mounting frenzy for Sandro's inevitable appearance. When he does come, they only look at one another.

On the empty train platform at the next station, Sandro is alone. She has restrained herself. He is a forlorn and slow moving figure.

In Messina, Sandro, searching for the journalist, encounters a street riot touched off by Gloria Perkins. She is an American "celebrity," a sex bomb who can be had for fifty thousand lira. Her appearance on the streets of Messina, dressed in a scanty outfit so tightly-fitting that the seam of her skirt splits (revealing a black garter and a piece of her thigh) has been the immediate cause of the riot. With this scene, Antonioni dramatizes what he seems to regard as the frenzied sexual appetites of male Italians—a theme that is central to his story because, as we will see,

Sandro's attraction to Claudia is at least partly motivated by the same destructive lust and he will turn to this same Gloria Perkins at the end of the film.

B. THE MONTALTOS'S VILLA

On the terrace of the Montaltos's sumptuous villa are gathered the yachting party: Julia, Corrado, Claudia, Patrizia, and Raimondo. Also present are Patrizia's husband, Ettore, the Princess Montalto, and Goffredo, the young prince. Nothing has changed with them: their conversation is still brittle, desultory, and caustic; their actions still evidence massive boredom. Only Claudia's behavior reflects the recent trauma of Anna's disappearance. She has searched the neighboring islands and found nothing. We learn from Ettore now that Sandro works for him as a kind of estimator and that Sandro is needed for a project that Ettore is currently negotiating. That is Ettore's main concern; Anna's fate is not on his mind. What is on Julia's mind is the young prince, who, she points out to Claudia, is a painter. Her flirtation with the seventeen-year-old boy is designed to get back at her husband Corrado, but it does not seem to be having an effect.

C. THE DOUBLE

In her room in the villa, Claudia sits, idly and playfully trying on a series of rings. Music is heard in the background, an ominous theme, mainly on the flute. She is wearing a bare-shouldered black dress and her hair is upswept. Tiring of the ring game, she throws the rings on the bed and goes to the window. She sees something that she wants to see more of and runs out the door. Cut to a wood-paneled room. She passes through here and out onto a white rooftop terrace. From inside the room we watch as she leans over the railing. We cut to a shot over her shoulder. A chauffeur emerges from a limousine carrying a box that he proceeds to take into the house. Julia and Goffredo pass by. Julia takes his arm: "I admit I'm curious," she says, of his painting. From inside the wood-paneled room again, we see Claudia turn away and move toward us. The suggestion has been made that she has been expecting to see Sandro.

Now inside Patrizia's room, we see Patrizia as she walks toward the mirror, wearing a blond wig, patting it into place. She hangs another wig, a black one, on a corner of the mirror. Claudia enters, smiling. A new musical theme is heard, this one a satirical little jazz motif, playful, sophisticated, light. Claudia comes behind the mirror, leans over, exchanges a few casual remarks with Patrizia about the dinner they are to attend, and just as casually removes the black wig from its place before going out of frame. Now we see her in the mirror as she slips it on and primps. Cut to a medium shot of her as she does some more primping and posing, joking in the same mood as the music. In this same shot,

Patrizia enters the frame, to conclude as an alert viewer does, that Claudia looks like a "different person." Claudia goes to her chair, picks up a shawl and her bag and poses with the ring—holding her hand straight out as if displaying it. Then she joins Patrizia and removes the wig. Patrizia fluffs her hair. They start out. We cut to the corridor outside, where Patrizia and Claudia part company. Claudia comes part way toward camera, wig in hand, and then, realizing that she still has it, hands it back to Patrizia.

But the point has been well made. Claudia, at this point, is on the verge of supplanting Anna in Sandro's affections—in his life—if we cannot use the first word with honesty. Antonioni has visualized the dramatic point by using the wig. Moreover, Claudia's forgetting that it was in her hand suggests the depth of her attachment to the darker identity of her false friend, the fact that the wish is entirely unconscious—but nevertheless real.

There follows a scene in which Julia manages to entice Goffredo into seducing her. Antonioni skillfully weaves Claudia into the scene, up to the point at which the actual seduction begins, so that there can be no mistake that she is a witness to the event. It is central to Antonioni's method that Claudia be exposed to such events. The reader will recall that Claudia has recently witnessed another kind of seduction on the train; that she has permitted herself to be kissed by Sandro on the yacht; that very early in the film she waited downstairs while Anna and Sandro made love (and that, in that scene, we saw her understanding of that fact). All these things constitute subtle pressure on her; soon she will succumb and move toward a nervous expression of her own sexuality.

That Claudia's life—and indeed Sandro's as well as every other individual's—is linked to the corrupt stain that Antonioni sees in society at large is made clear when she and Sandro visit the druggist. There, we see another little drama of neurotic sexuality—and both Claudia and Sandro see it too. The druggist had been quoted in the newspaper to the effect that someone resembling Anna had purchased tranquilizers from him. Now he tells Sandro he cannot remember. But his wife is also present and her remarks are enough to reveal her relationship to her husband. The druggist has a philanderer's impulse and his wife says as much. When the interview with Sandro is over, they move outside. At this moment, Claudia arrives—in time to hear that the couple has been married a mere three months and to note the man's visual appraisal of her (Claudia's) body. The druggist tells them that he thinks Anna took the bus to Noto. As if the stage had been set for his action, Sandro now removes Claudia's suitcase from the chauffeur-driven car and puts it into his own. Both get into the car; Sandro smiles. They are together at last, on the pretext of searching further for Anna.

FIGURE 16–4. *Claudia's joy.* (*Courtesy Janus Films.*)

D. NOTO

Claudia and Sandro drive into a brand new but deserted town (near Caltanisetta). The architecture is white, austerely modern, even interesting. But it is now empty and echoing. It frightens Claudia. We see a long shot as the car pulls away: the buildings loom up before us; modern life, the shot seems to say, is just so vacant.

We cut from there to a shot of Claudia, joyful, laughing, against a sky full of problematic shapes (Figure 16–4). The back of Sandro's head rises up into the frame. They embrace. They kiss, sinking to the ground. From above, we watch them as, sprawled out on the grass, they make fervent love to one another. The little sequence is all done in close-ups, nine shots (including a long shot of a passing train) detailing their erotic attentions to each other's faces, but principally to Claudia's. His fingers on her lips, the elongation of her neck as she bends over his face, the dropping, curved line of her pearls: all these suggest a great deal, the full release of erotic love. We should note that the first shot in the sequence is a close match to the composition of the frame of an important shot in the love scene in Sandro's apartment between him and Anna. We are meant to make the connection. Claudia is in a mood that does not match Anna's, however. Clearly, there is here more pure joy than in Anna's lovemaking. Nevertheless, Antonioni wants us to understand that the experience is not entirely a positive one for Claudia. He accomplishes this by means of the train that startles them as it passes very close by, its whistle blowing shrilly. The mechanical worm is the image evoked.

In the town square of Noto proper is the Hotel Trinacria, where, if she is anywhere, Anna will most likely be. They come here together, but Claudia cannot go inside. She is too much exposed by her feelings for Sandro. What if Anna should be there? Sandro goes in alone and Claudia waits in the square. But it, too, is unnerving. The square is filled with the men of the town. In the context of Italian life in Sicily in 1960—and perhaps even today—a respectable young woman does not appear alone under such circumstances. Claudia is therefore taken to be something else and is the object of hungry-eyed scrutiny. She flees from the frank stares of the crowd of men (it is a startling scene because of the sheer weight of the numbers of men who do the staring, arrayed as they are on the effective architectural form of the square, and the frankness of their sexual interest). Sandro, coming down the steps of the hotel, follows her into an art supply store where Claudia blurts out her feelings of guilt and shame and her ethical misgivings over her conduct. The scene ends with Sandro remarking that he has never before known a woman who wants to see things as clearly as Claudia does.

THE ROOF

Claudia and Sandro are sightseeing and come here, to the roof of a church (onto which they are led by a nun), to look out over the architecturally interesting town. Here among the bells and the bell ropes, Sandro reveals to Claudia the deep disappointment in his professional life: he yearns to become a creative artist, an architect, once again; but to do it he must stop working for Ettore as a mere estimator. Claudia is touched by the revelation and affirms her faith that Sandro is capable of making beautiful things. But they have been watching the baroque buildings set around the Noto square and Sandro uses them to analyze his own position: the age is not an age that wants beautiful things. (The buildings, to him, are unreal "stage settings.") It was different when the square of Noto was built. Then, again with his impulsiveness in the foreground, he suddenly asks Claudia to marry him. The question angers and frightens Claudia. She is confused. The wish to see things clearly that Sandro had ascribed to her is now, she understands, merely a wish, not a reality. She does not know what to say. Accidentally, she leans on a bell rope. She is surprised. She looks up. She grabs another, higher pitched. Sandro pulls one, too. Suddenly, the mood is changed. Claudia is happy, as she hears bells from other churches answering theirs. Together, they look off toward the source; then Claudia comes to him, happily.

The scene marks their deepening attachment and the continued quality of that attachment: they are not well tuned. Claudia seeks a steady unfolding of the relationship—always with Anna on her mind; Sandro's selfishness is always at the forefront of his consciousness. Giving way to his impulses is his way of dealing with his unhappiness.

CLAUDIA'S DANCE

From the roof, we have cut to a street scene: a sound truck makes its way through the streets with its loudspeaker blaring a popular love song. A man scatters leaflets through the sun roof. We cut to the hotel room shared by Claudia and Sandro where we find Claudia singing the song.

We are in a medium shot, looking across an unmade bed to the other side, where Claudia is searching for something. Finally, she locates her stocking and flings herself backward onto the bed. She is dressing and her mood is joyous. Her shapely leg shoots straight up in the air and she seems vibrant with this good feeling. Sandro's voice is heard asking if she is ready. Her response is to get up and dance across the room to where he is, camera panning with her.

Sandro simply does not have her high spirits and the contrast between his impatience to get going and her mood of playful happiness is striking. In fact, his mood is compatible with the sordidness of the cheap hotel room and this visual effect makes her dancing and posing all the more poignant. She continues to clown, throwing things desperately out of

FIGURE 16–5. *In the hotel room: An indifferent Sandro versus a playful Claudia.* (*Courtesy Janus Films.*)

drawers as she looks for her clothing. Sandro moves to the doorway, telling her he is going. But she moves quickly to intercept him, still playful, and in the same mood poses against the doorway, blocking it. Now we see them in a medium two-shot at the doorway (Figure 16–5). Claudia, still playful, poses; rolls away a bit. Her dialogue is fanciful. He will be missing a leg if he leaves without her. He must make extravagant protestations of his love. For a moment, he relents; the camera pans them back to the middle of the room, where he sits. A series of medium close-ups and over-the-shoulder shots record their next moments. First there is Sandro sitting in a medium close-up as the music continues and Claudia continues to sing along; his smile fades, as if he were profoundly distracted. A close-up follows of the back of Claudia's head: she turns, still smiling, asking if he loves her. But then she sees the look of distraction on his face and her smile fades. She knows he will not answer this truthfully. Over her shoulder, we see him again; the mood is the same. She sits at his feet, sinking back on her heels. "Why?" must she hear it, he wants to know. He smiles again, his mood rising but still, as we can see, shallow.

He touches her hair and rises. She does not respond when he asks if he will see her later. At the door, he stops and smiles at her again. Camera stays on the door as he leaves and we see his shadow move off and out of frame. Cut back to Claudia as she sits on the floor. For a moment, she remains in her thoughtful frame of mind, then she smiles to herself and rises.

The scene marks the first phase of Claudia's full understanding of Sandro's situation. As yet she is not prepared to absorb its full implications, and, as we will see, Antonioni suggests that whether she ever will or not is a moot question. Certainly for us the situation is clear.

Sandro goes alone to the cathedral square where his frustration is exacerbated by the museum's being closed to visitors. He wanders toward the easel of an artist who is working on a delicate (and superb) ink drawing of a shell-concave niche in the shadow of the Chiesa Madre and, in a fit of real jealousy, deliberately knocks an ink bottle onto the drawing. A fist fight is narrowly averted and he returns to the hotel. There, he finds Claudia consulting the landlady about Anna's possible whereabouts and takes her gently away from the conversation and into their room. Inside, he first goes out onto the balcony, then closes the shutters against the painfully intrusive facade of the Immacolata church. All the tensions of Sandro's immediate mental state, compounded perhaps by the frustration of the incident in the square and his previously having experienced the range of Claudia's playfulness, come together and get impulsively expressed in a need for sex. But his approach is crude and urgent and her sensitivities are considerable; she refuses his advances. Now their relations look more and more like Sandro's and Anna's. Claudia insists that they must return to a serious posture of concern for Anna. They must continue the search. They start to pack.

IV. The End

But we see a transition shot, Claudia and Sandro driving in his roadster, and then we are in the hotel in Taormina, where the yachting party, the augmented group we saw on the terrace of the Montaltos's villa, is assembled. Antonioni does not say where Claudia's determination to continue the search for Anna has gone. We can assume, however, that it has been as forgotten as it seems.

Antonioni sketches the new situation at the hotel with a few subtle strokes. While Sandro registers, Claudia wanders through the crowded public rooms. She is restless, uncertain. She locates Patrizia, whose comment that Claudia looks well is clearly her cynical acknowledgment that she knows of Claudia's relationship with Sandro. Sandro rejoins Claudia and kisses Patrizia's hand, the old charm returned. They start up to their rooms and on the stairs there is an exchange between Patrizia and Claudia that confirms what we had observed earlier: Claudia remarks that her childhood had been "poor." She is not a member of this class.

In their rooms, Sandro and Claudia are a comfortable couple. Claudia can clown around a little; Sandro gets ready for business as usual with Ettore (although Claudia reminds him of his stated intention to "drop Ettore," he shrugs it off). We hear music now, the same urgent theme that we heard over the titles and on the island. It signals another cycle; a return to an old state of affairs is in the offing.

Again, Sandro speaks of his past. Significantly, he had once wanted to become a diplomat (the profession of Anna's father), but now owns "two flats." Claudia says she is too tired to speak of that situation, but that she will do so later. For now she intends to sleep while Sandro goes down to join the others. Sandro tucks her into bed. They play a little game ("tell me you love me") and Sandro leaves.

The sequence to this point has featured a series of shots that emphasize the engulfment of Claudia and Sandro in this special environment. The camera has tracked after them and tracked in front of them, picturing them always being drawn deeper and deeper into the runnel-like corridors of the hotel; it is as if they were being drawn into this milieu by a powerful force beyond their control.

We are watching a medium shot of a string orchestra, featuring mandolins and guitars, playing in a crowded room. As Sandro walks into the shot, we pan with him as he goes toward a bar in the background. The room is crowded with people milling about, talking and drinking. Sandro orders a drink, picks it up and downs it. In the same shot, he walks toward camera, into a medium profile shot, lighting a cigarette. As he looks around, we catch a glimpse of Gloria Perkins, whom we had seen cause a riot in Messina. She looks at Sandro. He gives her an uninterested glance. Both walk away.

We cut to a shot of a woman looking at a painting on a landing. The painting depicts a young woman breast feeding a lecherous old man. Sandro enters the frame; he puffs his cigarette, looks at the painting for a second, and smiles at the woman. He puts out his cigarette, noticing someone in the crowd. He moves out of frame. The woman looks after him with interest.

We cut again to Ettore, seated and talking to a companion. He rises as Sandro enters the frame. They shake hands. Ettore wants to introduce him to some people, but Sandro, as we have seen, is in a restless, searching mood. Although he agrees, he wants to look around first. Ettore affirms that he (Sandro) will be at his disposal in the morning, to work for him. Before Sandro can reply, Ettore leaves him; the deed is done, we feel. Sandro has surrendered to his old ways. Now he looks up and sees Gloria Perkins again. This time their eyes lock onto one another. Now we cut to a reverse angle, from above, of Gloria Perkins's shoulder. With a provocative slide of the shoulder she moves off. In the background, Sandro continues to look after her for a moment; then he goes off, too, toward another room.

Sandro enters a darkened room. Light flickers from a source to his left; sounds emerge from the same area. It is a television set. For a moment, he sits in a chair, his head in his hands. Then he makes a decision and rises determinedly, leaving the room.

Cut to a close-up of Claudia's hand on her pillow. It stirs slightly and camera pans to her face, as she turns over, moving in her sleep; then she awakens. Because the space beside her is empty, she checks the time. Then she moves out of bed and into Sandro's room. We watch from her room and see her through two doorways as she takes one of his shirts from his suitcase, and hugs it to herself; she smells it and kisses it. Then she wanders back and reads a magazine.

Claudia's restlessness matches Sandro's—but for quite different reasons. As dawn edges onto the land, she is up and dressed—in black, as she had been on the train. She runs to Patrizia's room, looking for Sandro, hoping he is with Ettore. But he is not. Claudia voices to Patrizia her fear that Anna is back. Metaphorically, she is correct. She herself, the replacement for Anna, is on the verge of being replaced.

A series of four shots watch her running down corridors (as she did in going to Patrizia's room) and through elaborate doorways and arches in search of Sandro. Everywhere the debris of the previous night's festivities stands stale and dreary in her way, half-empty glasses, ash trays, even dead evergreens on the floor. Finally, she walks to the end of an immense dining room—she has heard sounds.

We cut to a shot over her shoulder. A couple is obviously locked in an embrace, making love on the couch. Sandro's head rises; he sees her; Gloria Perkins turns her head. A close-up shows us Claudia, stunned, rocked with what she is seeing. A two-shot of the couch: Sandro hides his head in shame; Gloria Perkins is angry. Back to Claudia: she backs away, shaking her head. She turns and runs. We see it in long shot.

At the couch, Sandro watches her go. He stands and brushes away Gloria Perkins's reaching, caressing hand. Sandro is alone in the frame. The woman's silky hand is whitely seen on his dark sleeve, and her voice is heard: she asks for a souvenir. With contempt, he reaches into his pocket and drops some money on the couch. Then he moves off. We cut to the couch. The bills are between the woman's legs. She moves them snakily toward the bills and pulls them toward her with her feet.

Claudia runs out of the hotel courtyard and across an open piazza until she reaches an iron railing. She is near a ruined church with a bell tower, on the opposite side of the railing. Sandro comes out of the hotel, looking for her. Claudia watches the trees. She leans past the railing and begins to sob. She hears Sandro, stops, and tries to pull herself together. There is a long shot of Claudia standing by the railing, with the church in the background. Sandro passes in front of her and sinks down, disconsolately, on a bench in the foreground. Claudia moves slowly toward the back of the bench, coming up behind him. There is a close-up of Sandro, bent. Now a reverse angle, a low-angle close-up of Claudia. Calm now, she looks at him steadily, soberly. Back to him as he wipes his tears away; again, he cannot look at her, although now he tries. Back to her as her eyes look down. The final, mournful music begins.

Now we see her hand in close-up as it rests on the back of the bench. It starts to rise, hesitantly; it stops; the fingers clench into a fist. Another close-up of her face: a look of some insight seems to pass over her features. Close-up of her hand again: now, without hesitation, she raises it to touch the back of Sandro's head, to stroke his neck once, and then rests it across his head. The white fingers are on his black hair—a stunning image of ambiguous compassion. As the dissonant and mournful music gets louder and louder, we see a long shot of the scene. On the right, a vertical wall; on the left, a view out over the sea to Mount Etna, a dormant volcano. Fade out. Antonioni has agreed with an interpretation of this scene suggested by Georges Sadoul. "On one side of the frame is Mount Etna in all its snowy whiteness, and on the other is a concrete wall. The wall corresponds to the man and Mount Etna corresponds somewhat to the situation of the woman. Thus the frame is divided exactly in half; one half containing the concrete wall which represents the pessimistic side, while the other half showing Mount Etna represents the optimistic.

"But I really don't know if the relationship between these two halves will endure or not, though it is quite evident the two protagonists will remain together and not separate. The girl will definitely not leave the man; she will stay with him and forgive him. For she realizes that she, too, in a certain sense is somewhat like him." ("A Talk," in ibid., p. 223.) But what then?

Style and Approach

The most striking and perhaps troublesome stylistic feature of *L'Avventura* is Antonioni's habit of preserving fictional time. That is, if it takes a character eight seconds to walk down a corridor, then we experience eight seconds of screen time. We are offered no relief from what other film makers might conceive of as the "boring" passage of time in relatively insignificant action. The pace of the film is thus not made false to the pace of the action. For Antonioni, these passages of fictive time are "real." For us, they are heavy with suspenseful pressure. What lies beyond the next turn in the corridor? What will the next panning motion of the camera reveal? Antonioni has said that "every day, every emotional encounter rises to a new adventure" (ibid., p. 223), to which we might add that in the case of his characters, every moment is for them an adventure. Thus, the preservation of fictional time is a technique, in his hands, that expresses the impulsiveness of his people. Any moment in the duration of time may bring new, and, hence, significant, action. In a sense that is *The Adventure*.

Permitting his actors to play each moment fully provides the space for Antonioni to permit this kind of fictional time to elapse. It is, thus, a means of permitting his camera to roam over the environment. As we have pointed out, the environment is essential, and one example will make the point clear. In the Noto episode, when Sandro returns to the hotel, just before he attempts to make love to Claudia (and she repulses him), Antonioni permits Sandro to move out onto the terrace in inchoate restlessness; because he does not foreshorten the scene, he is able to follow Sandro with his camera and show us the façade of the Immacolata church. This juxtaposes the figure of Sandro against the church—as if it were a kind of reproach to him. Such effects are frequent throughout the film.

But central to the style of the film is virtually everything connected to the iconography of the frame: staging and composition and the texture of the pictorial surface. We have already alluded to one framing device— that is, to characters looking away from one another. To this we should add another framing pattern: a frequent use of characters' backs as initial images in a sequence, or, as in the final scene, as punctuation and a statement of ambiguity. Profiles are also frequent. All these framing and compositional methods are set to work most often in Antonioni's in-depth photography. Deep focus is used with iron control, austere and classical. And the purpose he has most in mind is the expression of his theme of noncommunication. Thus, the visual motif of Claudia seen through pairs of doorways in long shots or running through corridors is also intended to express the same idea. The difference is that she is seen encountering what is on the other side of the doors; *she* is able, as far as anyone, to communicate.

We have already alluded to Antonioni's careful attention to the aesthetic of the black and white pictorial surface (see "Analysis of Major Sequences," p. 405). It is well to repeat here that this kind of gray scale deployment is in force throughout and accounts for the elegant and austere beauty of his visual imagery. When we consider that the frame is here especially alive by virtue of the fact that Antonioni rarely, if ever, resorts to a series of matching cuts and that complementary angles are always framed a little differently in order to enhance the visual interest of the frame, and add to this our understanding of how well he controls the black and white tonalities, we can understand the visual vitality. The painterly composition of the next-to-the-last shot in the film, Claudia's white hand on Sandro's black hair, made up as it is almost entirely of *masses* of black and white, amply illustrates the point.

Antonioni uses music sparingly in this film. The score is the work of Giovanni Fusco, who, except for *La Notte, Blow-Up* and *Zabriskie Point*, has provided the scores for all of the director's films. For *L'Avventura*, Antonioni requested a "very small orchestra: a clarinet, a saxophone, and something resembling a percussion ensemble." As to the kind of music he wanted, it was to be jazz, but not really jazz. He told Fusco to "imagine how they would have written a jazz piece in the Hellenic era if jazz had existed then." (From "The Adventure in *L'Avventura*," by Tommaso Chiaretti, trans. Salvator Attanasio, reprinted in ibid., p. 208.)

Thus, the jazz sounds one hears in the film are astringent in texture. For example, there is the high-spirited yet satiric little theme for clarinet and piano we hear under the scene at the Montaltos's villa when Claudia is dressing up for the party. The excitement and the satiric comment conveyed by this music enhance and underscore Claudia's similar feelings: it puts us in touch with her emotional mood in ways that the visual images alone could not. We hear similar music throughout the Sicilian section, rising and falling in tempo, doing the same kinds of underscoring. The music asserts its relationship to the film. For Antonioni that is the proper function of film music. The director considers music to be a part of the total sound one experiences in the film, as much an element of sound as the actor's voice. Thus, we do not hear music here as emotional conditioning, to prepare us to feel what the images alone cannot make us feel and know.

Antonioni is as sparing and equally effective in his use of natural sound. A repeated natural sound he uses is footsteps. Antonioni can create tensions of extraordinary subtlety and attention-catching intensity with the variety of such sounds (depending on the surface underfoot) he manages to employ. An example is Claudia's footsteps in the hotel in the final sequence. But the student of *L'Avventura* will also be struck by the number and variety of vehicular sounds that are heard here. Boats, cars, trains, trucks, and aircraft are all used to punctuate scenes, to raise or lower tensions, and even to parallel characters' moods. Indeed, these frequently comment on the action—as when the train whistle is heard over the silence of Claudia and Sandro's love-making. Moreover, there are numerous subtle employments of other natural sounds: the rustle of garments, dogs barking at a distance, birds.

Finally, to a student of films in the mid-1970s, a word should be said about the stylistic aplomb with which Antonioni has staged his love scenes. It may be difficult to realize the kinds of censorious regulations that existed when *L'Avventura* was made. The fact is, however, that there were many, and these could have been a disaster to a film in which erotic, physical love-making between the sexes is so important. Using these limitations, then, Antonioni has done magnificently well. The three love-making scenes (between, respectively, Anna and Sandro, Claudia and Sandro, and Sandro and Gloria Perkins) are all shot with the actors fully clothed (at least Sandro is always clothed; Anna is allowed to strip down to a slip, the ultimate limit of undress in 1960). These love scenes are not only able to convey the simple fact that the participants are making love—despite the clothing, evidence to the contrary—but also to convey the erotic flavor of the interactions. This is accomplished through their stylistic dimensions, the absolute accuracy in selecting details; the bodies are arranged and the emphases determined—by duration of the shot, among other things—in such a way as to produce the desired effect.

If there is a motto for the style and approach Antonioni uses here it would be partly in his own words: "I prefer to work in a dry manner, to say things with the least means possible." ("A Talk," in ibid., p. 231); but also perhaps partly in ours: that in the case of this film, "less" is "more."

CHAPTER 17

Il Posto

[The Sound of Trumpets]

Directed by ERMANNO OLMI

It is better to wear out one's shoes than one's sheets.

—Genoese proverb—

The world of labor and the people who work. . . . I think I shall never tire of this extraordinary theme that summarizes a heap of others.

—Ermanno Olmi, quoted in *Italian Cinema* by Pierre Leprohon, Trans. Roger Greaves and Oliver Stallybrass, New York and Washington, 1972.

CAST
DOMENICO	*Sandro Panzeri*
ANTONIETTA	*Loredana Detto*

CREDITS
DIRECTOR	*Ermanno Olmi*
SCENARIO	*Ermanno Olmi*
DIRECTOR OF PHOTOGRAPHY	*Lamberto Caimi*
EDITOR	*Carla Colombo*
ART DIRECTOR	*Ettore Lombardi*
PRODUCER	*Titanus/The 24 Horses*

1961   Black and white   90 minutes

Perspective on Neorealism

"Photography and the cinema . . . are discoveries that satisfy, once and for all and in its very essence, our obsession with realism." (André Bazin, "The Ontology of the Photographic Image," in *What is Cinema?*

selected and translated by Hugh Gray, Berkeley and Los Angeles, 1967, p. 12.) Bazin defines further the quarrel over realism in art by laying bare a confusion "between the aesthetic and the psychological" (ibid.): "between true realism, the need that is to give significant expression to the world both concretely and in its essence, and the pseudorealism of a deception aimed at fooling the eye (or for that matter the mind); a pseudorealism content in other words with illusory appearances." (Ibid.)

Realism, a term useful not only in describing phases of creativity in the plastic arts but in all the arts, has a special applicability and a special meaning when used to describe movies; this is so precisely because we have an insatiable appetite for that which duplicates actuality and because cinematography invariably does this—even where the work is not in the realist mode.

Nevertheless, realism is a convention, and like any other convention, it is called into ascendancy in the arts by a complex of cultural factors. Modern realism (as well as the cinematic neorealism we will be discussing in a moment) probably conceived itself in reaction against the prevailing romanticism of the arts in the first third of the nineteenth century. Against the search for the ideal and the celebration of the imagination's other-worldliness that characterized romanticism, realism posed the depiction of the actual and the celebration of this world. Such writers as Flaubert and Hardy, George Eliot, Ibsen and Stephen Crane and the painters Daumier and Millet all worked in the realistic vein. Yet, in analyzing their and other works of realist art, we find that the tendency toward mimetic reprsentation is not all there is to realism.

The realist convention embraces three general categories: it is (1) a method of representation, (2) a philosophical and political attitude and (3) a circumscribed subject matter. In addition to its method of representation, realist art is generally democratic in political temperament and philosophically pragmatic. Concerned with the here and now, realism places special value on the immediate life of the individual and on his journey through a particular time and place; the ordinary experience of this environment regulates human existence. Moreover, realistic subject matter is closely related to these ideas: it is also the here and the now, the everyday, the average, the urgently quotidian. It is the ultimate subject matter of bourgeois or working-class travail—that is, how to live in an imperfect world that presses down on one's possibilities for dignified survival. Realism uses its faithful method of representation to express the political and philosophical attitudes implicit in its subject matter.

As we have noted with reference to André Bazin, the cinema is a medium uniquely suited to satisfy our obsession with realistic representation. A large measure of our satisfaction with the cinema as art lies here exactly: all movies are, to some degree, realistic. To a significant degree, the cinema cannot escape this attribute.

But cinematic neorealism as a convention and a genre is properly and specifically located in the works generated by Italian cinema from roughly 1942 to around 1950. (Neorealism (new realism) is probably so-called to mark its having come after the nineteenth-century origins of realism in the other arts.) And the originator of this convention is Roberto Rossellini and his important films, *Open City* (*Roma, Città Aperta*, 1945) and *Paisan* (*Paisà*, 1946). [It is true that Rossellini and other neorealist directors were greatly influenced by Luchino Visconti's *Ossessione* (1942), but it was Rossellini who brought neorealism to its consummate form and it was he who brought the whole movement to worldwide attention. On the other hand, Visconti soon left it for other, more lyrical forms. For a very detailed and authoritative account of the movement and of Visconti's place in it, see Pierre Leprohon, *The Italian Cinema*, translated by Roger Greaves and Oliver Stallybrass, New York, 1972, pp. 85–124.]

Open City, which introduced neorealism, is the bitter story of the squalid and brutal last days of the Nazi occupation of Rome in 1944. It was made almost concurrently with the events it depicts (events based, in fact, on true models, with which Rossellini had been acquainted). The skeleton of the film is a struggle to resist tyranny, but its flesh is much more. As much as it portrays heroism, so does it uncover squalor, and its method is unswervingly to depict the actuality of a great city and its peoples in all their tragedy, humor, ugliness, and confusion. The grandeur that was Rome is a special source of irony in that we see this bitter drama played out against the crumbling, war-torn remains of a civilization that stands for balance and order. The politics of *Open City* are ultimately democratic (not least in its reconciliation of priest and worker). Its lesson is the centrality of experience, its method—as we have suggested—is to render truth pitilessly. It is a film that moves us toward the contemplation of new social arrangements; its cry of suffering and strength encourages us.

Rossellini's film has a legendary history. Made on a shoestring with a budget so low that the director did not see rushes until shooting was nearly completed, it opened to unanimously unfavorable reviews at home but swept the world a few months afterward. It is a film whose poverty was turned into a virtue and a powerfully discernible style: elaborate studio interiors gave way to the squalor of Rome's street locations; lighting was often rough and crude, often restricted to what still photographers call available light; actors were recruited off the streets (to play alongside the music hall comedians Anna Magnani and Aldo Fabrizzi); and the documentary camera style was the dominant one. The audience was encouraged, by the force of this cinematic style, to experience the felt life of the characters and their environment. That is the essential style of all of Italian neorealism. It can be seen at work in the films of a number of other Italian directors, in the work, for example, of Vittorio DeSica. *Shoeshine* (*Sciuscià*, 1946) was made in the same year as *Paisan* and DeSica's justly famous *Bicycle Thief* (*Ladri di Biciclette*, 1949) may just be the masterpiece of the neorealist films of the whole postwar period. The tradition has been worked by Alberto Lattuada (for example, *Il Bandito*, 1946 and *Senza Pietà*, 1948) and Pietro Germi (*In Nome della Legge*, 1949 and *Il Camino della Speranza*, 1950). It is virtually certain, as we will see, that Ermanno Olmi owes a great deal to this tradition.

Story and Characterization

The story is simply this: Domenico, a young man of perhaps seventeen, sets out one morning for the center of the Milan business district from his crowded, working-class home in the nearby suburb of Medo in order to be interviewed and examined for a job with a large, industrial firm. At the all day session in the firm's office (it, the firm, is never given a name), he meets a girl of about his own age, Antonietta, and is immediately attracted to her.

He is offered and accepts a job as an errand boy with an "outside unit" of the "Technical Section" until such time as an opening for a clerk develops; then he will be promoted. Domenico settles into the job and, as he does so, looks around, trying to locate Antonietta, who has also been hired, as a typist. But he has no luck in finding her.

Meanwhile, we are given impressionistic glimpses into the lives of a set of clerks, some mature, some elderly, all of whom work in the same room in the Technical Section.

Around Christmas time, Domenico runs into Antonietta in a corridor outside her office; she too had wondered about him. She asks him if he intends to go to the company's annual New Year's Eve dance. He is guarded in his reply, but on New Year's Eve he goes to the party in great anticipation of seeing her. She does not show up, and Domenico gets drunk and carouses with the other company employees.

Immediately after this, one of the clerks dies—a secret novelist, in fact —and Domenico receives the promotion he had been waiting for. As we last see him, he is occupying the rearmost desk in the section ("a matter of seniority," as the chief whispers discreetly) and staring toward the ever-loudening sound of the mimeograph machine, signaling that he has at last achieved . . . ?

The characterization—embodied in the acting of this entirely nonprofessional cast—is very simple and directs our attention to Domenico and Antonietta, two adolescents being introduced to the faceless prospects of the modern, urban job scene. Olmi's sympathy and respect for these two is quite extraordinary, for there is not a moment in the film when either is depicted sentimentally or seen to be without enormous dignity or utterly winning reserve.

Each is innmocent without being stupid, attuned to his social context but not conformist, sweet but not cloying, ambitious but not materialistic—although Antonietta appears to have been better socialized to depend for her pleasure on what she can acquire. Antonietta is the one who likes "sporty things"; she is the one who window shops on her lunch hour, and it is she who has already determined how much money she needs to earn to make her happiness complete. This fits her more mature point of development; it is Antonietta who thinks the name Domenico suits its owner because like it, he too is a "bit old-fashioned." Antonietta knows how to pique a boy's interest. "I never see you anymore," she says when she meets him in the hall, although he has been feverishly looking for her for some time.

Domenico, on the other hand, is great with innocence; he is pure, decent, attentive to his parents' authority and his brother's junior status vis-à-vis himself. It is the burden of the film to suggest what Domenico may become by surrounding him with a rich set of supporting characters, characters of all age ranges, so that the repeated notion that Domenico will have a job for "life" registers with the viewer and connects in our minds with the revelations of the older people we meet: there but for the grace of a few years' time goes Domenico.

Thus, the impressionistic portraits of the clerks are most important to our grasping the total impact of the film. Each is sketched in quick acid to give us the range of possibilities, to suggest what happens when the life has been ground out of a human being by the mechanical and meaningless work inflicted on him by modern industrial society. The woman who is late—she has had to neglect her children—is fated to move into late middle age with the grieving knowledge that her son is a handsome thief; Don Luigi is a miser, made friendless by his inability to move beyond self-interest (an impulse fostered in him by the low wages he receives, the chronic lack of wherewithal of workers such as he); the tenor ritually lives out as an amateur what he never had the courage or the opportunity to try to make his life's work: he is reduced to trying to sing the wrong aria at the wrong time (that is, from *Othello* on New Year's Eve); another clerk is a narcissistic adulterer; and another is a secret novelist, nearsighted, timid, close to death, dead.

These are the possibilities for a mature life in store for the developing Domenico. By placing him in juxtaposition to these lives, by having him wait for the *opportunity* to become a clerk like the others, Olmi makes it clear that their fate is probably Domenico's.

Themes and Interpretations

The title of the film in Italian is *Il Posto*, or "The Job," as if that were its subject. We should not be misled by the *Sound of Trumpets* into forgetting the crushing irony of the Italian title. For the latter suggests the real theme of the film, that in this particular Italian society a job is more important than whoever holds it and the holder will invariably reflect this as he grows old in his job. At every stage of his maturation, young boy, young man, mature man, middle-aged man, or old, retired man, he will seem less and less the inheritor of the possibilities with which he began.

Olmi's focus on young Domenico and his surrounding the boy with a rich panoply of characters of all ages allows this theme to be dramatized with special force.

But there are other, equally poignant, themes that emerge from the film. Almost as important is the corollary idea that if the worker is robbed of all possibility, he is especially robbed of the chance to develop fruitful interpersonal relations. In the case of Domenico and Antonietta this is apparent all through the film, to the very end. Domenico, thrust into a hostile and competitive business world long before he is prepared to survive it, is unable to develop his relations with Antonietta. She, on the other hand, is equally inept at furthering whatever chances they might have to come together. The same theme is dramatized by the same kinds of failures the other characters experience.

This is especially the case in the relations between Domenico's parents; the strange piece of maneuvering that precedes Domenico's bolting out of the house in order to attend the party is the epitome of their interactions: they cannot agree on letting the boy go, so they must resort to gestures of deception.

Similarly with the others: nobody really knows anybody else, especially when it comes to the strength of each one's secret aspirations or conduct. Thus, the tenor and his amateur performances, the adulterous woman and the neighbor who must not know her secret, the novelist who must hide in darkness the terrible impulse to write.

And thus the need to earn money for the purposes of a bare subsistence —this is the necessity that robs human beings of their possibilities and of each other and reduces them to the status of figures like the old retiree, who nevertheless continues to sit in an out-of-the-way place in a corridor of the Technical Section, and whose only satisfaction is to beat the others down the stairs to lunch. The themes dramatized here are the hard stuff of realist art. It is time to look at its particular dimensions.

Analysis of Major Sequences

I. The Test

The opening shot is of considerable duration and registers a revealing little scene as Domenico's Father leaves for work. The shot begins on Domenico, asleep on his side on a cot. As the shot widens and swings past the bed, we can see that Domenico's bed is in the kitchen of his family's working-class apartment and that his Father is just putting on his coat, here in the predawn darkness, getting ready to go to work. At the same time, Domenico's Mother is pouring wine from a large into a smaller bottle for the Father to drink with his lunch.

Now the Father goes to the window near Domenico's bed, takes a brush from the shelf and brushes his hair. He takes a step toward Domenico to wake him up. But the Mother intervenes. He can get up later. The Father is satisfied, but insists that in that case the Mother must be the one to remind Domenico that he must "do his best today." The Mother replies that "he's not a baby. He knows what he has to do." As the Father packs his lunch, he wants to make the point again: "Opportunities like this don't come up every day." Still on the same shot, the Father is ready to go. Can he get Mother some olive oil on his way home? He can. But what brand? The same as she always uses. Now he's ready, and he goes.

With simple, economical strokes, Olmi has sketched in the family background and the relations of the parents, subtly enough: Mama rules the roost, manipulating Father here as she will do later on when Domenico wants to go out to the New Year's Eve dance. He simultaneously marks the importance of this day in Domenico's life, and he does so in a single shot in which the camera moves and pans to accommodate the action. It is as if the cramped quarters of the family will permit no other method of shooting this part of their lives together. Moreover, the action is filled out by a small but revealing touch. Father doesn't know the family brand of olive oil. He needs to be told. It is the same brand and the life is the same, too. The Father need have no worry about Domenico: he *will* do his best; he can do nothing else.

After a brief transition (it consists of Domenico's looking up and a camera movement to follow the look and observe at the window the changing light), there is a simple title shot, followed by the words: "For those who live in and around Milan, in Lombardy, that city is, primarily, a place to work," over the shot as it pans away from the window to pick up the Mother's scolding of Franco, her younger son, with whom she carries on this dialogue on the other side of the door that divides the kitchen from the rest of the apartment.

Franco brings more light into the room as he enters with his books to do his Mother's bidding: to get his homework done before school. This awakens Domenico. He begins to take pot shots at his brother for using his, Domenico's, strap on Franco's schoolbooks. His attitude is harsh, authoritarian, and Olmi shoots the little scene by analyzing it in alternating close-ups of the actors—as if to confirm their separateness from each other and the fact that Domenico is undertaking some new authoritarian role this day. Perhaps it is a harsh emblem of his growing up. Or perhaps it is, as the Mother says when she intervenes to break up the quarrel, that they are simply boys, fighting as, it seems to her, they *always* do. But, she also says that Domenico need not carry on so. "You're a big boy now," and because he is going to "work" and not to school, he won't need the strap any more.

Cut to the same shot we saw register his Father's departure from work. In it, Domenico and Franco leave the house; Mother has to give Domenico his official envelope—he's still a little irresponsible, she charges. Bundling the boys out the door, she iterates a sentiment that is one of Olmi's central themes. "If you manage to get in there, you'll have a job for life." But it is a piece of naturalistic dialogue. Olmi characteristically will not stop to register it in dramatic ways: no close-ups, no musical stings.

On the balcony of the building, as the boys walk toward camera and away from their door, Mother follows them: has her elder son got a handkerchief? Has he enough money? They argue over his barely adequate one thousand lira as camera takes the boys down into the street and across a sunlit expanse away from the rather monotonous row of workers' houses they live in. As they turn a corner, camera begins to lead them, and although the Mother is now out of sight, the argument continues. Domenico won't go back for the extra money she is *now* willing to give him. (But when Franco returns for it, she insists that she wants "change" that evening.) When Franco returns with the money, camera follows them down a narrow street. They prance along together, a couple of energetic boys on their way; but when a horse and cart comes along, a perfect opportunity, only Franco scoots on to the back and hitches a ride; Domenico continues to walk along with dignity: as his mother had reminded him, he is a big boy now.

At the train station and on the train itself, Domenico is constantly reminded of his changed status, for both are filled with young people his age all going to school. From his facial expressions, we can tell that he is aware that things have changed. He is not altogether pleased.

Two shots effect a transition from the train to the lobby of the company building. One shows Domenico emerging from the pitch black of the station in Milan into a broad sweep of sunshine; the light hurts his eyes. He squints up, a special gesture that we see associated with him in this film, and we cut to what he sees: a panning shot of the dazzling façade of the building: sunlight gleams brilliantly off the metal and glass. Cut to the self-consciously modernistic lobby, a high-angle shot that sees him coming through the door and going to the information desk. He is tentative, but the guard is firm, and he is directed to the fourth floor. Even after he asks for reassurance, he is again directed to the "personnel" office.

Here, Olmi juxtaposes two swift, natural, and revealing scenes that we like to discuss as *touches*, for that word very adequately captures what is being discussed: a sure hand has done its work economically, with only a touch of the substance of its medium.

The first occurs as Domenico approaches the desk. As he hands over his envelope the two uniformed men leap to their feet. For a split second, Domenico thinks *he* has caused this behavior, but then a new shot shows us that they have risen in response to the entrance of the "Boss," a character we will see later on and who now commands the most servile gestures of respect from the two men in the lobby. One of them, the one with the cap, the one in full uniform then, hustles alongside the Boss, takes his coat, hat, and briefcase and, with a gesture born of years of practice, manages to usher him into the waiting elevator before joining him carrying all the Boss's paraphernalia. The remaining uniformed man turns to Domenico: "May I help you?"

After Domenico goes, we see the second touch: a man in late middle-age, respectably dressed, comes to the information desk and asks for help in finding the "welfare office." The guard seems not to understand the term, so the man makes it plainer: "The place where they give money to the poor."

As soon as he says this, we are up on the fourth floor watching Domenico come timidly through one of the thousand doors he will open in this building. And the touches have done their work. They have pictured Domenico right in the thick of his environment and colored his own existence thereby: the "company" is also a welfare office, a place that gives money to the poor—who nevertheless still need money, that's how little they get. Moreover, Domenico's status is made abundantly clear by the entrance of the "Boss" and the kind of deference he received. It is a crushing example of where Domenico stands in the hierarchy, yet the whole is accomplished within the naturalistic context of the film.

Here on the fourth floor we watch Domenico enter a door; camera frames the scene by enclosing it in a square pane of yet another door, through which Domenico will come. We see him ask an attendant something, his back is to us; then he turns and comes directly toward camera. Now camera tracks back and leads him through the framing door and along a lengthy corridor. He is wary, alert, on his guard, but not tentative; the mood of the moment is important, because this shot that leads him reminds us that he is actually being led to the "job" of the Italian title, and that this leading is fraught with significance for his fate. We will see several times in this early part of the film that he is similarly led by a backward tracking camera and the general meaning of the visual symbol is as we have outlined.

At the end of the corridor, where the light is appropriately low key and gloomy (as if he were being led along a narrow channel without clear sight of what was in store for him) and where he encounters just two people, both indifferent, he comes to another attendant's desk. It is the third he has so far encountered during his brief time in this formidable building. Here we encounter again one of the director's naturalistic touches that manages to symbolize much even as it adds richly to the realistic atmosphere. An errand "boy" (of some thirty-five years) in uniform (the same uniform that Domenico will wear later on, for he starts his career in the same job) is explaining to his fellow errand boy, seated at the desk, that he has just told off his superior, an "idiot" who "started shouting" as soon as he had entered the office. "I may be an errand boy," he had told him, "but you're a boor" (and we have cut to a reverse angle to see this man). He wasn't hired as his superior's servant and his duties do not include buying bread for the superior's lunch. In fact, he concludes, he (the errand boy) had "won" this little encounter, because the way he had stood up to the superior had rendered the latter speechless: "He didn't say a word."

The story the errand boy tells and the vehemence with which he tells it combine to produce an effect both comic and pathetic; for, of course, his status is exactly as low as his superior wishes to make it (even as low as a servant) and his only recourse to such a humiliating state of affairs is the little scene he now plays out with his fellow-worker, that is, his only recourse is this way of telling about the encounter in an exaggerated version. He could not have been so rough on so mighty a superior and won so complete a victory. (The same motif will be repeated later; we will see other employees *say* how angry or independent they *intend* to be with a superior and then we will watch as the bravado disappears in a welter of timidity and deference to a high status to which they can only hopelessly and helplessly pay homage.)

Domenico is directed to a waiting room and starts toward it. From inside the door we see him enter and immediately stop where he is, back against the door. In this medium shot, another applicant, standing up, is included in the left-hand portion of the frame, and as soon as Domenico has let the door close behind him, a third applicant enters the frame from camera right and occupies a standing position such that Domenico is framed between the two standing men. He seems smaller than either man because the perspective that has him in the background of the shot reduces him in size relative to the others (although not to the two seated figures, one on either side).

The framing is intentional and illustrates one of Olmi's important stylistic strengths: throughout the film we will be impressed with his rigorous and sometimes elegant framing, a skill that will extract from his scenes a great deal by way of meaning and meaningful relations.

Cut to a reverse angle, showing the rest of the room, as Domenico's eyes start moving, indicating that he is looking over his environment. The shot pans about the room where more than a dozen others, much like Domenico, except that they are older, alternately stand and sit in the available light of the room—gray morning light enters the room from a windowed wall at the rear. Now back to a close-up of Domenico; his eyes are the remarkable feature here, as they will be in all the remarkable reaction shots we will see of him throughout. They register an exact degree of discomfort and deference. Cut to a pair of applicants standing near him; one of them lights a cigarette and does not know what to do with his burnt out match. He puts it in his pocket. The cut is brief, but the detail is large. It is one of many by means of which Olmi suggests relations between people and between people and symbolic objects.

This has been a moment of just waiting, here in the waiting room, and just two shots have registered the silence: the close-up of Domenico and the two-shot that included the man with the match. Later we will discuss Olmi's use of screen time versus actual time (see pp. 456–457).

As we cut back to the medium shot of Domenico at the door we hear voices outside and the door is pushed part way open. We can only glimpse pieces of the speakers, but clearly we can tell that a woman and her son have been escorted here by someone who works for the firm and with whom the woman has some acquaintance. Whatever the degree of this acquaintance, it registers importantly on the applicants, for as she enters in an expensive fur coat and solidly middle-class appurtenances, an applicant sitting in the right-hand portion of the frame immediately leaves his seat in deference to her. She sits, accepting it as her due, and collars her son to stand beside her.

The entrance of this woman and what she stands for (influence with the powers that be, quite beyond the hopes of the others waiting here) touches off a wave of unease among the other applicants. Bravely, they discuss among themselves the *real* influence on their possibilities of being hired—that is, the examinations and what these will reveal of their aptitudes. However, they are not entirely convincing in this dialogue. One fears what they fear: that influence will be important. Nevertheless, the experience registers on Domenico, as a couple of tight close-ups reveal. At that moment the company test supervisor enters (Figure 17–1).

The deference shown this lower-echelon company employee is related to the deference shown the woman whose son is an applicant and as the test supervisor calls off the names of the applicants there is perhaps the only indelicate touch in Olmi's film. When the woman's son's name is called she answers for him. There are a couple of cuts showing the curious responses of the others in the room—their responses are too much in unison, too general.

A sequence of nine shots takes supervisor and group from the waiting room to where they undergo their first examination. We should stop to note, briefly, that in the second of these, as the group walks along the street (they are going to another building), we see them in long shot and see an old bum ask "What's going on?" The entire group files past, all except Domenico, who is compelled to answer, "Examinations. . . ." But the bum wants to know why, and by now the group has left the frame. Domenico is hesitant, but his simple goodness and humanity prevail. "For jobs," he replies, and starts to follow the others. For his pains, he is used as a comic straight man. "For jobs?" says the bum, "That's a laugh!" Again, Olmi has managed one of his touches. At once, the realistic texture is enhanced and a meaningful symbolic value is added: what good are these jobs, the encounter with the bum seems to ask.

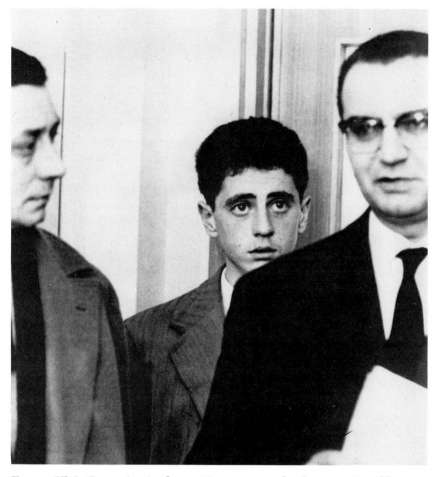

FIGURE 17–1. *Domenico in the waiting room on the first morning. (Courtesy Janus Films.)*

The remainder of the transitional shots are surely ironic, as they take us through a marvelous Italian Renaissance palazzo. Across a colonnade whose imposing verticals seem to dwarf the group, they proceed up an ornately carved staircase. Again Olmi's mastery of composition asserts itself. The second of the stairway shots presses home the incongruity of these figures against the aristocratic background. Olmi has managed to block most of the left-hand portion of the frame with a mass of black, separated from the detailed scene by a curving contour. The irony is all in the visual experience. But there is more: for they must proceed through the baroque splendor of a drawing room with polished parquet floors, giant mirrored walls, and carved relief plasterwork. From a high angle, we see them file through. Lingering at the rear is a middle-aged woman. The sun makes gleaming bars of light across the floors. She stops. Cut to a shot over her shoulder: for a brief second she toys with her hair and imagines—what?

The room in which the first test takes place is a high-domed, converted chapel. The irony generated in this scene is strong, for the applicants are given an hour to solve a ludicrously easy problem: from a roll of copper wire 520 centimetres in length, ¾ is cut ("repeat," says the examiner, "520"). Four fifths of the balance is then cut off, and the question is: How much remains? (Curiously enough, the answer is 26—not the 24 that both Domenico and Antonietta arrive at.) What is ironic is that all the candidates take the full hour and some still are engaged in calculations as the examiner declares the time to be up. Only Domenico seems to have finished early, a fact signified for us by an elegant transitional shot used to cover the passage of time. After a close-up of Domenico, the seventeenth shot of this thirty-shot scene, we cut to a shot that pans up the wall and catches the central chandelier and the dome; camera then pans right to left some 90° and we cut again to a close-up of Domenico, his head held high, as if what we have just seen of the ceiling was what he was looking at.

Lunch hour follows directly after a two-shot sequence in the examination room: close-up of Domenico looking at Antonietta; close-up of Antonietta: what he sees, his first glimpse of her.

Domenico is not entirely out of place in the crowded cafeteria where he takes his lunch; although he is squeezed in at a rear table and his neighbor shoves a newspaper in his face, he is not displeased with the food and is treated to an unexpected comic turn when a man opposite him borrows the newspaper and begins to mumble the headlines out loud ("Man Strikes Old Mother," "Man Tries to Kill Wife . . . he chased across the field with an ax," "Temperatures Are Falling," "Snow in the Alps"). Besides, Antonietta sits at the end of his table, and although he does not speak to her here he manages to announce at the cashier's desk that he too had taken the exam.

This gives him an opening and later (signaled by a dissolve from the restaurant), but still during lunch hour, he rushes across a crowded downtown street to be near her and strike up a casual conversation.

This scene proceeds by a series of shots of the two young people taken from inside the window displays of the various stores into which they look as they stroll. Domenico finds her at the window of a store that sells musical instruments. Casually, he joins her. We see them from a camera position inside the window and so are looking out toward them and the street. The traffic in the background seems very close to them.

Olmi appears to be shooting this entire sequence, the lunch hour, with long focal length lenses. The important property of this lens is that it foreshortens perspective, diminishing the distance between objects in the foreground and background. In other words, when the characters are photographed in the streets by using long lenses, background and foreground are made to seem closer to one another than they actually are. In the case of this sequence, Antonietta and Domenico appear to be closer to buildings and traffic—cars and trucks and buses—than they actually are. They seem slapped up against the other objects in the streets and appear to be closely linked metaphorically as well as actually to their environments.

Encouraged by a little half smile of Antonietta's, Domenico begins to speak and they walk off together, exchanging the barest pieces of information: they both live in the suburbs; he thinks the cafeteria food was not bad, she thinks it was poor—especially because of the odor it leaves on one's clothing (the odor of "fried food," as she says). This she remedies with an intimate little gesture: she gives both a touch of her perfume. We have been registering the scene in moving two-shots, camera either leading them or maintaining an oblique angle to them.

They cross the street at a quiet corner and exchange answers to the problem of the copper wire. (No subtitle is provided here; Antonietta says, "*venti quattro*," when Domenico asks for her answer.) They also show sympathy for one of the men who, according to Domenico "forgot the formula" for obtaining the answer. Antonietta nods and notes that he was married, too. Antonietta asks what job Domenico hopes to get: "Clerk," he answers. She seems quite content with whatever her lot might be, for although she took a commercial diploma (she had originally wanted to study languages but "got bored"), a woman's lot is to get married.

Now they arrive at another store. The mannequin in the window wears a flashy trench coat. Antonietta admires it. She "goes" for "sporty clothes," and Domenico will remember her preference, for it will become his own. He will ask for such a coat, but his mother will deny him the opportunity to buy one. Later, when he gets his first paycheck, he will buy one very much like it and hope to get the girl thereby; but it is only in modern American advertising that such sexual myths are still supposed to hold good and Domenico's magic coat will fail him.

We cut from a medium shot of the macho mannequin to a shot from inside an automobile agency, looking out the store window as Antonietta leads Domenico into the frame. He is saying what we might expect in this materialistic fantasy: that is, if he gets the job, he'll buy a motorcycle. As they walk past the agency, we see more of the gleaming machines in the foreground and hear him boast a little of having driven his Father's motorbike "several times." (We will not see his Father having any such vehicle—not even the "pedal bike" that Antonietta suspects it is.)

The next store is an appliance store, completing the cycle of things uppermost in the youngsters' minds.

Antonietta says she would be quite happy to earn about thirty-five thousand lira per month. (In 1961, thirty-five thousand lira would have been worth approximately $50.) Domenico is not sure what it is "possible" for him to earn. But he repeats his Father's information that even though the big firms don't pay very much, employment with them provides one with a job "for life." We may recall that this same notion was passed on to him earlier that morning and we note that an obedient son has been perfectly socialized: the values of his parents are firmly in his mind.

The series of shots from inside the store windows has called our attention to Olmi's preferred lighting texture. He works in a style reminiscent of what still photographers call available light—that is, the light from whatever source is near the subject. The style precludes the use of artificial light sources. During this series Olmi is not working in that style, but the frame *looks* that way. This is because Caimi, the photographer, has simulated the technique. The natural source of light in these shots is the light from the window displays and the sunlight behind the subjects, in the street. The background light is, thus, far more powerful and the subjects are always backlit. Their faces appear darker than we are used to seeing in films where realism is not quite so important.

Antonietta smells coffee and Domenico takes the hint. He invites her to have a cup and they enter the café. At the counter, Domenico is awkward, but bravely goes through with his order. His reward is that the counterman calls him "sir," and Antonietta is impressed enough to remark on it (Figure 17–2). Nevertheless, Domenico's awkwardness is evident; he drops his spoon on the way to join Antonietta at the table and gawkily stands up (while she sits) all through the drinking. In fact, he cannot de-

FIGURE 17–2. *Antonietta and Domenico having coffee. (Courtesy Janus Films.)*

cide what to do with his cup, until he looks over at another customer and sees that one simply pushes it away. He does so and they leave.

The scene has extraordinary freshness and delicacy and immediacy. From the moment Antonietta asks "Are you paying?" we become more and more aware that we are watching a significant moment in Domenico's development: almost without knowing it, without asking for it, he is having his first real date. And yet, in another sense, Domenico is perfectly conscious of what is happening, learning more every moment.

They wind up on a street corner watching a flurry of new downtown Milan construction. The noise is horrendous, the machinery brutal, and their positions awkward; but there is sunlight, too, and the freshness of their budding relationship; these things hold them in spite of the ugliness of the urban machine, until a bystander mentions that it is 2:30 and they realize that they must hurry back to the firm.

Here begins Olmi's equivalent of a chase, for their passage back is fraught with all the danger that is the hero and heroine's lot in a more conventional chase. If they are late, it will go against them. They run furiously through the difficult streets, through temporary passages, past prisonlike skeletal constructions, and in the streets when the sidewalks have been preempted. At last they come to a corner; they must cross; the traffic is horrendous. The scene is shot with extra-long lenses so that they appear to be virtually on top of the cars that flash ominously by. Domenico deftly threads his way across, but when he arrives, he discovers that Antonietta is still on the other side, frightened by the barrage of traffic. Bravely and without hesitation, he rushes back to get her; he takes her hand and runs her across to safety. But they still have a way to go, and now that Domenico has done his manly duty, Olmi permits him to hold Antonietta's hand: it is a just reward and Olmi signifies this fact by cutting to a series of moving shots with a green background. The park that they run through is the image, perhaps the climax, of their closeness.

As they were running through the park they were stopped and warned that it is forbidden to run on the grass. The fact that they were late, hence thoughtless, counts for nothing. Similarly, the applicant who is late is warned by the Supervisor to "take an earlier bus," and the Woman who is reprimanded for persistent lateness by the Boss is warned about *her* habits (Figure 17–3); in the world of work, there can only be rules—not accidental human behavior: there is no room for such a thing.

Back at the firm, we watch a series of comic medical and psychological tests. The scene between Domenico and his psychologist-examiner is a gem of realistic and comic accuracy. "Are you tormented by itching?" "Have you ever been dismissed from a job for drunkenness?" Even Domenico is amused and shows no self-consciousness in laughing.

It is night. We see a massive doorway; it is barred and reminds us of a prison door. Beside it, Domenico waits, obviously for Antonietta, who soon emerges, pleased that he has waited. "It's early," he says. But then

FIGURE 17–3. *At the Boss' desk: Domenico and the Woman who is chronically late. (Courtesy Janus Films.)*

FIGURE 17–4. *Antonietta and Domenico walking home. (Courtesy Janus Films.)*

again, it is always early when time has no meaning. Here, for Domenico, it has lost its value, because he has become completely caught up in the image that is Antonietta (Figure 17–4).

They walk along the darkened streets, camera leading them, discussing how each made out. They recall that each had been interviewed by the same psychologist in his long white coat, the one who had administered the knee bends in the physical examination. The light still comes from store windows: we are reminded by a sudden image: a huge, pot-bellied man stands by a brightly lit window in which are displayed giant bottles of wine. They come to another corner. Domenico offers to buy Antonietta a stick of gum from a sidewalk vending machine. She accepts. But the machine will not deliver the gum. He shakes it. No luck. He is told by a storekeeper to stop, or he will break the machine. "They stole ten lira from you," Antonietta says. But so will all the city's machinery steal from both of them.

They decide to walk to the station together; each finds out where the other lives, and here, for the first time in the film, as Antonietta asks Domenico's name, we hear background music. To name something is to give it a solidity and a reality that it cannot otherwise have, and it is as if here, with *"Für Elise"* tinkling on the piano in the background, Olmi tells us that the romance—at least the romance in Domenico's heart—has taken root.

Antonietta is her real name, but the first one she offers is "Magali." A boy in her neighborhood had not liked "Antonietta" and had named her Magali. Domenico, however, likes "Antonietta," though she doesn't care much for his middle name, which is "Trieste," in honor of that city's passing over into Italian hands around the time he was born.

They reach the corner where she will board her bus. The nighttime traffic is bustling with workers on their way home. A moment passes, registered in a series of glowing close-ups of each and recording also the new feelings alive in them. Antonietta reconsiders: "'Domenico' suits you . . . You're a bit old-fashioned, too"—like the name. Her bus comes and she says goodby, holding out the promise that "maybe we'll meet again." Ever the realist Domenico cannot think beyond work: "If they hire us . . ." he replies, despite his obvious state of enchantment with her. The issue is an important one; he cannot think of her beyond the context of the job and this will become a clear issue in her mind later on. We see her at the window of her bus as it roars by in the night, and this provides a transition to the window of his train.

We are outside looking in, watching him walk through a deserted car, traveling with him. He is in a marvelous mood and he is singing: "Bye bye, my baby/Just one last kiss before you go,/To last me forever and ever . . . /This is our last night together./We must part, as you know./Like a fairy tale, beginning 'once upon a time'." So delirious is his mood that he fails to notice what Olmi shows us, the uncoupling of his car from the rest of the train. It is very late when he finally arrives home, but he is still singing to the skies.

II. The Job

Domenico's father is pleased that his son is to be employed at the firm. The following day (presumably, for the time scheme is not entirely clear in the film), Domenico's mother prepares him for the job by seeing that he has a new coat; but the trench coat, the style that Antonietta had expressed a preference for, is too expensive; they settle for a plainer model. Then in the darkness of another morning—much resembling the first one we saw—Domenico leaves with his father for Milan and the job, traveling on the same train. This time it is filled with workers, not students.

Still eager to see Antonietta, who has by this point in the film become virtually a symbol for all the good things, all the pleasures, in life, he meets her in the waiting room along with the other successful applicants. They are separated when assigned to different jobs, and one of the cinematic high points of this section of the film occurs when Domenico is taken to the office of the "Boss." (The Boss in given neither name nor designation; he appears to be the same "Boss" we saw at the outset being fawned over in the lobby by the two lobby attendants. In any case, neither name nor designation is the least bit necessary: Olmi's artful drama tells us everything about his power, grandiosity, and crushing impersonality.)

It is not until the end of the scene that the Boss so much as looks at Domenico, but for us the whole of this exquisite piece of filmmaking is summed up in a single shot: from behind the great man's desk, at the level of the desk top, we see Domenico seated in the middleground, in the mid-left portion of the frame, the Boss's secretary is on the right, and the arms of the Boss himself are at the left edge of the frame, as an errand boy enters in the background, bearing a tray on which sits a cup of coffee. As Domenico watches in wide-eyed astonishment (and we can see this on his face through the use of depth-of-field photography), the arms of the secretary take the tray from the errand boy and place it down near the Boss's busy hands (they are signing documents; this is important activity, says the shot); carefully, she sugars it, stirs the cup, and lifts her hands free. The Boss leans forward, after his hands pick up the cup—without the loss of a beat in the routine of what he is doing— and drinks. He did not even have to look to see: he knew the coffee would be there. Domenico, the figure around whom this power ritual takes place, is intended to be seen taking his place in this system of hierarchical relations; and the effect is devastating.

Domenico is placed in the charge of Sartori, an errand boy in his thirties. Here he begins to be exposed to cynicism. But now we are introduced to what is in store for Domenico: the clerk's section (where, as the Boss had made clear, Domenico will eventually be placed). Dramatically, this is most appropriate—the juxtaposition of this material with Domenico's introduction to Sartori is richly effective.

We are introduced to five clerks, first as they are seated at their desks going about routine tasks on a routine day and, directly afterward, by means of a richly effective piece of cinematic impressionism, in revealing scenes of each one's private life.

First, and perhaps most important, is a nearsighted clerk, whom we have seen bent grotesquely over his desk, his eyes virtually touching the surface, at work on some grinding little clerical task. In his room, we see him literally fighting for light, presumably against the greedy parsimony of his landlady. By listening at doors—both of them—he eventually outwits her. With cunning, he douses all the lights and then drapes a small desk lamp with a handkerchief. Again, he bends to write, his face close to the hot little pool of light. Later, we will learn that he had been at work on a novel! The crushed spirit of art, its death registered in the death of this man (which creates the clerkship for Domenico), is one of Olmi's most mournful symbols.

A man is his late thirties, whom we had seen at his desk self-consciously combing his hair, is seen again involved with his hair; a woman is cutting it, as he luxuriously reads his newspaper. When a neighbor comes to her door and our man leaps to his feet to hide in the bathroom, we learn that the woman is married, and that he is probably an adulterer in addition to being a narcissist.

Don Luigi, whose name we have been given only because it suited a messenger in the office to give it with a twist of irony, had been at his desk frugally and elegantly clipping his cigarettes in half. Now we see him propped against a pillow, in bed, still smoking, reading a paper; he barely listens as his landlady comes to the doorway and tells him that someone, a buyer, had called that day to make an offer for a valuable set of magazines Don Luigi had inherited. As we dissolve away from his disinterested figure, we think we have seen a great miser.

Now we are in a neighborhood cafe where amateurs of the opera gather together. A clerk we had seen making a lot of noise in cleaning out his desk and rearranging his things, a sixty-year-old man, is called to the podium to sing a tenor aria from *I Puritani*. As he makes his way to the podium, a bystander marvels that at sixty he should still be singing the Bellini opera. He sings. It is not entirely unpleasant.

Cut to the apartment occupied by the elderly woman who had entered the Boss's office during Domenico's interview to explain why she had been late three times that month. She eats delicately what appear to be small bites of bread. Lurking near the foyer is a handsome and dissolute looking young man. The doorbell rings. As he opens it and a neighbor enters, he hurries out; we hear the neighbor ask for his mother.

The neighbor delivers some food, urges the woman not to bother re-paying her if she has no "change." But the woman insists. She goes to her purse. We see an insert of it: empty.

Back at the clerk's section, this woman is crying. One of the other clerks remarks that if he had had such a son he would have killed him by now. We gain the impression that her son stole the money from her purse.

In any case, the common themes in these lives, penury, adultery, nar-cissism, self-congratulatory singlemindedness (of the tenor who persists in one repeated activity), secrecy, unrecognized art, and shame all are dramatized with a sharpness and economy that are quite remarkable. Their placement at this point in the structure of Olmi's film suggests that they are in store for Domenico.

Domenico eventually gets his errand boy's uniform—in which, says Sar-tori, he looks like a "general"—his first paycheck, and his trench coat, but he has no luck in locating Antonietta until Christmas week.

III. Promotion

We see another of those endless corridors and Domenico coming to-ward us. He is delivering mail to this section. So he stops at the mail desk and leaves his bundle, but not before surreptitiously including the Christmas card we had seen him write a short while before. As he starts to go, a door opens and Antonietta emerges. Now we begin to see the scene in a series of alternating medium close-ups.

It is pertinent to note that Domenico has, at this point, finally suc-ceeded in finding Antonietta; because he did not know her last name (as we found out from him earlier, when he spoke to an old woman in the restaurant) we can only conclude that he must have worked hard (and surreptitiously) to locate her. Of course, she has done no such thing with respect to him; so she is surprised to see him and wants to know where he is working. Moreover, she adds, "I didn't recognize you—in that," the errand boy's uniform (although, ironically, he is also wearing the kind of trenchcoat she admired so much). Self-consciously he quickly removes his cap and begins to defend himself, assuring her that it is only a matter of an opening before he will be a clerk. Her thrust about his uniform was a cruel one and he shows us his vulnerability to it. Fur-thermore, we are confirmed in a suspicion that this relationship is entirely one-sided when Antonietta next asserts "I'm in the typing office." It is at once an assertion of superiority and a failure to recognize that of course he knows very well where she works.

Now she quite openly begins to fan what she may think is a lack of interest on his part by saying "I never see you anymore," and when he persists in relating their relations to the work situation ("I leave fifteen minutes later at night . . . and go to lunch an hour earlier"), asks him if he intends to go to the company's New Year's Eve dance. She speculates that her mother will let her attend; after all, "we're friends and coworkers." Just then, as Domenico replies, "Yes, it would be fun," her supervisor happens along the corridor, an elderly woman walking straight toward us. She is embarrassed and nods as the woman walks by, throwing a disapproving look over her shoulder. The encounter is ended as far as Antonietta is concerned. She hates to be caught talking in a corridor. She slips into her room, but pops out a moment later to say "Merry Christmas." The door closes behind her and we leave the scene on a close-up of thoughtful Domenico, not wanting to leave.

We have cut back to the kitchen of Domenico's house. The Mother washes the dinner dishes while Father reads his paper. Franco has been invited to watch TV at a friend's house and, as he goes, receives the admonition "Don't stay too long—it's a sign of bad manners." We have as yet no idea that it is New Year's Eve and cannot tell much about time from the series of cuts showing Domenico, with his father in the foreground, and his mother at the sink. In these, mother and son speak urgently but voicelessly to each other; something is being kept from the Father. Now camera pans slightly away from Domenico so that his father is featured in the shot and he is off screen. Father looks off right, toward Mother; and he begins to speak with only his lips; his face, he thinks, is hidden from Domenico by his slightly raised newspaper. A silent set of urgencies passes between Father and Mother. At last, the Father nods his head. From another angle, we see Father rise and fold his paper; then he turns and carefully enters the bathroom.

Just as soon as he is in, Domenico leaps to his feet, grabs his coat and races out past his mother. Without causing him to break stride in his dash out the door, she presses money into his hand: "Here! Don't get in too late!" And no sooner is the door closed then Father emerges from the bathroom. "At his age I wasn't allowed out at night," he says, resuming his seat and taking up his paper; "not even on New Year's Eve!" But the Mother answers, "He's not just 'out.' It's a company dance." The Father answers wearily: "Sure, another scheme for getting out. . . . They're always right. They wear you down arguing . . . and then goodby."

The behavior of the participants in this scene is worth analyzing, for the assumptions beneath the outward behavior must be understood. The signals passed between Domenico and his Mother on the one hand and the Mother and Father on the other suggest a very complicated set of arrangements whereby authority, nominally in the hands of the Father, has relaxed or modified its usual standards through the Mother's mediation. It is hard to imagine that Domenico is unaware that his Mother has made this arrangement with the Father, although Olmi does not show us this awareness, specifically. Certainly he does show us, in the weary, nostalgic regrets expressed by the Father after Domenico has gone, that something has been eroded in the Father's authority, in his way of living and bringing up his children. There is something *not* being passed on (although earlier we pointed out what *was* being passed on.) The point is to understand what effect these arrangements have had (or will have) on Domenico, and we suggest that the duplicity, the seeming clandestineness, will register strongest and that Olmi, although he is not entirely clear in this scene and in those that conclude his film, comes down hardest against the installation of slippery forms of human behavior in the young.

Domenico has left the house and gone briskly walking the usual way toward the train to Milan. Now, of course, it is dark; a lone bike rider passes him.

Cut to a series of three soft-focus shots of the sky in which fireworks are exploding. As we cut into a tram, we see Domenico with his hand cupped to his eye and his face pressed to a window: we have been watching what he sees. The tram rocks along toward the party and the shot widens, as Domenico, sensing that he is near his stop and filled with the anticipation that he will soon see Antonietta, rises and comes toward camera, toward the front of the tram. As he does this, we see a white-haired old gentleman rise from his seat with a small dog in his arms. Can this image be a pictorial allusion to one of Olmi's neorealist predecessors in Italian cinema: a reference to the old man and his dog in De Sica's *Umberto D?*

Domenico strains his eyes out into the night, searching for the stop; a man, apparently drunk very early in the evening, begins to sing incoherently. Domenico eyes him with suspicion and looks around uncomfortably to see if anyone else feels as he does about this dissolute activity. Cut to a medium close-up of a man blowing on a party favor, the air from his mouth extending a long paper tube across the screen.

Domenico arrives in the anteroom of the hall where the party will take place. He is greeted effusively by several *maître d's*. The confusion on his face is absolute, as they try hats on him, ask him if he's alone, and generally overwhelm him with their determination to see him begin celebrating. They have been paid to perform this function and he cannot be allowed to get away without their ministrations.

Finally, because he is alone, Domenico is given a bottle of wine (according to the rules, had he been with a girl, he would have gotten no wine). Then, fitted with a proper hat, carrying a party horn and his bottle of wine, he nods his head in thanks and starts out toward camera.

At this point we see the most devastating cut in the film, a transition that a spectator feels in his viscera. It is an immense long shot of a long, narrow room, on the left side of which are tables and on the right a row of columns. Across the vast distance, Domenico enters. We stay on this shot for the next minute and a half or more. We stay at this distance, too, because discretion is required. The pace at which Domenico comes toward us (he never gets much bigger than about one half screen height) is telling enough: he is immensely disappointed and very much ill at ease to be here. Only another couple is with him in the hall, and they are seated at the lower left-hand corner of the frame, silent. Finally, he reaches a table some three of four tables away from the couple and after a painful moment of looking about, sits down, coat and all, as the shrill and swinging sounds of a violin and piano begin. Then he opens his coat. He decides that he must remove it. He does so. All this while, Olmi permits screen time to coincide with fictional time, so we endure the discomfort along with Domenico in an almost physical way. Finally, he is settled, and we cut to a medium shot of the boy.

Now Olmi begins a series of cuts to analyze the gathering celebration. We see the band. We see the couple close up. They are elderly co-workers, not married to one another, apparently, and they are eager to get Domenico to join them; he has a bottle of wine and they do not. We see the scene as it develops. Domenico's face is a meticulous instrument for registering all the emotional colors of a boy at his first such affair. And all the while he looks over his shoulder, waiting for Antonietta.

The party sequence is divided into three distinct phases by two particular events. The first phase in Domenico's arrival, his shy entrance to the empty hall, his diffidence, and his anticipation of Antonietta's arrival. This phase ends when Domenico observes one of the women at the party as she begins to flirt with a man other than her escort. As the flirtation proceeds, it seems to get serious. Olmi is delicate in indicating that Domenico is moved by seeing this—a woman deserting her escort—but its effect on the young man is unmistakable. Once he sees the switch in the woman's affections, he seems more resigned to Antonietta's not coming and begins to get mildly interested in the party.

But he does not get fully into the spirit of things, nor does the party generate its own bacchanalian character, until midnight, when the new year is ushered in, and the master of ceremonies announces that husbands and fiancés are permitted to kiss their women on the lips. Domenico is urged to drink and a second later is out on the dance floor, taking part in a wild melee of communal dancing. His hat at an ever more rakish angle, he claps his hands, as "Finiculi, Finicula" gets louder and louder, and dances and leaps about with abandonment. There is a cut to a reveler at a table: he blows his horn in the face of the abandoned escort (whose woman had started the flirtation), but the escort doesn't think it funny.

Cut now, on a change of sound to dead silence, to the clerk's room back at the company. We are on a medium shot of the elderly woman clerk (whose son had stolen her money); she is staring at something, and as camera pans left to right, we see the other clerks standing in a silent frieze: they are all staring at what we cannot see in the foreground. We cut to a longer shot, from the front of the room, and now we see the empty desk of the novelist at which the others have been staring.

Olmi then offers a five-shot series of dissolves, all views of the novelist's now empty rented room, to impress us with emptiness. The notion of absence easily conveys the information that he has died. The next shot after the dissolves is a medium shot of the tenor and the clerk's section chief as they go through the contents of the novelist's desk, assigning some things to the company and some things as the personal property of the former occupant.

A quick cut to Domenico after a few seconds of this activity is a close-up of the boy; he is in profile, staring left. It is as if the shot were informing us that he is connected to this activity, and as we shall see this is the case.

The two men come to a bundle of papers. "Chapter 18," one of them reads. "I'd say it was personal," says the other. It is the touch that tells us exactly what the nearsighted clerk had been doing at night, hunched over his desk in his lonely room. And his death is significant on the symbolic level; art is snuffed out by this life.

As the contents of the desk are finally accounted for, we cut again to Domenico. He is asked to come in. Now we see him carrying a clerk's set of desk top paraphernalia (pencils, stapler, and so on), in a clerk's civilian clothing. He sits at the vacated desk and his action provokes a stormy response from the last man in the row, the clerk with the faulty light bulb. He is incensed that the "last one in" has been the first one "promoted"; the desk closest to the section chief is considered a mark of status. Like the uniformed errand boy we saw very early in the film, he works himself up into a rage and tells his nearest co-worker that he intends to quit, to at least angrily tell off the "unfair chief."

But he cannot manage so much. He marches up front and tells the chief what he thinks; but there is no anger in him; only a plea. And it is enough. The chief asks Domenico to move back, a "matter of seniority" (Figure 17-5). Domenico complies readily, and there is a rush among the three others clerks behind him to move up one desk apiece: Don Luigi, the white-collared girl, and the man with the faulty bulb all rush to transfer the contents of their desks. Domenico takes his few things and retreats to the rear.

We cut for a moment back to the chief's desk; he and the tenor are preparing a package of the novelist's belongings.

Then we cut back to a close-up of Domenico at his new desk. Slowly, without enthusiasm or interest, he starts to arrange his things. The light is in his eyes; he adjusts the lamp away from his face. He looks up.

We cut back to the chief's desk. The package of the novelist's belongings, neatly tied, is tossed by the chief up on top of a supply cabinet. The chief dusts off his hands.

We cut to a medium shot of a mimeograph machine operator working beside the chief's desk. Throughout the scene he has been in the background, preparing to run off a stencil. Now he is ready. Slowly and stead-

FIGURE 17–5. *A matter of seniority: Domenico and the Chief. (Courtesy Janus Films.)*

ily he turns the crank handle; the noise begins, becomes monotonous, and soon starts to grow louder and louder.

Cut to the last shot of the film: a tight close-up of Domenico at his desk. The light is muddy; his eyes are dark. He is staring at the mimeograph machine operator. It is a deadly blank stare. And the sound grows louder and louder: in its mechanical beat is the sound of a human heart.

Style and Approach

As we suggested in "Perspective" and, as we hope has been made clear by the "Analysis of Sequences," Olmi is very much in the direct line of Italian neorealism. Thus, a whole group of important stylistic elements in *Il Posto* derive from this influence (and from Olmi's early work as a documentarist).

These are (1) the use of locations rather than studio interiors; (2) the employment of a cast of nonprofessional actors; and (3) the nontheatrical character of the lighting.

The flat, low-key lighting of the first scene sets the tone for the lighting style of the film. The kitchen of Domenico's flat is thus seen to be a relatively dark, ill-defined place where light itself is a luxury. This refusal to dramatize with light is rigorously observed. Thus, as they walk along the streets of Milan window shopping, Domenico and Antonietta

remain partly in silhouette because the most intense light source is behind
them.

The lighting is also important in affording a viewer access to the experience the characters go through in their daily routines. The dawn
light in which Domenico goes with his father to Milan is exactly realized
—a matter of sitting on location and waiting for it—and gives us a sense
of what it means to be awake and traveling at that hour. Similarly, the
light in the waiting room where the job applicants are gathered is an
exact duplication of time and place.

The locations contribute to this exact rendering: the examination room
in the palazzo, the restaurant where the youngsters eat lunch, the kitchen
of Domenico's home, and the building where he works—are all actual
locations and together they give the film its distinctive look. In *Il Posto*
nothing has been manufactured especially for the film, as in *La Ronde*,
for example, where everything has been made for it. The contrast between the two is instructive.

As for the characters, the use of nonprofessional actors in the roles
is responsible for the spontaneity and freshness of the performances by
which character is realized. It is Olmi who creates the vivid but tightly
controlled gestural life they add to the film—his feeling for the nuanced
expressions of everyday life is precise—but it is the purity of the acting
that accounts for the cohesive view we get of the working-class types in
the film. Faces, movement, and natural comic responses are all untouched
by acting techniques; there are no false moves, no histrionics, no bravura
performances.

To enhance the realistic style of his film Olmi often works artfully with
screen time. That is, he is not averse to permitting a scene simply to
"play," without dialogue, action, or music being employed to make a
point. Two examples will make clear how Olmi permits screen time (the
time that elapses as the viewer watches) to equal fictional time (the duration of fictional action).

One example is found in the scene in the waiting room where the job
applicants first gather. Domenico enters and looks about; we see what
he sees; and then we see him again. Perhaps seven seconds elapse before
two men nearby begin to speak, but Olmi permits those seven seconds to
play over a close-up of Domenico. Screen time equals fictional time and
we get a profound sense of what Domencio feels in the scene simply by
being given the opportunity to watch and imagine.

The best example is in the party scene, immediately following the cut
from where Domenico gets his party hat and his bottle of wine. In the
long shot from the bandstand we watch Domenico enter for more than
ninety seconds. Time itself is both dramatic and revealing here and all
that is needed to allow us to enter fully into the experience is time. And
here we get it in abundance, living the life of the character along with
him.

Finally, the point should be made that there are other stylistic elements in *Il Posto* that are more theatrical in character. There is, for example, the strongly staged quality of the compositional and framing skills, an element of technique that Olmi uses with great effect. There is also the impressionism of the sketches of the clerks' lives. But in pointing out these theatrical elements we do not qualify our judgment that the film is essentially a piece of neorealist cinema art; for realism too, as we have noted, is a form of art and not a denotion of its absence. Olmi has been nothing here if not a consciously working artist. No viewer of *Il Posto* can imagine otherwise.

CHAPTER 18

Jules and Jim

Directed by FRANÇOIS TRUFFAUT

Assumptions of the New Wave
. . . .
6. Our continuous re-creation in every act is the condition of our freedom. But such a continuous freedom demands total responsibility for all that we are, have been, and are to be. It is only theoretically possible to live up to such a rigorous ideal . . . .

—Gabriel Pearson and Eric Rhode, "Cinema of Appearance," in *Focus on Shoot the Piano Player*, Leo Braudy, ed., Englewood Cliffs, N.J., 1972, p. 35.

I like everything that muddles the trail, everything which sows doubts . . . I enjoy unexpected details, things that prove nothing, things that show how vulnerable men are.

—François Truffaut, quoted in Roy Armes, *The French Cinema Since 1946. Volume 2: The Personal Style*, 2nd ed., London and New Jersey, 1972, p. 69.

CAST

CATHERINE	*Jeanne Moreau*
JULES	*Oskar Werner*
JIM	*Henri Serre*
THÉRÈSE	*Marie Dubois*
GILBERTE	*Vanna Urbino*
SABINE	*Sabine Haudepin*
ALBERT	*Boris Bassiak*
1ST CUSTOMER IN CAFÉ	*Jean-Louis Richard*
2ND CUSTOMER IN CAFÉ	*Michael Varesano*
DRUNKARD IN CAFÉ	*Pierre Fabre*
ALBERT'S FRIEND	*Danielle Bassiak*
MERLIN	*Bernard Largemains*
MATHILDE	*Elen Bober*
NARRATOR	*Michel Subor*

CREDITS

DIRECTOR	*François Truffaut*
SCENARIO	*François Truffaut and Jean Grualt, based on a novel by Henri-Pierre Roché*

C R E D I T S (Continued)

Director of Photography (in Franscope)	*Raoul Coutard*
Editor	*Claudine Bouche*
Music	*Georges Delerue; the song "Le Tourbillon" composed by Bassiak*
Sound	*Temoin*
Producer	*Les Films du Carosse/SEDIF*
1961	Black and white 104 minutes

Perspective: The New Wave

Contemporary French cinema owes its considerable international reputation largely to the work of Alain Resnais, Jean-Luc Godard, and François Truffaut. But these are not the only names to be mentioned in this connection. The richly productive period that began with Claude Chabrol's *Le Beau Serge* (1958) witnessed the emergence of a host of brilliant young film makers. We are thinking, for example, of Jacques Rivette, Agnés Varda, Claude Lelouch, Chris Marker, Jean-Pierre Melville, Louis Malle, Georges Franju, and Jacques Demy. With their works, French cinema has taken on a new dimension—quite a different one from the great cinematic heritage of their chronological predecessors: that is, Jean Vigo, René Clair, Jean Renoir, Max Ophuls, Jean Cocteau, René Clément, Robert Bresson, and Jacques Tati.

In trying to understand the work of the younger film makers, it is essential to consider the development of their careers as feature film directors. With the exception of a few such as Alexandre Astruc, Roger Vadim, and Louis Malle, none of the directors from Resnais to Demy served conventional apprenticeships as assistant directors or writers in commercial cinema. For this reason—at least in part—their work is remarkably free from the slick, confectionary aspects of pre-World War II French (and American) commercial cinema. On the other hand, the majority of these directors *did* spend time either in making short films or working on documentaries (or both). (Truffaut, for example, had made—before producing his first feature film, *The 400 Blows* (1959)—the short films *Une Visite* (1954), *Les Mistons* (1957), and, with Godard, *Une histoire d'eau* (1958). Varda made a number of shorts; Resnais spent eleven years making shorts, most of which were documentaries, including the superb, *Night and Fog* (1955); and Louis Malle's first credit appeared on a documentary of Jacques Cousteau's.) This experience frequently lends to their work an air of *cinéma vérité:* their films tend to have a hand-held look, a roughness of texture and a cinematic style influenced by solutions employed in low-budget short or documentary films.

Given the opportunity to direct feature length dramatic films, these directors were permitted from the beginning to make personal statements in their work. Usually under thirty when these opportunities arose, the directors' personal impulses were valued and they did not need to first win this freedom from reluctant producers by making strings of commercial successes (the usual sequence of events in the life of a feature film director). As Truffaut put it, prophetically, in 1957, "The film of tomorrow seems to me even more personal than a novel, individual and autobiographical, like a confession or a private diary." (Quoted on the title page of *French Cinema Since 1946: Volume Two: The Personal Style,* by Roy Armes, 2nd ed., London and New Jersey, 1970.)

Finally, and perhaps most important for these developing careers, a number of them had been film critics before becoming film directors. Under the tutelage of André Bazin, co-founder in 1951 (with Jacques Doniol-Valcroze) of the *Cahiers du Cinéma,* Chabrol, Godard, Truffaut, Rivette, and Rohmer all wrote extensively on film: they reviewed films, interviewed film makers, and contributed impressive theoretical essays to the *Cahiers* and to *Arts,* among others. They were even able to write speculative essays on films they *might* one day make as directors. Indeed, each thought of himself essentially as a director whose time was about to come.

Theirs was a total devotion to cinematic art. And they worked on each other's films as actors, writers, editors, even producers. But in no way did their devotion show itself so much as in their immersion in the history of this young art. This they were able to do through the auspices of the remarkable Cinemathéque Française. Founded in 1936, the Cinemathéque owns some sixty thousand prints of films by virtually all the world's significant film artists. Thus, the young French directors were able to steep themselves in film through repeated screenings of the work of artists from Lumiére to Murnau and from Vigo to Welles. Thus, at least the so-called Cahiers group (Truffaut, Godard, Chabrol, Rivette, and Rohmer) literally sees the world in terms of movies. As one film historian points out:

For this reason we find Godard defining his aims in *Le Mepris (Contempt)* as being "to film an Antonioni subject in the manner of Hawks or Hitchcock," and Truffaut declaring: "I reason in relation to the cinema and I believe that what my different films have in common is that they are the outcome of my reflections about other existing films and also about those I have shot. (Ibid., p. 44.)

In this way they learned the most important lessons of their craft, and their works abound in pictorial "quotations" from the work of their most respected predecessors. Their works look as if the directors understood that they are the heirs of a long tradition; indeed, nothing cinematic is alien to them.

In looking for a representative whose work exemplifies the style of the group—as we have discussed it—we could do no better than to select

François Truffaut and his *Jules and Jim*. The work dramatizes a deeply personal statement; it has the look and the manner of *cinéma vérité* and eschews slick commercialism; and it is a piece of cinema deeply informed by the past.

Story and Characterization

Just before World War I, Jules, a German, and Jim, a Frenchman, meet and become friends. When they meet Catherine, who seems to them an ideal come to life, she becomes Jules's girl friend. The three share good times together. Then, just before the war breaks out, Jules takes Catherine back to Germany and marries her.

After the war, Jim visits them, only to find that though they have had a child, Sabine, Catherine has been unfaithful to Jules and seems to be writing her own rules of conduct. Encouraged by Jules, Jim develops a re-relationship with Catherine that ends when she miscarries Jim's child.

Some years later, Jules and Catherine return to France, where they run into Jim. They go for a ride in Catherine's car and find themselves enjoying an aperitif in a small auberge. Then, as Jules watches in horror, Catherine takes Jim for a ride and deliberately drives the car off the end of a bridge and into a river, drowning both Jim and herself.

These are the bare bones of the narrative. And to be sure the details we have omitted tend to make this account skeletal. But what gives the film its real life is no mere matter of detail. It lies much deeper. And we will begin with the characters.

Although the film is named after the men, its center is Catherine, around whom they circle irresistably. But what exactly is the source of Catherine's attractiveness to the two men? Whence comes her utter domination of their lives? She is, first, a conception and an ideal. To Jules and Jim she fits a universal form, the form of a statue whose picture they saw and whose actuality in stone they traveled to an Adriatic island merely to glimpse. The transition from stone to flesh, however, cannot be accomplished, though under the burden of this attempted transformation they meet her, relate to her, and finally find their friendship ended by her (through Jim's death).

She comes into their lives under the aegis of art; and perhaps it is fair to say that they create her by investing her with the properties that both attract them to her and divide them from each other. And Catherine, being human, cannot resist her own apotheosis.

Thus, from the beginning she commands Jules and Jim and her mere wishes become elevated to the level of a philosophical program: freedom. Because they give her carte blanche, she becomes convinced of her own grandiose stature and her death ends with her immersion in the two elements with which she is constantly identified in the film, water

(Catherine of the seashore, Catherine of the Seine) and fire (Catherine burning letters, Catherine of the burning passion): drowning and cremation. Yet, she is also associated with earth and air—in her airy freedom and in her role as a kind of Earth mother to all men.

Which is all well and good—metaphorically. What else is she? On the level of the film's psychological action, she is willful, intense, impulsive, passionate, commanding, and, through Truffaut's delicate handling of its depiction, obviously a dynamic and satisfying sexual partner. In any case, Jeanne Moreau's tired beauty has an erotic suggestibility that is more than enough to convey the point.

Yet, to speak of her sexuality is to see that her vaunted freedom is no freedom at all. When all is said and done, she is hedged about with rules of her own devising that seem more like a child's code of justice. Thus, she considers herself a sexual Solomon when she decides to sleep with a former lover in order to "balance out" Jim's continuing to see Gilberte in Paris; she does the same when Jules's mother "offends" her on the eve of their wedding. Here her freedom seems more like self-serving anarchy.

Similarly, her attitude toward motherhood belies her program of liberation. On the one hand, she has a rather conventional need to be with Sabine, to fulfill her role as mother. On the other hand, however, having a child by Jim is an issue fraught with tension. It is as if the success or failure of procreation by this lover were a kind of magic talisman, a portent of the future.

All this is enough to capture our heroes' devotion; they do not see the child in the woman. But what of them?

Jules and Jim are effectively contrasted from the outset. They are light and dark, German and Frenchman, translator and poet, Sancho Panza and Don Quixote. Jules is shy and ineffective with women (although this is a bit difficult to imagine, considering Oskar Werner's handsome charm), while Jim is represented as so much more successful with them that he becomes Jules's mentor in the matter and tries to fix him up with a number of women. Indeed, Jim is in a sense ruthless with women; witness, for example, Jules's plea when he brings Jim to see Catherine: "Not this one, Jim, right?" Witness also the way Jim *uses* the faithful Gilberte throughout.

Jules, on the other hand, is naive. He is unable to see through Thérèse, so that when he takes her home his first thought is to make *separate* sleeping arrangements for the two of them. To emphasize Jules's conventionality, we are shown his dependence on his hourglass, the large, ticking clock, placed prominently in the Rhine chalet (where he also keeps his beloved hourglass), and his touching attention to speaking French without a trace of an accent. Jules thus appears to be the more vulnerable of the two; shy, passive, and inarticulate at first, he longs for the inner security that a conventional life may bring. However, under the heady influence of Bohemian Paris, it is Jules who, at the first luncheon with

Catherine, proposes the toast to "abolish all formalities." Generally, thereafter, he tries to join the game of going against convention; but he is not good at it.

Jim, who declares to Catherine that he feels "the need for adventures, for risks," appears to be the stronger of the two. He has the discipline to pursue a career and he does not break off completely with Gilberte, who can supply for him what Jules would like to have from Catherine. In fact, he almost marries Gilberte. In the end, however, he succumbs to Catherine's fatal command to join her in the car—without hesitation. The romance in Jim's soul *seems* to be under more constraints than it is in Jules's. In fact, one of the reasons why the voice-over narration has access to Jim's (but not to Jules's) inner thoughts is to allow us to follow the track of Jim's seeming good sense—his sense of reality; we are, of course, misled by such an impression of Jim.

For it is Jules who comes to a realistic appraisal of Catherine's character, and it is he who explains it to Jim after the war. (Jim *might* also have done so, for he had remarked, before the war, that Catherine was "for all men." He had known she was a poor risk in a marriage. But apparently he forgot the insight.) Jules is fully aware of how he and Jim have created their goddess, while Jim is simply helpless in the face of it. Where Jules is willing to settle for any arrangement so long as he can worship Catherine from close range—knowing *exactly* what that arrangement will cost him—Jim is still deluded into thinking he can "tame" Catherine into a conventional relationship. This is a crucial difference between the friends. Ultimately, Jim's refusal to see Catherine clearly enough will cost him his life.

Yet, despite this and other differences, what matters in the characters of Jules and Jim is that confronted by Catherine neither can resist her. In this they are the same, and Truffaut has done much to emphasize this similarity.

For example, both are artistic types; Jim writes, but Jules quotes and is much influenced by poetry. More important symbolically and in the context of the romantic aura Truffaut surrounds them with is that we see both of them using letters to convey their deepest feelings and carry on their most intimate relationships. This element dramatizes their detachment from flesh-and-blood reality, just as their relations to the pictures and the statue emphasize the mental character of their relationship with Catherine. In addition, Jim's story of the soldier whom he knew to have carried on a great romance by means of letters also dramatizes this idea. Truffaut further emphasizes the similarity between Jules and Jim by structuring Albert into his film. For this is no simple love triangle he has made. Catherine does not simply play Jules off against Jim, or vice versa (although she does do this once); rather, she impulsively uses Albert against both of them, as if they were one. Nor does Albert feel about her as do Jules and Jim. Although Albert is willing to marry her and become the father of little Sabine, only Jules and Jim worship her as a goddess.

The meaning of their helplessness lies in the ultimate source of Catherine's attractiveness: for Jules and Jim she is the incarnation of anarchy. She is not only the embodiment of instinctual but also of social liberation. At the stage of their lives with which the film begins, Jules and Jim are asking the universal questions of youth: Who am I and what may I do in this world? What are the limits of my behavior? The answers they would like are "I am a free man. I can do whatever appeals to me at any given moment." That answer exists in the person of Catherine.

Themes And Interpretations

The major theme of the film is the inability of Jules, Jim, or Catherine to abandon a stage of youthful idealism. In the face of the inevitable encroachment of that reality that is the fateful consequence of human growth and development, these three hold fast to romance, to fantasy, and to youth. Truffaut dramatizes this visually in one special way: none of the protagonists seems to age, even though the time frame of the action takes us from 1912 to a period defined by the images we see on the screen of the Ursuline Cinema (Nazis burning books) as somewhere in the early 1930s. (Only Catherine shows the slightest sign of aging: she wears glasses after the war, a delicate touch signifying perhaps that she is slightly older than the men.) The main issue is, thus, a longing for an illusory freedom, a freedom that, in the ordinary course of events, must be surrendered.

But here the passage of years, the need to make a living, and the demands of career and family life do not succeed in altering the choices made by Jules and Jim. Consequently, Catherine, who is the personified creation of their youthful modalities, is similarly unable to change as life makes its demands. The result is tragedy, made more poignant by the brilliance and gaiety of their youthful behaviors.

Thematically, this spontaneous gaiety is seen as preferable to an adult modality that is hardly even presented for contrast. Friendship between men—always, it seems, doomed by a woman's entrance onto the scene— spontaneous behavior by both sexes, and the beauty of both culture *and* nature are all minor themes that are personally stated in Truffaut's unique manner and, intertwined with the major theme, they combine to produce an extremely complex, bittersweet artwork.

Analysis of Major Sequences

1. The Opening

Over a dark screen we hear Catherine's voice: "You said to me: I love you. I said to you: wait. I was going to say: take me. You said to me: go away." This opening moment belongs, significantly, to Catherine's ambivalent impulses; it, and the final notes of the music we hear at the end, from Catherine's song, suggest that the men are caught in a vise that literally *is* Catherine and her ambivalence. It is a matter that requires some recollection on the part of the viewer, for the effect of this opening is soon dispelled.

The screen lights up and we begin the visuals on a breathless note of lively action. Brash and exhilarating music accompanies a series of quick cuts (whose frames, however, are not always filled with subject movement; some of the effect is provided by the movement—the pace—of the editing); these project us into a simpler world than our own, pre-World War I Paris, a period synonymous with innocence and possibility. The images under the titles are significant. They give us quick symbolic summaries of mood and tone: Jules and Jim rummaging in a costume chest; Jules and Jim exchanging elaborate greetings over a passage through a gate; an enormous close-up of Catherine; the two friends walking in a sunlit countryside with two young women; little Sabine—an ironic cupid —throwing a dart, followed by a swish pan to her target; Jules and Jim fighting a mock duel with broomsticks; Jules and Jim playing at the blind man and the cripple; Jules's hourglass; a piece of a Toulouse-Lautrec poster; Albert playing the guitar; Jules walking with Sabine on a grassy meadow. The pace of the cutting and the incessant round of activity that follows the titles do not flag; the rushing words of the narration

FIGURE 18–1. *A pictorial allusion: Homage to Jean Renoir.* (*Courtesy Janus Films.*)

and the images of friendship and comic action, the sheer intensity of what we see all bespeak youth, affection, freedom, and spontaneity. We become caught up in it. We care about these two young men and are swept along into their situation by the manner in which their lives are presented to us: the voice-over narration compressing time and detailing the growth of the relations between Jules and Jim—and especially Jim's unsuccessful attempts to fix Jules up with a woman. The expressive image that epitomizes this sequence is a brief but telling shot of Jules, Jim, and one of the young women leisurely rowing on the Seine. Framed by a willow on the bank, we recognize a direct quote of an opulent romantic image from Jean Renoir's *Une Partie de Compagne* (1936) and it makes the point well (Figure 18–1).

After Jules visits the prostitute with the watch strapped round her ankle, Jules and Jim meet Thérèse.

She comes into their lives in a whirl of panning shots and dissolves, casual introductions, mistaken identity (she continually fails to get their names straight, calling Jim "Jules" and vice versa), and her trademark: the steam engine act, in which she imitates a puffing billy with the aid of a lit cigarette smoked at the wrong end. She winds up at Jules's place because Jim has a date with Gilberte. But as casually as she enters their lives, she leaves them.

The event takes place in a small café (a well-used setting in which several significant scenes take place). As Thérèse, Jules, and Jim enter, the men hang back, engaged in a serious discussion. Thérèse finds a table and the three are seated, with the men still arguing. Here, Thérèse's unsuitability for Jules is underscored by the subject of their conversation: Shakespeare. We may note here that, later on in the film, when Jules is extolling Catherine's virtues to Jim, he observes that *she* teaches Shakespeare to those she is drawn toward. But Thérèse, utterly ignored by the men, quickly spots a likely prospect. She asks Jules for coins to pay for the music and moves to the mechanical piano, followed by her prospect. From him she gets a cigarette and goes into her steam engine act. This time there is no 360° pan as there was to accompany this act of hers in Jules's apartment. Instead, she puffs for a moment, then takes her escort's arm and starts out.

The camera follows them out the door and past the café window then swish pans to a two-shot of Jules and Jim. Jules, seeing them go, is inclined to go after Thérèse, but Jim holds his arm. Not at all heartbroken over her departure, Jules acknowledges that he doesn't "have any luck in Paris" and starts to talk about his German girl friends. He produces photographs of two of them. We see the photographs in close-up. They, and the woman's face Jules starts to draw on the table top as he speaks of being in love with being in love, foreshadow the pictures they will see in the next sequence, the ones of the statue that will stir them most deeply. Here, visuals and music and setting and composition (as well as splendid acting by Marie Dubois and Oskar Werner) contribute to our sense of this milieu: clearly things happen here on an unconventional level. Our protagonists are young, experimental, and comically self-conscious. In his flat and expressionless voice, the narrator tells us that Jim was so taken with Jules's drawing that he wanted to buy the table, but that the proprietor would only sell them by the dozen. We see, as the scene ends, Jim arguing fruitlessly with the proprietor but, most importantly, searching after some ideal that is hardly to be articulated now.

Before leaving this sequence we should note that Thérèse serves an important function in the film. She is one of the women with whom Catherine can be compared. Her game is casual, lighthearted promiscuity; she exploits her own sexuality in order to achieve pleasure, but for her such pleasure consists only in a variety of experiences. Unlike Catherine, as we will see, she has no sense of her own importance, no depths; she does not make rules, she only breaks one (fidelity) repeatedly. Thus, the breathless catalogue of her extraordinary sexual adventures, which Jim listens to with distracted attention, later on in the film in this same café, is very much like her steam engine act: an amusement and nothing more.

At the lower end of the scale of female sexuality is the girl, Denise, whom Jim's Acquaintance introduced to him—again in this same café—after he had heard Thérèse's catalogue. The Acquaintance (as he is designated in the script) literally knocks on Denise's head with his knuckles. "She's not stupid," he says, "she's hollow." She won't talk because, he continues, "she's a thing." This is because she's "unadulterated sex," a woman who is exploited because her need is precisely and only that: to be used sexually. The image of Denise is a horrifying one, almost as horrifying as the sight of Jim's and Catherine's bones emerging from the crematory fire, and we see in it the same symbol of harsh reality.

II. The Creation of Catherine

Catherine is born for them in Albert's studio, where they see the slides of the statue. Here the camera work is conventional until Jules, Jim, and Albert's woman friend are seated watching a brilliantly lit magic lantern screen. Then, as Albert comments, he flashes on a series of slides of rather ancient statues, two of which are badly decomposed. Finally, *the* statue appears. This one seems modern and depicts a very beautiful woman. It resembles, we think (although we have not located it exactly), a work by Maillol. The flashing screen examines this head in detail: zooms into eyes and lips, full front and profile. Albert begins to move on to the next one, but Jim asks to see the Maillol again. This time the process is repeated: many angles close up on the head. From the last close-up of the head, there is a very fast dissolve—virtually a cut—to the site where the statue is on exhibition: an outdoor garden on an Adriatic island. The narrator tells us of their decision to go to see it at once and notes that the men wore identical suits.

But the transition is worth commenting on. From the light-dazzled screen to the sun-bleached island is a transition so subtly, yet swiftly, effected that it could go unnoticed. But in that moment is the relation between wish and deed in the mind of the young: one is a mere light flicker away from the other.

On the island, as the narrator reports, "They were speechless. They had never met such a smile. If they ever met it, they would follow it." Thus, in their minds, wish and deed are virtually one: they are ripe to meet Catherine now. And the visual style makes clear their intoxication. There is a series of panning shots from one statue to another until the camera comes to rest on the Maillol. After this there is a series of cuts from tracking shot to dizzying tracking shot, around and past and back and forth in front of the enticing head, mimicking the emotional states of the white-suited viewers.

The transition between this island scene and the actual meeting with Catherine is the gymnasium scene. Here the action suggests the state of the men's minds. The gymnasium, filled with jousting contestants, among whom Jules and Jim are prominent, seems more than a gymnasium. The shouting, moving, posing figures, stylized as they are, suggest rather knights preparing for a serious contest for milady's favors (Figure 18–2).

FIGURE 18–2. *Jules and Jim jousting. (Courtesy Janus Films.)*

After a few moments, Jules and Jim stop to catch their breath. Just before they do the alert student can catch on the sound track Jules's voice shouting, "*Tu es* a gentleman, Jim!" Jim now produces an exerpt from his novel. His account of "Jacques" and "Julien" and the "fairy-tale atmosphere" in which their friendship develops describes also "Julien's last novel." It is a self-conscious recapitulation of Jim's friendship with Jules and he takes the trouble to identify the pair with Don Quixote and Sancho Panza. We need not inquire who is whom. We need only see that the friends are in this scene made to be symbolic members of a latter-day court of love: friends, combatants, poets, lovers.

They run to the shower where, as they wash, Jules announces that three women are coming to dinner and that he expects Jim to be there. The camera moves closer to Jules as he speaks and, as he finishes, tilts up to the shower head—as if anticipating that the expected dinner guests will come from a fruitful height.

We dissolve now to the courtyard of Jules's apartment. Jules and Jim sit at a table set for dinner. Three women start down the stairs toward the men. They leap up and start forward to greet them. The first two women come slowly, preceding the third, who is of course Catherine. Now the camera begins to indicate the relation between Catherine and the ideal of the statue. There is a zoom in to a tight close-up as she lifts her veil; a rapid editing pace accompanies the next eight shots, close-ups, profiles, inserts of eyes, lips and nose, the whole cutting order recapitulating the shot pattern Jules and Jim had seen in Albert's studio.

There is next a cut to a head-and-shoulders close-up of Jules. As he proposes a toast, camera pulls back to reveal the dinner guests seated at table. Jules proposes that they "abolish all formalities forever" and "instead of linking arms in the usual way . . . touch feet under the table." As he sits, this last direction is carried out; there is an immediate cut to a shot of the feet under the table showing the men's and women's shoes touching. The narrator tells us that Jules removes his foot quickly but that Jim permits his to continue touching Catherine's—until *she* breaks off contact. The camera tilts up to the level of the table top, again framing all the guests. Jules looks at Catherine. They drink and laugh and, as we see how they radiate vital good feelings toward each other, the screen is blacked out by a rectangular mask, isolating the pair in the upper portion of the frame. Magic.

The little byplay with the feet under the table reveals the differences in Jules's and Jim's temperaments. Perhaps Catherine learns these differences too.

III. Catherine Takes Charge

"For a month," says the narrator, "Jim disappeared completely." This is an error in the subtitles. The title should read "Jules" not "Jim." The narration is spoken over a scene showing Jules and Jim back at their gymnasium, both having massages. Jules urges Jim to visit him and Catherine.

There is a cut to the two friends climbing the stairs to Catherine's flat. It is a well-lit spiral staircase. As they go up, Jules says that Catherine is "anxious to know you better." Then, as if realizing the implications of what he has said, Jules pauses. The camera angle is from Jim's lower level, looking up at Jules, who says, significantly, "Not this one, Jim, right?"

Inside Catherine's bedroom, we see her, dressed in her nightgown with a shawl over her shoulders, looking out a window overlooking the staircase. She moves to the door to greet the friends. Jules kisses her cheek sedately and Jim shakes her hand. As they sit, she goes behind a screen to change clothes. We get a quick cut from a low-angle camera of Catherine's legs slipping into a pair of trousers. Almost immediately she emerges from behind the screen. It is still another piece of quick magic, this transformation. Now she is dressed in a disguise as Chaplin's *The Kid*, a tough but appealing little street urchin. Camera pans with her as she moves toward the men. Jim inspects her critically and decides her femininity is too blatant; as she examines herself in a hand mirror, Jim suggests a moustache. He takes up her cosmetic pencil and begins to draw it on. Music starts, a comically orchestrated burst of a zany tune, in the quick tempo of the silent films. Approving Jim's work, Catherine hangs up the mirror and, as a final touch, accepts a cigar from Jim.

We should note here that neither of the men is shocked at this little game. The whole mood is so light that they readily take it for a lark.

On the street, Catherine looks fine. The cap pulled down to one side adds the perfect touch. She slinks along roguishly and finally meets her test: a man emerging from a urinal with an unlit cigarette casually asks for a light. She supplies it. "Thank you, sir," says the man, and the test has been a success.

There is a dissolve to a shot of the three friends descending a flight of stairs leading to a footbridge over some railroad tracks. The narrator comments that "she enjoyed her disguise. The men were moved. It was a strange symbol." The success of the disguise is a subtle matter, but not so strange. It is a complex symbol of Catherine's gathering mastery over the men. On the one hand, it demonstrates her mastery over the environment: she can pass for a man on the streets of Paris. On the other hand, it is an example of her imaginative power, her daring and her enterprise. With it, she has even managed to transcend her sexual identity.

So powerful is the effect of this seemingly casual moment in the film— and its art lies in its actually *being* casual: comic, playful, and light-hearted—that, immediately afterward, Catherine sits down at the bottom of the steps and issues her first direct command to the men:

JIM: I think it's raining.

A train whistle is heard.

CATHERINE: Let's go to the seashore. We go tomorow.

There is no discussion here and a close-up of Catherine at this moment reveals the absolute authority in her face.

Needless to say, she wins the foot race across the bridge. She cheats by jumping the gun at the start and the camera indicates her leadership by tracking along with her as she runs. Moreover, now there is no music, no comedy, only the sound of heavy breathing, indicating the strain and seriousness of the contest.

The scene is a visual summary of a continuing pattern. For once at the seashore, it is Catherine who mandates their return to Paris; and during the seashore sequence, when Jules asks her to marry him, it is she who decides for both of them, evaluating not just her own, but also Jules's position. Only the outbreak of a world war interferes with her command over their movements.

The economy with which Truffaut dramatizes this state of Catherine's domination is apparent on the terrace of the villa they rent in the south of France. Immediately preceding this scene, we have been watching as Jules, Jim, and Catherine bicycled back from the beach. A dissolve from this bike-riding scene ends on a close-up of a table top on the terrace where a game of dominoes is in progress. As a hand reaches into the frame to move a piece, the shot widens and camera tilts up to feature her. Now the frame has Jim on the left, Catherine in the middle, seated against the wall of the villa, and Jules's hands on the domino pieces at the right. We cut to a matching shot: now Jules on the right, Catherine still in the middle background, and only Jim's hands on the left. Seated beside a small bust of Napoleon, Catherine—at the apex of a triangle, dominating the men in this visual pattern—notes that the men are absorbed in their game. She starts to speak:

CATHERINE: At fifteen I was in love with Napoleon. I dreamt I met him in a lift. He made love to me then left me. Poor Napoleon. . . . I was taught "Our Father who art in heaven." I thought it meant "art." I imagined my father with an easel, painting in Paradise. [Pause.] I believe I've said something funny, at least amusing. You might try to smile.

The dialogue is extraordinary. It belongs, in Roche's novel, to another, minor, character. But Truffaut saw how apt it was for Catherine, for it is revealing about her in every way. Napoleon, apart from whatever other associations we might make on hearing his name, literally stands for France to a Frenchman. He *is* the state. Catherine's dream is that she met this grandiose figure quite by accident. Then "he" made love to her, but *she* controls the situation by pitying him with that "poor Napoleon!" The shift from passive to active here parallel's the experiences of Jules and Jim with her. She was at first passive with them, too, and is now actively controlling.

But neither Jules nor Jim responds to her story of Napoleon. Nor do they respond to her joke. At this point, she is furious, and starts to scratch her back, thinking to offer them something they might not be able to resist: her body. "Will anyone present scratch my back?" Jules, still absorbed in the game (and still held in the same shot), replies, without looking at her, "The Lord scratches those who scratch themselves." But before he can finish his aphorism, she is up and coming toward Jules. As he finishes she slaps his face. Jules is stunned, as we cut to a close-up to witness his reaction to the slap. For a moment he glares at her, then bursts out laughing.

At this, Truffaut's camera playfully swings in a little panning arc over to Jim, who joins in the laughter, then with the same movement over and up to Catherine. Now Catherine is held in close-up as she speaks. She reminds them that before she met them she never laughed, but they have taught her the art. As she demonstrates the variety of looks on her face before and after, these looks are caught in freeze frames (Figure 18–3). The frozen frames are superb in capturing her visual allure and

FIGURE 18–3. *Catherine telling her dream of Napoleon. (Courtesy Janus Films.)*

remind us once again of the lantern slide images of the statue, the statue itself, and the shots of Catherine when they first met her in Jules's courtyard.

The scene very accurately details the precise relations between the three. It dramatizes her character exactly and theirs by a kind of negative indirection. That is, *they* become known by the way they respond in unison to *her*. Moreover, the visual pattern of the composition shows their exact emotional relations to Catherine.

On another rainy day at the seaside villa, Catherine decrees their return to Paris. There, Jim receives an advance from a book publisher and, to celebrate, takes them all to the theater. This scene, too, dramatizes Catherine's dominance, but less quietly than the scene on the terrace.

The scene begins in the balcony of the theater as the curtain falls. Catherine, sitting between the men, applauds along with them, but as they shoot glances at one another, she becomes suspicious and examines first one then the other. These small gestures prepare us once again for Catherine's determined intervention in their relations.

Now we cut outside to the dark night, where they are seen in a three-shot, with Catherine leading them down a flight of stone stairs from the quayside to the river bank of the Seine. This is a visual expression of an emotional theme (that is, Catherine leading them through life), and we have seen it before during the *Kid* scene. Now we note that Catherine has removed her suit jacket and has it slung over her shoulder.

CATHERINE: I still like that girl. She wants to be free. She invents her own life.

With these words, we recognize that while Catherine may be speaking of the play, she is also describing herself. (Catherine herself is, as the film in general and this scene in particular indicates, a highly theatrical creation. It is, moreover, not too farfetched to suggest that the "Swedish" play they have just seen is one of Strindberg's and to speculate further that the "Austrian" play Jim translates after the war may be Schnitzler's *La Ronde*. Both works allude satisfactorily to Catherine in that many of Strindberg's heroines share Catherine's destructive qualities, whereas Schnitzler's mirror her capricious infidelities.) The emotional drama of the scene resides in this identification.

But Jim does not agree with Catherine's assessment of the heroine and thinks it "a confused play." Thus ensues a conflict over their respective reactions to the play, with Catherine on one side and Jules and Jim on the other. It reaches a first aclimax when Jim challenges certain logical relations in the play, to which Catherine replies, "That's all you can think of." Jules answers with an indictment: "Yes. And you help us think of it."

Catherine is really annoyed now, and to indicate her emotional separation from the men, Truffaut separates them physically. Where we had,

FIGURE 18–4. *After the theater: Just before Catherine's leap. (Courtesy Janus Films.)*

before this outburst, camera leading them all in a three-shot, we now have two separate moving shots: one leads Catherine as she now ascends the parapet and teeters along its edge (Figure 18–4); and the other leads Jules and Jim as Jules, stirred up, begins to denounce women. They pay no special attention to Catherine's position on the parapet and Jim tries, unsuccessfully, to soften Jules's heated tirade. Jules spouts Baudelaire on the "abomination" called woman. Catherine has had all she can take.

CATHERINE: You're a pair of fools!
JIM: I don't approve of what Jules says at 2 in the morning. . . .

A close-up captures Catherine's blazing anger. "Then protest!" she says. A very quick cut to the two men records Jim's very casual, "I protest."

But it is not enough. Carefully, Catherine lifts her veil, drops her coat, and plunges into the Seine. The men are, of course, dumbfounded, shocked, frightened, and captured as they rush down to the water's edge and reach out toward her helplessly. As we see a medium shot from the water, with Catherine swimming delicate strokes in the silver moonlight, the narrator comments and Truffaut cuts back and forth between the rescue and her lonely hat on the waters:

NARRATOR: Jim never forgot that jump. He drew it the next day from his mind's eye. He admired Catherine as he blew her an invisible kiss. He didn't worry. He held his breath for her . . . Catherine's smile never changed after her triumph.

They haul her out of the water and into a taxi.

On the way home in the taxi, Catherine, her hair drying in strings, sits between them, an utterly triumphant smile on her face. The narrator is correct: it never changes. Like the slap she administered to Jules on the terrace, this piece of "liberated" impulsive behavior has also conquered. With it she has controverted and thus neutralized Jules's tirade, frightened him, and captured Jim's admiration completely. As Jim is about to leave the taxi, it is no longer "monsieur" but "just Jim" and she asks if they can meet at a café the following day.

Jim is only a little late for their meeting, but she is even later, and they do not see each other again until after the war.

IV. After the War: A Reunion

The images of war are mainly old newsreel clips. They depict trench warfare in considerable detail and they belong to the category of harsh reality: they conveniently divide the film into two parts and indicate that time is passing, bringing with it new demands on our protagonists. The new state of affairs after the war is marked by, in general, a more subdued pattern of visual images than we have seen in the prewar section. The camera is quieter, the pace of the editing slower, and the whole tone of exuberance is much reduced.

Nevertheless, when Jim arrives by train at the Rhine chalet where Jules and Catherine are living, the opening shots of the sequence are long shots from a helicopter. These seem to us to have a double effect, as do other helicopter shots used in these postwar sequences. They seem to produce in us the sense that we are watching the action from a cosmic perspective, and they establish a visual pattern that reminds us of the livelier style of the prewar section.

Now when Jim, Catherine, and Sabine arrive at the chalet from the train station, the subdued style still prevails (for a while, as we will see). Accompanied by long, drawn-out phrases of music (discordant, seeming to strain for resolution), the three walk through the lovely wood and approach the chalet from the subjective camera's point of view. Jules waits at the foot of the stairs leading to the terrace. The music rises as he and Jim share a mutual embrace.

A sedate panning shot around the chalet's ground floor interior precedes their entrance. To the loud ticking of the clock, we move slowly along the walls, noticing the clock and noticing also the Picasso that Jim had given to Catherine before the war (just before they had gone to the theater). Then they enter, all feeling the strangeness of their long separation. The camera holds on a three-shot as they do, angled toward the rocker and the couch where they will sit. Catherine leaves the frame to remove her hat and fetch a bottle and glasses. Jim sits on the couch while Jules occupies the rocker with Sabine on his lap. (Later on, as we will see, the rocker becomes a kind of symbolic seat of Catherine's favor; thus, it will be occupied in turn by Jules, Jim, and Albert, as each occupies a central place in Catherine's affections.) There is an awkward silence, emphasized by the creaking of the rocker as Jules goes rhythmically back and forth. Jim declines a drink, Jules refuses a cigarette ("I stopped smoking when I started to love plants"). We now cut from the steady three-shot and see them separately, as if isolated, in consecutive close-ups. Then we go back to the three-shot as Jules breaks the silence: "An angel is passing by."

Jim takes out his watch, looks at it, then replies in deadpan:

JIM: Yes. It's twenty past one. Angels always do at twenty past.
JULES: I didn't know that.
CATHERINE: Neither did I.

There is more silence, with the camera also remaining still.

JIM: At twenty past and twenty to as well.

Touched by the fairy tale, Jules (seen now in close-up), grinning widely, breaks the silence: "So you won the war, you louse!" Whereupon the camera takes its cue from the change of mood Jules's remark has provoked and executes one of those characteristic little swing pans, linking these three together; it pans to Jim ("I'd rather have won this") then to Catherine. As if she canot permit this relaxation of the tension to blossom further, Catherine suggests lunch.

As they move to the table and are seated by Catherine, we hear the subdued strains of what we will call the joyous theme. This melodic theme was heard first at the seashore accompanying the happiest moments of their carefree lives: their walk in the woods, bicycling to the sunlit beach, and so on. Its return here seems to signal a restoration of some of that same prewar mood.

Then the camera follows Catherine as she goes to the kitchen and the men embark on a conversation. In the kitchen, Catherine takes a soup tureen from the maid and returns with it to the table. Thus we are reminded that she is still central, placed somehow between and at the same time above the two men, the nourisher. When she reaches the table, a pair of successive close-ups of Jules and Jim is used for each man's discussion of his vocational life. These are remarkable in that they are closer angles on each than we have heretofore seen, and this is consonant with the closeness of reality to their lives, as the subject matter of the dialogue indicates:

JULES: I'm doing a book on dragonflies. I am writing it for a publisher. Catherine is illustrating it. Even Sabine helps. She goes with me into the swamps. I am going to build a pond in the garden.

After a close-up of Sabine rubbing her eyes, he continues:

JULES: One day, perhaps, I may become literary and write a love novel with insects as its characters. I have a bad tendency to specialize. I admire your versatility, Jim.

Jules is fully revealed in these words and in the veiled intensity with which he speaks them. His concentration on insects suggests multiple significance: first, it indicates his struggle to achieve order and control in his life. Dragonflies can be studied, organized, and classified. Limited in this way, they represent his achieving order outside himself to compensate for the disorder and lack of control in his personal life, where control is exercised by Catherine. At the same time, his literary speculation that he might someday write a "love novel with insects as its characters" suggests a wish to achieve detachment from love. This can be achieved by substituting insects for humans. And, finally, something about his association with insects has the effect of reducing *him* in size.

Moreover, the tail end of Jules's speech is a kind of a metaphor and has less to do with authorship than with the choice of a mate. For it is Jules who has a "bad tendency to specialize" in Catherine. Jules admires Jim's apparent lack of ties to her.

Jim, on the other hand, describes his career as a kind of enforced act of extreme disorder:

JIM: Oh, I'm a failure. Sorel, my teacher, taught me all I know.

This would be Albert Sorel (1846–1906), a noted French historian, whose principal work studied the effects of the French revolution on European politics. The mention of his name invokes no special allusive meaning, perhaps because his name is not well known. But the effect of liberation on institutions is an appropriate theme to link to Jim.

JIM: I told him I wanted to be a diplomat. "Do you have money?" No. "Can you honestly add an illustrious name to your own?" No. "Then forget about diplomacy." But what can I become? "Curious." That's no

career. "Not yet. Travel, write, translate. Learn to live anywhere, beginning now. There's a future in it. The French have ignored the world
for too long. A [news]paper will always pay for your fun."

Jim's ambition had been to lead a professional life at once patterned and
orderly but also filled with the need to be reticent and circumspect.
Sorel's suggestions and evaluations are distinguished by realism, and that
is the direction that Jim's professional life has taken. To be "curious"
squares well with his need for "adventure" and "risks" and in Catherine
he has found a subject to engage his curiosity fully.

As usual, Catherine, in this scene, has the last words:

CATHERINE: Jules thinks you have a bright future. So do I, but it may not
be spectacular.

After Catherine shows Jim around the chalet (significantly, she shows
him her and Jules's separate bedrooms), she points out through the window the inn where Jim will be staying. Its actual distance in the long
shot is farther than the metaphorical distance between Jim and Catherine.
That distance is narrowing.

The reunion seems complete, when, next, Jules, Jim, Catherine, and
Sabine move off the terrace and into the surrounding fields. We hear the
"joyous" theme full up now, and it reminds us of the prewar mood. We see
more of the irrepressible play that had characterized their activities then.
This time, Jim rolls down a hillside with Sabine in his arms.

As the four move farther off into the countryside, there is a dissolve
to the terrace where we see the men playing dominoes once again. This
is the game at which they used to spend much time, a symbol of their
harmless, playful competition. Now the shot reverberates in our memories,
for there is a pan over to the wall of the house, against which Catherine
is sitting with Sabine at her side. Before the war, at the seaside villa,
we saw a similar configuration: Catherine at the apex of a triangle
dominating the men at the bases. The earlier scene pointed up Catherine's
authority over the men. The present scene does the same, only now the
situation is more complex; Sabine is now part of Catherine's and Jules's
family.

Camera pulls back now, as if to emphasize the complicated new triangle. Then, in close-up, Catherine kisses Sabine and announces her bed-
time. The narrator comments: "Jim felt something was wrong."

After Sabine has been put to bed, Jules takes Jim into his room and
confirms his friend's premonition. Catherine has been unfaithful to him;
she has stayed away months at a time. He is no longer her husband, but
wants to remain close to her at all costs. A short while before the wed-

ding, Catherine, because Jules's mother had slighted her in some way, squared accounts by sleeping with an old lover. Jules is bewildered, shaken.

In his room at the inn, Jim prepares for bed and the Narrator comments: "Jim was not surprised. He recalled Jules's mistakes with other girls." Jim is prepared to enter the fray.

V. *Ménage à Trois*

The next night, Jules and Jim are sitting with Catherine and Sabine in the living room of the chalet. As Catherine takes Sabine up to bed, she pauses in the doorway to ask Jim if he would be free to speak to her later on. There is a close-up of Jim as he shoots a questioning glance at Jules. Only after Jules's close-up signifies *his* agreement does Jim agree. When she returns to the living room, the men are discussing the war again and, when Jules makes an innocent remark about Jim's acquaintance with German beer, Catherine erupts with a chauvinistic catalogue of French wines. They are superior. But it is all just an opportunity to intrude between the friends. Challenging Jim to "catch me," she runs outside into the darkness.

Outside, Jim catches her by a large old oak tree, and as the camera closes in on them from full figures to medium close-up, the two of them move forward toward camera. Now camera leads them at an acute angle as we see one of the lengthiest shots in the film: it is longer than two minutes. The scene consists of a long speech by each of them, and although there are a couple of cuts toward the middle of Catherine's monologue—at a point where they turn to go back toward the chalet and the camera no longer leads but follows them—the effect of the whole is of one continuous, smoothly flowing shot.

Catherine's story is by far the longer of the two and with it Truffaut engages our sympathy for her. It is, after all, probably the first time she has told it to a sympathetic listener and she tests Jim's sympathy at the outset by requiring him to acknowledge that he will not judge her when he hears her story.

What she has to say suggests that the war had had something to do with her estrangement from Jules. She also confirms our impression that Jules's passive nature attracted her and goes on to say that "my daughter attracted me like a magnet" and caused her to return to the family fold after a long "holiday" with a lover. But she insists that she must have her freedom and that her having given Jules a child entitles her to it.

Jim's story, by contrast, is nostalgic. It recounts their prewar times together and only adds that "he always knew Jules could never hold Catherine." When Jim leaves her, near dawn, he is well on his way to acknowledging and acting on his desire for her, although the narrator comments significantly, "Was Jim acting for Jules, or for himself? He never knew." As for Catherine, "perhaps she encouraged him, but she revealed her goals only when she achieved them."

Albert arrives the next day and Jim tells him and Jules his story of the soldier who fell in love through a long impassioned exchange of letters. Catherine and Albert perform their song (see "Style and Approach," p. 485).

Inevitably, Jim and Catherine come together. Catherine summons him for that fateful meeting by a devious method. She wants to read a book he has borrowed from Jules. The book is Goethe's *Elective Affinities* (in which there is also adultery, the cremation of lovers, and a level of psychological action). Jules calls Jim at the inn to urge his returning it at once. He also encourages Jim on the phone: "Marry her and let me be near her, Jim. Don't think of me as an obstacle."

Later that night, as we hear long phrases of romantic music, we see Jim approach the chalet carrying the book. He mounts the terrace and comes to the door. The shot widens to include Catherine, standing inside the doorway, clad in her nightgown. She opens the door, takes him by the hand, and leads him through the darkness of the chalet to a similar setting, another window-paned doorway. Here we see them in a tight, profiled close-up; silhouetted against the moonlit window, Jim traces her profile with his fingers. Wordlessly, they embrace, as an insect crawls slowly across one of the window panes.

Two dissolves from here feature Catherine's radiant face lying on a pillow. ("Their first embrace lasted all night.") From the last of these, there is a pan to her desk where we see the Goethe book and then to the window looking out on a pastoral dawn. The narrator comments: "Jim was a prisoner. No other woman existed."

At Catherine's insistence, Jim moves into the chalet, and for a time there exists there a chaste ménage à trois, chaste in that Jules enjoys no sexual relations with Catherine. Only once does she, perhaps by reflex action, attempt to seduce Jules, but his resistance, together with Jim's annoyance, dissuade her from further attempts. Reality, in the form of Jim's newspaper assignments, intrudes after a time, and Jim departs for Paris, leaving Catherine in Jules's care.

At this point, the new pair of lovers plans to marry (after Catherine's divorce from Jules) and set up their little household (including Jules) on a permanent basis. The important understanding grows between them that they will sanctify their love by having children together.

In Paris, Jim explains his plans to Gilberte and then has the encounters with Thérèse and Denise previously discussed (see p. 467).

When he returns from Paris, he finds that Catherine has been away, having an affair as "repayment" for Jim's staying with Gilberte in Paris. She enjoins him against making love that night; they could not be sure of the paternity of a child if she became pregnant. For the issue of a child has now taken on great intensity. When she fails to become pregnant after a prolonged period of time, they visit specialists to discover the cause. The doctors advise patience, but Catherine has little of it.

One night, she refuses to sleep in the same room with Jim. The attempt to bear Jim's child has become a trial to her. She cannot bear undergoing the "test." Jim agrees to a three-month separation and Catherine goes from their bedroom into Jules's. There we see her in a most poignant moment. Shattered by her own ideals, which seem to equate womanhood with fecundity in some magical way, she collapses into Jules's arms and tearfully accepts his protestations of undying affection. For a moment we think that Catherine is undergoing a transformation. Her reference to "growing old together" deceives us into thinking she might now elect to live a more realistic life. But this is an illusion.

Seeing Jim off again, they have occasion to spend the night in a hotel room (Figure 18–5). One last desperate bout of love-making ensues; they part, and, while Jim is in Paris, we learn through an extended sequence of letter exchanges that she is pregnant and once again eager for his return. Just as suddenly as this new mood overtakes her, however, another mood grips her when she miscarries and Jules writes to Jim that Catherine's love for him has died with the child.

VI. The End

The end of the film is, in its way, quite as theatrical as the beginning. Some years after Jules's letter ends Jim's affair with Catherine, the two

FIGURE 18–5. *Jim and Catherine in the hotel room. (Courtesy Janus Films.)*

friends meet again in front of their old gymnasium. They are delighted to meet once again. Jules and Catherine have moved to an old mill on the Seine not far from Paris, and *Jim* suggests a meeting the following day.

There follows a scene that has been expunged from the version distributed in the United States (see p. 93 of the screenplay). It takes place at Jim's flat, where he is living with Gilberte and where Jules comes to call. The men pay dominoes and Jules speaks of Catherine. She has purchased a revolver and is in a morbid frame of mind. She knows Jules is making this visit and she invites Jim and Gilberte for a drive in her car. Jim declines for Gilberte, accepts for himself and, significantly, insists on changing hats with Jules as the scene ends. The act reinforces their identification with one another: to Catherine they are one and the same. (Although the scene supplies certain missing logical connections—that is, it accounts for Catherine's suicidal frame of mind and prepares us for her pulling a gun on Jim a few minutes later—it is superfluous. Without it, Catherine's capriciousness rises to effective heights.)

The first car ride with Catherine is a scene that recapitulates the pattern of her behavior toward Jules and Jim throughout the film. The images in this sequence invariably feature Catherine leading the men. She leads them down the steps of the mill to her car (where we see intercuts of her hands on the controls); leads them out of the car to the *auberge* where they lunch with Albert (even her stopping to remove a pebble from her shoe—a lovely touch—stops the men from moving); and she leads them as they are about to leave the restaurant. The quiet denouement of this sequence, the way she quietly departs from Jules and Jim to take Albert's arm, is an ominous portent of things to come.

Catherine's dawn visit to Jim in her car and his subsequent appearance in her bedroom constitute a parody of movie melodrama that somehow seems appropriate. The bedroom scene might have been made under the influence of D. W. Griffith's dictum that "all you need to make a movie are a gun and a girl."

From the balcony of the mill, we watch as she takes Jim in through the French doors. She leads him to the bed and tells him to lie down. He does not. There is something he must tell her. It is an acute psychological analysis of her state of mind: she is living out a fantasy. He will marry Gilberte after all (although he lets slip an explanation of why he will soon respond to her last, fatal command; his promise to marry Gilberte, he says, "can be postponed").

From a pattern of quiet static shots and a single moving shot following Jim as he speaks, we are suddenly thrust into a furious montage. As a sweetly melodic strain of music segues into a more melodramatic tempo, Catherine cries "What of *me*?!" and pulls a gun. "You shall die, Jim!" We see inserts: close-up of the gun; her hand locking the door; a piece of a struggle; their hands at the gun; Jim wrenching it free; the window;

reverse angle as Jim leaps through. Music rises. Our last shot sees Jim on the far side of the mill pond, gun in hand, running hard away from Catherine.

Cut to a panning shot of the clouds. The narrator announces the time frame: "Several months later . . ." and we are in the Ursulines Cinema in Paris. On screen, Nazis are burning books; a way of life is ending. Jim watches impassively. Now we notice Jules and Catherine in the theater several rows behind Jim. Jules points him out to Catherine and then throws a spitball to get his attention. The boyishness has not changed. He responds at once and they go out to the lobby. For once the narrator's evaluation of Jim's inner state is inaccurate: "Jim was glad to see Jules and to see that Catherine left him cold."

Because she is trying "not to leave them alone," Catherine suggests a ride and takes them in her car. She drives fast and "carelessly" until they stop at another country café. As Jules and Jim converse over an aperitif, she intrudes for the last time. "I've something to tell you, Jim. Will you come with me?" Jim does not hesitate. He leaves Jules alone in the frame. Pan to Catherine. "Watch us, Jules." In the car, Jim is calm, expressionless, Catherine is half smiling. Is it a triumphant look? A series of cuts back and forth, as Jules rises, noticing with slow horror—as we do—the end: off the bridge and into the river in slow motion.

At the cemetery, Truffaut quietly takes us through the steps leading to the lovers' cremation and the interment of their ashes. Neither we nor Jules is spared each realistic detail. In the procession of images from casket to fire—to the horror of the bones emerging and the close-up of the bones being ground to ash with mortar and pestle—to crypt is an inexorable picture of a final reality too soon endured. To the end, Catherine challenges the natural order of things. "Catherine wanted [her ashes] to be cast to the winds, but it was not permitted." Reality triumphs over Catherine. But as Jules, who is "relieved" that it is over at last, walks out of the cemetery, the music we hear is "Le Tourbillon," Catherine's song. At least one final victory, then, is Catherine's.

Style and Approach

The characteristic stylistic feature of *Jules and Jim* is the sum total of the visual resources it exploits. That is to say, Truffaut uses in medley virtually every resource the medium knows: montage, full-shot framing, simple panning, tilting, zoom shots, 360° pans, masking shots, close-ups, long shots (many from a helicopter), the hand-held camera, tracking shots backward and forward, freeze frames and even, from the silent cinema, a burlesqued title card. Moreover, Truffaut takes very seriously indeed the adjective in the phrase "motion pictures." Therefore, there is constant movement in his visual images, particularly in the first part of the film (before the war). This motion comes from a variety of sources: camera movement, the movement of actors and objects (trains, bikes, boats, cars) within the frame, and the pace of the editing.

It is this movement, together with the narrative movement resulting from sudden switches of mood, tone, and action, that serves to characterize the irrepressible behavior of our young protagonists. Used sparingly after the war, it continues to maintain the illusion that they have not grown older and need not respond to reality's demands.

The voice-over narration is an integral part of the cinematic style. It serves several important functions: (1) the narrative commentary leaves the visual images free of the necessity to summarize developing relations and to compress time. Because the strength of the medium lies in its capacity to picture present-tense action, such a device is crucial in a film whose action spans twenty years; (2) it also summarizes character where such analysis needs the refinement that a wordless picture cannot supply, or where it depends on having access to the character's past; (3) its flat and expressionless tonalities suggest a mature onlooker, an observer whose balanced witness makes the headlong tragic rush of the film more poignant; (4) it gives us access to Jim's but not Jules's inner thoughts, and thus charts for us the progress of his potentially tragic involvement with Catherine. Thus, the narration, by pointedly contrasting visual, vocal, and characterological textures, furnishes the film with a kind of poetry.

One quality that has been almost universally ascribed to *Jules and Jim* is its lyricism. Contributing to this is its use of music, another integral component of the cinematic style. Rarely does Truffaut use the score to counterpoint the emotional content of the visual images; instead, music is used here to enhance the visual rhythms synergistically, often adding an element of movie wit by recapitulating, as in *The Kid* scene, the tempos and comic orchestrations of silent movies.

Music to enhance visual rhythms is often a particular theme associated with the sheer physical exuberance of the trio. For example, what the viewer might recognize at once is the particularly melodious "joyous" theme. We hear it first at the seashore villa. When they set off through the woods on the first brilliant morning after their arrival, the theme creeps up and under. It enhances the spontaneous style of the visuals, which capture their carefree and joyous play. Later, we hear it used more subtly at the reunion of the three after the war; it is also recognizable as Jim rolls down the hill with Sabine in his arms.

A special theme is assigned to Catherine and it is used with special effectiveness. This is Bassiak's song "Le Tourbillon," which is integrated into the film's dramatic texture. This is the song "composed" by Catherine and Albert that she sings to his guitar accompaniment on camera at the Rhine chalet. The fact that Catherine works on the song suggests something about her character: her wish to create. Moreover, it enhances the impression that there is something fanatical in her search for a certain freedom of creative expression. In addition, and perhaps more important, the song lyrics capture and repeat the thesis of action between Catherine and all her men:

> She had eyes, eyes of opal.
> They fascinated me.
> Her pale face was an oval.
> What a fatal *femme* was she.
>
> ❖ ❖ ❖
>
> We met with a kiss,
> A hit then a miss.
> It wasn't all bliss.
> And we parted.
> We went our ways
> In life's whirlpool of days.
>
> I saw her again one night.
> Again, she was an enchanted sight.
>
> ❖ ❖ ❖

This repetetive gain and loss is underscored by the repetetive rhythms of the melody. In addition, this the melody, as we have noted before, is played at the conclusion of the film. It accounts for Catherine's symbolic presence and signals her victory over both Jules and Jim even as her ashes are interred.

There also are occasions when music is used to interpret an otherwise ambiguous state of affairs between characters. For example, when Jim returns to the Rhine chalet late one night to return Jules's copy of *The Elective Affinities*, we know that he has been thinking more and more of his attraction to Catherine, but we do not know just how far she has gone in the same direction. Thus, when Jim approaches through the darkened forest—in the static camera angle from inside the chalet—and moves toward us we hear a sonorously romantic theme, something Mahlerian, which immediately suggests the proper emotional note we can expect to hear in the characters' interaction.

Music is used more frequently than natural sound. Only occasionally does Truffaut care about sounds; he does not go to special lengths to provide a generally realistic image by painstakingly laying in a full sound track. But there are moments when we should pay special attention to the effective sounds used. One of these, the race across the bridge, features only the sounds of breathing, and, together with the consistent use of a close-up of Catherine, emphasizes Catherine's overpowering presence. Later, in her room, Truffaut counterpoints the sound of the vitriol steaming down the sink with romantic music to produce a textural effect. The clock and the rocker in the Rhine chalet also produce powerful natural sound impressions that enrich the cinematic texture.

There is much more in the film that limitations of space and a sense of proportion have prevented our discussing. We have, for example, failed to mention a number of Truffaut's symbolic ideas. The commentary on nationalism inherent in the characters' French and German nationalities is only one of these.

Nevertheless, the riches of the work have been suggested. It remains now to summarize its significance, and that is not an easy task. For one thing, *Jules and Jim*, unlike, say, *The Rules of the Game* or, better, *L'Avventura* and *The Seventh Seal*, encourages us in two different ways at once. The last-named films are visual incitements to think and to understand—that is their principal effect on us—but *Jules and Jim* invites us to revel in its good feeling, to fantasize along with it, while it impels us to use thought in a not quite satisfactory effort to *understand*.

The effort is not satisfactory because it has been made too difficult for us to ever arrive at a singular sense of what the action *means*. Truffaut himself has said "There are two themes: that of the friendship between the two men, which tries to remain alive, and that of the impossibility of living *à trois*. The idea of the film is that the couple is not satisfactory but there is no alternative." (Ibid., p. 170.) Truffaut's canon reveals that he is, indeed, concerned with the theme of the problematic form of the couple relationship. Marriage, for Truffaut, is always beset with inevitable and destructive conflict.

Yet, it seems to us that his *Jules and Jim* goes beyond his statement of theme. To be sure it is concerned with that friendship of which he speaks, but his marriage partners have based their marriage on ideals that cannot be sustained and his *ménage à trois* is never really achieved. Rather, he seems concerned with a larger set of issues: with youth and age, idealism and reality, and the psychology of the liberated woman and her superiority over the passive male. All these issues ally his thought with a broader context and force us to see his film as a masterly dramatization of all these ideas, beautifully intertwined into a single pattern.

This frees us to enjoy his spectacularly affective cinema and to note that *Jules and Jim* has made a double contribution. It has been important in showing the way for others to exploit those visual resources of cinema that produce Truffaut's affective quality, and its subject matter has been liberating and has cleared the way for serious discussions of similar subjects.

CHAPTER 19

Notes on Six Films

Forbidden Games

[Jeux Interdits]

Directed by RENÉ CLÉMENT

The identification of director with spectator was, he insisted, the key to style, to his own perfectionist methods of montage; it demanded absolute discipline, it demanded an "agencement des plans," a constant sense of scene that would provide the clearest, the most effective explanation.

Lotte H. Eisner. "Style of René Clément" (Part I). *Film Culture* (September 1957), p. 21.

CAST

PAULETTE	*Brigitte Fossey*
MICHEL	*George Poujouly*
FATHER DOLLE	*Lucien Hubert*
MOTHER DOLLE	*Suzanne Courtal*
GEORGE DOLLE	*Jacques Marin*
BERTHE DOLLE	*Laurence Badie*
FATHER GOUARD	*Andre Wasley*
FRANCIS GOUARD	*Amedee*
JEANNE GOUARD	*Denise Peronne*
THE PRIEST	*Louis Sainteve*

CREDITS

DIRECTOR	*René Clément*
PRODUCER	*Robert Dorfmann*
SCENARIO	*Jean Aurenche, Pierre Bost, and René Clemént, based on a story by François Boyer*

CREDITS (Continued)

DIRECTOR OF PHOTOGRAPHY	*Robert Juillard*
ART DIRECTOR	*Paul Bertrand*
MUSIC	*Narcisco Yepes*
EDITOR	*Robert Dwyre*

Silver Film   1952   Black and white   90 minutes

The setting of *Forbidden Games* is France in World War II, during the German invasion. In the opening scene a column of refugees is strafed by planes. The parents of a five-year-old girl, Paulette, are killed. The child, bewildered and frightened, wanders into the countryside clutching the body of her dog (Figure 19–1).

She is found by an eleven-year-old farm boy, Michel. He takes her home and persuades his parents to let her stay. The two children become completely attached to each other and observe together the events in the farmhouse. These include the death of Michel's brother and a love affair between his sister and a young man from the adjoining farm who has deserted from the army. Unfortunately for the lovers, Michel's family, the Dolles, and that of the young man, the Gouards, have been involved for years in a feud.

FIGURE 19–1. *Paulette fondles the body of her dog killed in an air raid. (Courtesy Janus Films.)*

FIGURE 19–2. *Paulette and Michel admire the crosses in the cemetery while on their way to the burial of Michel's brother. (Courtesy Janus Films.)*

The two children, left to their own devices, devise a macabre game. It begins with the burial of Paulette's dog and is inspired by the funeral of Michel's brother (Figure 19–2). They cultivate a graveyard in an old mill, filling it with the bodies of dead animals found in the fields. At the girl's instigation Michel steals crosses from the local church and cemetery to decorate their private graveyard.

Eventually the thefts are traced to the boy. He agrees to return the crosses on the condition that his parents allow Paulette to remain. His father breaks this promise and the girl is taken away (Figure 19–3). In a rage of righteous indignation and sorrow at the loss of his playmate, Michel destroys the crosses.

In the last scene of the film Paulette is in a refugee center. Once again frightened and bewildered, she hears someone call out the name Michel. We see her disappear into the crowd as she searches for the only love and security that she has known since the death of her parents.

Forbidden Games is usually described as a "war film." The horrors of war are made vividly concrete for us in the opening sequence; war hovers over the farm like a threatening storm, and its ramifications are evident in the terrible "games" the children play. The film, however, transcends such a simple categorization, for it also deals with the love between two children, the ways in which children transform reality into fantasy, and the stubbornness and stupidity adults are capable of in their relationships (the feud between the two families contains in microcosm the same hatred and willful misunderstanding that leads to wars between nations). The most fundamental theme of the film, we feel, is the conflict between the imaginativeness and integrity of childhood and the pragmatism and dishonesty of the adult world.

Paulette is a victim of the war, but her wounds are internal. It is an irony of the film that this sweet, lovely child should devise a game of death more terrifying to us than the actual, painful demise of a young man. After all, what is more outrageous than the perversion of the essential innocence of childhood by the cruelties of adults? Twice security and love are taken from Paulette. First it is by a machine operated by a man that indiscriminately spews destruction and kills her parents. Then she is taken from the Dolle family by a well-meaning but impersonal bureaucratic system. And Father Dolle, for practical reasons, acquiesces to this rape of the child's emotions. In the last poignant scene in which Paulette runs into a crowd in response to a false hope that there is someone there who cares for her, we realize that she is not only the victim of war, but also of the modern world's indifference to the needs of the individual.

The girl appears to be the main character in the film, but in our opinion Michel is of greater interest. Paulette's love for him is basically childish—it is selfish and demanding. He is mature enough, however, to realize that love involves giving. Although his imagination is kindled by the grave-

FIGURE 19–3. *Paulette is taken away by the authorities. (Courtesy Janus Films.)*

yard game, it is for the sake of his beloved that he steals, knowing far better than Paulette that he is committing a crime for which he may have to pay heavily.

It is his feelings for the girl that lead him into conflict with the adult world and an understanding of its duplicity. He was aware that the thefts of the crosses would eventually bring the retribution of his parents and the priest upon his head. In his innocence, however, he could not believe that his father would lie: to promise to keep Paulette if Michel would return what he had stolen and then to allow the girl to be taken away. Faced with this betrayal, he could either submit to his father's authority as a child would or express his outrage at this violation of his integrity and the respect due to an individual of any age by destroying the crosses. He chooses the latter path with the punishment it entails. He loses his beloved and his naiveté, but in the process takes a giant step toward adulthood.

René Clément has directed this film with unobtrusive brilliance. The opening sequence of the attack on the column of refugees could have been a cinematic cliché. Instead, with its superb counterpoint of shots of a group with those of individuals, it is one of the most vivid of this type of sequence that we have experienced in any film. In addition, the director's reputation for meticulous attention to details is sustained by shots of the interior of the farmhouse. Whatever the setting, however, Clément can manipulate his camera to achieve intensely dramatic effects, as in the scene in which Michel throws the crosses into the river and, at the very end of the film, when Paulette hears Michel's name called.

Forbidden Games is a memorable film that reminds us of the innocence and vulnerability of childhood, while also making us more aware of how cruel and irresponsible adults so often are in dealing with that fragile world.

Shoot the Piano Player

[Tirez sur le Pianiste]

Directed by FRANÇOIS TRUFFAUT

I refused to be a prisoner of my first success. I discarded the temptation to renew that success by choosing a great subject. I turned my back on what everyone waited for and I took my pleasure as my only rule of conduct. You won't find any exposition scene in Piano Player *(nothing useful: everything is there for my pleasure as a film maker and I hope your pleasure as a spectator).*

. . .

I know that the result seems ill-assorted and the film seems to contain four or five films, but that's what I wanted.

François Truffaut. (Quoted in "Should Films Be Politically Committed," a discussion by the director with members of the French Federation of Cine-Clubs, reprinted in *Focus on Shoot the Piano Player*, ed. by Leo Braudy, Englewood Cliffs, N.J., 1972, p. 134.)

CAST

CHARLIE KOHLER/EDOUARD SAROYAN	*Charles Aznavour*
LÉNA	*Marie Dubois*
THÉRESA	*Nicole Berger*
CLARISSE	*Michèlle Mercier*
PLYNE	*Serge Davri*
MOMO	*Claud Mansard*
FIDO	*Richard Kanayan*
CHICO	*Albert Rémy*
RICHARD	*Jacques Aslanian*
ERNEST	*Daniel Boulanger*
LARS SCHMEEL	*Claude Heymann*
PASSERBY WHO HELPS CHICO	*Alex Joffé*
SINGER IN CAFÉ	*Boby Lapointe*
MAMMY	*Catherine Lutz*

CREDITS

DIRECTOR	*François Truffaut*
PRODUCER	*Pierre Braunberger*
ADAPTION	*François Truffaut and Marcel Moussy*
	from the novel Down There *by David Goodis*
	(published in France under the title Tirez sur le pianiste*)*
SCRIPT AND DIALOGUE	*François Truffaut*
DIRECTOR OF PHOTOGRAPHY	*Raoul Coutard*
EDITORS	*Claudine Bouché and Cécile Decugis*
ART DIRECTOR	*Jacques Mely*
SOUND	*Jacques Gallois*
MUSIC	*George Delerue (who also plays the piano for Aznavour).*
	The song "Dialogues d'amoureux," composed by Félix Leclerc and sung by Leclerc and Lucienne Vernay;
	the song "Vanille et framboise," composed and sung by Boby Lapointe.

1960   Black and White   84 minutes

A concert pianist and a night club piano player; a wife who is a waitress to support him (and who later dies a suicide) and a supportive mistress who is also a waitress (and who is later killed); the concert impressario is after his wife, the night-club owner is after his girl; Charlie looks into a mirror in the men's room of the café when we first see him and later, on the farm, he looks into a cracked shaving glass—toward the end, when we last see him: in between, he plays the piano and looks in the mirror; inner commentary and outer action—what can all this mean?

Surely it cannot mean that we are watching a formless and/or a meaningless pastiche. On the other hand, Truffaut is surely correct: he has found what he was "looking for": "the explosion of a genre (the detective film) by mixing genres (comedy, drama, melodrama, the psychological film, the thriller, the love film, etc.)" (Ibid.)

Truffaut's film does not rely on "neat" plot exposition and/or clearly enunciated thematic materials. But the plot, complex as it is and interrupted as it is, exploded by changes of tone, mood, and feeling—just when the spectator thinks he knows what's happening, just as he thinks he has settled comfortably into a groove—delivers a complex of thematic meaning nevertheless. For Edouard Saroyan-Charlie Kohler is seen to be caught up in themes of entrapment and escape, freedom and responsibility, experience and pain, love and happiness.

That the vagaries of mere existence lead to pain as well as pleasure, to irony and slapstick comedy, is articulated and dramatized by the very first scene. A man, running in desperation through the dark fog of a Paris night, is panting; the drama is urgent: we are told by the clacking of his heels on the wet pavement. Then what happens? Bam! He has a comic

Figure 19–4. *The tranquility of Charlie and Lena. (Courtesy Janus Films.)*

FIGURE 19–5. *Plyne and Lena: Charlie about to intervene. (Courtesy Janus Films.)*

encounter with a lamppost. A hand reaches into the frame—as if the jig were up. But no. It's just a passerby, someone wanting to help. The two of them walk along the street chatting, kidding around, discussing marriage of all things!

Truffaut's style *is* surprise—if we had to name it in a single word, and nowhere do the surprising solutions to existential problems come at us with greater stylistic surprise than in his *Shoot the Piano Player*. People run out on one another—Edouard runs out on Theresa, Charlie splits from Lena—and this is matched by the inversion of time, for example. Action goes forward and flashbacks run in the same direction. White cuts through black—a single spotlight stabbing through a field of black, moving toward that gorgeous ride from Paris up into the mountains: highway lights, reflections on windshields, brilliant sun, brilliant snow; black and white, snow and the dreary darkness of people against it. The crackling vitality of the visuals is surprisingly managed at every turn, and yet at every turn these visual details reinforce the themes.

Truffaut's camera, seemingly so alive and restless (as, in *Jules and Jim*, it not only seems but is), is paradoxically most often employed in a grand series of medium shots; at other places, he deliberately slows things down —in frame and camera movement—as if the contemplative modality were being urged on us by the visual patterns. Thus, the philosophy of discontinuity—as one cirtic has it—is susceptible in Truffaut's film to a more

FIGURE 19–6. *Charlie and Plyne: Life and death. (Courtesy Janus Films.)*

continuous perception. For one must surely come to some such judgment of Charlie/Edouard as has Truffaut and Oscar Wilde before him; such a judgment is probably responsible for David Goodis's original title: "Please do not shoot the pianist. He is doing his best."

Knife in the Water

[Noz W Wodzie]

Directed by ROMAN POLANSKI

I want my film to be done so the people who see it have the impression it was done without effort. But, of course, there is a lot of effort behind it, a lot of struggle. And as for realism, the only way to seduce people into believing you—whether they want to or not—is to take painstaking care with the details of your film, to make it accurate. Sloppiness destroys emotional impact.

Roman Polanski. Quoted in Joseph Gelmis, "Roman Polanski," *The Film Director as Superstar.* New York, 1970, p. 146.

CAST

ANDRZEJ	*Leon Niemczyk*
CHRISTINE	*Jolanta Umecka*
THE YOUNG MAN	*Zygmunt Malanowicz*

CREDITS

DIRECTOR	*Roman Polanski*
PRODUCER	*Stanislaw Zylewicz*
SCENARIO	*Jerzy Skolimoski, Jakub Goldberg, and Roman Polanski*
DIRECTOR OF PHOTOGRAPHY	*Jerzy Lipman*
MUSIC	*Krzysztof Komeda*
SOUND	*Halina Paszkowska*
EDITOR	*Halina Prugar*

Polski Film   1962   Black and white   94 minutes

———

Roman Polanski's international reputation is based primarily on such films as *Repulsion, Cul-de-sac,* and *Rosemary's Baby.* Many critics, however, believe that to date his finest cinematic achievement was his first feature length film, *Knife in the Water.* Although the director limited himself to three characters in a confined setting (or perhaps even because of these self-imposed restrictions), he attained a degree of subtlety of characterization, multilevel meaning, and a tightness of structure and style that, in our opinion, is not to be found in his later, often self-indulgent films.

The story line is deceptively simple. A middle-aged sports writer, Andrzej, and his young wife, Christine, are driving to a lake for a day of sailing. They pick up a hitchhiker (listed in the credits only as "The Young Man"). When they arrive at the pier, Andrzej impulsively invites the boy to join them.

An intense rivalry develops between the older man—worldly, confident, and an experienced sailor—and the youth—poor, insecure, and a novice at sailing (Figure 19–7). The wife is aware of the role she plays in their conflict, but she feigns indifference.

During one confrontation, Andrzej knocks his guest overboard. The young man seems to disappear under the water. The two on board the boat recall that he had said that he could not swim, and they desperately search for him. Andrzej swims to shore to notify the police. While he is away, the young man, who has been hiding behind a buoy, returns to the boat and eventually makes love with Christine (Figure 19–8). The two return to shore, but the boy leaves before the boat docks at the pier.

Andrzej is waiting. He says that he has not gone to the police because he did not take the keys to their car when he entered the water. Soon they are driving. Christine announces that the young man is safe and that

FIGURE 19–7. *A contest of knife-throwing skill between the Young Man and Andrzej. Christine is an observer. (Courtesy Janus Films.)*

she has been unfaithful to her husband. Andrzej does not—or at least he says he does not—believe her. He stops the car at a crossroads. One way leads to the police, the other home. The film ends with Andrzej trying to reach a decision.

The motives and actions of each of the three characters are influenced not only by individual needs, but also by the presence of the others. Andrzej is a financial success, proud of his material possessions, including his car, his boat—and his wife. Underneath his gruff, domineering exterior, however, he is unsure of himself, particularly in his relationship to his wife (there are undercurrents of sexual frustration involved). This is masterfully conveyed in the opening scene with a minimum of dialogue through facial expressions and tense silences.

The young man is a challenge to the middle-aged sports writer. He wants to prove his physical superiority and the value of experience to his wife, the boy, and, perhaps most of all, to himself. At the same time he has a grudging admiration and secret envy of the young man's adventurousness and open future. At first in small ways and then with increasing seriousness and maliciousness, he tests himself and the youth.

The young man's supposed drowning poses a terrible dilemma for Andrzej. If he does not go to the police, then he must admit that his self-confidence and sophistication are a façade covering a moral cowardice.

On the other hand, if he accepts his wife's version of what happened, he has been defeated sexually, an area in which a man of his age and type is most insecure.

Christine is the most passive of the three. Although her lovely body and attractive face emanate sex like the scent of an erotic perfume, she seems to be passionless. Her seduction of the young man is more mechanical than felt. One senses that she is watching her husband and waiting: there are some scores that she is going to settle. Her opportunity comes when she returns to shore and confronts her husband with the truth. As she sits in the car, she watches with a small smile Andrzej's inner conflict.

Polanski depicts in *Knife in the Water* a sterile marriage in which two

FIGURE 19–8. *The Young Man and Christine make love while Andrzej is away. (Courtesy Janus Films.)*

people know each other well enough for each to strike at the other's most vulnerable defenses. Like a magician who attracts our attention with his right hand while his left is actually doing the manipulating, Polanski puts the rivalry of the two men in the foreground while he is revealing in subtle ways a corrupt relationship.

The young man, the intruder, gains the most from the boat trip. At first he is bewildered and defensive as Andrzej baits him, but he soon fights back. In the end, the trip becomes for him a *rite de passage* from which he emerges a man.

Polanski has isolated his three characters on a boat in a vivid setting of sky and water. This confined space not only brings the characters physically and emotionally close together, but also allows the director to use his camera to focus our attention on individual objects. These soon assume symbolic dimensions. A saucepan handle, a game of pick-a-stick, an alarm clock, a bathrobe (first worn by Andrzej, then the boy), and a compass all transcend their utility and become means by which hidden emotions and ambiguous relationships are revealed. Of particular significance is the young man's knife. A dangerous game involving it at which the boy is adept establishes his first genuine challenge to Andrzej (Figure 19–9); its use saves the boat from floundering on shallows; the husband's

FIGURE 19–9. *The Young Man challenges Andrzej to play a dangerous game with his knife. (Courtesy Janus Films.)*

appropriation of the knife and later disposal of it precipitate the fight that results in the younger man being knocked into the water. That it is a phallic symbol is obvious, but it is also an objective correlative for the powers of youth that finally triumph over tyrannical authority.

A symbolic version of the Oedipus myth, a portrayal of a sterile marriage, a description of an experience from which a young man emerges an adult, and a commentary on the futility of replacing inner strength and confidence with the ownership of material objects and arrogant authority—all are valid interpretations of *Knife in the Water,* and others are possible. This film is, in fact, a rich cinematic experience that reveals new veins of meaning each time one delves into it.

The Servant

Directed by JOSEPH LOSEY

I don't regard my work as being particularly pessimistic because I think pessimism is an attitude that sees no hope in human beings or life in general, that has no compassion therefore; and to have compassion, I strongly believe you have to examine the worst, the most tragic, the most crucifying aspects of life as well as the most beautiful ones, and also the things that corrupt life, distort it, destroy it.

Joseph Losey (Quoted in Georges Sadoul, *Dictionary of Film Makers,* trans., ed. and updated by Peter Morris, Berkeley and Los Angeles, 1972, p. 157b.)

CAST

BARRETT	*Dirk Bogarde*
VERA	*Sarah Miles*
SUSAN	*Wendy Craig*
TONY	*James Fox*
LADY MOUNSET	*Catherine Lacey*
LORD MOUNSET	*Richard Vernon*
SOCIETY WOMAN	*Ann Firbank*
OLDER WOMAN	*Doris Knox*
BISHOP	*Patrick Magee*
CURATE	*Alun Owen*
SOCIETY MAN	*Harold Pinter*

CREDITS

DIRECTED BY	*Joseph Losey*
PRODUCER	*Joseph Losey and Norman Priggen for Springbok/Elstree*
SCENARIO	*Harold Pinter, from a story by Robin Maugham*
DIRECTOR OF PHOTOGRAPHY	*Douglas Slocombe*
PRODUCTION DESIGNER	*Richard MacDonald*
ART DIRECTOR	*Ted Clements*
MUSIC	*John Dankworth*
EDITOR	*Reginald Mills*

1963   Black and white   115 minutes

The Servant is a cinematic example of what Losey calls examining the
"worst." Its plot is relatively simple: Tony, the blond scion of a potent
and privileged class, has purchased a charming eighteenth-century house
in Chelsea, but he needs help with it. Becasue he is too old for a nanny
and not quite ready for a wife, he requires a proper servant and he gets
—well, whether or not he gets the proper one is a possible ambiguity of
meaning here. At any rate, he gets a darkly crafted character named Barrett, a gentleman's gentleman, whose ultimate task is to make life livable
for the helpless human being that Tony is revealed to be. He helps Tony
to fill the house elegantly with napery, books, furniture, silverware, and

FIGURE 19–10. *Tony—a moment with Susan. (Courtesy Janus Films.)*

FIGURE 19–11. *Vera and Barrett—attentive. (Courtesy Janus Films.)*

family portraits. A descendant of loyal servitors to this valet tradition, Barrett extends it in his work.

Tony's girl friend Susan, the wife for whom he is not yet ready, is also representative of that decency and goodness for which he is equally unprepared. Arrayed against her and the master is the servant Barrett: "My only ambition is to serve you . . . you know that." Barrett makes it clear to the viewer that he has more sinister intentions. He brings into the household a girl, posing as his sister, who quickly seduces Tony. Before Susan leaves, however, Barrett arranges the revelation that Vera, the "sister," is their common property and that she prefers Barrett to Tony. It is downhill all the way for Tony from this point onward. Servant becomes master and Tony's aristocratic possibilities for decadence get realized in a final orgy of degradation—for which Susan gets recalled, as if to twist the knife of debasement in the wound of Tony's carnal weakness.

As the slow, steady stain of corruption darkens the circle of our understanding, we come to see the sinister Barrett, played with extraordinary dark elegance by Dirk Bogarde, as some kind of mythic monster of evil, an Iago, an incontinently wise Mephisto—to whose Faust?—or a raging Caliban (even though his ugliness is not an issue). From the moment Barrett enters the house to discover Tony dozing in a camp chair—we note that the servant is awake and the master asleep—we are aware of

FIGURE 19–12. *Vera's service to Tony. (Courtesy Janus Films.)*

the pressure of the servant's evil mission, even though we cannot quite make out in so many words his exact motivation. Yet, it does not matter: evil *is* loose in the world and cannot be made to go away by the mere lighting of a match.

The homosexual implications, the heterosexual depravity, the struggles of servant and master, woman as good and woman as lynx—woman as evil—none of these faces of corrupt conflict gets in the way of our seeing also in this film that aristocracy must be reduced to a uselessly craven state by the iron competence of a rising middle class.

To be sure this is not Losey's major intention; for that, we need only *look* at his film. For the first element in his style is to allow his camera to roam over the faces of evil and to capture the inner (certainly here corrupt) light of material things: the glint of silverware on the side-boards, the great fires in the grates, the elegant rooms of the house, the mirrors, frames, corner mouldings. The stylistic insistence on this is further reinforced by the staging, the manner in which Losey's camera catches people in doorways and corners of rooms, the way it silkenly roams staircases and narrow passages—the better to give us a sense of the cramped position of the human beings caught up in this struggle. The bizarre ball game in which delicate statuary is shattered is also an emblem of the fragility of these cramped positions. In general, Pinter's halting surges of dialogue, incomplete yet breathingly suggestive, also enlarge this world.

Losey has managed to at once show us the "crucifying" *and* "the beautiful" and to somehow suggest that these are present together in all of us.

The Caretaker

Directed by CLIVE DONNER

The world is full of surprises. A door can open at any moment and someone will come in. We'd love to know who it is, we'd love to know exactly what he has on his mind and why he comes in, but how often do we know what someone has on his mind or who this somebody is, and what goes to make him and make him what he is, and what his relationship is to others?

Harold Pinter (Quoted in Martin Esslin, *The Peopled Wound: The Works of Harold Pinter*, Garden City, N.Y.: 1970, p. 31, and cited by John Lahr in the "Introduction" to his edition of *A Casebook on Harold Pinter's The Homecoming*, New York, 1971, p. xiii.)

CAST

MICK	*Alan Bates*
DAVIES	*Donald Pleasance*
ASTON	*Robert Shaw*

CREDITS

DIRECTED BY	*Clive Donner*
SCENARIO	*Harold Pinter, from his play*
DIRECTOR OF PHOTOGRAPHY	*Nicholas Roeg*
EDITOR	*Fergus McDonell*
PRODUCER	*Michael Birkett*

1963　　　　Black and white　　　113 minutes

This film, taken nearly verbatim from the classic piece of early Pinter, almost literally has no plot; things are revealed to be one way or another, but nothing really develops—except our growing horror and terror at what Pinter sees to be the contemporary status of relationships among us.

FIGURE 19–13. *Mick lashes out, taunting Davies. (Courtesy Janus Films.)*

Always happy to be let loose in the haunted confines of shabby London houses, Pinter here confines us to a single room of an unfinished, transitional hulk somewhere in the west of London. On a bitter winter's night, the hulking Aston—matching in bulk, stillness, and menace the house itself—brings home with him a derelict, Davies, who will later say (for what reason?) that his name is also Jenkins. Davies has been fired from some vague, menial employment at a "caff," and he has very nearly been involved in some sort of violent episode to the bargain. But Aston saves him and brings him to his junk filled room in his brother Mick's house. The latter, as lean and effusive as his brother is bulky and contained, is supposed to be a contractor of sorts, someone in the construction business. He has engaged his brother to "fix up" the house, to make apartments or other rentable living spaces out of what is now uninhabitable.

The film details what passes between these three and reveals to us the possibilities in such doings: old man Davies stays the night—and cannot leave, so mesmerized is he by the mute hospitality of Aston and so in

FIGURE 19–14. *The hysteria of Davies. (Courtesy Janus Films.)*

need is he, despite the ugly and bafflingly insecure gestures of his host, of accepting that hospitality. Aston is interested—can there be a better word?—in offering little kindnesses to the old man: he lends him a few bob, finds him a pair of shoes, rummages about to get him shoelaces; he makes up a snug little bed for the old fellow. Quarrelsome, ranting, puffed up with an importance long ago given up but not forgotten, Davies accepts all in a poor spirit. Even knowing that something is loose in that house that threatens him, he is still willing to stay on; indeed, at the end, he begs to do just that.

The dramatic triangle is made snug at the corners by the brothers, a strange pair: Robert Shaw (Aston) in his chilling recollection of shock treatments in a mental hospital, and Alan Bates in a series of wickedly contrived roles, filled with scorn and sneer, the sheer perversity of unmotivated malice, get a hold on the derelict. He asks both for shoes, both ask him to stay on as "caretaker" of the haunted house. He is to watch over the bucket catching rain from a leaky roof, an unconnected stove, a

Figure 19–15. *Aston, the Caretaker. (Courtesy Janus Films.)*

plaster Buddha, an immense collection of plain junk. But he makes noises at night; he stinks; he offends Aston and Mick will not side with him. He is asked to leave. We cannot say whether his pleading to stay on will meet with Aston's sympathy, but we fear the worst.

At a certain point, when he is asked to take the position, Davies assures

Aston that "I never been a caretaker before." The point of the film seems to be that none of the protagonists has in him the possibility of taking care of anything by way of a relationship. To be sure, there are, in Pinter's suavely understated language and his unremitting invention of situation, possibilties for verve, comedy, confrontation, and frustration, but nobody will ever become anything to anybody else. The music of human sympathy is capricious, its sources arbitrary, and its end a cold and heartless note.

Clive Donner has rendered all this with extraordinary invention, considering the dramatic limits of a stage play conceived for so limited a dramatic space. This has been achieved principally in the manipulation of light and shade—the film is dominated by the impression of elegant, liquid blacks and blindingly pure whites—the strong emphasis on absolute precision in composition, and the masterly control of performance. The room is small, the action mean, but the film is worth savoring.

Le Bonheur

[Happiness]

Directed by A G N É S V A R D A

In my films I always wanted to make people see deeply. I don't want to show things, but to give people the desire to see.

Agnés Varda. Quoted in Roy Armes, "Agnés Varda." *French Cinema Since 1946,* vol. 2 (New Jersey, 1970), p. 108.

CAST

FRANÇOIS	*Jean-Claude Drouot*
THÉRÈSE, HIS WIFE	*Claire Drouot*
GISOU, THEIR DAUGHTER	*Sandrine Drouot*
PIEROTT, THEIR SON	*Olivier Drouot*
EMILIE	*Marie-France Boyer*

CREDITS

DIRECTOR	*Agnés Varda*
PRODUCTION MANAGER	*Philippe Dussart*
SCENARIO	*Agnés Varda*

Director of Photography	*Jean Rabier and Claude Beausoleil*
Art Director	*Hubert Monloup*
Music	*W. A. Mozart*
Editor	*Janine Verneau*
Mag Bodard-Parc-Film 1965 Color	85 minutes

Le Bonheur is both a lovely film and a controversial one. The former quality derives from Agnés Varda's direction and exquisite use of color. The controversy is provoked by its plot.

François is happily married to Thérèse and both enjoy their two chil-

Figure 19–16. *François and Thérèse at home. (Courtesy Janus Films.)*

FIGURE 19–17. *François and Emilie in the young woman's apartment. (Courtesy Janus Films.)*

dren. Their home in the suburbs is crowded and homely (Figure 19–16); they fill it, however, with love and small pleasures. Thérèse is not unattractive but is worn with alternately taking care of a household and being a part-time seamstress. François is slim and handsome. He is liked by his fellow workers in a carpentry shop. The owner of the shop is an intimate friend as well as an employer. One of the chief pleasures of François and Thérèse is to picnic in the country. The first third of the film presents this contented pair with quiet simplicity.

Then François meets Emilie, a very attractive postal clerk. The two soon become lovers. Their mutual sensual pleasures are graphically portrayed (Figure 19–17). Emilie is willing to share her lover with his wife, for François makes clear, and obviously he is sincere, that he loves both women equally and would not want to hurt either one.

During a visit to the country, however, he tells his wife about Emilie. At first Thérèse is shocked and bitter, but she seems to accept the situation after he explains, as he did to his mistress, that one relationship does not diminish the other. They make love, but when François awakens, his wife is gone. After a frantic search, he discovers that she has drowned. No one can be sure if it is an accident or suicide, but the latter seems more likely. François's grief is genuine.

After a decent period of mourning he returns to Emilie and eventually they marry. And it works! She is accepted by the children and his friends. In the last scene, a parallel to one at the beginning of the film, François,

Emilie, and the children are at a picnic (Figure 19–18). He is clearly as content now with his new wife as he had been with Thérèse.

There are few complications in characterization. Our summary of the plot indicates almost as many of the nuances of characterization as the film offers. There is no indication that François is anything but completely honest in his feeling for the two women. Any doubts that Emilie has about the affair to which she has committed herself are minor. Thérèse has one moment of rage when she learns of her husband's infidelity, but the scene only lasts for a few minutes and then she disappears. We are given no insights into what tumultuous emotions grip her that could motivate the extreme of suicide.

Most critics have accepted Varda's film at face value and appreciated her lack of psychological overtones and a moralistic stance. Although she is regarded as an early member of "new wave" cinema, in this respect she is closer to a literary movement, that of the *le nouveau roman,* represented by the works of Alain Robbe-Grillet, Michel Butor, Claude Mauriac, and Nathalie Sarraute. The tenets of this movement include an emphasis on expression rather than content and a rejection by an author of any overt psychological, moralistic, or metaphysical comments on what happens to characters that become as much "things" as the objects that surround them. *Le Bonheur* can be considered as a cinematic rendering of a "new novel."

It is possible that Varda, who also wrote the scenario, is being ironic.

FIGURE 19–18. *A contented François with Emilie and the children on a picnic. (Courtesy Janus Films.)*

This is what one might expect from a female director who presents what can be described as every man's dream of good fortune and feminine submissiveness. We can discover, however, no evidence in the dialogue or visual effects that this was the director's intention. Either Varda is so subtle that most viewers miss her satire or she has met the challenge of being entirely objective in creating a story that would tempt most directors to suggest a moral judgment on François's incredible attitudes toward the proper relationship of men and women.

As a narrative, this film is intriguing but hardly of great significance. It is the director's exciting use of the camera and color that makes us want to see it repeatedly and to study it. We might not wholly agree with Judith Crist when in a review she called *Le Bonheur* one of the most beautiful films that she had ever seen, but from this perspective we believe that it has few rivals in the last two decades.

There are three main settings in the work, and each is presented with consummate skill. In the scenes in the country, Varda focuses on the beauties of nature with loving attention. A row of yellow flowers in the foreground of a shot or dark trees silhouetted against a pale blue sky demonstrates that the director has scrutinized the paintings of the French impressionists with care. And we feel during such shots some of the sheer aesthetic pleasure evoked by looking at a still life by Monet, Pissarro, Sisley, or Renoir.

The colors in François's and Thérèse's home are drab, predominantly browns and grays, with some objects that are vulgarly bright. Yet, the details of these rooms that the camera dwells on convey to us an atmosphere of domestic warmth. A man with his shirt off and a woman in a worn bathrobe could actually live in this setting.

On the other hand, Emilie's apartment is modern in style and decorated in cool colors, particularly shades of white. There is an aseptic quality to the rooms that makes an effective contrast to the passionate love-making that occurs there. It is in presenting François and Emilie together in bed that Varda proves that she can be as bold and artistic in photographing human beings as vivid settings.

The first reaction of most viewers after seeing *Le Bonheur* is a desire to argue with someone about its plot and characterization, but when the film is recalled in tranquility, its lyric loveliness is what lingers most in memory.

$\mathcal{B}$iographies and $\mathcal{F}$ilmographies

ANTONIONI, MICHELANGELO, (b. September 29, 1912) developed an early interest in films, worked as a theatre director, contributed film criticism to *Cinema* in the late thirties (and continued to write film criticism until the late forties) and worked, during the war, as an assistant to Marcel Carne and Roberto Rossellini. Antonioni also worked as a scenarist, collaborating with Ugo Betti, Giuseppe de Santis, Cesare Zavattini and Federico Fellini (on the latter's 1952 film, *Lo Sceicco Bianco,* for which he was also assistant director). From 1943 to 1950, he made some 7 documentary shorts. In 1950, he made his first feature, *Croanaca di un Amore.* Antonioni is noted for films in which individuals are seen being affected by the malaise of modern urban society, rootless, bored, drifting into unhappy love affairs and erotic encounters.

FILMOGRAPHY: SCRIPTS: Antonioni was co-author of the following: *I Due Foscari* (also by G. Campanile Mancinie, Mino Doletti, and Enrico Fulchignoni; directed by the latter. 1942); *Un pilota ritorna* (also by Rosario Leone, Ugo Betti, Massimo Mida, Gherardo Gherardi; directed by Roberto Rosselini. 1942); *Caccia Tragica* (also by Giuseppe de Santis, Carlo Lizzani, Cesare Zavattini, Corado Alvaro, Umberto Barbaro, Tullio Pinelli; directed by Giuseppe de Santis. 1947); *Lo Sceicco Bianco* (also by Federico Fellini and Tullio Pinelli; directed by Federico Fellini. 1952). SHORTS: *Gente del Po* (1943–47), *N.U./Nettezza Urbana* (1948), *L'Amorosa Menzogna* (1948–49), *Superstizione* (1949), *Sette Canne, un Vestito* (1950), *La Villa dei Mostri* (1950), *la Funivia del Faloria* (1950); FEATURES: *Croanaca di un Amore* (1950), *I Vinti* (1952), *La Signora Senza Camelie* (1953), *L'Amore in Citta* (1953; one episode), *Le Amiche* (1955), *Il Grido* (1957), *L'Avventura* (1960), *La Notte* (1960), *L'Eclisse* (1962), *Deserto Rosso* (Red Desert) (1964), *I Tre Volti* (1965: one episode, not released; negative destroyed by producer), *Blow-Up* (1966; English language), *Zabriskie Point* (USA, 1969), *The Passenger* (1974).

BERGMAN, INGMAR (b. 1918). The Swedish film director began his career in the arts as a playwright and theater director. In the latter area he achieved a national and then an international reputation as head of the Malmö City Theater (1952–1958) and of Sweden's national stage, the Royal Dramatic Theater in Stockholm (1963–1966). He has never completely deserted the theater, continuing to the present to direct plays and operas, and even branching out into radio and television. It is, however, as one of the world's most significant film directors that he is best known. His major films can be divided into four periods: (1) ten years characterized by an eclectic approach to film making (with the exception of the individual *Sawdust and Tinsel*), from *Crisis*, 1946, to *Smiles of a Summer Night*, 1955; (2) attainment of a unique style and approach, from *The Seventh Seal*, 1956, to *The Virgin Spring*, 1960; (3) a trilogy that explores the possibilities of an intimate, symbolic, austere type of cinema or "chamber film": *Through a Glass Darkly*, 1961, *Winter Light*, 1962, and *The Silence*, 1963; and (4) a return to the broader perspective of the second period, with innovative experiments in such techniques as the lengthy close-up and the use of color to reflect psychic states, *Persona*, 1966, to date. Bergman's films can be difficult, slow-moving, and obtuse, but few directors of our time have more effectively challenged the established limitations of the cinema medium or explored with greater perceptiveness the relations between the worlds of the conscious and the unconscious, the self and others, the physical and the metaphysical.

FILMOGRAPHY: SCRIPTS: *Torment* (*Hets*), (1944); *Last Pair Out* (*Sista Paret ut*), (1951); *Woman without a Face* (*Kvinna utan ansikte*), (1947); *Eva*, (1948); *Divorced* (*Franskild*), (1951), *Pleasure Garden* (*Lustgarden*), (1961). Bergman has written the scenarios for his own films, except for *Music in Darkness, Thirst, This Can't Happen Here*, and *The Virgin Spring*. FEATURES: *Crisis* (*Kris*), (1946); *It Rains on Our Love* (*Det Regnar pa var Kärlek*), (1946); *A Ship Bound for India* (*Skepp till Indialand*), (1947); *Music in Darkness* (*Musik i Mörker*), (1948); *Port of Call* (*Hamnstadt*), (1948); *Prison* (*Fängelse*), (1948); *Thirst* (*Törst*), (1949); *To Joy* (*Till Glädje*), (1950); *This Can't Happen Here* or *High Tension* (*Sant Händer inte Här*), (1950); *Summer Interlude* (*Sommarlek*), (1951); *Waiting Women* (*Kvinnors Väntan*), (1952); *Summer with Monika* or *Monika* (*Sommaren med Monika*), (1952); *Sawdust and Tinsel* or *The Naked Night* (*Gycklarnas Afton*), (1953), *A Lesson in Love* (*En Lektion i Karlek*), (1954); *Journey into Autumn* (*Kvinnodröm*), (1955); *Smiles of a Summer Night* (*Sommarnattens Leende*), (1955); *The Seventh Seal* (*Det Sjunde Inseglet*), (1956); *Wild Strawberries* (*Smultronstället*), (1957); *So Close to Life* or *Brink of Life* (*Nära Livet*), (1958); *The Magician* or *The Face* (*Ansiktet*), (1958); *The Virgin Spring* (*Jungfrukällen*), (1960); *The Devil's Eye* (*Djävulens Öga*), (1960); *Through a Glass Darkly* (*Sasom i en Spegel*), (1961); *Winter Light* (*Nattsvardsgästerna*), (1962); *The Silence* (*Tystnaden*), (1963); *Now about All*

These Women (*For atte inte Tala om Alla Dessa Kvinnor*), (1964);
Stimulantia, (1965: incomplete but one section released in 1967); *Persona*, (1966); *Hour of the Wolf* (*Vargtimmen*), (1968); *Shame* (*Skammen*), (1968); *The Rite* or *The Ritual* (*Riten*), (1969, for television); *A Passion* or *The Passion of Anna* (*En passion*), (1969); *Faro Document*, (1970); The Touch (1972); *Cries and Whispers* (*Viskningar och Ropswicht*), (1973); *Scenes from a Marriage* (1974).

CHAPLIN, CHARLES SPENCER (b. 1889). There can be little doubt that the most famous actor in the history of the motion picture is Charlie Chaplin, and the character most readily identified on the screen throughout the world is Charlie the tramp. The actor was born in a London slum and by the age of sixteen was a professional actor on the stage. He went on to gain a measure of acclaim as a comedian in English music halls (comparable to American vaudeville). In 1913 he came to the United States to join Mack Sennett's Keystone Company. He soon established himself as a major comic actor in movies, and it was at this time that Charlie the tramp was created. While still with Sennett, Chaplin began writing and directing one- and two-reelers. In 1918 he formed his own company, First National Film, and in 1923 was one of the founders of United Artists. It was while he was with the former that he produced his first feature film comedy, *The Kid*. After the advent of sound and a decade and a half of fabulous success, he abandoned the tramp character (although echoes of Charlie's character appeared in *The Great Dictator*). *Monsieur Verdoux* and *Limelight* were controversial but memorable dramas. His last two films ended his career with a decrescendo. Chaplin will always be remembered, however, for his greatest works, especially those in which he coordinated his talents as director, script writer, actor, producer, and, in the later films, composer of background music. As a director he was conservative, even reactionary, in his cinematic techniques, yet he used the camera efficiently and effectively. His scripts were often carelessly and unimaginatively written; however, some, such as the one for *The Gold Rush*, have been underestimated. It was as an actor that he was incomparable. His pantomime, his sly satirical touches, his ability to suggest the potential of tragedy in the most hilarious situation, his development of a character of infinite variety and subtle complexity—all combined to make Charlie Chaplin the greatest comedian that cinema has yet produced.

FILMOGRAPHY: SHORTS: Chaplin appeared in sixty-nine shorts between 1914 and 1923, including *The Star Boarder* (1914), *The Knockout* (1914), *A Night Out* (1915), *The Champion* (1915), *The Tramp* (1915), *Carmen* (1916), *The Floorwalker* (1916), *One A.M.* (1916), *The Pawnshop* (1916), *The Rink* (1916), *The Immigrant* (1917), *A Dog's Life* (1918), *Shoulder Arms* (1918), *The Pilgrim* (1923). FEATURES: *The Kid* (1921); *A Woman of Paris* (1923); *The Gold Rush* (1925); *The Circus* (1928);

City Lights (1931); *Modern Times* (1936); *The Great Dictator* (1940), *Monsieur Verdoux* (1947), *Limelight* (1952); *A King in New York* (1957); *A Countess from Hong Kong* (1967).

CLÉMENT, RENÉ (b. 1913). This distinguished French film maker began his career in cinema as a cameraman and director of documentaries. His first opportunity to create his own feature film, *The Battle of the Rails*, occurred while serving as technical adviser for Jean Cocteau's *Beauty and the Beast*. His early films undeservedly attracted little attention. With *Forbidden Games* and *Gervaise*, however, he became internationally known. His films of the 1960s, although always competently made, lack the intensity and visual clarity of his earlier works. He is predominantly eclectic in his style and approach to film making, but he has one noteworthy quality: an ability to evoke through a focus on details the atmosphere of a setting and the very texture of the lives of the characters who live in that environment.

FILMOGRAPHY: SHORTS: *Soigne ton gauche* (with Jacques Tati, 1937); *La Grand Chartreuse* (1937); *Arabie interdite* (consists of three documentaries, 1938); *La Bièvre* (1939); *Le Tirage* (1942); *Ceux du rail* (1942); *Toulouse* (1943); *La Grande Pastorale* (1943); *Chefs de demain* (1943); *Mountain* (1943). FEATURES: *Battle of the Rails* (*La Bataille du rail*), (1945); *La Père tranquille* (1946), *The Damned* (*Les Maudits*), (1947); *Le Mure di Malapurga* (1948); *Le Château de verre* (1950); *Forbidden Games* (*Jeux interdits*), (1952); *Knave of Hearts* (1954); *Gervaise* (1956); *The Sea Wall* or *This Angry Age* (*La Diga sul Pacifico*), (1958); *Plein Soleil* (1959); *Che Joia Vivere!* or *Quelle Joie de vivre!* (1961); *Le Jour et l'heure* (1963); *The Cage* or *Joy House* (*Les Félins*), (1963); *Is Paris Burning?* (*Paris brûle-t-il?*), (1966); *Ecrit sur le sable* (1966); *Rider in the Rain* (*Passager de la pluie*), (1969).

COCTEAU, JEAN (1889–1963). Few artists in this century have been as protean as this perennial *enfant terrible* of the arts. He was a poet, novelist, playwright, film director, essayist, and painter; he wrote scenarios for films, ballets, and operas. In whatever form he expended his prodigious talents and energies, he rejected the conventional and the cliché and joined the avant-garde of that medium. There are, however, certain recurrent themes in his works: the artist, misunderstood by society, is a *voyant* who explores the landscape of our inner world, in the process challenging reality and death; mystery and beauty are the instinctive languages of the artist; myth, dreams, and hallucinations are the repositories of the most profound "truths" about human nature. As a film director and script writer, he expressed these themes and others in visual terms. His *The Blood of a Poet* and *Testament of Orpheus* are classics of cinematic surrealism, a movement that he found more congenial than any other to his particular vision of the function and form of art. His other films are more accessible to intellectual interpretations, but all reveal his unique gift for creating mystery and beauty through illusionary effects.

FILMOGRAPHY: SCRIPTS: *Comédie du bonheur* (1942); *The Phantom Baron* (*Le Baron fantôme,* Cocteau contributed only the dialogue, 1943); *The Eternal Return* (*L'Eternal Retour*), (1943); *Les Dames du Bois de Boulogne,* (only dialogue, 1945); *Ruy Blas* (1947). FEATURES: *The Blood of a Poet* (*Le Sang d'un poète*), (1930); *Beauty and the Beast* (*La Belle et la Bête*), (1945); *The Eagle with Two Heads* (*L'Aigle à deux têtes*), (1947); *Les Parents terribles* (1948); *Orpheus* (*Orphée*), (1950); *Coriolan,* (16mm, not distributed commercially, 1950); *La Villa Santo-Sospir,* (16mm, not distributed commercially, 1952); *Testament of Orpheus* (*Le Testament d'Orphée*), (1960).

DONNER, CLIVE (b. 1926). Donner made his first film, a ten-minute work in 8mm, at the age of fourteen. A Londoner by birth, he spent his early years learning his craft as assistant editor to both Carol Reed and David Lean. Ultimately he worked at the Denham Studios and was responsible for editing such films as *I Am a Camera, Scrooge, The Purple Plain, Meet Me Tonight,* and *The Million Pound Note.* He has also worked for the J. Walter Thompson Company and has made a number of TV and documentary films. He is responsible for the widely acclaimed television documentary, *British Institutions,* and in 1960 created a 4½ hour series about India. He has also taught at the London School of Film Technique and made a number of films in Hollywood.

FILMOGRAPHY: FEATURES: *The Secret Place* (1957); *Heart of a Child* (1958); *Some People* (1962); *Nothing but the Best* (1963); *The Caretaker* (1963); *What's New Pussycat?* (1965); *Luv* (1966); *Here We Go Round the Mulberry Bush* (1967); *Alfred the Great* (1968).

KUROSAWA, AKIRA (b. 1910). Born in Tokyo, Kurosawa originally studied painting with the intention of earning a living as a commercial artist; but in 1936, answering a newspaper ad for assistant directors, he was hired by the PCL Studios (later the Toho Company) and began an apprenticeship under Kajiro Yamamoto. As assistant director, he worked on scores of films and, eventually, as part of his duties, wrote more than twenty scripts, many of which were filmed by other directors. Even after his debut as a director (in 1943), these scripts were being made into films. Since 1950 (and *Rashomon*), Kurosawa has been widely acclaimed as one of the world's master filmmakers.

FILMOGRAPHY: SCRIPTS: *Uma* (*Horses,* written with Kajiro Yamamoto, 1941); *Seishun no Kiryu* (*Currents of Youth*), (1942); *Tsubasa no Gaika* (*A Triumph of Wings*), (1942); *Dohyosai* (*Wrestling-Ring Festival*), (1944); *Appare Isshin Tasuke* (*Brava, Tasuke Isshin!*), (1945); *Hatsukoi* (*First Love*), a section of the omnibus film, *Yotsu no Koi no*

Monogatari (*Four Love Stories*), (1947); *Ginre no Hate* (*To the End of the Silver Mountains*, written with Kajiro Yamamoto, 1947); *Shozo* (*The Portrait*), (1948); *Jigoku no Kifujin* (*The Lady from Hell*), (1949); *Jakoman to Tetsu* (*Jakoman and Tetsu*), (1949; remade in 1964); *Akatsuki no Dasso* (*Escape at Dawn*), (1950); *Jiruba Tetsu* (*Tetsu "Jilba"*), (1950); *Tateshi Danpei* (*Fencing Master*), (1950); *Ai to Nikushime no Kanata* (*Beyond Love and Hate*), (1951); *Kedamono no Yado* (*The Den of Beasts*), (1951); *Ketto Kagiya no Tsuji* (*The Duel at the Key-Maker's Corner*), (1951); *Sugata Sanshiro*, (The first feature film directed by Kurosawa; remade under its original title in 1955; remade again in 1965, also under its original title and edited by Kurosawa); *Tekichu Odan Sanbyaku Ri* (*Three Hundred Miles through Enemy Lines*), (1957); *Sengoku Guntoden* (*The Saga of the Vagabond*, based on the original by Sadao Yamanaka, 1960); *Shichin no Samurai* (remade as the American film, *The Magnificent Seven*, 1961); *Rashomon* (remade as *The Outrage*, 1964); *Yojimbo* (remade in a pirated version, with Clint Eastwood, as *Per un pungo di dollari*, 1964). FEATURES: *Sanshiro Sugata* (1943); *The Most Beautiful* (*Ichiban Utsukushiku*), (1944); *Sanshiro Sugata-Part Two* (1945); *They Who Step on the Tiger's Tail* (*Tora no O o Fumu Otokotachi*, 1945, not released until 1952); *Those Who Make Tomorrow* (*Asu o Tsukuru Hitobito*), (1946); *No Regrets for Our Youth* (*Waga Seishun ni Kuinashi*), (1946); *One Wonderful Sunday* (*Subarashiki Nichiyobi*), (1947); *Drunken Angel* (*Yoidore Tenshi*), (1948); *The Quiet Duel* (*Shizukanaru Ketto*), (1949); *Stray Dog* (*Nora Inu*), (1949); *Scandal* (*Shubun*), (1950); *Rashomon* (1950); *The Idiot* (*Hakuchi*), (1951); *Ikiru* (*Living*), (1952); *Seven Samurai* (*Shichinin no Samurai*), (1954); *Record of a Living Being* (*Ikimono no Kiruku*), (1955); *The Throne of Blood* (*Kumonosu-jo*, 1957, based on Shakespeare's *Macbeth*); *The Lower Depths* (*Donzoko*), (1957); *The Hidden Fortress* (*Kakushi Toride no San-Akunin*), (1958); *The Bad Sleep Well* (*Warui Yatsu Hodo Yoku Nemuru*), (1960); *Yojimbo* (1961); *Sanjuro* (*Tsubaki Sanjuro*), (1962); *High and Low* (*Tengoku to Jigoku*), (1963); *Red Beard* (*Akahige*), (1965); *Dodesukaden* (1970).

LANG, FRITZ (b. 1890). The work of this very important film director falls into two periods: his years in Germany and those in the United States. He intended in his youth to emulate his father and become an architect. His training in this field laid the basis for his intense interest in the physical settings of his films and the meticulous care with which he planned each new one. It was during World War I that he began writing scenarios, and after the war he became a script writer and story editor. He directed his first film in 1919. In the 1920s he was soon recognized, with Murnau and Pabst, as one of the greatest of German silent film directors. He merged, as did many of his colleagues, a commitment to social criticism and a fascination with the ways revealed by expressionism of presenting cinematically the innermost levels of the human psyche. In 1931 he proved in *M* that he recognized that sound increased the dramatic potentials of motion pictures. The major script writer for that film was Thea von Harbou, who was Lang's wife. The two, however, disagreed in their attitudes toward Hitler. They parted in 1933, the year Hitler became chancellor of Germany. Thea von Harbou remained at home to become an ardent supporter of the Third Reich; Lang left for the United States. Lang's American films have been variously evaluated. Some critics point to *Fury, You Only Live Once, The Woman in the Window,* and *Clash by Night* as outstanding films. Others find in even these works only a faint echo of the cinematic genius who created *Destiny,* the Dr. Mabuse series, *Metropolis,* and *M.* The American films are definitely done with admirable craftsmanship and do carry to a new setting Lang's concern with the ramifications in human lives of fate and guilt and an instinctive sympathy for the underdog in any situation. It would seem, however, that Lang, as so many other European directors of his generation, had his artistic integrity and imaginativeness sapped by the commercialism and conservatism of bureaucratic Hollywood studios.

FILMOGRAPHY: SCRIPTS: *Die Hockzeit im Excentricclub* (1917); *Hilde Warren und der Tod* (1917); *Die Frau mit den Orchideen* (1919); *Die Pest in Florenz* (1919); *Das Indische Grabmal* (1921); *Totentanz* (1919); *Lilith und Ly* (1919); *Carola Hauser* (1921); *König Artus Tafelrunde* (1922). Lang was also co-script writer on most of the German films that he directed. FEATURES: *Halbblut* (1919); *Der Herr der Liebe* (1919); *Die Spinnen* (Part One—*Der Goldene See;* Part Two—*Das Brillandtenschiff;* 1919–1920); *Harakiri* (1919); *Das Wandernde Bild* (1920); *Vier um die Frau* (1920); *Destiny (Der Müde Tod),* (1921); *Dr. Mabuse der Spieler* (Part One—*Der Grosse Spieler;* Part Two—*Inferno;* 1922); *Die Nibelungen* (Part I—*Siegfrieds Tod;* Part Two—*Kriemhilds Rache;* 1924); *Metropolis* (1926); *Spione* (1928); *Die Frau im Mond,* 1929); *M* (1931); *Das Testament des Dr. Mabuse* (1933); *Liliom* (1933); *Fury* (1936); *You Only Live Once* (1937); *You and Me* (1938); *The Return of Frank James* (1940); *Western Union* (1941); *Man Hunt* (1941); *Hangmen Also Die* (1942); *The Ministry of Fear* (1943); *The Woman in the Window* (1944); *Scarlet Street* (1945); *Cloak and Dagger* (1946); *The Secret Beyond the Door* (1948); *House by the River* (1950); *An American Guerrilla in the Philippines* or *I Shall Return* (1950); *Rancho Notorious* (1951); *Clash by Night* (1952); *The Blue Gardenia* (1953); *The Big Heat* (1953); *Human Desire* (1954); *Moonfleet* (1955); *While the City Sleeps* (1956); *Beyond a Reasonable Doubt* (1956); *Das Indische Grabmal* (Part One—*Der Tiger von Eschnapur;* Part Two—*Das Indische Grabmal;* 1958); *Die tausend Augen des Dr. Mabuse* (1960).

LOSEY, JOSEPH (b. 1908). Losey was born in La Crosse, Wisconsin, and began his career as a theater critic in New York City in 1930. He later worked as a theater director for the Theater Guild and others, traveled widely in Europe (where he first became acquainted with the work of Bertolt Brecht, a continuing influence on his work), and in 1937 began his film work proper, supervising documentaries and educational films for such organizations as the National Youth Administration, the State Department and the Rockefeller Foundation. In 1939, he directed his first work, a short puppet film, and from 1943–1945 was under contract to MGM. In 1950, Losey, like so many others then under attack by the House Un-American Activities Committee (HUAC), was forced to go abroad, where he worked for some years under a pseudonym. This situation continued until 1957, when he finally emerged with a work under his own name (*Time Without Pity*). Since then he has grown steadily in stature as one of the most respected directors working on either side of the Atlantic.

FILMOGRAPHY: SHORTS: *Pete Roleum and His Cousins* (1939); *A Child Went Forth* (USA, 1941); *Youth Gets a Break* (USA, 1941); *A Gun in His Hand* (short, in the series, *Crime Does Not Pay*, USA, 1941); FEATURES: *The Boy With the Green Hair* (USA, 1948); *The Lawless/The Dividing Line* (USA, 1949); *The Prowler* (USA, 1950); *M* (remake; USA, 1950); *The Big Night* (USA, 1951); *Imbarco a Mezzanote* (*Stranger on the Prowl/Encounter;* Italy, 1951, under the pseudonym of Andrea Forzano); *The Sleeping Tiger* (Britain, 1954, under the pseudonym of Victor Hansbury); *A Man on the Beach* (a short, 1955); *The Intimate Stranger/Finger of Guilt* (1955, under the pseudonym of Joseph Walton); *Time Without Pity* (1957); *The Gypsy and the Gentleman* (1957); *Blind Date/Chance Meeting* (1959); *The Criminal/Concrete Jungle* (1960); *The Damned/These are the Damned* (1961); *Eva/Eve* (Italy, 1962); *The Servant* (Britain, 1963); *King and Country* (1964); *Modesty Blaise* (1966); *Accident* (Britain, 1967); *Boom* (1968); *Secret Ceremony* (1968); *Figures in a Landscape* (1970); *The Go-Between* (1971).

MURNAU, FRIEDRICH WILHELM (1888–1931). Murnau had a varied background in the arts before becoming a film maker in his late twenties. During his university years he studied painting and literature. Then he apprenticed himself to Max Reinhardt as an actor and assistant director. Once he did devote himself to cinema, beginning in 1919, he made up for lost time by directing twenty-one films in a dozen years. He soon demonstrated a unique combination of visual sensibility and sensitivity to dramatic values in a plot. As were most of his contemporaries in Germany, he was drawn to expressionism, but was too much of an individual to commit himself unconditionally to the movement. He used expressionistic techniques only when they served his purposes. His range was wide: from the world of the proletariat (*The Last Laugh*) to that of the nouveau riche (*Tartuffe*), from the city (most of his German films) to the country (*Sunrise* and *City Girl*) and even the South Seas *(Tabu)*.

He was most fascinated, however, by the demonic and corrupting or avenging spirits that rise from the dead or the unconscious. This interest in the satanic led him to search for new cinematic techniques to express the mysterious and elusive. He was not only innovative himself (*Nosferatu* was one of the first German films to have portions filmed outside of a studio), but he supported the revolutionary ideas of Carl Mayer, script writer extraordinary, and Karl Freund and Fritz Arno Wagner, his chief cameramen. After the immense popularity of *The Last Laugh*, he was invited by Fox Studios to make films in Hollywood. Even under adverse conditions, he was able to produce a masterpiece, *Sunrise*. His next two films were far less successful. With Robert Flaherty as associate director, he completed *Tabu*. Before the premier of this film he died in an automobile accident. Ranking film makers is a dubious practice, but there are few critics who would deny Murnau a place among at least the dozen most significant directors in the history of cinema.

FILMOGRAPHY: FEATURES: *The Child in Blue* (*Der Knabe in Blau*), (1919); *Satanas* (1920); *Longing* (*Sehnsucht*), (1920); *The Hunchback and the Dancer* (*Der Buchlige und die Tänzerin*), (1920); *The Two-Faced One* (*Der Januskopf*), (1920); *Afternoon . . . Night . . . Morning* (*Abend . . . Nacht . . . Morgen*), (1920); *They Walk in the Night* (*Der Gang in die Nacht*), (1921); *Marizza, Alias "The Smuggler Madonna"* (*Marizza, Genannt die Schmuggler-Madonna*), (1921); *Haunted Castle* (*Schloss Vogelöd*), (1921); *Nosferatu, A Symphony of Terror* (*Nosferatu, Eine Symphonie des Grauens*), (1922); *The Burning Acre* (*Der Brennende Acker*), (1922); *Phantom* (1922); *Expulsion* (*Die Austreibung*), (1923); *The Finances of the Grand Dukes* (*Die Finanzen des Grossherzogs*), (1924); *The Last Laugh* (*Der Letzte Mann*), (1924); *Tartuffe* (*Tartüff*), (1926); *Faust* (1926); *Sunrise* (1927); *Four Devils* (1928); *City Girl* or *Our Daily Bread* (1929); *Tabu* (1931).

OLMI, ERMANNO (b. 1931). Born in Bergamo, Italy, Olmi attended drama school and worked as an actor and producer in a number of Italian stage comedies and musicals. By 1953, however, he had begun to make the first of some thirty documentaries for Edison-Volta, for whom he also made his first full length film, *Il Tempo si è Fermato* (1959). As late as 1962, he also acted (in *Una Storia Milanese* by Eriprando Visconti), although he was by then an internationally known film director. His latest work has been made for television.

FILMOGRAPHY: SHORTS: *La Pattuglia di Passo San Giacomo* (1954); *Buongiorno Nature* (1955); *La Mia Valle* (1955); *Manon: Finestra 2* (1956); *Tre fili fino a Milano* (1958); *Il Pensionato* (1958); *Venezia, Città Modernà* (1958); *Alto Chiese* (1959); *Le Grand Barrage* (*Time Stood Still*), (1961). FEATURES: *Il Tempo si è Fermato* (1959); *Il Posto* or *The Job*), (1961); *I Fidanzati* (*The Fiancés*), (1962); *E Venne un Uomo* (*A Man Named John*), (1964); *Beata Gioventù* (for TV, 1967);

Un Certo Giorno (*One Fine Day*), (1969); *I Recuperanti* (*The Scavengers*, for TV, 1970); *Durante L'Estate* (for TV, 1970).

OPHULS, MAX (1902–1957). Born in Saarbrucken, Germany, Ophuls's real name was Max Oppenheimer. Beginning at the age of seventeen, he began a love affair with the theater and films that lasted all his life. His first experience was in the theater; as an actor and producer he was involved from 1919 to 1932 in more than two hundred productions. His film career began in 1930, when he began working as an assistant and dialogue director for Anatole Litvak. When Hitler came to power, he left Germany, having established himself as a director, and after working in France, Italy, and the Netherlands for seven years became a citizen of France in 1938. After the fall of France, he worked briefly in Switzerland and left for the United States in 1941. In Hollywood, he was out of work for four years but managed to make four unusual films there nevertheless. Returning to France in 1949, he made the last four—and probably the best—of his films. Ophuls died in Hamburg in 1957.

FILMOGRAPHY: FEATURES: *Dann schon lieber Lebertran* (Germany, 1930); *Die Lachende Erben* (Germany, 1931); *Die Verliebte Firma* (Germany, 1931); *Die Verkaufte Braut* (*The Bartered Bride*), (Germany, 1931); *Liebelei* (Germany, 1932); *Une histoire d'amour* (France, 1933; this is the French version, done with new close-ups, of his *Liebelei*); *On a volé un homme* (France, 1933); *La Signora di Tutti* (Italy, 1934); *Divine* (France, 1935); *Komedie om Geld* (*The Trouble with Money*), (Netherlands, 1936); *Ave Maria de Schubert* and *La Valse Brillante* (of Chopin), (two shorts, both made in France in 1936); *La Tendre ennemie* (France, 1936); *Yoshiwara* (France, 1937); *Werther* (France, 1938); *Sans lendemain* (France, 1939); *De Mayerling à Sarajevo* (France, 1940); *Vendetta* (USA, 1946; completed by Mel Ferrer and Howard Hughes); *The Exile* (USA, 1947); *Letter from an Unknown Woman* (USA, 1948); *Caught* (USA, 1948); *The Reckless Moment* (USA, 1949); *La Ronde* (France, 1950); *Le Plaisir* (France, 1951); *Madame de . . .* (France/Italy, 1953); *Lola Montès* (France/German Federal Republic, 1955).

POLANSKI, ROMAN (b. 1933). Polanski, before he left Poland, was recognized, with Jerzy Skolimowski, as one of the leading figures in the second wave of significant directors that emerged in his homeland after World War II. The first group consisted of Andrzej Munk, Andrzej Wajda, Jerzy Kawalerowiez, and others. One experience both groups shared was training at the celebrated Lodz School of Cinematography. Polanski entered the school after a number of years as a theater and film actor. Although he was an assistant to Munk, he turned, as did Skolimowsky, from the political preoccuptions of his predecessors (who as young men directly experienced World War II). *Knife in the Water,* Polanski's first feature film, is a penetrating study of a sterile marriage and a youth at the edge of adulthood. His direction in this work is restrained, with little of the cinematic bombast that seems to be epidemic among the leaders of the "Polish school," but there are undercurrents of sexual frustration and sadism. Polanski went to England and the United States to create his later films. A radical change occurred in his subject matter and approach to film making after leaving Poland. His major works, from *Repulsion* to *Macbeth,* are cinematic *grand guignol,* based on violence, witchcraft, and sexual perversities and obsessions. Characterization and themes are less important than nightmare effects. In creating images of horror, both real and imaginary, Polanski is a master. He also can be witty, if somewhat heavy-handed, in satirizing the hypocrisy and gullibility of human beings. Generally, however, his films (with the notable exception of *Knife in the Water*) disturb the surface of our emotions rather than move us deeply.

FILMOGRAPHY: SHORTS: *Break up the Party* (*Rozbijemy Zabawa*), (1957); *Two Men and a Wardrobe* (*Dwaj ludzie z szafa*), (1958); *When Angels Fall* (*Gdy spadaja anioly*), (1959); *The Lamp* (*Lampa*), (1959); *Le Gros et le maigre* (1961); *Mammals* (*Ssaki*), (1962). FEATURES: *Knife in the Water* (*Noz w Wodzie*), (1962); *Les Plus belles escroqueries du monde* (one episode in the film, 1963); *Repulsion* (1965); *Cul-de-sac* (1966); *The Dance of the Vampires* (1967); *Rosemary's Baby* (1968); *Macbeth* (1971); *Chinatown* (1974).

RENOIR, JEAN (b. 1894). The younger son of the great impressionist master, Auguste Renoir, Jean Renoir was born in Paris and early displayed an interest in ceramics. He worked at the craft some four years but was slowly immersing himself in films—a process that had begun in earnest some years previously while he was recovering from wounds suffered in World War I. (In that conflict, Renoir was at first a cavalryman but later switched branches and qualified as an aerial reconnaisance pilot.) The influence of two films, Erich von Stroheim's *Foolish Wives* and the Russian actor Mosjoukine's French-based *Le Brasier Argent* (directed by Alexander Volkov) persuaded him that he could find a place for himself in the world of films and he made his first one, finally, in 1924. Thereafter, Renoir's career developed steadily. In 1940, he emigrated to the United States and made six films there. Renoir is ranked among the very greatest of cinema masters for his poetic realism and his work has influenced a whole generation of French directors, including especially, François Truffaut. He is presently living in California.

FILMOGRAPHY: FEATURES: *La Fille de l'eau* (1924); *Nana* (1926); *Charleston* (1927); *Marquitta* (1927); *La Petite Marchande d'allumettes* (1928); *Tire-au-flanc* (1928); *Le Tournoi dans la cité* (1929); *Le Bled* (1929); *On purge bébé* (1931); *La Chienne* (1931); *La Nuit de carrefour* (1932); *Boudu sauvé des eaux* (1932); *Chotard et Cie* (1933); *Madame Bovary* (1934); *Toni* (1934); *Le Crime de Monsieur Lange* (1936); *Une partie de campagne* (1936; released 1946); *Les Bas-Fonds* (1936); *La*

Grande Illusion (1937); *La Marseillaise* (1938); *La Bête Humaine*
(1938); *La Règle du jeu* (1939); *La Tosca* (Italy, 1940; unfinished);
Swamp Water (USA, 1941); *This Land Is Mine* (USA, 1943); *Salute to
France* (USA, 1944); *The Southerner* (USA, 1945); *The Diary of a
Chambermaid* (USA, 1946); *The Woman on the Beach* (USA, 1947);
The River (India, 1951); *Le Carosse d'or* (France/Italy, 1952); *French
Cancan* (1954); *Elena et les hommes* (1956); *Le Déjeuner sur l'herbe*
(1959); *Le Testament du Dr. Cordelier* (*Experiment in Evil*, TV, 1959,
released in 1963); *Le Caporal épinglé* (1962); *Le Petit théâtre de Jean
Renoir* (1971; TV drama series).

TRUFFAUT, FRANÇOIS (b. 1932). Born in Paris, Truffaut was early turned
over to his grandmother and to studies at a lycée. Instead of studying,
however, he spent most of his time playing hookey and going to movies.
Thus, his passion for films and film making was apparent very early. At
sixteen he was caught stealing in order to finance a film club he had
founded. He was very early befriended by André Bazin, and, after a short
stint in the army (from which he deserted) and a subsequent punishment tour, he was briefly with the documentary film department of the
French Ministry of Agriculture. But his career really began in 1953,
when, fired by the ministry, he joined the staff of Bazin's *Cahiers du
Cinéma* and began to write regularly for that journal and for *Arts.* In
1955 he made his first short film, *Une visite,* and in the following year
worked as a research assistant for Roberto Rosselini on three unreleased
works. Since 1959, when his *400 Blows* won the Grand Prix at Cannes,
he has worked steadily as a film director and his work has been prominently identified with the new wave.

FILMOGRAPHY: SHORTS: *Une visite* (*A Visit*), (1955); *Les Mistons* (*The
Mischief Makers*), (1958); *Histoire d'eau* (co-directed with Jean-Luc
Godard, *History of Water*), (1959). FEATURES: *Les quatre cents Coups*
(*The 400 Blows*), (1959); *Tirez sur le pianiste* (*Shoot the Piano Player*),
(1960); *Jules et Jim* (1961); *Antonie et Colette* (an episode in the an-
thology film *L'Amour a vingt ans/Love at Twenty*), (1962); *La Peau
douce* (*Soft Skin*), (1964); *Fahrenheit 451* (Britain, 1966); *La mariée
était en noir* (*The Bride Wore Black*), (1967); *Baisers volés* (*Stolen
Kisses*), (1968); *La Sirène du Mississippi* (*Mississippi Mermaid*), (1969);
L'Enfant sauvage (*The Savage Child*), (1970); *Le Domicile conjugal*
(*Bed and Board*), (1970); *Les Deux Anglaises et le Continent* (*Two
English Girls*), (1971); *Une Belle Fille Comme Moi* (*Such a Gorgeous
Kid Like Me*), (1972); *La Nuit Américaine* (*Day for Night*), (1973).
Note: Truffaut has appeared as an actor in a number of films, most not-
ably in his own *L'Enfant sauvage* and *La Nuit Américaine.*

VARDA, AGNÉS (b. 1928). Varda was one of the first of the *nouvelle
vague* directors; in fact, her first feature, *La Pointe-Courte,* is often con-

sidered the first genuine "new wave" film. Her designation as a member of this movement is based on her willingness to abdicate the right to make moral and psychological judgments on her characters and her ability to suggest that the settings and objects that impinge on the lives of her characters reflect and influence their emotional states. Her main subject matter is the relationship between men and women, untouched by sociological and metaphysical concerns. It is, however, the beauty of her photography that usually most attracts viewers. Her experience as one of France's foremost still photographers has stood her in good stead. The composition and tonal values of individual shots are obviously planned with the greatest care. When color is added, the total effect can be breathtaking. Varda has not been a prolific director (six feature length films and a few shorts in almost two decades), but each of her works is an impressive creation by an acute sensibility and cinematic eye.

FILMOGRAPHY: SHORTS: *O saisons, O châteaux* (1957); *Opéra Mouffe* (1958); *Du côté de la côte* (1958); *La Cocotte d'Azur* (1959); *Salut les Cubains* (consists of still photographs, 1963); *Elsa* (for television, 1966); *Huey* (1968). FEATURES: *La Pointe courte* (1955); *Cleo from 5 to 7* (*Cléo de 5 à 7*), (1961); *Happiness* (*Le Bonheur*), (1965); *Les Créatures* (1966); *Loin de Vietnam* (in collaboration, 1967); *Lion's Love* (1969).

WAJDA, ANDRZEJ (b. 1936). Wajda was thirteen when Germany invaded Poland in 1939; three years later he joined the Resistance. At the end of the war he entered the Cracow Academy of Fine Arts to study painting. He left in 1950 and found his true metier at the School of Cinematography in Lodz. Soon he was directing shorts. His first three feature length films dealt with the activities of the Polish Resistance during the German occupation and focused on conflicts between leftist and rightist groups within the movement. This similarity of subject matter, and no other reason, has encouraged critics to label the films a trilogy. *Ashes and Diamonds*, the last of the three, is generally regarded as Wajda's finest work to date. The films that followed during the early 1960s were mostly period pieces, often diffuse in structure and frantic in style. With *Everything for Sale* (1968) and later works, however, he regained the vitality and exciting visual dynamics of his early films. Wajda, as with most of the early post-World War II Polish directors, has a social consciousness, but his preoccupation with political themes has not blinded him to the other emotional needs and frustrations of his characters, especially love and religion. More controversial has been his cinematic style. It is often described as "baroque," for he does not hesitate to place the weight of a plethora of visual symbols on a film and to use in a scene many special effects, unusual camera angles, and abrupt transitions between shots that many viewers find self-conscious, strained, and even gauche. On the other hand, in his latest work he seems to be moving toward a more controlled and discriminating cinematic language and rhetoric.

FILMOGRAPHY: SCRIPTS: *Three Stories* (*Trzy opowiesci*), (1953); *Roll Call* (*Apel poleglych*), (1956); his own *Ashes and Diamonds, Lotna, Samson, Everything for Sale,* and *Landscape after Battle.* SHORTS: *While You're Asleep* (*Kiedy ty spisz*), (1950); *Evil Boy* (*Zly cholpiec*), (1950); *Ilza Ceramics* (*Ceramika Ilzecka*), (1951); *I Go toward the Sun* (*Ide ku sloncu*), (1955); *Roly-Poly* (*Przekladaniec*), (for television, 1968). FEATURES: *A Generation* (*Pokolenie*), (1955); *Kanal* (1956); *Ashes and Diamonds* (*Popiol i Diamant*), (1958); *Lotna* (1959); *Innocent Sorcercers* (*Niewinni czarodzieje*), (1960); *Samson* (1961); *Siberian Lady Macbeth* (*Sibirska Ledi Magbet*), (1962); *The Ballmayer Interview* (*Wywidd z Ballmayerem*), (for television, 1962); *Another's Wife and Husband under the Bed*), (*Cudza zona i maz pod lozkiem*), (for television, 1962); *Ashes* (*Popioly*), (1965); *Gates to Paradise* (*Vrata raja*), (1967); *Everything for Sale* (*Wszstko na sprzedaz*), (1968); *Hunting Flies* (*Polowanie na muchy*), (1969); *Macbeth* (*Magbet*), (for television, 1969); *Landscape after Battle* (*Krajobraz po bitwie*), (1970); *The Birch Wood* (*Brzezina*), (1971).

Bibliography

There are so many easily accessible bibliographies of material on cinema in general, on theory, and on its history that we are not including such listings here. Instead we will mention half a dozen books in these categories that any student of the film will find invaluable.

Guidebook to Film, compiled and edited by Ronald Gottesman and Harry M. Geduld (New York, 1972) contains reliable information on books and periodicals (an annotated list); theses and dissertations about films; the names of museums, archive collections, film organizations and services; and other topics. *Dictionary of Films* by Georges Sadoul, translated, edited, and updated by Peter Morris (Berkeley, 1972) and *Dictionary of Film Makers* by Georges Sadoul, translated, edited, and updated by Peter Morris (Berkeley, 1972) are the most comprehensive and detailed compilations in dictionary form of films and film makers available in English. Many introductions to all aspects of film have been published. For the novice we recommend Ernest Lindgren's *The Art of the Film* (New York, 1970). The more sophisticated student should consult Siegfried Kracauer's *Theory of Film* (New York, 1960). In our judgment the best one-volume history of film is Gerald Mast's *A Short History of the Movies* (Indianapolis, Ind., 1971).

Material on individual films and directors is more difficult to locate. The following bibliographies should be useful to the reader who wants to obtain other views and background on the films that we have discussed in this book. We emphasize that these bibliographies, although fairly inclusive, are selected (for example, in most cases, we do not include film reviews) and confined to publications in English.

L'Avventura and Antonioni

ANTONIONI, MICHELANGELO. *L'Avventura: A Film by Michelangelo Antonioni.* From the film script by Michelangelo Antonioni, Elio Bartolini, and Tonino Guerra, New York, 1969. Contains a transcript of the film and much other valuable materials: an interview with Antonioni, a diary kept during shooting, and some valuable critical articles. For a list of other screenplays by Antonioni in print, see the bibliography in the next item.

527

CAMERON, IAN, and ROBIN WOOD. *Antonioni.* Praeger Film Library Series. New York, 1968.

COWIE, PETER. *Antonioni, Bergman, Resnais.* London, 1963.

GARIS, ROBERT. "Watching Antonioni." *Commentary,* **43** (April 1967), 86–89. Reply by P. Warshow, with rejoinder by Garis, *Commentary* **44** (Aug. 1967), 14–17.

GODARD, JEAN-LUC. "The Art of the Director: Godard Interviews Antonioni." *Cahiers du Cinéma in English* (Jan. 1966), 19–30.

———. "Interview." *Movie,* No 12 (Spring 1965), 31–34.

HERNACKI, THOMAS. "Michelangelo Antonioni and the Imagery of Disintegration." *Film Heritage,* **5** (Spring 1970), 13–21.

"Interview." *Cinema,* No. 100 (Nov. 1965), 51–61.

KINDER, MARSHA. "Antonioni in Transit." *Sight and Sound,* **36** (Summer 1967), 132–137.

LANE, JOHN FRANCIS. "Antonioni Diary: A Day-to-Day Record of Work on *The Eclipse.*" *Films and Filming,* **8** (March 1962), 11–12, 46.

———. "Oh! Oh! Antonioni." *Films and Filming,* **9,** (Dec. 1962), 58–66.

LAWSON, SYLVIA. "Notes on Antonioni." *The Sydney Cinema Journal,* No. 2 (Winter 1966), 9–18.

LEPROHON, PIERRE. *Michelangelo Antonioni: An Introduction.* Trans. by Scott Sullivan. New York, 1963.

LIBER, NADINE. "Antonioni Talks About His Work." *Life* (Jan. 27, 1967), 66–67.

REED, REX. "Interview with Antonioni." *The New York Times* (Jan. 1, 1967), Sec. II, p. 7. (Letter to the Editor by Antonioni critical of the interview, *The New York Times* (Jan. 15, 1967), Sec. II, p. 17.

SAMUELS, CHARLES THOMAS. "Interview with Antonioni" (Part I). *Vogue,* **155** (March 15, 1970), 96–97.

———. "Interview with Antonioni" (Part II). *Film Heritage,* **5** (Spring 1970), 1–12. The remainder of this issue is also devoted to Antonioni, principally to his *Zabriskie Point,* but see also the article listed by Hernacki.)

STRICK, PHILIP. *Antonioni.* Loughton, England, 1963.

———. "Antonioni Report." *Sight and Sound,* **43,** No. 1 (Winter 1973–1974), 30–31.

Ashes and Diamonds and Andrzej Wajda

"*Ashes and Diamonds*" (excerpts from reviews). *Filmfacts* (July 14, 1961), pp. 140–142.

AUSTEN, DAVID. "A Wajda Generation." *Films and Filming* (July 1968), pp. 14–19.

HIGHAM, CHARLES. "Grasping the Nettle: The Films of Andrzej Wajda." *Hudson Review* (Autumn 1965), pp. 408–414.

TOEPLITZ, KRZYSZTOF-TEODOR. "Wajda Redivivus." *Film Quarterly* (Winter 1969–1970), pp. 37–41.

WAJDA, ANDRZEJ. "Destroying the Commonplace." *Film Makers on Film Making.* Ed. by Harry M. Geduld. Bloomington, Ind., 1967.

———. *The Wajda Trilogy (Ashes and Diamonds, A Generation, Kanal).* Trans. and introduction by Boleslaw Sulik. Modern Film Scripts. New York, 1973.

Beauty and the Beast and Jean Cocteau

BAZIN, ANDRÉ. "Theater and Cinema— Part One." *What Is Cinema?* Berkeley, 1971, pp. 90–94.

COCTEAU, JEAN. *Cocteau on the Film: Conversations with André Fraigneau.* Trans. by Vera Traill. New York, 1954.

———. *Diary of a Film (La Belle et la Bête).* Trans. by Ronald Duncan. New York, 1950.

———. *The Journals of Jean Cocteau.* Ed., trans., and with an introduction by Wallace Fowlie. Bloomington, Ind., 1964.

———. *Two Screenplays: The Blood of the Poet, The Testament of Orpheus.* Baltimore, 1968.

———. *Three Screenplays: Orpheus, The Eternal Return, Beauty and the Beast.* New York, 1972.

FRAIGNEAU, ANDRÉ. *Cocteau.* Trans. by Donald Lehmkuhl. Evergreen Profile Books. New York, 1961.

GILSON, RENÉ. *Jean Cocteau: An Investigation into his Films and Philosophy.* Trans. by Ciba Vaughan. *Editions Seghers' Cinéma d'Aujourd'hui,* in English. New York, 1964.

OXENHANDLER, NEAL. "On Cocteau." *Film Quarterly* (Fall 1964), pp. 12–14.

———. "Poetry in Three Films of Jean Cocteau." *Yale French Studies* (Summer 1956), pp. 14–20.

TYLER, PARKER. "Beauty and the Beast." *Classics of the Foreign Film.* New York, 1962.

WALLIS, C. G. "The Blood of a Poet." *Kenyon Review* (Winter 1944), pp. 24–42.

Le Bonheur and Agnés Varda

ARMES, ROY. "Agnés Varda." *French Cinema since 1946,* v. 2. New York, 1970.

"*Le Bonheur*" (excerpts from reviews). *Filmfacts* (Aug. 1, 1966), pp. 138–139.

GOW, GORDON. "The Underground River." *Film and Filming* (March 1970), pp. 6–10.

SHIVAS, MARK. "*Cleo de 5 a 7* and Agnés Varda." *Movie* (Oct. 1962), pp. 32–35.

The Caretaker and Clive Donner

CAMERON, IAN and MARK SHIVAS. "What's New Pussycat: An Interview." *Movie,* **14** (Autumn 1965), 12–16.

DONNER, CLIVE. "A Free Hand." *Sight and Sound,* **28** (Spring 1959), 60–61.

———. "These Are The Most Selfish Actors of All." *Films and Filming,* **4** (April 1958), 7.

GOW, GORDON. "The Urge of Some People: Clive Donner Talks to Gordon Gow about his Transition from the Low Budget Film to the Epic." *Films and Filming,* **15** (July 1969), 4–8.

JOYCE, PAUL. "Nothing But The Best." *Film* (London), No. 45 (Spring 1966), 16–21.

PERKINS, V. F. "Clive Donner and Some People." *Movie,* **3** (Oct. 1962), 22–25.

TAYLOR, JOHN RUSSELL. "*The Servant* and *The Caretaker*." *Sight and Sound,* **33** (Winter 1963–1964), 38–39.

Forbidden Games **and René Clément**

ARMES, ROY. "René Clément." *French Cinema since 1946,* v. 1. New York, 1970.

EISNER, LOTTE H. "The Style of René Clément." *Film Culture* (Part I, Sept. 1947, p. 21; Part II, Oct. 1957, p. 11).

KOVAL, FRANCIS. "Interview with Clément." *Sight and Sound* (June 1950), pp. 149–151.

McVAY, DOUGLAS. "The Darker Side of Life: The Films of René Clément." *Films and Filming* (Dec. 1966), pp. 19–26.

The Gold Rush **and Charlie Chaplin**

AGEE, JAMES. "Comedy's Greatest Era." *Agee on Film.* New York, 1958.

BAZIN, ANDRÉ. "Charlie Chaplin." *What Is Cinema?* Trans. by Hugh Gray, Berkeley, 1967.

CAPP, AL. "The Comedy of Charlie Chaplin." *Atlantic Monthly* (Feb. 1950), pp. 25–29.

CHAPLIN, CHARLES. *Charlie Chaplin's Own Story.* Indianapolis, Ind., 1916.
——. *My Autobiography.* London, 1964.

Focus on Chaplin. Ed. by DONALD W. McCAFFREY. Film Focus Series. Englewood Cliffs, N.J., 1971.

HUFF, THEODORE. *Charlie Chaplin.* New York, 1951.

McDONALD, GERALD D., *et al. The Films of Charlie Chaplin.* New York, 1965.

MERYMAN, RICHARD. "Interview of Chaplin." *Life* (March 10, 1967), pp. 82–84, 88–94.

PAYNE, ROBERT. *The Great God Pan: A Biography of the Tramp Played by Charles Chaplin.* New York, 1952.

ROSEN, PHILIP. "The Chaplin World-View." *Cinema Journal* (Fall 1969), pp. 2–12.

SOLOMON, STANLEY J. "Accumulation as a Unifying Style: Chaplin's *The Gold Rush.*" *The Film Idea.* New York, 1972.

WILSON, EDMUND. "The New Chaplin Comedy." *New Republic* (Sept. 2, 1925), pp. 45–46.

YOUNG, STARK. "Charlie Chaplin." *New Republic,* (Feb. 8, 1928), pp. 358–359.

Jules and Jim, Shoot the Piano Player **and François Truffaut**

BLUESTONE, GEORGE. "The Fire and the Future." *Film Quarterly,* **20** (Summer 1967), 3–10.

BORDWELL, DAVID. "François Truffaut: A Man Can Serve Two Masters." *Film Comment,* **7** (Spring 1971), 18–23.

BRAUDY, LEO. "Hitchcock, Truffaut and the Irresponsible Audience." *Film Quarterly,* **21** (Summer 1968), 21–27.

BRODY, ALAN. "Jules and Catherine and Jim and Hedda." *Journal of Aesthetic Education,* **5** (April 1971), 91–102.

FISHER, RICHARD. "*Day for Night*: A Filmic Criticism," *Filmmakers Newsletter,* **7** (1974), 19–21.

Focus on Shoot the Piano Player. Film Focus Series. Ed. by Leo Braudy. Englewood Cliffs, N.J., 1972.

"François Truffaut—An Interview." Trans. by Paul Ronder. *Film Quarterly,* **17** (Fall 1963), 3–13. Trans. and abridged from *Cahiers du Cinéma,* No. 138 (Dec. 1962).

GRAMONT, SANCHE DE. "Life Style of Homo Cinematicus—François Truffaut." *The New York Times Magazine* (June 15, 1969), 12, 34–47.

GREENSPUN, ROGER. "Elective Affinities: Aspects of *Jules and Jim.*" *Sight and Sound,* **32** (Spring 1963), 78–82.

KINDER, MARSHA, and BEVERLE HOUSTON. "Truffaut's Gorgeous Killers." *Film Quarterly,* **17** (Winter 1973–1974), 2–10.

KLEIN, MICHAEL. "The Literary Sophistication of François Truffaut." *Film Comment,* **3** (Summer 1965), 24–29.

MALLOW, SAUL. "A Portrait of François Truffaut." *Filmmakers Newsletter,* **7** (1974), 23–27.

MARCORELLES, LOUIS. "Interview with François Truffaut." *Sight and Sound,* **31** (Winter 1961–1962), 35–37, 48.

MILLAR, GAVIN. "Hitchcock versus Truffaut." *Sight and Sound,* **38** (Spring 1969), 82–88.

PETRIE, GRAHAM. *The Cinema of François Truffaut.* New York and London, 1970.

SHATNOFF, JUDITH. "François Truffaut: The Anarchist Imagination." *Film Quarterly,* **16** (Spring 1963), 3–11.

WOOD, ROBIN. "Chabrol and Truffaut." *Movie* (London), No. 17 (Winter 1969–1970), 16–24.

Knife in the Water and Roman Polanski

BUTLER, IVAN. *The Cinema of Roman Polanski.* The International Film Guide Series. New York, 1970.

COWIE, PETER. "Polanski." *International Film Guide,* 1967. New York, 1966.

GELMIS, JOSEPH. "Roman Polanski." *The Film Director As Superstar.* New York, 1970.

GOW, GORDON. "Satisfaction—A Most Unpleasant Feeling." *Films and Filming* (April 1969), pp. 15–18.

HARRISON, ENGLE. "Polanski in New York" (also "Biography" and "Filmography"). *Film Comment* (Fall 1968), pp. 4–11.

MAYERSBERG, PAUL. "Polanski's Atmosphere." *New Society* (Jan. 30, 1969), p. 175.

MCARTHUR, COLIN. "Polanski." *Sight and Sound* (Winter 1968/69), pp. 14–17.

ROSS, T. J. "Roman Polanski, *Repulsion* and the New Mythology." *Film Heritage* (Winter 1968–1969), pp. 1–10.

WEINBERG, GRETCHEN. "Roman Polanski: An Interview." *Sight and Sound* (Winter 1963), pp. 32–33.

The Last Laugh and F. W. Murnau

EISNER, LOTTE. H. *Murnau.* Berkeley, 1973.

———. "Murnau and the Kammerspielfilm" and "The Evolution of the Costume Film: *Tartuffe.*" *The Haunted Screen: Expressionism in the German Cinema and the Influence of Max Reinhardt.* Berkeley, 1969.

Film Comment (Summer 1971), for "F. W. Murnau: An Introduction," by Gilberto Perez Guillermo (pp. 13–15), "*Sunrise*" by Molly Haskell (pp. 16–19), "*City Girl,*" by Richard Kozarski (pp. 20–22), and "*Tabu,*" by Robin Wood (pp. 23–27).

HUFF, THEODORE. *An Index to the Films of F. W. Murnau.* London, 1948.

KINDER, MARSHA, and BEVERLE HOUSTON, *"The Last Laugh." Close-up: A Critical Perspective on Film*. New York, 1972.

KRACAUER, SIEGFRIED. "Mute Chaos." *From Caligari to Hitler: A Psychological History of the German Film*. Princeton, 1947.

MURNAU, F. W. "The Ideal Picture Needs No Titles." *Theatre Magazine* (Jan. 1928), pp. 41–42.

TYLER, PARKER. *"The Last Laugh." Classics of the Foreign Film*. New York, 1962.

M and Fritz Lang

BAGAI, RAM. "Fritz Lang, Master of Mood." *Cinema Progress* (May–June 1938), pp. 10–11.

EISNER, LOTTE H. "The Fritz Lang Thriller" and "The Decline of the German Film." *The Haunted Screen: Expressionism in the German Cinema and the Influence of Max Reinhardt*. Berkeley, 1969.

JENSEN, PAUL M. *The Cinema of Fritz Lang*. The International Film Guide Series. New York, 1969.

———. *"M." Classics of the Film*. Ed. by Arthur Lenning. Wis., 1965.

KINDER, MARSHA, and BEVERLE HOUSTON. *"M." Close-up: A Critical Perspective on Film*. New York, 1972.

KRACAUER, SIEGFRIED. "Murderer Among Us." *From Caligari to Hitler: A Psychological History of the German Film*. Princeton, 1947.

LANG, FRITZ. "Happily Ever After." *Film Makers on Film Making*. Ed. by Harry M. Geduld. Bloomington, Ind., 1967.

———. *M*. Trans. by Nicholas Garnham. Classic Film Scripts. New York, 1968.

SARRIS, ANDREW. "Fritz Lang." *Film Culture* (Spring 1963), p. 14.

SOLOMON, STANLEY J. "Sound and Drama: Lang's *M*." *The Film Idea*. New York, 1972.

TYLER, PARKER. *"M." Classics of the Foreign Film*. New York, 1962.

Il Posto and Ermanno Olmi

BACHMANN, GIDEON. "Interview." *Nation*, **198** (May 25, 1964), 542–543.

———. "The New Italian Films." *Nation*, **198** (May 25, 1964), 540–542.

HOUSTON, PENELOPE. "Ermanno Olmi in London." *Sight and Sound*, **31** (Winter 1961/1962), 16.

———. "The Organisation Man." *Sight and Sound*, **33** (Spring 1964), 78–81.

"Interview." *Sequences*, No. 41 (April 1965), 55–59.

KAUFFMANN, STANLEY. "Fine Italian Hand." *The New Republic*, **150** (February 15, 1964), 34.

LANE, JOHN FRANCIS. "The Triumph of Italy's Realism." *Films and Filming*, **8** (December 1961), 38–39.

OLMI, ERMANNO. "A Conversation with John Francis Lane." *Sight and Sound*, **39** (Summer 1970), 148–152.

SOLOMOS, GEORGE PAUL. "Ermanno Olmi." *Film Culture*, **24** (Spring 1962), 35–36.

Rashomon and Akira Kurosawa

"Akira Kurosawa." *The East*, **1**, No. 6 (July 1965), 45–49.

ANDERSON, LINDSAY. "Two Inches off the Ground." *Sight and Sound*, **27**, No. 3 (Winter 1957–1958), 131–133; 160.

Focus on Rashomon. Ed. by Donald Richie. Englewood Cliffs, N.J., 1972.

Japanese Cinema: Film Style and National Character. Ed. by Donald Richie. New York, 1971.

"Kurosawa: Japan's Poet Laureate of Film." *Show Business Illustrated* (April 1, 1962), pp. 28–29.

LEYDA, JAY. "The Films of Kurosawa." *Sight and Sound*, **24** (Oct.–Dec. 1954), 74–78.

RICHIE, DONALD. *The Films of Akira Kurosawa*. 2nd ed. Berkeley and Los Angeles: 1970.

———. "Kurosawa on Kurosawa." *Sight and Sound*, **33** (Spring–Summer and Fall-Winter 1964), 200–203.

———. "A Personal Record." *Film Quarterly*, **14**, (Fall 1960), 20–30.

Rashomon: A Film by Akira Kurosawa. Consulting ed. Donald Richie. New York, 1969.

SILVERSTEIN, NORMAN. "Kurosawa's Detective-Story Parables." *Japan Quarterly*, **12** (July–Sept. 1965), 351–354.

La Ronde and Max Ophuls

ARMES, ROY. *French Cinema Since 1946: Volume One: The Great Tradition*. 2nd ed. London and New Jersey, 1970, 57–67.

ARCHER, EUGENE. "Ophuls and the Romantic Tradition." *Yale French Studies*, **17** (1956), 3–5.

Film Comment. One third of the entire issue, **7**, No. 2 (Summer 1971) is devoted to Ophuls. See especially, "Max Ophuls," by Andrew Sarris, 57–59.

MASON, JAMES, CHRISTIAN MATRAS, JACQUES NATÀNSON and PETER USTINOV. "Max Ophuls." *Sight and Sound*, **27** (Summer 1957), 49–50.

OLMI, ERMANNO. "My Experience." *Cahiers du Cinéma in English*, **1** (January 1966), 63.

REISZ, KAREL. "Ophuls and *La Ronde*." *Sequence*, **14** (1952), 33–35.

SARRIS, ANDREW. "Memory and Max Ophuls." *Moviegoer*, No. 3 (Summer 1966), 2–7.

WILLIAMS, F. "The Mastery of Movement: Max Ophuls." *Film Comment*, **5** (Winter 1969), 70–74.

The Rules of the Game, Grand Illusion and Jean Renoir

BAZIN, ANDRÉ. *Jean Renoir*. Ed. by François Truffaut. New York, 1973.

BERANGER, JEAN. "The Illustrious Career of Jean Renoir." *Yale French Studies*, **17** (Summer 1956), 27–37.

BRAUDY, LEO. *Jean Renoir: The World of His Films*. Garden City, N.Y., 1972.

CALLENBACH, ERNEST, and ROBERTA SCHULDENFREI. "The Presence of Jean Renoir." *Film Quarterly*, **14** (Winter 1960), 8–10.

CAREY, GARY. "The Renoir Experience." *Seventh Art*, **1** (Summer 1963), 16–17, 27–28.

COWIE, PETER. *Seventy Years of Cinema*. South Brunswick, N.J. and New York, 1969.

Dyer, Peter John. "Renoir and Realism." *Sight and Sound*, **29** (Summer 1960), 130–135.

Gilliatt, Penelope. "*Le Meneur de Jeu*." *The New Yorker* (23 Aug. 1969), 34–61.

Grand Illusion (Film Script). Trans. by Marianne Alexandre and Andrew Sinclair. New York, 1968.

Greenspun, Roger. "To Love a Renoir Movie Properly." *The New York Times* (Sept. 6, 1970), Sec. II, 1; 4.

"Interview." *Film* (Nov. 1966), 18–22.

"Interview with Jean Renoir." *Sight and Sound*, **37** (Spring 1968), 57–60.

Joly, J. "Between Theater and Life: Jean Renoir and *The Rules of the Game*." *Film Quarterly*, **21** (Winter 1967–1968), 2–9.

Kael, Pauline. *Kiss Kiss Bang Bang*. Boston, 1968.

Kerans, James. "Classics Revisited: *La Grande Illusion*." *Film Quarterly*, **14** (Winter 1960), 10–17.

Leprohon, Pierre. *Jean Renoir*. Trans by Brigid Elson. New York, 1971.

Marcorelles, Louis. "Conversation with Jean Renoir." *Sight and Sound*, **31** (Spring 1962), 78–83, 103.

Mast, Gerald. *Filmguide to Rules of the Game*. Bloomington, Ind. 1974.

Miller, Daniel. "The Autumn of Jean Renoir." *Sight and Sound*, **37** (Summer 1968), 136–141.

Rivette, Jacques, and François Truffaut. "Renoir in America: The French Director Thinks his Successes and Failures were His Own Doing." *Films in Review*, **5** (No. 1954), 449–456.

Rules of the Game (Film script). Trans. by John McGrath and Maureen Teitelbaum. New York, 1970.

Sesonske, Alexander. "Renoir: A Progress Report." *Cinema* (Beverly Hills), **6** (1970), 16–20.

The Servant and Joseph Losey

Brunius, Jacques. "Joseph Losey and *The Servant*." *Film*, No. 38 (Winter 1963), 27–30.

Callenbach, Ernest. "*The Servant*." *Film Quarterly*, **18**, No. 1 (Fall 1964), 36–38.

Durgnat, Raymond. "The Cubist Puritanism of Joseph Losey." *Film: The Magazine of the Federation of Film Societies*, No. 50 (Winter 1967–1968), 10–13.

Houston, Penelope, and John Gillett. "Conversations with Nicholas Ray and Joseph Losey." *Sight and Sound*, **30** (Autumn 1961), 182–187.

"Interview on *The Servant*." *Isis*, No. 1456, (Feb. 1, 1964).

Jacob, Gilles. "Joseph Losey, or The Camera Calls." *Sight and Sound*, **35** (Spring 1966), 62–67.

Leahy, James. "Joseph Losey and the Cinema of Violence." *Panorama Magazine, Chicago Daily News* (Jan. 28, 1967).

———. *The Cinema of Joseph Losey*. New York, 1967.

Losey, Joseph. "The Monkey on My Back," *Films and Filming*, **9** (Oct. 1963), 11:54.

———. "Ten Questions to Nine Directors: On *The Servant*." *Sight and Sound*, **33** (Spring 1964).